'Marco Longobardo's book demonstrates that while many of the post-WWII occupations are contested between the states involved, the *jus ad bellum* and self-defence, international humanitarian law and human rights law provide generally binding rules for the use of force. A particular strength of this book is thorough analysis of conventional law, custom, and jurisprudence combined with a sound assessment of the differences between law enforcement and the conduct of hostilities.'

> *Dieter Fleck*, former Director of International Agreements and Policy of the German Ministry of Defence, Member of the Advisory Board of the Amsterdam Center for International Law

'The law governing occupation may seem to be 'a sort of relic of another time', to borrow Dr Longobardo's words, but despite the evolution of international law it unfortunately still remains relevant. In a sense, this is the ultimate protection of human rights, where the occupying state must ensure rights and freedoms not of its own population but in a place where its presence, if legitimate at all, can only be temporary. Dr Longobardo's fine analysis of the use of armed force, especially through the lens of the human right to life, is a masterful scholarly contribution.'

> *William A. Schabas*, Professor of International Law, Middlesex University, and Professor of International Criminal Law and Human Rights, Leiden University

THE USE OF ARMED FORCE IN OCCUPIED TERRITORY

This book explores the international law framework governing the use of armed force in occupied territory through a rigorous analysis of the interplay between *jus ad bellum*, international humanitarian law, and international human rights law. Through an examination of state practice and *opinio juris*, treaty provisions, and relevant international and domestic case law, this book offers the first comprehensive study on this topic. This book will be relevant to scholars, practitioners, legal advisors, and students across a range of sub-disciplines of international law, as well as in peace and conflict studies, international relations, and political science. This study is intended to influence the way in which states use armed force in occupied territory, offering guidance and support in litigations before domestic and international courts and tribunals.

Marco Longobardo is a Research Fellow in Public International Law at the University of Westminster, where he also teaches public international law, international human rights law, and other related subjects. He undertook his doctoral studies at the Sapienza University of Rome and previously lectured at the University of Messina. He has published extensively on public international law in international peer-reviewed journals such as the *Journal of International Criminal Justice*, the *Heidelberg Journal of International Law*, and the *Netherlands International Law Review*.

The Use of Armed Force in Occupied Territory

MARCO LONGOBARDO

University of Westminster

CAMBRIDGE
UNIVERSITY PRESS

University Printing House, Cambridge CB2 8BS, United Kingdom

One Liberty Plaza, 20th Floor, New York, NY 10006, USA

477 Williamstown Road, Port Melbourne, VIC 3207, Australia

314-321, 3rd Floor, Plot 3, Splendor Forum, Jasola District Centre, New Delhi - 110025, India

79 Anson Road, #06-04/06, Singapore 079906

Cambridge University Press is part of the University of Cambridge.

It furthers the University's mission by disseminating knowledge in the pursuit of education, learning and research at the highest international levels of excellence.

www.cambridge.org
Information on this title: www.cambridge.org/9781108461498
DOI: 10.1017/9781108562027

© Cambridge University Press 2018

This publication is in copyright. Subject to statutory exception and to the provisions of relevant collective licensing agreements, no reproduction of any part may take place without the written permission of Cambridge University Press.

First published 2018
First paperback edition 2020

A catalogue record for this publication is available from the British Library

Library of Congress Cataloging in Publication data
NAMES: Longobardo, Marco, author.
TITLE: The use of armed force in occupied territory / Marco Longobardo.
DESCRIPTION: Cambridge [UK] ; New York, NY : Cambridge University Press, 2018. | Includes bibliographical references and index.
IDENTIFIERS: LCCN 2018012837 | ISBN 9781108473415 (hardback)
SUBJECTS: LCSH: Military occupation. | Military occupation damages. | Just war doctrine | Intervention (International law) | Humanitarian law. | International law and human rights. |
BISAC: LAW / International.
CLASSIFICATION: LCC KZ6429 .L66 2018 | DDC 341.6/6–dc23
LC record available at https://lccn.loc.gov/2018012837

ISBN 978-1-108-47341-5 Hardback
ISBN 978-1-108-46149-8 Paperback

Cambridge University Press has no responsibility for the persistence or accuracy of URLs for external or third-party internet websites referred to in this publication, and does not guarantee that any content on such websites is, or will remain, accurate or appropriate.

Ai miei genitori, Cinzia e Nicola
In ricordo di Lucio Dalla,
che mi avrebbe preso in giro,
e di Tiziana Saffioti,
che sarebbe stata orgogliosa di me

Contents

Foreword Professor Eyal Benvenisti		*page* xi
Acknowledgements		xiii
List of Abbreviations		xvii
Table of Cases		xxi
1	Scope of the Book	1
2	The Hostile Character of Occupation as Reflected by the Law of Occupation	20
3	The Applicability of *Jus ad Bellum* and Self-Defence to the Use of Armed Force in Occupied Territory	88
4	Armed Resistance against the Occupying Power in International Law	134
5	Law Enforcement and Conduct of Hostilities in Occupied Territory	165
6	The Regulation of the Use of Armed Force in Occupied Territory in Light of the Right to Life	241
7	General Conclusions	270
Select Bibliography		277
Index		315

Foreword

From the beginning, questions relating to the regulation of resistance against occupation have challenged the international law of occupation. Indeed, efforts to codify the law during the nineteenth century reached an impasse on the question of the right to resist an occupation, and codification was ultimately salvaged only by the Martens Clause, which was introduced to finesse the debate. But despite the centrality and ubiquity of the various legal issues related to the use of force in occupied territory, and the lack of scholarly agreement on key matters, academic efforts to clarify them remained scant.

Dr Marco Longobardo should therefore be praised for taking up the challenge of addressing the relevant questions in a thorough, uncompromising, and impartial way. His impressive study offers a comprehensive treatment of the various questions related to the legal regulation of the use of force in occupied territories. He combines careful study of state practice from the inception of the concept of occupation until our time together with a sensitive treatment of various legal sources, and above all, with an in-depth understanding of the unique nature of the role and powers of the occupying power under international law. Longobardo shows the ways in which the law of occupation, together with other rules of international law, has offered over time a highly sophisticated framework that has regulated and continues to regulate the use of armed force by the various actors in occupied territory.

Scholarly and diplomatic debates about the questions covered in this book will surely continue, given the conflicting positions of occupiers, occupied, and third parties, but Longobardo's comprehensive study, insightful analyses and important suggestions will no doubt influence these debates and hopefully resolve some of the outstanding disagreements.

Professor Eyal Benvenisti
Whewell Professor of International Law
University of Cambridge

Acknowledgements

In writing the acknowledgements for this book, I must admit that the line between personal and professional has collapsed during the last few years. Most of my academic encounters have become personal relationships that have outlasted the professional relationships from whence they grew. Although I have written this book over the last two years, I see now that its foundational research coincided with the early stages of my academic career, and impacted my personal life in the most profound manner. Accordingly, I feel the urge to express my gratitude to the people who played such a crucial role in my scientific and personal growth.

Throughout the writing of this book, I have been very lucky in the support and help I have received from many people. In particular, over the entire period from the selection of the topic to the publication of the book, I have benefitted from constant scientific and personal advice from Professors Paolo Benvenuti, Marcella Distefano, and Marco Roscini, who generously offered their knowledge, patience, and experience, as well as their time in reading the manuscript and providing me with their valuable comments. In addition, I wish to thank Professors Giulio Bartolini, Yoram Dinstein, Dieter Fleck, and Charles Garraway who read some chapters of the book and gave me insightful feedback. Moreover, I am indebted to professor Eyal Benvenisti, who has written a very generous foreword for this book. Ms Eden Oxley deserves my heartfelt thanks for having helped me at every step in revising and polishing the manuscript. Similarly, I wish to thank Tom Randall and the entire Cambridge University Press staff for their patient and competent support.

I first encountered the law of occupation when I was writing the final dissertation for my five-year master's Law degree at the University of Messina under the supervision of Professor Marcella Distefano. She introduced me to the study of international law and, since then, has always been a source of unlimited advice and support. To her, to Dr Livio Scaffidi Runchella, and to my 'academic sister', Dr Federica Violi, I owe a huge debt of gratitude regarding international law, funny meals, the hysterical organisation of activities, shared happiness, and hectic moments of panic-management.

Subsequently, for my PhD, I chose to concentrate on researching the law relating to the prolonged occupation of the Palestinian Territory at the Law School of the Sapienza University of Rome. During those years, I benefitted from the supervision of Professor Alessandra Lanciotti, and from the careful advice of both the director of the course, Professor Angelo Davì, and the other member of the board of supervisors, Professor Enzo Cannizzaro. Not only did they guide me through the exploration of the law of occupation, but many of their comments have also been incorporated into this book. Similarly, I was glad to include in this book some of the useful comments my dissertation received from the three external examiners (Professors Gianluca Contaldi, Maria Rosaria Mauro, and Alessandra Zanobetti) during my viva.

In addition, during my PhD, I spent two periods in London as a visiting researcher. During the first, in 2015, I had the privilege of working at Middlesex University under the supervision of Professor William Schabas; I thank him, along with Professors Joshua Castellino and Elvira Dominguez-Redondo, for having welcome me to Middlesex. The year after, in 2016, I returned to London as a visiting researcher at the University of Westminster, under the supervision of Professor Marco Roscini. That experience marked the beginning of a close collaboration with the University of Westminster, where, since January 2017, I have been proud to continue working as a Postdoctoral Research Fellow. Sometimes, I wonder whether Marco Roscini would have expected me to have been so shameless and rapacious in seeking his opinion and support. I still look to him for any relevant piece of advice, and I am very proud to be able to continue working with him.

Moreover, during the last five years, I have had the opportunity to discuss the topic of my research with a number of scholars and colleagues who I met in Rome, London, and at various academic events. Among others, I wish to thank Professors Giulio Bartolini, Eyal Benvenisti, Malgosia Fitzmaurice, Micaela Frulli, Lorenzo Gradoni, Vaios Koutroulis, Fabrizio Marongiu Buonaiuti, Maria Irene Papa, Marco Pertile, Paolo Picone, and Dr Aurora Rasi for the exchanges I had with them and for their advice. Similarly, I have enjoyed the friendship and camaraderie of a number of young colleagues with whom I shared and still share more than trite academic chit-chat (any reference to great food, countless drinks, commonplace academic fears, and great music is not coincidental).

It is worth mentioning that I conducted the research for this book in several libraries in Italy and in the United Kingdom. However, the library that most bore the weight of my many requests was the international law library of the School of Law at the Sapienza University of Rome. To the wonderful staff who manages that library, I owe my heartfelt thanks and humblest apologies.

Finally, I would not have accomplished anything in my life, let alone the writing of this book, without the unwavering support of my brother Luca and, in particular, my parents, Cinzia and Nicola, to whom this book is primarily dedicated.

The law herein is stated as of 20 December 2017. I retain full responsibility for any faults, errors, or omissions. Anything of worth in this book should be credited to my colleagues, family, and friends.

Abbreviations

ACHPR	African Charter on Human and Peoples' Rights
ACHR	American Convention on Human Rights
ArCHR	Arab Charter on Human Rights
ACmHPR	African Commission on Human and Peoples' Rights
ADI	*Anuario (español) de derecho international*
AFDI	*Annuaire français de droit international*
AJIL	*American Journal of International Law*
AP	Additional Protocol to the Four Geneva Conventions
CCPR	Human Rights Committee
CI	*La Comunità internazionale*
CJIL	*Chinese Journal of International Law*
CPA	Coalition Provisional Authority
CS	*Comunicazioni e studi*
DARS	Draft Articles on Responsibility of States for Internationally Wrongful Acts
DUDI	*Diritti umani e diritto internazionale*
ECHR	European Convention for the Protection of Human Rights and Fundamental Freedoms
ECJ	European Court of Justice
ECtHR	European Court of Human Rights
ED	*Enciclopedia del diritto*
EECC	Eritrea-Ethiopia Claims Commission
EJIL	*European Journal of International Law*
GA	General Assembly
GC	Geneva Convention
HCJ	High Court of Justice (Supreme Court of Israel)
HR	Hague Regulations
HRC	Human Rights Council

IACmHR	Inter-American Commission on Human Rights
IACtHR	Inter-American Court of Human Rights
ICC	International Criminal Court
ICCPR	International Covenant on Civil and Political Rights
ICESCR	International Covenant on Economic, Social and Cultural Rights
ICJ	International Court of Justice
ICLQ	*International & Comparative Law Quarterly*
ICRC	International Committee of the Red Cross
ICTR	International Criminal Tribunal for Rwanda
ICTY	International Criminal Tribunal for the Former Yugoslavia
IDF	Israel Defense Forces
IDI	Institut de droit international/Institute of International Law
ILJ	*International Law Journal*
ILM	*International Legal Material*
ILR	*International Law Reports* (formerly *Annual Digest and Reports of Public International Law Cases*)
ILS	*International Law Studies*
IMT	International Military Tribunal
IMTFE	International Military Tribunal for the Far East
IRRC	*International Review of the Red Cross*
IsLR	*Israel Law Review*
ITLOS	International Tribunal for the Law of the Sea
IYBR	*Israel Yearbook on Human Rights*
JCIL	*Journal of Comparative and International Law*
JCSL	*Journal of Conflict & Security Law*
JDI	*Journal du droit international*
JICJ	*Journal of International Criminal Justice*
JICL	*Journal of International and Comparative Law*
JIL	*Journal of International Law*
LGDJ	Librairie générale de droit et de jurisprudence
LJIL	*Leiden Journal of International Law*
LNTS	League of Nations Treaties Series
LQR	*Law Quarterly Review*
LR	*Law Review*
LRTWC	*Law Reports of Trials of War Criminals*
MLLWR	*Military Law & Law of War Review*
MPEPIL	*Max Planck Encyclopedia of Public International Law*
MPYUNL	*Max Planck Yearbook of United Nations Law*

NILR	*Netherlands International Law Review*
NJIL	*Nordic Journal of International Law*
OPT	Occupied Palestinian Territory
OTP	Office of the Prosecutor
RBDI	*Revue Belge de Droit International*
RCADI	*Recueil des cours de l'Académie de droit international de La Haye/Collected Courses of the Hague Academy of International Law*
RCGI	*Rivista della cooperazione giuridica internazionale*
RDI	*Rivista di diritto internazionale*
RDIPP	*Rivista di diritto internazionale privato e processuale*
RGDIP	*Revue Générale de Droit International Public*
RIAA	*Reports of International Arbitral Awards*
RSDIE	*Revue suisse de droit international et européen/Swiss Review of International and European Law*
SC	Security Council
SCSL	Special Court for Sierra Leone
SCT	*Studies in Conflict and Terrorism*
TRNC	Turkish Republic of Northern Cyprus
UN	United Nations
UNTS	*United Nations Treaty Series*
YIHL	*Yearbook of International Humanitarian Law*
YIL	*Yearbook of International Law*
YILC	*Yearbook of the International Law Commission*
ZaöRV	*Zeitschrift für ausländisches öffentliches Recht und Völkerrecht/ Heidelber Journal of International Law*

Table of Cases

A. INTERNATIONAL COURTS AND TRIBUNALS

1. *International Court of Justice*

Anglo-Iranian Oil Co Case (United Kingdom v. Iran) (Preliminary Objection)   p. 77
Application of the Convention on the Prevention and Punishment of the Crime of Genocide (Bosnia and Herzegovina v. Serbia and Montenegro)   p. 172, 211–213
Application of the International Convention on the Elimination of All Forms of Racial Discrimination (Georgia v. Russian Federation) (Order)   p. 66
Application of the International Convention on the Elimination of All Forms of Racial Discrimination (Georgia v. Russian Federation) (Preliminary Objections)   p. 77
Armed Activities on the Territory of the Congo (DRC v. Uganda)   p. 15, 29, 30, 44, 45, 55, 66, 76, 103, 105, 108, 155, 174, 224
Barcelona Traction, Light and Power Company, Limited (Second Phase Judgment)   p. 50, 84, 85
Constitution of the Maritime Safety Committee of the Inter-Governmental Maritime Consultative Organization, Advisory Opinion   p. 77
Continental Shelf (Tunisia v. Libyan Arab Jamahiriya)   p. 77
Corfu Channel Case (UK v. Albania)   p. 106
East Timor (Portugal v. Australia)   p. 12, 50, 85
Fisheries Jurisdiction (Spain v. Canada)   p. 77
Jurisdictional Immunities of the State (Germany v. Italy: Greece intervening)   p. 75, 116

Legal Consequences for States of the Continued Presence of South Africa in Namibia notwithstanding Security Council Resolution 276 (1970), Advisory Opinion   p. 10, 48, 49, 123, 150, 174

Legal Consequences of the Construction of a Wall in the Occupied Palestinian Territory, Advisory opinion   p. 2, 8, 11, 29, 43, 44, 45, 49, 50, 51, 56, 65, 68–70, 73, 76, 85, 93, 100, 103, 105, 109, 111, 112, 114, 115, 117, 132, 133, 150, 170, 216, 224, 260

Legality of the Use or Threat of Nuclear Weapons, Advisory Opinion   p. 66, 72, 73, 78, 79, 116, 150, 263

Military and Paramilitary Activities in and against Nicaragua (Nicaragua v. USA)   p. 74, 89, 102, 103, 106, 112, 119, 150, 212, 213, 217, 225

Obligation to Prosecute or Extradite (Belgium v. Senegal)   p. 84

Oil Platforms (Islamic Republic of Iran v. USA)   p. 89, 106, 120

Pulp Mills on the River Uruguay (Argentina v. Uruguay)   p. 106

Right of Passage over Indian Territory (Portugal v. India)   p. 74, 77

Western Sahara, Advisory Opinion   p. 13, 26

2. Permanent Court of International Justice

Legal Status of Eastern Greenland   p. 24

Lighthouses Cases between France and Greece   p. 40

The Case of SS Lotus (France v. Turkey)   p. 86, 87, 187

The Mavrommatis Palestine Concessions (Greece v. Great Britain) (Objection to the Jurisdiction of the Court)   p. 26

Treaty of Neuilly, Article 179, Annex, Paragraph 4 (Interpretation)   p. 127

3. International Tribunal for the Law of the Sea

Responsibilities and Obligations of States Sponsoring Persons and Entities with Respect to Activities in the Area, Advisory Opinion   p. 172

4. World Trade Organization Dispute Settlement Body

European Communities – Regime for the Importation, Sale and Distribution of Bananas, WT/DS27/R/USA   p. 75

Indonesia – Certain Measures Affecting the Automobile Industry, WT/DS54/R, WT/DS55/R, WT/DS59/R, WT/DS64/R   p. 75

Japan: Alcoholic Beverages II, WT/DS8/15 WT/DS10/15 WT/DS11/13   p. 53

5. Ethiopia-Eritrea Claims Commissions

Partial Award: Central Front – Eritrea's Claims 2, 4, 6, 7, 8, and 22   p. 15, 35, 174
Partial Award: Central Front – Ethiopia's Claim 2   p. 15
Partial Award: *Jus ad bellum* – Ethiopia's Claims 1–8   p. 15
Partial Award: Western and Eastern Fronts – Ethiopia's Claims 1 & 3   p. 15
Partial Award: Western Front, Aerial Bombardment and Related Claims – Eritrea's Claims 1, 3, 5, 9–13, 14, 21, 25, & 26   p. 15, 35

6. International Criminal Court

Gombo, Prosecutor v., ICC-01/05-01/08-3343, Judgment   p. 61, 211
Gombo, Prosecutor v., ICC-01/05-01/08, Decision Pursuant to Article 61(7)(a) and (b) of the Rome Statute on the Charges   p. 222
Katanga, Prosecutor v., ICC-01/04-01/07-3436, Trial Chamber, Judgment pursuant to Article 74 of the Statute   p. 15, 35, 61, 198, 211, 225, 229
Katanga, Prosecutor v., ICC-01/04-01/07-717, Pre-Trial Chamber I, Decision on the confirmation of charges   p. 15, 202, 225
Lubanga, Prosecutor v., ICC-01/04-01/06-803, Pre-Trial Chamber I, Decision on Confirmation of Charges   p. 15, 202, 211, 225
Lubanga, Prosecutor v., ICC-01/04-01/06, Trial Chamber, Judgment pursuant to Article 74 of the Statute   p. 15, 198, 211, 225, 229

7. International Criminal Tribunal for the Former Yugoslavia

Aleksovski, Prosecutor v., IT-95-14/1-A, Appeals Chamber   p. 211
Blaskic, Prosecutor v., IT-95-14-T   p. 30, 56
Delalić et al., Prosecutor v., IT-96-21-A, Appeals Chamber   p. 211
Delalić et al., Prosecutor v., IT-96-21-T, Judgment   p. 61
Kordić and Čerkez, Prosecutor v., IT-94-1-A   p. 211
Kunarac et al., Prosecutor v., IT-96-23-T&IT-96-23/1-T, Trial Chamber, Judgment   p. 64
Kupreškić, Prosecutor v., IT-95-16-T   p. 140
Martić, Prosecutor v., IT-95-11-R61   p. 141
Mladić, Prosecutor v., IT-09-92-T   p. 211
Naletilić and Martinović, Prosecutor v., IT-98-34-T, Trial Chamber Judgment   p. 15, 28, 30, 36, 37, 39, 55, 56, 199, 201
Prlić et al., Prosecutor v., IT-04-74A, Appeals Chamber   p. 15, 30, 35, 36, 201, 202

Tadić, Prosecutor v., IT-94-1-A, Appeals Chamber   p. 210, 211, 217, 225
Tadić, Prosecutor v., IT-94-1-T, Opinion and Judgment (Trial Chamber)   p. 30, 75, 234
Tadić, Prosecutor v., IT-94-1, Decision on the Defence Motion for Interlocutory Appeal on Jurisdiction   p. 128, 131, 222, 234, 237

8. Other International Criminal Courts and Tribunals

International Criminal Tribunal for Rwanda, Musema, Prosecutor v., ICTR-96-13-A, Trial's Chamber Judgment and Sentence   p. 222
International Military Tribunal (Nuremberg), Goering et al., Prosecutor v.,   p. 24, 177
International Military Tribunal (Tokyio), Hirota, Prosecutor v.,   p. 43
Special Court for Sierra Leone, Norman et al, Prosecutor v., SCSL-04-14-T, Decision on Motion of Acquittal,   p. 61
Special Court for Sierra Leone, Sesay et al., Prosecutor v., SCSL-04-15-T, Trial Judgment   p. 33, 34

9. European Court of Human Rights

Al-Jedda v. the UK (Application no. 27021/08)   p. 67, 69, 75, 184
Al-Saadoon and Mufdhi v. the UK (Application no. 61498/08)   p. 17, 67, 69
Al-Skeini et al. v. the UK (Application no. 55721/07)   p. 17, 45, 67, 68, 69, 198, 247, 249, 253
Armani Da Silva v. UK (Application no. 5878/08)   p. 246
Bankovič v. Belgium (Application no. 52207/99)   p. 68, 264
Catan et al. v. Moldova and Russia (Application nos 43370/04, 8252/05 and 18454/06)   p. 17
Chiragov et al. v. Armenia (Application no. 13216/05)   p. 15, 37, 67
Ergi v. Turkey (Application no. 40/1993/435/514)   p. 264
Finogenov et al. v. Russia (Application nos 18299/03 and 27311/03)   p. 244
Georgia v. Russia (Application no. 13255/07)   p. 67
Hassan v. the UK (Application no. 29750/09)   p. 67, 68, 78
Ilaşcu et al. v. Moldova and Russia (Application no. 48787/99)   p. 17, 69
Isayeva et al. v. Russia (Applications no. 57947/00, 57948/00, 57949/00)   p. 265
Isayeva v. Russia (Application no. 57950/00)   p. 265
Issa v. Turkey (Application no. 31821/96)   p. 69
Jaloud v. the Netherlands (Application no. 47708/08)   p. 67
Kaya v. Turkey, (Application no. 22535/93)   p. 246

Table of Cases   xxv

Khamzayev et al. *v.* Russia (Application no. 1503/02)   p. 264
Loizidou *v.* Turkey (Application no. 15318/89)   p. 12, 56, 67
Loizidou *v.* Turkey (Preliminary Objections) (Application no. 15318/89)   p. 68, 69
McCann *v.* UK (Application no. 18984/91)   p. 244, 246
Medvedyev et al. *v.* France (Application no. 3394/03)   p. 69
Ocalan *v.* Turkey (Application no. 46221/99)   p. 69
Sargsyan *v.* Azerbaijan (Application no. 40167/06)   p. 15, 37, 67
Solomou et al. *v.* Turkey (Application no. 36832/97)   p. 250
Tagayeva et al. *v.* Russia (Application no. 26562/07 and others)   p. 246
Varnava et al. *v.* Turkey (Application nos 16064/90, 16065/90, 16066/90, 16068/90, 16069/90, 16070/90, 16071/90, 16072/90 and 16073/90)   p. 67, 78, 264

10. *Inter-American Court of Human Rights*

Bámaca-Velásquez *v.* Guatemala   p. 71, 79
Inter-state Petition IP-02 Aisalla Molina (Ecuador *v.* Colombia) (Admissibility)   p. 79
Las Palmeras *v.* Colombia (Preliminary Objections)   p. 67, 71
Mapiripán Massacre *v.* Colombia   p. 67, 71, 79
Montero-Aranguren et al. *v.* Venezuela (Preliminary Objection, Merits, Reparations, and Costs)   p. 244
Santo Domingo Massacre *v.* Colombia   p. 67, 79
Velásquez Rodríguez *v.* Honduras (Merits)   p. 245
Zambrano Vélez et al. *v.* Ecuador (Merits, Reparations, and Costs)   p. 244

11. *Inter-American Commission on Human Rights*

Abella *v.* Argentina   p. 67, 70, 71, 79
Contreras et al. *v.* El Salvador (Admissibility)   p. 79
Decision on Request for Precautionary Measures (Detainees at Guatanamo Bay, Cuba   p. 67
Ribón Avila *v.* Colombia   p. 67
Salas et al. *v.* United States   p. 67

12. *African Commission on Human and Peoples' Rights*

Commission Nationale des Droits de l'Homme et des Libertés *v.* Chad   p. 246

Democratic Republic of Congo v. Burundi, Rwanda, Uganda   p. 67, 80
Zimbabwe NGO Human Rights Forum v. Zimbabwe   p. 246

13. Human Rights Committee

Domínguez v. Paraguay   p. 243
Suárez de Guerrero v. Colombia   p. 243
Umateliev v. Kyrgyzstan   p. 243

14. European Court of Justice

A et al. (C-158/14)   p. 180, 181
Council v. Front Polisario (C-104/16 P)   p. 13

15. Other Arbitral Tribunals

Affaire Chevreau (France v. Royaume-Uni)   p. 170
Affaire de la Dette Publique Ottomane (Bulgaria, Iraq, Palestine, Transjordan, Greece, Italy, and Turkey)   p. 40, 48
Affaire Relative à l'Or de la Banque Nationale d'Albanie (USA, France, Italy, and UK)   p. 50
Dispute between Argentina and Chile concerning the Beagle Channel   p. 77
German-Belgian Mixed Arbitral Tribunal, Milaire v. État Allemand   p. 175
Iran-United States Claims Tribunal, INA Corporation v. Island of Palmas (Netherlands, USA)   p. 77
Southern Bluefin Tuna (New Zealand-Japan, Australia-Japan)   p. 77

B. NATIONAL COURTS AND TRIBUNALS

Australia, High Court, Mabo v. Queensland No. 2   p. 24, 26
Belgium, Court of Appeal of Liège, Bourseaux v. Krantz   p. 48
Canada, Supreme Court, R v. Finta   p. 30
Denmark, Eastern Provincial Court, In re Hoffmann   p. 144
East Timor, Court of Appeal, Prosecutor General v. Dos Santos   p. 12
France, Court of Appeal of Paris, Clement v. Agent Judiciaire du Trésor Publi   p. 30
France, Military Court, Strasbourg, In re Wagner et al.   p. 177

Germany, British Zone of Control, Control Commission Court of Criminal Appeal, Prosecutor General *v.* Grahame   p. 24, 57
Greece, Court of Appeal of Thrace, L *v.* N   p. 48
Greece, Court of First Instance of Corfu, V *v.* O   p. 170
Greece, Criminal Court of Heraklion, In re G   p. 30
India, Supreme Court, Rev Mons Sebastiao Francisco Xavier dos Remedios Monteiro *v.* The State of Goa   p. 39
Israel, A and B *v.* State of Israel (CrimA 6659/06, CrimA 1757/07, Crim A 8228/07 and Crim A 3261/08)   p. 223
Israel, Abu Aita et al. *v.* Regional Commander of the Judea and Samaria Area et al. (HCJ 69/81)   p. 172
Israel, Ahmed et al. *v.* Prime Minister et al. (HCJ 9132/07)   p. 37
Israel, Ajuri et al. *v.* IDF Commander et al. (HCJ 7015/02)   p. 11, 52
Israel, Al-Bassiouni *v.* Prime Minister (HCJ 9132/07)   p. 94, 223
Israel, Almadani *v.* Minister of Defence (HCJ 3451/02)   p. 92
Israel, Barake *v.* Minister of Defence (HCJ 3114/02, 3115/02, 3116/02)   p. 202
Israel, Beit Sourik Village Council *v.* The Government of Israel (HCJ 2056/04)   p. 11, 55, 57, 132, 175, 202, 260, 261
Israel, Bethlehem Municipality *v.* The State of Israel (HCJ 1890/03)   p. 57
Israel, Gaza Coast Local Council *v.* The Knesset (HCJ 1661/05)   p. 11
Israel, Adalah *v.* GOC Central Command, IDF (HCJ 3799/02)   p. 84
Israel, Hess et al. *v.* Commander of the IDF Forces in the West Bank (HCJ 10356/02)   p. 57
Israel, Jam'iat Iscan Al-Ma'almoun *v.* IDF Commander (HCJ 393/82)   p. 2, 11, 52, 57, 173
Israel, Mara'abe *v.* The Prime Minister of Israel (HCJ 7957/04)   p. 57, 100, 132, 202
Israel, Marab et al. *v.* IDF Commander (HCJ 3239/02)   p. 179
Israel, Military Court of Appeals, Military Prosecutor *v.* Sergent Elor Azaria   p. 248
Israel, Military Court of the Central District, Military Prosecutor *v.* Sergent Elor Azaria   p. 248
Israel, Military Court Sitting in Ramallah, Military Prosecutor *v.* Omar Mahmud Kassem et al.   p. 145, 208, 209, 212
Israel, Physicians for Human Rights et al. *v.* IDF Commander of Gaza (HCJ 4764/04)   p. 140
Israel, Physicians for Human Rights *v.* Prime Minister (HCJ 201/09)   p. 223
Israel, Public Committee against Torture in Israel *v.* Israel (HCJ 769/02) ('Targeted Killings case')   p. 8, 77, 146, 195, 202, 223, 255, 257, 266, 267

Israel, Qawasmeh et al. *v.* IDF Commander et al. (HCJ 5290/14, 5295/14 and 5300/14)   p. 183
Israel, The Christian Society for the Holy Places *v.* Minister of Defence et al. (HCJ 337/71)   p. 52
Israel, Tsemel et al. *v.* Minister of Defence et al. (HCJ 102/82)   p. 35
Italy, Court of Appeal, Turin, Baffico *v.* Calleri   p. 144
Italy, Court of Cassation, Procuratore Generale della Repubblica *v.* Daki, Bouyahia e Toumi   p. 180
Italy, Court of Cassation, In re Scarpato   p. 30
Italy, Court of First Instance of Rome, Society Italiana per il Gas *v.* Mirabella   p. 43
Italy, Supreme Military Tribunal, In re Keppler   p. 138, 212
Italy, Supreme Military Tribunal, In re Lepore   p. 38
Malaysia, Elli anak Masing *v.* The King   p. 48
Netherlands, Council for the Restoration of Legal Rights, D'Escury *v.* Levensverzekerings-Maatschappij Utrecht Ltd   p. 141
Netherlands, Special Court of Cassation, In re Flesche   p. 24
Netherlands, Special Court of Cassation, In re Hoffmann   p. 190
Netherlands, Special Court of Cassation, In re Policeman Voleva   p. 190
Netherlands, Special Court of Cassation, In re Van Kampen   p. 190
Netherlands, Special Court of Cassation, In re Vogt   p. 182
Netherlands, Special Court, The Hague, In re Rauter   p. 140, 144, 147
Netherlands, Special Criminal Court, Arnhem, In re Heinemann   p. 138, 182
Netherlands, Special Criminal Court, The Hague, In re Contractor Work   p. 139, 175
Netherlands, Special Criminal Court, The Hague, In re van Huis   p. 139, 175
Norway, Eidsivating Lagmannsrett (Court of Appeal), In re Bruns   p. 144
Poland, Voivodship Court for the Voivodship of Warsaw, In re Koch   p. 177
Russia, Constitutional Court, Decision no. 6-P   p. 56
South Africa, Supreme Court, S *v.* Mogoerane et al. (TPD)   p. 219
South Africa, Supreme Court, S *v.* Sagarius en andere   p. 219
UK, British Military Court, Hamburg, In re Lewinski   p. 137
UK, British Military Court, Hamburg, In re Tesch et al. (Zyklon B case)   p. 177
UK, British Military Court, In re Sandrock et al.   p. 182
UK, British Military Court, Luneburg, In re Kramer et al.   p. 177
UK, Court of Appeal, Hesperides Hotels *v.* Aegean Turkish Holidays   p. 12

Table of Cases

UK, High Court of Justice, Amin v. Brown, Decision on Preliminary Question   p. 133

UK, High Court of Justice, Queen's Bench Division, Divisional Court, Al Skeini et al. v. Secretary of State for Defence   p. 190, 191

UK, House of Lords, Kuwait Airways Corp v. Iraq Airways Co (Nos 4 & 5)   p. 14

USA, Court of Appeals 9th Circuit, Cobb v. United States   p. 48

USA, District Court D Utah, Central Division, Aboitiz & Co v. Price   p. 170

USA, District of Columbia, Qualls et al. v. Rumsfeld et al., Memorandum and Order denying 5 Motion for Preliminary Injunction   p. 133

USA, Military Tribunal Nuremberg, In re Krupp   p. 48

USA, Military Tribunal, In re Ohlendorf et al.   p. 203

USA, Military Tribunal, Nuremberg, Willelm List et al. (Hostages case)   p. 29, 35, 38, 57, 169, 177, 178, 201, 204

USA, Supreme Court, American Insurance Company v. Canter   p. 23

USA, Supreme Court, Fleming v. Page   p. 22

USA, Supreme Court, Ford v. Surget   p. 33

USA, Supreme Court, Hamdan v. Rumsfeld   p. 215

USA, Supreme Court, Keely v. Sanders   p. 36

USA, Supreme Court, Ochoa v. Hernandez y Morales   p. 169

USA, Supreme Court, US v. Rice   p. 22

USA, Supreme Court, Zivotofsky v. Kerry   p. 56

1

Scope of the Book

Our houses are packed with Prussians to feed ... They give us nothing much to complain of, outside of the bitter lament of having to submit to foreigners.[1]

1.1. INTRODUCTION TO THE USE OF ARMED FORCE IN OCCUPIED TERRITORY

In 2011, the ICRC attempted to attract attention to the issue of the use of armed force in occupied territories, affirming that '[a]nother challenge raised by recent examples of occupation is the identification of the legal framework governing the use of force by an occupying power ... [T]here is a need to clarify how the rules governing law enforcement and those regulating the conduct of hostilities interact in practice in the context of an occupation'.[2] The purpose of this book is to clarify the legal framework regarding the use of armed force in occupied territory. Such a legal analysis appears even more necessary now since, in December 2017, during the very weeks in which this book has been finalised, violence has resumed once again in the OPT[3] as a response to the US decision to recognise Jerusalem as the Israeli capital.[4]

---

[1] Stéphane Audoin-Rouzeau, *1870: la France dans la Guerre* (Armand Colin 1989) 262, quoted by Karma Nabulsi, *Traditions of War: Occupation, Resistance and the Law* (Oxford University Press 1999) 37.

[2] ICRC, *International Humanitarian Law and the Challenges of Contemporary Armed Conflicts*, report presented at the 31st International Conference of the Red Cross and Red Crescent, Geneva, 2011, Doc 31IC/11/5.1.2, 28–9.

[3] See Nidal al-Mughrabi, 'Israeli Troops Kill Three Palestinians, Wound Scores in Protests over Jerusalem', *Reuters* (15 December 2017), available at uk.reuters.com/article/uk-israel-palestinians/israeli-troops-kill-three-palestinians-wound-scores-in-protests-over-jerusalem-idUKKBN1E91TQ

[4] See 'President Donald J. Trump's Proclamation on Jerusalem as the Capital of the State of Israel', 6 December 2017, www.whitehouse.gov/briefings-statements/president-donald-j-trumps-proclamation-jerusalem-capital-state-israel/

In occupied territories, occupying powers frequently employ armed force in order to maintain order or to fight against forces opposing the occupation. Similarly, armed groups – both those affiliated to the ousted sovereign and those not – may attempt to bring the occupation to an end by resorting to armed activities. This book explores the international law framework pertaining to the use of armed force in occupied territories on the basis of a thorough analysis of state practice and *opinio juris*, treaty provisions, international and domestic case law, and other relevant sources.

From a *jus ad bellum* perspective, the fact that a situation of occupation is normally created after an exercise of armed force by one or more states in the process of invading and taking control over another territory[5] renders obvious the link between the use of armed force and occupation. For instance, the Israeli occupation of the OPT commenced with the Israeli invasion of those territories during the international armed conflict with Egypt, Jordan, and Syria – commonly referred to as the 'Six-Day War'.[6] Similarly, the occupation of Iraq in 2003 by an US-led coalition was triggered by the so-called operation Iraqi Freedom.[7] Accordingly, the use of armed force is often the precursor for an occupation.[8] Moreover, the GA's definition of aggression,[9] the definition of the crime of aggression embodied in the ICC Statute,[10] and international case law,[11] coupled with state practice,[12] all demonstrate that the occupation of

---

[5] This is the most widely accepted definition of occupation. The next chapter will clarify further this definition.

[6] See ICJ, *Legal Consequences of the Construction of a Wall in the Occupied Palestinian Territory*, Advisory opinion, 9 July 2004, para. 73; HCJ 393/82 *Jam'iat Iscan Al-Ma'almoun v. IDF Commander*, 37(4) PD 785, 792, para. 10, unofficial English translation available at www.hamoked.org/items/160_eng.pdf

[7] See Letter dated 8 May 2003 from the Permanent Representatives of the United Kingdom of Great Britain and Northern Ireland and the United States of America to the United Nations addressed to the President of the Security Council, 8 May 2003; UNSC Res. 1483 (2003), 22 May 2003, preambular para. 13.

[8] For more on invasion and occupation, see *infra*, Section 2.3.2.

[9] See UNGA Res. 3314 (XXIX), 14 December 1974, Annex: Definition of Aggression, Art. 3: 'Military occupation, however temporary resulting from [an] invasion or attack' is considered to be an act of aggression. See also UNSC Res. 674 (1990), 29 October 1990, preambular, which defines the invasion and occupation of Kuwait as a direct threat to international peace and security.

[10] See ICC Statute, 2187 *UNTS* 90, amendments in A-38544 *UNTS*, Art. 8 bis(2)(a), which also define the crime of aggression by quoting the aforementioned passage of UNGA Res. 3314 (XXIX).

[11] See EECC, *Partial Award: Jus Ad Bellum – Ethiopia's Claim 1–8* (19 December 2005) 26 RIIA, 457, 467, para. 16 ('Eritrea violated Article 2, paragraph 4, of the Charter of the United Nations by resorting to armed force to attack and occupy Badme').

[12] See Italian Stato Maggiore della Difesa, Manuale di diritto umanitario (SMD-SG-014 1991) ('Italian Military Manual') section 21.1.

1.1. Introduction to the Use of Armed Force in Occupied Territory 3

a territory is constantly considered to be a violation of the prohibition of the use of force embodied in Article 2(4) UN Charter.

However, the use of armed force may be explored also in the context of an existing occupation. Indeed, in times of occupation, it happens quite frequently that the occupying powers or armed groups with or without allegiance to the ousted sovereign resort to armed force. For instance, in recent times, hostilities between Palestinian armed groups and Israel in the Gaza Strip and the West Bank have been commonplace.[13] Similarly, the CPA, the body that administered occupied Iraq between 2003 and 2004, had to use armed force in order to maintain order and address insurgency. If one assumes that these territories are or were under occupation, as it is commonly held, there is room to wonder which are the rules governing these and other episodes in which armed force was employed after the occupation had already been established.

This book explores the use of armed force in occupied territory through the interplay of mainly three branches of international law: *jus ad bellum*, international humanitarian law,[14] and international human rights law. After

---

[13] The most recent and large-scale events are the so-called operations Cast Lead (December 2008–January 2009), Pillar of Clouds (November 2012), and Protective Edge (June–July 2014) against the Gaza Strip. Facts and figures about these conflicts differ significantly on the basis of the sources employed. For the official Israeli positions, see Israel, *The Operation in Gaza 27 December 2008 –18 January 2009: Factual and Legal Aspects* (July 2009), available at www .mfa.gov.il/MFA_Graphics/MFA%20Gallery/Documents/GazaOperation%20w%20Links .pdf; IDF, Military Advocate General's Corps, Operation 'Pillar of Defense' (14–21 November 2012), available at www.law.idf.il/sip_storage/FILES/0/1350.pdf; Israel, *The 2014 Gaza Conflict 7 July–26 August 2014: Factual and Legal Aspects* (May 2015), available at www.mfa.gov.il/ ProtectiveEdge/Documents/2014GazaConflictFullReport.pdf. For some non-governmental Palestinian views, see Al-Haq, *'Operation Cast Lead': A Statistical Analysis* (August 2009), available at www.alhaq.org/attachments/article/252/gaza-operation-cast-Lead-statistical-analysis%20 .pdf; Al-Haq, *Voices From the Gaza Strip: A Year After Operation 'Pillar of Defense'* (21 November 2013), available at www.alhaq.org/documentation/weekly-focuses/757-voices-from-the-gaza-strip-a-year-after-operation-pillar-of-defense; Al-Haq, *Divide and Conquer: A Legal Analysis of Israel's Military Offensive against the Gaza Strip* (2015), available at www.alhaq.org/publications /DIVIDE.AND.CONQUER.pdf. The UN HRC dispatched a number of fact-finding missions, which reported on these three conflicts, emphasising both factual and legal aspects: *Human Rights in Palestine and Other Occupied Arab Territories: Report of the United Nations Fact-Finding Mission on the Gaza Conflict*, A/HRC/12/48, 25 September 2009 ('Goldstone Report'); Report of the United Nations High Commissioner for Human Rights on the Implementation of Human Rights Council Resolutions S-9/1 and S-12/1 – Addendum: Concerns Related to Adherence to International Human Rights and International Humanitarian Law in the Context of the Escalation Between the State of Israel, the De Facto Authorities in Gaza and Palestinian Armed Groups in Gaza that Occurred from 14 to 21 November 2012, A/HRC/22/35/Add.1, 4 July 2013; Report of the Detailed Findings of the Commission of Inquiry on the 2014 Gaza Conflict, A/HRC/29/CRP.4, 24 June 2015 ('2014 Gaza Report').

[14] In this work, the expressions 'international humanitarian law', '*jus in bello*', and 'law of armed conflict' are employed interchangeably as synonyms. On this terminology, see Robert Kolb, 'Human Rights and Humanitarian Law' in *MPEPIL online* (2013) para. 1.

an overview of the law of occupation and the inherent hostile character of situations of occupation (Chapter 2), this book assesses the relevance of *jus ad bellum* with regard to the use of armed force in occupied territory (Chapter 3), and the legitimacy of armed resistance against the occupying power (Chapter 4). This book goes on to analyse the use of armed force under the law of occupation: after having described the interplay of law enforcement and conduct of hostilities in occupied territory (Chapter 5), the book addresses the regulation of the use of armed force in light of the right to life in occupied territory (Chapter 6). At the end, the book provides some general conclusions (Chapter 7).

1.2. AN OVERVIEW ON INTERNATIONAL SCHOLARSHIP REGARDING THE USE OF ARMED FORCE IN TIMES OF OCCUPATION

Although the broader topic of the law of occupation has attracted significant attention in international law scholarship, particularly in the aftermath of occupations around the world that have made this issue increasingly relevant, post-WWII international scholarship has overlooked the issue of the regulation of the use of armed force in occupied territories for many years. Only in the last decade had some scholarship on this specific topic appeared. However, a comprehensive study on the use of armed force in occupied territory has not been published yet.

It is possible to divide contributions of international scholarship on the law of occupation into different phases, which follow the developments of the existing law and the main challenges in state practice. Although such a partition is inevitably imprecise, it serves as a helpful framework for the existing scholarship on occupation. The first phase of international scholarship on occupation started during the nineteenth century, when a number of classical authors began to outline the main features of the law of occupation,[15] contributing to the development of this branch of law and to its first international codification in 1899 and 1907.[16] This phase lasted until the end of WWII – even if, between the two world wars, many scholars appeared particularly concerned with providing legal justification for the acts of some occupying powers,[17] or to

---

[15] See, e.g., August W. Heffter, *Das Europäische Völkerrecht der Gegenwart* (Schroeder 1844), French translation by Jules Bergson, *Le droit international de l'Europe* (Cotillon 1873) 304–5; Pasquale Fiore, *Trattato di diritto internazionale pubblico* vol. III (3rd edn, Unione Tipografica Editrice 1891) 258–87; Antoine Pillet, *Les lois actuelles de guerre* (Rousseau 1898) 237–72.

[16] On the origin and evolution of the law of occupation, see *infra*, Section 2.2.

[17] This is the case with several Italian authors who tried to justify the Italian annexation of Ethiopia and Albania between WWI and WWII (e.g., Riccardo Monaco, 'Le recenti annessioni

1.2. Overview on International Scholarship

assess the legality of some specific occupations.[18] In this phase, some authors focused on the use of armed force in the occupied territory, in particular with reference to the legality of armed resistance against the occupying power.[19] However, after the end of this phase, academic interest in the use of armed force in occupied territory progressively dwindled.[20]

A second phase started after WWII, when a renewed interest in the law of occupation brought a number of authors to write interesting analyses of the law of occupation in light of the most recent practice; these pieces of scholarship are still very important in order to understand the law of occupation.[21] Despite their significance, general works on the occupation in this

---

territoriali al Regno d'Italia e il problema del diritto interlocale' (1941) 2 *Stato e diritto* 188, 190–2; Manlio Udina, 'Lo smembramento della Jugoslavia' (1941) 5 *Diritto internazionale* 3, 6–13). For an accurate analysis of these positions, see Giulio Bartolini, 'The Impact of Fascism on the Italian Doctrine of International Law' (2012) 14 *Journal of History of International Law* 237, 255 and 271–2.

[18] See, e.g., Ernst H. Feilchenfeld, *The International Economy Law of Belligerent Occupation* (Carnegie Endowment for International Peace 1942); Ernst Fraenkel, *Military Occupation and the Rule of Law: Occupational Government in the Rhineland 1918–1923* (Oxford University Press 1944).

[19] See, e.g., Platon De Waxel, *L'armée d'invasion et la population* (Kruger 1874); Bartholomew Sherston Baker, *Halleck's International Law* vol. II (C. K. Paul & Co. 1878) 444–79; Lassa Oppenheim, 'The Legal Relations between an Occupying Power and the Inhabitants' (1907) 37 LQR 363, and 'On War Treason' (1917) 33 LQR 266; Charles De Visscher, 'L'occupation de guerre' (1918) 34 LQR 72.

[20] On the decline of scholarly attention to this topic, see Frédéric Mégret, 'Grandeur et déclin de l'idée de résistance à l'occupation: réflexions à propos de la légitimité des "insurgés"' (2008) 41 RBDI 382.

[21] Some of these works are specifically devoted to the law of occupation. See Francesco Capotorti, *L'occupazione nel diritto di guerra* (Jovene 1949); Doris Appel Graber, *The Development of the Law of Belligerent Occupation 1863–1914: A Historical Survey* (Columbia University Press 1949); Alessandro Migliazza, *L'occupazione bellica* (Giuffrè 1949); Gerhard von Glahn, *The Occupation of Enemy Territory: A Commentary on the Law and Practice of Belligerent Occupation* (University of Minnesota Press 1957); Giorgio Cansacchi, 'Occupazione bellica' in *Novissimo Digesto Italiano* vol. XI (UTET 1965) 744. See also, from a wider geopolitical perspective, Carl Schmitt, *Der Nomos der Erde im Völkerrecht des Jus Publicum Europaeum* (Duncker & Humblot 1950), English translation by G. L. Ulmen, *The Nomos of the Earth* (Telos Press 2006). Extensive analyses of the law of occupation are present in the most important treatises such as Hersh Lauterpacht, *Oppenheim's International Law. A Treatise*, vol. II: *Disputes, War and Neutrality* (7th edn, Longmans 1952) 432–56; Giorgio Balladore Pallieri, *Diritto bellico* (2nd edn, Cedam 1954) 300–41; Paul Guggenheim, *Traité de Droit international public* vol. II (Georg & Cie 1954) 460–92; Julius Stone, *Legal Controls of International Conflict* (Rinehart and Co. 1954) 651–732; Myres S. McDougal & Florentino P. Feliciano, *Law and Minimum World Public Order: The Legal Regulation of International Coercion* (Yale University Press 1961) 731–832; Angelo Piero Sereni, *Diritto internazionale, vol. IV: Conflitti internazionali* (Giuffrè 1965) 2000–37; Hans Kelsen, *Principles of International Law* (2nd edn, Holt, Rinehart and Winston 1966) 139–49; Georg Schwarzenberger, *International Law as Applied by International Courts and Tribunals* vol. II (Stevens & Sons 1968) 163–358.

phase focus on the use of armed forces in occupied territory only under the umbrella of the relation between the occupying power and the inhabitants of the occupied territory; references to the use of armed force in these works usually focus on the legality of the atrocities committed during the Nazi occupation, such as collective punishment, the taking of hostages, and retaliations against civilians.[22]

The third phase began with the Israeli occupation of the OPT in 1967 and lasted until 2003. During this period, the law of occupation was at the centre of a number of new studies, with both a general focus as well as a specific concern with particular occupations – e.g., the Israeli occupation of the OPT and the Iraqi occupation of Kuwait.[23] Notwithstanding the ongoing relevance of some of these studies to a full appreciation of the law of occupation, they generally neglected to address the issue of the use of armed forces during occupations. Although some writers touched upon this topic in relation to the so-called Palestinian intifadas in 1987 (First Intifada) and 2000 (Second Intifada), they tended to focus specifically on the boundaries of the right to fight for national self-determination[24] and on the consequences of the measures undertaken by the occupying powers for the involved individuals,[25] rather

---

[22] E.g., these aspects are addressed by Capotorti, *L'occupazione*, 114–18; Lauterpacht, *Oppenheim's International*, 448–51; Stone, *Legal Controls*, 702–4; McDougal & Feliciano, *Law*, 790–808.

[23] See, e.g., Yoram Dinstein, 'The International Law of Belligerent Occupation and Human Rights' (1978) 8 IYBR 104; Carlo Curti Gialdino, 'Occupazione bellica' in *Enciclopedia del Diritto*, vol. XXIX (Giuffrè 1979) 720; Michael Bothe, 'Occupation, Belligerent' in Rudolf Bernhardt (ed.), *Encyclopedia of Public International Law* vol. IV (North-Holland 1982) 64; Adam Roberts, 'What Is a Military Occupation?' (1984) 55 British YIL 251; Eyal Benvenisti, *The International Law of Occupation* (Princeton University Press 1993). Among the works specifically addressing the occupation of the OPT, see Allan Gerson, *Israel, the West Bank and International Law* (Frank Case 1978); Esther Cohen, *Human Rights in the Israeli-Occupied Territories, 1967–1982* (Manchester University Press 1985); Adam Roberts, 'Prolonged Military Occupation: The Israeli-Occupied Territories since 1967' (1990) 84 AJIL 44; Emma Playfair (ed.), *International Law and the Administration of Occupied Territories* (Clarendon Press 1992); David Kretzmer, *The Occupation of Justice: The Supreme Court of Israel and the Occupied Territories* (State University of New York Press 2002). On the situation of occupied Kuwait, see Walter Kälin, *Human Rights in Times of Occupation: The Case of Kuwait* (Law Books of Europe 1994).

[24] See Natalino Ronzitti, *Le guerre di liberazione nazionale e il diritto internazionale* (Pacini Editore 1974) 48–9, 125–6; Richard A. Falk & Burns H. Weston, 'The Relevance of International Law to Palestinian Rights in the West Bank and Gaza: In Legal Defense of the Intifada' (1991) 32 Harvard ILJ 129; Michael Curtis, 'International Law and the Territories' (1991) 32 Harvard ILJ 457; John Quigley, *The Case for Palestine: An International Law Perspective* (2nd edn, Duke University Press 2005) 189–205.

[25] See James A. Demotses, 'Israeli Actions in Response to the Intifada: Necessary Security Measures or Violations of International Law?' (1992) 16 *Suffolk Transnational Law Review* 92; Amy J. Koreen, 'The Palestinian Uprising of December 1987: An Examination under International Humanitarian Law' (1992) 37 *Touro Journal of Transnational Law* 197; Shane Darcy, 'Punitive

1.2. Overview on International Scholarship

than on the issue of the use of armed force within occupied territory from a broader perspective.

However, the majority of scholarship addressing the law of occupation has been published since 2003, when the US and UK occupation of Iraq inspired new interest in the law of occupation[26] – a group of rules which were previously considered by some commentators a sort of relic of another time, only applicable to the very specific case of the OPT.[27] In this last phase, even the specific topic of the use of armed force in occupied territory attracted some attention, both in specific articles[28] and in the framework of more general works.[29] There are many factors at the basis of this shift. First, in the ICJ's

---

House Demolitions, the Prohibitions of Collective Punishment, and the Supreme Court of Israel' (2003) 21 Penn State International LR 477.

[26] On the occupation of Iraq, see, e.g., Adam Roberts, 'The End of Occupation: Iraq 2004' (2005) 54 ICLQ 27; Andrea Carcano, *L'occupazione dell'Iraq nel diritto internazionale* (Giuffrè 2009); Eyal Benvenisti & Guy Keinan, 'The Occupation of Iraq: A Reassessment' (2010) 86 ILS 263; Andrea Carcano, *The Transformation of Occupied Territory in International Law* (Brill 2015). For other authoritative works on the law of occupation in general, published in this phase, see Aldo Amirante, *Occupazione Bellica* (Edizioni Scientifiche Italiane 2007); Gregory H. Fox, *Humanitarian Occupation* (Cambridge University Press 2008); Yutaka Arai-Takahashi, *The Law of Occupation: Continuity and Change of International Humanitarian Law, and Its Interaction with International Human Rights Law* (Martinus Nijhoff 2009); Yoram Dinstein, *The International Law of Belligerent Occupation* (Cambridge University Press 2009); Robert Kolb & Sylvain Vité, *Le droit de l'occupation militaire: Perspectives historiques et enjeux juridiques actuelles* (Bruylant 2009); Christine Chinkin, 'Laws of Occupation' in Neville Botha, Michèle Olivier, & Delarey van Tonder (eds.), *Multilateralism and International Law with Western Sahara as a Case Study* (Unisa Press 2010) 167; Vaious Koutroulis, *Le début et la fin de l'application du droit de l'occupation* (Pedone 2010); Alessandra Annoni, *L'occupazione 'ostile' nel diritto internazionale contemporaneo* (Giappichelli 2012); Eyal Benvenisti, *The International Law of Occupation* (2nd edn, Oxford University Press 2012); Tristan Ferraro (ed.), *Expert Meeting: Occupation and Other Forms of Administration of Foreign Territory* (ICRC 2012); Philip Spoerri, 'The Law of Occupation' in Andrew Clapham & Paola Gaeta (eds.), *The Oxford Handbook of International Law in Armed Conflict* (Oxford University Press 2014) 182; Marco Sassòli, 'Concept and the Beginning of Occupation' in Andrew Clapham, Paola Gaeta, & Marco Sassòli (eds.), *The 1949 Geneva Conventions: A Commentary* (Oxford University Press 2015) 1390; Hanne Cuyckens, *Revisiting the Law of Occupation* (Brill 2017); Aeyal M. Gross, *The Writing on the Wall: Rethinking the International Law of Occupation* (Cambridge University Press 2017).

[27] See Davis P. Goodman, 'The Need of Fundamental Change in the Law of Occupation' (1985) 37 Stanford LR 1573.

[28] This topic has been explored from a general perspective primarily by Kenneth Watkin, who authored the 'Maintaining Law and Order during Occupation: Breaking the Normative Chains' (2008) 41 IsLR 175, and 'Use of Force during Occupation: Law Enforcement and Conduct of Hostilities' (2012) 94 IRRC 267. See, also, Iris Canor, 'When *Jus ad Bellum* Meets *Jus in Bello*: The Occupier's Right of Self-Defence against Terrorism Stemming from Occupied Territories' (2006) 19 LJIL 129; Mégret, 'Grandeur'.

[29] See Arai-Takahashi, *The Law*, 297–325; Dinstein, *The International Law*, 89–107; Kolb & Vité, *Le droit*, 345–66; Annoni, *L'occupazione*, 224–39; Ferraro, *Expert Meeting*, 109–19; Spoerri, 'The Law', 200–5.

Wall opinion in 2004, the Court addressed the issue of whether the occupying power may invoke *jus ad bellum* rules, and, in particular, self-defence, in response to armed attacks from within the occupied territory.[30] Second, in 2006, the Supreme Court of Israel delivered an important judgment on extrajudicial killings,[31] which attracted a lot of attention to the issue of the extrajudicial use of lethal force both within and outside of occupied territories (so-called targeted killings).[32] Third, as already demonstrated by the Second Palestinian Intifada and then confirmed by the aforementioned three Gaza military operations in 2009 (operation Cast Lead), 2012 (operation Pillar of Clouds), and 2014 (operation Protective Edge),[33] the OPT is not pacified at all, but rather, both Israel and the Palestinians continue to engage in armed activities. Finally, the occupation of Iraq functioned as a bench test for strategies

---

[30] *Wall* opinion, paras. 138–42. For a preliminary overview of the issues raised by the Court regarding this question, see Ruth Wedgwood, 'The ICJ Advisory Opinion on the Israeli Security Fence and the Limits of Self-Defense' (2005) 99 AJIL 52; Sean D. Murphy, 'Self-Defense and the Israeli *Wall* Advisory Opinion: An *Ipse Dixit* from the ICJ?' (2005) 99 AJIL 62; Iain Scobbie, 'Words My Mother Never Taught Me: "In Defense of the International Court"' (2005) 99 AJIL 76; Olivier Corten, 'L'applicabilité problématique du droit de légitime défense au sens de l'article 51 de la Charte des Nations Unies aux relatons entre la Palestine et Israël' (2012) 45 RBDI 67.

[31] HCJ 769/02 *Public Committee against Torture in Israel v. Israel*, unofficial English translation in (2007) 46 ILM 375 (*'Targeted Killings* case'). For some interesting remarks, see Giulio Bartolini, 'Le eliminazioni mirate di appartenenti a gruppi terroristici al vaglio della Corte suprema d'Israele' (2007) 1 DUDI 623; Paolo Benvenuti, 'Judicial Review nella guerra al terrorismo nella decisione della Corte suprema israeliana sui targeted killings' (2007) 19 *Diritto pubblico comparato ed europeo* XIII; Antonio Cassese, 'On Some Merits of the Israeli Judgment on Targeted Killings' (2007) 5 JICJ 339; Marko Milanovic, 'Lessons for Human Rights and Humanitarian Law in the War on Terror: Comparing *Hamdan* and the Israeli *Targeted Killings* Case' (2007) 89 IRRC 373.

[32] See, e.g., Nils Melzer, *Targeted Killings in International Law* (Cambridge University Press 2008); Giulio Bartolini, 'I *targeted killings* di appartenenti a gruppi terroristici tra diritto internazionale umanitario e diritti umani' in Pietro Gargiulo & Maria Chiara Vitucci (eds.), *La tutela dei diritti umani nella lotta e nella guerra al terrorismo* (Editoriale Scientifica 2009) 273; Claire Finkelstein, Jens David Ohlin, & Andrew Altman (eds.), *Targeted Killings: Law and Morality in an Asymmetrical World* (Oxford University Press 2012); Roland Otto, *Targeted Killings and International Law* (Springer 2012).

[33] The legality of these operations has been analysed extensively by legal scholarship. Further references will be provided where specifically relevant. Just to mention some works at this stage, see Gabriella Venturini, 'L'operazione militare di Israele contro Gaza e il diritto internazionale umanitario' (2009) 3 DUDI 309; Luisa Vierucci, 'Sul principio di proporzionalità a Gaza, ovvero quando il fine non giustifica i mezzi' (2009) 3 DUDI 319; Andreas Zimmermann, 'Abiding by and Enforcing International Humanitarian Law in Asymmetric Warfare: The Case of Operation Cast Lead' (2011) 31 Polish YIL 47; Laurent Trigeaud, 'L'opération Bordure protectrice menée par Israël dans la Bande de Gaza (8 juillet – 26 août 2014)' (2014) 60 AFDI 171; Sharon Weill & Valentina Azarova, 'The 2014 Gaza War: Reflections on *Jus Ad Bellum, Jus in Bello,* and Accountability' in Annyssa Bellal (ed.), *The War Report: Armed Conflict in 2014* (Oxford University Press 2015) 360.

regarding the use of armed force in occupied territory; the counterinsurgency policy employed therein attracted significant attention from scholars.[34]

However, the issue of the use of armed force during an occupation remains still largely underexplored given that, to the best knowledge of this author, there is no comprehensive work studying this topic from *jus ad bellum*, international humanitarian law, and international human rights law perspectives. The present book aims to fill this lacuna in international scholarship.

1.3. THE PRACTICE OF THE OCCUPATION

In the course of this book, there are many references to international practice regarding the law of occupation. Although the status of occupying power is not per se derogatory from an international humanitarian law perspective,[35] in the second half of the twentieth century the term 'occupation' became a synonym for 'oppression' of a people;[36] consequently, the occupying powers in many cases deny this status in order to avoid the attached stigma and the resulting legal obligations. Despite the fact that the application of the law of occupation is not a consequence of any proclamation of occupation,[37] this attitude proves problematic in assessing which situations must be seen as occupations and, thus, as sources of state practice regarding the use of armed force in occupied territory.

Taking into account states' reluctance to qualify themselves as occupying powers, this subsection outlines some situations that may be reasonably considered to be occupations on the basis of states' and international organisations' practice, the case law of international and domestic tribunals, and the opinion of qualified legal scholarship. This section takes into account in particular events that have occurred since 1949, when the law of occupation experienced an important evolution thanks to the adoption of the GC IV.[38] This list of situations that may be considered to be occupations is not intended to be complete – it is presented only for the specific purpose of circumscribing

---

[34] See, e.g., William Banks, *Counterinsurgency Law: New Directions in Asymmetric Warfare* (Oxford University Press 2013); Ganesh Sitaraman, *The Counterinsurgent's Constitution: Law in the Age of Small Wars* (Oxford University Press 2013); Kenneth Watkin, *Fighting at the Legal Boundaries: Controlling the Use of Force in Contemporary Conflict* (Oxford University Press 2016).

[35] Dinstein, *The International Law*, 1.

[36] On the relationship between the law of occupation and the principle of self-determination of peoples, see *infra*, Sections 2.4.2 and 4.3.1.

[37] See *infra*, Section 2.3.1.

[38] Convention (IV) relative to the Protection of Civilian Persons in Time of War, Geneva, 12 August 1949.

the practice employed to study the issue at the heart of this book. Other situations may qualify as occupation if the circumstances required by the law of occupation are met.[39]

The refusal of South Africa to withdraw its forces and allow the local inhabitants to exercise their right of self-determination in Namibia created one of the first internationally acknowledged post-WWII occupations. Since 1920, Namibia (under the name of South West Africa) was administered by South Africa under a mandate of the League of Nations.[40] However, in 1966, the GA, which had replaced the League of Nations with respect to its role regarding the administration of non-self governing territories, terminated the mandate.[41] The refusal of South Africa to withdraw from the area and to allow the self-determination of the local people was constantly condemned by the UN. For instance, the SC repeatedly qualified the situation as an occupation and requested the withdrawal of South African troops.[42] In addition, the ICJ was involved in a number of proceedings regarding the legality of the South African presence in Namibia, and finally, in 1971, the Court clearly affirmed that Namibia was under occupation[43] – a conclusion that is shared by many scholars.[44] The occupation of Namibia ended only in 1990.

Common practice regarding occupation derives from the Israeli occupation of the OPT, which commenced in 1967 after the Six-Day War.[45] The OPT comprises the West Bank, East Jerusalem, and the Gaza Strip. Before the Israeli occupation, these territories did not comprise any existing state; rather they had been placed first under the British Mandate over Palestine,[46] and had

---

[39] To the best knowledge of this author, the most complete overview of situations that may be qualified as occupations is performed by Benvenisti, *The International Law*.

[40] Mandate for German South West Africa, 17 December 1920, reprinted in Solomon Slonim, *South West Africa and the United Nations: An International Mandate in Dispute* (The John Hopkins University Press 1973) 369.

[41] See UNGA Res. 2145 (XXI), 27 October 1966.

[42] See UNSC Res. 264 (1969), 20 March 1969, preabular para. 5; UNSC Res. 269 (1969), 12 August 1969, para. 3.

[43] *Legal Consequences for States of the Continued Presence of South Africa in Namibia notwithstanding Security Council Resolution 276 (1970)*, Advisory opinion, 21 June 1971, paras. 118–19.

[44] See, e.g., Roberts, 'What Is', 291–2; Roberts, 'Prolonged Military Occupation', 49–50; Benvenisti, *The International Law*, 67.

[45] For different accounts on this conflict, see J. R. Gainsborough, *The Arab-Israeli Conflict* (Gower 1986) 126–79; John Quigley, *The Six-Day War and Israeli Self-Defense: Questioning the Legal Basis for Preventive War* (Cambridge University Press 2013).

[46] League of Nations, Mandate for Palestine and Memorandum by the British Government Relating to Its Application to Transjordan, Approved by the Council of the League of Nations on 16 September 1922, CPM 466. The legal problems surrounding this Mandate and its impact on the ongoing Israeli-Palestinian conflict are beyond the purview of this book. On the Mandate and the status of the OPT before the Israeli occupation, see, generally, W. Thomas

then been occupied by Egypt and Jordan.[47] Despite some early acknowledgements,[48] the government of Israel has not formally recognised that the OPT is occupied.[49] However, this assumption is firmly established in the case law of the Supreme Court of Israel.[50] Similarly, the most important judicial and non-judicial international institutions, including the ICJ, consider the OPT to be occupied by Israel.[51] This view is almost unanimously shared by scholars.[52] As already mentioned, the practice of the Israeli occupation is particularly relevant for this work since Israel and the Palestinians have both often resorted to armed force, as in the aforementioned 1987 and 2000 Palestinian intifadas and in the 2009, 2012, and 2014 military operations in the Gaza Strip. In addition, in December 2017, new armed confrontations occurred when some

---

Mallisson & Sally V. Mallisson, *The Palestine Problem in International Law and World Order* (Longman 1986); Peter Malanczuk, 'Israel: Status, Territory and Occupied Territories' in Bernhardt (ed.), *Encyclopedia*, 149; Giancarlo Guarino, *La questione della Palestina nel diritto internazionale* (Giappichelli 1994); James Crawford, 'Israel (1948–1949) and Palestine (1988–1999): Two Studies in the Creation of States' in Guy S. Goodwin-Gill & Stefan Talmon (eds.), *The Reality of International Law: Essays in Honour of Ian Brownlie* (Clarendon Press 1999) 95. More recently, see the essays collected in Nigel Rodley, Yuval Shany, & Yaël Ronen (eds.), 'Special Issue on the Palestine Mandate' (2016) 49 IsLR 285.

[47] See Dinstein, *The International Law*, 13.

[48] See the statement of the then legal advisor Theodor Meron, 'Opinion: Settlement in the Administered Territory' (18 September 1967), para. B, reprinted in Iain Scobbie & Sarah Hibbin, *The Israel-Palestine Conflict in International Law: Territorial Issues* (SOAS 2009) 116.

[49] See, e.g., Ministry of Foreign Affair, Disputed Territories – Forgotten Facts About the West Bank and Gaza Strip (1 February 2013), available at mfa.gov.il/MFA/MFA-Archive/2003/Pages/DISPUTED%20TERRITORIES-%20Forgotten%20Facts%20About%20the%20We.aspx. See also the Levy Commission Report on the Legal Status of Building in Judea and Samaria (21 June 2012), unofficial English translation available at israelipalestinian.procon.org/sourcefiles/The-Levy-Commission-Report-on-the-Legal-Status-of-Building-in-Judea-and-Samaria.pdf. The Israeli government's position is based on the article by Yehuda Z. Blum, 'The Missing Reversioner: Reflections on the Status of Judea and Samaria' (1968) 3 IsLR 279, as demonstrated by Eyal Benvenisti, 'An Article That Changed the Course of History?' (2017) 50 IsLR 269.

[50] See, e.g., *Jam'iat Iscan Al-Ma'almoun* case, 792; HCJ 1661/05 *Gaza Coast Local Council v. The Knesset*, 59(2) PD 481, 558–9; HCJ 2056/04 *Beit Sourik Village Council v. The Government of Israel*, 58(5) PD 807, para. 1, unofficial English translation available at elyon1.court.gov.il/Files_ENG/04/560/020/A28/04020560.A28.pdf; HCJ 7015/02 *Ajuri et al. v. IDF Commander et al.*, 125 ILR 537, para. 22.

[51] *Wall* opinion, para. 78. This position has been restated by UNGA Res. 56/204, 22 February 2002; UNGA Res. 69/93, 16 December 2014; UNSC Res. 608, 14 January 1988; UNSC Res. 726, 6 January 1992; UNSC Res. 1322, 7 October 2000; UNSC Res. 2334, 23 December 2016. See also Peter Maurer (as President of the ICRC), 'Challenges to International Humanitarian Law: Israel's Occupation Policy' (2012) 94 IRRC 1504.

[52] For some counterarguments, though few in number and not very sound, see Blum, 'The Missing Reversioner'; Meir Shamgar, 'The Observance of International Law in the Administered Territories' (1971) 1 IYHR 262; Hani Sayed, 'The Fictions of the Illegal Occupation in the West Bank and Gaza' (2014) 16 *Oregon Review of International Law* 79.

Palestinians leaders called for a new intifada in response to the US decision to recognise Jerusalem as the capital of Israel.[53]

Another example of long-term occupation is the Turkish occupation of Northern Cyprus, which began in 1974 as a consequence of a *coup d'etat* organised by the Greek military junta.[54] Despite the Turkish claims that the TRNC is an independent state, no other state has recognised its statehood. Moreover, the UN SC declared 'legally invalid' the creation of the TRNC[55] and deplored the 'secessionist acts in the occupied part of the Republic of Cyprus'.[56] Accordingly, the area must be considered under occupation, as confirmed by the case law of the ECtHR.[57]

Likewise, East Timor was under occupation from 1975 – when it was invaded by Indonesia after Portugal had relinquished its colonial control over the area – to 1999. The invasion was condemned by the SC and only Australia recognised the alleged annexation claimed by Indonesia.[58] The ICJ described the Indonesian authority as occupation.[59] Likewise, the Commission for Reception, Truth and Reconciliation in East-Timor concluded in 2006 that East Timor was under occupation on the basis of the military authority exercised by Indonesia through its mixed military and civilian administration.[60] A similar conclusion was reached by the Timorese domestic courts[61] and authoritative scholars.[62]

In addition, an attempt to annex a territory over which a state has no claim, even in the aftermath of another state's occupation and withdrawal from the territory, amounts to occupation. This is the ongoing situation of

---

[53] See Bethan McKernan, 'Jerusalem Latest: Hamas Calls for New Palestinian Uprising against Israel after Donald Trump Announcement', Independent (7 December 2017), available at www.independent.co.uk/news/world/middle-east/jerusalem-latest-hamas-israel-donald-trump-intifada-palestine-palestinians-capital-a8096411.html

[54] See UK, Court of Appeal, *Hesperides Hotels* v. *Aegean Turkish Holidays* (23 May 1977), 73 ILR 9, 15–16.

[55] UNSC Res. 541 (1983), 18 November 1982, para. 2.

[56] UNSC Res. 550 (1984), 11 May 1984, preamble.

[57] See ECtHR, *Loizidou* v. *Turkey* (Application no. 15318/89), 18 December 1996, para. 56; *Cyprus* v. *Turkey* (Application no. 25781/94), 10 May 2001, para. 77. See, also, Kypros Chrysostomides, *The Republic of Cyprus: A Study in International Law* (Kluwer Law International 2000); Benvenisti, *The International Law*, 188–94; Maria Chiara Vitucci, *Sovranità e amministrazioni territoriali* (Editoriale Scientifica 2012) 63–76.

[58] UNSC Res. 384 (1975), 22 December 1975; UNSC Res. 389 (1976), 22 April 1976.

[59] See *Case Concerning East Timor (Portugal* v. *Australia)*, 30 June 1995, para. 13.

[60] See Commission for Reception, Truth and Reconciliation in East-Timor, Final Report, January 2006, part 4.

[61] See East Timor, Court of Appeal, *Dos Santos* v. *Prosecutor General* (15 July 2003), 138 ILR 604, 609.

[62] See, e.g., Antonio Cassese, *The Self-Determination of Peoples: A Legal Reappraisal* (Cambridge University Press 1996) 226–7; Benvenisti, *The International Law*, 172–7.

Western Sahara. Until 1975, the area was administered by Spain, which finally relinquished its control under the pressure of the international community; in particular, the right to self-determination of the local Sahrawi people had attracted lots of support and was acknowledged by a pivotal ICJ advisory opinion.[63] However, after the Spanish withdrawal and notwithstanding an agreement between Spain, Morocco, and Mauritania regarding the partition of the area between the two latter states, Morocco gained control over the whole country, claiming to have annexed it.[64] Since this annexation is contested by the international community[65] and by the Frente Popular de Liberación de Saguía el Hamra y Río de Oro (POLISARIO) – the national liberation movement fighting for the self-determination of the Sahrawis, which had declared the creation of the Sahrawi Arab Democratic Republic in 1976[66] – the authority exercised by Morocco over Western Sahara falls into the definition of occupation.[67] To date, despite the presence of a UN peacekeeping mission in the area whose aim has been to facilitate the peace process,[68] the situation remains unresolved and tensions between the parties are common.[69]

When the Soviet troops intervened in Afghanistan in 1978, the country was placed under occupation.[70] Indeed, the URSS allegedly intervened on the invitation of Babrak Karmal, who, however, was not in a position to issue such

[63] *Western Sahara*, Advisory opinion, 16 October 1975.
[64] On these events, see Thomas M. Franck, 'The Stealing of the Sahara' (1976) 70 AJIL 694.
[65] The SC condemned the Moroccan takeover in Res. 380 (1975), 6 November 1975. Similarly, the GA urged Morocco to withdraw from the area through Res. 34/37 (1979), 21 November 1979, para. 6. Very recently, the ECJ declared that the Western Sahara is not part of the Moroccan territory in the case *Council v. Front Polisario*, C-104/16 P, 21 December 2016, paras. 81–108.
[66] POLISARIO is the 'representative of the people of Western Sahara' according to UNGA Res. 34/37 (1979), 21 November 1979, para. 7. For more on the POLISARIO, see Luigi Condorelli, 'Le droit international face à l'autodéterminacion du Sahara Occidental' (1978) 33 CI 396.
[67] See UNGA Res. 34/37 (1979); European Parliament, Directorate-General for External Policies, Policy Department, *Occupation/Annexation of a Territory: Respect for International Humanitarian Law and Human Rights and Consistent EU Policy* (25 June 2015) 39–40. See, also, Tullio Treves, *Diritto internazionale: problemi fondamentali* (Giuffrè 2005) 183–4; Chinkin, 'Laws'; Benvenisti, *The International Law*, 171–2; Martin Dawidowicz, 'Trading Fish or Human Rights in Western Sahara' in Duncan French (ed.), *Statehood and Self-Determination* (Cambridge University Press 2013) 272; Ben Saul, 'The Status of Western Sahara as Occupied Territory under International Humanitarian Law and the Exploitation of Natural Resources' (2015) 27 *Global Change* 301.
[68] UN Mission for the Referendum in Western Sahara, established by UNSC Res. 690 (1991), 29 April 1991.
[69] See the Statement attributable to the Spokesman for the Secretary-General on Western Sahara, 25 February 2017, available at www.un.org/sg/en/content/sg/statement/2017-02-25/statement-attributable-spokesman-secretary-general-western-sahara
[70] See Michael W. Reisman & James Silk, 'Which Law Applies to the Afghan Conflict?' (1988) 82 AJIL 459, 481–2; Benvenisti, *The International Law*, 180.

an invitation, since he was not involved in the government of Afghanistan at that time.[71] The Soviet control over Afghanistan lasted until 1988, and was condemned by the GA,[72] the Islamic Conference, and many states, all of which requested the URSS to withdraw from the area.[73]

Sometimes occupations have been so apparent that the entire international community has acknowledged them outright, such as in the case of Kuwait. After the Iraqi invasion of Kuwait in August 1990,[74] the SC condemned the invasion and requested the withdrawal of Iraqi forces, simultaneously affirming Iraqi responsibilities under the law of occupation.[75] In this case, 'the illegality of the purported annexation and the applicability of the law of occupation were obvious and, indeed, were immediately recognised as such by the international community'.[76] The intervention of an international coalition put to an end the Iraqi occupation; for some time in the course of the relevant military operations, a small portion of Iraq fell under the coalition's occupation.[77]

As addressed in the next chapter, an occupation may exist even in cases of authority exercised through allegedly independent bodies.[78] The ongoing situation of the Nagorno-Karabakh is a clear example of this kind of occupation. This area is a portion of Azerbaijan that, since 1992, has been under the control of the so-called Nagorno-Karabakh Republic, a puppet regime created by the Armenian minority and held in place with the support of the Armenian government.[79] Accordingly, as suggested by most international organisations,[80]

---

[71] Ibid., 177.
[72] See UNGA Res. ES-6/2 (1980), 14 January 1980 (annually reaffirmed until the Soviet withdrawal).
[73] For an overview of the reactions, see the intelligence memorandum of the US Central Information Agency, Worldwide Reaction to the Soviet Invasion of Afghanistan, February 1980 (approved for release on 7 November 2006), available at www.cia.gov/library/readingroom/docs/CIA-RDP81B00401R000600190013-5.pdf
[74] On these events, see Georg K. Walker, 'The Crisis over Kuwait, August 1990–February 1991' (1991) 1 *Duke JCIL* 25; Ugo Villani, *L'ONU e la crisi del Golfo* (3rd edn, Cacucci 2005) 19–93.
[75] UNSC Res. 662 (1990), 9 August 1990; UNSC Res. 664 (1990), 18 August 1990; UNSC Res. 666 (1990), 13 September 1990; UNSC Res. 674 (1990), 29 October 1990.
[76] Benvenisti, *The International Law*, 170. On the illegality of the Iraqi annexation, see also UK, House of Lords, *Kuwait Airways Corp v. Iraq Airways Co.* (Nos. 4 & 5) [2002] 2 AC 883, 1099, 1199.
[77] US, Office of the Legal Adviser United States Department of State, *Digest of United States Practice in International Law, 1991–1999* (International Law Institute 2005) 2078.
[78] See *infra*, Section 2.3.1.
[79] See Sylvain Vité, 'Typology of Armed Conflicts in International Humanitarian Law: Legal Concepts and Actual Situations' (2009) 91 IRRC 69, 74–5; Bogdan Ivanel, 'Puppet States: A Growing Trend of Covert Occupation' (2015) 18 YIHL 43, 45.
[80] See, e.g., UNSC Res. 884 (1993), 12 November 1993; UNGA Res. 62/243 (2008), 14 March 2008; Council of Europe Parliamentary Assembly, Res. 1416 (2005); OSCE, Report of the OSCE Minsk Group Co-Chairs' Field Assessment Mission to the Occupied Territories of

it seems that the situation should be regarded as an occupation,[81] notwithstanding the contrary view advanced by the ECtHR in its case law.[82]

Between the 1990s and the first years of the new millennium, international case law considered a number of areas as being occupied. For instance, during the armed conflicts following the dissolution of the former Yugoslavia, some territories fell under occupation, as confirmed by the ICTY.[83] Similarly, during 1998–2000 the armed conflict between Eritrea and Ethiopia, some areas were placed under occupation by both belligerents,[84] as acknowledged by the EECC.[85] Likewise, it is uncontroversial that some portions of DRC territory (e.g., the province of Ituri) were occupied by Uganda from 2001 to 2003, as acknowledged by the ICJ[86] and the ICC.[87]

Conversely, the classification of Afghanistan in 2001 as an occupied country is more troublesome. Without entering the debate regarding the legality in light of *jus ad bellum* of the operation Enduring Freedom, allegedly launched in response to the September 11 terrorist attacks,[88] from an international

---

Azerbaijan Surrounding Nagorno-Karabakh, 24 March 2011, executive summary available at www.osce.org/mg/76209?download=true

[81] See Vité, 'Typology', 75: Heiko Krüger, *The Nagorno-Karabakh Conflict: A Legal Analysis* (Springer 2010) 104–5; Natalino Ronzitti, *Il conflitto del Nagorno-Karabakh e il diritto internazionale* (Giappichelli 2014) 37–42; Spoerri, 'The Law', 183.

[82] See *Chiragov and Others v. Armenia* (Application no. 13216/05), 16 June 2015, para. 96; *Sargsyan v. Azerbaijan* (Application no. 40167/06), 16 June 2015, para. 94. For some critical remarks on these decisions with regard to the issue of the existence of an occupation, see Gross, *The Writing*, 110–13.

[83] See, e.g., *Prosecutor v. Naletilić* et al., Trial Chamber Judgment, IT-98-34-T, 31 March 2003; *Prosecutor v. Prlić* et al., IT-04-74A, Appeals Chamber, 29 November 2017.

[84] For more on this, see Andrea Gioia, 'The Belligerent Occupation of Territory' in Andrea de Guttry, Harry G. Post, & Gabriella Venturini (eds.), *The 1998–2000 War between Eritrea and Ethiopia* (TMC Asser Press 2009) 351; Terry D. Gill, 'The Law of Belligerent Occupation: The Distinction between Invasion and Occupation of Disputed Territory', in de Guttry, Post, & Venturini (eds.), *The 1998–2000 War between Eritrea and Ethiopia*, 365.

[85] See, e.g., EECC, *Partial Award: Central Front – Eritrea's Claims 2, 4, 6, 7, 8 & 22* (28 April 2004), 26 RIAA 115; EECC, *Partial Award: Central Front - Ethiopia's Claim 2* (28 April 2004), 26 RIAA 155; EECC, *Partial Award: Western Front, Aerial Bombardment and Related Claims – Eritrea's Claims 1, 3, 5, 9–13, 14, 21, 25 & 26* (19 December 2005) 26 RIAA 291; EECC, *Partial Award: Western and Eastern Fronts – Ethiopia's Claims 1 & 3* (19 December 2005), 26 RIAA 351.

[86] *Armed Activities on the Territory of the Congo (DRC v. Uganda)*, 19 December 2005, para. 178.

[87] See *Prosecutor v. Lubanga*, ICC-01/04-01/06-803, Pre-Trial Chamber I, Decision on Confirmation of Charges, 29 January 2007, para. 220; *Prosecutor v. Lubanga*, ICC-01/04-01/06, Trial Chamber, Judgment pursuant to Article 74 of the Statute, 14 March 2012, para. 557; *Prosecutor v. Katanga*, ICC-01/04-01/07-717, Pre-Trial Chamber I, Decision on the confirmation of charges, 30 September 2008, para. 239; *Prosecutor v. Katanga*, ICC-01/04-01/07-3436, Trial Chamber, Judgment pursuant to Article 74 of the Statute, 7 March 2014, para. 1202.

[88] See, among many others, Luigi Condorelli, 'Les attentats du 11 septembre et leurs suites: où va le droit international?' (2001) 105 RGDIP 829; Olivier Corten & François Dubuisson, 'Operation "liberté immuable": une extension abusive du concept de légitime défense' (2002) 106

humanitarian law perspective it should be noted that the US-led coalition took control over certain areas of the country (e.g., Kabul), and that the authority in these areas was very soon transferred to a local government pursuant to the Agreement on Provisional Arrangements in Afghanistan Pending the Re-Establishment of Permanent Government Institutions.[89] However, it remains unclear whether this 'light footprint'[90] exercised by the international community in order to facilitate a change of regime in the area amounts to occupation. Many scholars support this idea,[91] whereas others fail to analyse the international humanitarian law aspects of the conflict in Afghanistan through the lens of the law of occupation.[92] Other scholars explicitly deny that Afghanistan was occupied because, *inter alia*, the UN has not been concerned with Afghanistan as a situation of occupation and because the states parties to the coalition have not claimed the rights stemming from a situation of occupation.[93] However, for the purpose of this book, Afghanistan is considered to have been occupied until the restoration of Afghani sovereignty through the election of President Karzai.[94] Since that day, the consent of the newly elected Afghani

---

RGDIP 51; Marco Frigessi di Rattalma, 'Qualche riflessione sull'azione bellica in Afghanistan e la legittima difesa' in Andrea Giardina & Flavia Lattanzi (eds.), *Studi di diritto internazionale in onore di Gaetano Arangio-Ruiz* vol. III (Editoriale Scientifica 2003) 1623; Giorgio Gaja, 'Combating Terrorism: Issues of *Jus ad Bellum* and *Jus in Bello*: The Case of Afghanistan' in Wolfgang Benedek & Alice Yotopoulos-Marangopoulos (eds.), *Anti-Terrorist Measures and Human Rights* (Brill 2004) 161; Christine Gray, *International Law and the Use of Force* (3rd edn, Oxford University Press 2008) 198–207; Yoram Dinstein, *War, Aggression and Self-Defence* (6th edn, Cambridge University Press 2017) 243–4.

[89] This document was adopted on 5 December 2001 (S/2001/1154). On the independence granted to the local government after the adoption of this document, see Ivan Ingravallo, 'L'azione internazionale per la ricostruzione dell'Afghanistan' (2004) 59 CI 525, 534–5.

[90] For a discussion on the soft approach adopted by the US-led coalition and the international community towards the regime change in Afghanistan, see Carsten Stahn, *The Law and Practice of International Territorial Administration: Versailles to Iraq and Beyond* (Cambridge University Press 2008) 352–63.

[91] See, e.g., Marco Sassòli, 'Use and Abuse of the Laws of War in the "War on Terrorism"' (2004) 22 *Law and Inequality* 195, 209; Paolo Picone, 'Le autorizzazioni all'uso della forza tra sistema delle Nazioni Unite e diritto internazionale generale' (2005) 88 RDI 5, 56–62; David Weissbrodt & Amy Bergquist, 'Extraordinary Rendition and the Humanitarian Law of War and Occupation' (2007) 47 Virginia JIL 295, 304–6; Kolb & Vité, *Le droit*, 172–7; Benvenisti, *The International Law*, 187–8.

[92] For instance, there is no reference to the law of occupation in Robert Cryer, 'The Fine Art of Friendship: *Jus in Bello* in Afghanistan' (2002) 7 JCSL 37; Françoise J. Hampson, 'Afghanistan 2001–2010' in Elizabeth Wilmshurst (ed.), *International Law and the Classification of Conflicts* (Oxford University Press 2012) 242.

[93] See Joan Fitzpatrick, 'Jurisdiction of Military Commissions and the Ambiguous War on Terrorism' (2002) 96 AJIL 345, 349; Carcano, *The Transformation*, 372.

[94] According to one author (Gary D. Solis, 'Law of War Issues in Ground Hostilities in Afghanistan' (2009) 85 ILS 219, 229), the US occupation ended before the creation of the new government, when the Interim Authority was established.

1.3. The Practice of the Occupation

government and the support of the UN SC for the presence of foreign troops prevent the definition of the situation as occupation.[95]

The situation of Iraq between 2003 and 2004 is different. Following the highly criticised US-led invasion through the operation Iraqi Freedom,[96] the United States and the United Kingdom acknowledged their responsibilities as occupying powers,[97] and the SC took the view that Iraq was under occupation.[98] Accordingly, there is no doubt that Iraq between 2003 and 2004 was under occupation,[99] and thus, the situation of Iraq during those years is a valuable source of state practice regarding the use of armed force in occupied territories. This assumption is not challenged by the fact that the occupation of Iraq presents some features that are peculiar for the law of occupation, and which are examined, when relevant, in subsequent chapters.

Finally, it is sometimes argued that Russia occupied some areas of neighbouring states after 1992. First, it is sometimes contended that, since 1992, the Moldavian area of Transnistria has been under Russian occupation, in the form of a puppet government entirely dependent on Russia.[100] The ECtHR has affirmed that the control exercised by Russia is sufficient to trigger the application of the ECHR without entering into the debate over whether the area is occupied or not.[101] Second, some scholars contend that Russia also

---

[95] See John F. Murphy, 'Afghanistan: Hard Choices and the Future of International Law' (2009) 85 ILS 79, 94; David Turns, 'Jus ad Pacem in Bello? Afghanistan, Stability Operations and the International Laws Relating to Armed Conflict' 85 ILS 387, 399; Marco Sassòli, 'The International Legal Framework for Stability Operations: When May International Forces Attack or Detain Someone in Afghanistan?' 85 ILS 431, 433.

[96] The majority of scholars, including this author, support the idea that this operation was a blatant violation of *jus ad bellum*. See, e.g., Maurizio Arcari, 'L'intervention armée contre l'Iraq et la question de l'autorisation du Conseil de Sécurité' (2003) 19 ADI 5; Olivier Corten, 'Iraqi Freedom: peut-on admettre l'argument de l' "autorisation implicte" du Conseil de Sécurité?' (2003) 36 RBDI 205; Paolo Picone, 'La guerra contro l'Iraq e le degenerazioni dell'unilateralismo' (2003) 86 *RDI* 329; Sean D. Murphy, 'Assessing the Legality of Invading Iraq' (2003–4) 92 *The Georgetown Law Journal* 173; Villani, *L'ONU*, 136–49; Gray, *International Law*, 216–22. Contra, see Dinstein, *War, Aggression*, 347–51.

[97] See Letter dated 8 May 2003.

[98] UNSC Res. 1483 (2003), 22 May 2003; UNSC Res. 1546 (2004), 8 June 2004.

[99] See, e.g., ECtHR, *Al-Saadoon and Mufdhi v. the UK* (Application no. 61498/08), 30 June 2009, paras. 3 and 87; *Al-Skeini* et al. v. *the UK* (Application no. 55721/07), 7 July 2011, paras. 12 and 143; ICC, OTP, Response to Communications Received Concerning Iraq (9 February 2006) 7; ICC, OTP, Report on Preliminary Examination Activities 2014 (2 December 2014) paras. 46–8 (acknowledging the status of occupying power pursuant to the aforementioned SC resolutions and the UK and US letter to the SC); ICC, OTP, Report on Preliminary Examination Activities 2015 (12 November 2015) paras. 30–2 (acknowledging the status of occupying power pursuant to the aforementioned SC resolutions and the UK and US letter to the SC).

[100] For a convincing explanation of this, see Ivanel, 'Puppet', 48–51.

[101] See *Ilaşcu* et al. v. *Moldova and Russia* (Application no. 48787/99) 8 July 2004, paras. 382, 392–3; *Catan* et al. v. *Moldova and Russia* (Application nos 43370/04, 8252/05 and 18454/06), 19 October 2012, paras. 111–12.

occupied the Georgian provinces of Abkhazia and South Ossetia during the 2008 armed conflict between Russia and Georgia.[102] In the aftermath of the conflict, these two entities declared their independence from Georgia, albeit gaining scant recognition by the international community, while Russian troops still remain stationed in the two areas on the basis of some agreements with the local administrations.[103] The situation should not be qualified as occupation if one recognises the statehood of these two entities.[104] Conversely, if they are not considered to be independent states, as seems to be the attitude of the international community due to their dependence on Russian troops and founding, then the areas should be considered under occupation, as affirmed very timidly by a EU fact-finding mission[105] and by the ICC.[106] A similar situation exists in the Crimean peninsula as of March 2014, when some representatives of the Russian minority organised a referendum and declared the secession from Ukraine and the annexation to Russia.[107] The international community has not recognised the secession;[108] instead the EU and many states have adopted sanctions against Russia as a consequence of the illegality of Crimea's annexation.[109] Moreover, Russia has been accused of having

[102] This is the official position of Georgia (see ICJ, *Application Instituting Proceedings, Application of the International Convention on the Elimination of All Forms of Racial Discrimination (Georgia v. Russian Federation)*, 12 August 2008, para. 78). See also Natia Kalandarishvili-Mueller, 'On the Occasion of the Five-year Anniversary of the Russian-Georgian War: Is Georgia Occupied?', EJIL: Talk!, 1 October 2013 and 'The Status of the Territory Unchanged: Russia's Treaties with Abkhazia and South Ossetia, Georgia', *Opinio Juris*, 20 April 2015.

[103] Benvenisti, *The International Law*, 196.

[104] On the lack of the elements of statehood and international recognition regarding these entities, see Olivier Corten, 'Déclarations unilatérales d'indépendance et reconnaissances prématurées: du Kosovo à l'Ossétie du sud et à l'Abkhazie' (2008) 112 RGDIP 721; Antonello Tancredi, 'Neither Authorized nor Prohibited? Secession and International Law after Kosovo, South Ossetia and Abkhazia' (2008) 18 Italian YIL 37.

[105] Independent International Fact-Finding Mission on the Conflict in Georgia (IIFFMCG), Report, Vol. II, September 2009, paras. 370–9 (affirming that the responsibility for maintenance of law and order is upon Russia, notwithstanding its denial that it is an occupying power).

[106] See Situation in Georgia, ICC-01/15-12, Pre-Trial Chamber I, Decision on the Prosecutor's request for authorisation of an investigation, 27 January 2016, para. 27.

[107] See Letter dated 19 March 2014 from the Permanent Representative of the Russian Federation to the United Nations Addressed to the Secretary-General, A/68/803-S/2014/202, 20 March 2014. On the legality of this referendum, see Antonello Tancredi, 'Crisi in Crimea, referendum ed autodeterminazione dei popoli' (2014) 8 DUDI 480; Anne Peters, 'The Crimean Vote of March 2014 as an Abuse of the Institution of the Territorial Referendum', in Christian Calliess (ed.), *Liber Amicorum für Torsten Stein zum 70. Geburtstag* (Nomos 2015) 278.

[108] See, e.g., UNGA Res. 68/262 (2014), 27 March 2014; UNGA Res. 71/205 (2017), 1 February 2017.

[109] The majority of scholars have suggested that the annexation was not supported by the principle of self-determination of peoples but, rather, was a breach of some fundamental international law rules (such as the ban of the use of force, the principle of self-determination

contributed to the secession of Crimea from Ukraine and of having influenced the outcome of the referendum through the use of armed force, particularly through agents conducting covert actions in the area before, during, and after the referendum.[110] If these allegations prove sound, there is room to argue that Crimea is under Russian occupation,[111] as suggested by Ukraine,[112] the GA,[113] and the ICC OTP.[114]

All of these situations are valuable sources of state practice that are employed in the following chapters in order to explore the legal framework governing the use of armed force in occupied territories.

---

of peoples itself, and the Ukraine's territorial integrity). See, among many others, Théodore Christakis, 'Self-Determination, Territorial Integrity and Fait Accompli in the Case of Crimea' (2015) 75 ZaöRV 75; Peter Hilpold, 'Ukraine, Crimea and New International Law: Balancing International Law with Arguments Drawn from History' (2015) 14 CJIL 237; Jure Vidmar, 'The Annexation of Crimea and the Boundaries of the Will of the People' (2015) 16 *German Law Journal* 365.

[110] See ICC, OTP, Report on Preliminary Examination Activities (2016), 14 November 2016, para. 155. For a discussion on this topic and further evidence, see Maurizio Arcari, 'Violazione del divieto di uso della forza, aggressione o attacco armato in relazione all'intervento militare della Russia in Crimea?' (2014) 8 DUDI 473; Antonello Tancredi, 'The Russian Annexation of the Crimea: Questions Relating to the Use of Force' (2014) 1 *Zoom In – Questions of International Law* 10; Veronika Bílková, 'The Use of Force by the Russian Federation in Crimea' (2015) 75 ZaöRV 27; Thomas D. Grant, *Aggression against Ukraine: Territory, Responsibility, and International Law* (Palgrave Macmillan 2015).

[111] See, e.g., the French position expressed in S/PV.712, 5–6; Office of the UN High Commissioner for Human Rights, Situation of Human Rights in the Temporarily Occupied Autonomous Republic of Crimea and the City of Sevastopol (Ukraine), 27 September 2017, para. 36; European Parliament, Directorate-General for External Policies, *Occupation/Annexation*, 25–7. See, also, Michael Bothe, 'The Current Status of Crimea: Russian Territory, Occupied Territory or What?' (2014) 53 MLLWR 99; Robin Geiß, 'Russia's Annexation of Crimea: The Mills of International Law Grind Slowly but They Do Grind' (2015) 91 ILS 425, 443–7.

[112] See, e.g., the statements made by Ukraine in the Letter Dated 3 October 2016 from the Permanent Representative of Ukraine to the United Nations Addressed to the Secretary-General, A/71/540-S/2016/839, 11 October 2016; Letter Dated 14 September 2016 from the Permanent Representative of Ukraine to the United Nations Addressed to the Secretary-General, A/71/379-S/2016/788, 15 September 2015.

[113] See UNGA Res. 71/205 (2017), paras. 1–2.

[114] OTP, Report on Preliminary Examination Activities (2016) para. 158.

2

The Hostile Character of Occupation as Reflected by the Law of Occupation

An occupation regime ... is the rule of a foreign government which does not even pretend to represent the will of the governed population. No ethnic ties, no shared traditions, no voluntary act of political confidence unite the rulers and their subjects. Indeed, each mistrusts the other.[1]

2.1. INTRODUCTION

This chapter analyses the situation of occupation and its realities. First, the chapter explores the emergence of the concept of occupation as a distinct situation from that of annexation, particularly in light of the practice of European states after the French Revolution. The chapter then describes the nature of the occupation as a fact that triggers the application of a number of duties and powers commonly referred to as the law of occupation. An occupation, in a nutshell, is the establishment of a foreign, hostile authority over a portion of territory; accordingly, this chapter explains who can exercise such an authority, when such an authority begins, and when it ends. The chapter moves on to explore the law of occupation and, in particular, its 'openness' to other areas of international law. Moreover, the chapter explores the basic tenets of the law of occupation, i.e., the distinction between occupation and annexation and the temporariness of occupation. The temporary nature of the occupation is what shapes the norms regarding the powers and duties conferred by the law upon the occupying power. This chapter addresses particularly the issue of the application of international human rights law in occupied territory and the interplay between international human rights law and international humanitarian law. The law of occupation as a whole demonstrates considerable tension between the fact that the situation of occupation is established in

[1] Fraenkel, *Military Occupation*, 205.

the course of an international armed conflict and thus is hostile in character, and the need for the occupying power to take over as temporary administrator of the occupied territory, through the same means that the ousted sovereign would have employed had it remained in control of the area. This tension is pivotal to understanding the complexities of the use of armed force in occupied territory.

2.2. ORIGIN AND DEVELOPMENT OF THE LAW OF OCCUPATION

Since international law has evolved rapidly with the evolution of international relations across the centuries, isolating a study regarding the law of occupation from the broad evolution and changes that have occurred in international law would be incorrect. As the following sections briefly explain, the law of occupation is mainly concerned with the protection of the sovereignty of the ousted sovereign formerly governing the occupied territory, and the protection of civilians dwelling in the occupied territory, taking into due account the occupying power's security as well. To understand both of these principles at the origin of the law of occupation, and the evolution they faced and still face, it is necessary to refer also to the broader international law backdrop from which the law of occupation originates.

The law of occupation is a product of a legal system based on state sovereignty that originated in the 1648 Peace of Westphalia, the clichéd birthdate of modern international society and of modern international law, according to many scholars.[2] When referring to the Westphalian model of international law, usually scholars refer to a legal system based on sovereign states that are the main subjects of that system, and whose sovereignty is the source of every international law rule.[3] From this perspective, every limitation imposed upon states regarding the extent of their sovereignty aims to protect other states' sovereignty.[4]

---

[2] See Fiore, *Trattato* vol. I, 26. This opinion is shared by modern treatises such as Antonio Cassese, *International Law* (2nd edn, Oxford University Press 2005) 24; Gideon Boas, *Public International Law* (Edward Elgar 2012) 8–9; Andrea Gioia, *Manuale di diritto internazionale* (5th edn, Giuffrè 2015) 4. On the debate regarding whether the Peace of Westphalia was a true turning point in international law and in the creation of the modern concept of sovereignty, see, e.g., Randall Lesaffer, 'The Classical Law of Nations (1500–1800)' in Alexander Orakhelashvili (ed.), *Research Handbook on the Theory and History of International Law* (Edward Elgar 2011) 408, 409–10.
[3] See Emer De Vattel, *Le droit des gens* vol. I (London 1758) 21.
[4] According to Gerry Simpson, 'International Law in Diplomatic History' in James Crawford & Martti Koskenniemi (eds.), *The Cambridge Companion to International Law* (Cambridge University Press 2012) 25, 31–2:

Although classical international lawyers considered occupation as a means to annex new portions of territory on the basis of the Roman tradition regarding conquest,[5] in the years of the French Revolution and the Napoleonic Wars, the idea that occupation is different from annexation became popular in *political* discourse regarding the right of self-determination of peoples.[6] However, the distinction between occupation and annexation became accepted as *law* only at the beginning of the nineteenth century, after the Congress of Vienna (1815) denied the validity of the annexations that had occurred during the Napoleonic wars.[7] During these years, notwithstanding the contrary opinion of some US judgements,[8] a range of decisions from French courts clearly affirmed that the mere fact of occupation gained *manu militari* was not sufficient to transfer sovereignty over the occupied territory to the occupying power.[9] Soon, some

---

The Treaties [of Westphalia] confirmed the supplanting of centralised imperial power by a judicial arrangement of autonomous sovereigns ... A small number of sovereigns within Europe were accorded legal equality in their external relations and, most important, in their internal political and religious arrangements ... Westphalia expressly rejected ... the idea that inter-state relations, and in particular war, can be organised on the basis of some sort of centrally enforced accountability for illegal acts ... Westphalia rejected justice and righteousness as an organising principle of the international (European) legal order. Instead, sovereignty became its own justification.

[5] See Alberico Gentili, *De Iure Belli Libri Tres* vol. III (London 1612), English translation by John C. Rolfe (Clarendon Press 1933) 304; Hugo Grotius, *De jure belli ac pacis libri tres* (Paris 1625), English translation by Francis W. Kelsey, *On the Law of War and Peace* Vol. III (Oceana 1964) 667; De Vattel, *Le droit*, vol. II, 171.

[6] The French Constitution of 3 September 1791, chapter VI, declared that: 'La Nation française renonce à entreprendre aucune guerre dans la vue de faire des conquêtes, et n'emploiera jamais ses forces contre la liberté d'aucun peuple' (text available at www.conseil-constitutionnel .fr/conseil-constitutionnel/francais/la-constitution/les-constitutions-de-la-france/constitution-de-1791.5082.html). For an historic survey on this period, see Peter M. R. Stirk, 'The Concept of Military Occupation in the Era of the French Revolutionary and Napoleonic Wars' (2015) 3 *Comparative Legal History* 60.

[7] For example, Art. C(3) of the Final Act of the Congress of Vienna affirms that: 'Le Prince Ludovisi Buoncompagni conservera pur lui et ses Successeurs légitimes, toutes les propriétés que sa Famille possédait dans la principauté de Piombino, dans l'ile d'Elbe ses dépendances, *avant l'occupation de ces pays par les troupes Françaises*, en 1799' (text in Henry Wheatom, *Elements of International Law* (3rd edn, Lea & Blanchard 1846) 639) (emphasis added).

[8] US Supreme Court, *US* v. *Rice* (1819) 17 US 246; US Supreme Court, *Fleming* v. *Page* (1850) 50 US 603.

[9] Challine reports that in 1812 the Court de cassation applied this principle to a complex issue regarding the validity of the law promulgated by the King of Naples in the occupied territory of the Papal States, later occupied by France. Similarly, the same principle was applied by the Court de cassation in 1818 regarding the French occupation of Catalonia, and in other subsequent decisions (see Paul Challine, *Le droit international public dans la jurisprudence française de 1789 à 1848* (Loviton 1934) 116–19, 122–5).

2.2. Origin and Development of the Law of Occupation

prominent scholars began to advance this argument in their writings as well.[10]

In this context, between 1874 and 1889, the law of occupation was codified with the main aim of protecting the interests of certain European states that were seeking to preserve their sovereignty in case of the loss of control of one or more portions of their territory due to an armed conflict.[11] Consequently, one pillar of the law of occupation even today is that the occupying power does not acquire sovereignty over the occupied territory, nor is it to be considered owner of the public property located therein. In the original view, however, the non-annexation principle was inapplicable if the occupation concerned the entire territory of a state and if that state surrendered unconditionally, as its international legal personality would have been cancelled by the occupation, and the surrender would have been considered a rejection of any claim under the law of occupation (*debellatio*).[12] According to the US Supreme Court, '[t]he usage of the world is, *if a nation be not entirely subdued*, to consider the holding of conquered territory as a mere military occupation until its fate shall be determined at the treaty of peace'.[13] It is unclear whether the doctrine of *debellatio* has ever reached the status of customary international law.[14]

---

[10] According to Lauterpacht and Benvenisti, the first author who made a distinction between military occupation and annexation was Heffter (see Lauterpacht, *Oppenheim's International Law*, 432–3; Benvenisti, *The International Law*, 27–8).

[11] The first codification ever of the law of occupation is embodied in the Instructions for the Government of Armies of the United States in the Field, 24 April 1863, (so-called Lieber Code, text in Dietrict Schindler & Jiri Toman (eds.), *The Laws of Armed Conflicts* (Martinus Nijhoff 1988) 3), which was a military manual adopted to regulate the American Civil War. At the international level, the first attempt to codify the law of occupation was the Manual on the Laws of War on Land, Oxford, 9 September 1880 (Oxford Manual), a private codification conducted by the IDI. Subsequently, some States adopted the Project of an International Declaration concerning the Laws and Customs of War, Brussels, 27 August 1874, a non-binding document that is the outcome of a conference among fifteen European States (hereinafter: Brussels Declaration). Later, during the First Hague Peace Conference of 1899 the Regulations concerning the Laws and Customs of War on Land were adopted, annexed to the Convention (II) with Respect to the Laws and Customs of War on Land, The Hague, 29 July 1899. These last treaty provisions were subsequently slightly revised in 1907, when they were readopted in the Regulations concerning the Laws and Customs of War on Land, annexed to the Convention (IV) respecting the Laws and Customs of War on Land, The Hague, 18 October 1907 (HR).

[12] For early views on *debellatio*, see Capotorti, *L'occupazione*, 68–71; Migliazza, *L'occupazione*, 53–73; von Glahn, *The Occupation*, 273–90.

[13] US Supreme Court, *American Insurance Company v. Canter* (1828) 26 US 511, 542 (emphasis added).

[14] For instance, some Italian scholars invoked the doctrine of *debellatio* to argue that the Italian annexations of Ethiopia (1936) and Albania were valid (1939) (see Monaco, 'Le recenti'). The doctrine was also invoked in relation to the status of Germany after WWII by some domestic courts (see, e.g., Germany, British Zone of Control, Control Commission Court of Criminal

This need to protect the sovereignty of the occupied states was envisaged only as applicable in relation to European states. Those same states reserved for themselves the right to augment their own territory by occupying areas in other continents as happened in the Americas, Africa, and Asia. Obviously, these territories were inhabited by people organised in human communities, often with a high degree of organisation. However, to be able to conquer these areas, European states used to declare them *terrae nullius*, and then to annex them.[15] It is noteworthy that a prominent theorist has suggested that modern international society was born from the different regulations of these kinds of occupation.[16] Nonetheless, even if limited to the European states, the law of occupation was an important turning point since, for the first time, international law severed the link between effective control of a territory and sovereignty over that area, well before some elements of international practice would have suggested that legal concerns do play a role in territorial changes.[17]

Appeal, *Grahame v. Director of Prosecutions* (26 July 1947), 14 ILR 228, 233; Holland, Special Court of Cassation, *In re Flesche* (17 February 1949), 16 ILR 266, 292); however, it was ruled out by the IMT as inapplicable to Germany (*In re Goering* et al. (1 October 1946), 13 ILR 203, 220).

[15] See PCJI, *Legal Status of Eastern Greenland*, 5 September 1933, PCIJ Series A/B, No. 53, 44–64. This practice is well described by the High Court of Australia in *Mabo v. Queensland No. 2*, (1992) 175 *Commonwealth Law Reports* 1, 32 (par Justice Brennan):

> The European nations parcelled out the territories newly discovered to the sovereigns of the respective discoverers, provided the discovery was confirmed by occupation and provided the indigenous inhabitants were not organized in a society that was united permanently for political action. To these territories the European colonial nations applied the doctrines relating to acquisition of territory that was *terra nullius*. They recognized the sovereignty of the respective European nations over the territory of 'backward peoples' and, by State practice, permitted the acquisition of sovereignty of such territory by occupation rather than by conquest. Various justifications for the acquisition of sovereignty over the territory of 'backward peoples' were advanced. The benefits of Christianity and European civilization had been seen as a sufficient justification from mediaeval times. Another justification for the application of the theory of *terra nullius* to inhabited territory ... was that new territories could be claimed by occupation if the land were uncultivated, for Europeans had a right to bring lands into production if they were left uncultivated by the indigenous inhabitant.

On this kind of occupation, see, generally, Roberto Ago, *Il requisito dell'effettività dell'occupazione in diritto internazionale* (Anonima Romana Editore 1934).

[16] This is the well-known theory advanced by Schmitt, *Der Nomos*. On the relevance of Schmitt's theories in the study of contemporary law of occupation, see Nehal Bhuta, 'The Antinomies of Transformative Occupation' (2005) 16 EJIL 721.

[17] The interplay between the principle of effectiveness and the principle of legality with regard to allegedly unlawful territorial situations is beyond the purview of this book. See, generally, Enrico Milano, *Unlawful Territorial Situations in International Law – Reconciling Effectiveness, Legality and Legitimacy* (Brill 2005); Salvatore Zappalà, 'Can Legality Trump Effectiveness

2.2. Origin and Development of the Law of Occupation

The relationship between the law of occupation and sovereignty evolved further on the basis of the changes that affected the concept of sovereignty within the state in times of peace, such as those limitations brought about by the raising of the principle of self-determination of peoples,[18] the adoption of universal and regional human rights conventions,[19] the consequent progressive erosion of the principle of the *domaine réservé*,[20] the ongoing shift from bilateralism to community interests in international relations,[21] and the entire evolution of the international legal order.[22] In this new legal and political environment, the idea that the occupation of a territory does not lead to its annexation became more acceptable since this view was in line with many other international law rules, particularly that of the principle of self-determination of peoples and the prohibition of the use of force in international law, which led to the demise of the concept of conquest.[23] These same developments suggest that contemporary international law does not recognise any situation of *debellatio*,[24] and that 'the rule protecting State personality against illegal

---

in Today's International Law?' in Antonio Cassese (ed.), *Realizing Utopia: The Future of International Law* (Oxford University Press 2012) 105.

[18] Although the principle of self-determination of peoples became a legal rule only after WWII, it has more ancient political and philosophical roots which may have influenced the formation of the law of occupation. On the origins of this principle, see generally Cassese, *Self-Determination*, 11–140.

[19] See generally Menno T. Kamminga & Martin Scheinin (eds.), *The Impact of Human Rights Law on General International Law* (Oxford University Press 2009).

[20] This principle is today enshrined in Art. 2(7) UN Charter. However, this principle has been progressively eroded and today it is well accepted that states may be held accountable for their conduct in their domestic jurisdiction. For more on this, see Benedetto Conforti & Carlo Focarelli, *The Law and Practice of the United Nations* (6th edn, Brill 2016) 167–89.

[21] See, e.g., Bruno Simma, 'From Bilateralism to Community Interest in International Law' (1994) 250 RCADI 217.

[22] According to Benvenisti, 'the concept of occupation can be seen as the mirror-image of the concept of sovereignty' and the changes in the way sovereignty is currently constructed 'also affect[] the law of occupation by modifying the restrictions on the occupant's exercise of authority' (Benvenisti, *The International Law*, 21). For more on the relationship between occupation and sovereignty, see Martti Koskenniemi, 'Occupation and Sovereignty: Still a Useful Distinction?' in Ola Engdahl & Pål Wrange (eds.), *Law at War: The Law as It Was and the Law as It Should Be* (Brill 2008) 163.

[23] On this topic, see the thorough analysis of Sharon Korman, *The Right of Conquest: The Acquisition of Territory by Force in International Law and Practice* (Clarendon Press 1996).

[24] Since the end of WWII, there has been no claim of *debellatio* in state practice. Some have argued that the doctrine of *debellatio* could have applied to Iraq in 2003 (see Russel Buchan, *International Law and the Construction of the Liberal Peace* (Hart 2013) 210), but the SC affirmed clearly that it was a case of occupation (UNSC Res. 1483 (2003), 22 May 2003, preambular para. 13, and para. 5). For the opinion, shared by most scholars, that *debellatio* is no longer in line with contemporary international law, see Korman, *The Right*, 223–4; Kolb & Vité, *Le droit*, 96; Arai-Takahashi, *The Law*, 39–40; Benvenisti, *The International Law*, 56–7, 163–4; Michael N. Schmitt, 'Debellatio' in MPEPIL (2009) para. 15; Carcano, *The*

annexation has acquired a peremptory character, reflecting the peremptory character of the rules relating to the use of force'.[25] Incidentally, it should be noted that this process led also to the demise of the occupation of territory outside Europe as a means of territorial acquisition since, today, it is well accepted that only areas genuinely devoid of inhabitants may be considered to be *terrae nullius*[26] – a now almost entirely obsolete concept that has no relevant place in contemporary international law.[27]

In addition, from its origins, the law of occupation has been concerned with the protection of individuals. In the beginning, the law protected mainly individual rights and, in particular, private property in occupied territory. This concern may be explained on two different levels. First it could be seen as indirectly protecting state sovereignty since, according to a very traditional conception of international law, any alleged mistreatment relating to individuals should be considered an act against their national state's sovereignty.[28] However, the origins of the rules pertaining to individual protection in occupied territory may be better addressed in the context of the development of the principle of distinction between civilians and combatants.[29] According to De Vattel, the conqueror seizes on public property of the defeated state, while private individuals are permitted to retain their property.[30] Similarly, Rousseau

---

Transformation, 114. Although Dinstein admits the existence of the doctrine of *debellatio*, he appears sceptical of its applicability to Germany at the end of WWII, and does not provide any other example of state practice (Dinstein, *The International Law*, 2, 33, 50).

[25] James Crawford, *The Creation of States in International Law* (2nd edn, Oxford University Press 2006) 704.

[26] See ICJ, *Western Sahara* opinion, 80–1.

[27] See High Court of Australia, *Mabo v. Queensland No. 2*, 41–2. See also Bothe, 'Occupation', 64; Alain Pellet, 'The Palestinian Declaration and the Jurisdiction of the International Criminal Court' (2010) 8 *JICJ* 981, 995; James Crawford, *Brownlie's Principles of Public International Law* (8th edn, Oxford University Press 2012) 220.

[28] For instance, this principle is at base of the rule of diplomatic protection, which was originally envisaged as an action meant to protect states' rights rather than individuals' rights (see PCIJ, *The Mavrommatis Palestine Concessions (Greece v. Great Britain) (Objection to the Jurisdiction of the Court)* 30 August 1924, PCIJ Series A No. 2, 12). However, in contemporary international law there is a progressive interplay between the rules on treatment of foreigners and diplomatic protection on the one hand, and the protection of human rights on the other (see, e.g., Enrico Milano, 'Diplomatic Protection and Human Rights before the International Court of Justice: Re-fashioning Tradition?' (2004) 35 Netherlands YIL 85; Maria Irene Papa, 'Protezione diplomatica, diritti umani e obblighi *erga omnes*' (2008) 91 RDI 669; ILC, Draft Articles on Diplomatic Protection with Commentaries (2006), A/61/10, sub Art. 1, para. 5).

[29] On the historical development regarding the distinction between combatants and civilians, see Francesco Salerno, 'Il nemico "legittimo combattente" all'origine del diritto internazionale dei conflitti armati' (2009) 38 *Quaderni Fiorentini* 1417; Alexander Gillespie, *A History of the Laws of War* vols. I–II (Hart 2011).

[30] De Vattel, *Le droit*, 176.

2.2. Origin and Development of the Law of Occupation

advocated that 'même en plein guerre, un prince juste s'empale bien, en pays ennemi, de tout ce qui apartment au public, mais il respecte la personnel et les biens des particuliers'.[31] From this perspective, as suggested by a leading commentator,[32] the protection of some basic individual rights in occupied territory – principally property rights – may be considered a consequence of a new approach towards war, according to which 'la guerre n'est point une relation d'homme à homme, mais une relation d'État à État, dans laquelle les particuliers ne sont enemis qu'accidentellment'.[33]

Likewise, the protection of individuals in occupied territory has faced a certain evolution. Because the law codified at the beginning of the nineteenth century proved unable adequately to protect individuals who had fallen into the hands of occupying powers during WWI and WWII, states adopted new rules, which are today embodied in the 1949 GC IV.[34] Its provisions regarding the protection of civilians in occupied territory form an integral part of the law of occupation, and have been complemented by those embodied in the subsequent 1977 AP I.[35] All these new norms were intended as the response to a new conception of the way in which wars, *rectius*, armed conflicts, were to be conducted. This new conception, based on the so-called principle of humanity,[36] led to a general 'humanisation' of international humanitarian law[37] that also affected the law of occupation.

---

[31] Jean-Jacques Rousseau, *Contrat social ou principes du droit publique* (2nd edn, Bureaux de la Publication 1865), Livre 1, IV.
[32] Benvenisti, *The International Law*, 24.
[33] Charles Maurice de Talleyrand-Périgord, 'Letter to Napoleon', 20 November 1806, quoted by Benvenisti, *The International Law*, 24.
[34] During WWII, many territories were occupied by the Axis Powers, the Soviet Union, and the Allies. However, on most occasions they failed to comply with the law of occupation (Benvenisti, *The International Law*, 140–3, 164–6).
[35] Protocol Additional to the Geneva Conventions of 12 August 1949, and relating to the Protection of Victims of International Armed Conflicts, 8 June 1977 (AP I).
[36] The principle of humanity has been a supplemental source of international humanitarian law since 1899. It is embodied in the so-called Martens Clause, a provision according to which:

> En attendant qu'un Code plus complet des lois de la guerre puisse être édicté, les Hautes Parties contractantes jugent opportun de constater que, dans les cas non compris dans les dispositions réglementaires adoptées par Elles, les populations et les belligérants restent sous la sauvegarde et sous l'empire des principes du droit des gens, tels qu'ils résultent des usages établis entre nations civilisées, des lois de l'humanité et des exigences de la conscience publique.

(HR, preambular para. 8; a slightly different version is embodied in Art. 1(1) AP I).
[37] The word is borrowed from the famous work of Theodor Meron, 'The Humanization of Humanitarian Law' (2000) 94 AJIL 239. See also Theodor Meron, *The Humanization of International Law* (Brill 2006) 1–89. On this process, see also Alessandro Migliazza, 'L'évolution de la

Accordingly, in the analysis of the current law of occupation, especially with regard to situations that are not fully coincident with those the drafters of the relevant conventions had in mind, one must take into account the evolution of international law in general, and international humanitarian law in particular.

2.3. OCCUPATION AS A FACT

2.3.1. *The Factual Elements of the Definition of Occupation*

In the discourse regarding occupation, very often there is some confusion between two different things: the very real situation of occupation versus the legal regulation of that situation (often referred to as the law of occupation). As a fact, occupation is as old as international relations; however, as a body of law, occupation is relatively recent, as argued in the preceding section.[38] To determine whether the law of occupation is applicable, it is first necessary to verify whether a situation of occupation exists.[39] The relationship between the fact and the law of occupation, in a nutshell, can be summarised as follows: every time there is (*sein*) the fact of the occupation, the international legal order demands (*sollen*) the application of the institute of occupation, i.e., the law of occupation.[40] Accordingly, the occupation is not merely a fact, but a fact relevant to international legal order since it triggers the applicability of a number of international rules.[41] In the words of one observer, occupation 'is a fact recognized and regulated by international law, not an institution created by it'.[42] Consequently, the idea that the factual nature of occupation prevents from scrutinising its legality under international law is incorrect,[43] and there is no need to construct a 'normative approach' to the law of occupation.[44]

---

réglementation de la guerre à la lumière de la sauvegarde des droits de l'Homme' (1972) 137 RCADI 141.

[38] Accordingly, this author does not share the view according to which '[l]a *occupatio bellica* de un territorio extranjero es *una institución jurídica* tan antigua como las relaciones entre los pueblos' (Luis Maside Miranda, 'Cuestiones relativas a la *occupatio bellica*' (2004) 8 *Anuario da Facultade de Dereito da Universidade da Coruña* 461 (second emphasis added)).

[39] See ICTY, *Prosecutor v. Naletilić*, para. 211.

[40] See the US Department of Defense, Law of War Manual, June 2015 (Updated December 2016), section 11.2.

[41] See Balladore Pallieri, *Diritto*, 304–5; Sereni, *Diritto*, 2002.

[42] Christopher Greenwood, 'The Administration of Occupied Territory in International Law' in Playfair (ed.), *International Law*, 241, 250.

[43] This idea was advanced by Meir Shamgar, 'Legal Concepts and Problems of the Israeli Military Government: The Initial Stage' in Meir Shamgar (ed.), *Military Government in the Territories Administered by Israel 1967–1980* (Hebrew University of Jerusalem Press 1982) 13, 43.

[44] The idea that a normative approach to the law of occupation is a development needed to overcome the factual nature of the occupation is purported by Gross, *Writing*, 2–4, who, however,

2.3. Occupation as a Fact

Because the applicability of the law of occupation follows the fact of the occupation, it is irrelevant whether the occupation was established in violation of international law, as emphasised in a number of international decisions.[45] Indeed, on the basis of the principle of equality of belligerents, international humanitarian law, including the law of occupation, is applicable to every belligerent in the same way, irrespective of the legality of their actions under *jus ad bellum* or other international law rules.[46]

Article 42 HR embodies a tentative definition of occupation.[47] According to the authoritative French text, '[u]n territoire est considéré comme occupé lorsqu'il se trouve placé de fait sous l'autorité de l'armée ennemie. L'occupation ne s'étend qu'aux territoires où cette autorité est établie et en mesure de s'exercer'.[48] This definition, which reflects customary international law,[49] is not concerned with the way in which an occupation commences: normally, it is preceded by an invasion, but the occupation may also be created by other occurrences.[50] What is relevant is that a state of occupation is established in fact in any way. The key elements of the occupation may be summarised

---

    overestimates the value of some statements of political actors regarding the factual nature of occupation; indeed, Gross should rely more on the fact that occupation as a fact does not imply that there is no law regulating the occupation, but rather, that the fact of the occupation is the situation triggering the application of the law of occupation.

[45] See US Military Tribunal, Nuremberg, *Willelm List* et al. (19 February 1948), (1948) 9 LRTWC 34, 59 (*Hostages* case); DRC v. *Uganda*, para. 173; DRC v. *Uganda*, Separate opinion of Judge Kooijmans, para. 58. See also Netherlands, Special Court, *Re Christiansen* (12 August 1948), 15 ILR 412, 413. For an isolated contrary view, see Rotem Giladi, 'The Jus Ad Bellum/Jus In Bello Distinction and the Law of Occupation' (2008) 41 IsLR 246.

[46] According to AP I, preambular para. 4, international humanitarian law 'must be fully applied in all circumstances to all persons who are protected by those instruments, *without any adverse distinction based on the nature or origin of the armed conflict or on the causes espoused by or attributed to the Parties to the conflict*' (emphases added). See also common Art. 1 GCs, according to which States Parties 'undertake to respect and ensure respect for the present Convention *in all circumstances*', and common Art. 2 GCs, according to which the Conventions 'apply to *all cases* of declared war or of any other armed conflict' as well as to '*all cases* of partial or total occupation of the territory of a High Contracting Party' (emphases added). For more on this principle, see Vaios Koutroulis, 'And Yet It Exists: In Defence of the "Equality of Belligerents" Principle' (2013) 26 LJIL 449, and, with specific reference to situations of occupation, *Les relations entre le* jus contra bellum *et le* jus in bello: *étanchéité absolue ou vases communicants?* (PhD Dissertation, Université Libre de Bruxelles 2011) 221–54 (chapter on file with the author).

[47] 'This definition is not at all precise, but it is as precise as a legal definition of a fact such as occupation can be', observes Lauterpacht, *Oppenheim's International Law*, 435.

[48] The official English text does not emphasise as well the factual nature of occupation: 'Territory is considered occupied when it is actually placed under the authority of the hostile army. The occupation extends only to the territory where such authority has been established and can be exercised'.

[49] *Wall* opinion, para. 79; DRC v. *Uganda*, para. 172. See also US Military Manual, section 11.2.2.

[50] For instance, in the DRC v. *Uganda* case, the ICJ found that the Congolese province of Ituri has been under Ugandan occupation (para. 176) following the DRC's withdrawal of consent regarding the presence of Ugandan troops in the Congolese territory (para. 53).

as follows: the exercise of authority by one state engaged in an international armed conflict against another state, over one part of the territory of the latter; loss of authority by the latter over that part of territory; and lack of consent by the state whose territory is controlled.[51] It should be noted that, according to Article 2(2) GC IV, a territory may be placed under occupation even if there is no armed resistance from the sovereign and the people of that territory (*occupatio pacifica*);[52] however, this does not mean that the sovereign of the occupied country consented to the occupation, but rather, that it suffered the duress of occupation without resorting to armed force.[53]

States may exercise their authority over the occupied territory through other formally autonomous entities or through armed groups controlling that territory.[54] In these cases, the acts of the puppet regime or of the armed group exercising authority over the territory should be considered as acts of the sponsor state, which is actually an occupying power.[55] As the ICTY clearly affirmed, the occupying power's 'authority may be exercised by proxy through *de facto* organised and hierarchically structured groups. The rationale behind this is that states should not be allowed to evade their obligations under the law of occupation through the use of proxies'.[56]

There is nothing in Article 42 HR preventing an international organisation from creating a situation of occupation[57] as long as the aforementioned factual requirements of the occupation are met,[58] as today is held by most scholars.[59]

---

[51] See *DRC v. Uganda*, 173: Ferraro, *Expert Meeting*, 17–23; Sassòli, 'Concept', 1393–4.
[52] 'The Convention shall also apply to all cases of partial or total occupation of the territory of a High Contracting Party, even if the said occupation meets with no armed resistance.'
[53] See Dinstein, *The International Law*, 31–2, 35.
[54] See ICTY, *Prosecutor v. Blaskic*, IT-95-14-T, 3 March 2000, para. 149; *Prosecutor v. Naletilić*, paras. 181–8, 197–202; *Prosecutor v. Prlić* et al., para. 322.
[55] See ICTY, *Prosecutor v. Tadic*, IT-94-1-T, Opinion and Judgment (Trial Chamber), 7 May 1997, para. 584. See also Greece, Criminal Court of Heraklion, *In re G* (1 January 1945), 12 ILR 437, 439; France, Court of Appeal of Paris, *Clement v. Agent Judiciaire du Trésor Public* (10 February 1961), 41 ILR 478, 479–80; Canada, Supreme Court, *R v. Finta* (24 March 1994), 102–3, available at www.asser.nl/upload/documents/DomCLIC/Docs/NLP/Canada/RcFinta_SupremeCourt_24-3-1994-EN.pdf.
[56] *Prosecutor v. Prlić* et al., para. 322.
[57] Art. 42 HR pertains to the action of a 'hostile army', without mentioning a 'state'.
[58] The Italian Court of Cassation held that the presence of foreign troops on Italian territory after the armistice between Italy and the Allied Force under UN auspices in the aftermath of WWII constituted a form of occupation by the UN since the Italian Court failed to attach the due importance to the Italian consent to that presence (Italy, Court of Cassation, *Re Scarpato* (14 July 1951), 18 *ILR* 625, 627).
[59] See D. W. Bowett, *United Nations Forces: A Legal Study of United Nations Practice* (Stevens and Sons 1964) 490–1; Claude Emanuelli, *Les action militaires de l'ONU et le droit international humanitaire* (Wilson et Lafleur Itée 1995) 40; Sylvain Vité, 'L'applicabilité du droit international de l'occupation militaire aux activités des organisations internationales' (2004)

2.3. Occupation as a Fact

Notwithstanding the fact the HR do not mention this possibility, and although international organisations may not become parties to the HR and to the GC IV,[60] international organisations involved in armed conflicts are bound by customary international humanitarian law, as demonstrated by UN practice,[61] and, accordingly, they must respect the law of occupation as customary law if a situation of occupation is created. Arguably, an authorisation of the use of force by the SC under Chapter VII of the UN Charter[62] may result in a situation of occupation,[63] as confirmed by the SC Resolution 1970 (2011), which authorised states to use armed force to protect civilians in Libya 'while excluding a foreign occupation force of any form on any part of Libyan territory'.[64]

In actual practice, however, it becomes difficult to find cases in which international organisations have created situations of occupation:[65] for instance, the UN, the international organisation more frequently involved in armed

---

86 IRRC 9, 20; Robert Kolb, Gabriele Porretto, & Sylvain Vité, *L'application du droit international humanitaire et des droits de l'homme aux organisations internationales. Forces de paix et administrations civiles transitoires* (Bruylant 2005) 217–21; Stahn, *The Law*, 467–71; Arai-Takahashi, *The Law*, 587; Kolb & Vité, *Le droit*, 99–105; Hans-Peter Gasser & Knut Dörmann, 'Protection of the Civilian Population' in Dieter Fleck (ed.), *The Handbook of International Humanitarian Law* (3rd edn, Oxford University Press 2013) 231, 267; Benvenisti, *The International Law*, 63; Spoerri, 'The Law', 191; Sassòli, 'Concept', 1408.

[60] See Art. 6 1907 Hague Convention IV (to which the HR are annexed) and Art. 155 GC IV, according to which only 'Powers' (i.e., 'states') may adhere to these conventions.

[61] See the UN Secretary-General's bulletin 'Observance by United Nations forces of international humanitarian law', 6 August 1999. On the bulletin, see Luigi Condorelli, 'Le azioni dell'ONU e l'applicazione del diritto internazionale umanitario: il bollettino del Segretario generale del 6 agosto 1999' (1999) 92 RDI 1049; Paolo Benvenuti, 'Le respect du droit international humanitaire par les forces des Nations Unies: la circulaire du Secrétaire Général' (2001) 105 RGDIP 355; Tristan Ferraro, 'The Applicability and Application of International Humanitarian Law to Multinational Forces' (2013) 95 IRRC 561.

[62] Since the UN Member States have never made available to the SC their own troops to create a 'UN army' pursuant to Art. 43 UN Charter, the SC has dispatched enforcement missions under Chapter VII by authorising member States to use armed force in certain circumstances. On this topic – beyond the purview of this chapter – see, generally, Niels Blokker, 'Is the Authorization Authorized? Powers and Practice of the UN Security Council to Authorize the Use of Force by "Coalitions of the Able and Willing"' (2000) 11 EJIL 541; Picone, 'Le autorizzazioni'; Linos-Alexandre Sicilianos, 'Entre multilatéralisme et unilatéralisme: l'autorisation par le Conseil de sécurité de recourir à la force' (2009) 339 RCADI 9.

[63] See Vité, 'L'applicabilité', 20; Dinstein, *The International Law*, 37.

[64] UNSC Res. 1970 (2011), 26 February 2011, para. 4.

[65] Some authors have argued that the Nato Kosovo Force dispatched in Kosovo after the 1999 armed conflict and operating pursuant to UNSC Res. 1244 (1999), 10 June 1999, should have been considered a force of occupation (see John Cerone, 'Minding the Gap: Outlining KFOR Accountability in Post-Conflict Kosovo' (2001) 12 EJIL 469; Benvenisti, *The International Law*, 292–8). However, other publicists reject this claim (see, e.g., Kolb, Porretto, & Vité, *L'application*, 225, 227; Enrico Milano, *Formazione dello Stato e processi di State-Building nel diritto internazionale: Kosovo 1999–2013* (Editoriale Scientifica 2013) 153–62).

conflicts, usually assumes authority over a portion of territory on the basis of some form of consent from the territorial state or the local population, as in the case of peacekeeping missions.[66] Moreover, although the direct administration of portions of territory by the UN may resemble situations of occupation,[67] there are significant differences between the two scenarios.[68] Even authors supporting the idea that the authority of the UN territorial administrations derives from their occupation of a territory rather than from consent[69] argue that the two situations are too different to be treated in the same way.[70] More significantly, state practice and *opinio juris* regarding the application of the law of occupation to UN administrations is inconsistent.[71] However, as long as these UN administrations are supported by some kind of consent from the territorial sovereign or, in cases of territories not constituted as states, from representatives of the local population, the law of occupation is not applicable *de jure*.[72] Practically, the UN may decide to govern a directly administered

[66] Consent is still today the most important element in distinguishing between peacekeeping and peace enforcement operations (see Micaela Frulli, *Le operazioni di peacekeeping delle Nazioni Unite: continuità di un modello normative* (Editoriale Scientifica 2012)). The element of consent has been interpreted in different ways: at an earlier stage, peacekeeping missions were dispatched in international armed conflict and, consequently, the SC required the consent of every state involved (see Antonietta Di Blase, 'The Role of the Host State's Consent with Regard to Non-Coercive Actions by the United Nations' in Antonio Cassese (ed.), *United Nations Peace Keeping: Legal Essays* (Sijthoff & Noordhoff 1978) 55); however, in response to the increasing involvement of peacekeepers in non-international armed conflicts, the SC has considered it necessary to request only the consent of the territorial state in which the mission was to be deployed, sometimes seeking the consent of non-state actors as a matter of policy rather than to fulfill a legal requirement (see Giorgio Gaja, 'Use of Force Made or Authorized by the United Nations' in Christian Tomuschat (ed.), *The United Nations at Age Fifty. A Legal Perspective* (Nijhoff 1995) 39, 51; Alfonso J. Iglesias Velasco, 'El marco jurídico de las operaciones de mantenimiento de la paz de Naciones Unidas' (1/2005) *Foro, Nueva época* 127, 144–5; Ian Johnstone, 'Managing Consent in Contemporary Peacekeeping Operations' (2011) 18 *International Peacekeeping* 168, 171–2; Frulli, *Le operazioni*, 72–9).
[67] On the similarities between UN transitional administration and foreign occupation, see Steven R. Ratner, 'Foreign Occupation and International Territorial Administration: The Challenges of Convergence' (2005) 16 EJIL 695; Ralph Wilde, *International Territorial Administration* (Oxford University Press 2008) 355–6.
[68] For a detailed analysis, see Conforti & Focarelli, *The Law*, 327. See also Rosalyn Higgins, Philippa Webb, Dapo Akande, Sandesh Sivakumaran, & James Sloan, *Oppenheim's International Law: United Nations* vol. II (Oxford University Press 2017) 1088.
[69] See Simon Chesterman, *You, The People. The United Nations, Transitional Administrations, and State-Building* (Oxford University Press 2004) 152–3.
[70] Ibid., 6–7.
[71] For instance, Australia acknowledged that it was bound by the HR and GC IV during the operation in Somalia, while the USA refused to acknowledge the same (see Stahn, *The Law*, 472).
[72] See UK Military Manual, section 11.1.2. The Italian Military Manual qualifies as occupied territory any territory placed under the control of a peacekeeping mission or a multilateral

2.3. *Occupation as a Fact* 33

territory to a certain extent in conformity with the law of occupation de facto, even if the situation is not an actual occupation, thanks to the similarities between the two situations.[73]

Typically, a situation of occupation may not be established in a non-international armed conflict.[74] It is clear that the drafters of the relevant conventions had in mind situations in which occupations were created on territories outside the boundaries of the occupying power.[75] Indeed, the state fighting against an armed group is the sovereign of its own territory and has the right to maintain its own territorial integrity.[76] Less clear is the reason why insurgents controlling portions of territory should not be considered subject to the law of occupation. According to the SCSL, it is not true that 'limiting the applicability of the law of occupation to international armed conflicts deprives civilian populations under the control of internal insurgent groups of the protections they would be afforded if they were under the occupation of a foreign power', since 'as is evident from

---

international force, but emphasises that this kind of occupation is regulated case by case by the rules embodied in the international mandate that has originated it (section 50). See also Marco Sassòli, 'Droit international pénal et droit pénal interne: le cas des territoires se trouvant sous administration internationale' in Marc Henzelin & Robert Roth (eds.), *Le droit pénal à l'épreuve de l'internationalisation* (Bruylant 2002) 119, 144; Erika De Wet, 'The Direct Administration of Territories by the United Nations and Its Member States in the Post-Cold War Era: Legal Bases and Implications for National Law' (2004) 8 *MPYUNL* 291, 326–9; Kolb, Porretto, & Vité, *L'application*, 225–7; Vité, 'L'applicabilité', 22–3; Picone, 'Le autorizzazioni', 55, fn. 144; Ivan Ingravallo, *Il Consiglio di sicurezza e l'amministrazione diretta dei territori* (Editoriale Scientifica 2008) 155–7; Stahn, *The Law*, 471–3. *Contra*, see Noemi Corso, 'A props de l'applicability du droit de l'occupation militaries aux forces des Nations Unies' (2013) 23 RSDIE 609.

[73] See Vité, 'L'applicabilité', 29–33; Kolb, Porretto, & Vité, *L'application*, 227–32; Rüdiger Wolfrum, 'International Administration in Post-Conflict Situations by the United Nations and Other International Actors' (2005) 9 MPYUNL 649, 695; Ingravallo, *Il Consiglio*, 157; Charles Garraway, 'Occupation Responsibilities and Constraints' in Howard M. Hensel (ed.), *The Legitimate Use of Military Force* (Ashgate 2008) 263, 268; Stahn, *The Law*, 474–8; Arai-Takahashi, *The Law*, 604–7; Ferraro, *Expert Meeting*, 33–4.

[74] See US Supreme Court, *Ford v. Surget* (1878) 97 *US* 594, 614; SCSL, *Prosecutor v. Sesay* et al., SCSL-04-15-T, Trial Judgment, 2 March 2009, paras. 982–8. See also US Military Manual, section 11.1.3.3.

[75] See Roberts, 'What Is', 255:

Taking the conventions as a whole, it is evident that the concept of military occupation remains essentially international in character. At the heart of almost all treaty provisions and legal writings regarding occupations is the image of the armed force of a State exercising some kind of coercive control or authority over inhabited territory outside the accepted international frontiers of their State ... The [GCs] give rather few hints about its possible relevance in any analogous situations which may arise within a State.

[76] Dinstein, *The International Law*, 34–4; Sassòli, 'Concept', 1415; Noam Zamir, *Classification of Conflicts in International Humanitarian Law* (Edward Elgar 2017) 77–8.

its general requirements, Additional Protocol II was designed to regulate situations where insurgent groups exercise control over part of the territory of a State'.[77] In truth, states have been reluctant to consider insurgents to be occupying powers in the territory they control in order not to lend to their de facto administration any appearance of legitimacy.[78] However, when, in certain circumstances, an *international* armed conflict arises between a state and an armed group, then a situation of occupation can be created and the law of occupation may be applicable. For instance, occupations can be created in armed conflicts between states party to the AP I and groups fighting for the self-determination of peoples in cases of colonial domination, alien occupation, or racist regimes, pursuant to Article 1(4) AP I.[79] Moreover, situations of occupation can be created in armed conflicts between a state and insurgents as long as the state has recognised the insurgents' belligerency, thus transforming the non-international armed conflict into an international armed conflict.[80] However, it is clear that armed groups stationing within the territory of a state with its consent are not occupying the area in the sense of the law of armed conflict.[81]

Going back to the most frequent scenario – occupations carried out by states – since the condition of occupation is a fact, '[m]ere proclamation of occupation is insufficient to bring an occupation into existence'[82] and '[t]erritory may be occupied even though no proclamation of occupation has been issued'.[83] In practice, states are reluctant to acknowledge their position as occupying powers, which is a source of a number of legal obligations as well as cause of widespread stigma in international relations.[84] Thanks to

[77] *Prosecutor* v. *Sesay* et al., para. 983. One author argued that the law of occupation should be changed to be applicable to armed groups controlling portions of territory in non-international armed conflicts to grant more protection to individuals placed under their authority (see Sandesh Sivakumaran, 'Re-envisaging the International Law of Internal Armed Conflict' (2011) 22 EJIL 219, 245–7).
[78] See Benvenisti, *The International Law*, 61 (supporting the idea that insurgents may create situations of occupation subject to the law of occupation); Sassòli, 'Concept', 1415; Zamir, *Classification*, 78.
[79] See Roberts, 'What Is', 293; Dinstein, *The International Law*, 34. For the application of this rule in situations of occupation, see *infra*, Section 5.5.3.2.
[80] Dinstein, *The International Law*, 34. For more on this rule, see Yoram Dinstein, *Non-International Armed Conflicts in International Law* (Cambridge University Press 2014) 108–13. The first codification ever of the law of occupation, the Lieber Code, was a military manual specifically addressing the American Civil War.
[81] Accordingly, it is technically not correct that Hezbollah 'occupies' the Southern part of Lebanon, as suggested by Israel (see S/PV.5489, 6).
[82] US Military Manual, section 11.4.
[83] Ibid., section 11.2.4.
[84] See Koskenniemi, 'Occupation', 164.

the factual nature of occupation, the extent of time the authority is exercised over a territory is irrelevant to the existence of an occupation *as a fact*,[85] even if a certain degree of stability is necessary to fully comply with the law of occupation.[86]

2.3.2. *The Issue of the Authority Required for the Establishment of an Occupation*

The debate regarding whether a territory is occupied or not focuses mainly on the degree of authority exercised by the hostile state in order to occupy the territory. It is commonly held that 'actual authority' pursuant to Article 42 HR is synonymous with 'effective control', and that, accordingly, the occupation itself means effective control of foreign territory.[87] However, it is worth pointing out that a number of states prefer to employ the word 'authority' that is embodied in treaty law,[88] and that the ICTY explicitly endorsed the employment of the text of 'actual authority' rather than that of 'effective control'.[89]

The main problem is determining when the authority may be considered to be effective. To answer this question, the ICTY provided some guidelines that may help to determine whether the authority of the occupying power has been fully established:

---

[85] According to the Supreme Court of Israel, '[I]f the military force gained effective and practical control over a certain area, it is immaterial that its presence in the territory is limited in time or that the intention is to maintain only temporary military control' (HCJ 102/82 *Tsemel* et al. v. *Minister of Defence* et al. (1983), quoted by Benvenisti, *The International Law*, 200).

[86] EECC, *Partial Award, Western Front, Aerial Bombardment and Related Claims, Eritrea's Claims 1, 3, 5, 9–13, 14, 21, 25, & 26*, 307 (partially contradicting what the EECC had affirmed in EECC, *Partial Award, Central Front–Eritrea's Claims 2, 4, 6, 7, 8, & 22*, 136).

[87] See *Hostages* case, 56; ICC, *Prosecutor v. Katanga*, Judgment pursuant to Art. 74 of the Statute, ICC-01/04-01/07, 7 March 2014, para. 1179; Report of the Independent International Fact-Finding Mission on the Conflict in Georgia vol. II (September 2009), 304. See also Curti Gialdino, 'Occupazione', 721; Bothe, 'Occupation', 65; Dinstein, *The International Law*, 42–3; Benvenisti, *The International Law*, 43.

[88] See Canada, Ministry of National Defence, Law of Armed Conflict at the Operational and Tactical Level (13 August 2001) section 1203; España, Ministerio de Defensa, Orientaciones. El Derecho de los Conflictos Armados (OR7-004, 2nd edn, 2007) vol. I, section 2.7.a.(2) (Spanish Military Manual); France, Ministère de la Défense, Manuel du droit des conflits armés (2013) 88 (French Military Manual); Germany, Federal Ministry of Defence, Law of Armed Conflict Manual, May 2013, section 527. See also Italian Military Manual, section 32; UK Ministry of Defence, The Joint Service Manual of the Law of Armed Conflict (JSP 383 2004) section 11.3 (UK Military Manual); US Military Manual, section 11.2.2.1 (these three last manuals, however, employ the word 'control' in describing the exercise of the occupying power's authority in subsequent paragraphs).

[89] See *Prosecutor v. Prlić* et al., para. 317, fn. 964.

– the occupying power must be in a position to substitute its own authority for that of the occupied authorities, which must have been rendered incapable of functioning publicly; – the enemy's forces have surrendered, been defeated or withdrawn. In this respect, battle areas may not be considered as occupied territory. However, sporadic local resistance, even successful, does not affect the reality of occupation; – the occupying power has a sufficient force present, or the capacity to send troops within a reasonable time to make the authority of the occupying power felt; – a temporary administration has been established over the territory; – the occupying power has issued and enforced directions to the civilian population.[90]

From this interesting case law it is clear is that the occupying power is not required to control every parcel of the occupied territory, but 'it is sufficient that the occupying force can, within a reasonable time, send detachments of forces to enforce its authority within the occupied district'.[91] Indeed, '[n]o conquering army occupies the entire territory conquered. Its authority is established when it occupies and holds securely the most important places, and when there is no opposing governmental authority within the territory. The inability of any other power to establish and maintain governmental authority therein is the test'.[92] Accordingly, rebel forces' sporadic successes in controlling some areas in the occupied territory are not sufficient to terminate the occupation.[93] All in all, the assessment of the authority exercised over the occupied territory should be conducted case by case. Indeed, the degree of authority required for the occupation is flexible,[94] since it may vary according to the actual circumstances of the occupied territory; for instance, a thinly inhabited area may require a less intense degree of control to be considered occupied.[95]

Two main issues regarding the effectiveness of the authority are particularly thorny. First, it is debatable whether troops with boots on the ground are necessary to maintain a situation of occupation. The positive view was advocated by the Supreme Court of Israel in relation to the status of the

---

[90] *Prosecutor v. Naletilić*, para. 217 (references omitted); *Prosecutor v. Prlić* et al., para. 320 (references omitted).
[91] US Military Manual, section 12.2.2.1.
[92] US Supreme Court, *Keely v. Sanders* (1878), 99 US 441, 447.
[93] For more on this, see *infra*, Section 5.4.3.
[94] See Andrea Gattini, 'Occupazione bellica' in Sabino Cassese (ed.), *Dizionario di diritto pubblico* (Giuffrè 2006) 3889, 3891; Dinstein, *The International Law*, 43–4.
[95] US Military Manual, section 12.2.2.1.

Gaza Strip after the withdrawal of the Israeli forces in 2005, pursuant to the so-called Disengagement Plan.[96] In this Court's opinion, because Israel lost effective control over the Gaza Strip after the withdrawal of its troops, Israel is no longer bound by the law of occupation.[97] However, no treaty provision refers explicitly to the presence of troops as a condition for the existence of a situation of occupation, and the ICTY only referred to the presence of foreign troops as *one of the factors* that may contribute to demonstrate the establishment of foreign authority.[98] The contrary view held by the ECtHR in two recent decisions was not very well argued, and the Court failed to demonstrate that the presence of foreign troops is a constitutive element of occupation.[99] Indeed, if a hostile state manages to maintain its authority over the occupied territory even in the absence of its own troops on the ground, then the situation should be considered an occupation. In the case of the Gaza Strip, Israel maintains total control over the borders of the area, the territorial sea, the airspace, and the supplies of water and electricity.[100] Accordingly, on the basis of the consideration that occupation is a fact, there is room to argue that the Gaza Strip is under Israeli occupation after

---

[96] For an Israeli view on the Disengagement Plan, see the statement available on the website of the Israeli Ministry of Foreign Affairs, at www.mfa.gov.il/mfa/foreignpolicy/peace/guide/pages/israels%20disengagement%20plan-%20renewing%20the%20peace%20process%20apr%20 2005.aspx. For the Palestinian view, see the statement of the Palestine Liberation Organization (PLO), Negotiations Affairs Department, *The Israeli "Disengagement" Plan: Gaza Still Occupied*, September 2005, available at www.nad-plo.org/etemplate.php?id=8. For a description of the situation of the Gaza Strip under international law after the Israeli withdrawal, see generally Iain Scobbie, 'Gaza', in Wilmshurst (ed.), *International Law*, 280.

[97] See HCJ 9132/07 *Ahmed* et al. v. *Prime Minister* et al., 30 January 2008, para. 12, unofficial English translation at elyon1.court.gov.il/Files_ENG/07/320/091/n25/07091320.n25.pdf. Some scholars support the view that the Gaza Strip is no longer occupied, such as Yuval Shany, 'Faraway, So Close: The Legal Status of Gaza after Israel's Disengagement' (2005) 8 YIHL 369; Elizabeth Samson, 'Is Gaza Occupied? Redefining the Status of Gaza under International Law' (2010) 25 American University ILR 915; Hilly Moodrick-Even Khen, 'Having It Both Ways: The Question of Legal Regimes in Gaza and the West Bank' (2011) 16 *Israel Studies* 55; Solon Solomon, 'Occupied or Not: The Question of Gaza's Legal Status after the Israeli Disengagement' (2011) 19 Cardozo JICL 59; Benvenisti, *The International Law*, 211–12; Hanne Cuyckens, 'Is Israel Still an Occupying Power in Gaza?' (2016) 63 NILR 275.

[98] *Prosecutor v. Naletilić*, para. 217.

[99] See *Chiragov* et al. v. *Armenia*, para. 96; *Sargsyan* v. *Azerbaijan*, paras. 94 and 143–4. It should be noted that these paragraphs apparently rely on the opinion of very renown experts mentioned in the footnotes of the decisions; however, at a close analysis, most of these authorities suggest more flexible and cautious approaches (see Marko Milanovic, 'European Court Decides That Israel Is Not Occupying Gaza', EJIL: Talk!, 17 June 2015).

[100] See the Report on the Situation of Human Rights in the Palestinian Territories Occupied by Israel since 1967, 21 January 2008, A/HRC/7/17, para. 11.

the withdrawal of Israeli troops,[101] as affirmed by a number of international institutions.[102]

The second problem is whether, during the phase of invasion, there is sufficient authority to consider the invaded territory to be occupied. On the basis of relevant international case law and state practice, it appears that the fact of occupation is not coincident with that of invasion, which are two distinct phases of an armed conflict.[103] Accordingly, the application of the law of occupation is not triggered by mere invasion.[104] However, in practice, it may be difficult to identify the moment in which an invasion becomes an occupation. As suggested, a viable solution is considering that '[o]nce an invader has gained control over a part of an invaded territory, the law of occupation applies, even if the movement forward that precedes such control is continuing in other parts of the territory'.[105] However, it should be noted that *some* rules of the law of occupation may be triggered by circumstances that are different from the fact of occupation. This is the case of some rules of the GC IV, which may be applicable to individuals falling into the hands of the enemy during an

---

[101] This view is shared by the majority of scholars. See, e.g., Alain Bockel, 'Le retrait israélien de Gaza et ses conséquences sur le droit international' (2005) 51 AFDI 16, 23; Geneviève Bastid Burdeau, 'Les références au droit international' in SFDI, *Les compétences de l'Etat en droit international* (Pedone 2006) 161, 168; Alain Bockel, 'Gaza: le processus de paix en question' 55 AFDI 173, 180–3; Dinstein, *The International Law*, 278; Victor Kattan, 'Operation Cast Lead: Use of Force Discourse and *Jus ad Bellum* Controversies' (2009) 15 Palestine YIL 95, 107; Shane Darcy & John Reynolds, 'An Enduring Occupation: The Status of the Gaza Strip from the Perspective of International Humanitarian Law' (2010) 15 JCSL 211, 235; John Quigley, *The Statehood of Palestine: International Law in the Middle East Conflict* (Cambridge University Press 2010) 225; Vaios Koutroulis, 'Of Occupation, *Jus ad Bellum* and *Jus in Bello*: A Reply to Solon Solomon's "The Great Oxymoron: *Jus in Bello* Violations as Legitimate Non-Forcible Measures of Self-Defense: The Post-Disengagement Israeli Measures towards Gaza as a Case Study"' (2011) 10 CJIL 897, 909–10; Annoni, *L'occupazione*, 54; Zimmermann, 'Abiding', 53; Orna Ben-Naftali, 'Belligerent Occupation: A Plea for the Establishment of an International Supervisory Mechanism' in Cassese (ed.), *Realizing*, 538, 542; Otto, *Targeted Killings*, 509; Vitucci, *Sovranità*, 32–3; Julia Grignon, 'The Geneva Conventions and the End of Occupation' in Clapham, Gaeta, & Sassòli (eds.), *The 1949 Geneva Conventions*, 1575, 1593–6.

[102] See UNGA Res. 64/94, 19 January 2010, para. 4; Report of the United Nations Fact-Finding Mission on the Gaza Conflict, A/HRC/12/48, 25 September 2009, paras. 273–9; Report of the International Fact-finding Mission to Investigate Violations of International Law, Including International Humanitarian and Human Rights Law, Resulting from the Israeli Attacks on the Flotilla of Ships Carrying Humanitarian Assistance, A/HRC/15/21, 22 September 2010, paras. 63–6; 214 Gaza Report, paras. 26–31. See also ICC, OTP, Situation on Registered Vessels of Comoros, Greece and Cambodia – Art. 53(1) Report, 6 November 2014, paras. 27–9; Maurer, 'Challenges', 1506.

[103] See *Hostages* case, 55–6; Italy, Supreme Military Tribunal, *In re Lepore* (19 July 1946), 13 ILR 354, 355; US Military Manual, section 11.1.3.1.

[104] Ibid., section 11.1.3.

[105] Michael Bothe, 'Effective Control during Invasion: A Practical View on the Application Threshold of the Law of Occupation' (2012) 94 IRRC 37, 40.

2.3. Occupation as a Fact

invasion, even if the occupation under Article 42 HR is not established yet.[106] This position has achieved a certain amount of support in international case law[107] as well as in state practice,[108] even if it is not entirely definitive.[109] However, this does not mean that the GC IV embodies a different definition of occupation from that codified by Article 42 HR[110] but, rather, that some of the rules pertaining to the law of occupation may be triggered by authority exercised upon individuals.[111]

2.3.3. The Termination of Occupation

The termination of the state of occupation is a matter of fact as well.[112] Despite the lack of treaty provisions regarding the way an occupation ends, it could be

---

[106] According to Pictet, 'So far as individuals are concerned, the application of [GC IV] does not depend upon the existence of a state of occupation within the meaning of Art. 42 referred to above. The relations between the civilian population of a territory and troops advancing into a territory, whether fighting or not, are governed by the present Convention' (Jean Pictet (ed.), *Commentary to IV Geneva Convention* (ICRC 1958) 60). For a modern support to this theory, see Marco Sassòli, 'A Plea in Defence of Pictet and the Inhabitants of Territories under Invasion: The Case for the Applicability of the Fourth Geneva Convention during the Invasion Phase' (2012) 94 IRRC 42.

[107] This position was quoted with approval by the ICTY, *Prosecutor v. Naletilić*, paras. 219–23.

[108] For instance, there is a very cautious endorsement in the US Military Manual, section 11.1.3.1. ('as a matter of policy').

[109] See, e.g., Marten Zwanenburg, 'Challenging the Pictet Theory' (2012) 94 IRRC 30.

[110] See *Prosecutor v. Naletilić*, paras. 215–16; India, Supreme Court, *Rev Mons Sebastiao Francisco Xavier dos Remedios Monteiro v. The State of Goa* (26 March 1969), *All India Reporter*, (1970) 329 SC 87. See also Tristan Ferrarro, 'Determining the Beginning and End of an Occupation under International Humanitarian Law' (2012) 94 IRRC 133, 136–9. The idea of a different definition of occupation was advanced by S. D. Dikker Hupkes, *What Constitutes Occupation? Israel as the Occupying Power in the Gaza Strip after the Disengangement* (EM Meijers Instituut 2007) 32–3, 52–3.

[111] For some convincing arguments, see Dinstein, *The International Law*, 40.

[112] On this basis, the present author does not share the opinion of some commentators, according to whom the Gaza Strip is no longer occupied, but remains subject to the law of occupation nonetheless, due to different *normative* tests applied to the termination of the occupation. Although a thorough analysis of these theories is clearly beyond the purview of this work, they may be summarised as follows. First, on the basis of the principle of self-determination of peoples, it has been suggested that the law of occupation would apply to a territory even after a loss of actual authority, until the said territory had reached full and complete self-determination; the supporter of this opinion considers that the Gaza Strip has no longer achieved its self-determination and, accordingly, Israel would be bound to the law of occupation to fill a gap of responsibility (Iain Scobbie, 'An Intimate Disengagement: Israel's Withdrawal from Gaza, the Law of Occupation and of Self-Determination' (2004-5) 11 *Yearbook of Islamic and Middle Eastern Law* 3; for some counterarguments, see Koutroulis, *Le début*, 256–9). A second theory moves from the fact that, under Art. 4 of the Declaration of Principles on Interim Self-Government Arrangements between Israel and the PLO (13 September 1993, text in 32 ILM 1525) and under Art. 31(7) of the Israeli-Palestinian Interim Agreement on the West Bank

inferred that as soon as one of the elements of the definition of occupation is no longer present, then the situation of occupation ends.[113] In general, there is a trend to consider that, once the occupation is firmly established, temporary loss of control or decreasing intensity of control do not terminate the occupation: indeed, there is a presumption of continuation of the occupation which aims to prevent occupying powers from slightly reducing their control in order to escape their obligations under the law occupation. Accordingly, the factual changes that produce the end of a situation of occupation must be firmly ascertained, paying due attention to the fact that the actual authority of the occupying power may last on the occupied territory even after it relinquished boots-on-the-ground control.

There are a number of occurrences that may terminate the fact of occupation. First, occupation may end because the ousted sovereign regain control over the territory – in cases of successful uprising of the population of the occupied territory or withdrawal of the occupying power – or because a peace treaty terminating the hostile character of the foreign authority has been concluded – e.g., authorising the presence of the foreign troops or ceding the occupied territory to the occupying power.[114] Arguably, such a treaty should be concluded between a *restored* sovereign and the occupying power not to be considered invalid pursuant to Article 52 of the 1969 Vienna Convention on the Law of Treaties (VCLT).[115]

---

and the Gaza Strip (28 September 1995, text in 37 ILM 557), the West Bank and the Gaza Strip should be regarded as an indivisible territorial unity; this opinion suggests that until the occupation had ended in both areas, the Gaza Strip and the West Bank must be considered occupied notwithstanding any Israeli withdrawal (see PLO, *The Israeli "Disengagement" Plan*, section E; Nicholas Stephanopoulos, 'Israel's Legal Obligations to Gaza after the Pullout' (2006) 31 Yale JIL 524, 525–37).

[113] See UK Military Manual, section 11.7; US Military Manual, section 11.3.1; Kolb & Vitè, *Le droit*, 150. For more on the termination of occupation, see Koutroulis, *Le début*, 156–287; Dinstein, *The International Law*, 270–3; Adam Roberts, 'Occupation, Military, Termination of' in *MPEPIL* online (2009); Eyal Benvenisti, 'The Law on the Unilateral Termination of Occupation' in Andreas Zimmermann & Thomas Giegerich (eds.), *Veröffentlichungen des Walther-Schücking-Instituts für Internationales Recht an der Universität Kiel* (Kiel University Press 2009) 371; Konstantinos Mastorodimos, 'How and When Do Military Occupations End?' (2009) 21 Sri Lanka JIL 109; Ferraro, 'Determining'.

[114] In two cases regarding the Greek acquisition of territory in the aftermath of the collapse of the Ottoman Empire, international case law made a distinction between the period in which Greece should have been considered to be an occupying power, and the subsequent phase in which Greece had acquired sovereignty over certain areas pursuant to some treaties (among which the Treaty of Lausanne, 24 July 1923, 28 LNTS 12). See *Affaire de la Dette Publique Ottomane (Bulgaria, Irak, Palestine, Transjordan, Greece, Italy and Turkey)*, 18 April 1925, 1 RIAA 529; PCIJ, *Lighthouses Cases between France and Greece*, 17 March 1934, 62 PCIJ Reports, Series A/B, 4.

[115] Vienna Convention on the Law of Treaties, 23 May 1969, 1155 UNTS 331 (VCLT).

Second, the occupation may end because a new legitimate government arises in the occupied territory *pendente occupatione*, giving its consent to the presence of foreign troops. These phenomena are viewed with some suspicion in international relations since the occupying power may create a puppet regime in the attempt to free itself from the duties under the law of occupation. Accordingly, there is a presumption against the independence of local governments created *pendente occupatione*.[116] The new entity, in order not to be considered an organ of the occupying power, must demonstrate that it is effective and independent.[117] In recent practice, there is a trend to consider a local government born under occupation to be legitimate when it represents the local population of the occupied country, is freely elected, and its coming into power is supported by the UN, as in the case of Afghanistan in 2002.[118] In these cases, the consent of the new valid government prevents foreign authority from being considered hostile and, thus, from creating an occupation.

Finally, SC Resolution 1546 (2004), a binding Chapter VII decision that declared the end of the occupation in Iraq well before the factual situation of the occupation had changed, raises grave concerns regarding the factual test for the termination of an occupation.[119] Clearly, the SC may not change reality by passing a resolution;[120] if this isolated episode were to be consolidated in international practice it might be possible to conclude that the SC could alter the *applicability of the law of occupation*, disregarding the underlying factual situation.[121] Arguably, '[i]t is premature to draw all-embracing general conclusions from the single – and singular – instance'.[122]

[116] Crawford, *The Creation*, 76.
[117] Capotorti, *L'occupazione*, 109–10; Curti Gialdino, 'Occupazione', 735; Marco Longobardo, 'Lo Stato di Palestina: emersione fattuale e autodeterminazione dei popoli prima e dopo il riconoscimento dello status di Stato non membro delle Nazioni Unite' in Marcella Distefano (ed.), *Il principio di autodeterminazione dei popoli alla prova del nuovo millennio* (CEDAM 2014) 9, 18.
[118] See Sassòli, 'The International Legal Framework', 433.
[119] UNSC Res. 1546 (2004), para. 2.
[120] According to Roberts, 'Iraq is clearly not a case of an occupation coming to an end when an occupying power withdraws from a territory, or is driven out of it ... [T]he factual situation will not change overnight' (Roberts, 'The End', 46). It has been suggested that resolution may be read as just a declaration of a change in the situation of Iraq that in fact did not occur: 'This statement is a mere anticipation of a future event. If that anticipation should be proved wrong by the facts – by the very operation of effectiveness – IHL and occupation law would continue to apply inasmuch as the ordinary conditions for their applicability are met' (Robert Kolb, 'Occupation in Iraq since 2003 and the Powers of the UN Security Council' (2008) 98 IRRC 29, 46).
[121] See, e.g., US Military Manual, section 11.1.2.5. As it was noted, 'in the eye of *the law* the occupation formally came to a close by June 30 despite *the fact* that the coalition forces were still exercising administrative authority in certain areas of Iraq' (Benvenisti & Keinan, 'The Occupation', 269) (emphases added).
[122] Dinstein, *The International Law*, 273.

2.3.4. One Occupation or Many Kinds of Occupations?

Taking into account the factual nature of the occupation it is possible to solve also a terminological issue. Treaties, military manuals, and pieces of scholarship employ different expressions such as 'occupation', 'military occupation', 'belligerent occupation', and so on. Are there different kinds of occupation that correspond to these labels?

In the past, many authors have tried to classify a variety of types of occupation in light of the additional factual circumstances occurring in different occupations. Indeed, it is possible that some occupations differ with respect to certain details. For instance, while some occupations occur without meeting armed resistance, others are characterised by the presence of ongoing hostilities between the belligerents outside the occupied territory. Such a difference may be employed to classify different kinds of occupations.[123]

However, this author believes that similar classifications are not very helpful, since they do not reflect the application of different legal regimes. They are mainly descriptive: the fact of the occupation comprises the elements of the hostile character of the foreign authority, the exercise of foreign authority without legal title, and the loss of authority of the sovereign. These are the *basic* elements of the occupation as a fact, which are sufficient to trigger the application of the law of occupation. It may happen that other *additional* factual elements characterise specific occupations. However, as long as the basic elements exist, those situations fall into the definition of occupation. It is comforting that the author who classified seventeen types of occupation affirmed that these classifications are 'not mutually exclusive: a given occupation might well fit into two or more of the categories at the same time, and/or at different times ... – a reminder of the artificiality of these categories. The list ... represents just one attempt at distillation and improvisation'.[124]

For these reasons, since the definition of occupation appears to be flexible enough to encompass every kind of occupation, in the present book, the word 'occupation' will be employed with regard to any kind of occupation. Similarly, the expressions 'occupation', 'military occupation', and 'belligerent

---

[123] For instance, the ongoing presence of hostilities between the belligerents would qualify an occupation as 'belligerent' rather than as 'military' according to McDougal & Feliciano, *Law*, 733.

[124] See Roberts, 'What Is', 260. Already in 1949, Migliazza noted that the law of occupation is unitary even if it has to deal with a number of different situations, and that, accordingly, the duties and powers of the occupying power should be considered flexible (Migliazza, *L'occupazione*, 63).

occupation' should be read as interchangeable, as confirmed by recent state practice.[125]

2.4. ... AND OCCUPATION AS LAW

2.4.1. *The Law of Occupation as an Open System*

As already noted, the law of occupation is a component of international humanitarian law. As in other branches of international humanitarian law, the law of occupation is at the same time binding *qua* customary international law and *qua* treaty law. The main international instruments regarding the law of occupation are the aforementioned 1907 HR, which reflects customary international law,[126] the GC IV, which largely reflects customary international law,[127] and some provisions embodied in the AP I, whose customary status is a matter of debate.[128] It should be noted that the rules of these instruments that are embodied in the parts explicitly devoted to the occupation should not be applied exclusively. Other provisions embodied in the same instruments but not directly pertaining to the law of occupation might seem to be applicable, in particular when the provisions pertaining to the occupation does not regulate certain situations.[129]

In addition to HR, GC IV, and AP I, other international humanitarian law treaties contain rules regarding the law of occupation. For instance, in the field of the protection of cultural property in times of armed conflict, the law

---

[125] According to the US Military Manual: 'Military occupation is also called belligerent occupation ... This manual uses the terms "military occupation," "belligerent occupation," and "occupation" to refer to situations governed by the law of belligerent occupation' (section 11.1.1.1).

[126] See IMTFE, *In re Hirota* (12 November 1948), 15 ILR 356, 366; *Wall* opinion, para. 89. See also Italy, Court of First Instance of Rome, *Society Italiana per il Gas* v. *Mirabella* (15 June 1948), 15 ILR 606, 607.

[127] See, generally, Theodor Meron, 'The Geneva Conventions as Customary Law' (1987) 81 AJIL 348.

[128] On this debate, see Antonio Cassese, 'The Genova Protocols of 1977 on the Humanitarian Law of Armed Conflict and Customary International Law' (1984) 3 *UCLA Pacific Basin Law Journal* 55; Dieter Fleck, 'The Protocols Additional to the Geneva Conventions and Customary International Law' (1990) 29 MLLWR 497; Christopher Greenwood, 'Customary Law Status of the 1977 Geneva Protocols' in Astrid J. M. Delissen & Gerald Jacob Tanja (eds.), *Humanitarian Law of Armed Conflict: Challenges Ahead: Essays in Honor of Frits Kalshoven* (Martinus Nijhoff 1991) 93; Fausto Pocar, 'To What Extent Is Protocol I Customary International Law?' (2002) 78 ILS 337.

[129] Section 6.3.2.1 touches on the issue of the relationship between rules regarding the conduct of the hostilities and the law of occupation in cases of resumption of hostilities.

of occupation is complemented by Article 5 of the 1954 Convention for the Protection of Cultural Property in the Event of Armed Conflict,[130] Article I of its 1954 First Protocol,[131] and Article 9 of its 1999 Second Protocol.[132] The occupying power must apply all these rules in a manner consistent with the rules embodied in the HR, GC IV, and AP I.[133]

However, the application of the law of occupation does not bar the application of other branches of international law. With respect to customary international law, the ICJ has affirmed that the principle of self-determination of peoples, which is embodied in some treaty provisions as well, is applicable in times of occupation.[134] Similarly, the principle of permanent sovereignty over natural resources, which originated from economical self-determination and gained customary status,[135] should be considered applicable in times of occupation,[136] notwithstanding the contrary opinion of the ICJ.[137] This conclusion is consistent with the law of occupation's rules pertaining to the protection

---

[130] 249 UNTS 240.
[131] 249 UNTS 358.
[132] 2253 UNTS 212.
[133] On the protection of cultural property in the occupied territory, see Manlio Frigo, 'La protezione dei beni culturali nei territori occupati. Il divieto di esportare i beni culturali da un territorio occupato e gli obblighi di restituzione', in Paolo Benvenuti & Rosario Sapienza (eds.), *La tutela internazionale dei beni culturali nei conflitti armati* (Giuffrè 2007) 103.
[134] See *Wall* opinion, para. 88. The relevance of the principle of self-determination with regard to the use of armed force in occupied territory is explored *infra*,. Sections 4.3.1 and 5.5.3.2.
[135] The ICJ recognised the customary status of this principle in *DRC v. Uganda*, para. 244. This principle was first proclaimed by a number of resolutions of the GA, for instance, by UNGA Res. 1803 (XVII), 14 December 1962; UNGA Res. 2158 (XXI), 25 November 1966; UNGA Res. 3171 (XXVIII), 17 December 1973; UNGA Res. 3201 (S-VI), 1 May 1974; UNGA Res. 3281 (XXIX), 12 December 1974. For more on this principle, see Ian Brownlie, 'Legal Status of Natural Resources in International Law' (1979-I) 162 RCADI 249; Manlio Frigo, 'La sovranità permanente degli Stati sulle risorse naturali' in Paolo Picone & Giorgio Sacerdoti (eds.), *Diritto internazionale dell'economia* (Franco Angeli 1982) 245; Nico J. Schrijver, *Sovereignty over Natural Resources: Balancing Rights and Duties* (Cambridge University Press 1997); Valentina Zambrano, *Il principio di sovranità permanente dei popoli sulle risorse naturali tra vecchie e nuove violazioni* (Giuffrè 2009); Marc Burgenberg & Stephan Hobe (eds.), *Permanent Sovereignty over Natural Resources* (Springer 2015).
[136] This is the opinion of most commentators. See, e.g., Antonio Cassese, 'Powers and Duties of an Occupant in Relation to Land and Natural Resources' in Playfair (ed.), *International Law*, 419, 426; Iain Scobbie, 'Natural Resources and Belligerent Occupation: Mutation Through Permanent Sovereignty' in Stephen Bowen (ed.), *Human Rights, Self-Determination and Political Change in the Palestinian Occupied Territories* (Kluwer Law 1997) 221, 247–53; Schrijver, *Sovereignty*, 143–60; Emanuele Cimiotta, 'Conflitto armato nella Repubblica Democratica del Congo e principio della sovranità permanente degli Stati sulle proprie risorse naturali' in Aldo Ligustro & Giorgio Sacerdoti (eds.), *Problemi e tendenze del diritto internazionale dell'economia: Liber amicorum in onore di Paolo Picone* (Editoriale Scientifica 2011) 55, 76–8; Mara Tignino, *L'eau et la guerre: éléments pour un régime juridique* (Bruylant 2011) 259.
[137] *DRC v. Uganda*, para. 244.

of public and private property, which are applicable to natural resources as well.[138]

As a matter of treaty law, the occupying power must not alter the application of international treaties in force in the occupied territory before the occupation, as they fall into the broad interpretation of the word 'law' in Article 43 HR,[139] and thus they are part of the law applicable to the occupied territory. In addition, recent international case law has consistently held that the occupying power is bound by its international human rights treaty obligations in times of occupation, unless it has invoked the derogation clauses embodied in some of those treaties with regard to derogable rights.[140] Indeed, states, international organisations, and international courts and tribunals have become aware that treaties regarding international human rights law continue to apply during armed conflict, and that states are bound by those same conventions when they undertake certain activities beyond their own borders; accordingly, scholars and courts have been discussing how to interpret and simultaneously apply international humanitarian law and international human rights law while avoiding normative conflicts. This issue is addressed in Section 2.5.[141]

Moreover, the law of occupation itself allows the occupying power and the representatives of the population of the occupied territory to conclude agreements in order to implement and complete the law of occupation. According to Article 7 GC IV, '[i]n addition to the agreements expressly provided for in [the Convention], the High Contracting Parties may conclude other special agreements for all matters concerning which they may deem it suitable to make separate provision.' The only limitation is that these agreements must not 'adversely affect the situation of protected persons, as defined by the present Convention, nor restrict the rights which it confers upon them',[142] as confirmed by Article 47 GC IV.[143] If these agreements are concluded between two

---

[138] See Cassese, 'Powers'; Scobbie, 'Natural Resources'; Marco Pertile, *La relazione tra risorse naturali e conflitti armati nel diritto internazionale* (CEDAM 2012) 171–214; Marco Longobardo, 'The Palestinian Right to Exploit the Dead Sea Coastline for Tourism' (2015) 58 German YIL 317.

[139] See Theodor Meron, 'The Applicability of Multilateral Conventions to Occupied Territories' (1978) 72 AJIL 542.

[140] See *Wall* opinion, para. 106; *DRC v. Uganda*, para. 216; ECtHR, *Al Skeini v. UK*, para. 138.

[141] See *infra*, Section 2.5.

[142] Art. 7 GC IV.

[143] According to Art. 47 GC IV, 'Protected persons who are in occupied territory shall not be deprived, in any case or in any manner whatsoever, of the benefits of the present Convention ... by any agreement concluded between the authorities of the occupied territories and the occupying power'.

subjects of international law, as in the case of the so-called Oslo Accords,[144] the agreements concluded in the 1990s between the State of Israel and the movement of national liberation, the Palestine Liberation Organization (PLO),[145] they are international treaties.[146] Accordingly, pursuant to Articles 7 and 47 GC IV, the rules embodied in these agreements bind Israel and the PLO as long as they do not conflict with the law of occupation.[147]

Finally, the law of occupation may be integrated by binding SC resolutions, as was the case for the US and UK occupation of Iraq in 2003 and 2004. The occurrence of normative conflicts between these resolutions and the law of occupation raises some concerns regarding which of the two sources should prevail. Two lines of argument may be advanced. According to a first view, since the SC acting pursuant to Chapter VII may not violate the law of occupation – as the latter will prevail as a matter of *lex specialis*[148] or even

---

[144] The most important agreements forming the Oslo Accords are the following: Declaration of Principles on Interim Self-Government Arrangements, 13 September 1993; Agreement on Gaza Strip and Jericho Area, 4 May 1994; Israeli-Palestinian Interim Agreement, 28 September 1995; Protocol Concerning the Redeployment in Hebron, 17 January 1997; Wye River Memorandum, 23 October 1998; Agreement on Movement and Access, 15 November 2005 (all these agreements are available via www.mfa.gov.il). For an overview, see Raja Shehadeh, *From Occupation to Interim Accords: Israel and the Palestinian Territories* (Kluwer Law 1997); Geoffrey R. Watson, *The Oslo Accords: International Law and the Israeli-Palestinian Agreements* (Oxford University Press 2000).

[145] On the treaty-making power of national liberation movements, see Claude Lazarus, 'Le Statut International des Mouvements de Libération Nationale à l'Organisation des Nations Unies' (1974) 20 AFDI 173, 198–9; Julio A. Barberis, 'Nouvelles questions concernant la personnalité juridique international' (1983) 179 RCADI 145, 259–64; Cassese, *Self-Determination*, 169; M. Angeles Ruiz Colomé, *Guerras civiles y guerras coloniales* (Eurolex 1996) 41–86.

[146] This is the opinion of most commentators: Eyal Benvenisti, 'The Israeli-Palestinian Declaration of Principles: A Framework for Future Settlement' (1993) 4 EJIL 542, 544–5; Fabio Marcelli, 'Gli accordi fra Israele e OLP nel diritto internazionale' (1994) 77 RDI 430, 464; Peter Malanczuk, 'Some Basic Aspects of the Agreements between Israel and the PLO from the Perspective of International Law' (1996) 7 EJIL 485, 488–92; Crawford, 'Israel', 120–1; Watson, *The Oslo Accords*, 55–102. *Contra*, see Christine Chinkin, 'Normative Developments in the International Legal System' in Dinah Shelton (ed.), *Commitment and Compliance: The Role of Non-Binding Norms in the International Legal System* (Oxford University Press 2000) 21, 26; Benedetto Conforti, *Diritto internazionale* (10th edn, Editoriale Scientifica 2014) 15–16.

[147] On Arts. 7 and 47 GC IV, the most complete study is the one by Robert Kolb, 'Etude sur l'occupation et sur l'article 47 de la IVeme Convention de Genève du 12 août 1949 relative à la protection des personnes civiles en temps de guerre: le degré d'intangibilité des droits en territoire occupé' (2002) 10 African YIL 267. The Israel–PLO agreements have been considered in conflict with these provisions by John Quigley, 'The PLO–Israeli Interim Agreements and the Geneva Civilians Convention' in Bowen (ed.), *Human Rights*, 25.

[148] See Terry D. Gill, 'Legal and Some Political Limitations on the Power of the UN Security Council to Exercise Its Enforcement Powers under Chapter VII of the Charter' (1995) 26 Netherlands YIL 33, 171.

jus cogens[149] – then the law of occupation should prevail. A more pragmatic approach, based on the willingness of states to implement SC binding resolutions even when they are in conflict with other treaty obligations pursuant to Article 103 UN Charter,[150] and on the fact that there are insufficient routes to bring a complaint regarding the validity of SC resolutions,[151] suggests that the law of occupation may be derogated by SC decisions.[152] This last option seems more in line with the practice followed during the occupation of Iraq.

Accordingly, it is clear that the law of occupation has many 'strata',[153] and that the law of occupation is strictly related to international humanitarian law beyond the law of occupation, and to international law more generally. This interplay of different legal systems should be borne in mind when describing the main features of the law of occupation, the administrative powers of the occupying powers, and the use of armed force in occupied territory.

---

[149] Picone, 'Le autorizzazioni', 57. For the characterisation as *jus cogens* of some provisions of the law of occupation, see Kolb & Vité, *Le droit*, 250–60. However, international humanitarian law in general is not considered a source of *jus cogens* by other authors, such as Rafael Nieto-Navia, 'International Peremptory Norms (*Jus Cogens*) and International Humanitarian Law' in Lal Chand Vohrah, et al. (eds.), *Man's Inhumanity to Man: Essays on International Law in Honour of Antonio Cassese* (Kluwer Law International 2003) 595.

[150] According to Art. 103 UN Charter, 'In the event of a conflict between the obligations of the Members of the United Nations under the present Charter and their obligations under any other international agreement, their obligations under the present Charter shall prevail.' For an in-depth analysis of this provision see Jean-Marc Thouvenin, 'Article 103' in Jean-Pierre Cot, Alain Pellet, & Mathias Forteau (eds.), *La Charte des Nations Unies: commentaire article par article* vol. II (3rd edn, Economica 2005) 2133; Lorenzo Gradoni, 'Il lato oscuro dell'articolo 103 della Carta delle Nazioni Unite' in Massimo Meccarelli, Paolo Palchetti, & Carlo Sotis (eds.), *Le regole dell'eccezione. Un dialogo interdisciplinare a partire dalla questione del terrorismo* (eum 2011) 263; Andreas Paulus & Johann Ruben Leiß, 'Article 103' in Bruno Simma, et al. (eds.), *The Charter of the United Nations. A Commentary* vol. II (3rd edn, Oxford University Press 2012) 2110; Robert Kolb, 'L'article 103 de la Charte des Nations Unies' (2013) 367 RCADI 9.

[151] The ICJ has no direct jurisdiction on the validity of the SC resolutions (see, generally, Maria Irene Papa, *I rapporti tra la Corte internazionale di giustizia e il Consiglio di sicurezza* (CEDAM 2006)). However, some international regional courts and some domestic tribunals have challenged the applicability of SC decisions in cases of conflicts with fundamental human rights; for an analysis of the relevant case law – beyond the purview of this work – see, among many others, Pasquale De Sena, 'Le Conseil de sécurité et le contrôle du juge' in Joël Rideau, et al. (eds.), *Sanctions ciblées et protections juridictionnelles des droits fondamentaux dans l'Union européenne* (Bruylant 2010) 43; Antonios Tzanakopoulos, *Disobeying the Security Council: Countermeasures against Wrongful Sanctions* (Oxford University Press 2011); Maïa-Oumeïma Hamrouni, 'Les juridictions européennes et l'article 103 de la charte des Nations Unies' (2017) 120 RGDIP 769.

[152] See US Military Manual, section 11.1.2.5; Charles H. D. Garraway, 'The Duties of the Occupying Power: An Overview of the Recent Developments in the Law of Occupation' in Julia Race & Patrick Sutter (eds.), *Facets and Practices of State-Building* (Martinus Nijhoff 2009) 179, 186–92.

[153] This expression is borrowed from Dinstein, *The International Law*, 4.

2.4.2. The Distinction between Occupation and Annexation, and Its Corollaries

Although the main feature of the law of occupation – that the occupied territory is not annexed by the occupying power because of the actual authority exercised therein – is not clearly specified in the HR, this rule is implicit in Article 43 HR, which regulates the occupying power's administration. According to this provision, '[l]'autorité du pouvoir légal ayant passé *de fait* entre les mains de l'occupant ...'.[154] As affirmed by a leading commentator, Article 43 HR 'protects the separate existence of the State, its institutions, and its laws'.[155] More explicitly, Article 47 GC IV affirms that '[p]rotected persons who are in occupied territory shall not be deprived, in any case or in any manner whatsoever, of the benefits of the present Convention by any change introduced ... by any annexation ... of the whole or part of the occupied territory'. Similarly, Article 4 AP I reaffirms that '[n]either the occupation of a territory nor the application of the Conventions and this Protocol shall affect the legal status of the territory in question'. As already mentioned, the difference between annexation and occupation was first recognised by domestic courts,[156] and became firmly rooted in international[157] and domestic case law after WWI.[158] This principle is also consistently affirmed by most military manuals.[159]

In addition, the prohibition on annexation regarding occupied territory is consistent with and reinforced by two fundamental rules of international law. First, the prohibition of annexation is a corollary of the prohibition of the use of force under Article 4(2) UN Charter. Indeed, the inadmissibility of the acquisition of territory by war has been affirmed on a number of occasions by the SC[160] and GA,[161] it is embodied in regional agreements such as the Charter

---

[154] Emphasis added. According to the English text, 'The authority of the legitimate power having in fact passed into the hands of the occupant ...'

[155] Pictet (ed.), *Commentary to IV Geneva*, 273.

[156] See *supra*, Section 2.2.

[157] See *Affaire de la Dette Publique Ottomane*, 555; US Military Tribunal Nuremberg, *In re Krupp* (31 July 1948), 15 ILR 620, 622; *Namibia* opinion, Dissenting Opinion of Judge Sir Gerald Fitzmaurice, para. 85, fn. 58.

[158] See Greece, Court of Appeal of Thrace, *L v. N* (1 January 1947), 14 ILR 242; Belgium, Court of Appeal of Liège, *Bourseaux v. Krantz* (24 June 1948), 15 ILR 526, 527; Malaysia, *Elli anak Masing v. The King* (22 March 1948) 15 ILR, 586; US Court of Appeals 9th Circuit, *Cobb v. United States* (11 June 1951), 18 ILR 549, 552.

[159] See US Military Manual, section 11.4; UK Military Manual, section 11.9; French Military Manual, 17.

[160] See, e.g., UNSC Res. 242 (1967), 22 November 1967, preamb. para. 2; UNSC Res. 2334 (2016), 23 December 2016.

[161] UNGA Res. 2625 (XXV), Declaration on Principles of International Law Concerning Friendly Relations and Co-operation among States in Accordance with the Charter of the United

2.4. ... and Occupation as Law

of the Organization of American States,[162] and it is considered to be well rooted in customary international law, according to the ICJ.[163] Second, the prohibition of annexation is also consistent with the principle of self-determination of peoples, which is applicable even in situations of occupation. Pursuant to this principle, '[a]ll peoples have the right of self-determination. By virtue of that right they freely determine their political status and freely pursue their economic, social and cultural development'[164] – something that would obviously be hampered if a transfer of sovereignty over a territory controlled *manu militari* were allowed by international law.[165]

The prohibition on annexation is reinforced by the fact that states are under a duty not to recognise unlawful situations created in violation of fundamental rules of international law.[166] This duty is mentioned by the ICJ[167] and confirmed by Article 41 DARS.[168] This rule is fully applicable to annexation following an occupation, as affirmed by the SC, which did not recognise the Israeli annexation of East Jerusalem,[169] and by the ICJ, which considers every state to be under a duty not to recognise illegal situations created in the OPT.[170] It is clear that the duty not to recognise such an illegal annexation is based on the fact that the prohibition of use of force, at least the prohibition of aggression, and the principle of self-determination of peoples – the rules

---

Nations, 24 October 1960, para. 10; UNGA Res. 42/22, Declaration on the Enhancement of the Effectiveness of the Principle of Refraining from the Threat or Use of Force in International Relations, 18 November 1987, para. 10.

[162] See Art. 21: 'No territorial acquisitions or special advantages obtained either by force or by other means of coercion shall be recognized' (Bogotá, 30 April 1948, text in 119 *UNTS* 3).

[163] *Wall* opinion, para. 87.

[164] Common Art. 1 ICESCR/ICCPR.

[165] See Korman, *The Right*, 225–30.

[166] For a detailed overview of state practice and *opinio juris*, see Korman, *The Right*, 234–48.

[167] *Namibia* opinion, paras. 122–5.

[168] DARS, with Commentaries (2001), A/56/10. On this duty, see, generally, Giuliana Ziccardi Capaldo, *Le situazioni territoriali illegittime nel diritto internazionale* (Editoriale Scientifica 1977); John Dugard, *Recognition and the United States* (Cambridge University Press 1987); Milano, *Unlawful Territorial Situations*; Stefan Talmon, 'The Duty Not to "Recognize as Lawful" a Situation Created by the Illegal Use of Force or Other Serious Breaches of a *Jus Cogens* Obligation: An Obligation without Real Substance?' in Christian Tomuschat & Jean-Marc Thouvenin (eds.), *The Fundamental Rules of the International Legal Order: Jus Cogens and Obligations Erga Omnes Obligations* (Martinus Nijhoff 2006) 99; Martin Dawidowicz, 'The Obligation of Non-Recognition of an Unlawful Situation' in James Crawford, Alain Pellet, & Simon Olleson (eds.), *The Law of International Responsibility* (Oxford University Press 2010) 683.

[169] See UNSC Res. 476 (1980), 30 June 1980, paras. 2–3; UNSC Res. 478 (1980), 30 August 1980.

[170] *Wall* opinion, para. 146. The Court does not refer directly to East Jerusalem, as that area was beyond the scope of the requested opinion. However, the Court had previously defined the illegal situation created by the construction of a barrier in the West Bank and its related Israeli settlements as a de facto annexation (para. 121).

that accompanied the evolution of the law of occupation – are *jus cogens* and produce obligations *erga omnes*.[171]

The prohibition on unilateral annexation of the occupied territory implies, as corollary, the fact that the occupation is inherently a temporary situation since the occupied territory should be returned to the ousted sovereign at the end of the occupation. With reference to the ancient Roman rule of *postliminium*, it has been argued that at the end of the occupation the restored sovereign has the right to abrogate legislation passed by the occupying power in violation of international law because of its invalidity.[172]

The temporariness of the occupation does not mean that the occupation must be short; rather, it implies that the occupation must terminate at a certain point. As has been suggested, the word 'temporary' 'can mean both "not permanent; provisional" and "lasting only a short time; transitory." In situations of belligerent occupation, "temporary" means first of all "not permanent; provisional." It reflects the idea that a belligerent occupation does not change the status of the occupied territory but merely suspends the exercise of the ousted sovereign's rights over the said territory'.[173]

Various provisions of the law of occupation confirm that the state of occupation is not permanent and that the occupied territory must be returned to the ousted sovereign. First, it should be noted that the occupying power does not acquire ownership of public goods and natural resources pursuant to Article 55 HR; rather, the occupying power has the same rights of the usufructuary, i.e., it may enjoy the fruits of public property, but it is prevented from completely depleting it or alienating it. Second, pursuant to Article 43 HR, the occupying power must not alter, 'unless absolutely prevented', the law in force in the occupied territory before the occupation. Finally, pursuant to Article 49(6) GC IV, the occupying power must not transfer its own population into

---

[171] The prohibition on the use of force was considered to be *jus cogens* by the ILC (see (1966-II) YILC 258; DARS, 112) and a source of obligations *erga omnes* by the ICJ (*Barcelona Traction, Light and Power Company, Limited, Second Phase Judgment*, 5 February 1970, para. 34). The principle of self-determination of peoples was recognised as *jus cogens* by the ILC ((1966-II) YILC 258; DARS, 113) and as a source of obligations *erga omnes* by the ICJ (*Case Concerning East Timor*, para. 29; *Wall* opinion, para. 88). For an overview of the conceptual distinction between *jus cogens* and obligations *erga omnes*, see Paolo Picone, 'The Distinction between *Jus Cogens* and Obligations *Erga Omnes*' in Enzo Cannizzaro (ed.), *The Law of Treaties beyond the Vienna Convention* (Oxford University Press 2011) 411.

[172] See *Affaire Relative à l'Or de la Banque Nationale d'Albanie (Etats-Unis d'Amérique, France, Italie, Royaume-Uni de Grande-Bretagne et d'Irlande du Nord)*, 12 RIAA 13, 40.

[173] Vaios Koutroulis, 'The Application of International Humanitarian Law and International Human Rights Law in Situation of Prolonged Occupation: Only a Matter of Time?' (2012) 94 IRRC 165, 167.

the occupied territory[174] since this would create an alteration in the demographic balance of that territory that would hampered the restitution to the ousted sovereign.[175]

Article 6(3) GC IV does not alter the temporariness of the occupation. According to this provision, in case of occupation, the application of some provisions of the convention 'shall cease one year after the general close of military operations'. This provision was applied by the ICJ to the OPT with regard to the construction of the Israeli security fence, or wall.[176] To this regard, it should be noted that, although Article 3(b) AP I seems to abrogate Article 6(3) GC IV,[177] Israel is not party to the AP I and, consequently, the ICJ was correct not to examine the issue of the relationship between these two rules.[178] However, the Court received criticism regarding the application of Article 6(3) GC IV because this provision seems to be inapplicable due to the ongoing military operations in the OPT. Apparently, the ICJ 'read the term "general close of military operations" and referred to such operations "leading to the occupation"',[179] while, instead, the provision refers to military operations

[174] According to the ICJ, the practice of transferring the occupying power's population into the occupied territory, coupled with the measures employed to grant their security, may create 'a "fait accompli" on the ground that could well become permanent, in which case ... it would be tantamount to de facto annexation' (*Wall* opinion, para. 121). See also the Memorandum of Herbert J. Hansell, Legal Adviser of the US Department of State, on the Legality of Israeli Settlements in (1978) *Digest of United States Practice in International Law* 1575. For more on Art. 49(6), which has been invoked especially in relation to the Israeli occupation of the OPT, see Jean Salmon, 'Les colonies de peuplement israéliennes en territoire palestinien occupé au regard de l'avis consultatif de la Cour internationale de Justice du 9 juillet 2004' in Andreas Fischer-Lescano et al. (eds.), *Frieden in Freiheit, Peace in liberty, Paix en liberté – Festschrift fur Michal Bothe zum 70. Geburtstag* (Nomos 2008) 285; Christian Tomuschat, 'Prohibition of Settlements' in Clapham, Gaeta, & Sassòli (ed.), *The 1949 Geneva Conventions*, 1551; Theodor Meron, 'The West Bank and International Humanitarian Law on the Eve of the Fiftieth Anniversary of the Six-Day War' (2017) 111 AJIL 357, 372–4. See also the essays collected in the 'Symposium on Revisiting Israel's Settlements' (2017) 111 AJIL Unbound 29.
[175] See UNSC Res. 2334 (2016), para. 1. According to Pictet, this rule 'is intended to prevent a practice adopted during the Second World War by certain Powers, which transferred portions of their own population to occupied territory for political and racial reasons or in order, as they claimed, to colonise those territories. Such transfers worsened the economic situation of the native population and endangered their separate existence as a race' (Pictet, *Commentary to IV Convention*, 283). See also Catriona Drew, 'Self-Determination, Population Transfer and the Middle East Peace Accords' in Bowen (ed.), *Human Rights*, 119, 140–66.
[176] *Wall* opinion, para. 125.
[177] See German Military Manual, section 536.
[178] Whether a rule of customary international law of the same content of Art. 3(b) AP I emerged and abrogated Art. 6(3) GC IV is a matter of debate that should have deserved a clarification by the ICJ. On the status of Art. 3(b) AP I and its relationship with Art. 6(3) GC IV, see Grignon, 'The Geneva Conventions', 1582–5.
[179] Orna Ben-Naftali, '"A la Recherche du Temps Perdu": Rethinking Article 6 of the Fourth Geneva Convention in the Light of the Legal Consequences of the Construction of a Wall

occurring during the occupation as well.[180] The preparatory works of the GC IV demonstrate that states had different views on this provision.[181] However, interpreting the GC IV in light of its aim and object, that is the protection of civilians, one has to conclude that the ICJ's creative interpretation is not correct[182] as confirmed by the case law of the Supreme Court of Israel that applies some provisions of the GC IV which would not be applicable pursuant to Article 6(3).[183] However, it should be noted that Article 6(3) GC IV, when applicable, does not mean that an occupation must last for a maximum of one year, nor does it imply that the occupation automatically ends after one year.

Especially with regard to the occupation of the OPT, the temporariness of the occupation is challenged by the fact that some occupations last a long amount of time. The Supreme Court of Israel has argued that the law of occupation should apply differently in cases of so-called prolonged occupations,[184] an expression that is mentioned by some SC resolutions.[185] However, there is nothing in treaty law allowing a different interpretation of the law of occupation in cases of prolonged occupation, nor is it clear after how many years an occupation would become 'prolonged'.[186] In the absence of new treaty law regarding what constitutes a prolonged occupation,[187] an analysis of uniform state practice and *opinio juris* is necessary to verify whether international customary law regulates prolonged occupations differently from those lasting for a short time. However, it should be noted that '[a]ttempts by Israel to propound the idea that the occupation does not fit into those rules have been firmly and consistently rejected by states as well

---

in the Occupied Palestinian Territory Advisory Opinion' (2005) 38 IsLR 212, 214. See also Ardi Imseis, 'Critical Reflections on the International Humanitarian Law Aspects of the ICJ Wall Advisory Opinion' (2005) 99 AJIL 102, 106; Grignon, *The Geneva Conventions*, 1579.

[180] On the occurrence of hostilities during occupation, see *infra*, Section 5.4.

[181] See the debate in the *Final Record of the Diplomatic Conference of Geneva of 1949* vol. II/A, 623–35.

[182] See Ferraro, *Expert Meeting*, 75; Iain Scobbie, 'Prolonged Occupation and Article 6(3) of the Fourth Geneva Convention: Why the International Court Got It Wrong Substantively and Procedurally', EJIL: Talk!, 16 June 2015.

[183] See HCJ 7015/02 *Ajuri et al. v. IDF Commander*, para. 17 (discussing the applicability of Art. 78 GC IV, which would be inapplicable pursuant to Art. 6(3)).

[184] See HCJ 337/71 *The Christian Society for the Holy Places v. Minister of Defence et al.*, 26(1) PD 574, 582; HCJ 393/82 *Jam'iat Iscan Al-Ma'almoun v. IDF Commander*.

[185] See UNSC Res. 471 (1980), 5 June 1980; UNSC Res. 476 (1980), 30 June 1980.

[186] For more on this, see Richard A. Falk, 'Some Legal Reflections on Prolonged Israeli Occupation of Gaza and the West Bank' (1989) 2 *Journal of Refugee Studies* 40; Roberts, 'Prolonged Military Occupation'; Koutroulis, 'The Application'; Iain Scobbie, 'International Law and the Prolonged Occupation of Palestine', 22 May 2015, available at papers.ssrn.com/sol3/papers.cfm?abstract_id=2611130.

[187] For such a proposal, see Itay Epshtain, 'Setting a Time Limit: The Case for a Protocol on Prolonged Occupation', 11 May 2013, available at phap.org/system/files/article_pdf/Epshtain-ProlongedOccupation_0.pdf

by the [UN]. In these circumstances it was impossible for new customary rules to evolve in the matter: unilateral statements by one state are not sufficient to form a customary rule'.[188] Neither does recourse to the rule on evolutionary interpretation of treaties embodied in Article 31(3)(b) VCLT[189] demonstrate that the law of occupation must be interpreted in a different way with respect to prolonged occupations. Indeed, the practice of just one state is insufficient: this rule refers to a 'concordant, common and consistent sequence of acts or pronouncements which is sufficient to establish a discernible pattern implying the agreement of the parties regarding [the] interpretation' of a treaty.[190] Arguably, the prolonged character of the occupation is a factual element that must be taken into account in the interpretation of existing rules, rather than a normative element relevant for the emergence of new rules pertaining to the occupation.[191]

Accordingly, it is clear that the occupying power's authority over the occupied territory does not result in a transfer of sovereignty; rather, it must be seen as a temporary situation, at the end of which the ousted sovereign should be restored. This conclusion shapes the entire discipline pertaining to the occupying power's administration.

2.4.3. The Administration of Occupied Territory

This subsection summarises the main features of the occupying power's duty to administrate the occupied territory. Section 5.3 analyses in greater detail the aspects more closely linked to the issue of the use of armed force in the occupied territory, such as measures regarding the maintenance of public order in the occupied territory.

The authority gained *manu militari* by the occupying power allows it to administer the occupied territory. Despite early views to the contrary,[192] the

---

[188] Cassese, 'Powers', 419–20.
[189] According to this rule, in the interpretation of a treaty 'any subsequent practice in the application of the treaty which establishes the agreement of the parties regarding its interpretation' should be taken into account. On this interpretive criterion, see, among many others, Giovanni Distefano, 'L'interprétation évolutive de la norme internationale' (2011) 115 RGDIP 373; Pierre-Marie Dupuy, 'Evolutionary Interpretation of Treaties: Between Memory and Prophecy' in Cannizzaro (ed.), *The Law*, 123; Georg Nolte, *Treaties and Subsequent Practice* (Oxford University Press 2013); Erik Bjorge, *The Evolutionary Interpretation of Treaties* (Oxford University Press 2014); Luigi Crema, *La prassi successiva e l'interpretazione del diritto internazionale scritto* (Giuffrè 2017).
[190] WTO, *Japan: Alcoholic Beverages II, Report of the Appellate Body* (4 October 1996) (WT/DS8/AB/R, WT/DS10AB/R, WT/DS11/AB/R) 13 (references omitted).
[191] See Koutroulis, 'The Application', 276–80; Longobardo, 'The Palestinian Right', 326–7.
[192] See, e.g., George B. Davis, *The Elements of International Law, with an Account of Its Origin, Sources and Historical Development* (3rd edn, Harper & Brothers 1908) 329; Oppenheim, 'The Legal Relations'.

exercise of governmental functions by the occupying power is not a question of fact, but is, rather, based on the law of occupation itself. According to Article 43 HR, '[l]'autorité du pouvoir légal ayant passé de fait entre les mains de l'occupant, celui-ci prendra toutes les mesures qui dépendent de lui en vue de rétablir et d'assurer, autant qu'il est possible, l'ordre et la vie publics en respectant, sauf empêchement absolu, les lois en vigueur dans le pays'.[193] This rule is normally considered to be the most important provision regarding powers and duties of the occupying power.[194] Its paramount role in the regulation of the use of armed force in the occupied territory is addressed in Section 5.5.

The administration of the occupying power is like a hydra with two heads: on the one hand, as with every government of a modern state, the occupying power must take into account the interests of the local population as a matter of both public order and economic life; on the other, the occupying power must respect the prerogatives of the ousted sovereign and must care for its own security, which is likely endangered by the hostility of the local population. It is undeniable that 'at the heart of all occupations exists a potential – if not an inherent – conflict of interest between occupant and occupied'.[195] Julius Stone correctly points out that '[e]very belligerent occupation involves, psychologically speaking, various shadings of the conflict of legal orders and supporting ethical allegiances'.[196] This conflict of interests assume dramatic proportions in light of the general environment in which occupations usually occurs, i.e., international armed conflicts with the subsequent temporary denial of a people's exercise of self-determination. As has been suggested, '[a]ll occupiers are likely to have an uneasy relationship with any remaining governmental institutions during the period of occupation (it is, after all, termed a belligerent occupation). By their very nature, occupations engender an antagonistic

---

[193] The official English translation reads as follows: 'The authority of the legitimate power having in fact passed into the hands of the occupant, the latter shall take all the measures in his power to restore, and ensure, as far as possible, public order and safety, while respecting, unless absolutely prevented, the laws in force in the country.' However, the word 'safety' is a clear error of translation. Since the only authoritative text is the French one, the English version of Art 43 HR should be read as referring to 'civil life', rather than 'safety'. See Edmund H. Schwenk, 'Legislative Power of the Military Occupant under Article 43, Hague Regulations' (1945) 54 Yale Law Journal 393; Benvenisti, The International Law, 68; Yoram Dinstein, 'Legislation under Article 43 of the Hague Regulations: Belligerent Occupation and Peacebuilding', Program on Humanitarian Policy and Conflict Research Harvard University, 1 Occasional Paper Series (Fall 2004) 2, available at www.hpcrresearch.org/sites/default/files/publications/OccasionalPaper1.pdf

[194] 'Article 43 is a sort of mini-constitution for the occupant administration' according to Benvenisti, The International Law, 69.

[195] Benvenisti, The International Law, 3–4.

[196] Stone, Legal Controls, 726.

relationship'.[197] These tensions colour the entire regulation regarding the administration of the occupied territory, including the use of armed force by the occupying power.

Whether the establishment of an administration is a duty for the occupying power has been debated. It should be noted that the existence of such an administration is not a constitutive element of a situation of occupation, as confirmed by the case law of the ICTY, which lists the establishment of a temporary administration as only one of the factors suggesting that a situation of occupation exists, rather than as a requirement.[198] The same position was held by the Supreme Court of Israel when it affirmed that the occupation 'do[es] not depend on the establishment of a particular organizational framework in the form of military administration'.[199] Similarly, the lack of such an administration does not excuse the occupying power from its responsibilities, as affirmed by the ICJ.[200] On this basis, the debate regarding the duty to establish an administration after the beginning of the occupation is moot: an efficient administration is the most effective way for the occupying power to fulfil its obligations under Article 43 HR, but the lack of such administration is not per se unlawful, as long as the occupying power fulfils its responsibilities in other ways.

In addition, there is no formal requirement regarding the administration of the occupying power. First, the occupying power may provide for an exclusively military administration, as in the entire OPT during the early stage of the Israeli occupation[201] and, still today, in certain areas of the West Bank,[202] as well as in Iraq in 2003-4.[203] Second, the occupying power may decide to establish a civil administration, as Israel did in 1981, when the military commander appointed a 'Head of the Civilian Administration'.[204] Third, the occupying

---

[197] Buchan, *International Law*, 208-9.
[198] *Prosecutor v. Naletilić*, para. 217.
[199] HCJ 102/82 *Tzemel* et al. v. *Minister of Defence* et al., 37(3) PD 365, English translation quoted by Shany, 'Farewell', 376.
[200] *DRC v. Uganda*, para. 173.
[201] See Law and Administration Proclamation, 7 June 1967, (1971) 1 *IYHR* 419. For more on this early stage, see Mona Rishmawi, 'The Administration of the West Bank under Israeli Rule' in Playfair (ed.), *International Law*, 267, 271-5.
[202] See *Beit Sourik* case, para. 23.
[203] See the Coalition Provisional Authority (CPA): Origin, Characteristics, and Institutional Authority (Report for the US Congress, 6 June 2005) 14. For more on the CPA, see Carcano, *The Transformation*, 147-59.
[204] See Israel Military Order No. 947 Concerning the Establishment of a Civilian Administration, available at www.israellawresourcecenter.org/israelmilitaryorders/fulltext/mo0947.htm. For more on this stage, see Joel Singer, 'The Establishment of a Civil Administration in the Areas Administered by Israel' (1982) 12 *IYHR* 259; Rishmawi, 'The Administration', 275-81.

power may decide to transfer part of the administration to representatives of the occupied population, as in the case of the OPT after the creation of the PNA;[205] in this case, the occupation does not end as long as the occupying power maintains authority over the administration,[206] as confirmed by the ICJ and the Supreme Court of Israel which considered the OPT to be occupied even years after the establishment of the PNA.[207] Fourth, the occupying power may create an administration that is presented as autonomous, but that can be classified as a puppet regime, i.e., a regime acting on behalf of another state and controlling a portion of territory;[208] in these circumstances, the acts of the puppet regimes should be considered the same as acts of the sponsor state, which is actually an occupying power – as in the case of the TRNC, whose territory the international community still considers to be occupied by Turkey.[209] Finally, the occupying power may, in violation of the duty not to annex the occupied territory, simply extend its administration to an occupied territory invoking a right to annex it – as in the cases of East Jerusalem[210] and Crimea.[211]

However, the source of authority for the administration of the occupied territory is always military in character.[212] Indeed, '[i]t is immaterial whether the government over an enemy's territory consists in a military or civil or mixed administration. Its character is the same and the source of its authority the same. It is a government imposed by force, and the legality of its acts is determined by the law of war'.[213]

---

[205] See Agreement on Gaza Strip and Jericho Area, Cairo, 1994, 33 ILM 622, Art. 3 ('transfer of authority') and Art. 5 ('jurisdiction').
[206] See Bastid-Burdeau, 'Les références', 169–70; Dinstein, *The International Law*, 57–8.
[207] See *Wall* opinion, para. 77; *Best Sourik* case, para. 23.
[208] See ICTY, *Prosecutor v. Blaskic*, IT-95-14-T, 3 March 2000, para. 149; *Prosecutor v. Naletilić*, paras. 181–8, 197–202.
[209] See ECtHR, *Loizidou v. Turkey*, para. 44. See also UNSC Res. 541 (1983), 18 November 1983, S/RES/541; UNSC Res. 550 (1984), 11 May 1984, S/RES/550.
[210] See Basic Law: Jerusalem, Capital of Israel, 30 July 1980, Art. 1 (English text available at www.knesset.gov.il/laws/speciaL/eng/basic10_eng.htm). On the status of East Jerusalem, in particular after the SC's declarations regarding the invalidity of the annexation, see Antonio Cassese, 'Legal Considerations on the International Status of Jerusalem' (1986) 3 Palestine YIL 13; Ruth Lapidoth, 'Jerusalem and the Peace Process' (1994) 28 IsLR 402; Alfonso J. Iglesias Velasco, 'El Estatuto jurìdico-internacional de Jerusalén' (1999) 48 *Afers Internacional* 75; Ugo Villani, 'Lo status di Gerusalemme nel diritto internazionale' (1999) 54 CI 217. See also US Supreme Court, *Zivotofsky v. Kerry* (8 June 2015), 167 ILR 708.
[211] Federal Constitutional Law, on Admitting to the Russian Federation the Republic of Crimea and Establishing within the Russian Federation the New Constituent Entities of the Republic of Crimea and the City of Federal Importance Sevastopol, 21 March 2014. The annexation was ratified by the Russian Constitutional Court with decision no. 6-P of 19 March 2014, Rossiykaya Gazeta, *Federal Issue* No. 6335.
[212] Greenwood, 'The Administration', 253.
[213] US Military Manual, section 11.8.6.

The main duties conferred upon the occupying powers by Article 43 HR are the maintenance of public order and civil life in the occupied territory, and the duty not to change, unless this is absolutely prevented, the law already in force before the occupation in the occupied territory. The restoration and securing of public order encompasses 'responsibility for preserving order, punishing crime, and protecting lives and property within the occupied territory',[214] the duty to restore and ensure civil life regards the 'whole social, commercial and economic life of the community',[215] and 'a variety of aspects of civil life, such as the economy, society, education, welfare, health, [and] transport'.[216]

As stated by the Supreme Court of Israel, in the maintenance and securing of public order and civil life, the occupying power 'is not allowed to consider the national, economic and social interests of his own state, inasmuch as such interests have no effect on his security interest in the area or the interest of the local population'.[217] Since Article 49(6) GC IV prohibits the transfer of population of the occupying power in the occupied territory, Article 43 HR must be coherently interpreted as referring only to the population of the occupied territory – which enjoy the status of protected persons under Article 4 GC IV.[218] Consequently, the case law of the Supreme Court of Israel according to which the occupying power pursuant to Article 43 HR has to balance the interests of the local Palestinian population with those of the Israeli settlers[219] is in conflict with international humanitarian law.[220]

---

[214] *Hostages* case, 57.

[215] Germany, British Zone of Control, Control Commission, Court of Criminal Appeal, *Grahame v. Director of Prosecutions*, 232.

[216] HCJ 393/82 *Jam'iat Iscan Al-Ma'almoun v. IDF Commander*, 37(4) PD (1983) 785.

[217] Ibid., 794–5.

[218] According to Art. 4 GC IV, '[p]ersons protected by the Convention are those who, at a given moment and in any manner whatsoever, find themselves, in case of a conflict or occupation, *in the hands of a Party to the conflict or Occupying Power of which they are not nationals*' (emphasis added).

[219] See *Beit Sourik* case, paras. 36–44; HCJ 10356/02 *Hess et al. v. Commander of the IDF Forces in the West Bank*, 58(3) PD 443, unofficial English translation available at http://elyon1.court .gov.il/files_eng/02/970/104/115/02104970.r15.pdf, para. 8 ('The local population for this purpose includes both the Arab and Israeli inhabitants'); HCJ 1890/03 *Bethlehem Municipality v. The State of Israel*, PD 59(4) 736, unofficial English translation available at www.law.idf .il/sip_storage/FILES/2/352.pdf, paras. 16–17; HCJ 7957/04 *Mara'abe v. The Prime Minister of Israel*, 60(2) PD 477, unofficial English translation available at http://elyon1.court.gov.il/ Files_ENG/04/570/079/A14/04079570.A14.pdf, paras. 27–32.

[220] Aeyal M. Gross, 'The Construction of a Wall between The Hague and Jerusalem: The Enforcement and Limits of Humanitarian Law and the Structure of Occupation' (2006) 19 LJIL 393, 418, and 'Human Proportions: Are Human Rights the Emperor's New Clothes of the International Law of Occupation?' (2007) 18 EJIL 1; Martti Koskenniemi, 'Occupied Zone: A Zone of "Reasonableness?"' (2008) 41 IsLR 13; Marco Pertile, 'Il principio di proporzionalità tra diritto umanitario e diritti umani' in Adriana Di Stefano & Rosario Sapienza (eds.), *La tutela dei diritti umani e il diritto internazionale* (Editoriale Scientifica 2012) 159, 194–204.

The need to pursue the interests of the protected persons allows the occupying power to adopt positive measures to maintain and secure public order and civil life. However, the occupying power must implement Article 43 HR without altering, *sauf empêchement absolu*, the laws in force in the territory before the beginning of the occupation – the so-called conservationist or continuity principle.[221] There are two ways to reconcile the conservationist principle with the duties to maintain and secure public order and civil life. First, Article 43 HR allows the occupying power to undertake positive measures to maintain and secure public order and civil life. For instance, with regard to measures aiming to foster the economy of the occupied territory, the occupying power has to undertake some actions to fulfil Article 43 HR as long as it does not violate the law already in force in the territory.[222] Since the occupying power is not the sovereign, its duty to ensure stability and development of economic life in the occupied territory must be implemented while respecting the laws in force in the territory and, above all, in a manner consistent with the interests of the legitimate sovereign.[223] Second, Article 64 IV CG allows the occupying power to alter the law in force in the occupied territory 'to fulfil its obligations under the present Convention, to maintain the orderly government of the territory, and to ensure the security of the occupying power, of the members and property of the occupying forces or administration, and likewise of the establishments and lines of communication used by them'. Notwithstanding an authoritative different view that posits that Article 64 GC IV may be constructed as a separate, wider regime,[224] and despite the fact that this provision expressly refers only to penal legislation, Article 64 GC IV has been constantly interpreted as applicable to every kind of legislation adopted to fulfil Article 43 HR.[225] Since, pursuant to Article 154 GC IV, the Convention is 'supplementary to Sections II and III of the [HR]', the *empêchement absolu* should be read as encompassing the need to fulfil the GCs, to maintain order in the occupied territory, and to ensure the security of the occupying power and its members.[226] In other

---

[221] See Fox, *Humanitarian Occupation*, 233–7; Kristen E. Boon, 'Obligations of the New Occupier: The Contours of a *Jus Post Bellum*' (2009) 31 *Loyola of Los Angeles International & Comparative Law Review* 60.
[222] Longobardo, 'The Palestinian Right', 326–30.
[223] Alain Pellet, 'The Destruction of Troy Will Not Take Place' in Playfair (ed.), *International Law*, 169, 186.
[224] See Benvenisti, *The International Law*, 95–102.
[225] See Joyce A. C. Gutteridge, 'The Geneva Conventions of 1949' (1949) 26 *British YIL* 294, 324. See also Pictet (ed.), *Commentary to IV Geneva*, 335.
[226] For more on this, see *infra*, Section 5.3.

words, Article 64 GC IV complements Article 43 HR.[227] The clause regarding the *empêchement absolu* is commonly invoked to justify the occupying power's abrogation of illegal provisions that are in conflict with fundamental rules of international law, such as those at the basis of the Nazi regime in Germany and the Ba'ath party in Iraq; the abrogation of those systems met mainly with consensus at the international level and is generally considered legal since such heinous regimes are incompatible with the goals of the law of occupation[228] and pose serious threats to the security of the occupying power.[229] Although some states and authors have recently advocated that more extensive changes in the legal system of the occupied territory may be lawful under certain conditions (so-called transformative occupation), state practice clearly demonstrates that no other changes may be introduced beyond the boundaries of Article 43 HR and Article 64 GC IV.[230]

As the next subsection explains how, in administering the occupied territory, the occupying power must take into account the international human rights obligations incumbent upon it. However, the need to fulfil human rights obligations may not be used to overthrow the limits bestowed on the occupying power by Article 43 HR and Article 64 GC IV. International human rights law must be applied in a way not inconsistent with the law of occupation.[231] This outcome is consistent with the object and purpose of the law of occupation, and in particular of Article 43 HR and Article 64 GC IV: the occupying power is allowed to govern the occupied territory while preserving the rights of the ousted sovereign and the well-being of the local population. The occupying power is not in a position to implement international human rights obligations in order to transform the occupied territory in a way that would create a permanent change in the legal regime of that area; on balance, the occupying power may legitimately fulfil those human rights obligations that were freely chosen by the ousted sovereign when in control of that territory. Coherently, the law of occupation itself provides for the basic needs of the population of the occupied territory in a way

---

[227] Consequently, this author does not share the view according to which Art. 64 GC IV 'replaced the positive test proposed in Article 43 of the Hague Regulations' (Spoerri, 'The Law', 194).
[228] See Lauterpacht, *Oppenheim's International Law*, 446–7; Arai-Takahashi, *The Law*, 109–11.
[229] See McDougal & Feliciano, *Law*, 770.
[230] For more on this issue, see Adam Roberts, 'Transformative Military Occupation: Applying the Laws of War and Human Rights' (2006) 100 AJIL 580; Vaios Koutroulis, 'Mythes et réalités de l'application du droit international humanitaire aux occupations dites "transformatives"' (2007) 40 RBDI 365; Carcano, *The Transformation*.
[231] This assertion is addressed in more detail infra, Section 2.5.

consistent with the customary core of human rights law,[232] compelling the occupying power to provide the population of the occupied territory with food and medical supplies,[233] healthcare,[234] clothing and shelter,[235] care and education of children,[236] civilian defence services,[237] spiritual assistance,[238] protection of workers,[239] and relief.[240]

Not only is the occupying power prevented from changing the law of the occupied territory, but it must preserve the pre-existing administration as well. With regard to the administration of the justice, which is examined in more details in a subsequent chapter,[241] it should be noted that 'the tribunals of the occupied territory shall continue to function in respect of all offences covered by' the law of the occupied territory before the occupation,[242] which operates along with the military courts established by the occupying power to adjudicate breaches of the provisions enacted by the occupying power to guarantee its own security.[243]

The occupying power's administration must comply with the basic principles on occupation as enshrined in Article 43 HR and, with regard to specific topics, in other provisions of the law of occupation. For instance, the rules pertaining to private and public property are based on the assumption that the occupying power is not the legitimate sovereign of the occupied territory, and that the territory must be returned to the restored sovereign at the end of occupation in conditions similar to those existing at the beginning of the occupation. Accordingly, the aforementioned Article 55 HR compels the occupying power to act as an usufructuary of public property, preventing the occupying power from completely depleting natural resources or alienating other public property.[244] Moreover, the occupying power may only 'take possession of

---

[232] See Flavia Lattanzi, 'Il confine fra diritto internazionale umanitario e diritti dell'uomo' in Giardina & Lattanzi (eds.), *Studi*, 1985, 1988.
[233] Art. 55 GC IV.
[234] Arts. 56 and 57 GC IV.
[235] Art. 69(1) AP I.
[236] Art. 50 GC IV.
[237] Arts. 63 and 64(2) AP I.
[238] Art. 58 GC IV.
[239] Art. 52 GC IV.
[240] Arts. 59–63 GC IV.
[241] See *infra*, Section 5.3.2.
[242] Art. 64 GC IV.
[243] See Art. 66 GC IV.
[244] For more on this, see Scobbie, 'Natural Resources', 221; Cassese, 'Powers'; Anicée van Engeland, 'Protection of Public Property' in Clapham, Gaeta, & Sassòli (eds.), *The 1949 Geneva Conventions*, 1535.

2.4. ... and Occupation as Law 61

cash, funds, and realizable securities which are strictly the property of the State, depots of arms, means of transport, stores and supplies, and, generally, all movable property belonging to the State which may be used for military operations'.[245] In addition, both public and private property may be destroyed only 'where such destruction is rendered absolutely necessary by military operations',[246] and both public and private property are protected from pillage.[247] Finally, Article 46 HR specifically affirms that '[p]rivate property cannot be confiscated' unless it consists of war materials pursuant to Article 53(2) HR (which can be seized, but must be restored or compensated at the end of the occupation).[248]

Similarly, with regard to taxation, Article 48 HR provides that the occupying power may collect taxes in the interest of the occupied state under the obligation 'de pourvoir aux frais de l'administration du territoire occupé dans la mesure où le Gouvernement légal y était tenu', while new taxes may be imposed only 'pour les besoins de l'armée ou de l'administration'.[249] Similarly, in the actual collection of contributes, '[i]l ne sera procédé, autant que possible, à cette perception que d'après les règles de l'assiette et de la répartition des impôts en vigueur'.[250] It is a matter of debate whether the occupying power may levy new taxes;[251] the most correct solution is to assess the legality of new legislative acts regarding contributions – including some alterations in the existing tax system strictly to maintain and ensure the public life in the occupied territory – against Article 43 HR.[252]

---

[245] Art. 53(1) HR.
[246] Art. 53 GC IV.
[247] See Arts. 28 and 47 HR, and Art. 33(3) GC IV. 'Pillage' encompasses both private and public property, according to the ICTY, *The Prosecutor v. Zejnil Delalić* et al., IT-96-21-T, Judgment, 16 November 1998, para. 590; SPSL, *Prosecutor v. Norman* et al., SCSL-04-14-T, Decision on Motion of Acquittal, 21 October 2005, para. 102; ICC, *Prosecutor v. Katanga*, para. 115.
[248] For more on the protection of private property in occupied territory, see Noemi Corso, 'Occupazione militare e tutela della proprietà privata' in Di Stefano & Sapienza (eds.), *La tutela*, 115; Yutaka Arai-Takahashi, 'Protection of Private Property' in Clapham, Gaeta, & Sassòli (eds.), *The 1949 Geneva Conventions*, 1515.
[249] Art. 49 HR.
[250] Art. 51 HR (emphasis added).
[251] For example, they are generally prohibited according to most military manuals (Italian Military Manual, section 35; UK Military Manual, section 11.31; US Military Manual, section 11.22.1.2). For an overview of the different options, see Gerhard von Glahn, 'Taxation under Belligerent Occupation' in Playfair (ed.), *International Law*, 341, 350–1.
[252] Ibid., 352–4.

2.5. THE LAW OF OCCUPATION AND INTERNATIONAL HUMAN RIGHTS LAW

2.5.1. Preliminary Remarks

The issue of the relationship between the law of occupation and international human rights law is linked to the aforementioned open character of the law of occupation. The application of international human rights law in times of occupation has received extensive attention in international scholarship. In the past, the debate regarding the application of human rights in occupied territory did not focus on the application of international human rights law instruments along with international humanitarian law, but rather, the issue was mainly addressed through the framework of the protection international humanitarian law provides for individual rights in times of occupation.[253] More recently, the discourse on the contextual application of these two branches of international law has changed: the debate has been framed in the context of the wider debate regarding the so-called fragmentation of international law,[254] and many authors have discussed whether the old law of occupation may be complemented, updated, and rendered even more 'human' through the application of international human rights law standards, particularly in the context of the occupations of the OPT and Iraq.[255]

---

[253] See Dinstein, 'The International Law'; John Dugard, 'Enforcement of Human Rights in the West Bank and Gaza Strip' in Playfair (ed.), *International Law*, 461.

[254] On this debate see, generally, Report of the Study Group of the ILC (finalised by Martti Koskenniemi), Fragmentation of International Law: Difficulties Arising from the Diversification and Expansion of International Law, A/CN.4/L.682 (13 April 2006). See also Pierre-Marie Dupuy, 'L'unité de l'ordre juridique international' (2002) 297 *RCADI* 9; Tullio Treves, 'Fragmentation of International Law: The Judicial Perspective' (2007) 23 CS 821; Benedetto Conforti, 'Unité et fragmentation du droit international: "Glissez, mortels, n'appuyez pas"!' (2007) RGDIP 5; Mario Prost, *The Concept of Unity in Public International Law* (Hart 2012); Mads Andenas & Eirik Bjorge (eds.), *A Farewell to Fragmentation: Reassertion and Convergence in International Law* (Cambridge University Press 2015).

[255] See John Quigley, 'The Relation between Human Rights Law and the Law of Belligerent Occupation: Does an Occupied Population Have a Right to Freedom of Assembly and Expression?' (1989) 12 *Boston College International and Comparative Law Review* 1; Eyal Benvenisti, 'The Applicability of Human Rights Conventions to Israel and to the Occupied Territories' (1992) 26 IsLR 24; Jochen A. Frowein, 'The Relationship between Human Rights Regimes and Regimes of Belligerent Occupation' (1998) 28 IHYR 1; Orna Ben-Naftali & Yuval Shany, 'Living in Denial: The Application of Human Rights in the Occupied Territories' (2004) 37 IsLR 17; Danio Campanelli, 'The Law of Military Occupation Put to the Test of Human Rights Law' (2008) 90 IRRC 653; Ralph Wilde, 'Complementing Occupation Law: Selective Judicial Treatment of the Suitability of Human Rights Norms' (2009) 42 IsLR 80; Arai-Takahashi, *The Law*, 401–607; Noam Lubell, 'Human Rights Obligations in Military Occupation' (2012) 94 IRRC 317; Tristan Ferraro, 'The Law of Occupation and Human Rights Law: Some Selected Issues' in Robert Kolb & Gloria Gaggioli (eds.), *Research Handbook on Human Rights and Humanitarian Law* (Edward Elger 2013), 273.

It is undeniable that international humanitarian law and the law of occupation specifically are far from perfect in regulating the administration of the occupied territory and that they afford the occupying power a great degree of largess in dealing with the use of armed force in the occupied territory. Even the effort to humanise the law of occupation through the adoption of the GC IV must be put in proper context: GC IV has been adopted with short-term occupations in mind.[256] It follows that the application of international human rights law has been envisaged, especially in times of prolonged occupation, as a way to force the occupying power to administer the occupied territory in the interests of the local population.[257] In this view, the tension between the governmental character of the occupying power and its hostile nature is reproduced in the legal framework envisaged for the occupied territory: international human rights law, the law usually applicable between governments and governed individuals, and international humanitarian law, the law specifically pertaining to hostile relations between belligerents. However, the cohabitation between these two branches in times of occupation presents many challenges which are relevant also for the use of armed force in occupied territory.

This section summarises the main principles regarding the application of international human rights law in occupied territory. First, it demonstrates that international human rights law is applicable in armed conflict and binds occupying powers' conduct in the occupied territory. The section goes on to explore the possibility of normative conflicts between the two branches, and the solutions offered by international law. Finally, it is suggested that the application of international human rights law introduces an element of variability that requires a case by case assessment of the legal framework in every occupation. All these notions are relevant for the identification of the legal framework applicable to the use of armed force in occupied territory.

2.5.2. The Application of International Human Rights Law in Occupied Territory

The application of international human rights law in times of armed conflict and occupation has been extensively debated.[258] The first issue is whether

---

[256] See supra Section 2.4.2.
[257] See Roberts, 'Prolonged Military Occupation', 70–4.
[258] The international scholarship on this topic is too vast to be indicated here. In addition to other works specifically mentioned in this chapter, see René Provost, *International Human Rights and Humanitarian Law* (Cambridge University Press 2002); Anna Guellali, 'Lex specialis, droit international humanitaire et droits de l'homme: leur interaction dans le nouveaux conflits armés' (2007) 111 RGDIP 539; Roberta Arnold & Noëlle Quénivet (eds.), *International*

international human rights law is per se applicable in situations of armed conflict or, rather, whether states have decided to regulate armed conflict only through international humanitarian law.

International human rights law and international humanitarian law have different origins and, traditionally, have been considered applicable in very different contexts. International humanitarian law originated in international law to regulate the interstate phenomenon of war, and it is concerned with the delicate balance between the belligerents' interest in winning a war – often labelled as 'principle of necessity' – and the international law community's interest in limiting the impact of the hostilities on civilians and persons hors de combat – often labelled as 'principle of humanity'.[259] Conversely, human rights law originated in domestic (constitutional) law to regulate the relationship between the sovereign and its own subjects, and only later was it transposed in international law.[260] Accordingly, it is easy to understand that the two sets of rules are inspired by different goals because international humanitarian law was envisaged to deal with the enemy in the context of armed conflict while international human rights law normally regulates the peacetime relationships between a sovereign and the individuals under its jurisdiction. In recent times, these two branches have been increasingly converging owing to the adoption of the AP I, which refers clearly to human rights standards.[261]

Humanitarian Law and Human Rights Law Towards a New Merger in International Law (Brill 2008); Françoise J. Hampson, 'The Relationship between International Humanitarian Law and Human Rights Law from the Perspective of a Human Rights Treaty' (2008) 90 IRRC 549; Alexander Orakhelashvili, 'The Interaction between Human Rights and Humanitarian Law: Fragmentation, Conflict, Parallelism, or Convergence?' (2008) 19 EJIL 125; Orna Ben-Naftali (ed.), *International Humanitarian Law and International Human Rights Law: Pas de Deux* (Oxford University Press 2011); Kolb, 'Human Rights'; Kolb & Gaggioli (eds.), *Research Handbook*; Gilles Giacca, *Economic, Social and Cultural Rights in Armed Conflict* (Oxford University Press 2014); Gerd Oberleitner, *Human Rights in Armed Conflict: Law, Practice, Policy* (Cambridge University Press 2015); Andrea Clapham, 'The Complex Relationship between the 1949 Geneva Conventions and International Human Rights Law' in Clapham, Gaeta, & Sassòli (eds.), *The 1949 Geneva Conventions*, 701; Darragh Murray, *Practitioners' Guide to Human Rights Law in Armed Conflict* (Elizabeth Wilmshurst, Francoise Hampson, Charles Garraway, Noam Lubell, & Dapo Akande (consultant eds.)) (Oxford University Press 2016).

[259] For more on this, see *infra*, Section 6.3.

[260] On the evolution of international humanitarian law and international human rights law, see, generally, Robert Kolb, 'The Relationship between International Humanitarian Law and Human Rights Law: A Brief History of the 1948 Universal Declaration of Human Rights and the 1949 Geneva Conventions' (1998) 38 IRRC 409; Provost, *International Human Rights*, 1–10.

[261] See Art. 75 AP I; ICTY, *Prosecutor v. Kunarac* et al., IT-96-23-T&IT-96-23/1-T, Trial Chamber, Judgment, 22 February 2001, para. 467. On the convergence between international humanitarian law and international human rights law, see, generally, Edoardo Greppi, 'Diritto internazionale umanitario dei conflitti armati e diritti umani: profili di una convergenza' (1996) 51 CI 473; Paolo Benvenuti, 'La tutela dei diritti umani e il diritto internazionale umanitario' in Di Stefano & Sapienza (eds.), *La tutela*, 53; Kolb, 'Human Rights'.

2.5. The Law of Occupation and International Human Rights Law

However, there are still radical differences between international human rights law and international humanitarian law which are relics of their different origins:[262] for instance, the deprivation of an individual's life is ordinarily under international humanitarian law if that person is a combatant, while it is an exceptional circumstance under international human rights law. This issue is one of the most relevant for the discourse regarding the use of armed force in occupied territory.[263]

On the basis of the different origins and features of international human rights law and international humanitarian law, in the past some authors denied the applicability of international human rights law in times of armed conflict.[264] However, only few governments[265] and scholars[266] still uphold this view. Conversely, today, due to a significant evolution in international case law, there is no doubt that international human rights law continues to apply in times of armed conflict and occupation, alongside international humanitarian law. Indeed, this conclusion is supported by a strong textual element: many international human rights law conventions embody provisions relating to the possibility to derogate certain obligations in times of armed conflict; these provisions confirm that the drafters of international human rights law conventions considered them, absent the derogation, to be applicable during

---

[262] On the differences between the two bodies, see Lattanzi, 'Il confine'; William A. Schabas, '*Lex Specialis?* Belt and Suspenders? The Parallel Operation of Human Rights Law and the Law of Armed Conflict, and the Conundrum of *Jus ad Bellum*' (2007) 40 IsLR 592.

[263] See *infra*, Chapter 6.

[264] See, e.g., Jean Pictet (ed.), *Humanitarian Law and the Protection of War Victims* (Sijthoff 1975) 15:

> Humanitarian law is valid only in the case of armed conflict while human rights are essentially applicable in peacetime, and contain derogation clauses in case of conflict. Moreover, human rights govern relations between the State and its own nationals, the law of war those between the State and enemy nationals. There are also profound differences in the degree of maturity of the instruments and in the procedure for their implementation. The Geneva Conventions are universal and of a mandatory nature. This is certainly not the case with human rights instruments. The system of supervision and sanctions also differs. Thus the two systems are complementary, and indeed they complement one another admirably, but they must remain distinct, if only for the sake of expediency.

[265] See the Israeli position quoted in the *Wall* opinion, paras. 110–12. After a long struggle against the extraterritorial application of human rights, recently, the US has accepted that the UN Convention against Torture is applicable extraterritorially and during armed conflict (see Opening Statement by Mary E. McLeod, Acting Legal Adviser US Department of State Committee Against Torture, 12–13 November 2014, available at geneva.usmission.gov/2014/11/12/acting-legal-adviser-mcleod-u-s-affirms-torture-is-prohibited-at-all-times-in-all-places/)

[266] For one notable exception, which regards situations of occupation, see Michael J. Dennis, 'Application of Human Rights Treaties Extraterritorially in Times of Armed Conflict and Military Occupation' (2005) 99 AJIL 119.

armed conflict and occupations.[267] More straightforwardly, the existence of a state of war – i.e., the outdated condition for the application of international humanitarian law – does not bar the application of the UN Convention against Torture pursuant to its Article 2(2),[268] while the UN Convention on the Rights of the Child embodies a provision explicitly dedicated to the protection of children's rights in armed conflict.[269] Accordingly, nothing in the text of international human rights law conventions suggests that they are not applicable in times of armed conflict and occupation.

The ICJ gave a significant stimulus regarding the application of international human rights law in times of armed conflict and occupation, affirming in the *Nuclear Weapons* opinion, in the *Wall* opinion, and in the *DRC v. Uganda* case that, in principle, international human rights law does not cease to apply in times of armed conflict.[270] Similarly, in the case *Georgia v. Russia*, the ICJ seemed to be ready to analyse the application of the International Convention on the Elimination of All Forms of Racial Discrimination in times of armed conflict,[271] even if the case never reached the merits stage.[272] Finally, at the time this chapter was written, there was another pending case before the ICJ regarding the application of the same international human rights law conventions in the conflict between Ukraine and Russia.[273] It is noteworthy that the ICJ found that the *Wall* opinion and the *DRC v. Uganda* case regarded

---

[267] See, e.g., Art. 4 ICCPR; Art. 15 European Convention for the Protection of Human Rights and Fundamental Freedoms (ECHR) (text in 213 *UNTS* 222). For more on these derogations, see Roslyn Higgins, 'Derogations under Human Rights Treaties' (1976–7) 48 British YIL 281; Ilaria Viarengo, 'Deroghe e restrizioni alla tutela dei diritti umani nei sistemi internazionali di garanzia' (2005) 88 RDI 955; Giuseppe Cataldi, 'Le deroghe ai diritti mani in stato di emergenza' in Laura Pineschi (ed.), *La tutela internazionale dei diritti umani: norme, garanzie, prassi* (Giuffrè 2006) 752; Francesco Seatsu, 'On the Interpretation of Derogation Provisions in Regional Human Rights Treaties in Light of Non-Binding Sources of International Humanitarian Law' (2011) 4 *Inter-American and European Human Rights Journal* 3.

[268] Art. 2(2) Convention against Torture (text in 1465 *UNTS* 85): 'No exceptional circumstances whatsoever, *whether a state of war or a threat of war*, internal political instability or any other public emergency, may be invoked as a justification of torture' (emphasis added).

[269] Art. 38 Convention on the Rights of the Child, text in 1577 *UNTS* 3. The international human rights law protection of children in armed conflict is widened by the Optional Protocol to the Convention on the Rights of the Child on the Involvement of Children in Armed Conflict (text in 2173 *UNTS* 222), which, inherently, is a human rights instrument applicable in times of armed conflict.

[270] See *Legality of the Use or Threat of Nuclear Weapons*, Advisory Opinion, 8 July 1996 ('*Nuclear Weapons* opinion') para. 25; *Wall* opinion, para. 106; *DRC v. Uganda*, para. 216.

[271] *Application of the International Convention on the Elimination of All Forms of Racial Discrimination (Georgia v. Russian Federation)*, Order, 15 October 2011.

[272] Ibid., Judgments on Preliminary Objections, 1 April 2011.

[273] *Application of the International Convention for the Suppression of the Financing of Terrorism and of the International Convention on the Elimination of All Forms of Racial Discrimination (Ukraine v. Russian Federation)*, Application Instituting Proceedings, 16 January 2017.

2.5. The Law of Occupation and International Human Rights Law 67

situations of occupations. Similarly, some territories likely have been occupied in the armed conflicts between Russia and Georgia and Russia and Ukraine.[274]

The CCPR affirmed the applicability of the ICCPR in times of armed conflict and occupation on a number of occasions.[275] A similar practice has been followed by the ECtHR with regard to the ECHR,[276] by the IACmHR[277] and the IACtHR[278] with regard to the ACHR, and by the ACmHPR with regard to the ACHPR.[279] Accordingly, there is a general consensus among judicial and quasi-judicial international law institutions regarding the applicability of international human rights law conventions in situations of armed conflict and occupation.

A second issue regards whether international law conventions bind States in actions undertaken outside their borders.[280] To answer this question it should be noted that many international law conventions embody provisions regarding their scope of application, according to which they are applicable

---

[274] See *supra*, Section 1.3.

[275] See, e.g., CCPR, *General Comment* no. 29, 31 August 2001, para. 3; *General Comment* no. 31, 26 May 2004, para. 11; *General Comment* no. 35, 16 December 2014, para. 64; *Draft General Comment* no. 36, July 2017, para. 67, available at www.ohchr.org/EN/HRBodies/CCPR/Pages/GC36-Article6Righttolife.aspx. For more on this practice, see Vito Todeschini, 'The ICCPR in Armed Conflict: An Appraisal of the Human Rights Committee's Engagement with International Humanitarian Law' (2017) 35 *Nordic Journal of Human Rights* 203, 208–19.

[276] See *Loizidou v. Turkey*; *Cyprus v. Turkey*; *Varnava et al. v. Turkey* (Applications nos. 16064/90, 16065/90, 16066/90, 16068/90, 16069/90, 16070/90, 16071/90, 16072/90, and 16073/90), 19 September 2009; *Al-Saadoon and Mufdhi v. UK*; *Al Skeini et al. v. UK*; *Al-Jedda v. the UK* (Application no. 27021/08), 7 July 2011; *Chiragov et al. v. Armenia*; *Sargsyan v. Azerbaijan*; *Georgia v. Russia* (Application no. 13255/07), 3 July 2014; *Hassan v. UK* (Application no. 29750/09), 16 September 2014; *Jaloud v. the Netherlands* (Application no. 47708/08), 20 November 2014.

[277] See IACmHR, *Salas et al. v. United States* (14 October 1993) (1993) Annual Reports IACHR 312, para. 6; *Abella v. Argentina* (18 November 1997), Report no. 55/97, OEA/Ser.L/V/II.95. Doc.7rev; *Ribón Avila v. Colombia* (13 April 1998) OEA/Ser.L/V/II.98doc.6rev; *Decision on Request for Precautionary Measures (Detainees at Guatanamo Bay, Cuba)* (12 May 2002), (2002) 41 ILM 532.

[278] See *Las Palmeras v. Colombia* (4 February 2000) (Preliminary Objections), IACtHR Series C No. 67; *Mapiripán Massacre v. Colombia* (15 September 2005), IACtHR Series C No. 134; *Santo Domingo Massacre v. Colombia* (30 November 2012) IACtHR Series C No. 259.

[279] See *Democratic Republic of Congo v. Burundi, Rwanda, Uganda* (23 May 2003), Report no. 227/99, paras. 64–5, available at www.achpr.org/files/sessions/33rd/comunications/227.99/227_99_democratic_republic_of_congo__burundi_rwanda_uganda.pdf).

[280] This topic has been explored by vast academic literature. See, among many others, Pasquale De Sena, *La nozione di giurisdizione statale nei trattati sui diritti dell'uomo* (Giappichelli 2002); Fons Coomans & Menno Kamminga (eds.), *Extraterritorial Application of Human Rights Treaties* (Intersentia 2004); Marko Milanovic, *Extraterritorial Application of Human Rights Treaties: Law, Principles, and Policy* (Oxford University Press 2011); Samantha Besson, 'The Extraterritoriality of the European Convention on Human Rights: Why Human Rights Depend on Jurisdiction and What Jurisdiction Amounts To' (2012) 25 LJIL 857; Karen Da Costa, *The Extraterritorial Application of Selected Human Rights Treaties* (Brill 2012); Nehal Bhuta (ed.), *The Frontiers of Human Rights: Extraterritoriality and Its Challenges* (Oxford University Press 2016).

where states exercise their jurisdiction.[281] State jurisdiction means the capacity of governmental conduct to affect the individual enjoyment of a right,[282] and it is related to 'the relationship between the individual and the State in relation to a violation of any of the rights', protected by international human rights law conventions.[283] While state jurisdiction is primarily exercised within a state's own borders,[284] 'the concept of "jurisdiction" ... is not restricted to the national territory of the High Contracting Parties' and, in particular circumstances, 'international law does not exclude a State's exercise of jurisdiction extra-territorially, the suggested bases of such jurisdiction'.[285] In these cases, international human rights law is applicable to state conduct.[286]

The notion of jurisdiction is linked to the extraterritorial control exercised over a portion of territory or a person. It is clear that in situations of occupation states exercise jurisdiction outside their borders, since a situation of occupation is, *par définition*, actual authority over a portion of foreign territory. Following the CCPR practice, the ICJ held that 'while the jurisdiction of States is primarily territorial, it may sometimes be exercised outside the national territory. Considering the object and purpose of the [ICCPR], it would seem natural that, even when such is the case, states parties to the Covenant should be bound to comply with its provisions'.[287] Similarly, according to the ECtHR, the ECHR is applicable

> when as a consequence of military action – whether lawful or unlawful – [a contracting state] exercises effective control of an area outside its national territory. The obligation to secure, in such an area, the rights and freedoms set out in the Convention derives from the circumstance of such control, whether it be exercised directly, through its armed forces, or through a subordinate local administration.[288]

Since occupation is based on effective control, the situation of occupation creates a presumption of exercise of extraterritorial jurisdiction, so that '[w]here

---

[281] See, e.g., Art. 1 ECHR; Art. 2(1) ICCPR; Art. 1 ACHR; Art. 2(1) UN Convention against Torture.
[282] See De Sena, *La nozione*, 231.
[283] CCPR, *Sergio Euben Lopez Burgos v. Uruguay*, 6 June 1979, A/36/60, para. 12(1).
[284] See ECtHR, *Bankovič v. Belgium* (Application no. 52207/99), 12 December 2001, para. 59. See also *Al-Skeini*, para. 131.
[285] *Loizidou v. Turkey* (Preliminary Objections) (Application no. 15318/89), 23 March 1995, para. 62.
[286] See also *Wall* opinion, paras. 109 and 111.
[287] Ibid., para. 109.
[288] See *Loizidou v. Turkey* (Preliminary Objections), para. 62. See also *Cyprus v. Turkey*, paras. 77–8; *Al-Skeini*, para. 138; *Hassan v. the UK*, paras. 75–80.

the fact of such domination over the territory is established, it is not necessary to determine whether the contracting state exercises detailed control over the policies and actions of the subordinate local administration'.[289] Accordingly, states must apply their international human rights law obligations in times of occupation, which are situations of exercise of extraterritorial jurisdiction.[290]

It should be noted that the same approach regarding the extraterritorial application of human rights law has been taken also with regard to international human rights law conventions that do not refer to jurisdiction. For instance, the ICJ observed that although the ICESCR 'contains no provision on its scope of application', however, 'it is not to be excluded that it applies both to territories over which a State party has sovereignty and to those over which that State exercises territorial jurisdiction',[291] concluding that Israel is bound by ICESCR as well.[292] The ICJ's conclusion on this point was based on the observation of the UN Committee on Economic, Social and Cultural Rights, which had considered the ICESCR binding upon Israel in the OPT with no reference to jurisdiction.[293] Accordingly, there is a clear judicial and quasi-judicial trend that considers international human rights law instruments to be applicable extraterritorially in times of armed conflict and occupation.[294]

---

[289] *Loizidou v. Turkey* (Preliminary Objections), para. 62. See also *Al-Skeini*, para. 138.

[290] According to the ECtHR, there is an extraterritorial exercise of jurisdiction not only in cases of occupation, but also in other cases of territorial control, such as incursions during military operations (see *Issa v. Turkey* (Application no. 31821/96), 16 November 2004), indirect control of foreign governments (*Ilascu v. Moldova and Russia* (Application no. 48787/99), 8 July 2004, paras. 382–92), and the presence of foreign troops pursuant to SC authorisations (*Al Jedda v. UK* (Application no. 27021/08), 7 July 2011, para. 86). Moreover, the Court found that a State exercises extraterritorial jurisdiction in some cases of personal control, such as during operation in the high sea (*Medvedyev et al. v. France* (Application no. 3394/03), 29 March 2010, paras. 66–7; *Hirsi v. Italy* (Application no. 27765/09) 23 February 2012, paras. 74–82), during arrests (*Ocalan v. Turkey* (Application no. 46221/99), 12 May 2005, para. 91), in the management of detention facilities (*Al-Saadoon v. UK*, para. 88), and in other cases. For more on this topic, see De Sena, *La nozione*; Milanovic, *Extraterritorial Application*; William A. Schabas, *The European Convention on Human Rights: A Commentary* (Oxford University Press 2015) 92–112.

[291] *Wall* opinion, para. 112.

[292] Ibid.

[293] See Concluding observations of the Committee on Economic, Social and Cultural Rights: Israel, E/C.12/1/Add.27 (4 December 1998), para. 8.

[294] Interestingly, the ICJ affirmed that some 'provisions of [the Convention on the Elimination of All Forms of Racial Discrimination] generally appear to apply, like other provisions of instruments of that nature, to the actions of a State party when it acts beyond its territory' (*Application of the International Convention on the Elimination of All Forms of Racial Discrimination*, para. 109). Since this Convention has no clause pertaining to its geographical scope of application, it could be argued that the ICJ implied that every international human rights law convention is suitable to extraterritorial application.

While, on the basis of the aforementioned judicial evolution, today it is undisputed that, in situations of occupation, the occupying power is bound by the international human rights law conventions it had ratified, it should be noted that the issue is quite different with regard to *customary* international human rights law. First, the fact that a rule is customary in nature does not imply that it is applicable extraterritorially; this conclusion could only derive from the analysis of state practice and *opinio juris* regarding its scope of application. Notwithstanding the contrary view of some authors,[295] most commentators[296] and at least one military manual[297] confirm the view that even customary international human rights law is applicable extraterritorially. However, the main issue surrounding customary international human rights law is the lack of consensus regarding which rules of international human rights law have reached customary status.[298] This uncertainty makes it difficult to scrutinise the occupying power's conduct under customary international humanitarian law. However, the core of international human rights law that is usually considered customary in nature is protected as well by international humanitarian law, which is fully applicable to the occupying power.[299] Interestingly, although the official Israeli position denies the applicability of international human rights law to the OPT,[300] Israel has committed to respect customary international human rights law pursuant to the Oslo Accords. According to the Agreement on Gaza Strip and Jericho Area, 'Israel and the Palestinian Authority shall exercise their powers and responsibilities pursuant to this Agreement with due regard to *internationally-accepted norms and principles of human rights* and the rule of law';[301] similarly, the Interim Agreement provides that 'the Palestinian Police and the Israeli military forces shall

[295] See, e.g., Milanovic, *Extraterritorial Application*, 3–4.
[296] See Noam Lubell, *Extraterritorial Use of Force against Non-State Actors* (Oxford University Press 2010) 233–5; Watkin, *Fighting*, 151.
[297] US Department of Defence, *Operational Law Handbook* (2015) Section IV.B.1.
[298] On customary international human rights law, see Theodor Meron, *Human Rights and Humanitarian Norms as Customary Law* (Oxford University Press 1989); Bruno Simma & Philip Alston, 'The Sources of Human Rights Law: Custom, *Jus Cogens*, and General Principles' (1988–9) 12 Australian YIL 82; Richard B. Lillich, 'The Growing Importance of Customary International Human Rights Law' (1995–6) 25 Georgia JICL 1; Pasquale De Sena, 'Prassi, consuetudine e principi nel campo dei diritti dell'uomo. Riflessioni internazionalistiche' (2014) 34 *Ragion pratica* 511; Hugh Thirlway, 'Human Rights in Customary Law: An Attempt to Define Some of the Issues' (2015) 28 LJIL 495.
[299] See IACmHR, *Abella v. Argentina*, para. 158: 'The American Convention, as well as other universal and regional human rights instruments, and the 1949 Geneva Conventions share a common nucleus of non-derogable rights and a common purpose of protecting human life and dignity'.
[300] See *Wall* opinion, paras. 110–12.
[301] Art. 14 Agreement on Gaza Strip and Jericho Area.

exercise their powers and responsibilities ... with due regard to *internationally-accepted norms of human rights and the rule of law, and shall be guided by the need to protect the public, respect human dignity and avoid harassment*'.[302]

Accordingly, it is well-established today that international human rights law is fully applicable in situations of occupation. Occupying powers must respect both international humanitarian law and international human rights law. This complex legal framework may present some challenges in cases of discordant provisions in the two bodies of international law.

2.5.3. Governing the Relationship between International Human Rights Law and International Humanitarian Law in Occupied Territory

The aforementioned case law and quasi-judicial practice demonstrate that international humanitarian law and international human rights law must apply cumulatively. Accordingly, the application of one branch of international law, in principle, does not cause the inapplicability of the other. Very clearly, the CCPR affirmed that '[w]hile, in respect of certain Covenant rights, more specific rules of international humanitarian law may be specially relevant for the purposes of the interpretation of Covenant rights, both spheres of law are complementary, not mutually exclusive'.[303]

Textual references in both international human rights law and international humanitarian law conventions support the cumulative application of international human rights. For instance, Article 29(b) ACHR states that '[n]o provision of this Convention shall be interpreted as ... restricting the enjoyment or exercise of any right or freedom recognized by virtue of the laws of any State Party or by virtue of another convention to which one of the said states is a party'.[304] Similarly, Article 53 ECHR provides that '[n]othing in this Convention shall be construed as limiting or derogating from any of the human rights and fundamental freedoms which may be ensured under the laws of any High Contracting Party or under any other agreement to which it is a party'. However, the ECtHR never clarified whether the

---

[302] Art. 11(1), Annex I, Interim Agreement.
[303] *General Comment* no. 31, para. 11.
[304] Text in 114 *UNTS* 143. According to the IACmHR, this rule *requires* the Commission to apply international humanitarian law rather than the Convention if this results in a 'higher standard of protection' for individual rights (*Abella v. Argentina*, para. 166). However, this interpretation has been challenged by the IACtHR, which has considered that the American Convention 'has only given the Court competence to determine whether the acts or the norms of the States are compatible with the Convention itself, and not with the 1949 Geneva Conventions' (*Las Palmeras v. Colombia*, para. 33; see also *Bámaca-Velásquez v. Guatemala* (Merits) (25 November 2000), IACtHR Series C No. 70, paras. 207–8; *Mapiripán Massacre v. Colombia*, para. 115).

reference to 'any of the human rights and fundamental freedoms which may be ensured under ... any other agreement' encompasses also international humanitarian law instruments, especially since Article 53 ECHR has been employed extremely rarely.[305] More clearly, Article 38(1) of the UN Convention on the Rights of the Child prescribes that 'States Parties undertake to respect and to ensure respect for rules of international humanitarian law applicable to them in armed conflicts which are relevant to the child', adding a number of further obligations in the subsequent paragraphs.

With regard to international humanitarian law, it should be noted that Article 72 AP I affirms that its rules are 'additional to the rules concerning humanitarian protection of civilians and civilian objects in the power of a Party to the conflict contained in the [GC IV] as well as to *other applicable rules of international law relating to the protection of fundamental human rights during international armed conflict*'.[306] According to some authoritative commentators, this provision would refer to the application of international human rights law as well.[307] Similarly, some authors have suggested that the fact that Article 7 GC IV admits the conclusion of special agreements between the belligerents that positively affected protected persons should be read as allowing the application of international human rights law along with international humanitarian law.[308]

However, in cases in which international humanitarian law and international human rights law appear to regulate a particular type of conduct differently, the relationship between international human rights law and international humanitarian law triggers some theoretical and practical issues. Absent any derogations, which may avoid similar situations, there could be problems of occupying powers' facing an unclear legal framework. Although it is true that the convergence between these two branches of international law have progressively reduced the risk of a normative conflict, in light of the genetic differences between international human rights law and international humanitarian law, their contextual application may pose some problems.

The main point of reference in this regard is the case law of the ICJ. In the *Nuclear Weapons* opinion, the ICJ affirmed that the right to life in armed conflict should be interpreted in light of international humanitarian law, which

---

[305] See Schabas, *The European Convention*, 904.
[306] Emphases added. See also the Preamble of AP II ('international instruments relating to human rights offer a basic protection for the victims' of non-international armed conflict').
[307] See Yves Sandoz, Christophe Swinarski, & Bruno Zimmermann (eds.), *Commentary on the Additional Protocols of 8 June 1977 to the Geneva Conventions of 12 August 1949* (Martinus Nijhoff 1987) 842–3.
[308] See Arai-Takahashi, *The Law*, 424–5; Annoni, *L'occupazione*, 129.

2.5. The Law of Occupation and International Human Rights Law 73

is considered to be *lex specialis*.[309] It should be noted that this was one of the first times the relationship between these two branches of international law was regulated with reference to the *lex specialis* principle, which immediately become mainstream in legal scholarship.[310]

However, this reference to the principle *lex specialis derogat generalis* is not entirely correct for a number of reasons. First, since international human rights law was considered applicable during armed conflict by the drafters of the most relevant conventions – who included derogation clauses to avoid the regular course of events, i.e., the application of the conventions even in wartime – it is difficult to understand why international humanitarian law would be more apt, and thus would deserve to prevail as *lex specialis*.[311] More correctly, in the *Wall* opinion, the ICJ affirmed that:

> As regards the relationship between international humanitarian law and human rights law, there are thus three possible situations: some rights may be exclusively matters of international humanitarian law; others may be exclusively matters of human rights law; yet others may be matters of both these branches of international law. In order to answer the question put to it, the Court will have to take into consideration both these branches of international law, namely human rights law and, as *lex specialis*, international humanitarian law.[312]

This paragraph may be interpreted as suggesting that during an occupation or armed conflict, international humanitarian law may be the *lex specialis* prevailing over international human rights law, giving no hint as to how to discern between the different situations. In this regard, some have cautioned that the comparison between international human rights law and international humanitarian law must be narrow and specific: if a normative conflict exists between two provisions and cannot be solved through interpretation, then

---

[309] See *Nuclear Weapons* opinion, para. 25.

[310] For a thorough analysis of the scholarship before and after the *Nuclear Weapons* opinion with regard to the interplay between international human rights law and international humanitarian law, see Marko Milanovic, 'The Lost Origins of *Lex Specialis*: Rethinking the Relationship between Human Rights and International Humanitarian Law' in Jens David Ohlin (ed.), *Theoretical Boundaries of Armed Conflict and Human Rights* (Cambridge University Press 2016) 78, 82–103.

[311] See Andrea Bianchi, 'Dismantling the Wall: The ICJ's Advisory Opinion and Its Likely Impact on International Law' (2004) 47 German YIL 343, 371–2; Annoni, *L'occupazione*, 125–6; Jean D'Aspremont & Elodie Tranchez, 'The Quest for Non-Conflictual Coexistence of International Human Rights Law and Humanitarian Law: Which Role for the *Lex Specialis* Principle?' in Kolb & Gaggioli (eds.), *Research Handbook*, 241–2.

[312] *Wall* opinion, para. 106.

that specific *generalis* provision may be discarded in favour of the *specialis* one, without discarding the entire application of international human rights law in case of unavoidable conflicts.[313]

Second, the *lex specialis* principle normally applies when two conflicting provisions have the same scope of application. Typically, this is the case in the relationship between customary law and treaty law, where treaty law is considered the manifestation of contracting states' will to regulate in a different way a matter already disciplined by customary international law.[314] Similarly, when two treaty provisions of the same system are identical in scope, the more specific provision is applicable instead of the other as *lex specialis*,[315] as happens also in certain circumstances with regard to the use of armed force in occupied territory.[316] On the contrary, since the scopes of international humanitarian law and international human rights law are different, as are the conditions of application of these two branches of international law, it is not possible to apply the *lex specialis* principle in order to discard the application of international human rights law: *lex specialis* is a technique envisaged to solve normative conflicts within the same system, whilst the normative conflict between international humanitarian law and international human rights law involves two different branches, both of which may be considered *lex specialis* in relation with international law as a whole.[317]

Third, the application of the *lex specialis* principle is possible only when a normative conflict exists. However, there is no clear definition of what a normative conflict is in international law. According to a narrow view, adopted inter alia by the WTO dispute settlement bodies, a normative conflict exists only with regard to 'clashes between obligations ... *where those obligations are*

---

[313] See, e.g., Bianchi, 'Dismantling', 373; Dinstein, *The International Law*, 88; Iain Scobbie, 'Principle or Pragmatics? The Relationship between Human Rights Law and the Law of Armed Conflict' (2010) 14 JCSL 449, 456–7; Marko Milanović, 'A Norm Conflict Perspective on the Relationship between International Humanitarian Law and Human Rights Law' (2010), 14 JCSL, 459, 462–5.

[314] See, e.g., *Right of Passage over Indian Territory (Portugal v. India)*, Judgment, 12 April 1960, 44; Case Concerning Military and Paramilitary Activities in and against Nicaragua (*Nicaragua v. USA*), Judgment, 27 June 1986, para. 274. See also state practice and case law collected by Anja Lindroos, 'Addressing Norm Conflicts in a Fragmented Legal System: The Doctrine of *Lex Specialis*' (2005) 74 NJIL 27, 49–52.

[315] See *Dispute between Argentina and Chile*, para. 36.

[316] See *infra*, Section 6.3.2.1.

[317] This assumption was advanced with regard to the similarly uneasy relationship between international trade law and international human rights law by Conforti, 'Unité', 13–14; Andreas Ziegler & Bertram Boie, 'The Relationship between International Trade Law and International Human Rights Law' in Erika De Wet & Jure Vidmar (eds.), *Hierarchy in International Law: The Place of Human Rights* (Oxford University Press 2012) 272, 290; Erika De Wet & Jure Vidmar, 'Conflitti tra paradigmi internazionali: gerarchia versus integrazione sistemica' (2015) 20 *Ars interpretandi* 119, 131.

2.5. The Law of Occupation and International Human Rights Law 75

mutually exclusive in the sense that a Member cannot comply with both obligations at the same time, and (ii) the situation where *a rule in one agreement prohibits what a rule in another agreement explicitly permits*'.[318] Accordingly, situations in which there is a rule contained in one treaty prohibiting a certain conduct, and another rule contained in another treaty putting forward more stringent conditions to perform that same conduct, should not be classified as conflicts since the obligations arising from the two treaties 'can both be complied with at the same time without the need to renounce explicit rights or authorizations'.[319] Similarly, the ICJ affirmed that there is no normative conflict between the right to reparation from gross violations of international human rights law and international humanitarian law vis-à-vis state immunity, since states could seek alternative ways to grant reparations without infringing state immunity.[320] Finally, the ECtHR held that a permissive norm of international humanitarian law does not constitute an 'obligation' from which a normative conflict with the ECHR may arise.[321] Under this definition of normative conflict,[322] it is difficult to envisage a conflict between international humanitarian law and international human rights law since a state could respect both branches by refraining from adopting a certain conduct which is *permissible* (not mandatory) under one of them and prohibited by the other.

However, recent scholarship demonstrates a trend to enlarge the definition of normative conflicts so as to encompass also situations in which normative conflicts exist where the obligations originating from two applicable norms, if applied, would be logically inconsistent.[323] The supporters of this solution argue that the narrow concept of normative conflict resolves automatically in the prevalence of commands over permissions, creating a hierarchy that

---

[318] *European Communities – Regime for the Importation, Sale and Distribution of Bananas*, WT/DS27/R/USA (22 May 1997) para. 7.159 (references omitted, emphases added). See also *Indonesia – Certain Measures Affecting the Automobile Industry*, WT/DS54/R, WT/DS55/R, WT/DS59/R, WT/DS64/R (2 July 1998), para. 5.169.

[319] *European Communities*, para. 7.160.

[320] *Jurisdictional Immunities of States (Germany v. Italy: Greece intervening)*, 3 February 2012, para. 94. For an analysis of this case from the perspective of norm conflict resolution, see Ulf Linderfalk, 'The Principle of Rational Decision-Making as Applied to the Identification of Normative Conflicts in International Law' (2013) 73 ZaöRV 591.

[321] See ECtHR, *Al Jedda v. UK*, para. 107 (with reference to Art. 78 GC IV regarding internment).

[322] This definition is supported by many authors. See, e.g., Wilfred Jenks, 'The Conflict of Law-Making Treaties' (1953) 30 British YIL 401, 426; W. Czaplinski & G. Danilenko, 'Conflict of Norms in International Law' (1990) 21 NILR 3, 12; Wolfram Karl, 'Treaties, Conflict Between' in Bernhardt (ed.), *Encyclopedia* vol. IV, 935, 936; Seyed-Ali Sadat-Akhavi, *Methods of Resolving Conflicts between Treaties* (Brill 2003) 5.

[323] See the Report of the Study Group of the ILC, paras. 23–4 (with the caveat that while a broader concept of conflict does 'not lead into logical incompatibilities between obligations upon a single party, [it] may nevertheless also be relevant for fragmentation').

is not supported by international law.[324] Obviously, if one supports this broad concept of normative conflicts, conflicts between international humanitarian law and international human rights law are more likely to occur, and the state under the two conflicting obligations may only choose to breach one command on the basis of another permission, shifting the problem to the plan of international responsibility.[325]

For all these reasons, constructing the relationship between international human rights law and international humanitarian law in terms of *lex specialis*, with international humanitarian law prevailing over international human rights law in cases of normative conflicts, appears incorrect.

However, the *lex specialis* debate is probably moot. The ICJ itself, one year after its mention of the *lex specialis* principle in the *Wall* opinion, reaffirmed its position regarding the interplay between international human rights law and international humanitarian law verbatim, with the only significant omission being that of the sentence regarding *lex specialis*.[326] Many scholars have argued that this omission should be seen as proof that the ICJ itself no longer relies on the *lex specialis* principle,[327] rather favouring the contextual application of the two branches of law in a cumulative way, consistently with the case law of other international courts and tribunals and the practice of international monitoring mechanisms that have applied international human rights law in context regulated by international humanitarian law. The disappearance of any reference to *lex specialis* should be read as a ticket back to the well-established step-by-step process regarding apparent conflicts of norms. Contrary to the ICJ's opinion, the *lex specialis* principle is not an interpretive rule, but rather a rule pertaining to the solution of normative conflicts, according to which, when it is impossible to solve normative antinomies through interpretation, the rule most directly pertinent to a specific situation should

---

[324] See Joost Pauwelyn, *Conflict of Norms in Public International Law* (Cambridge University Press 2003); Erich Vranes, 'The Definition of "Norm Conflict" in International Law and Legal Theory' (2006) 17 EJIL 395. The narrow concept on normative conflict is considered applicable only in the WTO system by Lindroos, 'Addressing', 58.

[325] See James Crawford & Penelope Nevill, 'Relations between International Courts and Tribunals: The "Regime Problem"' in Margaret A. Young (ed.), *Regime Interaction in International Law: Facing Fragmentation* (2012) 235, 236–7: 'When we cannot [interpret our way out of conflict], the rather frail way we resolve conflict is to remit it to the black box of state responsibility: in effect, conflict becomes a matter of remedies or reconciliation of "competing breaches" through circumstances precluding wrongfulness or through the vagaries of availability of remedies'.

[326] *DRC v. Uganda*, para. 216.

[327] See, e.g., Kolb & Vité, *Le droit*, 334; Milanovic, 'A Norm Conflict'; 464; Annoni, *L'occupazione*, 126; Vitucci, *Sovranità*, 55.

2.5. The Law of Occupation and International Human Rights Law

apply instead of another that is discarded.[328] Accordingly, the reference to *lex specialis* as a tool of interpretation is misleading. Rather, it would be possible to refer to the *lex specialis* principle only after having attempted to interpret in a coherent way two apparently conflicting norms.

In addressing apparent conflicts, the interpreter must take into account the specificity of each situation. There are areas not covered by international human rights law or by international humanitarian law, as recognised by the ICJ; in these fields, obviously, only one system would apply and there is no risk of normative conflicts.[329] In cases of overlapping between the scope of application of international human rights law and international humanitarian law, states must try to reconcile apparently conflicting provisions through the interpretive criteria. Since there is a duty to interpret treaties so that their provisions may be effectively applied,[330] some authors have spoken about the existence of a presumption against normative conflicts.[331] Accordingly, apparent conflicts must be solved first pursuant to Article 31(3)(c) VCLT, which requires to take into consideration, as part of the context of a provision, 'any relevant rules of international law applicable in the relations between the parties' (so-called technique of systemic integration). Through this rule it is possible to interpret international human rights law and international humanitarian law in a

---

[328] See, e.g., ICJ, *Right of Passage over Indian Territory*, 44; *Dispute between Argentina and Chile concerning the Beagle Channel*, 21 RIAA 53, paras. 36 and 38; ICJ, *Case Concerning Continental Shelf (Tunisia v. Libyan Arab Jamahiriya)*, Judgment, 24 February 1982, para. 24; Iran-United States Claims Tribunal, *INA Corporation v. Iran* (Decision of 12 August 1985), (1985-I) 8 *Iran-US CTR* 378; *Southern Bluefin Tuna (New Zealand-Japan, Australia-Japan)*, 23 RIAA para. 52.
    For this position in legal scholarship, see the classical authors Grotius, *De iure* , Book II, Chap. XVI, Sect. XXIX, 428; De Vattel, *The Law* vol. I, Book II, Chap. XVII, para. 316. More recently, see Jean Salmon (ed.), *Dictionnaire de droit international public* (Bruylant 2001) 652; Pauwelyn, Conflict, 409; D'Aspremont & Tranchez, 'The Quest', 223, 225, and 235.

[329] See *Targeted Killings* case, para. 18. For instance, international humanitarian law does not regulate the right of freedom of expression; accordingly, this right is wholly regulated by international human rights law even in times of armed conflict (Murray, *Practitioners' Guide*, 102–3).

[330] See ICJ, *Anglo-Iranian Oil Co. Case (United Kingdom v. Iran)* (Preliminary Objection), Judgment, 22 May 1952, 105; *Constitution of the Maritime Safety Committee of the Inter-Governmental Maritime Consultative Organization*, Advisory Opinion, 8 June 1960, 160; *Fisheries Jurisdiction (Spain v. Canada)*, Judgment, 4 December 1998, para. 52; *Application of the International Convention on the Elimination of All Forms of Racial Discrimination (Georgia v. Russian Federation)* (Preliminary Objections), 1 April 2011, paras. 133–4. For more on the rule of effectiveness in treaty interpretation, see Oliver Dörr, 'Article 31 – General Rule of Interpretation' in Oliver Dörr & Kirsten Schmalenbach (eds.), *Vienna Convention on the Law of Treaties: A Commentary* (2nd edn, Springer 2018), 559, 565–7.

[331] See, generally, Michael Akehurst, 'The Hierarchy of the Sources of International Law' (1974–5) 47 British YIL 273, 275; Pauwelyn, *Conflict*, 240–4.

coherent way, avoiding the construction of conflicting obligations and specifying the meaning of provisions embodied in each branch.

This process is the one followed by the ICJ in the *Nuclear Weapons* opinion, which was wrongly labelled as *lex specialis*.[332] In dealing with the interpretation of 'the right not arbitrarily to be deprived of one's life' under Article 4 ICCPR, the Court affirmed that '[t]he test of what is an arbitrary deprivation of life ... falls to be determined by ... the law applicable in armed conflict which is designed to regulate the conduct of hostilities'.[333] The ICJ thus employed international humanitarian law in order to interpret, in a coherent way, an international human rights law provision (the term 'arbitrary'). Even if the ICJ did not mention systemic integration pursuant to Article 31(3)(c) VCLT, it is clear that this paragraph is based on that interpretive rule, rather than constituting an example of conflict resolution.

The ICJ is not isolated in this pattern. For instance, after an initial reluctance, in the most recent cases, the ECtHR has employed international humanitarian law as an instrument to interpret the ECHR in situations involving armed conflicts and occupations.[334] In the *Varnava* case, the Court held that the ECHR 'must be interpreted in so far as possible in light of the general principles of international law, *including the rules of international humanitarian law*'.[335] In the *Marguš* case, the Court interpreted Article 4 of Protocol no. 7 regarding *ne bis in idem* in light of the international humanitarian law regimes applicable to serious violations of the GCs.[336] In the *Hassan* case, the Court emphasised that, pursuant to Article 31(3)(c) VCLT, 'the Convention must be interpreted in harmony with other rules of international law of which it forms part. This applies no less to international humanitarian law'.[337] The Court went further, stressing the fact that '[the GCs], intended to mitigate the

---

[332] In this case, a kind of 'renvoi teqnique' operated, according to Robert Kolb & Robert Hyde, *An Introduction to the International Law of Armed Conflicts* (Hart 2008) 271–2; Edoardo Greppi, 'To What Extent Do the International Rules on Human Rights Matter?' in Fausto Pocar, Marco Pedrazzi, & Micaela Frulli (eds.), *War Crimes and the Conduct of Hostilities: Challenges to Adjudication and Investigation* (Edward Elgar 2013) 38, 42.

[333] *Nuclear Weapons* opinion, para. 25.

[334] On the influence of international humanitarian law on the ECtHR's case law, see, generally, Gloria Gaggioli & Robert Kolb, 'A Right to Life in Armed Conflicts? The Contribution of the European Court of Human Rights' (2007) 37 IYHR 115; Andrea Gioia, 'The Role of the European Court of Human Rights in Monitoring Compliance with Humanitarian Law in Armed Conflict' in Ben-Naftali (ed.), *International Humanitarian Law*, 201; Linos-Alexandre Sicilianos, 'L'articulation enter droit international humanitaire et droits de l'homme dans la jurisprudence de la Cour européenne des droits de l'homme' (2017) 27 RSDIE 3.

[335] *Varnava v. Turkey*, para. 185.

[336] See *Marguš v. Croatia* (Application no.) 27 May 2014. See also Sicilianos, 'L'articulation', 14, 4455/10.

[337] *Hassan v. the UK*, para. 102.

2.5. The Law of Occupation and International Human Rights Law 79

horrors of war, were drafted in parallel to the [ECHR] and enjoy universal ratification'.[338]

Similarly, on a number of occasions the IACmHR and the IACtHR have applied the ACHR in light of the relevant international humanitarian law provisions. For instance, in the *Abella* case, the Commission affirmed that it 'must necessarily look to and apply definitional standards and relevant rules of humanitarian law as sources of authoritative guidance in its resolution of this and other kinds of claims alleging violations of the American Convention in combat situations'.[339] Similarly, the Commission stated that the application of provisions of the ACHR 'is informed by the provisions of international humanitarian law for internal hostilities'.[340] Furthermore, following the *lex specialis* reference in the *Nuclear Weapons* opinion, the Commission affirmed that, in certain circumstances, 'the test for evaluating the observance of a particular right, such as the right to liberty, *in a situation of armed conflict may be distinct from that applicable in time of peace*. In such situations, international law, including the jurisprudence of this Commission, dictates that it may be necessary to *deduce the applicable standard by reference to international humanitarian law*'.[341] The Commission clarified that '[i]n this way, although the *lex specialis* with respect to acts taking place in the context of an armed conflict is [international humanitarian law], this does not mean that international human rights law is inapplicable'.[342] Significantly, the IACtHR affirmed that 'relevant provisions of the Geneva Conventions may be taken into consideration as elements for the interpretation of the American Convention'[343] and that the international human rights law and international humanitarian law 'complement each other or become integrated to specify their scope or their content'.[344] Following the *Nuclear Weapons* opinion, the IACtHR affirmed that the text regarding the arbitrary deprivation of life in a non-international armed conflict must be constructed on the basis of international humanitarian law.[345]

---

[338] Ibid.
[339] See *Abella v. Argentina*, para. 161.
[340] See *Avila v. Colombia*, para. 135.
[341] *Decision on Request for Precautionary Measures* (emphases added). See also *Contreras et al. v. El Salvador* (Admissibility) (23 February 2005), para. 20 (available at cidh.org/annualrep/2005eng/ElSalvador708.03eng.htm).
[342] *Inter-state Petition IP-02 Franklin Guillermo Aisalla Molina (Ecuador v. Colombia)* (Admissibility) (21 October 2010), OEA/Ser.L/V/II.140.Doc.10, para. 122.
[343] *Bámaca-Velásquez v. Guatemala*, para. 209. See also *Mapiripán Massacre v. Colombia*, para. 115.
[344] *Mapiripán Massacre v. Colombia*, para. 115. See also *Santo Domingo Massacre v. Colombia*, para. 187.
[345] See *Eduardo Nicolas Cruz Canchez v. Peru* (17 April 2015), IACtHR Series C No. 292, paras. 272–3.

Finally, the ACmHPR affirmed that international humanitarian law 'constitute[s] part of the general principles of law recognised by African States' which may be relevant as 'subsidiary measures to determine the principles of law, other general or special international conventions, laying down rules recognized by African States' that must be taken 'into consideration in the determination of [a] case' regarding the application of the ACHPR.[346] Similarly, in the *General Comment no. 3* to the ACHPR, the Commission affirmed that '[i]n armed conflict, what constitutes an "arbitrary" deprivation of life during the conduct of hostilities is to be determined by reference to international humanitarian law'.[347]

From the aforementioned case law and quasi-judicial practice, it is clear that, today, international human rights law and international humanitarian law should apply, as far as possible, in a coherent way during armed conflicts and occupations. However, this coherent interpretation should not blur the existence of separate obligations under international human rights law and international humanitarian law. Simply, in contemporary armed conflicts, belligerents' actions must comply with *international humanitarian law interpreted in light of the applicable rules of international human rights law* as well as with *international human rights law interpreted in light of the applicable rules of international humanitarian law*.[348] The interpretation should focus, case by case, on the specific rules of the two systems allegedly in conflict, which are the objects of two separate acts of interpretation that should be performed taking into account the existence of the other rule pursuant to Article 31(3)(c) VCLT.[349] However, international human rights law and international humanitarian law obligations do not conflate; rather, they may constitute different sources of international responsibility in cases of violations if a military action does not comply with both branches of international law simultaneously.[350]

---

[346] *Democratic Republic of Congo v. Burundi, Rwanda, Uganda*, para. 70.
[347] ACmHPR, *General Comment no. 3*, 4–18 November 2015, para. 32, available at www.achpr.org/files/instruments/general-comments-right-to-life/general_comment_no_3_english.pdf
[348] Accordingly, as already mentioned, the Supreme Court of Israel has been severely criticised because it conflated international human rights standards and international humanitarian law in a number of decisions in order to reduce the protection afforded by the law of occupation to the local population of the OPT. See *supra*, Section 2.4.3, and the references mentioned therein.
[349] See IACmHR, *Inter-state Petition IP-02 Aisalla Molina*, para. 121.
[350] See Orakhelashvilli, 'The Interaction', 168; Christof Heyns, Dapo Akande, Lawrence Hill-Cawthorne, & Thompson Chengeta, 'The International Legal Framework Regulating the Use of Armed Drones' (2016) 65 ICLQ 791, 821–2.

2.5.4. Variable Geometries with Regard to the Use of Armed Force in Occupied Territory

The contextual application of international humanitarian law and international human rights law in times of occupation may produce an unintended consequence: the application of international human rights law, and its interpretive value, may be different on the basis of the international human rights obligations that are binding upon the occupying power. Accordingly, there is no entirely identical legal framework applicable to every occupation, as well as in the matter of the use of armed force in occupied territory.

With regard to international humanitarian law, the law of occupation and, in particular, the rules affecting the use of armed force, are binding upon all the states since they are customary in nature and because of the universal ratification of the GC IV. Similarly, customary international human rights law, whatever its content is, binds every state. However, the situation is different with regard to international human rights law.

Indeed, an initial distinction should be drawn between states parties to the same conventions and states that are not parties to the same conventions. For instance, in the case of the occupation of Iraq, the two main components of the CPA, the USA and the United Kingdom, had to follow different legal standards as only the United Kingdom was party to the ECHR.[351] Just to narrow the scope to the use of armed force, on the one hand, the USA had to comply with international humanitarian law obligations interpreted in light of ICCPR, and with ICCPR obligations interpreted in light of applicable international humanitarian law, but on the other hand the United Kingdom had to comply with international humanitarian law obligations interpreted in light of ICCPR *and of ECHR*, and with ICCPR *and ECHR* obligations interpreted in light of applicable international humanitarian law. Thanks to the general convergence between international human rights law treaties and the cross-fertilisation between international human rights law judicial and quasi-judicial bodies,[352] the practical differences likely have a light impact on the applicable legal framework. However, some differences

---

[351] The CPA is referred to here just as an example. On the complex issue of the allocation of responsibility between individual states and the CPA itself, see Stefan Talmon, 'A Plurality of Responsible Actors: International Responsibility for Acts of the Provisional Coalition Authority in Iraq' in Phil Shiner & Andrew Williams (eds.), *The Iraq War and International Law* (Hart 2008) 185. For a broader view on the issue of joint responsibility in situations of occupation, see Enrico Milano, 'Occupation' in André Nollkaemper & Ilias Plakokefalos (eds.), *The Practice of Shared Responsibility* (Cambridge University Press 2017) 733.

[352] On this topic, see generally the essays collected in Carla Buckley, Alice Donald, & Philip Leach (eds.), *Towards Convergence in International Human Rights Law: Approaches of Regional and International Systems* (Brill 2017).

should be taken into account: for instance, the right to life is non-derogable in times of armed conflict under the ICCPR,[353] while the ECHR allows derogation for 'lawful acts of war'.[354] However, as explained Section 6.2, this difference does not hamper the applicability of ICCPR in occupied territory since it in *renvoie* to international humanitarian law to determine which deprivations of the right of life are arbitrary. Similarly, the USA and the United Kingdom had different views on the death penalty in occupied Iraq because the United Kingdom is party to Protocols 6 and 13 ECHR, which prohibits the death penalty.

A second element of differentiation is the possibility of invoking derogation clauses. In principle, two occupying powers may be subject to the same international humanitarian law and international human rights law obligations, but if one of the two formally derogates from some conventional international human rights law obligations, the legal frameworks applicable to the two states are slightly different.

It follows that, while international humanitarian law obligations are the same for every occupying power, there could be differences regarding the applicable international human rights law. Accordingly, international human rights law injects a variable into the law of occupation that should require a case by case assessment to determine the legal framework applicable in the occupied territory, including that regulating actions involving the use of armed force.

2.6. CONCLUSIONS: THE FUNCTION OF THE LAW OF OCCUPATION

Although the occurrence of occupation has been described as 'a natural phenomenon in war',[355] international law treats situations of occupation as exceptional circumstances in which it is necessary to allocate rights and responsibilities beyond the normal order based on sovereign states.[356] As has been suggested, 'an occupation presents the international order with the challenge of the exceptional: the severance of the link between sovereignty and effective control entailed in an occupation, suspends the normal order as it relates to the occupied territory'.[357] The occupying power is not the representative of the occupied state as in the Roman institute of the *negotiorum gestio*,[358] but rather, the legal orders of the occupying power and of the occupied state

---

[353] See Art. 4(2) ICCPR.
[354] See Art. 15(2) ECHR.
[355] Dinstein, *The International Law*, 1.
[356] This dichotomy is well described in the *Island of Palmas* case (Netherlands, USA), 4 April 1928, 2 RIAAA 829, 838–40.
[357] Ben-Naftali, 'Belligerent Occupation', 540.
[358] For this theory, see Mario Marinoni, 'Della natura giuridica dell'occupazione bellica' (1910) 5 RDI 181.

2.6. Conclusions: The Function of the Law of Occupation

are applicable at the same time in the occupied territory,[359] thanks to the international law of occupation that allocates duties and responsibilities between the two legal orders, providing some limits and faculties to the occupying power's exercise of governmental powers.[360] Apparently, in occupied territory a number of legal systems are applicable: the law of the occupied territory, which must be respected by the occupying power and regulates most aspects of daily life; the rules adopted by the occupying power, such as military orders regarding the maintenance of public order and civil life; and international law, which plays a double role since, on the one hand, both customary international law and treaty law regulate the law of occupation, and on the other, the occupying power must respect even in time of occupation its own international obligations pursuant to international customary law and treaty law, especially in the field of human rights. The law of occupation provides the tools to navigate this apparent maze.

Accordingly, the law of occupation may be summarised as that branch of international humanitarian law dealing with the delicate equilibrium between different interests when, as a consequence of an international armed conflict, a hostile state is required to govern a portion of territory. The interests at stake changed with the evolution of the law of occupation and of the international community in general. Clearly, the rules first codified in the HR mainly concern the legal interests of two subjects: the state acting as an occupying power and the ousted sovereign of the occupied territory. Accordingly, in case of *debellatio*, when one of these two international subjects disappears, the law of occupation was no longer applicable. However, the legal interests of states have changed in light of the broader evolution of international law, as reflected by state practice and the law codified in GC IV and AP I. States have become progressively aware that the law of occupation has been shifting from protection of sovereign interests to protection of the local population, especially since WWII. For instance, the US Military Manual describes the law of occupation as involving 'a complicated, trilateral set of legal relations between the occupying power, the temporarily ousted sovereign authority, and the inhabitants of occupied territory'.[361] The UK Military Manual goes beyond and does not refer to the ousted sovereign; rather it affirms that: '[t]he military occupation of territory establishes a special relationship between the occupying power and the civilian population of the area, involving,

---

[359] See Roberto Ago, 'Occupazione bellica dell'Italia e Trattato Lateranense' (1946) 2 CS 130, 143; Capotorti, *L'occupazione* 57–61; Balladore Pallieri, *Diritto*, 312–15.
[360] See Pietro Ziccardi, 'Occupazione bellica ed amministrazione della giustizia' (1948) *Temi* 488.
[361] US Military Manual, section 11.4 (quoting Stone, *Legal*, 694) (emphasis added). See also Garraway, 'Occupation', 278; Gasser & Dörmann, 'Protection', 266.

on each side, certain rights and duties'.[362] The focus on the protection of the local population is confirmed by the Supreme Court of Israel, according to which 'safeguarding of the lives of the civilian population is a central value in the humanitarian law applicable to belligerent occupation'.[363] However, even this scheme is quite reductive since it does not take into account other states not directly involved in the occupation. In fact, some rules pertaining to occupation confers duties and rights to states that are neither the occupied state nor the occupying power. For instance, Articles 59–63 AP I allow third states and international organisations to bring relief to the population of the occupied territories under certain conditions. Similarly, pursuant to Article 47 GC IV, the status of the occupied territory may not be altered by special agreements between the occupying power and third states.[364] Arguably, the law of occupation does not affect the legal interests of the occupying power and the occupied state alone. Rather, the customary law of occupation imposes obligations *erga omnes*, that is 'obligations of a State towards the international community as a whole',[365] while treaty law pertaining to the law of occupation should be regarded as obligations *erga omnes partes*, that is, obligations 'that each State party [to a treaty] has an interest in compliance with ... in any given case'.[366] Even if obligations *erga omnes* and obligations *erga omnes partes* are different,[367] they overlap in the case of the law of occupation since the GC IV was ratified by every state in the world.

Several elements of the law of occupation support the view that these rules embody obligations *erga omnes* and *erga omnes partes*. First, it is well known that common Article 1 GCs require all states parties 'to respect and to ensure respect for the present Convention[s] in all circumstances'; most

---

[362] UK Military Manual, section 11.1.1.
[363] HCJ 3799/02 *Adalah* v. *GOC Central Command, IDF* (6 October 2005), 145 ILR 407, para. 23.
[364] See Alessandro Migliazza, 'Occupazione bellica' in *Enciclopedia Giuridica* vol. XXI (Treccani 1990) 1, 5–6. Already in 1942, one author had noted that also other states' rights and duties were affected by the occupation (Feilchenfeld, *The International*, 9).
[365] *Case concerning the Barcelona Traction*, para. 33.
[366] *Questions Relating to the Obligation to Prosecute or Extradite (Belgium v. Senegal)*, Judgment, 20 July 2012, para. 68.
[367] Generally on obligations *erga omnes* and *erga omnes partes*, see Maurizio Ragazzi, *The Concept of International Obligations Erga Omnes* (Oxford University Press 1997); Linos-Alexandre Sicilianos, 'The Classification of Obligations and the Multilateral Dimension of the Relations of International Responsibility' (2002) 13 EJIL 1127; Christian J. Tams, *Enforcing Obligations Erga Omnes in International Law* (Cambridge University Press 2005); Santiago Villalpando, *L'émergence de la communauté internationale dans la responsabilité des États* (PUF 2005); Christian Tomuschat & Jean-Marc Thouvenin (eds.), *The Fundamental Rules of the International Legal Order: Jus Cogens and Obligations Erga Omnes* (Brill 2006); Giorgio Gaja, 'The Protection of General Interests in the International Community' (2012) 364 RCADI 9; Paolo Picone, *Comunità internazionale e obblighi erga omnes* (3rd edn, Jovene 2013).

2.6. Conclusions: The Function of the Law of Occupation

commentators have argued that the expression 'ensure respect' indicates the existence of legal interests in the implementation belonging to every state and to the international community as a whole,[368] as acknowledged by the ICJ in relation to some provisions of the law of occupation.[369] Second, the law of occupation derives in part from and has evolved thanks to the emergence of two other core principles of international law, the principles of prohibition against the use of force and of self-determination of peoples, which impose obligations *erga omnes*, as confirmed by the ICJ.[370] Third, this perspective sheds some light on a conceptual problem relating to situations of occupations where the occupied territory did not belong to any formed state before the beginning of the occupation, such as in the case of the OPT in 1967 and East Timor in 1975. When these occupations began, these territories were not part of any existing state. Accordingly, in a bilateral perspective, there were no subjects of international law holding the rights that corresponded to the occupying powers' duties,[371] especially because, at that time, individuals were not considered subjects of international law,[372] while peoples were seen only

---

[368] See, e.g., Luigi Condorelli & Laurence Boisson De Chazournes, 'Quelques remarques à propos de l'obligation des États de «respecter et faire respecter» le droit international humanitaire «en toutes circonstances»' in Christophe Swinarski (ed.), *Études et essais sur le droit international humanitaire et sur les principes de la Croix-Rouge en l'honneur de Jean Pictet* (ICRC 1984) 17; Paolo Benvenuti, 'Ensuring Observance of International Humanitarian Law: Function, Extent and Limits of the Obligation of Third States to Ensure Respect for International Humanitarian Law' (1989–90) *Yearbook of the International Institute of Humanitarian Law* 27; Laurence Boisson De Chazournes & Luigi Condorelli, 'Common Article 1 of the Geneva Conventions Revisited: Protecting Collective Interests' (2000) 82 IRRC 67; Robin Geiß, 'The Obligation to Respect and to Ensure Respect for the Conventions' in Clapham, Gaeta, & Sassòli (ed.), *The 1949 Geneva Conventions*, 111; Jean-Marie Henckaerts, 'Article 1: Respect and Ensure Respect' in ICRC, *Updated Commentary on the First Geneva Convention* (ICRC/ Cambridge University Press 2016) 35. *Contra*, see Carlo Focarelli, 'Common Article 1 of the 1949 Geneva Conventions: A Soap Bubble?' (2010) 21 EJIL 125.

[369] *Wall* opinion, para. 159. See also Bianchi, 'Dismantling', 378–83; Marco Pertile, '"Legal Consequences of the Construction of a Wall in the Occupied Palestinian Territory": A Missed Opportunity for International Humanitarian Law?' (2004) 14 Italian YIL 121, 153–8; Alexander Orakhelashvili, 'Legal Consequences of the Construction of a Wall in the Occupied Palestinian Territory: Opinion and Reaction' (2006) 11 JCSL 119, 128–34.

[370] See *Barcelona Traction* case, para. 34; *East Timor* case, para. 29; *Wall* opinion, paras. 88 and 155.

[371] With regard to the OPT, this opinion was advanced, for instance, by Blum, 'The Missing Reversioner'.

[372] For an overview on the debate whether international humanitarian law confers rights directly upon individuals, see Provost, *International Human Rights*, 27–34; Paola Gaeta, 'Are Victims of Serious Violations of International Humanitarian Law Entitled to Compensation?' in Ben-Naftali (ed.), *International Humanitarian Law*, 305, 319; Pierre D'Argent, 'Non-Renunciation of Rights Provided by the Conventions' in Clapham, Gaeta, & Sassòli (eds.), *The 1949 Geneva Conventions*, 145.

as beneficiaries of the principle of self-determination conferred by states.[373] On these bases, at a time when there was no general consensus on the possibility that individuals had rights under international law, one may wonder which were the legal subjects that held the rights correspondent to those occupying powers' duties under the law of occupation. The answer is the international community as a whole since the law of occupation embodies obligations *erga omnes* and *erga omnes partes*.

Consequently, the law of occupation does not create a mere trilateral relation. Rather, the law of occupation pertains to multilateral legal relations between the ousted sovereign, the occupying power, the population of the occupied territory (per se or as beneficiaries, if one rejects the idea that individuals may be have rights under international humanitarian law), and every state in the international community, which may be directly addressed by some provisions of the law of occupation or, more generally, has a legal interest in other states' compliance with these rules.

Finally, the law of occupation is a normative system with a peculiar mix of permissive and prohibitive features. Indeed, international humanitarian law as codified by the HR is often considered to be a prohibitive system, that is, a group of rules prohibiting certain conduct while allowing states to do whatever is not expressly prohibited.[374] This approach is rooted in the concept of sovereignty, which would allow states to undertake every action not expressively prohibited by international law.[375] In such a context, international humanitarian law does not confer proper 'rights' on the occupying power, but rather, powers or faculties of actions on the belligerents, without imposing correlative duties to accept and tolerate the action imposed on the other party.[376] However, in more recent times, the progressive humanisation of international humanitarian law has partially transformed this normative system into a permissive system, wherein conduct that is not specifically prohibited may be nonetheless illegal if it infringes upon rights conferred to individuals.[377] With

---

[373] Crawford, *The Creation*, 116 and 126.
[374] On the debate regarding the permissive or prohibitive character of international humanitarian law, in light of the relevant normative evolution, see, generally, Robert Kolb, *Advanced Introduction to International Humanitarian Law* (Edward Elgar 2014) 17–21.
[375] This idea is often called 'Lotus principle' since it was affirmed by the PCIJ, *The Case of SS Lotus (France v. Turkey)*, 7 September 1927, Series A no. 10, 18.
[376] Kolb, *Advanced Introduction*, 18. A clear example of this is the regulation of intelligence collection during armed conflicts; intelligence collection is admissible under Art. 24 HR, even if the enemy has the faculty to contrast it and to prevent and punish it under certain circumstances (such as in the case of espionage, which is considered such a harmful for of intelligence collection that spies can be denied the status of prisoners of war under Art. 46(1) AP I).
[377] See Kolb, *Advanced Introduction*, 19–21.

2.6. Conclusions: The Function of the Law of Occupation

regard to the law of occupation, it is not possible to conclude that the law of occupation is an entirely prohibitive or permissive system either. Rather, the rules of the law of occupation may be divided into three groups: first, there are some norms imposing duties on the occupying power, such as the duty to restore and ensure public order and civil life pursuant to Article 43 HR; second, there are some norms that allow the occupying power to undertake certain conduct, such as Article 48 HR that permits the occupying power to collect taxes; third, there are some rules that constitute non-transgressible prohibitions on the occupying power's action.[378] Since the law of occupation is concerned with the protection of the interests of the ousted sovereign, it prohibits every activity that could lead to the annexation of the occupied territory and to the confusion between the provisional government of the occupying power and the legitimate government of the ousted sovereign. Indeed, in principle the ousted sovereign's sovereignty, which the law of occupation preserves as legally relevant notwithstanding the lack of effectiveness over the occupied territory, would prevent the occupying power from undertaking governmental functions. In other words, the occupied state's sovereignty would in principle prevent another state from exercising its own sovereignty upon the occupied territory; however, the law of occupation constitutes the permissive title to do so.[379] Accordingly, the law of occupation restrains the occupying power's conduct in order to preserve the interests of the ousted sovereign and the local population, providing for explicit permissions each time the occupying power is required to undertake a responsibility (such as those related to the administration of the occupied territory). However, those of the occupying power are not 'rights' technically speaking, but rather 'faculties'.

In conclusion, the different interests and legal regimes concerned by the occupation are reflected in the delicate balance between the hostile character of the occupation and its governmental-like quality, provided by the law of occupation. Such a balance determines and governs the rules pertaining to the use of armed force in occupied territory, which are analysed in the following chapters.

---

[378] See Capotorti, *L'occupazione*, 141–4.
[379] This conclusion is supported by the *Lotus* case itself, wherein, after having declared the *Lotus* principle, the Court affirmed that 'the first and foremost restriction imposed by international law upon a State is that – failing the existence of a permissive rule to the contrary – it may not exercise its power in any form in the territory of another State' (PCIJ, *The Case of SS Lotus*, 18).

3

The Applicability of *Jus ad Bellum* and Self-Defence to the Use of Armed Force in Occupied Territory

Etenim cum inter bellum et pacem medium nihil sit, necesse est tumultum, si belli non sit, pacis esse.[1]

3.1. INTRODUCTION

One can easily understand the need to resort to armed force in times of occupation in light of the elements of the situation of occupation, i.e., the exercise of authority over a territory from a hostile power, normally as a result of armed conflict. Similarly, the law of occupation itself tries to strike a balance between the authority exercised by the occupying power and the fact that this authority is not to be assimilated to that of the ousted sovereign. Consequently, the occupation is likely perceived as a foreign domination by the inhabitants of the occupied territory, while the ousted sovereign, if there is one, may be willing to regain control over the territory temporary placed under foreign authority.

This chapter explores whether the rules of *jus ad bellum*, i.e., the rules concerning the resort to armed force, are relevant for the use of armed force in the occupied territory, focusing particularly on Article 2(4) UN Charter (the ban on the use of armed force in international relations) and Article 51 UN Charter (self-defence), as well as on some other alleged rules of customary international law where they appear applicable to situations of occupation.

The chapter focuses first on the *jus ad bellum* as legal justification for the use of armed force by the occupying power, and then on its relevance for the force employed by the occupying state and the inhabitants of the occupied territory. In particular, the ICJ's case law on this issue, as well as the academic

[1] Cicero, *In M Antonium, Oratio Philippica Octava*, para. 1(4).

debate surrounding this case law, is critically analysed to demonstrate that the proposed explanations about the applicability or inapplicability of *jus ad bellum* in times of occupation are not conclusive.

Finally, the chapter concludes with a novel explanation of why *jus ad bellum* rules are largely inapplicable to the use of armed force in the occupied territory. This explanation is based on the preservation of a state of ongoing armed conflict in the occupied territory owing to the situation of occupation itself.

3.2. *JUS AD BELLUM* JUSTIFICATIONS FOR THE USE OF FORCE BY THE OCCUPYING POWER

3.2.1. *The Role of Self-Defence in State Practice Regarding Occupation*

As mentioned, the legitimacy of recourse to armed force by the occupying power in the occupied territory has not been explored for many years. The most recent debate on the role of *jus ad bellum* in the context of occupations originated mainly from the discourse about the right of self-defence of the occupying power. According to Article 51 UN Charter, '[n]othing in the present Charter shall impair the inherent right of individual or collective self-defence if an armed attack occurs against a Member of the United Nations, until the Security Council has taken measures necessary to maintain international peace and security'. The ICJ has consistently held that this provision largely reflects international customary law, and that the response in self-defence must be proportionate, necessary, and immediate.[2] However,

---

[2] See, e.g., *Nicaragua v. USA* para. 194; *Case Concerning Oil Platforms (Islamic Republic of Iran v. USA)*, Judgment, 6 November 2003, para. 43. For some seminal works on this topic, see Hans Kelsen, *The Law of the United Nations* (Stevens & Sons 1950) 791–805; Derek William Bowett, *Self-Defence in International Law* (Manchester University Press 1959); Ian Brownlie, *International Law and the Use of Force by States* (Clarendon Press 1968) 214–308; Pierluigi Lamberti Zanardi, *La legittima difesa nel diritto internazionale* (Giuffrè 1972); Linos-Alexandre Sicilianos, *Les réactions décentralisées à l'illicite* (LGDJ 1990) 291–336; Thomas M. Franck, *Recourse to Force: State Action against Threats and Armed Attacks* (Cambridge University Press 2002); Antonio Cassese, 'Article 51' in Jean-Pierre Cot, Alain Pellet, & Mathias Forteau (eds.), *La Charte des Nations Unies: commentaire article par article* vol. II (3rd edn, Economica 2005) 1329; Natalino Ronzitti, 'The Expanding Law of Self-Defence' (2006) 11 JCSL 343; Christine Gray, *International Law and the Use of Force* (3rd edn, Oxford University Press 2008); James A. Green, *The International Court of Justice and Self-Defence in International Law* (Hart 2009); Olivier Corten, *The Law against War: The Prohibition on the Use of Force in Contemporary International Law* (Hart 2010) 401–94; Tom Ruys, '*Armed Attack*' *and Article 51 of the UN Charter* (Cambridge University Press 2011); Dinstein, *War, Aggression*, 195–327; Christopher Greenwood, 'Self-Defence' in *MPEPIL* online (2011); Alessandra Lanciotti & Attila Tanzi (eds.), *Uso della forza e legittima difesa nel diritto internazionale*

since there is no reference in the text of this provision to its applicability in situations of occupation, in order to verify whether an occupying power has the right of self-defence against armed attacks originating from within the occupied territory, this chapter will analyse the relevant state practice, which must be taken into account in the interpretation of Article 51 UN Charter.[3]

First, it should be noted that state practice should be confined to those situations in which states recognise themselves to be occupying powers, irrespectively of the fact that the lack of acknowledgement of the situation of occupation does not preclude the application of the law of occupation. Indeed, it is normal that states rejecting their status as occupying powers would not invoke self-defence to justify their use of force in those territories. In situations in which an occupying power considers itself to have annexed the occupied territory, then it would not invoke self-defence to resort to armed force in that territory since no state needs self-defence as a legal basis to justify the use of force within its own territory.[4] Similarly, in cases of occupations through puppet regimes, the occupying power would justify its use of armed force on different bases, for instance, on the basis of the request of the puppet regime.[5] Accordingly, there is no state practice regarding the invocation of self-defence in those situations, which obviously should be considered occupations even without the acknowledgement of this characterisation by the occupying power. Actually, the EU fact-finding mission investigating the 2006 armed conflict between Georgia and Russia analysed the relationship between South Ossetia, Abkhazia, Georgia, and Russia in light of *jus ad bellum* and self-defence during the 2006 armed conflict; however, since the mission failed to consider South Ossetia and Abkhazia occupied by Russia, its conclusions, somewhat unconvincing as they are, are not particularly relevant for this analysis.[6] Consequently, the only two situations that may be used

---

contemporaneo (Jovane 2012); Albrecht Randelzhofer & Georg Nolte, 'Article 51' in Bruno Simma et al. (eds.), *The Charter of the United Nations: A Commentary* (3rd edn, Oxford University Press 2012) 1397; Paolo Picone, 'L'insostenibile leggerezza dell'art 51 della Carta dell'ONU' (2016) 99 RDI 7.

[3] See Art. 31(3)(b) VCLT. For more on this criterion, see *supra*, Section 2.5.3.

[4] See Corten, *The Law against War*, 127–35; Michael N. Schmitt, 'Responding to Transnational Terrorism under the *Jus ad Bellum*: A Normative Framework' in Michael N. Schmitt & Jelena Pejic (eds.), *International Law and Armed Conflict: Exploring the Faultlines* (Martinus Nijhoff 2007) 157, 169; Oliver Dörr, 'Use of Force, Prohibition of', in *MPEPIL online* (2015) para. 21.

[5] This is the argument advanced by Russia to justify the use of armed force in South Ossetia and Abkhazia (see IIFFMCG, Report, vol. II, 263–94).

[6] With regard to *jus ad bellum*, the fact-finding mission considered South Ossetia and Abkhazia as two entities short of statehood but independent (IIFFMCG, Report, vol. II, 227–94). The application of *jus ad bellum* and self-defence embodied in the report met with harsh criticisms (see, e.g., Christian Henderson & James A. Green, 'The *Jus ad Bellum* and Entities Short of Statehood in the Report on the Conflict in Georgia' (2010) 59 ICLQ 129).

3.2. Jus ad Bellum *Justifications*

as sources of state practice are the occupation of Iraq and, especially in the last decades, that of the OPT. However, this paragraph demonstrates that this practice is extremely thin.

With regard to the occupation of Iraq, to the best of this author's knowledge, the CPA never invoked the right to self-defence to justify the use of armed force against attacks originating from within the occupied Iraq. Indeed, even in the aftermath of terrorist attacks, the USA never invoked self-defence against the insurgents in Iraq, and other states did not address the problem of the security of the CPA in the framework of *jus ad bellum*.[7] States referred only to the need of the restored future government of Iraq to be able to defend itself: for instance, the USA affirmed that 'as it resumes full control of its affairs, Iraq will need a military for self-defence. Accordingly, we have started training the new Iraqi army.'[8] Moreover, there is no reference to self-defence in the documents of the CPA,[9] nor in the US field manual adopted after the security situations experienced by the USA in the occupied Iraq and Afghanistan,[10] even though this manual is explicitly applicable to situations of occupations.[11] Accordingly, it is possible to affirm that the occupation of Iraq does not provide any evidence of state practice regarding the exercise of self-defence by the occupying power in the occupied territory.

The situation of the OPT is different. Israel is the only occupying power that has invoked self-defence to justify its use of armed force in occupied territory. Consequently, a detailed analysis of Israel's claims and the reaction of other states will help develop greater understanding of the applicability of *jus ad bellum* in times of occupation. At a close scrutiny, Israeli practice does not appear decisive.

In the framework of the Second Intifada, Israel justified the so-called operation Defensive Wall in response to a series of Palestinian terrorist attacks in 2002 on the basis of self-defence: 'Israel has no choice other than to act in accordance with its *right to self-defence* and to take the action that it deems

---

[7] See S/PV.4812, in the aftermath of a terrorist attack against UN facilities.
[8] Ibid., 3. See also S/PV.4869, 4 and the Memorandum from Ambassador Bremer for the Secretary of Defense Rumsfeld, Dissolution of the Ministry of Defense and Related Entities, 19 May 2003, reprinted in Stefan Talmon (ed.), *The Occupation of Iraq, vol. II: The Official Documents of the Coalition Provisional Authority and the Iraqi Governing Council* (Hart 2013) 811.
[9] These documents, along with other extremely interesting sources, are reprinted in Talmon (ed.), *The Occupation*.
[10] See Watkin, 'Use of Force', 283.
[11] US Army Marine Counterinsurgency Field Manual, US Field Manual No. 3–24 (December 2006), section 1–2.

necessary to defend its citizens from violence and terror'.[12] This justification, notwithstanding the support of the Supreme Court of Israel,[13] has met with mixed reactions from other states.[14] For instance, the operation was considered an act of aggression by China,[15] Syria,[16] Algeria,[17] Libya,[18] Qatar,[19] Djibouti,[20] Jordan,[21] Iraq,[22] Iran,[23] Morocco,[24] Cuba,[25] Saudi Arabia,[26] Egypt,[27] Yemen,[28] South Africa,[29] United Arab Emirates,[30] Malaysia,[31] and Palestine itself,[32] which, consequently, implicitly rejected the self-defence argument. A second group of states, including of France,[33] Mauritius,[34] Mexico,[35] Norway,[36] Pakistan,[37]

---

[12] See Letter dated 1 April 2002 from the Permanent Representative of Israel to the United Nations addressed to the Secretary-General, UN Doc S/2002/337 (emphasis added). See also the declarations before the SC of the Israeli representative: 'We will exercise our basic right of self-defence and target the vast terrorist infrastructure that the Palestinian Authority continues to nurture and sustain in its territory' (S/PV.4503, 6) and 'Israel has no choice but to exercise its right and duty under international law to defend ourselves. This is a right that any State would exercise under the conditions that we have been facing' (S/PV.4506, 6).

[13] See HCJ 3451/02 *Almadani v. Minister of Defence*, 25 April 2002, para. 9, unofficial English translation available at www.legal-tools.org/doc/9b58f0/pdf/: 'Israel finds itself in the middle of difficult battle against a furious wave of terrorism. Israel is exercising its right of self defense. See The Charter of the United Nations, art. 51. This combat is not taking place in a normative void'.

[14] For a detailed analysis, see François Dubuisson, 'L'applicabilité du droit de légitime défense dans les rapports entre Israël at le Territoire palestinien occupé' in Jean-Philippe Kot (ed.), *Palestine and International Law, New Approaches* (Birzeit University Press 2011) 89, 99–101.

[15] S/PV.4503, 16.
[16] Ibid., 18.
[17] Ibid., 20.
[18] Ibid., 21 and S/PV.4506, 14.
[19] S/PV.4503, 22.
[20] Ibid., 23.
[21] Ibid., 25.
[22] Ibid., 26.
[23] Ibid., 27.
[24] Ibid., 30.
[25] Ibid., 32.
[26] Ibid., 33 and S/PV.4506, 17.
[27] S/PV.4506, 8.
[28] Ibid., 13.
[29] Ibid., 16.
[30] Ibid., 21.
[31] Ibid., 23.
[32] S/PV.4503, 5; S/PV.4506, 3.
[33] S/PV.4503, 9.
[34] Ibid., 10.
[35] Ibid., 14.
[36] Ibid., 19.
[37] Ibid., 29.

3.2. Jus ad Bellum *Justifications*

Spain,[38] Chile,[39] and Brazil,[40] criticised the *quomodo* of the Israeli response on the basis of the principle of proportionality both under *jus ad bellum* and *jus in bello* – leaving open the question of their opinion regarding the justification of self-defence. Finally, the USA supported Israel's claim of a right to self-defence, simultaneously cautioning the political consequences of an armed response against the Palestinian leadership,[41] while Bulgaria acknowledged 'Israel's right to respond to terror' without qualifying it univocally as self-defence.[42]

Similarly, Israel invoked self-defence with regard to the construction of the wall in the West Bank. Israel claimed before the UN GA that:

> A security fence has proven itself to be one of the most effective non-violent methods for preventing terrorism in the heart of civilian areas. The fence is a measure wholly consistent with *the right of States to self-defence enshrined in Article 51* of the Charter. International law and Security Council resolutions, including resolutions 1368 (2001) and 1373 (2001), have clearly recognized the right of States to use force in self-defence against terrorist attacks, and therefore surely recognize the right to use non-forcible measures to that end.[43]

The issue of self-defence in relation to the Israeli wall was addressed by the 2004 *Wall* opinion. Leaving aside for a moment the Court's findings on this issue, which will be analysed in the next subsection, the remarks on self-defence made by some states participating in the proceedings are extremely relevant. The possibility of Israel relying on self-defence in relation to armed groups' attacks originating from the OPT was rejected by Palestine,[44] Saudi Arabia,[45] Malaysia,[46] Belize,[47] Jordan,[48] and the League of Arab States.[49] In the aftermath of the *Wall* opinion, some states criticised the Court for not having taken into proper account the Israeli right to self-defence:[50] for instance,

---

[38] S/PV.4506, 10.
[39] Ibid., 15.
[40] Ibid., 25.
[41] S/PV.4503, 12: 'We understand that Israel has a right to self-defence, but we call on Prime Minister Sharon and his Government to carefully consider the consequences of their actions'.
[42] Ibid., 15.
[43] A/ES-10/PV.21, 20 October 2003, 6 (emphasis added).
[44] Written Statement Submitted by Palestine, 30 January 2004, paras. 530–4; Oral Statement of Palestine, 23 February 2004, CR 2004/1, 44–5
[45] Written Statement of the Kingdom of Saudi Arabia, 30 January 2004, paras. 31–4.
[46] Written Statement of Malaysia, 30 January 2004, paras. 146–9.
[47] Oral Statement of Belize, 24 February 2004, CR 2004/3, paras. 41–3.
[48] Oral Statement of Jordan, ibid., para. 9.
[49] Oral Statement of the League of Arab States, 25 February 2004, CR 2004/5, 29–30.
[50] For an overview, see Dubuisson, 'L'applicabilité', 105–7; Corten, 'L'applicabilité', 86–7.

the Netherlands pointed out that '[t]he European Union recognize[s] Israel's security concerns and its right to act in self-defence'[51] and the USA strongly advocated for the applicability of Article 51 UN Charter.[52] On the other hand, Djibouti supported the idea that Israel could not rely on self-defence,[53] and the final resolution refers to 'the right and the duty to take actions in conformity with international law and international humanitarian law to counter deadly acts of violence against their civilian population in order to protect the lives of their citizens', without mentioning self-defence under *jus ad bellum*.[54]

Since these two episodes, scholars have analysed Israeli claims of acting in self-defence in relation to the three aforementioned military operations in the Gaza Strip.[55] However, on closer scrutiny, there are some reasons to doubt the actual relevance of these episodes as manifestation of state practice regarding the occupying powers' right to self-defence under Article 51 UN Charter in response to armed attacks originating from within the occupied territory.

Indeed, Israel seems to have softened its reliance on an autonomous right to self-defence pursuant to Article 51 UN Charter or international customary law pertaining to *jus ad bellum*. With regard to operation Cast Lead (2009), Israel, before the UN SC, affirmed that the operation was launched in response to rockets and mortars fired from the Gaza Strip pursuant to Article 51 UN Charter.[56] The Supreme Court of Israel supported this view.[57] However, in the official document in which Israel explained to the international community the facts and law pertaining to the operation, Israel asserted that its right to respond to rockets fired from the Gaza Strip was based on the existence of an ongoing conflict with Hamas.[58] The justification of self-defence pursuant to Article 51 UN Charter was advanced only as a suppletive legal basis for the operation.[59] Although 'the Gaza Operation was justified as an act of self-defence', '[i]n any case, Israel's right to use force against Hamas was triggered years ago, when Palestinian terrorist organisations, including Hamas, initiated the armed conflict which is still ongoing. The current operation was another regrettable stage

---

[51] A/ES-10/PV.27, 8.
[52] See A/ES-10/PV.25, 2; A/ES-10/PV.27, 4.
[53] Ibid., 2.
[54] See GA Res. ES-10/15 (2004), 2 August 2004, preambular para. 16.
[55] See Dubuisson 'L'applicabilité', 102–5; Corten, 'L'applicabilité', 87–99; Kattan, 'Operation', 98–102; Weill & Azarova, 'The 2014', 362–70.
[56] Identical letters dated 27 December 2008 from the Permanent Representative of Israel to the United Nations addressed to the Secretary-General and to the President of the Security Council, 27 December 2008, S/2008/816. See also S/PV.6060, 6.
[57] See HCJ 9132/07 *Al-Bassiouni* v. *Prime Minister*, 30 January 2008, unofficial English translation available at elyon1.court.gov.il/Files_ENG/07/320/091/n25/07091320.n25.pdf, para. 20.
[58] Israel, *The Operation in Gaza*, para. 67.
[59] Ibid., para. 68; see also paras. 69–71.

3.2. Jus ad Bellum *Justifications* 95

in this conflict'.[60] It seems to this author that Israel's reliance on self-defence is secondary with respect to the argument of the existence of an ongoing armed conflict – a justification that will be analysed in Section 3.4. It should be noted that the Israeli view is, however, based on the wrong assumption that at that time 'the Gaza Strip is neither a State nor a territory occupied or controlled by Israel', but, rather, the case would be based on '*sui generis* circumstances'.[61]

The Israeli invocation of self-defence as the legal basis to resort to armed force with regard to the operation received the endorsement of some states, including Italy,[62] Vietnam,[63] Belgium,[64] Croatia,[65] the USA,[66] Benin,[67] Panama,[68] the Netherlands,[69] and Denmark,[70] which, however, appeared reluctant to explicitly invoke Article 51 UN Charter.[71] Other states contested the operation on the basis of its disproportionate character, without entering into the debate over whether Israel could have invoked self-defence.[72] However, a number of states, including Libya,[73] Egypt,[74] Venezuela,[75] Jordan,[76] Nicaragua,[77] Kuwait,[78] Tunisia,[79] Bolivia,[80] Pakistan,[81] Maldives,[82] Lebanon,[83]

---

[60] Ibid., para. 72.
[61] Israel, *The Operation in Gaza*, para. 30. Similarly, a commentator supported the Israeli claim of self-defence on the basis of this alleged *sui generis* status of the Gaza Strip (see Solon Solomon, 'The Great Oxymoron: *Jus In Bello* Violations as Legitimate Non-Forcible Measures of Self-Defense: The Post-Disengagement Israeli Measures towards Gaza as a Case Study' (2010) 9 CJIL 501).
[62] S/PV.6060, 13.
[63] Ibid. (condemning the operation as disproportionate).
[64] Ibid., 17.
[65] Ibid.
[66] S/PV.6063, 5.
[67] A/ES-10/PV.35, 3.
[68] Ibid., 7.
[69] Ibid., 16.
[70] Ibid., 17.
[71] See Koutroulis, 'Of Occupation', 909–10.
[72] South Africa (S/PV.6060, 9); France (S/PV.6060, 9); Costa Rica (S/PV.6060, 16); Burkina Faso (A/ES-10/PV.35, 5); Cyprus (A/ES-10/PV.35, 18); Malta (A/ES-10/PV.35, 20).
[73] S/PV.6060, 7–8.
[74] Ibid., 18.
[75] A/ES-10/PV.34, 4.
[76] Ibid., 7–8.
[77] Ibid., 11.
[78] Ibid., 13.
[79] Ibid., 16.
[80] Ibid., 19.
[81] Ibid., 22.
[82] Ibid., 26
[83] A/ES-10/PV.35, 20.

and the entire Non-Aligned Movement[84] denied Israel's claim regarding self-defence. Self-defence was excluded as a justification by the international fact-finding mission dispatched by the League of Arab States,[85] as well as by the mission dispatched by the HRC.[86]

With regard to the operation Pillar of Clouds (2012), Israel invoked the defensive nature of its action, but it did not mention Article 51 UN Charter.[87] The Israeli claim was considered to be without grounds by many states, including, among others, Palestine,[88] Egypt,[89] Cuba,[90] Syria,[91] Malaysia,[92] Iran,[93] Pakistan,[94] Saudi Arabia,[95] Morocco,[96] Turkey,[97] Jordan,[98] and Bahrain.[99] Other states condemned the operation as indiscriminate and disproportionate without entering the debate regarding Israeli entitlement to invoke self-defence, as in the cases of Indonesia[100] and Russia.[101] However, a few states supported

---

[84] Statement by the Coordinating Bureau of the Non-Aligned Movement on the Non-Compliance by Israel with Security Council Resolution 1860 (2009) and the Escalation of the Israeli Military Aggression against the Gaza Strip, 15 January 2009, A/63/679-S/2009/36.
[85] See Letter dated 1 October 2009 from the Permanent Observer of the League of Arab States to the United Nations, addressed to the President of the Security Council, S/2009/537, paras. 408–11.
[86] See Goldstone Report, para. 1883.
[87] See Identical Letters from the Permanent Representative of Israel to the United Nations addressed to the Secretary-General and the President of the Security Council, 23 November 2012, S/2012/870. See also IDF, Operation 'Pillar of Defense', 2.
[88] A/67/PV.44, 3.
[89] A/67/PV.47, 1.
[90] Ibid., 3.
[91] Ibid., 5.
[92] Ibid., 6.
[93] Ibid., 8.
[94] Ibid., 13.
[95] See the official declaration 'Saudi Arabia Condemns the Israeli Assaults on Gaza Strip' available at www.spa.gov.sa/viewstory.php?newsid=1049764.
[96] According to news reports. See 'Morocco Strongly Condemns Israel's Military Operation in Gaza' NZweek, 16 November 2012, available at www.nzweek.com/world/morocco-strongly-condemns-israels-military-operation-in-gaza-25466/.
[97] According to news reports. See Raphael Ahren, 'Egypt, Jordan, Turkey and Russia Chorus Condemnation of Israel's Resort to Force, US Leads Western Supporters' *The Times of Israel* 15 November 2012, available at www.timesofisrael.com/egypt-jordan-turkey-and-russia-chorus-condemnation-of-israels-resort-to-force-us-leads-western-supporters/.
[98] Ibid.
[99] See 'Minister of State for Foreign Affairs Affirms Bahrain's Position in Supporting the Palestinian Case', 11 November 2012, available at www.mofa.gov.bh/Default.aspx?tabid=7824&ItemId=2102.
[100] A/67/PV.44, 7.
[101] According to news reports. See Ahren, 'Egypt, Jordan, Turkey and Russia Chorus Condemnation of Israel's Resort to Force, US Leads Western Supporters'.

the Israeli right of self-defence: Denmark,[102] Italy,[103] the Netherlands,[104] Germany,[105] the USA,[106] and Bulgaria[107] openly voiced their support.

With regard to the operation Protective Edge (2014), Israel claimed that its action was defensive in nature, but it failed to invoke the right of self-defence consistently. For instance, there is no mention to a right of self-defence in the notification sent to the SC regarding the launch of the operation, where Israel simply noted that 'Hamas has taken responsibility for the barrage of rockets, and the Israeli government will now fulfil its responsibilities by defending its citizens. The Israeli Government will put a stop to these terrorist attacks; it is our duty as a responsible government to do so'.[108] Conversely, before the SC, Israel claimed that it had 'launched a self-defence operation, called Protective Edge, to counter the attacks, to defend our citizens',[109] without mentioning Article 51 UN Charter. More significantly, in the report prepared by the Ministry of Foreign Affairs to explain the legal and factual aspects of the operation, Israel reiterated the position according to which the primary legal basis of the operation was the existence of an ongoing armed conflict with Hamas:

> The confrontation between Israel and these terrorist organisations in the Gaza Strip satisfies the definition of armed conflict under international law. *The 2014 Gaza Conflict was simply the latest in a series of armed confrontations*, precipitated by the continuing attacks perpetrated by Hamas and other terrorist organisations against Israel. After previous periods of intense fighting (including in 2009 and 2012), Hamas agreed to ceasefires, each of which it later breached, leading to Israel's resumption of responsive military action to defend its population from attacks. *Hamas's attacks leading up to the 2014 Gaza Conflict were thus part of a larger, ongoing armed conflict*. But even if one were not to consider the 2014 Gaza Conflict part of a continuous armed conflict justifying Israel's use of force both previously

---

[102] A/67/PV.44, 18.
[103] Ibid., 19.
[104] See the press release 'Timmermans Condemns Rocket Attacks on Israel from Gaza', 13 November 2012, available at www.government.nl/latest/news/2012/11/13/timmermans-condemns-rocket-attacks-on-israel-from-gaza.
[105] According to news reports. See Ahren, 'Egypt, Jordan, Turkey and Russia Chorus Condemnation of Israel's Resort to Force, US Leads Western Supporters'.
[106] See 'Remarks by President Obama and Prime Minister Shinawatra in a Joint Press Conference', 18 November 2012, available at obamawhitehouse.archives.gov/the-press-office/2012/11/18/remarks-president-obama-and-prime-minister-shinawatra-joint-press-confer.
[107] See the statement of the Minister of Foreign Affair, available at www.mfa.bg/en/events/73/4/539/index.html.
[108] Identical letters from the Permanent Representative of Israel to the United Nations addressed to the Secretary-General and the President of the Security Council, S/2014/474, 7 July 2014.
[109] S/PV.7214, 6. See also S/PV.7220, 8–9.

and during this time, Hamas's armed attacks against Israel in 2014 would independently qualify as an armed attack triggering Israel's inherent right of self-defence.[110]

Accordingly, Israel seems to rely primarily on the existence of an ongoing armed conflict with Hamas as the main legal justification of the operation Protective Edge, while self-defence is only invoked as a secondary legal basis.

Again, the Israeli operation met with mixed reactions.[111] A number of States, including Palestine,[112] Syria,[113] Jordan,[114] Lebanon,[115] Egypt,[116] Saudi Arabia,[117] Pakistan,[118] Morocco,[119] Malaysia,[120] Algeria,[121] Ecuador,[122] Namibia,[123] Nicaragua,[124] Turkey,[125] Bolivia,[126] Democratic People's Republic of Korea,[127] Indonesia,[128] Maldives,[129] Quatar,[130] Iran,[131] El Salvador,[132] Venezuela,[133] Cuba,[134] Kazakhstan,[135] and Kuwait,[136] considered the Israeli action to be illegal and not based on self-defence. On the contrary, the USA,[137] the United Kingdom,[138] Rwanda,[139]

---

[110] Israel, *The 2014 Gaza Operation*, paras. 66–7 (emphases added).
[111] For an overview, see Trigeaud, 'L'opération', 186–8.
[112] S/PV.7214, 5.
[113] S/PV.7216, 12.
[114] S/PV.7220, 10; S/PV.7222, 11.
[115] S/PV.7222, 29.
[116] Ibid., 32.
[117] Ibid., 32–3.
[118] Ibid., 34.
[119] Ibid., 35.
[120] Ibid., 36.
[121] Ibid., 41.
[122] Ibid., 41.
[123] Ibid., 43.
[124] Ibid., 45.
[125] Ibid., 46.
[126] Ibid., 47.
[127] Ibid., 48–9.
[128] Ibid., 50.
[129] Ibid.
[130] Ibid., 52.
[131] Ibid., 55.
[132] Ibid., 59.
[133] Ibid.
[134] Ibid., 62.
[135] Ibid., 65.
[136] Ibid., 68.
[137] S/PV.7220, 10; S/PV.7222, 12.
[138] S/PV.7220, 15; S/PV.7222, 17.
[139] Ibid., 20.

Luxembourg,[140] Nigeria,[141] Australia,[142] Chad,[143] Lithuania,[144] Norway,[145] Canada,[146] Bangladesh,[147] and Jamaica[148] supported with different views the Israeli right to self-defence.

From these manifestations of state practice and *opinio juris*, it is clear that Israel steadfastly believes that it has the right to respond to the rockets and mortars fired from the Gaza Strip through armed force, to protect its own citizens and territory. However, Israel is less consistent about whether to base this right on the *jus ad bellum* right to self-defence or on the existence of an ongoing armed conflict.

More generally, an analysis of the occupations of Iraq and OPT demonstrates that there is little support in state practice and *opinio juris* regarding the occupying powers' right to self-defence pursuant to Article 51 UN Charter. Indeed, the Israeli claims met with strong criticisms: Arab states, Latin American states, and many African and Asian states have consistently rejected the invocation of self-defence, while fewer, mainly Western states, have supported them. Accordingly, it is impossible to consider that the occupying power's recourse to self-defence in the occupied territory is supported by uniform practice or accepted as law by the generality of states.

3.2.2. *The Role of Self-Defence in the Case Law of the ICJ or, A Few Lines Creating a Huge Debate*

In 2004, despite the scarcity of State practice, the question of the occupying powers' right to self-defence pursuant to Article 51 UN Charter in occupied territories was addressed by the ICJ in its advisory opinion regarding the legality of a wall (or fence)[149] built by Israel in the West Bank. As mentioned, Israel

---

[140] S/PV.7222, 9.
[141] Ibid., 20.
[142] Ibid., 24.
[143] Ibid., 26.
[144] Ibid., 27.
[145] Ibid., 51.
[146] Ibid., 60.
[147] Ibid., 61 ('We do not deny Israel's right to exist in peace or to self-defence. But we strongly condemn its practice of routinely killing innocent Palestinians under various pretexts. It is unfortunate that Israel has been using the pretext of self-defence to kill people living under its own occupation').
[148] Ibid., 68.
[149] For the almost entirely pointless debate between Israel and other states and international actors regarding the correct name of that construction (wall, barrier, fence, or what else), see Eugenia López-Jacoiste Díaz, 'Algunas reflexiones sobre la Opinión Consultiva sobre el Muro de Israel: la solución está en Ramalla y Gaza y no en la Haya o Manhattan' (2004) 20 ADI 467, 468 fn. 3.

had claimed before the UN GA that the barrier was a self-defence measure,[150] and the UN Secretary-General, in his Report prepared pursuant to the request of advisory opinion, had emphasised that the Israeli position was based on Article 51 UN Charter and SC resolutions 1368 (2001) and 1373 (2001).[151]

The ICJ dedicated only two paragraphs of its opinion to the problem of self-defence. After having quoted Article 51 UN Charter, the Court dismissed the relevance of self-defence with regard to the legality of the wall. According to paragraph 139 of the ICJ's opinion,

> Article 51 of the Charter thus recognizes the existence of an inherent right of self-defence in the case of armed attack by one State against another State. However, Israel does not claim that the attacks against it are imputable to a foreign State. The Court also notes that Israel exercises control in the [OPT] and that, as Israel itself states, the threat which it regards as justifying the construction of the wall originates within, and not outside, that territory. The situation is thus different from that contemplated by Security Council resolutions 1368 (2001) and 1373 (2001), and therefore Israel could not in any event invoke those resolutions in support of its claim to be exercising a right of self-defence. Consequently, the Court concludes that Article 51 of the Charter has no relevance in this case.

This paragraph sparked a significant debate: immediately, three judges of the ICJ criticised this paragraph in their individual opinions,[152] and the Supreme Court of Israel very soon voiced its disagreement, affirming that it 'find[s] this approach of the [ICJ] hard to come to terms with'.[153]

Paragraph 139 of the ICJ's opinion can be interpreted in at least two ways: the ICJ may have addressed the inapplicability of self-defence against attacks from non-state actors *tout court* or, rather, may have considered this rule to be inapplicable in the specific situation of an occupation. The confusion is exacerbated by the fact that the ICJ advanced two quite different reasons for denying the applicability of the self-defence rule: on the one hand, the ICJ affirmed that only states can launch armed attacks and trigger a response in self-defence; on the other, the Court said that the fact that the occupied territory is placed under occupation per se excludes the application of self-defence.

Regardless of the merits of these two arguments, the ICJ should have argued more conclusively on this pivotal point, to clarify international law with regard

---

[150] See *supra*, Section 3.2.2.
[151] A/ES-10/248, 24 November 2003, para. 6 (emphasis added).
[152] See *Wall* opinion, Separate Opinion of Judge Higgins, paras. 33–5; Separate Opinion of Judge Kooijmans, paras. 35–6; Declaration of Judge Buergenthal, paras. 5–6.
[153] *Mara'abe v. The Prime Minister of Israel*, para. 23.

to a topical issue. Rather, the Court preferred to offer a 'telegraphic',[154] 'foggy and ambiguous'[155] *'ipse dixit'*.[156]

To better study this issue, the different arguments are hereby analysed separately.

3.2.3. Scholarly Interpretations of the Wall Opinion's Paragraph Pertaining to Self-Defence

3.2.3.1. The Use of Force by the Occupying Power in the Framework of the Debate Regarding the Use of Force against Non-State Actors

Since the wall was allegedly built in order to respond against attacks from Palestinian armed groups, the ICJ's rejection of the Israeli right to self-defence has been interpreted as the ICJ's official position regarding the possibility of invoking self-defence against non-state actors in any circumstances. Due to the importance of this topic in contemporary international law, it is necessary to summarise briefly this issue.

Article 51 UN Charter does not state explicitly that the author of the attack must be a State to claim self-defence. However, Article 51 UN Charter is commonly read in conjunction with Article 2(4) UN Charter, according to which '[a]ll Members shall refrain in their international relations from the threat or use of force against the territorial integrity or political independence of any state, or in any other manner inconsistent with the Purposes of the United Nations'.[157] Since only states may become members of the UN,[158] most authors consider that the system created by Articles 2(4) and 51 UN Charter is applicable only to the use of force between two or more states.[159] Similarly, the GA's

---

[154] Scobbie, 'Words', 87.
[155] Bianchi, 'Dismantling', 376.
[156] Murphy, 'Self-Defense', 62.
[157] It is impossible to acknowledge the almost unlimited scholarship on Art. 2(4). Just to mention very few pivotal studies, see Brownlie, *International Law*, 112–22; Nico J. Schrijver, 'Article 2, Paragraphe 4' in Cot, Pellet & Forteau (eds.), *La Charte*, 437; Gray, *International Law*, 30–66; Corten, *The Law against War*; Dinstein, *War, Aggression*, 89–98; Oliver Dörr & Albrecht Randelzhofer, 'Article 2(4)' in Simma et al. (eds.), *The Charter*, 200; Mary Ellen O'Connell, 'The Prohibition of the Use of Force' in Nigel D. White & Christian Henderson (eds.), *Research Handbook on International Conflict and Security Law* (Edward Elgar 2013) 89; Dörr, 'Use'; James Crawford & Rowan Nicholson, 'The Continued Relevance of Traditional Rules and Institutions Relating to the Use of Force' in Mark Weller (ed.), *The Oxford Handbook of the Use of Force in International Law* (Oxford University Press 2015) 86; Nico J. Schrijver, 'The Ban on the Use of Force in the UN Charter' ibid., 465.
[158] See Art. 4(1), UN Charter.
[159] See Ruiz Colomé, *Guerras*, 90; Villani, *L'ONU*, 21; Corten, *The Law against War*, 126–97; Sergio Marchisio, *L'ONU: il diritto delle Nazioni Unite* (2nd edn, Il Mulino 2012) 62–3;

Declaration on Principles of International Law concerning Friendly Relations and Co-operation among States (Declaration on Friendly Relations) affirms that '*[e]very State* has the duty to refrain in its international relations from the threat or use of force against the territorial integrity or political independence of *any State*',[160] while, more recently, the UN Secretary-General acknowledged that 'norms governing the use of force by non-State actors have not kept pace with those pertaining to States' and that the 'normative framework of the United Nations surrounding State use of force must be complemented by a normative framework of equal authority surrounding non-State use of force'.[161] Consequently, armed attacks launched by non-state actors that are not attributable to a state would fall outside the scope of the ban on the use of armed force under Article 2(4) UN Charter, and thus the victim state may not react in self-defence pursuant to Article 51.[162]

This interstate view on *jus ad bellum* finds support in the ICJ's case law. In its 1986 decision in the *Nicaragua* v. *USA* case, the ICJ affirmed that acts of violence used by armed groups do not amount to an armed attack under Article 51 UN Charter unless those acts are attributable to a state under the rules of international responsibility.[163] Although this statement opens the door to the debate regarding the attribution to a state of some non-state actors' attacks pursuant to customary international law,[164] nonetheless, in the

---

O'Connell, 'The Prohibition', 99–113; Dörr & Randelzhofer, 'Article 2(4)', 213–15; Dörr, 'Use', para. 21.

[160] GA Res. 2625 (XXV), 24 October 1970 (emphases added).

[161] Follow-up to the Outcome of the Millennium Summit, Note by the Secretary-General, 2 December 2004, A/59/565, paras. 159–60 (emphases added). See also the pertinent remarks by Mégret, 'Grandeur', 397–8.

[162] See Pierluigi Lamberti Zanardi, 'Indirect Military Aggression' in Antonio Cassese (ed.), *The Current Legal Regulation of the Use of Force* (Martinus Nijhoff 1986) 111, 112–16; Condorelli, 'Les attentats', 838–9; Corten & Dubuisson, 'Operation', 55; Andrea Gioia, 'Terrorismo internazionale, crimini di guerra e crimini contro l'umanità' (2004) 87 RDI 5, 47; Pierre Klein, 'Le droit international à l'épreuve du terrorisme' (2006) 321 RCADI 203, 370–410; Marco Sassòli, 'Terrorism and War' (2006) 4 JICJ 959, 962; Conforti & Focarelli, *The Law*, 314–15; Pietro Gargiulo, 'Uso della forza (diritto internazionale)' in *Enciclopedia del Diritto* (Giuffrè 2012) 1367, 1397–8, 1415–16; Randelzhofer & Nolte, 'Article 51', 1417–18; Giovanni Distefano, 'Use of Force' in Clapham & Gaeta (eds.), *The Oxford*, 545, 557–60.

[163] See *Nicaragua* v. *USA*, para. 193:

> The Court does not believe that the concept of 'armed attack' includes not only acts of armed bands where such acts occur on a significant scale but also assistance to rebels in the form of the provision of weapons or logistical or other support. Such assistance may be regarded as a threat or use of force, or amount to intervention in the internal or external affairs of other States.

[164] For more on this, see *infra*, Section 5.5.2.

context of self-defence, it narrows the application of Article 51 UN Charter to interstate armed attacks. Despite some criticisms,[165] the ICJ's reasoning in the *Nicaragua* v. *USA* case likely reflected the reality of international relations at the time of the adoption of the UN Charter, when attacks against states were seen as likely originating from other states. In this context, the *Wall* opinion's paragraph 139, wherein it affirms that 'Article 51 of the Charter thus recognises the existence of an inherent right of self-defence in the case of armed attack by one State against another State' would confirm this view.[166] Similarly, the decision of the ICJ not to engage with the topic of self-defence against non-state actors in its *DRC* v. *Uganda* case since 'the legal and factual circumstances for the existence of a right of self-defence by Uganda against DRC were not present'[167] has been interpreted by some observers as the ICJ's confirmation of the inapplicability of self-defence to armed attacks launched by non-state actors.[168] Finally, with regard to the 2008 declaration of independence of Kosovo, the Court affirmed that Article 2(4) UN Charter supports the principle of territorial integrity, which, by definition, is applicable only to states,[169] thus implicitly reaffirming the relation between the ban on use of force and interstate relations.[170] Indeed, there is significant state practice regarding states' condemnations of actions allegedly undertaken in self-defence against non-state actors.[171]

---

[165] See, for instance, Rosalyn Higgins, *Problems and Process: International Law and How We Use It* (Clarendon Press 1995) 250–1.

[166] This seems to be the interpretation given in the Separate Opinion of Judge Higgins, para. 33, in the Separate Opinion of Judge Kooijmans, para. 35, and in the Declaration of Judge Buergenthal, para. 6. See also the critical remarks of Raphaële Rivier, 'Conséquences juridiques de l'édification d'un mur dans le territoire palestinien occupé, Cour internationale de Justice, avis consultatif du 9 juillet 2004' (2004) 50 AFDI 292, 334–6; Wedgwood, 'The ICJ', 58; Murphy 'Self-Defense', 63.

[167] *DRC* v. *Uganda*, para. 147.

[168] This is, for instance, the opinion of Jörg Kammerhofer, 'The Armed Activities Case and Non-State Actors in Self-Defence' (2007) 20 LJIL 89, 105; Ruys, *Armed*, 483; Corten, 'L'applicabilité', 80. *Contra*, see Kimberley N. Trapp, 'Can Non-State Actors Mount an Armed Attack?' in Weller (ed.), *The Oxford*, 679, 689.

[169] *Accordance with International Law of the Unilateral Declaration of Independence in Respect of Kosovo*, Advisory Opinion, 22 July 2010, para. 80: 'The Court recalls that the principle of territorial integrity is an important part of the international legal order and is enshrined in the Charter of the United Nations, in particular in Article 2, paragraph 4'.

[170] See Olivier Corten, 'Territorial Integrity Narrowly Interpreted: Reasserting the Classical Inter-State Paradigm of International Law' (2011) 24 LJIL 87.

[171] See the reactions to the seventies and eighties raids of South Africa against non-state actors in neighbouring States (SC Res. 527 (1982), 15 December 1982; SC Res. 546 (1984), 6 January 1984; SC Res. 568 (1985), 21 June 1985); to the 1986 Israeli raid against the PLO basis in Tunis (SC Res. 573 (1985)), to the 1986 US raids against Tripoli (GA Res. 41/38, 20 November 1986), to the 1998 US bombing of some allegedly terrorist bases in Sudan (S/53/ 285, 25 August 1998 (Yugoslavia); S/1998/794, 24 August 1998 (Pakistan); S/1998/800, 24 August 1998 (Kuwait); S/1998/879, 22 September 1998 (Sudan); S/1998/894, 28 September 1998 (Lebanon)).

Conversely, some scholars argue that it is possible to invoke self-defence against non-state actors. These scholars tend to fall into two main categories of thought. One such body of scholarship asserts that the interstate character of self-defence is no longer in line with contemporary international law, while the other contends that the state which allows non-state actors to organise an attack from its territory and which tolerates their presence in its territory should be considered responsible for those acts.

The view arguing that the interstate character of self-defence is outdated emphasises that the law on self-defence evolved on the basis of new normative documents, and recent manifestations of state practice and *opinio juris*. Indeed, SC Resolutions 1368 (2001) and 1373 (2001), adopted in the aftermath of the September 11 attacks and invoked by Israel with regard to the wall, recognise 'the inherent right of individual or collective self-defence in accordance with the Charter' even in cases of terrorist attacks.[172] Moreover, in state practice, claims of self-defence against non-state actors have met less criticism after September 11 than before. For instance, in the cases of the 2001 US war against Afghanistan for its connection with Al Qaeda, the 2006 Israeli raid against Hezbollah in Lebanon, the 2007 and 2008 Turkish raids in Northern Iraq, the Kenyan raids in south Somalia, and the attacks of the US-led coalition against ISIS in Syria since 2014, the majority of the international community has not criticised the right to resort to self-defence, but rather, only the way in which self-defence was exercised or the existence of an actual armed attack by non-state actors justifying the response.[173] Arguably, the SC should not act as a global legislator according to the UN Charter,[174] and, thus, Resolutions 1368 (2001) and 1373 (2001) should not be viewed as legislative acts. However, since Article 51 UN Charter does not specify the author of the armed attack triggering the right of self-defence, it is possible to argue that states have interpreted Article 51 as also encompassing attacks from non-state actors in the most recent practice following 2001. This has been affirmed by some

---

[172] SC Res. 1368 (2001), 12 September 2011, preamble; Sc Res. 1373 (2001), 28 September 2001, preamble.
[173] It is not possible providing here all the details regarding these reactions. See the analysis of Ruys, *Armed*, 447–72.
[174] See, generally, Gaetano Arangio-Ruiz, 'On the Security Council's "Law-Making"' (2000) 83 RDI 609. For a broader discussion of this topic, see Catherine Denis, *Le pouvoir normative du Conseil de Security des Nations Unies: Portée et limites* (Bruylant 2004); Tullio Treves, 'The Security Council as Legislator' in Aristotle Constantinides & Nikos Zaikos (eds.), *The Diversity of International Law: Essays in Honour of Professor Kalliopi K. Koufa* (Brill 2009) 61.

ICJ judges[175] and authors,[176] and demonstrated by the adoption of the aforementioned resolutions.[177] To this end, the contrary view of the ICJ would not be an insurmountable obstacle, since ICJ case law, although extremely authoritative, is not a primary source of international law, as are treaty law and customary international law.[178]

Another opinion propounds the view that a state which allows non-state actors to organise an attack from its territory and which tolerates their presence in their territory should be considered responsible for those acts, pursuant to a different interpretation of the existing rules on attribution embodied in the DARS,[179] or because of the emergence of a special non-codified customary rule on attribution.[180] In these cases, the action in self-defence would not be directed against non-state actors per se, but rather against a state that is considered the author of the armed attack materially committed by a non-state actor. In order to better specify the content of rule, scholars have advanced the theory that the territorial state is responsible for the attacks of non-state actors located in its territory when

---

[175] According to *Wall* opinion, Separate Opinion of Judge Kooijmans, para. 35:

> The possibility to react in self-defence against non-State actors] is the completely new elements in these resolutions. This new element is not excluded by the terms of Article 51 since this conditions the exercise of the inherent right of self-defence on a previous armed attack without saying that this armed attack must come from another State even if this has been the generally accepted interpretation for more than 50 years.

See also *Wall* opinion, Declaration of Judge Buergenthal, para. 6; *DRC v. Uganda*, Separate Opinion of Judge Kooijmans, para. 28, and Separate Opinion of Judge Simma, para. 11.

[176] See, e.g., Thomas M. Franck, 'Terrorism and the Right of Self-Defence' (2001) 95 AJIL 839; Cassese, 'Article 51', 1352; Davis Brown, 'Use of Force against Terrorism after September 11th: State Responsibility, Self-Defence and Other Responses' (2003) 11 Cardozo JICL 1; Benjamin Langille, 'It's Instant Custom: How the Bush Doctrine Became Law after the Terrorist Attacks of September 11, 2001' (2003) 26 *Boston College International & Comparative Law Review* 145; Schmitt, 'Responding'; Dinstein, *War, Aggression*, 241–9; Alain Pellet, 'Response to Koh and Buchwald's Article: Don Quixote and Sancho Panza Tilt at Windmills' (2015) 109 AJIL 557, 562–3.

[177] For the contrary view, see Michael P. Scharf, *Customary International Law in Times of Fundamental Change: Recognizing Grotian Moments* (Cambridge University Press 2013) 206–210.

[178] See Arts. 38(1) (applicable law) and 59 (bindingness of the judgments) ICJ Statute.

[179] See, e.g., Sean D. Murphy, 'Terrorism and the Concept of "Armed Attack" in Article 51 of the U.N. Charter' (2002) 43 Harvard ILJ 41, 50–1; Carsten Stahn, 'Terrorist Acts as "Armed Attack": The Right to Self-Defense, Article 51 (1/2) of the UN Charter, and International Terrorism' (Summer/Fall 2003) 27 *The Fletcher Forum of World Affairs* 35, 51; Christian J. Tams, 'The Use of Force against Terrorists' (2009) 20 EJIL 359, 384–7.

[180] See Andreas Zimmermann, 'The Second Lebanon War: *Jus ad Bellum, Jus in Bello* and the Issue of Proportionality' (2007) 11 MPYUNL 99, 120.

it is 'unwilling or unable' to prevent and stop the attacks,[181] on the assumption that the territorial state would have violated its duty not to allow private actors to use its territory to harm other states.[182] Although this position has the advantage of allocating within a state international responsibility for an armed attack launched by a non-state actor, it is subject to some criticisms. One of the major problems with this argument is that it seems basically unfair to treat in the same way a state that is unwilling to prevent attacks originating from its territory and a state that would like, but it is unable to do so.[183] Moreover, self-defence is a legitimate response only in the case of a particular violation (an 'armed attack') of the prohibition on the use of force.[184] In the absence of any uniform *opinio juris* and state practice regarding a modification of the existing rules on attribution or the emergence of a new special rule in this field, the action in self-defence against non-state actors' armed attacks would be a response to the violation of another primary rule: the due diligence duty to prevent one state's territory from being used to bring harm to another state.[185] Considering the lack of prevention the new rule of attribution would be a wrong assumption, not only because the violation of a due diligence obligation of vigilance and prevention does not entail any attribution of private actors' conduct,[186] but also because, following this idea, the right of self-defence would become available in response to a violation of this other primary rule, which is not mentioned in Article 51 UN Charter. Finally, this view seems to overlap with the different idea that, notwithstanding the contrary dictum in the *Nicaragua* v. *USA* case, the state's tolerance of armed groups in their territory is a form of support that should fall under the definition of armed attack.[187]

---

[181] See Ashley S. Deeks, '"Unwilling or Unable": Toward a Normative Framework for Extraterritorial Self-Defense' (2012) 52 Virginia JIL 483.

[182] On the content of this duty, see *Arbitration on the Island of Palmas*, 839; *Corfu Channel Case (UK v. Albania)*, 9 April 1949 (Merits), 22; *Pulp Mills on the River Uruguay (Argentina v. Uruguay)*, 20 April 2010, para. 101.

[183] See Carlo Focarelli, *International Law as Social Construct: The Struggle for Global Justice* (Oxford University Press 2012) 369; Dawood I. Ahmed, 'Defending Weak States against the "Unwilling or Unable" Doctrine of Self-Defense' (2013) 9 JIL & International Relations 1.

[184] In *Nicaragua* v. *USA*, para. 195, the ICJ clarified the fact that not just any violation of the use of force entitles the victim state to respond in self-defence. For the contrary view, see *Case Concerning Oil Platforms*, Separate Opinion of Judge Simma, para. 12.

[185] See Gioia, 'Terrorismo internazionale', 47, fn. 106; Natalino Ronzitti, 'The 2006 Conflict in Lebanon and International Law' (2006) 16 Italian YIL 3, 6; Attila Tanzi, 'Riflessioni introduttive per un dibattito sull'uso della forza armata e la legittima difesa nel diritto internazionale contemporaneo' in Lanciotti & Tanzi (eds.), *Uso*, 1, 9; Enrico Milano, 'Il ricorso all'uso della forza nei confronti di attori non statali' in Lanciotti & Tanzi (eds.), *Uso* , 105, 130.

[186] For more on this, albeit in a different context, see Marco Longobardo, 'State Responsibility for International Humanitarian Law Violations by Private Actors in Occupied Territories and the Exploitation of Natural Resources' (2016) 63 NILR 251, 267–70.

[187] This was the idea already expressed in *Nicaragua* v. *USA*, Dissenting Opinion of Judge Jennings, 543. For a discussion of this issue, see Milano, 'Il ricorso', 122–5.

3.2. Jus ad Bellum *Justifications*

Other authors prefer to leave aside the right of self-defence, referring instead to other forms of self-help with analogous practical consequences. For instance, it has been argued that, since forcible actions against non-state actors do not fall into the prohibition on the use of armed force under Article 2(4) UN Charter, which is applicable only between states, then states can use armed force against non-state actors to protect their own interests without any limitation from the *jus ad bellum*.[188] This view is formally correct in relation to non-state actors per se,[189] but does not take into account the interests of the state in which those actors are located, which must be assessed in light of *jus ad bellum*.[190] A particular development of this view considers that states have a right to resort to forcible measures against non-state actors pursuant to an autonomous rule of customary international law that would have survived the adoption of the UN Charter.[191]

Whether it is possible to invoke self-defence or analogous forms of self-help against non-state actors remains controversial, especially with respect to the aforementioned problems regarding the violation of the sovereignty of the state in whose territory the non-state actors are based. Even if some states have argued that they were attacking only the non-state actors and not the territorial state as well,[192] in reality it is very difficult to argue that an attack against an armed group located in the territory of State A does not violate State's A territorial integrity (constituting an act of aggression against that state). According to some authors, the sovereignty of the state in whose territory the armed groups are based would be protected by rigorously applying the criteria of the necessity, proportionality, and immediacy of the response in self-defence.[193] Another author suggested that non-state actors can be attacked only in cases in which they control a significant portion of the state territory so that the

---

[188] See, e.g., Ruth Wedgwood, 'Responding to Terrorism: The Strikes against Bin Laden' (1999) 24 Yale JIL 568.
[189] However, while self-defence against a state's armed attack has the aim to repel the attack, actions allegedly undertaken in self-defence against non-state actors have the aim to destroy them; accordingly, these actions should not be labelled as self-defence (see Francesco Salerno, *Diritto internazionale: principi e norme* (4th edn, Cedam 2017) 236).
[190] See Canor, 'When', 138.
[191] Se Antonello Tancredi, 'Il problema della legittima difesa nei confronti di milizie non statali alla luce dell'ultima crisi tra Israele e Libano' (2007) 90 RDI 909, 995.
[192] See for instance the position of Turkey with regard to its raids in northern Iraq against members of the Kurdish Partîya Karkerén Kurdîstan (PKK), Verbal note dated 26 March 2008 from the Permanent Mission of Turkey to the United Nations Office at Geneva addressed to the secretariat of the Human Rights Council, 26 March 2008, A/HRC/7/G/15.
[193] See Kimberley N. Trapp, 'Back to the Basics: Necessity, Proportionality, and the Right of Self-Defence against Non-State Terrorist Actors' (2007) 56 ICLQ 141, 145–6; Tanzi, 'Riflessioni', 9–10; Milano, 'Il ricorso', 130–4; Ruys, *Armed*, 509.

attack would not infringe that state's sovereignty.[194] Moreover, it should be noted that self-defence is not only a right of states under *jus ad bellum*, but rather, also a circumstance precluding the wrongfulness of acts under Article 21 DARS. This provision does not refer to the violation of the prohibition on the use of force, since the exercise of self-defence is a right rather than a violation of Article 2(4) UN Charter,[195] but rather concerns other international law rules that are violated in the exercise of that right;[196] on this basis, it could be argued that the state acting lawfully in self-defence against non-state actors, if its response is proportionate, necessary, and immediate, can claim that the violation of the sovereignty of the state on whose territory the non-state actors are based is not a wrongful act pursuant to Article 21 DARS.[197]

However, as demonstrated by the preceding brief analysis, even if there is a certain trend in considering Article 51 UN Charter applicable in cases where non-state actors' conduct armed attacks,[198] the current law regarding the use of armed force in self-defence against non-state actors remains controversial, and very likely, the ICJ deliberately avoided pronouncing it in the *DRC v. Uganda* case.[199] However, it is submitted here that the issue of the use of armed force by the occupying power should not be addressed in the context on that debate.

Following the idea that the ICJ rejected the possibility of reacting in self-defence against non-state actors as a matter of principle, one may envisage the creation of different legal regimes – one based on *jus ad bellum* and one

---

[194] See Enzo Cannizzaro, 'Entités non-étatiques et régime international de l'emploi de la force: une étude sur le cas de la réaction israélienne au Liban' (2007) 110 RGDIP 333, 345–51, and *Diritto internazionale* (3rd edn, Giappichelli 2016) 53–5.

[195] See Commentary to the DARS, 74, para. 1.

[196] Ibid., para. 2: 'Self-defence *may justify non-performance of certain obligations other than that under Article 2, paragraph 4, of the Charter of the United Nations*, provided that such non-performance is related to the breach of that provision' (emphasis added).

[197] See Nicholas Tsagourias, 'Self-Defence against Non-State Actors: The Interaction between Self-Defence as a Primary Rule and Self-Defence as a Secondary Rule' (2016) 29 LJIL 801, 819–24; Federica I. Paddeu, 'Use of Force against Non-State Actors and the Circumstance Precluding Wrongfulness of Self-Defence' (2017) 30 LJIL 93, 106–14.

[198] This trend is not only supported by some emerging state practice, but it is also recognised by a number of non-binding academic documents such as the Institut de Droit International, Res. of 10 October 2007, para. 10; the *Chatham House Principles of International Law on the Use of Force by State in Self-Defence* (Chatham House 2005) 11; the *Leiden Policy Recommendation on Counter-Terrorism and International Law* (Leiden Grotius Centre 2010) para. 38. On the authoritativeness of these academic documents and their role in the ascertaining of international customary law, see Sandesh Sivakumaran, 'The Influence of Teachings of Publicists on the Development of International Law' (2017) 66 ICLQ 1.

[199] This is the conclusion of Gray, *International Law*, 202, and 'The Use of Force and the International Legal Order' in Malcolm D. Evans, (ed.), *International Law* (4th edn, Oxford University Press 2014) 618, 629; Crawford, *Brownlie's Principles*, 749.

unrelated to *jus ad bellum* – depending on whether the occupied territory was part of an existing state before the occupation or not, and whether the attack is attributable to an occupied state, if any. Applying the ICJ's majority opinion regarding the impossibility of invoking self-defence in the OPT since Palestine is not a state renders the ICJ's reasoning contradictory. Although the Court held that Palestine in 2004 was not a state, but rather a self-determination unit,[200] it granted Palestine some prerogatives that are typical to states in advisory proceedings. According to the Court, 'in light of General Assembly resolution A/RES/ES-10/14 and the report of the Secretary-General transmitted to the Court with the request, and taking into account the fact that the General Assembly has granted Palestine a special status of observer and that the latter is co-sponsor of the draft resolution requesting the advisory opinion', Palestine may 'submit to the Court a written statement on the question' and 'may also take part in the hearings'.[201] If the conundrum regarding self-defence was linked to the fact that Palestine was not a state, the ICJ would have fallen in a contradiction, admitting that Palestine was a state enough to participate in the proceedings, but not enough to mount an armed attack under Article 51 UN Charter, as acutely pointed out by Judge Higgins in her separate opinion.[202]

In addition, the ICJ's majority opinion on this point may have further unintended consequences in other situations of occupation. Indeed, the occupation of the OPT is a hard case since in 1967, at the beginning of the occupation, that area was not part of any existing state,[203] even if, more recently, many have argued that Palestine became a state as demonstrated by the GA's recognition of the Palestine status as 'non-member State' in 2012,[204]

---

[200] *Wall* opinion, para. 88.
[201] ICJ, *Legal Consequences of the Construction of a Wall in the Occupied Palestinian Territory*, Order, 19 December 2003, paras. 2–3.
[202] According to the *Wall* opinion, Separate Opinion of Judge Higgins, para. 34: 'Palestine cannot be sufficiently an international entity to be invited to these proceedings, and to benefit from humanitarian law, but not sufficiently an international entity for the prohibition of armed attack on others to be applicable. This is formalism of an unevenhanded sort.' On the participation of Palestine into proceedings before the ICJ, see generally Paolo Palchetti, 'La participation de la Palestine à la procédure devant la Cour internationale de Justice' in Thierry Garcia (ed.), *La Palestine: d'un etat non membre de l'organisation des Nations Unies a un etat souverain?* (Pedone 2015) 75.
[203] See *supra*, Section 1.3.
[204] See UN GA Res. 43/177, 15 December 1988. The view that Palestine is today a state is shared by a number of scholars: see Francis A. Boyle, 'The Creation of the State of Palestine' (1990) 1 EJIL 307; Eric David, 'Le statut étatique de la Palestine' (2009) 20 *I diritti dell'uomo. Cronache e battaglie* 42; John Quigley, *The Statehood*; Jean Salmon, 'La qualité d'Etat de la Palestine' (2012) 45 RBDI 13; Ghislain Poissonnier, 'La Palestine, État non-membre observateur de l'Organisation des Nations Unies' (2013) 140 JDI 427; Longobardo, 'Lo Stato di Palestina';

and its ability to participate in a number of international organisations and multilateral treaties.²⁰⁵ Reading *a contrario* the Court's dictum, one should admit that in cases of occupied territories belonging to a state before the occupation it is possible to invoke self-defence under Article 51 UN Charter. However, there is no evidence in state practice and *opinio juris* suggesting a different legal basis to the occupying powers' responses to armed attacks from within the occupied territory depending on whether the attacks are attributable to a (occupied) state or not.

Even admitting that in times of occupation self-defence may be invoked only against state actors, it would be impossible to attribute private actors' conduct to the occupied state on the basis of their unwillingness or inability to prevent them – not only because of the aforementioned critics to this theory, but also because in times of occupation the occupied state has lost its capacity to control its own territory, and thus cannot be held responsible for the violation of its duty to prevent that territory being used to bring harm to other states.²⁰⁶

Louis Balmond, 'Etat Palestinien' in Garcia (ed.), *La Palestine*, 5. *Contra*, see James Crawford, 'The Creation of the State of Palestine: Too Much Too Soon?' (1990) 1 EJIL 307; Yaël Ronen, 'Recognition of the State of Palestine: Still Too Much Too Soon?' in Christine Chinkin & Freya Baetens (eds.), *Sovereignty, Statehood and State Responsibility: Essays in Honour of James Crawford* (Cambridge University Press 2015) 229; Antonello Tancredi, 'Le droit a l'autodétermination du peuple Palestinien' in Garcia (ed.), *La Palestine*, 33.

²⁰⁵ Palestine was admitted first to UNESCO (see UNESCO, Press Release: General Conference Admits Palestine as UNESCO Member State, 31 October 2011, available at unispal.un.org/DPA/DPR/unispal.nsf/0/F32B83B0D5E6D75A8525793A004C8312), and then recognised by the GA as a UN 'non-member State'. Since UNESCO is a UN body, the UNESCO membership allows Palestine to participate in a huge number of multilateral treaties which, explicitly or implicitly, are open to ratifications by entities claiming statehood that are members of the UN or of UN bodies (for more on this, see Laurent Trigeaud, 'L'influence des reconnaissances d'Etat sur la formation des engagements conventionnels' (2015) 119 RGDIP 571). Consequently, Palestine has become a party to a huge number of international conventions, among which are all the main UN universal human rights treaties, the HR, the four GC, the two APs, and the ICC Statute. Despite this fact, some authors have argued that this process is not enough to fill alleged gaps in the Palestinian requirements of statehood (see Jure Vidmar, 'Palestine and the Conceptual Problem of Implicit Statehood' (2013) 12 CJIL 19; Marina Mancini, 'Conseguenze giuridiche dell'attribuzione alla Palestina dello status di Stato osservatore presso le Nazioni Unite' (2013) 96 RDI 100). This author believes that the wide participation of Palestine in international relations strengthens its already existing elements of statehood (see Marco Longobardo, 'La recente adesione palestinese alle convenzioni di diritto umanitario e ai principali trattati a tutela dei diritti dell'uomo' (2014) 1 *Ordine internazionale e diritti umani* 771, and 'Some Developments in the Prosecution of International Crimes Committed in Palestine: Any Real News?' (2015) 35 Polish YIL 109, 119–27).

²⁰⁶ See Scobbie, 'Words', 83; Canor, 'When', 142–3.

3.2.3.2. The Allegedly 'Internal' Character of the Force Employed by the Occupying Power as a Bar to the Application of Self-Defence

Another possible explanation of the ICJ's rejection of the self-defence argument can be found in consideration of the fact that the armed attacks against Israel do not possess an international character. According to the *Wall* opinion, '[t]he Court also notes that Israel exercises control in the [OPT] and that, as Israel itself states, the threat which it regards as justifying the construction of the wall originates within, and not outside, that territory.'[207] According to Judge Kooijmans, this was the Court's main reason for rejecting the Israeli position:

> The argument which in my view is decisive for the dismissal of Israel's claim that it is merely exercising its right of self-defence can be found in the second part of paragraph 139. The right of self-defence as contained in the Charter is a rule of international law and thus relates to *international* phenomena. Resolutions 1368 (2001) and 1373 (2001) refer to act of international terrorism as constituting a threat to *international* peace and security; they therefore have no immediate bearing on terrorist acts originating within a territory which is under control of the State which is also the victim of these acts. And Israel does not claim that these acts have their origin elsewhere.[208]

This position disentangles the issue of the use of force in occupied territory from the problem surrounding claims of self-defence against non-state actors in other circumstances. However, dismissing self-defence because it covers only 'international phenomena' and threats to 'international peace' necessarily implies that the use of armed force in the occupied territory is not international in character. It seems that, according to Judge Kooijmans, attacks from the occupied territory can be likened to the resort to force by insurgents within a state, which is addressed consistently without invoking self-defence.[209] In this regard, the rule according to which it is not possible to invoke self-defence in response to armed attacks originating from within the territory of a state is extended to every territory under the state's control.[210]

However, leaving aside the problem of whether to qualify the conflict between an occupying power and the population of the occupied country as international armed conflict or non-international armed conflict,[211] it is

---

[207] *Wall* opinion, para. 139.
[208] Ibid., Separate Opinion of Judge Kooijmans, para. 36 (emphases in the original).
[209] See Canor, 'When', 140.
[210] Ibid.; Victor Kattan, 'The Legality of the West Bank Wall: Israel's High Court of Justice v. the International Court of Justice' (2007) 40 *Vanderbilt Journal of Transnational Law* 1425, 1482, and 1485.
[211] This point will be discussed in detail, *infra*, Section 5.5.

necessary to recall that the basic tenet of the entire law of occupation is that the occupied territory *should not* be assimilated to the territory of the occupying power. The law of occupation prevents the occupying power from treating the occupied territory as if it were a portion of its own territory because the law assumes that the occupation is temporary and that the occupying territory must be returned to the ousted sovereign. Consequently, the use of armed force in the occupied territory cannot be considered an internal (or non-international, following Judge Kooijmans wording) employment of armed force. Correctly, Judge Higgins pointed out that this interpretation is at odds with the fact that the Court found that the OPT was not annexed by Israel and that it 'is certainly "other than" Israel'.[212] Apart from this fundamental objection, this kind of 'territorial test' seems at odds with the past ICJ's case law as well. In the *Nicaragua* v. *USA* case, the ICJ had held that armed groups controlled by other states may launch armed attacks from within the victim state's territory as long as the attacks have certain scale and effects.[213] From this perspective, the fact that the attacks originate from within a state's own territory would not bar the invocation of self-defence.[214] Consequently, although the opinion expressed by Judge Kooijmans is extremely interesting, in that it emphasises the impossibility of invoking self-defence in a situation of occupation, it is not possible to buy into Judge Kooijmans' reasoning fully because the basic tenet of the law of occupation is that the occupied territory cannot be assimilated into the territory of the occupying power.

3.2.3.3. The Alleged Inapplicability of Self-Defence on the Basis of the Lack of Statehood of the Targets of the Israeli Response

Although there are several faults in Judge Kooijmans' reasoning, the same premises emphasised in his separate opinion can be employed to further another argument based on the lack of statehood of *the targets of the Israeli response*. This position is different from the aforementioned debated issue of the lack of statehood of the *attackers*, and thus it deserves a separate analysis.

---

[212] *Wall* opinion, Separate Opinion of Judge Higgins, para. 34. See also Christian J. Tams, 'Light Treatment of a Complex Problem: The Law of Self-Defence in the *Wall* Case' (2005) 16 EJIL 963, 968–9; Schmitt, 'Responding', 169; Noam Lubell, 'The ICJ Advisory Opinion and the Separation Barrier: A Troublesome Route' (2005) 35 IYHR 283, 291–2; Arthur Watts, 'Israeli Wall Advisory Opinion (Legal Consequences of the Construction of a Wall in the Occupied Palestinian Territory)' in *MPEPIL online* (2007) para. 42.
[213] *Nicaragua* v. *USA*, para. 195.
[214] See Bianchi, 'Dismantling', 375–6.

3.2. Jus ad Bellum *Justifications*

To the best knowledge of this author, this perspective was addressed mainly by some scholars debating the 2014 Gaza armed conflict in the blogosphere. Following the suggestion that commentators should have dedicated more attention to the *jus ad bellum* dimension of that armed conflict,[215] one author analysed whether the Israeli actions against the Gaza Strip were in potential breach of Article 2(4) UN Charter.[216] Since this provision prohibits the use of armed force in the *international relations* of states and since Article 51 UN Charter is an exception to this rule, only conduct potentially in breach of Article 2(4) UN Charter may be justified under the rule of self-defence.[217] According to this view, if the Israeli use of force falls outside the scope of Article 2(4), then it cannot be qualified as self-defence.[218] In this sense, this perspective seems similar to that advanced by Judge Kooijmans with respect to his point that the armed force employed lacks 'internationality'. However, the last view considers that the use of armed force is not international on the basis of the targets of the defensive reaction of the occupying power. Determining the scope of Article 2(4) UN Charter is pivotal to substantiating this view. Following the aforementioned traditional, albeit not unchallenged, interpretation, according to which 'international relations' means 'interstate relations', that author concludes that the classification of the Gaza Strip as a state or a portion of state is crucial to determining whether Israel could have resorted to self-defence or, more precisely, whether the use of armed force by Israel was potentially in breach of Article 2(4) UN Charter and, thus, potentially justifiable under Article 51 UN Charter.[219]

The differences between this argument and that of the relevance of the status of the attackers (non-state actors *vs* states) are relevant. Following this line of reasoning, Israel would be entitled to react in self-defence against attacks launched by non-state actors based on the territory of a third state, since this reaction would be a breach of Article 2(4) UN Charter with regard to that third state, and thus it could in principle be justified as an act of self-defence.[220] For instance, following this idea, the Israeli invocation of self-defence against Hezbollah in 2006 would be legitimate because Israel was

---

[215] See Geir Ulfstein, 'More Focus on *Jus ad Bellum* in Gaza', *Just Security*, 12 August 2014.
[216] See Dapo Akande, 'Is Israel's Use of Force in Gaza Covered by the *Jus Ad Bellum*?', EJIL: Talk!, 22 August 2014.
[217] The ILC emphasised the relationship between Art. 2(4) and Art. 51 UN Charter in the DARS, commentary to Article 21, para. 1.
[218] Akande, 'Is Israel's Use'.
[219] Ibid. The author refers to the position of Corten, *The Law against War*, 126.
[220] See, in general terms, Marko Milanovic, 'Accounting for the Complexity of the Law Applicable to Modern Armed Conflicts' in Christopher Ford, Shane Reeves, & Winston Williams (eds.), *Complex Battlespaces: The Law of Armed Conflict and the Dynamics of Modern*

potentially in breach of Article 2(4) UN Charter with regard to Lebanon.[221] On the other hand, if one follows the different argumentation focused on the status of the attackers, Hezbollah's and Hamas's armed attacks should be treated equally since they are both non-state actors.

Although focusing on the nature of the target of the response emphasises the relevance not only of Article 51 UN Charter, but also that of *jus ad bellum* in its entirety, this focus fails to address the problem in light of the classification of the Gaza Strip as an occupied territory.[222] Rather, the piece discussing this perspective is a follow-up to another reflection based on the assumption that the Gaza Strip is no longer under occupation.[223] Even if the first author did not want to exclude the possibility that Gaza was under occupation from his analysis, he clearly concluded that 'before one assesses how the law of self-defence might apply to Israel's actions, one might first have to answer the question whether Palestine is a state'.[224] Conversely, this author considers that the occupied status of a territory is the most important element to be taken into account in the discourse surrounding the applicability of *jus ad bellum* in occupied territories, whereas the statehood of the occupied territory would be entirely irrelevant to the discourse regarding the occupying power's right of self-defence.

3.2.3.4. The Inapplicability of Self-Defence on the Basis of the *Lex Specialis* Principle

A fourth strand of reasoning around the *Wall* opinion suggests that the ICJ considered self-defence inapplicable since international humanitarian law would be the legal regime governing the occupying power's recourse to armed force. Accordingly, since *jus ad bellum* is a generic branch of law and the law of occupation is specifically concerned with situations of occupation, the latter should be applied as *lex specialis*, excluding the applicability of the former.[225]

Warfare (Oxford University Press, forthcoming) 7, draft available at papers.ssrn.com/sol3/papers.cfm?abstract_id=2963575

[221] It is not by chance that Israeli claims of self-defence with regard to the 2006 Lebanese armed conflict met a more solid support than similar claims regarding the armed conflicts against the Gaza Strip. See the discussion reported in S/PV.5511. See also Milano, 'Il ricorso', 108–9.

[222] There is no mention to the debate regarding the status of Gaza in that blogpost. The relevance of the situation of occupation for this problem has been emphasised only by the two comments of Dan Joyner posted on 23 August 2014 in response to the main blogpost.

[223] See Marko Milanovic, 'A Follow-Up on Israel and Gaza', EJIL: Talk!, 3 January 2009.

[224] Akande, 'Is Israel's Use'.

[225] See, e.g., Tams, 'Light Treatment', 970; Canor, 'When', 144–5; Weill & Azarova, 'The 2014', 368 (with implicit reference to this principle).

3.2. Jus ad Bellum *Justifications*

The Palestinian arguments advanced before the ICJ with respect to the legality of the wall support the position that the law of occupation regulates the use of armed force in the occupied territory, barring the application of *jus ad bellum*. In its written statement, Palestine argued that *jus ad bellum* was not applicable because the measures that may be adopted pursuant to the GC IV '*exhausts the legal rights of an occupying power*. A State may not use all of its powers under the [GC IV] and the Laws of War and then decide that those powers are inadequate and invoke the *more general* right of self-defence, which belongs to the *jus ad bellum*'.[226] Similarly, in his oral pleading on behalf of Palestine, Professor Georges Abi-Saab affirmed that *jus in bello* determined the legality of the wall 'as the *lex specialis* governing the ensuing situation regardless of the rules of the *jus ad bellum*.'[227]

This solution has many advantages and it is very close to the correct one. The conclusion that the resort to armed force by the occupying power is regulated by the *jus in bello* rather than by the *jus ad bellum* is sound, as will be explained meticulously in Section 3.4. Moreover, this solution implies that the ICJ, in the *Wall* opinion, did not want to state the law pertaining to self-defence against non-state actors in every circumstance, but rather it merely excluded the application of self-defence in times of occupation.[228] Finally, this view fully takes into account the specificities of the situation of occupation irrespectively of whether the occupied territory is situated in an existing state or not.

However, this view regarding *jus in bello* is not terminologically persuasive for its reference to the *lex specialis* principle. As discussed previously, the law of occupation is an open system, and other international law rules are in principle, applicable during an occupation.[229] As mentioned, the principle *lex specialis derogat generalis* is a rule pertaining to the solution of normative conflicts, according to which, when it is impossible to solve normative antinomies via interpretation, the rule most directly pertinent to a specific situation shall apply instead of another that should be discarded.[230] This rule implies that, in cases of normative conflicts that are not solvable through interpretation, states must choose which obligation to implement and which one to disregard on the basis of an evaluation of which rule can be considered more

---

[226] *Wall* opinion, Written Statement Submitted by Palestine, 30 January 2004, para. 534 (second emphasis added).
[227] Oral Statement of Palestine, 23 February 2004, CR 2004/1, 44.
[228] This is the interpretation of many authors. See Gray, *International Law*, 135; Milano, 'Il ricorso', 121.
[229] See *supra*, Section 2.4.1.
[230] See *supra*, Section 2.5.3.

specific in light of the specific situation to be regulated. However, the relationship between *jus in bello* and *jus ad bellum* is not that of two competing legal systems that are contextually applicable and, thus, potentially in conflict. Apart from a scant few authors who have suggested the need to conflate *jus ad bellum* and *jus in bello* evaluations,[231] the majority of scholars have consistently held that the two branches are separate, and therefore, that a military action must first comply with *jus ad bellum* and then must be scrutinised under *jus in bello*.[232] For instance, with regard to proportionality in relation to nuclear weapons, the ICJ affirmed that 'at the same time, a use of force that is proportionate under the law of self-defence, must, in order to be lawful, also meet the requirements of the law applicable in armed conflict which comprise in particular the principles and rules of humanitarian law'.[233] Similarly, the Court, after having affirmed that there is no autonomous rule prohibiting recourse to nuclear weapons, affirmed that the issue must be separately addressed under *jus in bello*.[234] It is not happenstance that, in the dispositive of the same advisory opinion, the ICJ addressed the legality of nuclear weapons under *jus ad bellum* and *jus in bello* in two separate sections.[235] Consequently, *jus ad bellum* and *jus in bello* apply in parallel, without any normative conflict which would trigger the application of the *lex specialis* principle.[236]

---

[231] See, with regard to the issue of proportionality, Enzo Cannizzaro, 'Contextualizing Proportionality: *Jus ad Bellum* and *Jus in Bello* in the Lebanese War' (2006) 88 IRRC 779, and 'Proportionality in the Law of Armed Conflicts' in Clapham & Gaeta (eds.), *The Oxford*, 332. In relation to the law of occupation, see Giladi, 'The *Jus*'.

[232] See US Military Manual, section 3.5. See also, among many others, François Buignon, '*Jus ad Bellum*, *Jus in Bello* and Non-International Armed Conflicts' (2003) 6 YIHL 167; Marco Sassòli, '*Ius ad Bellum* and *Ius in Bello* – The Separation between the Legality of the Use of Force and Humanitarian Rules to Be Respected in Warfare: Crucial or Outdated?' in Schmitt & Pejic (eds.), *International Law*, 241; Alexander Orakhelashvili, 'Overlap and Convergence: The Interaction between *Jus ad Bellum* and *Jus in Bello*' (2007) 12 JCSL 157; Jasmine Moussa, 'Can *Jus ad Bellum* Override *Jus in Bello*? Reaffirming the Separation of the Two Bodies of Law' (2008) 90 IRRC 963; Robert D. Sloane, 'The Cost of Conflation: Preserving the Dualism of *Jus ad Bellum* and *Jus in Bello* in the Contemporary Law of War' (2009) 34 Yale JIL 48; Dinstein, *War, Aggression*, 177–85; Keiichiro Okimoto, 'The Cumulative Requirements of *Jus ad Bellum* and *Jus in Bello* in the Context of Self-Defense' (2012) 11 CJIL 45.

[233] *Nuclear Weapons* opinion, para. 42.

[234] Ibid., para. 74.

[235] Ibid., para. 105(2)C e D.

[236] The parallel application of different sets of international rules also precludes the application of another rule pertaining to the solution of normative conflicts, the hierarchical principle, which in international law concerns only the normative conflicts between *jus dispositivum* and *jus cogens*. The ICJ referred to the parallel application of the rule on state immunity and the prohibition of international crimes in order to exclude the existence of a normative conflict which would have required the evaluation of the peremptory character of the prohibition of international crimes (see *Jurisdictional Immunities of the State*, para. 95).

Coming back to the use of armed force during an occupation, in theory there is nothing precluding the parallel application of *jus ad bellum* and *jus in bello* to the use of armed force by the occupying power. The occupying power's military actions should be separately scrutinised under the two sets of norms – *jus ad bellum* and the rules, enshrined in the law of occupation, pertaining to the occupying power's use of force.[237] From this perspective, military operations in occupied territory are subject to the same twofold test that must be conducted in relation to every military operation occurring outside the occupied territory.

Consequently, the fact that the law of occupation embodies some rules regarding the use of armed force by the occupying power does not necessarily mean that these rules prevail over *jus ad bellum* because they are more specific, because international humanitarian law usually applies in parallel (i.e., without creating normative conflicts) with *jus ad bellum*. Accordingly, the inapplicability of self-defence and *jus ad bellum* must be disentangled from the *lex specialis* principle and constructed on another basis pertaining to the specificities of the situation of occupation.

3.2.4. Provisional Conclusions

From the foregoing analysis of the relevant state practice it is possible to conclude that the majority of states do not support the view that the occupying power can invoke *jus ad bellum*, and in particular self-defence, in order to justify its resort to armed force in occupied territory. The only extant practice in favour of the invocation of *jus ad bellum* pertains to Israel; however, the majority of the international community rejected the Israeli invocations of self-defence against attacks originating from within the OPT, whereas the few Western states supporting this claim were often reluctant to qualify the Israeli actions as a manifestation of the right under Article 51 UN Charter.

The lack of similar practice regarding other occupations only serves to strengthen this conclusion that *jus ad bellum* and self-defence are inapplicable to the use of force by the occupying power in the occupied territory. Moreover, the ICJ itself endorsed – albeit briefly – this position in the *Wall* opinion. Unfortunately, the ICJ failed to explain why the occupying power

---

[237] *Contra* see Koutroulis, 'Of Occupation', who correctly considers that the separation between *jus in bello* and *jus ad bellum* bars *jus ad bellum* from overthrowing the limits imposed by *jus in bello* (910). However, the author fails to demonstrate why the separation between these two branches should lead to the application of *jus in bello* rules governing the use of armed force in the occupied territory only (908), rather than the cumulative application of the two branches. Arguably, the author implicitly supported the application of the *lex specialis* principle, but he never mentions that in his nonetheless thorough analysis.

cannot invoke *jus ad bellum*, and the opposite views embodied in some individual judges' opinions fail to shed sufficient light on this matter.

States and international scholarship alike have tried to justify the impossibility to apply *jus ad bellum* and self-defence on different grounds. Some have argued that this conclusion is the consequence of the general impossibility of invoking self-defence against non-state actors – one of the most debated issues in contemporary international law, where state practice is not coherent enough to provide a definitive answer. Other scholars have considered that *jus ad bellum* is inapplicable because armed attacks originating from within an occupied territory lack an international character; these scholars have instead argued that these attacks must be qualified as internal phenomena. A third stream of thought has considered that the occupying power cannot invoke self-defence since a response against non-state actors who are not based in the territory of a state falls outside the scope of the prohibition on the use of force in *international* relations. Finally, some authors have suggested that the use of force in occupied territory is regulated only by the law of occupation that is applicable as *lex specialis* instead of *jus ad bellum*.

However, all these conclusions fall short of providing a coherent and unique answer to the problem of the applicability of *jus ad bellum* to the use of force by the occupying power in the occupied territory. Indeed, some of these arguments distinguish between armed attacks originating from within a territory that is part of a state from attacks involving a territory that is not situated in any existing state, creating different regimes for the two situations. Moreover, some of these theories do not take into proper account the fact that an occupied territory must not be considered to be a portion of the occupying power's own territory, since the law of occupation, the ban on the use of armed force, and the principle of self-determination of peoples impose a duty to preserve the distinction between the occupied territory and the occupying power's own territory. Finally, the claim that the law of occupation prevails as *lex specialis* with regard to the regulation of the use of armed force is in conflict with the principle of separation between *jus ad bellum* and *jus in bello*.

Consequently, at the moment there is no completely satisfactory answer to the question of why the occupying power cannot invoke *jus ad bellum* even if state practice and *opinio juris* steadily support this view. Before providing an original answer to this question, this author considers useful to analyse the debate regarding the applicability of *jus ad bellum* to the armed force employed *against* the occupying power as well since it is submitted here that there is a unitary explanation regarding the (in)application of *jus ad bellum* to resort to armed force both *against* and *by* the occupying power.

3.3. JUS AD BELLUM JUSTIFICATIONS FOR THE USE OF FORCE AGAINST THE OCCUPYING POWER

3.3.1. *The Recourse to Self-Defence by the Occupied State*

After having examined the application of *jus ad bellum* to the occupying power's resort to armed force in the occupied territory, it is now necessary to move the analysis to the resort to armed force against the occupying power.

As an occupying power, a state may face armed attacks from different sources. On the one hand, the sovereign of the occupied territory may try to resume the hostilities in order to put an end to the occupation, through individuals that are either members of its own armed forces or who act under the direction and control of the occupied state. In such cases, the question addresses the potential of an occupied state to invoke *jus ad bellum* against the occupying power in the occupied territory. On the other hand, the occupied state may invoke *jus ad bellum* in order to regain control of its territory from outside the occupied area. In addition, the population of the occupied territory may resort to armed force against the occupying power without any link to the ousted sovereign. This may happen in the cases both of occupied territories formerly belonging to a state and of territories not situated into any state prior to the beginning of the occupation.

Doubtless, a state whose territory is invaded and placed under occupation is entitled to react in self-defence. Indeed, the occupation of a portion of territory is considered to be an aggression pursuant to the GA's definition of aggression[238] and the ICC Statute as revised in 2010.[239] Even if there is a certain debate regarding the differences between the terms 'armed attack' pursuant to Article 51 UN Charter and 'aggression' pursuant to Article 39,[240] the ICJ has considered the GA's definition of aggression relevant for the determination of the existence of an armed attack under customary international law.[241] Accordingly, situations of occupations are armed attacks entitling the victim state to react in self-defence. For instance, when Kuwait was occupied by Iraq in 1990, Kuwait was able to invoke collective self-defence in order to receive the help of the coalition of states that finally drove the Iraqi troops out of the country. Even in the absence of SC resolution 678 (1990),[242] the intervention of the coalition would have been lawful in principle, albeit with some

---

[238] UNGA Res. 3314 (XXIX), Art. 3.
[239] ICC Statute, Art. 8(2)(a).
[240] For an overview of this debate, see Ruys, *Armed*, 126–38.
[241] *Nicaragua v. USA*, para. 195.
[242] SC Res. 678 (1990), 29 November 1990.

restrictions, thanks to the Kuwaiti right of collective self-defence.[243] Similarly one author, after having considered that Argentina had illegally occupied the Falkland Islands in 1982, concludes that the UK reacted in self-defence in the military action to regain control over the islands.[244] This is also the position of Iran, according to which '[i]n the case of the invasion of another State's territory, in principle an attack still exists as long as the occupation continues', enabling the occupied State to invoke self-defence.[245]

From this perspective, self-defence may be invoked to justify resort to armed force *from outside the occupied territory*. For instance, if only a portion of one state is placed under occupation, that state may invoke self-defence to attack the occupying power in that area. This seems to be the case of the relationship between Georgia and Russia occupying South Ossetia in the 2008 armed conflict, even if the EU fact-finding mission failed to consider South Ossetia occupied by Russia, and found Article 51 UN Charter to be applicable to the relationship between Georgia and South Ossetia on the basis of the characterisation of South Ossetia as an entity claiming statehood rather than occupied territory.[246]

However, it should be noted that when an occupation is firmly established, the international community seems to disfavour recourse to armed force in self-defence. For instance, it is highly unlikely today that the international community would support an armed attempt by the Republic of Cyprus to regain control over North Cyprus after more than four decades of Turkish occupation. Rather, the international community is struggling to solve that dispute in a peaceful way, and the negotiations between the two parties have intensified since 2014.[247] Similarly, with respect to the occupation of Crimea,

---

[243] See Giorgio Gaja, 'Il Consiglio di sicurezza di fronte all'occupazione del Kuwait: il significato di un'autorizzazione' (1990) 73 RDI 696; Picone, 'Le autorizzazioni', 17–20; Marc Weller, *Iraq and the Use of Force in International Law* (Oxford University Press 2010) 34–40; Dinstein, *War, Aggression*, 325–6.

[244] See Anthony Aust, *Handbook of International Law* (2nd edn, Cambridge University Press 2010) 211. The status of the Falkland Islands as occupied territory is unclear since the UK accuses Argentina of having occupied the islands in April 1982, while Argentina accuses the UK to have occupied them since 1883 (see Michael Waibel, 'Falkland Islands/Islas Malvinas', in *MPEPIL online* (2011)).

[245] *Case Concerning Oil Platforms*, Iran's Reply, para. 7.47.

[246] See IIFFMCG, Report, vol. II, para. 238–51.

[247] See the Joint Declaration of the leaders of Greek and Turkish Cypriot communities, Nicos Anastasiades and Derviş Eroğlu, 11 February 2014, available at cyprus-mail.com/2014/02/11/joint-declaration-final-version-as-agreed-between-the-two-leaders/; the Joint Statement to the Press on behalf of the Greek Cypriot leader Mr Nicos Anastasiades and the Turkish Cypriot leader Mr Mustafa Akıncı, 14 September 2016, available at unficyp.unmissions.org/joint-statement-press-behalf-greek-cypriot-leader-mr-nicos-anastasiades-and-turkish-cypriot-leader;

even though Ukraine labelled the occupation as an act of aggression,[248] it did not react in self-defence;[249] instead, the SC has stressed, on a number of occasions, its support for a peaceful solution based on negotiations,[250] with the Package of measures for the Implementation of the Minsk agreements as the starting point.[251]

This increasing international trend towards peaceful resolution of occupation does not amount to a renunciation of the right to self-defence, which is not renounceable because of its inherent character.[252] However, this practice does suggest that, after the occupation is settled, an armed response is no longer available under the law of self-defence – at least once the parties have started negotiations or have resorted to other peaceful mechanisms of dispute resolution, which would render the armed response unnecessary.[253] The same conclusion cannot be held with regard to the criterion of immediacy since an occupation constituting an armed attack should be regarded as a continuous wrongful act[254] and, accordingly, an armed response *durante occupatione* would be in line with the criterion of immediacy.

The situation regarding the reaction in self-defence *from within the occupied territory* is different. Only states are entitled to react in self-defence. Article 51 UN Charter is very clear in this regard since it refers to 'the inherent right of individual or collective self-defence if an armed attack occurs against a Member of the United Nations', a status that only states can obtain. Accordingly, only the state with sovereignty over the occupied territory – if any – may invoke self-defence. Consequently, this rule, on the basis of Article 51 UN Charter, would be inapplicable to an occupied territory that did not belong to any state before the occupation, such as the OPT and East Timor,

---

and the Statement from the Conference on Cyprus, 12 January 2017, available at www.uncyprustalks.org/statement-from-the-conference-on-cyprus/. For the support of the SC to this peaceful solution based on negotiations, see UN SC Res. 2338 (2017), 26 January 2017.

[248] See A /68/PV.80, 1.

[249] The lack of proportion between the Russian military strength and Ukrainian military assets may be at the basis of this cautious approach. Indeed, there is no *duty* of an attacked state to react in self-defence; this is a *right* rather than an obligation (see Marco Roscini, 'On the "Inherent" Character of the Right of States to Self-Defence' (2015) 4 Cambridge JICL 634, 647–8).

[250] See SC Res. 2202 (2015), 17 February 2015.

[251] OSCE, Package of Measures for the Implementation of the Minsk Agreements, 12 February 2015, English translation available at peacemaker.un.org/sites/peacemaker.un.org/files/UA_150212_MinskAgreement_en.pdf.

[252] See Roscini, 'On the "Inherent" Character', 648–51.

[253] Ibid., 653.

[254] See DARS, commentary to Art. 14, para. 3.

or in cases in which the authors of the armed response do not have any link to the ousted sovereign.[255]

However, even states and entities claiming statehood as widely recognised as Palestine never invoked self-defence to justify recourse to armed force against the occupying power. For instance, with regard to the Turkish occupation of Northern Cyprus, the Republic of Cyprus invoked self-defence only in relation to hypothetical future attacks against portions of the Cypriot territory that were still not occupied, rather than invoking self-defence in relation to the situation of the occupied territory.[256] Analogously, Palestine has never invoked the right of self-defence with regard to the operations against Gaza despite the fact that, especially in 2014, Palestine considered itself to be a state.[257] Even those states that have condemned the Israeli operations as aggressions have endorsed this position by never affirming in the debates within the UN that Palestine has the right to react in self-defence against Israel, although they simultaneously acknowledged Palestinian statehood.[258]

Consequently, in state practice there are examples of reactions in self-defence only with regard to the force employed from outside the occupied territory. Moreover, state practice suggests that self-defence may be invoked only in the aftermath of the occupation's commencement since, once judicial or extrajudicial means of dispute resolution have been triggered, the resort to self-defence would no longer be considered necessary.

3.3.2. The Lack of Entitlement to Self-Defence of the Local Population of the Occupied Territory

While self-defence may be invoked by the ousted sovereign, the local population of a territory does not have a right to self-defence under *jus ad bellum*.

---

[255] See Mégret, 'Grandeur', 409.
[256] See Letter from the Permanent Representative of Cyprus to the United Nations addressed to the Secretary-General, S/1997/739, 29 September 1997:

> For exclusively *defensive* purposes, the Government of Cyprus proceeded with its decision to purchase the S-300 missile system, following the repeated threats by Turkey against Cyprus. Under Article 51 of the Charter, it is the right and the duty of the independent and sovereign Republic of Cyprus to take all necessary steps for its adequate defence, when the occupied part of Cyprus has become one of the most militarized areas in the world, as described in your reports, and when Cyprus is under direct military threat of Turkey (emphasis added).

See also Letter dated 29 September 1997 from the President of Cyprus addressed to the Secretary-General, S/1997/762, 1 October 1997.
[257] See S/PV.7214, 3–6.
[258] See Corten, 'L'applicabilité', 75–6.

Neither the local population of a territory not belonging to any state prior to the occupation nor non-state actors operating from within the occupied territory enjoy self-defence against the occupying power pursuant to *jus ad bellum*.

Indeed, during the decolonisation era, some authors have argued that the population of the occupied territory would be entitled to react in self-defence against the occupying power. Following this view, peoples whose self-determination is denied would have a right to self-defence against the oppressing states, since the denial of self-determination is equated to an armed attack, putting on the same level a state victim of an armed attack and a people whose self-determination is denied.[259] For instance, this view was advanced by Judge Ammoun in his Separate Opinion on the advisory proceeding regarding the South African occupation of Namibia; according to Judge Ammoun, some UNGA and UNSC resolutions, which stress the legitimacy of armed struggle against foreign dominations that oppress self-determination, necessarily imply that the oppressed peoples have the right to react in self-defence:

> [T]he Security Council [i]n its resolution 269 (1969), following the General Assembly, ... recognized 'the legitimacy of the struggle of the people of Namibia against the illegal presence of the South African authorities in the territory'; a legitimate struggle against what, if not against an aggression? This is a logical interpretation, no refutation of which is possible. It follows not only from the logic of things but also from the actual text of the Charter. For Article 51 only authorizes self-defence [*légitime défense*] or legitimate struggle in cases of response to armed attack [*agression armée*]. Thus once the Security Council proclaims the legitimacy of a defence or of a struggle against a foreign occupier, it is an armed attack [*agression armée*] which is in question, and the occupier's act cannot consequently be anything other than an aggression [*agression*].[260]

Similarly, SWAPO itself, with regard to its struggle against the occupation of South Africa, affirmed that:

> [Self-determination] is a right which accrues in favour of a people. If it is forcibly denied them, then, under article 51 of the Charter of the United

---

[259] See Aldo Bernardini, 'Iraq: illecita occupazione, resistenza popolare, autodeterminazione irakena' (2003) RCGI 29; Giuseppe Palmisano, 'Autodeterminazione dei popoli' in *Enciclopedia del Diritto, Annali*, vol. V (Giuffrè 2012), 128. For further references, see the critical analysis of John Dugard, 'The Organisation of African Unity and Colonialism: An Inquiry into the Plea of Self-Defence as a Justification for the Use of Force in the Eradication of Colonialism' (1967) 16 ICLQ 157, 168–87.

[260] See *Namibia* opinion, Separate Opinion of Vice-President Ammoun, 90. See also Christos Theodoropoulos, 'Support for SWAPO's War of Liberation in International Law' (1979) 26 *Africa Today* 39, 43.

Nations, they have a right to defend themselves and their territory; the more so, against an illegal occupier. A peoples liberation war can be clearly identified as defensive action within the meaning of the Charter.[261]

This idea is extremely important since, if it is considered correct, it would entitle a people under occupation not only to react as such against the occupying power, but also to invoke collective self-defence from other states.[262]

However, the argument that the local population of the occupied territory – even in the case of a national liberation movement that leads the resistance – would enjoy the right to self-defence against the occupying power is not convincing, since states and states alone are the only subjects of international law entitled to resort to self-defence. The wording of Articles 2(4) and 51 UN Charter is particularly clear in affirming that only states may react in self-defence.[263] In addition, contrary to the aforementioned problem of the value of armed attacks from non-state actors as conditions triggering the states' right to self-defence, there is no state practice and *opinio juris* at all affirming that the right of self-defence under *jus ad bellum* may be exercised by non-state actors. Consequently, only states may react in self-defence, in accordance with the rationale at the basis of the right of self-defence: indeed, the inherent character of self-defence is linked to the protection of the elements of a state, i.e., the effective and independent capacity of government, a permanent population, and a definite territory;[264] these elements, in particular the capacity of government with effectiveness and independence, are not present in movements of national liberation, nor can they be attributed to the population of the occupied territory itself.

---

[261] See the SWAPO's declaration quoted in John Dugard, 'SWAPO: The *Jus ad Bellum* and the *Jus in Bello*' (1976) 93 *South African Law Journal* 144, 144–5.

[262] Cassese, *Self-Determination*, 198.

[263] See Dugard, 'The Organisation', 171–7; Lamberti Zanardi, *La legittima difesa*, 187–8; Georges Abi-Saab, 'Wars of National Liberation in the Geneva Conventions and Protocols' (1979) 65 RCADI 438, fn. 8; Cassese, *Self-Determination*, 197–8, and 'Article 51', 1356; Corten, *The Law against War*, 138–47, and 'L'applicabilité', 77–80; Alberta Fabbricotti, 'Legittima difesa e autodeterminazione dei popoli' in Lanciotti & Tanzi (eds.), *Uso*, 255, 274–5.

[264] See Roscini, 'On the "Inherent" Character', 646–7. The tripartition of the elements of statehood was first envisaged by Georg Jellinek, *L'état moderne et son droit*, vol. II, *Théorie juridique de l'État* (Giard & Brière 1913) 17–71 (French translation by Georges Fardis), and embodied, with minor modifications, in Art. 1 of the Montevideo Convention on the Rights and Duties of States, 1933 (text in 165 LNTS 19). On the current relevance of these criteria for contemporary international law, see Crawford, *Creation*, 37–89.

State practice and *opinio juris* tend to preclude any argument that the population of an occupied territory enjoys the right to self-defence against the occupying power since states are reluctant to equate a situation of denied self-determination to an armed attack under Article 51 UN Charter. The reference to UNGA and UNSC practice in Judge Ammoun's opinion is misleading. In fact, no UNGA or UNSC resolutions ever affirmed that a people under occupation has a right to self-defence.[265] For instance, although at the time of the drafting of the Declaration on Friendly Relations some states suggested including a clause regarding self-defence against colonialism and other oppressive regimes,[266] the majority of states rejected these proposals, and no reference to self-defence against oppressing regimes was included.[267] In fact, this and other relevant resolutions, which will be analysed thoroughly in the following chapter, stress the legitimacy of armed struggle against an oppressive regime without referring to *jus ad bellum* rules.[268] Clearly, the lack to any reference to *jus ad bellum* is consistent with the view that *jus ad bellum* does not confer any rights on non-state actors.

It follows that only the ousted sovereign is entitled to self-defence in reaction to the occupation, while non-state actors located in occupied territory and the local population fall outside the scope of application of *jus ad bellum*. The legitimacy of their resort to armed force is analysed under the principle of self-determination of peoples in the following chapter.

3.3.3. *Provisional Conclusions*

When dealing with the legitimisation of employing armed force against the occupying power, a distinction between the occupation of portions of a state and the occupation of territory not belonging to any state must be made. Indeed, the reliance on *jus ad bellum* to justify the use of armed force against the occupying power in these two cases should be examined from different perspectives.

International law allows the state whose territory is occupied to use armed force in individual or collective self-defence since the occupation of a portion

---

[265] See Corten, *The Law against War*, 138.
[266] See the proposals at A/AC.125/L.16, 17 March 1966, 3; A/AC.125/L.21, 22 March 1966, 2; A/AC.125/L.23, 24 March 1966, para. B; A/AC.125/L.38/Add.1, 20 April 1966, para. 113; A/AC.125/12, 3 April 1970, para. 43; A/5746, 27 October 1964, paras. 83–5; A/6230, 27 June 1966, paras. 136–42.
[267] The reasoning behind the rejection is explained in A/5756, 27 October 1964, paras. 86–9; A/6230, 27 June 1966, paras. 143–53. For an accurate analysis of the preparatory works of this resolution with reference to the issue of self-defence, see Robert E. Gorelick, 'Wars of National Liberation: *Jus ad Bellum*' (1979) 11 Case Western Reserve JIL 71, 72–7.
[268] See *infra*, Section 4.3.1.

of territory is an armed attack pursuant to Article 51 UN Charter. Accordingly, a state whose territory is occupied can resort to armed force against the occupying power or ask other states to intervene. The typical example of this right is represented by the occupation of Kuwait by Iraq in 1990. Conversely, states do not rely upon self-defence to justify the resort to armed force from within the occupied territory, nor is there any state practice regarding the invocation of self-defence when the occupation is firmly established. In general, the international community seems to favour peaceful mechanisms of resolving existing occupations, and such mechanisms would render a response in self-defence unlawful because unnecessary.

With regard to territories not belonging to any states before the occupation, the local population may not invoke self-defence against the occupying power. This possibility is ruled out by Articles 2(4) and 51 UN Charter, which refer only to states, and was rejected during the preparatory works of the aforementioned resolutions of the GA regarding the duties and rights of states in connection with struggles for self-determination.

Consequently, state practice demonstrates that the rules of *jus ad bellum*, including the right of self-defence, do not play any relevant role with regard to the use of force against the occupying power. This conclusion is in line with the view that even the occupying power itself cannot invoke *jus ad bellum* rules. The following subsection explores why these rules are not applicable to armed force employed in contexts of occupation.

3.4. THE INAPPLICABILITY OF *JUS AD BELLUM* AND SELF-DEFENCE IN SITUATIONS OF OCCUPATION BECAUSE OF THE EXISTENCE OF A SITUATION OF ONGOING ARMED CONFLICT

The occupying power and the occupied state cannot rely on self-defence and *jus ad bellum* for the reason that they are already involved in an armed conflict. Even if actual hostilities have diminished down, the situation of occupation inherently preserves the existence of an armed conflict in the occupied territory, making the rules on *jus ad bellum* irrelevant.

The rules of *jus ad bellum* aim to regulate the resort to armed force in international law. Since the adoption of the UN Charter and of its Article 2(4), states must not resort to armed force as a matter of principle. Only in particular circumstances, i.e., the need to resort to proportionate and immediate self-defence against an armed attack, may states resort unilaterally to armed force. When an armed conflict is triggered, *jus ad bellum* ceases to function. From that moment on, international law is concerned only with how the armed conflict is conducted, i.e., the respect for *jus in bello* and – if applicable – international

3.4. Inapplicability of Jus ad Bellum and Self-Defence

human rights law.[269] Accordingly, during an ongoing armed conflict there is no need to justify every action on the basis of *jus ad bellum*: if State A and State B are involved in an armed conflict, there is no need to justify under *jus ad bellum* every single military operation State A wants to launch against State B. Rather, international law demands only that every operation respects international humanitarian law, whilst only the outbreak of the conflict and its effects may be scrutinised under *jus ad bellum*.[270]

In the past, this shift was made clear by the distinction between the law of peace and the law of war.[271] *Jus ad bellum* was considered to be part of the law of peace. When a state resorted to armed force, there was a shift in the relevant rules from the law of peace to the law of war (*jus in bello*). This shift was the product of the establishment of the so-called state of war, which was at the basis of the duties and rights of both belligerents and neutrals.[272] When the state of war was operating, *jus ad bellum* rules were no longer relevant – since they were part of the law of peace – and only *jus in bello* rules regulate the hostilities. To navigate this somewhat rigid dichotomy without creating uncertainty, the state of war was created mainly through a formal declaration (the declaration of war), which had the main task of determining the moment at which the law of peace was replaced by the law of war.[273]

Today, the theory of the state of war is no longer as relevant as it was in the past. Since the adoption of the UN Charter, the normal state in international relationship has been peace, while war has been a merely temporary exception. More recently, the way in which states conduct their hostilities has changed dramatically. Following the adoption of the GCs, the term 'armed conflict' has largely replaced 'war'.[274] Indeed, states today are involved in armed conflicts that do not need to be formally declared or acknowledged

---

[269] On the application of international human rights law in armed conflict and occupation, see *supra*, Section 2.5.

[270] This is the case of the works of the EECC, which examined only the outset of the armed conflict between Ethiopia and Eritrea under *jus ad bellum* (*Partial Award: Jus ad Bellum – Ethiopia's Claim 1–8*).

[271] This distinction has been applied by the PCIJ, *Treaty of Neuilly, Article 179, Annex, Paragraph 4 (Interpretation)*, Series A, no. 3, Judgment, 12 September 1924, 7.

[272] On the state of war, see Balladore Pallieri, *Diritto*, 3–34; Schwarzenberger, *International Law*, 59–106; Dinstein, *War, Aggression*, 32–6; Marina Mancini, *Stato di guerra e conflitto armato nel diritto internazionale* (Giappichelli 2009), and 'The Effects of a State of War or Armed Conflict' in Weller (ed.), *The Oxford*, 988; Natalino Ronzitti, *Diritto internazionale dei conflitti armati* (Giappichelli 2017) 146–9.

[273] See Art. 1 of the Hague Convention (III) Relative to the Opening of Hostilities, The Hague, 18 October 1907.

[274] See common Art. 2 GCs, and the explanations of Pictet (ed.), *Commentary to IV Geneva Convention*, 17–21. See also UK Military Manual, section 3.1.1.

by the belligerents in order to trigger the application of *jus in bello*; rather, international humanitarian law is binding as soon as states are placed, as a matter of fact, in a situation of armed conflict.[275] Furthermore, contemporary international law generally rejects the idea that an armed conflict results in the automatic cessation of application of the rules pertaining to peacetime; rather, today it is widely accepted that even in armed conflict those rules are still in force as long as they are not expressively derogated.[276]

Notwithstanding these developments, the theory of the state of war has not vanished entirely.[277] The theory has simply changed and evolved to adapt to the new normative environment, under the label of theory of the effects of an ongoing armed conflict.[278] Where an ongoing armed conflict exists,

> the only question to be asked under the rules of the *ius ad bellum*, the prohibition of the use of force, is: who started the whole conflict? The individual military action undertaken within the framework of the conflict can only be judged in the light of the *ius in bello*, but not by the yardstick of the *ius ad bellum* independently from the question which party violated the *ius ad bellum* by starting the conflict[279]

Thus, even today, there is no need to justify every military operation under *jus ad bellum* in an ongoing armed conflict.

---

[275] ICTY, *Prosecutor v. Tadić*, IT-94-1, Decision on the Defence Motion for Interlocutory Appeal on Jurisdiction, 2 October 1995, para. 70:

> An armed conflict exists whenever there is a resort to armed force between States or protracted armed violence between governmental authorities and organized armed groups or between such groups within a State. International humanitarian law applies from the initiation of such armed conflicts and extends beyond the cessation of hostilities until a general conclusion of peace is reached; or, in the case of internal conflicts, a peaceful settlement is achieved.

> According to Pictet, '[t]here is no need for a formal declaration of war, or for recognition of the existence of a state of war, as preliminaries to the application of the Convention. The occurrence of de facto hostilities is sufficient' (Pictet (ed.), *Commentary to IV Geneva Convention*, 20).

[276] See ILC, Draft Articles on the Effects of Armed Conflicts on Treaties, with commentaries (2011), Art. 3. This theme has been intensely debated in legal scholarship: see Arnold McNair, 'Les effects de la guerre sur les traités' (1937) 59 RCADI 527; Stone, *Legal*, 447–50; Schwarzenberger, *International Law*, 71–4; Mancini, *Stato*, 269–84; Ronzitti, *Diritto*, 149–52; Arnold Pronto, 'The Effect of War on Law – What Happens to Their Treaties When States Go to War' (2013) 2 Cambridge JICL 227.

[277] See Brownlie, *International Law*, 384–401.

[278] See Ronzitti, *Diritto*, 148; Mancini, 'The Effects', 1000–13.

[279] Michael Bothe, 'Terrorism and the Legality of Pre-emptive Force' (2003) 14 EJIL 234, 227.

3.4. Inapplicability of Jus ad Bellum and Self-Defence

The shift from war in the classical term and armed conflict has further obfuscated the issue of whether two states continue to be involved in hostilities or not, due to the demise of formal declarations of war[280] and the sliding overlapping between causes of suspension and of termination of hostilities.[281] Moreover, since the determination of the existence of an armed conflict is a matter of fact, it could be difficult for third states to gather the evidence needed to determine whether an armed conflict is ongoing, especially in situations wherein less intense hostilities exist – a common phenomenon today and one that is blurring the distinction between peacetime and wartime.[282]

All these considerations suggest great caution in invoking the theory of the existence of an ongoing armed conflict. In fact, states sometimes try to justify single episodes, in the framework of an ongoing armed conflict, with reference to *jus ad bellum*, even if this would not be strictly necessary.[283] One author has suggested that this practice would be clear evidence of the continuous relevance of *jus ad bellum* in an ongoing armed conflict.[284] In his opinion, this practice should be used as an evidence of the difficulty in establishing when an armed conflict starts and when it ends, with dangers of states relapsing to armed force in the absence of any *jus ad bellum* justification by invoking a never-ended past armed conflict.

However, states and scholars commonly employ the theory of the existence of an ongoing armed conflict. For instance, Israel has constantly justified its actions against neighbouring states such as Iran, Lebanon, and Syria under the existence of an ongoing armed conflict, even if the SC has often condemned these episodes under *jus ad bellum*.[285] Moreover, one author has suggested that the armed conflict between the US-led coalition and Iraq in 2003 did not need any *jus ad bellum* justification since those countries were still embedded in the state of war triggered by the 1990 Iraqi invasion of Kuwait and subsequent international intervention[286] – a conclusion that this author

---

[280] UK Military Manual, section 3.2.1.
[281] Armistices were once considered mere causes of suspension and became causes of termination only in the most recent practice (Dinstein, *War, Aggression*, 44–51).
[282] On the blurring of the distinction between the laws of war and peace, see Carsten Stahn, '"Jus ad Bellum", "Jus in Bello" … "Jus post Bellum"? – Rethinking the Conception of the Law of Armed Force' (2006) 17 EJIL 921; Charles H. D. Garraway, 'War and Peace: Where Is the Divide?' (2012) 88 ILS 93.
[283] See the practice collected by Christopher Greenwood, 'The Relationship between *Ius ad Bellum* and *Ius in Bello*' (1983) 9 *Review of International Studies* 221.
[284] Ibid.
[285] See William O'Brian, 'Reprisals, Deterrence and Self-Defense in Counterterror Operations' (1990) 30 Virginia JIL 421, 426.
[286] See Dinstein, *War, Aggression*, 326–7 and 347.

does not share, since the 1990 armed conflict clearly ended in 2003.[287] Most recent state practice has demonstrated that some states consider themselves to be involved in a never-ending armed conflict, as in the so-called global war against terrorism allegedly launched by the USA after September 11 and never concluded.[288]

These last examples clearly show that the doctrine of the ongoing existence of an armed conflict may be subject of abuses, and thus, it must be handled with care,[289] especially because it can be difficult to ascertain whether an *ongoing* armed conflict in fact existed. Leaving aside situations of occupation, states have two options when dealing with the resort of armed force: they may invoke the rules of *jus ad bellum* or, rather, they may try to demonstrate ongoing involvement in an armed conflict; in this last case, if that state wants to exclude the relevance of *jus ad bellum* rules after the outbreak of the conflict, it has to demonstrate case by case, on the basis of a strict analysis of the specific factual circumstances, that any subsequent attack is part of an ongoing and uninterrupted armed conflict. The absolute ban on the use of force in the UN Charter puts the burden of proof regarding the existence of this ongoing armed conflict on the attacking state.

However, it is submitted here that it is the situation of occupation that preserves the existence of an ongoing armed conflict in the occupied territory,[290] so that the *jus ad bellum* is irrelevant for the use of armed force in that area. In the words of the German Military Manual, a 'military occupation results in a state of international armed conflict. This also applies if hostilities have in general come to a final end'.[291] This happens even if hostilities occur after many years of relatively untroubled occupation when, absent the occupation, the new hostilities would not be considered as occurring during an existing armed conflict.[292] The existence of an ongoing armed conflict is *presumed* in

---

[287] See Bothe, 'Terrorism', 235.
[288] See, e.g., Legal Adviser Koh's Speech on the Obama Administration and International Law, March 2010, available at www.cfr.org/international-law/legal-adviser-kohs-speech-obama-administration-international-law-march-2010/p22300. This opinion is the subject of a number of criticisms. For an analysis of the most problematic issues, see Noam Lubell, 'The War (?) against A-Qaeda' in Wilmshurst (ed.), *Classification*, 421.
[289] According to one commentator, '[t]he notion of continuous armed conflict is a dangerous one, open to abuse' (Bothe, 'Terrorism', 236). In another author's view, '[t]his reasoning reflects [a] rather conservative view' (Eliav Lieblich, 'Reflections on the Israeli Report on the Gaza Conflict', *Just Security*, 24 June 2015).
[290] See Michael N. Schmitt, 'Iraq (2003 onwards)' in Wilmshurst (ed.), *Classification*, 356, 364–5: 'It must be understood that a state of international armed conflict continues during a belligerent occupation'.
[291] German Military Manual, section 535.
[292] *Contra*, see Milanovic, 'Lessons', 384.

3.4. Inapplicability of Jus ad Bellum and Self-Defence

situations of occupation, on the basis of the hostile character of the authority exercised by the occupying power.[293] This view is supported by the ICTY's case law, which recognised that, until the cessation of the hostilities, international humanitarian law applies to territory placed under the control of a belligerent party 'whether or not actual combat takes place there'.[294] Since the Court had affirmed that international humanitarian law applies when, de facto, an armed conflict exists,[295] the Court seems to imply that the control exercised by a belligerent over a portion of territory preserves the existence of an ongoing armed conflict.[296] Similarly, in the aftermath of the Six-Day War, the SC demanded the termination of occupation and the cessation of every state of belligerency, demonstrating that the occupation preserves the existence of a state of belligerency.[297] Although the maintenance of a prolonged state of armed conflict may raise some concerns, even critics of the theory of the existence of an ongoing armed conflict seems to exclude that these concerns may affect a situation of occupation[298] since the law of occupation tames the recourse to armed force by the occupying power beyond the boundaries normally imposed upon belligerents by international humanitarian law.[299]

Consequently, in situations of occupation, *jus ad bellum* is not applicable because of the existence of an ongoing armed conflict.[300] Indeed, in situations of occupation, the hostile relationship between the occupying power and the occupied territory is accompanied by the need not to create confusion between the occupying power's administration and the ousted sovereign. The law of occupation freezes the situation in limbo wherein the hostile character of the actual government is preserved, imposing heavy limitations on the occupying power's administration. In this circumstance, the occupation also preserves the state of ongoing armed conflict in the occupied territory.

---

[293] See the statement of the ICRC's representative during the drafting of the GV IV, *Final Record of the Diplomatic Conference of Geneva of 1949*, vol. II/A, 625.
[294] ICTY, *Prosecutor v. Tadić*, Decision on the Defence Motion, para. 70.
[295] Ibid.
[296] See Gioia, 'Terrorismo internazionale', 48–9.
[297] See SC Res. 242 (1967), 22 November 1967, para. 1.
[298] See Konstantinos Mastorodimos, 'The Character of the Conflict in Gaza: Another Argument towards Abolishing the Distinction between International and Non-International Armed Conflicts' (2010) 12 *International Community Law Review* 437, 453, who noted that: 'There is a serious policy and humanitarian reason to avoid classifying the overall situation in Palestine as an active armed conflict, *beyond, of course, the regime of military occupation*' (emphasis added).
[299] See *infra*, Sections 5 and 6.
[300] The majority of the experts convened by the ICRC excluded the relevance of *jus ad bellum* on the basis that 'the occupying power's authority to use force in the occupied territory is inherent to the state of occupation, since the latter constituted a form of armed conflict' (Ferraro, *Expert Meeting*, 111).

Consequently, 'the main question [is] not whether the occupying power could use force in occupied territory but rather when, and under what conditions and standards'.[301] Accordingly, in situations of occupation, the use of armed force is no longer linked to *jus ad bellum*, which has 'no relevance',[302] in the carefully worded opinion of the ICJ.[303] Rather, the law of occupation itself regulates the resort to armed forces, also allowing the occupying power to employ defensive measures.[304] Consequently, an occupying power may not lawfully claim self-defence as an additional instrument to protect its own interests under *jus ad bellum*[305] – a conclusion that does not rely on any particular view regarding the different issue of the right to self-defence against non-state actors.[306] Similarly, the use of armed force in occupied territory does not need any SC's authorisation since the faculty to resort to armed force is inherent in the situation of ongoing armed conflict.[307]

This position is supported by some state practice. For instance, as mentioned before, Israel justified the construction of the wall and the 2009 and 2014 operations against the Gaza Strip primarily on the basis of the existence of an ongoing armed conflict, invoking self-defence only as a supplementary justification.[308] Obviously, Israel was referring to an armed conflict that begun in 2000 rather than to the situation of occupation,[309] because its official position is that the Gaza Strip is no longer occupied. This assumption was also made by the Supreme Court of Israel at the time of the construction of the wall.[310]

Again, the existence of an ongoing armed conflict was acknowledged by some domestic judgments regarding the occupation of Iraq in 2003 and 2004.

---

[301] Ibid.
[302] *Wall* opinion, para. 139.
[303] See Raphaël Van Steenberghe, 'Self-Defence in Response to Attacks by Non-state Actors in the Light of Recent State Practice: A Step Forward?' (2010) 23 LJIL 183, 191.
[304] See *Wall* opinion, para. 141.
[305] See Vaughan Lowe, 'The Wall in the Occupied Palestinian Territory' in Laurence Boisson de Chazournes & Marcelo Kohen (eds.), *International Law and the Quest for Implementation: Liber Amicorum Vera Gowlland-Debbas* (Martinus Nijhoff 2010) 309, 311.
[306] Ibid.
[307] Accordingly, this author does not agree with the idea that UNSC Res. 1483 (2003) and Res. 1511 (2003) may be seen as an authorisation to use armed force within occupied Iraq (see Massimo Starita, 'L'occupation de l'Iraq, le Conseil de Sécurité, le droit de la guerre et le droit des peuples à disposer d'eux-mêmes' (2004) 108 RGDIP 883, 897–8). The relevant provisions of these resolutions – particularly paras. 13 and 14 of UNSC Res. 1511 (2003) – authorises *third States* to create a multilateral force, which is authorised to use armed force in the occupied territory. However, they do not refer to the armed force that the occupying powers may apply, even if, in fact, the multilateral force operated along with the occupying powers.
[308] See *supra*, Section 3.2.1.
[309] See Israel, *The Operation in Gaza*, para. 36; Israel, *The 2014 Gaza Operation*, para. 66.
[310] See *Beit Sourik Village* case, para. 2; *Mara'abe* case, para. 1.

3.4. Inapplicability of Jus ad Bellum and Self-Defence

In the case *Qualls* et al. v. *Rumsfeld* et al., the District Court of the District of Columbia affirmed the existence of a state of war between the USA and Iraq after the launching of the Iraqi Freedom operation.[311] Similarly, in the case *Amin v. Brown*, the British High Court of Justice affirmed the existence of a state of ongoing armed conflict (as distinct from the state of war) between the United Kingdom and Iraq at the time of the occupation.[312]

The ICJ case law does not contradict the conclusion that the situation of occupation freezes the existence of an ongoing armed conflict in the occupied territory, thereby preventing the parties from invoking *jus ad bellum* to justify specific military actions. In another passage of the *Wall* opinion, before engaging in the examination of the issue pertaining to self-defence, the Court affirmed that among 'the rules and principles of international law which are relevant in assessing the legality of the measures taken by Israel',[313] there is the ban on use of force and its corollary regarding the illegality of territorial acquisition resulting from the threat or use of force, as embodied in Article 2(4) UN Charter and in the Declaration on Friendly Relations, both reflecting international customary law.[314] However, this dictum only means that the principle of inadmissibility of conquest, at the basis of the law of occupation and entwined with the ban on the use of force, is applicable to the entire Israeli occupation of the OPT, including the areas affected by the route of the wall.[315]

On this basis, and not relying on the concept of *lex specialis*, is it possible to concur with those authors who have stressed that, in situations of occupation, the use of armed force by the occupying power does not fall under the scope of application of *jus ad bellum*, but rather, is regulated by international humanitarian law. Similarly, the use of force by the occupied state and by the population of the occupied territory is rooted in the existence of an ongoing armed conflict.

Consequently, the most applicable body of international law is international humanitarian law and, in particular, the law of occupation. Its relevance for the use of armed force in the occupied territory will be examined in the following chapters.

---

[311] US, District Court District of Columbia, *Qualls* et al. v. *Rumsfeld* et al., Memorandum and Order denying 5 Motion for Preliminary Injunction, 7 February 2005, 11, available at www.gpo.gov/fdsys/pkg/USCOURTS-dcd-1_04-cv-02113/pdf/USCOURTS-dcd-1_04-cv-02113-0.pdf.
[312] UK, High Court of Justice, *Amin v. Brown*, Decision on Preliminary Question (27 July 2005), [2005] EWHC 1670 (Ch), ILDC 375 (UK 2005), Chancery Division, para. 46.
[313] *Wall* opinion, para. 86.
[314] Ibid., para. 87.
[315] Ibid., para. 121.

4

Armed Resistance against the Occupying Power in International Law

E come potevamo noi cantare

con il piede straniero sopra il cuore,

fra i morti abbandonati nelle piazze

sull'erba dura di ghiaccio, al lamento

d'agnello dei fanciulli, all'urlo nero

della madre che andava incontro al figlio

crocifisso sul palo del telegrafo?[1]

4.1. INTRODUCTION

After having affirmed that *jus ad bellum* does not regulate the use of armed force in occupied territory, it is now necessary to analyse the legal framework regarding armed resistance against the occupying power. State practice demonstrates unequivocally that such armed resistance does in fact occur. Usually, this resistance raises very different emotional responses from the occupying power and the population of the occupied territory. The population of the occupied territory and its ousted sovereign typically sympathise with any armed resistance, despite the fact that the occupying power usually considers this same armed resistance to be illegal.

---

[1] Salvatore Quasimodo, 'Alle fronde dei salici', *Giorno dopo giorno* (Mondadori 1947). In English, these verses may be translated as follows: 'And how could we sing / with the foreign foot on our hearts, / among the dead abandoned in the squares / on the grass hard for the ice, to the lamblike cry / of children, to the black scream / of a mother who was going toward her son / crucified on a telegraph pole?' (author's translation).

This chapter explores the legitimacy of armed resistance against the occupying power under international law. The first subsection deals with the legitimacy of armed resistance under international humanitarian law and, in particular, the attitude of international humanitarian law towards the local population of the occupied territory with respect to the use of armed force. State practice demonstrates that international humanitarian law does not impose on the local population any duty of obedience to the occupying power. Conversely, international humanitarian law has evolved so as to recognise that, under certain circumstances, armed resistance against the occupying power is a form of lawful belligerency.

Other sources of international law also support the legitimacy of armed resistance against the occupying power. For instance, this chapter explores the legitimacy of armed resistance against the occupying power from the perspective of the principle of self-determination of peoples, which offers a high degree of legitimacy to armed resistance against the occupying power, especially when this resistance is conducted by national liberation movements that are representative of the local population of the occupied territory. In addition, the legitimacy of armed resistance against the occupying power may be inferred also from some states' reluctance to consider as terrorism, at an international level, conduct that occurs in situations of occupation.

4.2. THE LEGITIMACY OF ARMED RESISTANCE IN OCCUPIED TERRITORY UNDER INTERNATIONAL HUMANITARIAN LAW

4.2.1. *Preliminary Remarks*

Although international humanitarian law embodies only a portion of international law rules relevant to armed resistance against the occupying power, the legitimacy of armed resistance in occupied territory must be analysed first from the perspective of international humanitarian law, since situations of occupation are primarily addressed through *jus in bello*.

The problem of the legitimacy of armed resistance against the occupying power has amounted to an autonomous legal issue only since it was finally acknowledged that an occupation itself was not sufficient means to annex a territory. Before this turning point in international law, the problem of armed resistance against the occupying power was treated just as a form of rebellion against the new sovereign.[2]

---

[2] See Graber, *Development*, 70.

Notwithstanding the relevance of this topic for international humanitarian law, the codification of international humanitarian law conventions regarding the legitimacy of armed resistance in occupied territory met with significant difficulties due to disagreement among states. Most powerful states have attempted to affirm the illegality of any armed resistance against the occupying power, since their strength would likely place them in the role of occupying powers; conversely, smaller states that feared becoming victims of occupations have been vocal in emphasising the right to armed resistance against the occupying power.[3] According to one author, two different 'traditions of war' are at the basis of such a disagreement: 'martialism', which approaches the occupation from an interstate perspective and emphasises its extralegal dimension, and 'republicanism', which is based on justice in war, patriotism, and individual and national self-reliance, supporting the idea of a legitimate struggle against the occupying power even in cases of the defeat of the ousted sovereign.[4] The same author has argued that, between these two extremes, there is a third tradition of war called the 'Grotian tradition', based on the idea of codifying the law of war through international law; however, the codified nineteenth-century international law, based on the concept of state sovereignty and the divide between military and civilians, would have led to the same results as martialism, that is, favouring conquering armies.[5] This complex reconstruction, deserving praise in its own right as a unique endeavour with regard to the law of occupation, attracted some attention from international law scholars.[6] Indeed, even from a legal perspective, it is necessary to acknowledge the different ideologies and practical reasons behind states' positions regarding armed resistance in occupied territories to fully understand the evolution of relevant international humanitarian law.

The fact that codified international humanitarian law treats armed resistance after the establishment of the occupation in an entirely different way from armed resistance prior to the occupation deserves great attention. Prior to the establishment of the occupation, international humanitarian law recognises the legitimacy of the *levée en masse*, granting substantial protection to the individuals concerned. A *levée en masse* may be described as 'the

---

[3] See, generally, Graber, *Development*, 70–109. Further details are reported in the following subsections of this chapter.
[4] See the detailed descriptions of these models in Nabulsi, *Traditions*, 76–7, 80–127, 177–240.
[5] Ibid., 76 and 128–76.
[6] See, e.g., Ben Clarke, 'The Judicial Status of Civilian Resistance to Foreign Occupation under the Law of Nations and Contemporary International Law' (2005) 7 *University of Notre Dame Australia Law Review* 1.

spontaneous springing to arms of the population in defence of the country'.[7] Article 2 HR posits that '[t]he inhabitants of a territory *which has not been occupied*, who, on the approach of the enemy, spontaneously take up arms to resist the invading troops without having had time to organize themselves' should be regarded as combatants if they carry arms openly and if they respect international humanitarian law.[8] The legality of the *levée en masse* under international law is confirmed by a number of treaty provisions[9] and judicial decisions.[10] The justification of the *levée en masse* is often founded in the exceptionality of its occurrence,[11] in the fact that it would be a form of self-defence of the local population against an incoming occupation,[12] and, more correctly, in the metalegal consideration that the defence of the homeland in the face of an invasion should be considered just for patriotic reasons.[13] However, international law fails to take into account the relevance of all these considerations when the occupation is firmly established, without providing any satisfactory answer as to why these two very similar phenomena should be treated differently.

The difficulties of codifying international humanitarian law on armed resistance in occupied territory and states' ideological divergences regarding the relationship between the occupying power and the local population of the occupied territory are particularly manifest with regard to the existence of an alleged duty of obedience of the local population and with regard to the legality of armed resistance against the occupying power. In relation to these issues, the codified law should be taken into account both with regard to what it says and to what it does not explicitly regulate.

4.2.2. *The 'Duty of Obedience' of the Population of Occupied Territory*

In the nineteenth century and in the early decades of the twentieth century, especially before the codification of the law of occupation, a number of authorities suggested that the local population of the occupied territory would have a duty of obedience towards the occupying power. This duty would facilitate

---

[7] Morris Greenspan, *The Modern Law of Land Warfare* (University of California Press 1950) 62.
[8] Emphasis added.
[9] See, e.g., Art. 51 Lieber Code; Art. 10 Brussels Declaration; Art. 2(4) Oxford Manual; Art. 4(A)(6) GC III.
[10] See, e.g., British Military Court, Hamburg, *In re Lewinski* (19 December 1949), 16 ILR 509, 515.
[11] See Dinstein, *Conduct*, 57.
[12] Green, *The Contemporary Law*, 131.
[13] McDougal & Feliciano, *Law*, 546; Salerno, 'Il nemico', 1465.

the occupying power's maintenance of public order in the occupied territory. However, codified international law, relevant case law, and state practice all demonstrate that such a duty under international law in fact does not exist.

In the past, the existence of a duty of obedience towards the occupying power was usually explained as quasi-contractual relationship, wherein the local population was expected to exhibit obedience to the occupying power, and, in exchange, the occupying power was expected to respect the rights of the local population. For instance, according to Halleck, the occupying power would replace the ousted sovereign in the exchange between governmental protection and allegiance of the local population.[14] For his part, Fiore considered that a sort of 'moral contract' would exist between the local population and the occupying power, according to which the local population must obey the occupying power, which, in exchange, must protect the local population's rights.[15] Generally, many prominent authors endorsed the idea of a duty of obedience based on a quasi-contractual relationship,[16] which received the judicial support of some domestic case law.[17] However, other authors have rejected this contention on the basis that there could be no such quasi-contractual exchange between a state physically oppressing a territory and the local population, since they are ontologically placed in a hostile relationship.[18] Accordingly, some authors have argued that the obedience of the local population was merely the factual consequence of the effectiveness of the occupying power's repressive apparatus, rather than a duty imposed by international law.[19]

An alternate explanation for the existence of such a duty of obedience relied on the duty of every state to implement the law of occupation if it is party to the HR. According to this view, states bound by the law of

---

[14] See Sherston Baker, *Halleck's International Law*, 462–3.

[15] Fiore, *Trattato* vol. III, 260–1.

[16] See Alessandro Corsi, *L'occupazione militare in tempo di guerra* (Forzani & Co. 1882) 41–2; Jules Guelle, *Precis des lois de la guerre sur terre* vol. 1 (Pedone Laurel 1884) 129–30; Carlos Calvo, *Le droit international théorique et pratique* vol. IV (5th edn, Russeau 1896) 212–18; Pillet, *Les lois*, 200–1, 207–9; Albéric Rolin, *Le droit moderne de la guerre* vol. I (Albert Dewit 1920) 429; Paul Fauchille, *Traité de droit international public* vol. II (Russeau 1921) 210–211.

[17] See, e.g., Holland, Special Criminal Court, Arnhem, *In re Heinemann* (10 December 1946) 13 ILR 395, 396; Italy, Supreme Military Tribunal, *In re Keppler* (1953) 36 RDI 193, 195–9. See also Capotorti, *L'occupazione*, 79–83.

[18] See, e.g., the observations of De Waxel, *L'armée*, 72–3; William E. Hall, *A Treatise on International Law* (4th edn, Clarendon Press 1895) 493–9.

[19] See, e.g., Paul Pradier-Fodéré, *Traité de Droit International Public Européen* vol. VII (Pedone 1897) 695; Henri Bonfils & Paul Fauchille, *Manuel de droit international public* (7th edn, Rousseau 1914) 815.

occupation would have accepted in advance the possibility of an occupying power's administration over their territory based on Article 43 HR and, consequently, they would have provided an implicit acceptance of such a duty of obedience as the counterpart of the duty to restore and ensure public order in the occupied territory.[20] Following this approach, the duty of obedience is considered as a parcel of a more general duty to *pati* (suffer) the occupying power's authority.

However, the majority of contemporary scholars reject the existence of such a duty of obedience for a number of reasons.[21] First, the alleged duty of obedience is at odds with the codified law of occupation. According to Article 45 HR, which reflects customary international law,[22] '[i]l est interdit de contraindre la population d'un territoire occupé à prêter serment à la Puissance ennemie'. In addition, Article 68(3) GC IV observes that the 'death penalty may not be pronounced against a protected person unless the attention of the court has been particularly called to the fact that since the accused is not a national of the occupying power, *he is not bound to it by any duty of allegiance.*'[23] These two provisions clearly reveal that the law of occupation does not encompass any duty of obedience upon the local population of the occupied territory, as confirmed by a number of domestic decisions.[24]

Second, the idea of a synallagmatic relationship between the occupying power and the occupied state is untenable in light of the practice regarding the punishment of international crimes committed against the local population of occupied territory. For instance, war crimes trials regarding German and Japanese conduct during WWII have demonstrated that the protection of the local population of an occupied territory does not cease due to armed

---

[20] See the decision of the Belgian Supreme Court of 20 May 1916, quoted and criticised in De Visscher, 'L'occupation'. On the alleged duty of *pati* upon the ousted sovereign, see Annoni, *L'occupazione*, 239–45.
[21] See Richard R. Baxter, 'The Duty of Obedience to the Belligerent Occupant' (1950) 27 British YIL 235, 257–66; von Glahn, *The Occupation*, 45; Balladore Pallieri, *Diritto*, 316; Stone, *Legal Controls*, 725–6; Sereni, *Diritto*, 2020–1; Schwarzenberger, *International Law*, 173, 329; Greenwood, 'The Administration', 252; Annoni, *L'occupazione*, 224–5.
[22] Schwarzenberger, *International Law*, 173, fn. 52.
[23] Emphasis added. According to Pictet, 'The words "duty of allegiance" constitute an acknowledgment of the fundamental principle according to which the occupation does not sever the bond existing between the inhabitants and the conquered State' (Pictet, *Commentary to IV Convention*, 346). Very clearly Oppenheim affirms that '[i]nahabitants do not owe an atom of allegiance to the occupying power' (Oppenheim, 'On War', 273).
[24] See, e.g., Holland, Special Criminal Court, The Hague, *In re van Huis* (15 November 1946) 13 ILR 350; Holland, Special Criminal Court, The Hague, *In re Contractor Work* (15 July 1946) 13 ILR 353.

resistance.[25] Today, this assumption is rooted firmly in international law,[26] thanks to the general evolution of contemporary international humanitarian law, which is based on obligations *erga omnes* and *erga omnes partes*.[27] As a consequence, the application of the law of occupation may not be suspended or terminated due to a material breach of the relevant conventions by other parties, as affirmed by Article 60(5) VCLT, which refers to 'provisions relating to the protection of the human person contained in treaties of a humanitarian character, in particular to provisions prohibiting any form of reprisals against persons protected by such treaties'.[28] Similarly, countermeasures involving the violation of the law of armed conflict and affecting civilians, even in response to similar violations (so-called reprisals), are today forbidden by the GCs and AP I.[29] Accordingly, constructing the duty of obedience as the counterpart of the protection offered by the occupying power to protected persons in the occupied territory is incorrect since such protection is unconditional and satisfies the shared interests of the international community.

Nonetheless, some states still argue about the existence of a duty of obedience to the occupying power that would be something different from the duty of allegiance. For instance, the US Military Manual, after having mentioned a duty of 'strict obedience to the orders of the occupant' and that 'the occupying

---

[25] See, e.g., Holland, Special Court, The Hague, *In re Rauter* (4 May 1948) 15 ILR 500. See also Baxter, 'The Duty', 243.
[26] See, e.g., HCJ 4764 *Physicians for Human Rights et al. v. IDF Commander of Gaza*, 58(5) PD 385, paras. 10–12, unofficial English translation available at elyon1.court.gov.il/Files_ENG/04/640/047/A03/04047640.a03.pdf
[27] See *supra*, Section 2.6.
[28] It is undisputed that international humanitarian law conventions are covered by the definition of this provision. See Bruno Simma & Christian J. Tams, 'Article 60 – Convention de 1969' in Olivier Corten & Pierre Klein (eds.), *Les Conventions de Vienne sur le droit des traités: Commentaire article par article* (Bruylant 2006) 2131, 2157–61; Mark E. Villiger, *Commentary on the Vienna Convention on the Law of Treaties* (Martinus Nijhoff 2009) 746–7; Thomas Gigerich, 'Article 60' in Dörr & Schmalenbach (eds.), *Vienna Convention*, 1095, 1120–2.
[29] See Art. 46 GC I, Art. 47 GC II, Art. 13(3) GC III, Art. 33(3) GC IV, Art. 20, 51(6), 52(1), 53(c), 54(4), 55(2), and 56(4) AP I. See also Art. 50(1)(c) DARS. The customary character of the ban on reprisals against civilians has been debated by the ICTY with different positions in its case law (the ICTY declared the customary character of reprisals against civilians in some cases such as *Prosecutor v. Zoran Kupreškić*, IT-95-16-T, 14 January 2000, para. 531; *Prosecutor v. Milan Martić*, IT-95-11-R61, 8 March 1996, para. 10, while reversing its view in the decision *Prosecutor v. Milan Martić*, IT-95-11-T, 12 June 2007, paras. 464–8). Since some states still today consider that, under exceptional circumstances, civilians may be subject to reprisals in the course of hostilities (see Jean-Marie Henckaerts & Louise Doswald-Beck (eds.), *Customary International Humanitarian Law* vol. I (Cambridge University Press 2005) 520–2), the ICRC considers that the ban on reprisals against protected persons is customary in character (Henckaerts & Doswald-Beck (eds.), *Customary*, 519–20), while there is a strong trend towards the crystallisation of a customary ban on reprisals against civilians in the conduct of hostilities (Henckaerts & Doswald-Beck (eds.), *Customary*, 523).

power may demand and enforce from the inhabitants of occupied territory such obedience as may be necessary for the security of its forces, for the maintenance of law and order, and for the proper administration of the country', concludes that '[t]he inhabitant's obedience to the occupying power is generally distinguished from a duty of allegiance'.[30] This position, which recently received the endorsement of the ICRC,[31] requires some clarification in order to be understood properly. The law of occupation simply imposes on the occupying power the duty to maintain law and order in the occupied territory pursuant to Article 43 HR. However, this entitlement does not imply any duty of obedience upon the local population: even if 'international law permits a belligerent occupant to prohibit and punish, [it] *does not itself prohibit*[] conduct by the inhabitants' of the occupied areas which is hostile to him or which is inconsistent with the security of his forces or administration.'[32] Accordingly, 'their duty to obey does not ... arise from their own Municipal Law, nor from International Law, but from the Martial Law of the occupant to which they are subjected'.[33] Domestic case law supports this conclusion.[34] In this respect, one could share the view that 'the law of war requires a minimum cooperation between the occupying power and the inhabitants of the occupied territory'[35] only as long as it is understood that this 'degree of co-operation ... is a factual necessity if the laws are to work effectively; it is not rooted in an international law duty of obedience to the occupant'.[36] This view is confirmed by the UK Military Manual, according to which 'while the occupant is entitled to require obedience to lawful orders, it does not necessarily follow that failure to comply with such orders is illegal under the law of armed conflict'.[37]

4.2.3. *The Legality of Armed Resistance against the Occupying Power*

The issue of the legality of armed resistance against the occupying power is related to the topic of the existence of a duty of obedience. The main question is whether international humanitarian law prohibits armed resistance as

---

[30] US Military Manual, section 11.7.1.
[31] See Nils Melzer, *International Humanitarian Law: A Comprehensive Introduction* (ICRC 2016) 241.
[32] Baxter, 'The Duty', 266 (emphasis added).
[33] Lauterpacht, *Oppenheim's International Law*, 438–9. See also Oppenheim, 'The Legal Relationship', 368; Baxter, 'The Duty', 261.
[34] See Holland, Council for the Restoration of Legal Rights, *D'Escury v. Levensverzekerings-Maatschappij Utrecht Ltd* (30 April 1940) 15 ILR 572.
[35] Frédéric De Mulinen, *Handbook on the Law of War for Armed Forces* (ICRC 1987) para. 806.
[36] Greenwood, 'The Administration', 252.
[37] UK Military Manual, section 11.15.1.

such or, rather, only prescribes the way in which such a resistance must be conducted.

Although armed resistance against the occupying power, if successful, is a legitimate way to end an occupation,[38] Article 52(2) Lieber Code posited that international law prohibited the civilian population from acts of armed resistance.[39] Consequently, from the perspective of the Lieber Code, armed resistance fell within the territory of the alleged war crimes of 'war treason'[40] and 'war rebellion'.[41] This view is fully consistent with the fact that the Lieber Code was a domestic instrument envisaged to govern the conduct of hostilities between the US government and insurgents during the American Civil War; accordingly, it is not surprising that, in that scenario, the US government wanted to bar the local population of a territory formerly occupied by the rebels from undertaking armed resistance against the governmental forces should they regain control over the area.

However, since the only situation in which an occupation may arise in contemporary international law is during international armed conflicts, different interests are at stake than when the Lieber Code was adopted to regulate the conduct of hostilities in the American Civil War. Indeed, during the nineteenth century, occupying powers in Europe faced a number of acts of armed resistance by organised units in occupied territory, such as the French irregular forces (*francs-tireurs*) employed against the Prussian occupation forces in the Franco-Prussian War (1970–1).[42] When, after these events, the European states attempted to codify for the first time the rules of *jus in bello*, it was apparent that the Lieber Code's provision regarding the illegality of acts of armed resistance against the occupying power had become obsolete.[43]

---

[38] See De Waxel, *L'armée*, 73; De Visscher, 'L'occupation', 76; Giuseppe Barile, 'Tendenze e sviluppi della recente dottrina italiana di diritto internazionale pubblico (1944–1951)' (1952) 4 CS 397, 473.

[39] See, also, Francis Lieber, 'Guerrilla Parties, Considered with Reference to the Laws and Usages of War' in *Miscellaneous Writings* vol. II (Lippincott & Co. 1881) 277.

[40] 'War treason' may be defined as 'the commission of hostile acts, except armed resistance and possibly espionage, by persons other than members of the armed forces properly identified as such' within or outside the occupied territory (Baxter, 'The Duty', 244). For a discussion on 'war treason', see Baxter, 'The Duty', 253–7.

[41] According to Art. 85 Lieber Code, 'war rebels' are 'persons within an occupied territory who rise in arms against the occupying or conquering army, or against the authorities established by the same. If captured, they may suffer death, whether they rise singly, in small or large bands, and whether called upon to do so by their own, but expelled, government or not. They are not prisoners of war'. For a discussion of the concept of 'war rebellion', see Baxter, 'The Duty', 244–53.

[42] For a historical account, see Nabulsi, *Traditions*, 46–52.

[43] For a historical account of the codification of international humanitarian law on this issue, see Graber, *Development*, 79–91; W. J. Ford, 'Resistance Movements in Occupied Territory' (1956) 3 NILR 355; W. Thomas Mallison & R. A. Jabri, 'Juridical Characteristics of Belligerent

During the Franco-Prussian War, the status of *francs-tireurs* was uncertain: while the occupying power considered their actions in violation of *jus in bello*, other states argued that they deserved prisoner of war status due to their allegiance with the French Government-in-Exile.[44] This disagreement is reflected in subsequent relevant codifications, which remained silent on the issue of the legality of armed resistance against the occupying power. For instance, although the 1874 Brussels Declaration and the 1880 Oxford Manual affirm that organised militia and volunteer corps are legitimate combatants if they comply with certain requirements,[45] they mention situations of occupation only to concede the status of legitimate belligerents upon 'the population of a territory *which has not been occupied*, who, on the approach of the enemy, spontaneously take up arms to resist the invading troops without having had time to organize themselves' (*levée en masse*).[46] The silence surrounding the legality of armed resistance from the civilian population in occupied territory is explained by the disagreement between states taking different views on the legality of such an armed resistance. For instance, at the Brussels Conference, the Belgian representative declared that his country could not have voted for a provision depriving those civilians who conduct armed resistance against the occupying power of the prisoner of war status.[47] Similarly, the Russian delegate proposed that the local population of the occupied territory be considered prisoners of war if they took arms to defend the their country and complied with certain other requirements (conformation with *jus in bello*, responsible leadership, distinctive signs, carrying arms openly, minimum degree of organisation).[48] More straightforwardly, France suggested that any individual taken with arms in hand for the defence of their country and complying with *jus in bello* should be treated as a prisoner of war.[49] However, the opposition of other states resulted in the conference omitting any provision specifically dealing with civilian armed resistance in occupied territory, thus 'sanction[ing] the practice of leaving each state to do as it pleases'.[50]

Occupation and the Resort to Resistance by the Civilian Population: Doctrinal Development and Continuity' (1974) 42 *George Washington Law Review* 185, 190–219; Adam Roberts, 'Resistance to Military Occupation: An Enduring Problem in International Law' (2017) 111 AJIL Unbound 45.

[44] See David Turns, 'The Law of Armed Conflict (International Humanitarian Law)' in Evans (ed.), *International Law*, 821, 832.

[45] Art. 9 Brussels Declaration; Art. 2 Oxford Manual.

[46] Art. 10 Brussels Declaration (emphasis added).

[47] 'Actes de la Conférence Réuni à Bruxelles, 27 Julliet–27 Août 1874' in *Nouveau Recueil Général de Traités* 2nd Series vol. IV (1879–1880) 21, cited in Graber, *Development*, 73, fn. 15.

[48] Ibid., 115.

[49] Ibid.

[50] Ibid., 85.

A similar deadlock occurred during the negotiations of the HR, wherein the disagreement between different delegations led again to the exclusion of any reference to the legality of armed resistance against the occupying power.[51] The UK delegation suggested the adoption of a provision according to which nothing in the in the HR should be read as 'tending to lessen or abolish the right belonging to the population of an invaded country to fulfill its duty of offering by all lawful means the most energetic patriotic resistance to the invader'.[52] Despite any explicit reference to occupation and many doubts about the content of the expression 'lawful means', the proposed draft provision was rejected.[53] A similar fate was bestowed upon the Swiss proposal according to which 'no act of retaliation' could have been permitted against civilians raising arms against the occupying power.[54] Again, the question of the legality of such an armed resistance was left unresolved by any treaty provision, even if the delegates put the civilians participating in armed resistance 'under the protection and empire of the principles of international law, as they result from the usages established between civilized nations, from the laws of humanity and the requirements of the public conscience' pursuant to the Martens Clause.[55]

However, it is worth pointing out that neither of these instruments restated the Lieber Code's provision regarding the illegality of armed resistance under international law. Despite the failure to codify a rule on the legality of such an armed resistance, the lack of agreement among states on this point reveals that the Lieber Code's perspective was under significant strain and was not recognised as part of customary international law by very many states. In due time, the view that *jus in bello* does not prohibit civilian armed resistance against the occupying power became prevalent, as demonstrated by a number of domestic judgments.[56]

---

[51] For a fascinating account of this diplomatic deadlock, see Antonio Cassese, 'The Martens Clause: Half a Loaf or Simply Pie in the Sky?' (2000) 11 EJIL 187, 193–8.

[52] James Brown Scott (ed.), *The Proceedings of the Hague Peace Conferences: Translation of the Original Texts* (Carnegie Endowment for International Peace 1920) 550.

[53] Graber, *Development*, 88.

[54] Brown Scott (ed.), *The Proceedings*, 550.

[55] See Cassese, 'The Martens Clause' 187, 197–8; Eyal Benvenisti, 'Occupation, Belligerent' in *MPEPIL online* (2009) para. 20; Roberts, 'Resistance', 46.

[56] See Norway, Eidsivating Lagmannsrett (Court of Appeal), *In re Bruns* (Judgment of 20 March 1946), 13 ILR 390, 393; Italy, Court of Appeal, Turin, *Baffico v. Calleri* (Judgment of 5 January 1948), 15 ILR 424; Denmark, Eastern Provincial Court, *In re Hoffmann* (Judgment of 21 September 1948) 16 ILR 508; Holland, *In re Rauter*, 435. See, also, De Waxel, *L'armée*, 74.

4.2. Legitimacy of Armed Resistance

The subsequent codifications of *jus in bello* took WWII's emphasis on the role of armed resistance against the occupying power into account.[57] As George Scelles noted, the utility of armed resistance during WWII was 'considérable' and such a resistance 'peut être la seule ressource d'un gouvernement surpris par l'agression, obligé à l'exil et, pour un peuple, la seule façon de défendre son existence et son droit à disposer de lui-même'.[58] In 1949, the GCs recognised that participating in armed resistance against the occupying power is not a war crime. Indeed, according to Article 4(A)(2) GC III, '[m]embers of other militias and members of other volunteer corps, including those of organized resistance movements, belonging to a Party to the conflict and operating in or outside their own territory, *even if this territory is occupied*' are entitle to the protection of prisoners of war if they comply with the requirements of GC III.[59] Accordingly, this provision clarifies that resistance against the occupying power is not per se prohibited by international humanitarian law; rather, GC III acknowledges the legitimacy of armed resistance,[60] limiting at the same time the entitlement to the status of prisoners of war to only those combatants complying with certain criteria regarding their distinction from civilians.[61] Article 44(3) AP I goes on to posit that, when the nature of

---

[57] According to Richard R. Baxter, 'So-Called "Unprivileged Belligerency": Spies, Guerrillas and Saboteurs' (1951) 28 British YIL 323, 334–5,

> [r]esistance activities were an important instrument in the defeat of the Axis during the Second World War, and it is hardly possible to name an armed conflict which has taken place since the conclusion of those hostilities in which guerrillas have not played an important and often decisive role. Only a rigid legal formalism could lead to the characterization of the resistance conducted against Germany, Italy, and Japan as a violation of international law. Patriotism, nationalism, allegiance to some sort of political authority have replaced the desire for loot, which has traditionally been attributed to the guerrilla, in motivating civilians to take an active part in warfare.

[58] Georges Scelles, 'Observations' (1957-I) 47 *Annuaire de l'IDI* 578, 591.

[59] Emphasis added. These requirements are: '(a) being commanded by a person responsible for his subordinates; (b) that of having a fixed distinctive sign recognizable at a distance; (c) that of carrying arms openly; (d) that of conducting their operations in accordance with the laws and customs of war' (Art. 4(A)(2) GC III).

[60] See Anthony Roger, 'Combatant Status' in Elizabeth Wilmhurst & Susan Breau (eds.), *Perspectives on the ICRC Study on Customary International Humanitarian Law* (Cambridge University Press 2007) 101, 106.

[61] For more on the requirements for the prisoner of war status in occupied territory, see Marco Pertile, 'L'adozione di misure contro il terrorismo nei territori occupati: i poteri e gli obblighi delle potenze occupanti' in Gargiulo & Vitucci (eds.), *La tutela*, 295, 310–11. Clearly, the need to fight the occupying power in covert ways results in the fact that many acts of resistance are not carried out by individuals entitled to the prisoner of war status (see, e.g., Israel, Military Court Sitting in Ramallah, *Military Prosecutor v. Kassem* et al. (13 April 1969) 42 ILR 470, 482–3).

the hostilities make it impossible for combatants to distinguish themselves in accordance to GC III, nevertheless, they shall be considered combatants if they carry their 'arms openly: (a) during each military engagement, and (b) during such time as [they are] visible to the adversary while [they are] engaged in a military deployment preceding the launching of an attack in which [they are] to participate'. In light of the radical state disagreement on this rule, which was considered mainly applicable in occupied territory,[62] it is generally accepted that Article 44(3) AP I does not reflect customary international law.[63] However, should a combatant fail to comply with international humanitarian law criteria, they would not be entitled to the prisoner of war status, but nevertheless, their resistance would not be per se a violation of international law.[64]

The exploration of the legal framework applicable to civilian armed resistance is clearly beyond the purview of this book. However, suffice it to say that, according to Article 5(2) GC IV, those individuals involved in 'activity hostile to the security of the occupying power', when absolute military security so requires, may 'be regarded as having forfeited rights of communication' under GC IV. Article 45(3) AP I specifically abrogated this rule, affirming that, in occupied territory, 'any person who has taken part in hostilities, who is not entitled to prisoner-of-war status and who does not benefit from more favourable treatment in accordance with [GC IV] ... shall also be entitled, notwithstanding Article 5 [GC IV], to his rights of communication'. The existence of this specific regime fueled a debate regarding the creation of a third category beyond combatants and civilians, that of 'unlawful combatants', which would include also civilian armed resistance in occupied territory.[65] However, correctly, the Supreme Court of Israel affirmed that civilians involved in armed resistance against the occupying power still remain civilians under international humanitarian law.[66] The treatment provided to civilian armed resistance pursuant to the GC IV and AP I is, however, inapplicable to members of

---

[62] See Henckaerts & Doswald-Beck (eds.), *Customary* vol. I, 387–9; Ronzitti, *Diritto*, 180–1.
[63] See, generally, Dinstein, *Conduct*, 64.
[64] See Roberto Ago, 'Nota a *In re Keppler*' (1953) 36 RDI 200, 205–6; von Glahn, 'The Occupation', 55; Baxter, 'The Duty', 340; Ford, 'Resistance' 381–2; Clarke, 'The Judicial Status', 19–20.
[65] The existence of this third category was suggested by some authors and opposed by others. See, generally, Baxter, 'So-Called "Unprivileged Belligerency"'; Michael H. Hoffman, 'Terrorists Are Unlawful Belligerents, Not Unlawful Combatants: A Distinction with Implications for the Future of International Humanitarian Law' (2002) 34 Case Western Reserve JIL 227; Luisa Vierucci, 'Prisoners of War or Protected Persons *qua* Unlawful Combatants? The Judicial Safeguards to which Guantanamo Bay Detainees Are Entitled' (2003) 1 JICJ 284; Knut Dörmann, 'The Legal Situation of "Unlawful/Unprivileged" Combatants' (2005) 85 IRRC 45; Shlomy Zachary, 'Between the Geneva Conventions: Where Does the Unlawful Combatant Belong?' (2005) 38 IsLR 378.
[66] *Targeted Killings* case, para. 28.

the ousted sovereign's armed forces who fail to comply with the requirements for the prisoner of war status while involved in armed resistance against the occupying power.[67]

In light of the above considerations, the evolution of international humanitarian law demonstrates that there has been no ban on civilian armed resistance in occupied territory since the origins on the law of occupation. The fact that the Lieber Code is the only source that prohibits such an armed resistance is not relevant since the Lieber Code is not an instrument codifying international law regarding international armed conflicts and occupations that occur therein, but rather, a domestic piece of legislation that aimed to regulate armed conflicts between the US government and insurgents. On the contrary, the negotiations of the Brussels Conference and the Hague Conference demonstrate that many states considered that such an armed resistance was in fact legal. Today, the permissibility of this conduct is confirmed by the GC III, which clearly acknowledges that armed resistance against the occupying power is legitimate, providing as well for some requirements in order to allow the participants to enjoy the prisoner of war status.

In conclusion, contemporary international humanitarian law treats armed resistance in occupied territory as espionage: the activity is not per se prohibited, but the enemy against which it is directed has the right to fight it and to deprive the members of enemy resistance who do not comply with the proper requirements of the prisoner of war status.[68] Accordingly, the members of civilian armed resistance against the occupying power place themselves at risk of being punished for their conduct if they do not comply with international humanitarian law requirements on the prisoner of war status. However, from the perspective of the legitimacy of the armed resistance as such, international humanitarian law confirms that it is not prohibited. This conclusion is perfectly in line with the lack of any international law duty of obedience upon the population of an occupied territory.

4.2.4. Preliminary Conclusions

The stance of international humanitarian law regarding the legitimacy of armed resistance against the occupying power may appear ambiguous since

---

[67] See Sandoz, Swinarski, & Zimmermann (eds.), *Commentary*, 558. According to Art. 44(4) AP I, such combatants are not entitled to prisoner of war status, but they shall, nevertheless, be afforded 'protections equivalent in all respects to those accorded to prisoners of war' under GC III.
[68] The analogy between the espionage and armed resistance in occupied territory was first envisaged by the Special Court of The Hague in the case *In re Rauter*, 435.

the law of occupation does not address this issue directly. Although, in the past, this silence has been interpreted as implying a duty of obedience on the local population and the illegality of armed resistance, the previous subsections demonstrate that such claims do not withstand scrutiny. However, the silence of the law of occupation on these issues is perfectly in line with the entire rationale behind the law of occupation, while the inclusion of member of armed resistance (under certain circumstances) among lawful combatants demonstrates a general support for the legitimacy of armed resistance.

The law of occupation was drafted to regulate the conduct of the occupying power. Since 'the traditional assumption of the laws of war is that bad (or potentially bad) occupants are occupying a good country (or at least one with a reasonable legal system that operates for the benefit of the inhabitants)',[69] the drafters of the law of occupation focused their attention on the occupying power's conduct only. Even those provisions concerning with the protection of the ousted sovereign's interests – such as Article 55 HR on public property – are drafted as commands for the occupying power. The same is true with regard to the conduct of the local population of the occupied territory: despite the fact that the HR considers the local population as the beneficiary of some provisions regarding limits to the occupying power's administration[70] and the GC IV embodies some provisions regarding the 'rights' of the local population, the only conduct regulated is that of the occupying power. No command is placed on the local population. No command is placed upon the ousted sovereign. Apart from Article 47 GC IV – the only significant exception which prohibits the authorities of the occupied territory from reducing the protection offered by the convention to protected persons – the law of occupation does not regulate the conduct of the ousted sovereign or of the local population.

With this consideration in mind, the exclusion of any norm regarding the legality of armed resistance in occupied territory is understandable. Armed resistance falls outside the material scope of the law of occupation. It has already been explained that this silence is the result of disagreement among states. However, from the perspective of this study, it is important to emphasise that the law of occupation *acknowledges* the fact of armed resistance *without regulating* it. However, this lack of regulation does not imply that armed resistance is prohibited by international humanitarian law; rather, the basic prohibitive character of international humanitarian law suggest that the absence of any prohibition regarding armed resistance against the occupying

---

[69] Roberts, 'Transformative' 601.
[70] See, e.g., Art. 46 HR.

power should be read as an implicit affirmation that armed resistance is legitimate.[71] Similarly, the fact that, under certain circumstances, the members of armed resistance are not entitled to the prisoner of war status is not evidence of the illegality of armed resistance as such; rather, international humanitarian law permits a number of actions concerning the conduct of hostilities which, albeit permitted, may be opposed by the enemy and may lead to the loss of the prisoner of war status (such as in relation to espionage). This is the consequence of the fact that international humanitarian law does not confer 'rights', but rather 'faculties', which may be opposed by the other party.[72]

Accordingly, it is possible to conclude that international humanitarian law does not prohibit armed resistance against the occupying power, even if it is conducted by civilians. However, international humanitarian law does not provide a 'right' to participate in armed resistance either. Simply, armed resistance against the occupying power is a fact that is acknowledged by international humanitarian law conventions, which protect the participants in such activities as long as they comply with certain requirements regarding the entitlement to the prisoner of war status. The acknowledgement that, under certain circumstances, members of armed resistance movements are entitled to the status of prisoners of war strongly suggests that international humanitarian law supports the legitimacy of such an armed resistance, without, however, considering it to be a right.

4.3. OTHER INTERNATIONAL LAW SOURCES ON THE LEGITIMACY OF ARMED RESISTANCE IN OCCUPIED TERRITORY

4.3.1. *The Principle of Self-Determination of Peoples and the Fight against the Occupying Power*

Besides international humanitarian law, other branches of international law support the legitimacy of armed resistance against the occupying power. In particular, a number of scholars base the legitimacy of armed resistance against the occupying power on the principle of self-determination of peoples, one of the most important rules of international law whose role in contemporary international community is uncontested.

The principle of self-determination of peoples is enshrined, at a universal level, in the UN Charter as well as in the ICCPR and ICESCR.[73]

---

[71] On the permissive versus prohibitive character of international humanitarian law and of the law of occupation, see *supra*, Section 2.6.
[72] See *supra*, Section 2.6.
[73] See Arts 1(2) and 55 UN Charter; common Art. 1 ICCPR/ICESCR.

In addition, some regional conventions prescribe respect for the principle of self-determination of peoples.[74] However, the content of the principle of self-determination is not detailed in these instruments, but rather, must be reconstructed on the basis of state practice and *opinio juris*.[75] During the years of the decolonisation, the UN GA passed a number of resolutions with the aim of spelling out the content of the principle of self-determination. The most notable among these resolutions specifically address the topic of the legitimacy of armed resistance against oppressive regimes, including during situations of occupation. Accordingly, although these resolutions are not per se binding,[76] they provide useful evidence of the existence of customary international law, and are relevant for the interpretation of other existing rules.[77]

The principle of self-determination of peoples is applicable in situations of occupation as affirmed by the ICJ in relation to Namibia[78] and the OPT.[79] The principle of self-determination of people is both applicable *qua* treaty law – since it is embodied in common Article 1 ICCPR/ICESCR, which is applicable in situations of occupation[80] – and *qua* customary international law. Indeed, state practice demonstrates that situations of occupation are considered among those cases in which a people enjoys the right of self-determination. Various UN organs have held this position consistently in relation to most occupations, as in the cases of Namibia,[81] OPT,[82] East

---

[74] See, e.g., Art. 20 ACHPR; Art. 2 ArCHR.
[75] The academic literature on this principle is vast. Just to name a few important works, see Flavia Lattanzi, 'Autodeterminazione dei popoli' in *Digesto delle discipline pubblicistiche* (UTET 1987) 4; Gaetano Arangio-Ruiz, 'Autodeterminazione (diritto dei popoli alla)' in *Enciclopedia giuridica* (Treccani 1988) 1; Cassese, *Self-Determination*; Théodore Christakis, *Le droit à l'autodetermination en dehors de situations de décolonisation* (Pedone 1999); Karen Knop, *Diversity and Self-Determination in International Law* (Cambridge University Press 2002); Antonello Tancredi, 'Autodeterminazione dei popoli' in Cassese (ed.), *Dizionario*, 568; Stefan Oeter, 'Self-Determination' in Simma et al. (eds.), *The Charter*, 313; Giuseppe Palmisano, 'Autodeterminazione dei popoli' in *Enciclopedia del Diritto, Annali* vol. V (Giuffrè 2012) 81; James Summers, *Peoples and International Law* (2nd edn, Brill 2013). See also the essays collected in Christian Tomuschat (ed.), *Modern Law of Self-Determination* (Martinus Nijhoff 1993); French (ed.), *Statehood*; Distefano (ed.), *Il principio*; Fernando R. Tesón (ed.), *The Theory of Self-Determination* (Cambridge University Press 2016).
[76] See, generally, Gaetano Arangio-Ruiz, 'The Normative Role of the General Assembly of the United Nations and the Declaration of Principles of Friendly Relations: With an Appendix on The Concept of International Law and the Theory of International Organisation' (1972-III) 137 RCADI 409.
[77] See *Nicaragua* v. *USA*, paras. 188 and 191; *Nuclear Weapons* opinion, para. 70.
[78] *Namibia* opinion, paras. 52–3.
[79] *Wall* opinion, para. 88.
[80] See *supra*, Section 2.5.
[81] See, e.g., UNGA Res. 31/146 (1976), 20 December 1976, para. 1.
[82] See, e.g., UNGA Res. 3236 (XXIX) (1974), 22 November 1974, para. 1; UNGA Res. 67/19 (2012), 4 December 2012, para. 1.

4.3. Other International Law Sources

Timor,[83] Western Sahara,[84] Afghanistan (under Soviet occupation),[85] and Iraq.[86] From this extremely coherent state practice it is evident that a people under occupation have the right of self-determination under international law.[87] On this basis, some authors have argued that a situation of occupation is, inherently[88] or under certain circumstances,[89] a violation of the principle of self-determination of peoples, so that the occupation would be illegal. Although this issue is beyond the purview of the present research,[90] since the law of occupation applies irrespectively of the legality of the occupation itself, in many instances, such as regarding the prohibition against annexation, the law of occupation and the principle of self-determination of peoples protect the same legal interests. The situation of occupation does prevent the immediate realisation of self-determination, but the law of occupation preserves the self-determination of the population of the occupied territory as long as the occupation lasts.[91]

Since the principle of self-determination of peoples focuses on the process of resisting hostile oppression, this norm is particularly suitable for supporting the legitimacy of armed resistance against the occupying power.[92] Indeed, some scholars have suggested that the principle of self-determination of peoples modifies the application of existing rules of *jus ad bellum* in situations of occupation,[93] while others have argued that the principle of self-determination

---

[83] See, e.g., UNSC Res. 384 (1975), 22 December 1975, para. 1.
[84] See, e.g., UNGA Res. 34/37 (1979), 21 November 1979, para. 1.
[85] See, e.g., UNGA Res. 37/37 (1983), 29 November 1983, para. 2.
[86] See, e.g., UNSC Res. 1483 (2003), 22 May 2003, para. 4; UNSC Res. 1546 (2004), 8 June 2004, para. 3.
[87] For more on this, see Cassese, *Self-Determination*, 90–99, and *Diritto internazionale* (3rd edn, Il Mulino 2017, Micaela Frulli (ed.)) 167–9; Salerno, *Diritto*, 49–54.
[88] See, e.g., Cassese, *Self-Determination*, 55, 90–9; Youngjin Jung, 'In Pursuit of Reconstructing Iraq: Does Self-Determination Matter?' (2004–5) 33 *Denver JIL & Politics* 53.
[89] See, e.g., Orna Ben-Naftali, Aeyal M. Gross & Keren J. Michaeli, 'Illegal Occupation: Framing the Occupied Palestinian Territory' (2005) 23 Berkeley JIL 551, 565–70.
[90] For an accurate overview of international practice regarding illegal occupation, see Yaël Ronen, 'Illegal Occupation and Its Consequences' (2008) 41 IsLR 201.
[91] For more on this, see Pellet, 'The Destruction', 180–6; Jorge Cardona Llorens, 'Le principe du droit des peuples à disposer d'eux-mêmes et l'occupation étrangère' in *Droit du pouvoir, pouvoir du droit: Mélanges offerts à Jean Salmon* (Bruylant 2007) 855; Matthew Saul, 'The Impact of the Legal Right to Self-Determination on the Law of Occupation as a Framework for Post-Conflict State Reconstruction' in Noëlle Quénivet & Shilan Shah-Davis (eds.), *International Law and Armed Conflict* (TMC Asser 2010) 398; Cuyckens, *Revisiting*, 106–7.
[92] For a theoretical inquiry into the principle of self-determination of people as a 'right to resist', see Jens David Ohlin, 'The Right to Exist and the Right to Resist' in Tesón (ed.), *The Theory*, 70.
[93] See, e.g., George Bisharat et al., 'Israel's Invasion of Gaza in International Law' (2009) 38 Denver JIL & Policy 41, 67–70; Kattan, 'Operation', 110–17.

of peoples creates a special regime regarding the use of armed force in the context of occupations.[94]

These ideas find some ground in regional international human rights instruments. For instance, Article 20(2) ACHPR posits that '[c]olonized or oppressed peoples shall have the right to free themselves from the bonds of domination by resorting to any means recognized by the international community'. As emphasised in the case law of the ACmHPR, this provision does not confer a right to individuals, but rather, to peoples, in the context of the principle of self-determination of peoples.[95] Although this provision is broad enough to have sparked an interesting debate regarding the existence of a generic 'right to resist' oppressive regimes in international law,[96] for the purposes of this book, it is clear that the reference to colonised or oppressed peoples covers situations of occupation. More straightforwardly, the ArCHR embodies one provision entirely dedicated to situations of occupation; according to Article 2(4) ArCHR, '[a]ll peoples have the right to resist foreign occupation'. Again, the right to resist is described as a peoples' right rather than a human right in

---

[94] See Ronzitti, *Le guerre*, 72–103, and 'Resort to Force in Wars of National Liberation' in Antonio Cassese (ed.), *Current Problems of International Law* (Giuffrè 1975) 319, 329–53; Lattanzi, 'Autodeterminazione', 23–4; Dubuisson, *'L'applicabilité'*, 96–7.

[95] See the decisions commented in Shannonbrooke Murphy, 'Unique in International Human Rights Law: Article 20(2) and the Right to Resist in the African Charter on Human and Peoples' Rights' (2011) 11 *African Human Rights Law Journal* 465, 478–82.

[96] Ibid. In the past, many legal philosophers have suggested that individuals have a right to resist against a tyrannous regime, in particular in domestic settings, in light of the social contract at the base of the relationship between the government and the subjects (see, e.g., John Locke, *Two Treatises of Government* (1689) (London 1821) 364, 388; Samuel von Pufendorf, *Two Books of the Elements of Universal Jurisprudence* (1660), English translation by William Abbott Oldfather, Thomas Behme (ed.) (Liberty Fund 2009) 393). Although in the past this view was shared by some international lawyers (e.g., support for the existence of such a right to resist can be found in De Vattel, *Le Droit* vol. I, 298), most contemporary international human rights law instruments do not mention a human right to resist; e.g., the Universal Declaration of Human Rights acknowledges in its preamble the possibility to 'recourse, as a last resort, to rebellion against tyranny and oppression' in such a convoluted way that clearly demonstrate that the Declaration does not consider the 'right to resist' a proper right (UNGA Res. 217A (III), Universal Declaration of Human Rights, 10 December 1948, preamble para. 3). For more on the right to resist beyond situations of occupation – a fascinating topic that is outside the purview of this book – see Frédéric Mégret, 'Le droit international peut-il être un droit de résistance? Dix conditions pour un renouveau de l'ambition normative internationale' (2008) 39 *Études internationales* 39; Mélanie Dubuy, 'Le droit de résistance à l'oppression en droit international public: le was de la résistance à un régime tyrannique' (2014) 32 *Civitas Europa* 139; Olivier Corten, 'La rébellion et le droit international: le principe de neutralité en tension' (2014) 374 RCADI 53, 232–57; Gwilym David Blunt, 'Is There a Human Right to Resistance?' (2017) 39 *Human Rights Quarterly* 860; Jan Arno Hessbruegge, *Human Rights and Personal Self-Defense in International Law* (Oxford University Press 2017) 294–301.

the framework of the principle of self-determination of peoples.[97] The main reason behind the adoption of such a specific provision regarding resistance against the occupation is the ongoing occupation of former Arab territories (the OPT, the Golan Heights, some portions of South Lebanon) by Israel.

Another treaty often mentioned to support the legitimacy of armed resistance against the occupying power is AP I, which recognises the particular role of the struggle for self-determination in relation to the characterisation of these kinds of conflicts under *jus in bello*. According to Article 1(4) AP I, the rules pertaining to international armed conflicts apply also to

> armed conflicts in which peoples are fighting against colonial domination and *alien occupation* and against racist régimes in the exercise of their right of self-determination, as enshrined in the [UN Charter] and the [Declarations on Friendly Relations among States].[98]

Although this rule deserves attention in the study of the use of armed force in times of occupation, it is analysed in the section dealing with international humanitarian law since it pertains to the applicability of *jus in bello* rather than of *jus ad bellum*.[99]

As already mentioned, a number of GA resolutions may be interpreted to suggest that the principle of self-determination of peoples legitimises the resort to armed force against the occupying power by the population of the occupied territory. According to one such resolution, Resolution 1514 (XV) of 1960,

> all armed actions or repressive measures of all kinds directed against dependent peoples shall cease in order to enable them to exercise peacefully and freely their right to complete independence, and the integrity of the national territory shall be respected.[100]

The GA went further with the Declarations on Friendly Relations among States, in which it prohibited states from employing forcible means to deprive peoples of their basic rights. According to the Declarations,

> [e]very State has the duty to *refrain from any forcible* action which deprives peoples referred to in the elaboration of the principle of equal rights and self-determination of their right to self-determination and freedom and independence.[101]

---

[97] See Art. 2(1) ArCHR.
[98] Emphasis added.
[99] See *infra*, Section 5.5.3.2.
[100] UNGA Res. 1514 (XV) 1960, 14 December 1960, para. 4.
[101] UNGA Res. 2625 (XXV), 24 October 1970 (emphasis added).

More specifically, in a subsequent resolution, the GA affirmed:

> *The legitimacy of the struggle of peoples under colonial and alien domination* recognized as being entitled to the right to self-determination to restore to themselves that right by any means at their disposal; [recognized] the right of people under colonial and alien domination in the legitimate exercise of their right of self-determination *to seek and receive all kinds of moral and material assistance ...*[102]

Moreover, in the Declaration concerning Permanent sovereignty over natural resources, the GA '*support[ed] resolutely* the efforts of developing countries and of the *peoples of the territories under* colonial and racial domination and *foreign occupation in their struggles to regain effective control over their natural resources*'.[103] Accordingly, this resolution seems to support an armed struggle aimed at regaining control over natural resources located in the occupied territory.[104]

Furthermore, in its Definition of Aggression, the GA affirmed that '[n]othing in this Definition ... could in any way prejudice the right to self-determination, freedom and independence, ... nor *the right of these peoples to struggle to that end and to seek and receive support ...*'[105] The GA seems to be suggesting a right to self-help – if not explicitly self-defence – for peoples facing oppressions.

Similarly, in the Declaration on the Inadmissibility of Intervention and Interference in the Internal Affairs of States, the GA proclaimed that '[t]he duty of a State to refrain from any forcible action which deprives peoples under colonial domination or *foreign occupation* of their right to self-determination, freedom and independence',[106] while a subsequent resolution declared 'the legitimacy of the struggle of peoples for independence, territorial integrity, national unity and liberation from colonial and foreign domination and *foreign occupation by all available means, including armed struggle*'.[107]

On the basis of these resolutions, some authors consider that, in circumstances of denied self-determination, the oppressing state is prevented from

---

[102] UNGA Res. 2649 (XXV), 30 November 1970, paras. 1–2 (emphases added).
[103] UNGA Res. 3171 (XXVIII), 17 December 1973, para. 2 (emphases added).
[104] The ICJ recognised that the principle of permanent sovereignty over natural resources based on GA Res. 3171 (XXVIII) and on the GA resolutions is a rule of customary international law (*DRC v. Uganda*, para. 244). However, the Court never addressed the content of the principle and its corollaries such as the existence of rules pertaining to the recourse to armed force in order to regain control over natural resources.
[105] UNGA Res. 3314 (XXIX), para. 7 (emphasis added).
[106] UNGA Res. 36/103, 19 December 1981, principle II(d) (emphasis added).
[107] UNGA Res. 37/46, 3 December 1982, para. 22 (emphasis added).

resorting to armed force in order to maintain its domination, while third states would be under a duty not to assist the oppressing state in the perpetuation of its domination.[108] Some authors went further and argued that, when self-determination is denied, an oppressed people has an autonomous right to resort to armed force in order to achieve self-determination,[109] while third states would have the right to intervene *in a non-military way* in support of the people struggling to obtain self-determination without violating the principle of non-intervention.[110] This idea was particularly supported by Soviet scholars, who considered the denial of self-determination as creating an autonomous right to resort to armed force under *jus ad bellum*.[111]

In addition, thanks to the principle of self-determination, states may grant organised resistance groups a peculiar status under international law and the capacity to enter into relations with states as subjects of international law. This is the case for national liberation movements that fight against occupying powers, an idea that gained strong support in the UN during the Cold War. For instance, the GA recognised the PLO as 'the representative of the Palestinian people', inviting it to participate to GA meetings on the question of Palestine[112] with the status of observer[113] and giving it a number of additional procedural rights;[114] even the SC invited representatives from PLO to participate in some of its meetings concerning the situation of the OPT.[115] Similarly, the GA recognised POLISARIO as the 'representative of the people of Western Sahara',[116] and SWAPO as 'sole authentic representative of the Namibian people'.[117]

The ensemble of these treaty law provisions and GA resolutions seems to support the idea that armed resistance against the occupying power falls within the context of a legitimate struggle for self-determination. The repetition of resolutions concerning the legitimacy of armed resistance against

---

[108] See Abi-Saab, 'Wars', 371; Heather A. Wilson, *International Law and the Use of Force by National Liberation Movements* (Clarendon Press 1988) 135; Cassese, *Self-Determination*, 194–7; Ruiz Colomé, *Guerras*, 89; Palmisano, 'Autodeterminazione', 128.

[109] Wilson, *International Law*, 94; Cassese, *Self-Determination*, 197–8; Ruiz Colomé, *Guerras*, 97–9.

[110] Ronzitti, *Le guerre*, 123–41; Cassese, *Self-Determination*, 199–200; Ruiz Colomé, *Guerras*, 90. On the ban on an armed intervention by third states, see Dinstein, *War, Aggression*, 72–5.

[111] See Abi-Saab, 'Wars', 438, fn. 8.

[112] See UNGA Res. 3210 (XXIX), 14 October 1974. On the evolution of the PLO, see Giancarlo Guarino, 'The Palestine Liberation Organization and Its Evolution as a National Liberation Movement' (2008) 10 RCGI 13; Quigley, *The Statehood*, 133–48.

[113] See UNGA Res. 3237 (XXIX) (1974), 22 November 1974.

[114] See UNGA Res. 52/250 (1998), 7 July 1998.

[115] See, e.g., S/PV.2883, 30 August 1989.

[116] See UNGA Res. 34/37 (1979), 21 November 1979, para. 7.

[117] See UNGA Res. 31/146 (1976), 20 December 1976, para. 13.

the occupying power, the recognition of the international character of armed conflicts against the occupying power by the AP I,[118] and the procedural privilege conferred within the UN system to some national liberation movements contribute to the idea that the majority of states consider the struggle against the occupying power to be legitimate.[119] Although armed resistance in occupied territory under the principle of self-determination falls outside the scope of traditional *jus ad bellum*, which regulates mainly interstate relationship, however, the principle of self-determination of peoples offers a source of legitimacy. In other words, the end of the struggle against the occupying power, that is the full achievement of self-determination, is acknowledged by states, which treat armed resistance against the occupying power in a manner different from that of other armed resistance in different contexts.

However, the contours of the legitimacy of armed resistance against the occupying power are not clearly defined and have evolved over the course of decades. State practice and manifestations of *opinio juris* regarding the right of the population of an occupied territory to resort to armed force and to receive non-military assistance are scarce.[120] A strong disagreement among states is evident, especially since the debate on this topic has been monopolised by the armed struggle in the OPT, wherein states show polarised views in support of Israel or the Palestinians. Accordingly, the UN Secretary-General has to acknowledge that the existence of '[t]he right to resistance is contested by some'.[121]

Furthermore, the principle of self-determination may be invoked only by those armed resistance groups operating under the umbrella of a national liberation movement recognised as such by the GA. Clearly, not every resistance group against the occupying power falls into this category, since often the resistance is fragmented in conflicting armed groups that operate without central coordination. In addition, the decision to acknowledge an armed group fighting against an occupying power as a movement of national liberation is a highly political one, negotiated within the GA. Accordingly, it could happen that two armed resistance groups with identical features would not be both

---

[118] This author believes that Art. 1(4) AP I is not the decisive factor in order to consider the hostilities between the local population and occupying powers to be regulated by the law on international armed conflict, but rather, this conclusion is supported by other reasons that are explained *infra*, Section 5.5.3.2.

[119] See Jean D'Aspremont, 'La légitimité des rebelles en droit international' (Interest Group on Peace and Security – ESIL Heidelberg Meeting 2008) 5, available at papers.ssrn.com/sol3/papers.cfm?abstract_id=1266047

[120] See Gray, *International Law*, 63–4.

[121] Follow-up to the Outcome of the Millennium Summit, para. 160.

4.3. Other International Law Sources

considered legitimate enough to resort to armed resistance against the occupying power.

Moreover, the application of the principle of self-determination to support the legality of armed resistance against the occupying power is particularly advocated in cases of occupations created in violation of *jus ad bellum* and prolonged occupations, wherein the principle of self-determination of peoples would render lawful any armed resistance against the (illegal) occupation.[122] This approach would not contradict the principle of equality of belligerents, since the legality of the occupation under *jus ad bellum* would not affect the application of the law of occupation but, rather, of the principle of self-determination of peoples. Yet this solution is unconvincing because there is no evidence that, with regard to the application of the principle of self-determination of peoples, an occupation established under the legitimate exercise of armed force according to *jus ad bellum* is more excusable than a different occupation. Arguably, the constraints on self-determination posed by an occupation created during a self-defence action could not be justified in invoking self-defence as a circumstance precluding the wrongness of an act under Article 21 DARS; in fact, the principle of self-determination is *jus cogens* and, accordingly, no justification may be invoked when a *jus cogens* norm is violated.[123] In addition, the reference to the prolonged character of the occupation as a clear indication of the illegal character of the hostile authority is, albeit *prima facie* captivating, difficult to apply: in fact, it is not clear after how much time it would take for an occupation based on self-defence to become so prolonged that it triggers the legality of armed resistance. Accordingly, it is not easy to reconcile the principle of self-determination and occupations established in line with *jus ad bellum* without considering *jus ad bellum* (in the form of self-defence or SC's authorisation) prevailing on the principle of self-determination, notwithstanding the fact that both rules are *jus cogens*. One viable solution is offered by the direct link between the legitimate struggle for self-determination and the GA's recognition of the role of national liberation movements; it could be argued that the GA determines when an occupation is not justified under *jus ad bellum* or prolonged enough to trigger a legitimate armed resistance against the occupying power. In fact, practice shows that the GA has recognised the legitimacy of armed struggle conducted by national liberation movements only in cases of prolonged occupations and/or occupations not justified under *jus ad bellum* (OPT, Western Sahara, Namibia).[124]

---

[122] See, e.g., Bernardini, 'Iraq'; Carcano, *Transformative*, 448–9.
[123] See Art. 26 DARS.
[124] On the disagreement whether the occupation of the OPT started in the exercise of the Israeli right to self-defence, see *supra*, Section 1.3.

Additionally, the existence of an autonomous right to use armed force against the occupying power should be considered in relation with the fact that the occupying power is *not* prevented from employing armed force in the occupied territory. Instead, as explained in the subsequent chapters, the law of occupation confers upon the occupying power the duty and right to employ armed force in order to maintain public order and civil life under Article 43 HR.[125] Following the idea that the principle of self-determination of peoples would allow the population of the occupied territory to employ armed force, and bar the occupying power from using it,[126] one has to conclude that Article 43 HR is void because it conflicts with the principle of self-determination of peoples, which is a recognised *jus cogens* rule.[127] No state has ever supported this view, especially in light of the pivotal role of Article 43 HR with regard to the law of occupation.

Finally, it seems that the international community is in agreement in strongly supporting a peaceful solution for situations of occupation, requiring the national liberation movements to renounce the use of armed force. This trend is clearly demonstrated by the practice regarding the OPT. In this context, not only has the SC condemned the use of force by the Palestinians and Israel alike on a number of occasions,[128] but the PLO has also formally renounced the use of armed force as a means to end the occupation.[129] This position was further strengthened by the agreements concluded by the PLO and Israel in the 1990s, from which it is possible to conclude that, today, the Palestinian people may not claim a right to use armed force against Israel under the principle of self-determination of peoples as long as negotiations are actually being carried out by the parties.[130] The fact that the launch of a new intifada in December 2017 was justified on the basis of the stalemate in the peace talks (which were rendered moot by the US decision to recognise Jerusalem as the capital of Israel) and that the Palestinian leadership

---

[125] See *infra*, Sections 5 and 6.
[126] Dubuisson, 'L'applicabilité', 96–7.
[127] See Art. 53 VCLT.
[128] See SC Res. 242 (1967); 338 (1973), 22 October 1973, para. 3; Res. 1397 (2002), 12 March 2002; 1115 (2003), 22 November 2003 (referring to the duty to implement the document called 'A performance-based roadmap to a permanent two-state solution to the Israeli-Palestinian conflict' (S/2003/529, 7 May 2003)); Res. 1850 (2008), 16 December 2008; Res. 1860 (2009), 18 January 2009.
[129] See the Letter from Yasser Arafat to Prime Minister Rabin, 9 September 1993, available at www.mfa.gov.il/mfa/foreignpolicy/peace/guide/pages/israel-plo%20recognition%20-%20exchange%20of%20letters%20betwe.aspx
[130] See Robert P. Barnidge, Jr, *Self-Determination, Statehood, and the Law of Negotiation: The Case of Palestine* (Hart 2016).

denounced the accords concluded with Israel[131] supports the idea that there is a trend in international law favouring non-armed resistance against the occupying power, rather than armed resistance.

In conclusion, the principle of self-determination of peoples is undoubtedly a powerful tool supporting the legitimacy of resistance against the occupying power, especially when it is conducted by a national liberation movement recognised at the UN level as the legitimate representative of the oppressed people. However, it is difficult to identify a 'right to resist' pursuant to the principle of self-determination of peoples, especially in light of the instruments that the law of occupation confers on the occupying power to fight against armed resistance. In addition, contemporary international law discourages resorting to armed force against the occupying power. Nevertheless, and notwithstanding these important issues, the principle of self-determination of peoples should be seen as a source of legitimacy for the struggle against the occupying power.

4.3.2. *International Conventions against Terrorism and Resistance against the Occupying Power*

A further, albeit indirect, reference to the legitimacy of armed resistance against the occupying power may be found in the attitude of some states with regard to the adoption of counterterrorism conventions. State practice demonstrates that states are reluctant to define terrorism at a universal level and to conclude relevant conventions that are applicable in occupied territory because they do not want to sanction the activity of armed resistance against the occupying power. Accordingly, these states seem to support the view that armed resistance against the occupying power is legitimate.

The issue of the legitimacy of armed resistance against the occupying power is one of the main reasons why, at a universal level, there is no comprehensive convention defining what terrorism is. Indeed, in 1996 an Ad Hoc Committee was established by the GA with the mandate of 'developing a comprehensive legal framework of conventions dealing with international terrorism'.[132] However, during the negotiations for a Comprehensive Convention on International Terrorism, many Arab states requested the introduction of a clause excluding the application of such a convention to situations of

---

[131] See Tim Lister, 'For Palestinians, Trump's Jerusalem Move Is the End of the Peace Process', CNN (6 December 2017), available at edition.cnn.com/2017/12/06/middleeast/trump-jerusalem-israeli-palestinian-peace-process-intl/index.html.
[132] UNGA Res. 51/210 (1996), 17 December 1996, para. 9.

armed resistance against the occupying power.[133] This position was opposed by Western states, and the resulting deadlock is still blocking the adoption of such a convention.

Some existing conventions against terrorism do not apply in situations of armed resistance in occupied territory. Sometimes, states have reached this goal by excluding the application of these instruments to situations of armed conflict, wherein international humanitarian law regulates conduct that in peacetime falls within the definition of terrorism.[134] For instance, Article 12 of the UN International Convention against the Taking of Hostages posits that 'the present Convention shall not apply to an act of hostage-taking committed in the course of armed conflicts as defined in the Geneva Conventions of 1949 and the Protocols thereto', which remains regulated by international humanitarian law.[135]

Other conventions are less clear regarding their inapplicability in situations of occupation. For instance, Article 19(2) of the International Convention for the Suppression of Terrorist Bombings, posits that:

> The activities of armed forces during an armed conflict, as those terms are understood under international humanitarian law, which are governed by that law, are not governed by this Convention, and the activities undertaken by military forces of a State in the exercise of their official duties, inasmuch as they are governed by other rules of international law, are not governed by this Convention.[136]

Since there is no reference to armed resistance against the occupying power in this provision, but rather, the expressions 'armed forces' and 'military force of a State', which seem to exclude civilian resistance, many Arab states have not ratified this convention. Interestingly, upon ratification, Pakistan officially declared that 'nothing in this Convention shall be applicable to struggles, including armed struggle, for the realization of right of self-determination launched against any alien or foreign *occupation* or domination'.[137] Similar

---

[133] Report of the Ad Hoc Committee established by General Assembly resolution 51/210 of 17 December 1996, Eighth session (28 June–2 July 2004), A/59/37, Annex II, 10–11. See, also, Follow-up to the Outcome of the Millennium Summit, para. 160 ('The search for an agreed definition of [terrorism] usually stumbles on two issues ... The second objection is that peoples under foreign occupation have a right to resistance and a definition of terrorism should not override this right').

[134] For an overview on the relevant conventions, see Kimberley N. Trapp, *State Responsibility for International Terrorism* (Oxford University Press 2011) 105–21.

[135] Text in 1316 UNTS 205.

[136] Text in 2149 UNTS 256.

[137] Emphasis added. Text available at treaties.un.org/pages/ViewDetails.aspx?src=IND&mtdsg_no=XVIII-9&chapter=18&clang=_en

4.3. Other International Law Sources

declarations were also appended to the aforementioned UN Convention on the Taking of Hostages, such as that issued by Lebanon.[138] However, these declarations raised a significant number of objections from other state parties, which rejected them as contrary to the object and purpose of those conventions.[139]

The exclusion of situations of occupation from the scope of application of counterterrorism conventions does not mean that armed groups involved in resistance may resort to terrorism, but only that the conduct of armed resistance must be assessed under international humanitarian law only. In this regard, Article 12 of the UN International Convention against the Taking of Hostages has been described as a 'choice of law provision, which simply pointed to international humanitarian law as the applicable law in respect of activities of armed forces in an armed conflict'.[140] However, some other regional instruments exclude the struggle for self-determination and armed resistance against the occupying power from the very definition of terrorism, suggesting that no act of terrorism may exist in the context of the fight for self-determination.[141] This position is untenable as a matter of customary international law since, as affirmed by the SC and the GA on a number of occasions, acts of terrorism are prohibited in every context[142] and the sole fact of fighting for the self-determination of one people under occupation is not a legal justification for acts of terrorism.[143]

Indeed, international humanitarian law does not recognise the existence of terrorism as a status of individuals but, rather, prohibits some conduct that aims to spread terror among the population which, in peacetime, would be considered to be 'acts of terror' or 'terrorism' under different international law rules.[144] For instance, Article 33 GC IV prohibits 'all measures of

---

[138] Text available at treaties.un.org/pages/viewdetails.aspx?src=ind&mtdsg_no=xviii-5&chapter=18&lang=en

[139] For an overview on such declarations and objections, see Trapp, *State Responsibility*, 121–7.

[140] A/59/37, Annex II, para. 4.

[141] See, e.g., Art. 2(4) of the 1998 Arab Convention for the Suppression of Terrorism (adopted by the Arab League); Art. 2(1) of the 1999 Convention on Combating Terrorism (adopted by the Organisation of the Islamic Conference).

[142] See, e.g., UNGA Res. 49/60 (1994), 9 December 1994, para. 2; UNSC Res. 1269, 19 October 1999, para. 1; UNSC Res. 1566, 8 October 2004, para. 3.

[143] See Andrea Bianchi & Yasmin Naqvi, *International Humanitarian Law and Terrorism* (Hart 2011) 62–4; Raffaella Nigro, *La definizione di terrorismo nel diritto internazionale* (Editoriale Scientifica 2013) 38–42.

[144] See Orna Ben-Naftali & Keren R. Michaeli, 'We Must Not Make a Scarecrow of the Law: A Legal Analysis of the Israeli Policy of Targeted Killings' (2003) 36 Cornell ILJ 233, 270–1; Marco Pertile, 'Fighting Terror within the Law? Terrorism, Counterterrorism and Military Occupations' in Pocar, Pedrazzi, & Frulli (eds.), *War Crimes*, 276; Giulio Bartolini, 'I *targeted killings*', 278.

intimidation or of terrorism', while Article 51(2) AP I prohibits 'acts or threats of violence the primary purpose of which is to spread terror among the civilian population'. Since it is well established that armed groups must comply with international humanitarian law, as recognised in particular by the case law of international criminal tribunals,[145] the rules of *jus in bello* such as Article 33 GC IV and Article 51(2) AP I are the legal framework regulating armed resistance against the occupying power. Accordingly, excluding the application of counterterrorism conventions in armed conflict does not equate with the suggestion that acts of terror may be undertaken by armed resistance against the occupying power.[146]

In conclusion, international practice demonstrates that the Arab states are reluctant to impose at international level the domestic criminalisation of acts of terrorism if they occur in the course of armed resistance against the occupying power. However, this practice is countered by other significant state practice condemning terrorism whenever it occurs. With regard to the armed resistance against the occupying power, it is clear that acts of terror are already prohibited by international humanitarian law rules. However, for the limited purposes of this chapter, the Arab states' position regarding the scope of application of counterterrorism conventions may be seen as suggesting the legitimacy of armed resistance in occupied territory.

4.4. CONCLUSIONS

From the analysis conducted on the issue of armed resistance against the occupying power it is clear that international law is not at ease when dealing with this topic. International law appears unprepared to address in an effective way something that is clearly based upon metalegal motivations. Indeed, the defence of the homeland from the occupying power touches chords such as patriotism, heroism, and the spirit of sacrifice in those who rise in arms against the occupying power. The fact that international humanitarian law recognises

---

[145] The topic of respect for international humanitarian law by non-state actors is vast and has attracted significant of attention from academic literature. On this issue, which is beyond the purview of this book, see Sandesh Sivakumaran, 'Binding Armed Opposition Groups' (2006) 55 ICLQ 369; Cedric Ryngaert & Anneleen Van de Meulebroucke, 'Enhancing and Enforcing Compliance with International Humanitarian Law by Non-State Armed Groups: an Inquiry into some Mechanisms' (2010) 16 JCSL 443; Darragh Murray, 'How International Humanitarian Law Treaties Bind Non-State Armed Groups' (2015) 20 JCSL 101.

[146] On the relationship between terrorism and international humanitarian law, see, generally, Hans-Peter Gasser, 'Acts of Terror, "Terrorism" and International Humanitarian Law' (2002) 84 ICRC 547; Ben Saul, *Defining Terrorism in International Law* (Oxford University Press 2008) 271–313; Bianchi & Naqvi, *International Humanitarian Law*; Nigro, *La definizione*, 228–335.

such aspirations and motivations when dealing with an incoming occupation, as in the case of the *levée en masse*, while failing to acknowledge the same identical underlying reasons when an occupation is established seems contradictory. Obviously, such an outcome is not a coincidence, but rather, it reflects the interests of the powerful states that considered themselves likely to be occupying powers when international law was codified.

The difference between the views of smaller states versus more powerful states is particularly clear in the examination of international humanitarian law, which for a long time had no regulation on the legality of armed resistance at all due to disagreement among states. However, international humanitarian law has evolved so that today the existence of armed resistance in occupied territory is openly acknowledged, never prohibited, and even, under certain circumstances, entitles those involved in this activity to prisoner-of-war status. From a broader perspective, the absence of any regulation of armed resistance in the law of occupation is in line with the fact that the law of occupation only governs the conduct of the occupying power. However, in light of the generally prohibitive character of international humanitarian law, the silence of the law of occupation on the activities of the resistance should not be read as a source of illegality of armed resistance against the occupying power. Rather, during an occupation, armed resistance is a legitimate event, which, however, may be legitimately opposed by the occupying power. Accordingly, it is possible to conclude that international humanitarian law offers a source of legitimacy, even if not a proper right, to armed resistance against the occupying power.

A similar outcome can be inferred by reference to the principle of self-determination of peoples, a pivotal rule which is fully applicable in occupied territory. State practice demonstrates that the international community acknowledges that the people of an occupied territory – if it is organised in a national liberation movement that is representative of that people – has the faculty to resort to armed force. The sympathy of the international community is demonstrated by a number of procedural rights granted by the UN to these movements and by the fact that their struggles are considered to be legitimate by a number of important resolutions. However, one has to acknowledge that there is a clear trend favouring peaceful means of resistance and negotiations rather than armed resistance to put the occupation to an end. Accordingly, state practice regarding the legitimacy of such an armed resistance is restricted to those cases where the occupying power refuses to negotiate and maintain a territory under occupation for a long time. Nevertheless, the principle of self-determination of peoples is the main source of legitimacy of armed resistance against the occupying power.

Finally, some states have shown support for armed resistance against the occupying power by excluding the application of counterterrorism conventions to occupied territory. Nevertheless, acts of terrorism are prohibited by international humanitarian law applicable to the armed resistance against the occupying power. Accordingly, there is no right to resort to terrorism in the struggle against the occupying power at all. However, the declarations and views taken by these states during the negotiations of counterterrorism conventions are factual elements in support of the legitimacy of armed resistance.

In conclusion, international law does not recognise an actual 'right to resist' against the occupying power, since international law is the product of compromises between small states, which are afraid to be occupied, and powerful states, which are more likely to assume the role of occupying power. Nevertheless, international humanitarian law and the principle of self-determination of peoples show a clear support for the legitimacy of armed resistance against the occupying power, if it is exercised within the boundaries of international law.

5

Law Enforcement and Conduct of Hostilities in Occupied Territory

Be quite clear in your calculations, that two weeks earlier or later you will have an uprising. It always happens in a conquered country.[1]

5.1. INTRODUCTION

After having ruled out the relevance of the *jus ad bellum* in relation to the use of armed force in occupied territory and having assessed the legitimacy of armed resistance against the occupying power, it is necessary to examine other general issues regarding the use of armed force in occupied territory. In particular, this chapter explores why the law of occupation is considered the main legal framework in light of the different scenarios requiring the use of armed force that may arise in occupied territory. It is argued that the different situations requiring the use of armed force in occupied territory may be studied in the context of two different tasks incumbent upon the occupying power and involving the use of armed force: law enforcement and conduct of hostilities. This chapter analyses the legal regulations of these two paradigms, providing a novel perspective on the interplay between law enforcement and conduct of hostilities.

In particular, this chapter posits that the occupying power may resort to armed force in occupied territory only pursuant to international humanitarian law. Article 43 HR allows the occupying power to use armed force both in order to restore and ensure public order and to provide for its own security. However, Article 43 HR should not be read as a norm that widens the rights of the occupying power; rather, its function is to *restrict* the occupying power's faculty to resort to armed force to cases of the maintenance and restoration of public order only, and to provide for its own security.

---

[1] Napoléon Bonaparte, *Correspondance de L'Empéreur Napoléon Ier* (Panckoucke 1857–69) 12, 911, quoted by Nabulsi, *Traditions*, 41.

The chapter goes on to describe the international humanitarian law rules on the maintenance of public order in occupied territory. The law of occupation prescribes that the occupying power should not alter criminal provisions or public officials such as judges and police units, demonstrating that the occupying power is under a duty to restore and ensure public order through the same instruments that the ousted sovereign would have employed. This principle is explicit with reference to the criminal law system and judiciary; however, it is argued here that the same rationale applies to the use of armed force. Consequently, the occupying power must restore and ensure public order through law enforcement, the paradigm pertaining to the use of armed force within the domestic context. This operational model is characterised by a specific applicable legal framework based on international and domestic human rights law. This framework governs law enforcement in occupied territory as well.

Although the continuity principle regarding the maintenance of public order compels the occupying power to resort to law enforcement, it may happen that hostilities occur in occupied territory. This is not unusual in light of the fact that a situation of occupation is, by definition, an episode in an ongoing armed conflict. This chapter explores whether the occurrence of hostilities is compatible with a situation of occupation and clarifies why hostilities conducted in occupied territory must be governed by the law on international armed conflict.

Finally, this chapter addresses the topic of the interplay between the two paradigms of law enforcement and conduct of hostilities in occupied territory. After having reviewed the most significant solutions offered by scholars, this chapter argues that the principle of continuity embodied in Article 43 HR and related provisions regulate the interplay between the two paradigms. Accordingly, this chapter argues that the law of occupation prescribes the application of the law-enforcement paradigm as long as the ousted sovereign would have employed that paradigm. In other words, the switch to the conduct of hostilities is permitted only when an armed confrontation assumes such features that it would have been considered a non-international armed conflict absent the occupation. Indeed, only under such circumstances would the ousted sovereign have resorted to the conduct of hostilities paradigm.

5.2. DIFFERENT SITUATIONS REQUIRING THE USE OF ARMED FORCE IN OCCUPIED TERRITORY

When dealing with the issue of the use of armed force in occupied territory, it is possible to think that the clashes between the occupying power, on the one hand, and the local population of the occupied territory and the ousted sovereign, on the other, follow more or less the same pattern. However, history demonstrates that the reality is quite different. Indeed, the violence that may occur in occupied territories may be very different as to its origins, goals, scale, and effects. The law of occupation patently fails to acknowledge explicitly the fact that, in different occupations, the occupying power may have to resort to armed force on the basis of very different scenarios. In fact, the inherent conflict of the occupying power's administration, which is both a form of government and a hostile apparatus, raises the need to resort to armed force in different scenarios: as every government may over its own territory, the occupying power may need to employ armed force in order to fight crime and other public order disruptions while, at the same time, the occupying power may be required to face a resumption of hostilities meant to put the situation of occupation to an end.

Violence in occupied territory may be seen as a tool to force the occupying power to relinquish its control over that territory. Accordingly, the ousted sovereign may dispatch troops in the occupied territory or the local population may spontaneously organise resistance groups with the aim of expelling the occupying power from that area. In other cases, the resistance movements have their own goals that are different and distinct from those of the ousted sovereign, based on different ideological, religious, and political agendas.[2] For instance, with regard to resistance movements in occupied territory during WWII, it has been noted that in occupied Russian areas, the resistance fought to restore Russian sovereignty, while in the Balkans, Tito organised his partisans as a tool to establish a new political regime at the end of the occupation.[3] Similarly, during the Soviet occupation of Afghanistan, the Afghani resistance was fighting to restore the independence of its country,[4] while in the case of the resistance against the US-led occupation of Iraq, only some groups had ties with the former regime.[5]

Moreover, despite the clear link between violence in the occupied territory and the will of the local population to put the occupation to an end, which has been noted also by the UN Secretary-General,[6] the situation of occupation itself is not the only trigger to violence against the occupying power. For instance, during the Second Intifada, the desire to overthrow the Israeli occupation was only one of the reasons leading to the uprising, along

---

[2] For an overview of the practice prior to WWI, see Nabulsi, *Traditions*, 55–63.
[3] See John Shy & Thomas W. Collier, 'Revolutionary War' in Peter Paret (ed.), *Makers of Modern Strategy from Machiavelli to the Nuclear Age* (Princeton University Press 1986) 833.
[4] See, generally, W. Michael Reisman, 'The Resistance in Afghanistan is Engaged in a War of National Liberation' (1987) 81 AJIL 906.
[5] See Watkin, 'Use of Force', 279–83.
[6] See Follow-up to the Outcome of the Millennium Summit, paras. 21, 36, 145, and 148(a).

with personal, religious, economic, and social motives.[7] Similarly, during the occupation of Iraq, ordinary crime was almost as dangerous as insurgency from armed groups.[8]

In addition, international practice demonstrates that the scale of the violence the occupying power may face may vary depending on specific circumstances. For instance, the two Palestinian intifadas that bloodied the OPT in 1987 and in 2000 presented different features even though they were both examples of uprising against the occupying power. The First Intifada was characterised by 'popular street demonstrations and commercial strikes' in which demonstrators 'burned tires, threw stones and Molotov cocktails at Israeli cars, brandished iron bars, and waved the Palestinian flag'.[9] During the Second Intifada the violence had a decidedly different character, extending to guerrilla warfare against Israeli vehicles, ambushes, and the placement of improvised explosive devices targeting both civilians and combatants.[10] The two different uprisings posed different challenges to the occupying power, which in turn reacted in different ways: during the First Intifada, Israel 'used the full panoply of crowd control measures to quell the disturbances: cudgels, night sticks, tear gas, water cannons, rubber bullets and live ammunition',[11] while, during the Second Intifada, Israel employed more robust means and methods of warfare.[12]

Moreover, occupying powers may face different threats contextually in the same occupied territory. For instance, while Israel was engaged in the large-scale operation Cast Lead against the Gaza Strip in 2009, at the same time Israeli troops were involved in quelling demonstrations in the West Bank through interventions that ranged from incursions to search-and-arrest operations.[13] Similarly, the situation of occupied Iraq was described as a 'mosaic war', in which different kinds of uprisings and demonstrations were happening at the same time in different areas of the occupied territory.[14]

---

[7] See, e.g., Assaf Moghadam, 'Palestinian Suicide Terrorism in the Second Intifada: Motivations and Organizational Aspects' (2003) 65 SCT 65.

[8] See Amnesty International, *Iraq: Looting, Lawlessness and Humanitarian Consequences*, 10 April 2013, available at www.amnesty.org/en/documents/mde14/085/2003/en/, and *Iraq: The Need for Security*, 3 July 2003, available at www.amnesty.org/en/documents/mde14/143/2003/en/

[9] Avi Shlaim, *Israel and Palestine: Reappraisals, Revisions, Refutations* (Verso 2009) 32–3.

[10] See Sergio Catignani, *Israeli Counter-Insurgency and the Intifadas: Dilemmas of a Conventional Army* (Routledge 2008) 104–6; Benny Morris, *One State, Two States: Resolving the Israel/Palestine Conflict* (Yale University Press 2009) 150–1.

[11] Shlaim, *Israel*, 33.

[12] Catignani, *Israeli Counter-Insurgency*, 108.

[13] Goldstone Report, para. 1381.

[14] US Army Marine Counterinsurgency Field Manual, sections 1–37.

Even such a cursory glance at state practice demonstrates that situations in which the occupying power may resort to armed force are various and that, accordingly, the armed response may have different characteristics, case by case. In this respect, the situation of resistance in occupied territory is similar to that of the partisan in Carl Schmitt's analysis, according to which there are a variety of different triggers and motivations for partisans in different scenarios.[15]

This book considers the specific function that the occupying power has to perform on a case by case basis as the main element to take into account. First, the occupying power may resort to armed force in the context of the restoration and maintenance of public order. In this scenario, the governmental functions of the occupying power play a decisive role in the employment of armed force, which follows the law-enforcement paradigm. Second, the occupying power may be required to deal with the resumption of hostilities, where the force employed is similar to that typical of hostilities occurring during an armed conflict outside occupied territory.

5.3. LAW ENFORCEMENT AND THE MAINTENANCE AND RESTORATION OF PUBLIC ORDER IN OCCUPIED TERRITORY

5.3.1. *The Duty to Restore and Ensure Public Order in Occupied Territory and the Use of Armed Force*

The maintenance and restoration of public order is the main legal framework pertaining to the use of armed force in occupied territory. The regulation of these activities is embodied in Article 43 HR, according to which the occupying power 'prendra toutes les mesures qui dépendent de lui en vue de rétablir et d'assurer, autant qu'il est possible, l'ordre et la vie publics'. In the debate over the adoption of the 1874 Brussels Declaration, the Belgian delegate suggested that 'l'ordre publique' stays for 'la securité ou la sureté générale'.[16] Public order encompasses 'responsibility for preserving order, punishing crime, and protecting lives and property within the occupied territory'.[17] International law 'imposes upon the occupant the duty to maintain public order and to provide for the preservation of the rights of the inhabitants. The emphasis is upon

---

[15] See Carl Schmitt, *Theorie des Partisanen, Zwischenbemerkungzum Begriff des Politischen* (Duncker & Humblot 1963). This similarity has been noted by Marco Pertile, 'Fighting Terror', 276–7.
[16] Quoted in Benvenisti, *The International Law*, 77.
[17] *Hostages* case, 57. See, also, US, Supreme Court, *Ochoa v. Hernandez y Morales*, (1913) 230 US 139, 159, according to which the occupying power has the duty 'to do whatever … necessary to secure public safety, social order, and the guaranties of private property'.

public order and safety, and the welfare of the inhabitants'.[18] The occupying power's duties regarding public order encompass 'responsibility for ensuring the safety and security of the population in the occupied territory'[19] since 'the occupant cannot sit idly by if marauders pester the occupied territory, killing local inhabitants, even though no soldiers of the army of occupation get injured'.[20] The expression 'all the measures' encompasses the occupying power's resort to armed force.[21]

The occupying power's duty to restore and ensure public order under Article 43 HR also encompasses the occupying power's faculty to provide for its own security. Indeed, although the occupying power may not rely on *jus ad bellum*, it is not required to stand idle and 'turn the other cheek',[22] but rather, is entitled to respond to security threats pursuant to the law of occupation. This conclusion is clearly covered by the non-binding English text of Article 43 HR, according to which the occupying power must restore and ensure 'public order and safety'. As the ICJ acknowledged in the *Wall* opinion with regard to the OPT, Israel 'has to face numerous indiscriminate and deadly acts of violence against its civilian population. It has the right, and indeed the duty, to respond in order to protect the life of its citizens'.[23] The occupying power's faculty to defend itself and its own citizens was also acknowledged by the vast majority of states that took part in the aforementioned debates regarding the legality of some Israeli military actions in the OPT, even if, as a Section 3.2 showed, these states were reluctant to invoke the concept of self-defence. Moreover, this faculty has been long recognised both by international[24] and domestic case law,[25] and is acknowledged by Article 64 GC IV, according to which the law in force in the occupied territory may be altered if this is essential to 'ensure the security of the occupying power, of the members

---

[18] US, District Court D Utah, Central Division, *Aboitiz & Co. v. Price*, (D Utah 1951) 99 *Federal Supplement* 602, 610.
[19] This is the position of Mexico regarding occupied Iraq, as expressed in S/PV.4808, 5.
[20] Dinstein, 'The International Law', 111.
[21] Ibid., 112.
[22] Andreas Paulus, 'UN Missions and the Law of Occupation' in Andreas von Arnauld, Nele Matz-Lück, & Kerstin Odendahl (eds.), *100 Years of Peace through Law: Past and Future* (Duncker & Humblot 2015) 237, section II.3.
[23] *Wall* opinion, para. 141.
[24] See *Affaire Chevreau (France v. Royaume-Uni)*, 9 June 1931, 2 RIAA 1113, 1123: 'L'Arbitre estime ne pas pouvoir nier aux forces britanniques opérant en Perse le droit d'y prendre les mesures nécessaires pour se protéger contre des actes de la population civile qui seraient de nature à nuire aux opérations ou à favoriser l'ennemi'.
[25] See Greece, Court of First Instance of Corfu, *V v. O* (1 January 1947), 14 ILR 264, 265; US, District Court D Utah, Central Division, *Aboitiz & Co. v. Price*, 610 (international law 'has recognized the right of the protection of [the occupying power's] military interests and the exercise of police powers').

5.3. Law Enforcement and Public Order

and property of the occupying forces or administration'. This provision is a specification of the general rule embodied in Article 27(4) GC IV, according to which 'the Parties to the conflict may take such measures of control and security in regard to protected persons as may be necessary as a result of the war'.[26] It follows that the occupying power has the *faculty* to restore and ensure public order in its own interest, and the *duty* to do so in the interests of the population of the occupied territory and of the ousted sovereign. However, the law of occupation does not spell out precisely the conditions in which the occupying power may resort to armed force.[27]

There is no doubt that Article 43 HR provides occupying powers with legal obligations, and not only faculties, regarding the maintenance of public order. This conclusion is confirmed by SC Resolution 1483 (2003), in which the SC called upon the CPA 'to promote the welfare of the Iraqi people through the effective administration of the territory, including in particular working towards *the restoration of conditions of security and stability*'.[28] France explained this passage as follows: 'Security must be restored as soon as possible throughout the territory of Iraq. The resolution affirms the obligations of the occupying Powers in this area'[29] and '[p]ending the full restoration of Iraqi sovereignty, that responsibility falls first of all to the occupying Powers pursuant to international law'.[30] The CPA recognised this duty immediately in one of its first pieces of legislation, according to which the CPA 'shall exercise powers of government temporarily in order to ... restore conditions of security and stability'.[31] The fact that Article 43 HR embodies an obligation is also confirmed by the possibility to seek compensation for violations of the duty to restore and ensure public order.[32]

It is important to emphasise that the duty to restore and ensure public order is an obligation of means or conduct rather than an obligation of result,[33] as

---

[26] On the relationship between Art. 27(4) GC IV and the maintenance and restoration of public order in times of occupation, see Melzer, *Targeted Killing*, 157–64.
[27] See Garraway, 'Occupation', 277; Venturini, 'L'operazione', 317; Ferraro (ed.), *Expert Meeting*, 109–10.
[28] UNSC Res. 1483 (2003), para. 4 (emphasis added).
[29] France, S/PV.4761, 3–4.
[30] S/PV.4812, 6.
[31] CPA Regulation no. 1, 16 May 2003, available at govinfo.library.unt.edu/cpa-iraq/regulations/20030516_CPAREG_1_The_Coalition_Provisional_Authority_.pdf
[32] See UN Compensation Commission, *Governing Council Decision no. 9* (6 March 1992), 109 ILR 593, paras. 12–15.
[33] See Marco Sassòli, 'Legislation and Maintenance of Public Order and Civil Life by Occupying Powers' (2005) 16 EJIL 661, 664–5; Dinstein, *The International Law*, 91–2; Alexandra Perina, 'Legal Bases for Coalition Combat Operations in Iraq, May 2003-Present' (2010) 86 ILS 81, 84.

is clear from the words 'as far as possible' in Article 43 HR and as recognised by the Supreme Court of Israel.[34] In the case of an obligation of conduct, states must 'deploy adequate means, to do the utmost, to obtain [a] result'[35] employing the due diligence required by the duty; however, states may not be held responsible if, notwithstanding their diligent conduct, the result is not obtained.[36] Accordingly, if public order in the occupied territory is disrupted,

[34] See HCJ 69/81 *Abu Aita* et al. v. *Regional Commander of the Judea and Samaria Area* et al., 37(2) PD 197, para. 50(c), unofficial English translation available at www.hamoked.org/files/2011/290_eng.pdf:

> The drafters of the Regulations defining these duties did not use unequivocal and absolute language, but from the outset kept in mind the objective difficulties that might emerge from a change of government resulting from a military operation, when the new government continues to function as a military government which is of legal temporary character. Hence, the duties were defined as being conditional on what is possible (d'autant qu'il est possible). The degree of possibility of fulfillment of the duties is measured according to a complex of circumstances, that is, not only in the light of the needs of the territory, but also in the light of the legitimate needs of the military government.

[35] ITLOS, *Responsibilities and Obligations of States Sponsoring Persons and Entities with Respect to Activities in the Area*, Advisory opinion, 1 February 2011, para. 110. The distinction between obligations of means or conduct and obligations of result was introduced in the debate regarding the law of international responsibility by the special rapporteur Roberto Ago (draft Arts. 20 and 21 in Report of the International Law Commission on Its 29th Session, (1977-II) YILC 11). Even though Ago's proposal was not included in the DARS, the distinction between obligations of means or conduct and obligations of result has attracted the attention of many scholars (see Jean Combacau, 'Obligations de résultat et obligations de comportement: quelques questions et pas de réponse' in Daniel Bardonnet, Jean Combacau, Michel Virally, & Prosper Weil (eds.), *Mélanges offerts a Paul Reuter* (Pedone 1981) 181; Benedetto Conforti, 'Obblighi di mezzi e obblighi di risultato nelle convenzioni di diritto uniforme' in Tullio Treves, Fausto Pocar, Tullio Scovazzi, & Roberta Clerici (eds.), *Studi in memoria di Mario Giuliano* (Cedam 1989) 373; Pierre-Marie Dupuy, 'Reviewing the Difficulties of Codification: On Ago's Classification of Obligations of Means and Obligations of Result in Relation to State Responsibility' (1999) 10 EJIL 371; Antonio Marchesi, *Obblighi di condotta e obblighi di risultato: contributo allo studio degli obblighi internazionali* (Giuffré 2003); Constantin P. Economidés, 'Content of the Obligation: Obligations of Means and Obligations of Result' in James Crawford, Alain Pellet, & Simon Olleson (eds.), *The Law of International Responsibility* (Oxford University Press 2010) 371).

[36] See ICJ, *Application of the Convention on the Prevention and Punishment of the Crime of Genocide (Bosnia and Herzegovina v. Serbia and Montenegro)*, 26 February 2007, para. 430. On due diligence, see Riccardo Pisillo Mazzeschi, *'Due Diligence' e responsabilità internazionale degli Stati* (Giuffré 1989), and 'The Due Diligence Rule and the Nature of International Responsibility of States' (1992) 35 German YIL 9; José Fernando Lozano Contreras, *La nociòn de debida diligencia en derecho internacional public* (Atelier 2006); Timo Koivurova, 'Due Diligence', in *MPEPIL online* (2010); Joanna Kulesza, *Due Diligence in International Law* (Brill 2016); Maja Seršić,'Due Diligence: Fault-based Responsibility or Autonomous Standard?' in Rüdiger Wolfrum, Maja Seršić, & Trpimir M. Šošić (eds.), *Contemporary Developments in International Law: Essays in Honour of Budislav Vukas* (Brill 2016) 151.

5.3. Law Enforcement and Public Order

the occupying power may not be considered responsible as long as it manages to demonstrate that it has taken all the feasible measures in its power to restore and ensure public order.[37]

There are some differences between the duty to 'restore' and the duty to 'ensure' public order.[38] While the duty to 'ensure' public order is linked to the temporal dimension of the occupation since, as long as the occupation lasts, the occupying power must take every feasible measure to avoid disorders, the duty to restore public order mainly addresses the immediate aftermath of the occupation, when the invasion of the territory and the attempts to resist the incoming occupying power may have created chaos in the occupied territory.[39] For instance, at the beginning of the CPA's occupation, Iraq was in a situation of extreme chaos due to the dismantling of Saddam Hussain's regime and a general release of common criminals in 2002: in the aftermath of the invasion, a huge number of personal revenges, looting of private and public goods, kidnappings, and other violent activities occurred,[40] with an estimated 10,000 Iraqi civilians killed in the year following the US invasion.[41] At first, the Coalition troops failed to intervene, and the main cities of Iraq were systematically stripped of everything of value while the Coalition tried to establish its authority over Iraq.[42] However, once it had been established, the CPA attempted to restore public order through some ordinances that, on the one hand, required the dissolution of a number of former governmental entities such as the Ministry of Defence and related military organisations,[43] and on the other, sharply restricted the ability of the local population to carry arms.[44] It is likely that dismantling the Iraqi security and defence forces did not contribute the restoration of public order since they could have helped the CPA in dealing with the disorder and criminality.[45]

The occupying power replaces the ousted sovereign with regard to every duty concerning the restoration and maintenance of public order in occupied territory. For instance, the presence of UN personnel and facilities does not

---

[37] Sassòli, 'Legislation', 664; Longobardo, 'State Responsibility', 267–9.
[38] This distinction has been emphasised by the Supreme Court of Israel on a number of occasions. See e.g. *Abu Aita*, para. 50(c); *Jam'iat Iscan Al-Ma'almoun*, para. 18.
[39] See Benvenisti, *The International Law*, 78.
[40] See Amnesty International, *Iraq: Looting*, and *Iraq: The Need*. See, also, Phillip James Walker, 'Iraq and Occupation' in David H. Wippman & Michael Evangelista (eds.), *New Wars, New Laws? Applying Laws of War in 21st Century Conflicts* (Martinus Nijhoff 2005) 259, 269–74.
[41] David H. Bayley & R. M. Perito, *The Police in War: Fighting Insurgency, Terrorism, and Violent Crime* (Lynne Rienner Publishers 2010) 7.
[42] See ibid., 6.
[43] See CPA Order no. 2, 23 May 2003.
[44] See CPA Order no. 3, 31 December 2003.
[45] See Watkin, 'Use of Force', 280.

transfer the occupying power's responsibilities regarding the restoration and maintenance of public order to the UN,[46] but rather, the occupying power is in charge of the safety of UN facilities and property in occupied territory.[47] Moreover, the occupying power is responsible for the safety of foreign states' diplomatic missions located in occupied territory,[48] as demonstrated by the CPA's creation of units with the aim to protect diplomatic missions.[49] Furthermore, the occupying power has a duty of vigilance over private actors' conduct that may violate international humanitarian law and international human rights law.[50] Similarly, the occupying power replaces the sovereign with regard to the duty not to allow private actors to use the controlled territory to harm other states, as confirmed by the ICJ with regard to Namibia[51] and by state practice regarding the occupation of Iraq.[52]

In light of this duty to restore and ensure public order in the occupied territory, Article 43 HR is often considered to be the legal basis for the use of armed force by the occupying power in the occupied territory.[53] However, this assumption is not entirely accurate. As already explained, and *jus ad bellum* notwithstanding, the only source for the use of armed force in the occupied territory is the existence of a state of armed conflict that lasts until the end of the occupation.[54] Usually, international humanitarian law, along with other applicable international law rules, regulates the way (*quomodo*) in which military operations are conducted, not the possibility of launching

---

[46] See Report of the Secretary-General pursuant to paragraph 24 of Security Council resolution 1483 (2003), S/2003/715, para. 105.

[47] See the statements of Germany and China in the aftermath of an attack against UN facilities in Iraq, S/PV.4812, 8 and 9–10.

[48] See the remarks by China in S/PV.4812, 9–10 and the practice collected by Stefan Talmon, 'Diplomacy under Occupation: The Status of Diplomatic Missions in Occupied Iraq' (2006) 6 *Anuario Mexicano de Derecho Internacional* 461, 502–5.

[49] See CPA Order no. 27, 4 September 2003, section 2.6.

[50] See *DRC v. Uganda*, paras. 178 and 250. See also EECC, *Partial Award: Central Front – Eritrea's Claims* 2, 4, 6, 7, 8 *and* 22, para. 67. For an analysis of the basis of this kind of responsibility, see Longobardo, 'State Responsibility'.

[51] See *Namibia* opinion, para. 118:

> The fact that South Africa no longer has any title to administer the Territory does not release it from its obligations and responsibilities under international law towards other States in respect of the exercise of its powers in relation to this Territory. Physical control of a territory, and not sovereignty or legitimacy of title, is the basis of State liability for acts affecting other States.

[52] See the Joint Statement of Iraq's Neighboring States, 2 November 2003, in Talmon (ed.), *The Occupation*, 1453, 1454, para. 7.

[53] See, e.g., Capotorti, *L'occupazione*, 114–15.

[54] See *supra*, Section 3.4.

these operations (*an*), which is the concern of *jus ad bellum*. However, the situation of the occupied territory is different from other situations where hostilities are conducted since the occupying power is vested with governmental functions, and the population of the occupied territory is in the hands of the enemy *par définition*.[55] Accordingly, there is the need to further restrain the occupying power's potential to resort to armed force: this is the role of Article 43 HR and Article 64 GC IV, which impose additional limitations on the use of armed force by the occupying power with regard to the aim of the force employed. According to Article 43 HR and Article 64 GC IV, only armed force employed to restore and ensure public order in the occupied territory, as well as to guarantee the occupying power's security, is lawful. Force employed to other ends – even if, in principle, in line with the rules pertaining to the conduct of hostilities or applicable to law-enforcement operations – should be considered illegal.

Admittedly, state practice has afforded great latitude to occupying powers with respect to the invocation of Article 43 HR. However, there is a trend in international case law demonstrating that Article 43 HR should be read as *restricting* the occupying power's faculties with respect to those of a state involved in the armed conflict without controlling a portion of territory effectively. For instance, an arbitral tribunal affirmed that '[A]rticle 43 [HR] a pour objet non de mettre l'occupant au benefice d'un privilège ou d'un droit, mais, au contraire, de lui imposer une obligation'.[56] Similarly, a Dutch court clearly affirmed that this provision's aim 'was to *define* the limits of the exercise of the actual power of the occupant'[57] and that it was 'intended to *curtail* the powers of the enemy over occupied territory, and not to define its rights against the population'.[58] More recently, the Supreme Court of Israel affirmed that '[t]he discretion of the military commander is *restricted* by the normative system in which he acts, and which is the source of his authority',[59] since the law of occupation 'imposes conditions on the use of this authority'.[60]

Although Article 43 HR is not the 'source' of the entitlement to the use of armed force in occupied territory, this provision is crucial to understanding the legal framework applicable to every armed confrontation occurring

---

[55] See Art. 4 GC IV. See, also, ICTY, *Prosecutor v. Tadic*, Opinion and Judgment (Trial Chamber), para. 579.
[56] German-Belgian Mixed Arbitral Tribunal, *Milaire v. État Allemand*, (1923) 2 RDTAM 715, 719 (quoted in Arai-Takahashi, *The Law*, 103).
[57] Holland, Special Criminal Court, The Hague, *In re Contractor Work*, 353 (emphasis added).
[58] Holland, Special Criminal Court, The Hague, *In re van Huis*, 350 (emphasis added).
[59] *Beit Sourik*, para. 33 (emphasis added).
[60] Ibid. para. 34.

in the occupied territory. Its most visible role is prescribing the use of law-enforcement instruments to deal with the maintenance and restoration of public order, thanks to the government-like responsibilities this provision introduces in the hostile environment of the occupation.[61] Less well explored is the idea that Article 43 HR may be regarded as the norm for explaining the shift from law enforcement to the conduct of hostilities, again by virtue of the fine balance that this provision strikes between the governmental and the hostile characteristics of the occupying power's administration.[62]

In conclusion, the law of occupation is undoubtedly the main legal framework pertaining to the use of armed force in the occupied territory. However, rather than conferring on the occupying power the right to employ armed force, Article 43 HR and Article 64 GC IV limit the cases in which the occupying power may resort to armed force to the maintenance and restoration of public order, and to providing for its own security. Moreover, the law of occupation is useful to determine those cases in which the occupying power may resort to armed force in the context of law-enforcement operations, and those cases in which it may resort to hostilities.

5.3.2. *International Humanitarian Law Conventions and the Restoration and Maintenance of Public Order*

Before the adoption of the HR, international law allowed the occupying power to restore and ensure public order through whatever means, since the legality of the repression of the occupying power was considered to be outside the scope of international law.[63] The adoption of the HR did not change the legal framework significantly since the HR provided no indication of the way in which the occupying power could implement its duty to restore and ensure public order. Accordingly, the occupying power could adopt any measures in its power as long as it did not infringe on the few limitations imposed by the HR,[64] such as the respect for the allegiances of the local population pursuant to Articles 44 and 45 HR, the respect for the basic rights of the local population pursuant to Article 46 HR, and the ban on collective punishment under Article 50 HR. Outside the boundaries of these provisions, the occupying power was free to resort to any means to restore and ensure public order and

---

[61] This aspect is explored *infra*, Section 5.3.3.2.
[62] This assertion is argued in details *infra*, Section 5.6.2.
[63] See Calvo, *Le droit*, 218; Fiore, *Trattato* vol. III, 267.
[64] See Pertile, 'L'adozione', 300, with reference to the aforementioned tripartition of the norms of the law of occupation envisaged by Capotorti, *L'occupazione*, 141–4.

guarantee its own security.[65] Drastic means – such as reprisals against civilians and taking of hostages – were considered in line with customary international law,[66] and trials against members of the population of the occupied territory, if held, did not respect the rights of the accused.[67]

However, during WWII, Germany deliberately disregarded the HR provisions pertaining to the way in which an occupying power may ensure and restore public order and protect its own safety. The Nazi regime systematically violated all the main tenets of the law of occupation, especially the rights of the population of the occupied territories.[68] As demonstrated by the findings of domestic and international trials held after WWII, Germany adopted heinous means such as taking hostages, collective punishment, forcible transfers and deportations, reprisals against civilians, and many other brutal measures. These measures were not intended only to restore and ensure public order in the occupied territory, but rather, 'the mass murders and cruelties ... were part of a plan to get rid of whole native populations by expulsion and annihilation, in order that their territory could be used for colonisation by Germans'.[69] Accordingly, during the Nuremberg trial before the IMT[70] and before postwar domestic courts,[71] many Nazi officials were tried for war crimes related to serious violations of both HR rules on occupation and other applicable rules of *jus in bello*.

After these dramatic experiences, states decided to impose on occupying powers additional limits regarding the activity of restoration and maintenance of public order, mainly codifying principles and rules that had already been envisaged in the case law of the IMT and of domestic occupation and military courts. Since 1949, Article 49 GC IV has generally prohibited individual or mass forcible transfers and deportations of protected persons from occupied

[65] De Visscher, 'L'occupation', 77; Capotorti, *L'occupazione*, 114–18.
[66] See the state practice referred to by Stone, *Legal Controls*, 702–4; Nabulsi, *Traditions*, 22–36.
[67] See G. M. Spaight, *War Rights on Land* (MacMillan & Co. 1911) 349–50; Balladore Pallieri, *Diritto*, 318–19.
[68] For a description of the brutal means employed by Germany in occupied territory, see Raphael Lemkin, *Axis Rule in Occupied Europe: Laws of Occupation, Analysis of Government, Proposals for Redress* (Carnegie Endowment for International Peace 1944). On the missed application of the law of occupation by Germany during WWII, see Lauterpacht, *Oppenheim's International Law*, 448–51. On the lack of compliance with the law of occupation by most belligerents during WWII, see Benvenisti, *The International Law*, 131–66.
[69] US Military Tribunal at Nuremberg, *In re Von Leeb* et al. (1948), 12 LRTWC 1, 22.
[70] See, e.g., IMT, *In re Goering*; *Hostage* case.
[71] See British Military Court, Hamburg, *In re Tesch* et al. (*Zyklon B* case) (8 March 1946), 13 ILR 250; British Military Court, Luneburg, *In re Kramer* et al., (17 November 1945) 13 ILR 267; French Military Court, Strasbourg, *In re Wagner* et al. (3 May 1946), 13 ILR 385; Poland, Voivodship Court for the Voivodship of Warsaw, *In re Koch* (10 November 1959), 30 ILR 496.

territory; these measures may be adopted only for the temporary evacuation of a given area 'if the security of the population or imperative military reasons' so require, at the same time granting to the evacuated people their health, hygiene, nutrition, safety, and family unit, as well as the return to their land. Moreover, Article 51 GC IV reinforces the ban on enlisting people of the occupied territory to work for the occupying power, while Article 34 GC IV states that the taking of hostages is prohibited – an innovative rule, if one considers the failure of the US Military Tribunal at Nuremberg to rule out completely the possibility of an occupying power taking hostages to ensure order.[72]

Significantly, the drafters of the GC IV recognised that the main instrument to restore and ensure public order is criminal law and an effective judicial system. As has been suggested in the wake of the occupation of Iraq, '[t]he restoration of law and order rests in part on the development of a fully functioning and effective justice system'.[73] The main criminal law system and judicial apparatus that are tasked with the maintenance and restoration of public order in occupied territory are those of the occupied territory itself, pursuant to the continuity principle embodied in Article 43 HR and other related provisions.[74] This principle is confirmed by Article 64(1) GC IV, according to which the tribunals of the occupied territory remain in function and must apply the criminal law in force in the occupied territory. The criminal law in force in the occupied territory may have different origins; for instance, in the OPT, Israel has invoked security regulations adopted during the British Mandate in order to ensure public order and prosecute offenders, arguing that they had never been repealed and were thus law in force in the occupied territory under Article 43 HR.[75]

However, the conservation of the criminal law in force prior to the occupation is not absolute: under Article 64(1) GC IV, the criminal laws in force in the occupied territory may be 'repealed or suspended by the occupying power [only] in cases where they constitute a threat to its security or an obstacle to the application of the [GC IV]'. This was the case of the Iraqi criminal code and judicial systems, which had permitted egregious violations of human rights under Saddam Hussein's regime,[76] and which, accordingly, have been

[72] See *Hostage* case, 61.
[73] See the statement of UK in S/PV.4812, 5.
[74] See Burma, High Court of Judicature, *The King v. Maung Hmin* et al. (11 March 1946), 13 ILR 334, 336.
[75] See Israel, Military Court Sitting in Nablus, *Military Prosecutor v. Saad* et al. (1 November 1968), 47 ILR 476; Israel, Military Court Sitting in Ramallah, *Military Prosecutor v. Bakhis* et al. (10 June 1968), 47 ILR 484.
[76] On the atrocities of the Ba'athist judicial regime, see Human Rights Watch, *World Report 2005*, 467, available at pantheon.hrw.org/legacy/wr2k5/wr2005.pdf; Michael J. Kelly, 'Iraq and the Law of Occupation: New Tests for an Old Law' (2003) 6 YIHL 127, 139–42.

5.3. Law Enforcement and Public Order

repealed by the CPA.[77] The same continuity rationale is behind Article 54(1) GC IV, according to which 'the occupying power may not alter the status of public officials or judges in the occupied territories'. This provision is applicable to judges, prosecutors, and police officers; its role with regard to the use of armed force is discussed in a subsequent section.[78]

However, in the fields of public order and occupying powers' security, the GC IV widens the legislative powers conferred to the occupying powers. According to Article 64(2) GC IV, the occupying power may pass new legislation that is 'essential to enable the occupying power to fulfil its obligations under the present Convention, to *maintain the orderly government* of the territory, and to *ensure the security* of the occupying power, of the members and property of the occupying forces or administration'.[79] As has already been mentioned, this pivotal provision must be interpreted in light of Article 43 HR so that the 'empêchement absolu' clause in Article 43 HR should be read now as encompassing cases in which new legislation is essential in order to allow the occupying power to implement international humanitarian law, to restore and ensure public order, and to provide for its own security. However, new legislation is only an exceptional means to ensure public order, as demonstrated by the word 'essential' embodied in Article 64(2) GC IV. Accordingly, the burden of proof regarding the justification for the adoption of such measures rests on the occupying power.

Article 64(2) GC IV allows the occupying power to introduce new legislation in order to provide for its own security. In the practice of occupation, provisions explicitly criminalising violent activities against the occupying power are quite common. Very often these new laws passed by the occupying power are labelled as counterterrorism measures. The use of the expressions 'terrorism' and 'counterterrorism' may generate some confusion. As already noted, international humanitarian law does not recognise the existence of terrorism as a status but, rather, prohibits some conduct that aims to spread terror among the population which, in peacetime, are usually considered to be 'acts of terror' or 'terrorism'.[80] The aforementioned clauses, excluding the applicability of some international conventions on terrorism to actions occurring in situations of occupation,[81] do not prevent the occupying power from labelling as terrorism conduct against its security that may result in destabilisation of public order in occupied territory. Instead, the main aim of those counterterrorism

---

[77] See Order no. 7, 10 June 2003, and Order no. 31, 31 September 2003.
[78] See *infra*, Section 5.3.3.2.
[79] Emphases added. See also HCJ 3239/02 *Marab* et al. v. *IDF Commander*, 57(2) PD 349, para. 21, unofficial English translation available at www.hamoked.org/files/2012/3720_eng.pdf
[80] See, *supra*, Section 4.3.2.
[81] Ibid.

conventions is to impose a duty of domestic criminalisation regarding certain conduct; their clauses excluding the application in times of armed conflict and occupation simply exclude *the duty of criminalisation*, without, however, introducing a *duty not to criminalise* as terrorism such conduct.[82] In these cases, acts of armed resistance against the occupying power are not considered acts of terrorism *under international law*[83] but, rather, they may be punished by the new legislation enacted by the occupying power on the basis of the law of occupation. Accordingly, the recourse to the category of 'terrorism' is mainly a political choice that is not linked to the international law notions of terrorism embodied in international conventions. For instance, South Africa passed the Terrorism Act no. 83 in 1967 in order to address SWAPO's resistance in occupied Namibia,[84] and considered itself involved in a counterterrorism campaign.[85] On the other hand, the Supreme Court of Israel reasoned under the law of occupation and the category of the maintenance and restoration of public order pursuant to article 43 HR, invoking at the same time, and for mainly rhetorical reasons, the concept of terrorism.[86] Finally, the CPA failed to define as terrorists individuals from Iraq who threatened the public order in the occupied territory.[87] However, even courts of states different from the occupying power have considered some conduct disrupting public order in the occupied territory as terrorist in nature, as in the *Daki* case decided by the Italian Court of Cassation, which pertained to conduct that occurred in occupied Iraq.[88] For the purposes of this book, what is important to emphasise

---

[82] See ECJ, *A et al.*, C-158/14, 14 March 2017, para. 16. This position had already been suggested by Andrea Gioia, 'Terroristi o combattenti: un'alternativa credibile alla luce del diritto internazionale?' (2007) 29 *Ragion Pratica* 355, 360.

[83] See Saul, *Defining Terrorism*, 77–8.

[84] On this act and its judicial application, see Christina Murray, 'The Status of the ANC and SWAPO and International Humanitarian Law' (1983) 100 *South African Law Journal* 402, and 'The 1977 Geneva Protocols and Conflict in Southern Africa' (1984) 33 ICLQ 462.

[85] See Republic of South Africa, *Report of the Commission of Inquiry into Reporting of Security Matters Regarding the South African Defence Force and the South African Police Force* (1980) 70–1.

[86] See Pertile, 'Fighting Terror', 281–6.

[87] In some speeches, the US and UK leaders made a distinction between 'terrorists' (individuals infiltrating from outside Iraq) and 'insurgents' (individuals from within the country). See, e.g., Declaration on Iraq by President George W. Bush and Prime Minister Tony Blair, 20 November 2003, available at https://georgewbush-whitehouse.archives.gov/news/releases/2003/11/20031120-1.html; President Bush Addresses Nation, Discusses Iraq, War on Terror, 28 June 2005, available at https://georgewbush-whitehouse.archives.gov/news/releases/2005/06/20050628-7.html

[88] Italy, Court of Cassation, *Procuratore Generale della Repubblica c Daki, Bouyahia e Toumi* (17 January 2007), (2008) 44 RDIPP 812 (see the comments offered by Maria Chiara Noto, 'Le sanzioni del Consiglio di sicurezza e il terrorismo internazionale nella giurisprudenza penale nazionale: il caso *Daki*' (2008) 44 RDIPP 732; Gioia, 'Terroristi o combattenti'; Gabriele Della Morte, 'Sulla giurisprudenza italiana in tema di terrorismo internazionale'

is that, under the law of occupation, terrorism does not represent a separate issue, but rather, it should be addressed in the same way and under the same legal rules pertaining to the maintenance and restoration of public order.[89]

Moreover, the occupying power's ability to create new offences is not restricted only to the cases of Article 64(2) GC IV, but generally measures adopted with retaliatory intent or which could be applied disregarding procedural guarantees are forbidden. For instance, the occupying power has the duty to inform the population of the occupied territory regarding the existence of these new offences, which should not have retroactive effects.[90] The tribunals created by the occupying power in relation to new offences must be 'properly constituted, non-political military courts' located in the occupied territory,[91] and they must take in due consideration the fact that the accused is not a national of the occupying power.[92] These tribunals may pass death penalty judgments only in very specific cases,[93] 'provided that such offences were punishable by death under the law of the occupied territory in force before the occupation began',[94] and except for any person under eighteen.[95] These tribunals are forbidden from passing judgments regarding conduct occurred before the beginning of the occupation.[96]

With regard to the procedural rights of the accused, occupying power's tribunals may pass judgment only after 'regular' trials.[97] The need for a fair trial for the accused in the case of offences against the occupying power has been particularly evident in cases pertaining to the summary executions

---

(2009) 92 RDI 443). Similarly, although in the context of a non-international armed conflict, the ECJ affirmed that 'actions by armed forces during periods of armed conflict, within the meaning of international humanitarian law, may constitute "terrorist acts" *for the purposes of those acts of the European Union*' (ECJ, A et al., para. 97 (emphasis added); see Jose Antonio Valles Cavia, 'El concepto de acto terrorista y el comportamiento de fuerzas armadas durante un conflicto armado' (2017) 57 *Revista de Derecho Comunitario Europeo* 689).

[89] Accordingly, the distinction between terrorism and ordinary crimes supported by some authors (see, e.g., Katharina Parameswaran, 'The Use of Military Force and the Applicable Standards of Force Governing Police Operations in Occupied Territories' (2006) 45 MLLWR 249, 250) is only descriptive and does not entail different legal considerations.

[90] See Art. 65 GC IV.

[91] See Art. 66 GC IV. For more on this topic, see generally Kathleen Cavanaugh, 'The Israeli Military Court System in the West Bank and Gaza' (2007) 12 JCSL 197; Sharon Weill, 'The Judicial Arm of the Occupation: The Israeli Military Courts in the Occupied Territories' (2007) 89 IRRC 395; Yutaka Arai-Takahashi, 'Law-Making and the Judicial Guarantees in Occupied Territories' in Clapham, Gaeta, & Sassòli (eds.), *The 1949 Geneva Conventions*, 1421, 1429–36.

[92] See Art. 67 GC IV and Art. 68(2) GC IV.

[93] See Art. 68(2) GC IV.

[94] Art. 68(3) GC IV.

[95] Art. 68(4) GC IV.

[96] See Art. 70 GC IV.

[97] See Art. 71(1) GC IV.

of civilians during WWII, where courts have recognised the existence of such a right even in the absence of any specification in the HR.[98] Articles 71 through 75 GC IV provide a list of procedural rights that codify the basic judicial guarantees in the occupied territory. These guarantees should not be considered exhaustive, but rather, international human rights law provisions pertaining to the right of a fair trial and binding upon the occupying power should be applied in order to better clarify the meaning of a 'regular trial' under Article 71(1) GC IV.[99]

In addition, houses and buildings may not be demolished for law-enforcement purposes. According to Article 53 GC IV, '[a]ny destruction by the occupying power of real or personal property belonging individually or collectively to private persons ... is prohibited, except where such destruction is rendered absolutely necessary by military operations'. Since, as argued in a subsequent subsection, the expression 'military operations' refers to conduct of hostilities in occupied territory,[100] Article 53 GC IV prohibits any destruction of property during law-enforcement operations, while it permits such destruction in the conduct of hostilities if absolutely necessary.[101] It follows that the Israeli practice of demolishing civilian houses as a counterterrorism measure in law-enforcement operations is a violation of Article 53 GC IV and, likely, of a number of international human rights law provisions pertaining to the right to property.[102] Moreover, this practice, since it affects the rights of individuals residing with alleged terrorists, may amount to collective punishment, which is forbidden by a number of provisions of the law of occupation as well as by international human rights law.[103] Accordingly, support at the Supreme Court

---

[98] See, e.g., British Military Court for the Trial of War Criminals, *In re Sandrock* et al., 1 LRTWC 35, 44; Holland, Special Criminal Court, Arnhem, *In re Heinemann*, 396–7; Holland, Special Court of Cassation, *In re Vogt* (5 December 1949), 16 ILR 459, 460–1. See also Guelle, *Precis*, 130.

[99] See, generally, Yutaka Arai-Takahashi, 'Fair Trial Guarantees in Occupied Territory the Interplay between International Humanitarian Law and Human Rights Law' in Arnold & Quénivet (eds.), *International Humanitarian Law*, 455.

[100] See *infra*, Section 5.4.1.

[101] For more on this, see *infra*, Section 6.3.2.1.

[102] It is not possible to provide here a full account of this practice. See, among others, the assessment provided by John Quigley, 'Punitive Demolition of Houses: A Study in International Rights Protection' (1992–3) 5 *St Thomas Law Review* 359; Yoram Dinstein, 'The Israeli Supreme Court and the Law of Belligerent Occupation: Demolitions and Sealing off of Houses' (1999) 29 IYHR 285; Kretzmer, *The Occupation*, 145–64; Guy Harpaz, 'When Does a Court Systematically Deviate from Its Own Principles? The Adjudication by the Israel Supreme Court of House Demolitions in the Occupied Palestinian Territories' (2015) 31 LJIL 28.

[103] See Darcy, 'Punitive'.

level for the practice of demolishing civilian houses for the purpose of law enforcement raises some serious concerns.[104]

Finally, pursuant to Article 78(1) GC IV, '[i]f the occupying power considers it necessary, for imperative reasons of security, to take safety measures concerning protected persons, it may, at the most, subject them to assigned residence or to internment'. The provision goes on stating that these measures must be adopted in conformity with a procedure approved in advance by the occupying power, and that they should conform with GC IV, providing both a right of appeal and a system of periodic review.[105] Since this provision does not clarify the time limit of these temporary measures, it allows occupying powers to intern protected persons indefinitely until the general close of the hostilities,[106] as in the case of the practice of administrative detention conducted by Israel:[107] it has been reported that thousands of Palestinian are under detention without any trial,[108] while the Supreme Court of Israel did not order any of the detained to be released between 2000 and 2010, notwithstanding the reviews of over 300 cases.[109] The harshness of this regime, which provides scant guarantees for individuals who may be interned indefinitely without any conviction, is at odds with international human rights law standards regarding the principles of legality, individual freedom, and the right to a fair trial. In cases in which these rules are binding upon the occupying power, it is reasonable to conclude that a practice of administrative detention, theoretically in line with international humanitarian law, is unlawful nonetheless if

---

[104] HCJ 5290/14, 5295/14 and 5300/14, *Qawasmeh* et al. v. *IDF Commander* et al., 11 August 2014, unofficial English translation at www.hamoked.org/files/2014/1158616_eng.pdf. For some critical remarks, see Shane Darcy, 'Collective Punishment Receives a Judicial Imprimatur', EJIL: Talk!, 21 August 2014.
[105] See Art. 78(2) GC IV.
[106] According to Art. 133(1) GC IV, '[i]nternment shall cease as soon as possible after the close of the hostilities'.
[107] See Tyler Davidson & Kathleen Gibson, 'Expert Meeting on Security Detention Report: Speaker's Summary: Security Detention and Israel' (2009) 40 Case Western Reserve JIL 323, 356–62.
[108] See Hamoked & B'Tselem, *Without Trial: Administrative Detention of Palestinians by Israel and the Internment of Unlawful Combatants Law*, October 2009, available at www.btselem .org/sites/default/files2/publication/200910_without_trial_eng.pdf; B'Tselem, *Human Rights in the Occupied Territories: 2011 annual report*, available at www.btselem.org/sites/default/ files2/2011_annual_report_eng.pdf; EU, European Parliament, Directorate-General for External Policies of the Union, Israel's Policy of Administrative Detention (Policy Briefing May 2012), available at www.europarl.europa.eu/RegData/etudes/briefing_note/join/2012/491444/ EXPO-AFET_SP(2012)491444_EN.pdf
[109] See Shiri Krebs, 'Lifting the Veil of Secrecy: Judicial Review of Administrative Detentions in the Israeli Supreme Court' (2012) 45 *Vanderbilt Journal of Transnational Law* 639, 643.

it violates international human rights law.[110] The Supreme Court of Israel has also confirmed that international human rights law is relevant when assessing the legality of administrative detention.[111] Significantly, the ECtHR considered that administrative detention pursuant the GC IV and some SC resolutions is nonetheless subject to judicial scrutiny under the ECHR,[112] while the CCPR affirmed that administrative detention in occupied territory must comply with the rights guaranteed by the ICCPR.[113]

In conclusion, international humanitarian law offers scant indications regarding the implementation of the duty to restore and ensure public order. The HR and the GC IV attempt to constrain the brutality of the response of the occupying power, prohibiting its ability to resort to heinous practices such as collective punishment, the taking of hostages, and forcible transfers and deportations. However, apparently, they do not regulate the resort to armed force to restore and ensure public order.

5.3.3. Law Enforcement in Occupied Territory

5.3.3.1. The Function of Law Enforcement

The next subsections aim to demonstrate that law enforcement is the operational model and the normative regime primarily applicable to the use of armed force by the occupying power. Since the duty to restore and ensure public order coupled with the basic tenets of the law of occupation compel the occupying power to resort to law enforcement, preliminarily, a brief overview of the meaning of law enforcement and the legal framework governing it is necessary.

Even in peacetime, the maintenance of public order is not limited to the adoption of relevant legislation. One of the main means of ensuring public order is law enforcement. Law enforcement may be described both as an operational model and a legal paradigm. Since the operational model of law enforcement encompasses operations involving the use of armed force[114] that

---

[110] See Jelena Pejic, 'Procedural Principles and Safeguards for Internment/Administrative Detention in Armed Conflict and Other Situations of Violence' (2005) 87 IRRC 375, 377–80.
[111] HCJ 5591/02 *Yassin* et al. v. *Commander of the Ktziot Military Camp Ktziot Detention Facility* et al., 57(1) PD 403, para. 11, unofficial English translation available at www.hamoked.org/items/6600_eng.pdf
[112] See *Al Jedda* v. *UK*, paras. 107–9.
[113] See CCPR, Concluding observations of the Human Rights Committee: Israel (3 September 2010), para. 7.
[114] See, generally, Stuart Casey-Maslen & Sean Connolly, *Police Use of Force under International Law* (Cambridge University Press 2017) 2.

5.3. Law Enforcement and Public Order

are subject to the restraints of the pertinent legal paradigm, law enforcement plays a central role in the study of the use of armed force in occupied territory.

Although binding international legal instruments do not define law enforcement despite its importance in occupied territory, some soft law instruments shed light on its role. According to the UN Code of Conduct for Law Enforcement Officials, law enforcement refers to the exercise of police powers, including arrest and detention, by state officials.[115] Similarly, the European Code of Police Ethics refers to 'traditional public police forces or police services, or to other publicly authorized and/or controlled bodies with the primary objectives of maintaining law and order in civil society, and who are empowered by the state to use force and/or special powers for these purposes'.[116] These instruments render it possible to define law enforcement. For instance, Niels Melzer and Gloria Gaggioli define law enforcement as 'comprising all territorial and extraterritorial measures taken by a state or other collective entity to maintain or restore public security, law and order or to otherwise exercise its authority or power over individuals, objects, or territory'.[117] Similarly, Robert Kolb and Silvayn Vité take the view that police operations comprise two aspects: one judicial dimension, with the aim of ensuring respect for the law and prosecuting the authors of violations, and one administrative, with the aim of maintaining public order and implementing measures adopted by administrative or judicial authorities.[118]

Soft law instruments address law enforcement as a function,[119] an operational model at the disposal of states to ensure and restore public order. It follows that the actors performing a certain operation are not crucial to determine whether one operation falls into the law-enforcement model. Usually, civilian police agents are tasked with law-enforcement responsibilities and, due to the preponderant role of police in law enforcement during peacetime, law enforcement operations are very often defined as 'police operations'. However, in some cases, the military supplements police in this task; in this

---

[115] Code of Conduct for Law Enforcement Officials (annexed to GA Res. 34169, 17 December 1979), commentary to Art. 1.

[116] Council of Europe, Committee of Ministers, European Code of Police Ethics, Recommendation Rec(2001)10, 19 September 2001, 7.

[117] Nils Melzer & Gloria Gaggioli, 'Conceptual Distinction and Overlaps between Law Enforcement and the Conduct of Hostilities' in Terry D. Gill & Dieter Fleck (eds.), *The Handbook of the International Law of Military Operations* (2nd edn, Oxford University Press 2015) 63, 63.

[118] Kolb & Vité, *Le droit*, 348.

[119] See Ramón Martínez Guillem, 'La participación de fuerzas policiales en las operaciones de mantenimiento de la paz' in Consuelo Ramón Chornet (ed.), *El derecho internacional humanitario ante los nuevos conflictos armados* (Tirant lo Blanch 2002) 159, 167; Melzer, *Targeted Killing*, 87; Melzer & Gaggioli, 'Conceptual', 63–4.

event, the operational model is the same as for law enforcement conducted by police.[120]

International and domestic human rights law govern law enforcement. The function of law enforcement is inherent to the exercise of governmental powers; law enforcement is rooted in the vertical relationship between a government and individuals subject to its jurisdiction.[121] The monopoly of states with regard to the maintenance of public order through measures involving the use of armed force is balanced by the constraints embodied in international and domestic human rights law. The human rights law rules governing state conduct during law-enforcement operations originated in peacetime and, accordingly, are different from international humanitarian law rules pertaining to the conduct of hostilities. Although the law-enforcement legal paradigm is explored in the subsequent chapter, suffice it to say, here, that in light of international human rights law applicable during law-enforcement operations, the use of lethal armed force must be considered a last-resort measure.[122] Accordingly, the application of law enforcement in times of occupation poses significant challenges.

5.3.3.2. Law Enforcement as the Primary Paradigm Regarding the Use of Armed Force in Occupied Territories

Since the occupying power is vested with law-enforcement responsibilities, if it is required to use armed force, it has the duty to resort as far as possible to law enforcement in order to ensure and restore public order in occupied territory. This subsection demonstrates that, although the law of occupation is apparently silent regarding the way in which armed force must be used in the occupied territory, there is a presumption regarding the application of law enforcement that compels the occupying power to refrain from resort to the model of the conduct of hostilities. As a consequence, if hostilities occur in occupied territory, the occupying power bears the burden of proof to demonstrate that the law-enforcement model was not applicable.

As already noted, law enforcement is a function that is applicable to the vertical relationship between states and individuals under their jurisdiction. Although jurisdiction is primarily territorial, in situations of occupation, states exercise their jurisdiction extraterritorially *par définition*; consequently, occupying powers are required to deal with the vertical relationship between

---

[120] See Paul Tavernier, 'Le recours à la force par la police' in Christian Tomuschat, Evelyne Lagrange, & Stefan Oeter (eds.), *The Right to Life* (Brill 2010) 41, 46–8.
[121] See Melzer, *Targeted Killing*, 87.
[122] See *infra*, Section 6.2.1.

themselves and the individuals under their jurisdiction through law enforcement. Indeed, under certain circumstances, states may be permitted to conduct law-enforcement operations outside their own borders by a specific international law rule.[123] In situations of occupation, the permissive rule allowing law-enforcement operations in the occupied territory is Article 43 HR, which dictates the duty to restore and ensure public order and, at the same time, compels the occupying power to fulfil this responsibility through, primarily, the law already in force in the occupied territory. As already noted, Article 43 HR is completed by Article 64 GC IV.

Some authors have suggested that the different expression of 'security operation' should be employed for law-enforcement operations conducted in situations of armed conflict in order to distinguish them from peacetime law enforcement.[124] Indeed, law enforcement in armed conflict and occupation is sometime conceived more broadly than in peacetime, encompassing activities that are not typical of peacetime law enforcement, such as the detention of prisoners of war.[125] Thanks to the hostile relationship between the population of the occupied territory and the occupying power, law enforcement in occupied territory is similar to law-enforcement operations performed by peacekeepers in post-conflict situations, where law-enforcement operations may be conducted by organs perceived by the local population as alien or hostile.[126] However, setting aside the terminological dispute between law-enforcement and security operations, emphasis should be given to the fact that governing a territory and its inhabitants requires the exercise of a certain *function* that, in peacetime, is performed by the sovereign state while, in situations of occupation, is performed by the occupying power. In this author's view, there are not enough differences between the exercise of this function within a state and in situations of occupation to justify the use of a different terminology. Actually, the situation of occupation affects the legal framework pertaining to law-enforcement operations, which must take into account the aforementioned international humanitarian law limits regarding the maintenance and restoration of public order in occupied territory. However, the occupation does not alter the basic features of law enforcement.

With the exception of the paradigm regulating the conduct of hostilities between the ousted sovereign and the occupying power, the law of occupation demands the application of law enforcement as the preferential paradigm pertaining to the use of armed force in occupied territory. The aforementioned

---

[123] See PCIJ, *The Case of SS Lotus*, 18.
[124] Murray, *Practitioners' Guide*, 91.
[125] Melzer & Gaggioli, 'Conceptual', 65.
[126] Kolb & Vité, *Le droit*, 348, fn. 955.

rules regarding non-forcible means of maintenance and restoration of public order emphasise that the occupying power may resort to the same measures that the ousted sovereign would have employed. Indeed, the whole normative system regarding the maintenance of existing criminal law and officials distinctly demonstrates that the GC IV favours the application of criminal law as an instrument to ensure public order in the same circumstances and by the same institutions as before the beginning of the occupation. The governmental authority of the occupying power, albeit temporary in nature, requires the application of peacetime means to restore and ensure public order; this same rationale should be applied to forcible means of maintenance and restoration of public order.[127] In dealing with the maintenance of public order, states generally resort to armed force in the framework of law-enforcement operations. Accordingly, the occupying power, which is temporarily placed by the law of occupation, and in particular by Article 43 HR and Article 64 GC IV, in the shoes of the ousted sovereign, must use armed force in compliance with the law-enforcement paradigm in continuity with the maintenance of public order operated by the ousted sovereign.

The continuity between the law-enforcement activities of the ousted sovereign and that of the occupying power is demonstrated by a close scrutiny of the role of the local police in occupied territory. After the beginning of the occupation, usually the police units of the occupied territory are no longer performing their law-enforcement activity because of the dismantling of the ousted sovereign's governmental apparatus. In fact, the cessation of the function of the police officers of the occupied territory is one of the main threats to public order in the area. In theory, police units of the occupied territory may continue performing their function since they fall into the category of state officials who should keep conducting their functions pursuant to Article 54 GC IV.[128] However, the work of police units should be voluntary: Article 51(2) GC IV prevents the occupying power from requiring police to 'undertake any work which would involve them in the obligation of taking part in military operations', in particular with regard to 'measures aimed at opposing legitimate belligerent acts, whether committed by armed forces hostile to the occupying power, by corps of volunteers or by organized resistance movements'.[129] However, the maintenance in function of the local police is rather 'a particularly delicate matter',[130] both for the police themselves and for the occupying power: the former could feel a conflict of allegiance in serving under

[127] See Ferraro, 'The Law', 288.
[128] Pictet (ed.), *Commentary to IV Geneva Convention*, 307.
[129] Ibid.
[130] Ibid.

an enemy administration, while the latter would be reluctant to trust people belonging to the occupied territory with carrying arms and conducting such a delicate task as law enforcement. It is not happenstance that Article 51(2) GC IV provides that the occupying power may not 'in any way apply sanctions to or take any measures of coercion or discrimination against [officials or judges], should they abstain from fulfilling their functions for reasons of conscience', thus recognising the possibility of such a conflict of allegiances. The very idea, supported by some military manuals, that the local police may be *compelled* to perform its proper function with regard to ordinary crime[131] is contradicted by this provision, which prohibits any sanction for those police officers refusing to obey the orders of the occupying power. However, the GC IV does not bar the occupying power from *inviting* the police in the occupied territory to keep performing their function, and they are free to agree to do so. This is confirmed by state practice: for instance, at the beginning of the occupation of Iraq, the CPA did not dismantle entirely the Iraqi police,[132] but rather, invited those officials not involved with the former regime to resume their role;[133] however, since the highest echelons of the police had been dismissed due to their (actual or alleged) affiliation to the Ba'ath party, the effectiveness of the Iraqi police was seriously impaired.[134]

Nevertheless, the law of occupation restricts the latitude of the occupying power's faculty to employ the local police of the occupied territory. The occupying power is prevented from requiring local police to enforce those new pieces of legislation passed pursuant to Article 43 HR and Article 64(2) GC IV. Indeed, the idea that state officials, including police, must keep performing their functions in the occupied territory is in line with the conservationist principle, according to which the occupying power does not annex the occupied territory, but rather administers that area temporarily. Since the law of occupation requires the daily life of the occupied territory to be altered as little as possible, particularly in relation to the law in force and its judicial and extrajudicial implementation, requiring the local police of the occupied territory to implement *new* legislation would cause an alteration in the task

---

[131] See Italian Military Manual, section 49.5; UK Military Manual, section 10.20.2.2. The same position was advanced by Pictet (ed.), *Commentary to IV Geneva Convention*, 307.
[132] See generally Robert M. Perito, 'The Iraq Federal Police. US Police Building under Fire' (October 2011), available at www.usip.org/sites/default/files/SR291_The_Iraq_Federal_Police.pdf
[133] See the US declaration in S/PV.4812, 3, according to which '[t]ens of thousands of Iraqi police answered the call to return to work for the betterment of their country'.
[134] See Carcano, *The Transformation*, 241; Matt Sherman & Josh Paul, 'The Role of Police in Counterinsurgency Operations in Iraq, 2003–2006' in C. Christine Fair & Sumit Ganguly (eds.), *Policing Insurgencies: Cops as Counterinsurgents* (2014) 227, 230.

originally performed by the local police; similarly, such an involvement of the local police in the implementation of the occupying power's legislation could create confusion in the population of the occupied territory between temporary and exceptional commands enacted by the occupying power and the law passed by the ousted sovereign. Domestic case law confirms that the local police of the occupied territory have no duty to implement new legislation passed by the occupying power.[135]

In the practice of occupation, occupying powers have recognised openly the value of local police in the maintenance of public order and the role of law enforcement. For instance, during the Indonesian occupation of East Timor, the Indonesian military command recruited East Timorese civilians into civil defence forces for conventional territorial security roles, combat, surveillance, and intelligence tasks.[136] With regard to the OPT, the Israeli–PLO agreements envisaged a tight cooperation between the Palestinian police and Israeli armed forces. According to the Declaration of Principles, the primary responsibility for the maintenance of public order in some portions of the OPT rests upon the Palestinian police, while Israel is responsible only for the security of Israelis and external threats.[137] Moreover, according to the Interim Agreement, the Palestinian police 'shall be deployed and shall assume responsibility for public order and internal security for Palestinians',[138] coherently with the transfer to the PNA of the responsibility regarding maintenance of public order in some portions of West Bank and Gaza Strip.[139] Recently, the role of the Palestinian security forces has been acknowledged also by the SC.[140] Similarly, the CPA in Iraq considered the training of local police units to be one of the best instruments for maintaining public order,[141] while the SC has stressed in two resolutions the pivotal role of a new Iraqi police to maintain public order in the occupied Iraq.[142] The commonplace character of such practice confirms that law enforcement through local police is increasingly seen as the best option to restore and ensure public order.

---

[135] See Holland, Special Court of Cassation, *In re Policeman Voleva* (20 January 1947), 14 ILR 258, 258–9; Id, *In re Van Kampen* (12 March 1947) 14 ILR 259, 259–60; Id, *In re Hoffmann* (19 December 1951), 18 ILR 701, 702.
[136] Commission for Reception, Truth and Reconciliation in East-Timor, Final Report, January 2006, part 4, paras. 92–3.
[137] See Art. 8 Declaration of Principles.
[138] Art. 10(3) Interim Agreement. See also Art. 4(1), Annex I, Interim Agreement.
[139] According to Art. 5(2)(a), Annex I, Interim Agreement, '[t]he Council will … assume the powers and responsibilities for internal security and public order in Area A'.
[140] See UNSC Res. 2334 (2016), preamb para. 7.
[141] See UK, High Court of Justice, Queen's Bench Division, Divisional Court, *Al Skeini et al. v. Secretary of State for Defence*, [2004] EWHC 2911 (Admin), para. 43.
[142] See UNSC Res. 1511 (2003), para. 16; UNSC Res. 1546 (2004), para. 14.

However, some law-enforcement operations in occupied territory are conducted directly by the occupying power through its own armed forces or by police units created within the army.[143] For instance, during the occupation of Namibia and the fighting against the movement of national liberation SWAPO and its military branch, South Africa employed its own police as main tool to address resistance actions until 1974:[144] at the beginning of the occupation, the police were the only corp officially employed in the maintenance of public order, since South Africa had argued that its actions were based on its mandatory powers, which did not encompass the detachment of military forces;[145] subsequently, with the involvement of the South African armed forces, law-enforcement responsibilities were shared between the army and the police, with special tasks bestowed upon the police unit called *Koevoet*,[146] which, in particular, was required to enforce a number of criminal provisions that punished conduct of armed resistance under the label of terrorism.[147] Similarly, in occupied Iraq, law-enforcement operations conducted by the British army have been described as comprising 'patrols, arrests, anti-terrorist operations, policing of civil demonstrations, protection of essential utilities and infrastructure and protecting police stations'.[148] In general, military units *normally tasked with law-enforcement operations in peacetime* are nonetheless particularly fit to perform law enforcement in occupied territories,[149] as demonstrated by the Italian Military Manual, which prescribes that the security of the occupying power should be assigned mostly to the *Carabinieri*, despite the fact that this military law-enforcement unit operates mainly in peacetime law enforcement within the Italian territory.[150]

Accordingly, state practice demonstrates that occupying powers tend to ensure and restore public order through the local police of the occupied territory or directly through the deployment of occupational units usually

---

[143] Police units created within the armed force are not considered civilians (US Military Manual, section 4.23.2).

[144] See Richard Dale, 'The Armed Forces as an Instrument of South African Policy in Namibia' (1980) 18 *The Journal of Modern African Studies* 57, 67; Lieneke Eloff de Visser, 'Winning Hearts and Minds: Legitimacy in the Namibian War for Independence' (2013) 24 *Small Wars & Insurgencies* 712, 719.

[145] See Richard Dale, 'Melding War and Politics in Namibia: South Africa's Counterinsurgency Campaign, 1966–1989' (1993) 20 *Armed Forces and Society* 7, 10–11.

[146] See de Visser, 'Winning', 719–20; Kersti Larsdotter, 'Fighting Transnational Insurgents: The South African Defence Force in Namibia, 1966–1989' (2014) 37 SCT 1024, 1030.

[147] Terrorism Act no. 83 in 1967, text available at disa.ukzn.ac.za/sites/default/files/pdf_files/leg19670621.028.020.083.pdf. See also Dale, 'The Armed Forces', 66.

[148] UK, High Court of Justice, *Al Skeini* et al. v. *Secretary of State for Defence*, para. 43.

[149] Sassòli, 'Legislation', 668.

[150] See Italian Military Manual, section 47.

employed in law-enforcement activities during peacetime. This practice confirms the idea that the law of occupation not only requires the maintenance of the criminal law system and judiciary to restore and ensure public order, but that the conservationist principle demands the use of armed force at the same conditions of the ousted sovereign, that is, with reference to the maintenance of public order, law enforcement.

Another argument suggests that the preference for law enforcement creates also a legal presumption regarding the recourse to law enforcement. Since the occurrence of hostilities in the occupied territory is a clear breach of public order, the occupying power has a duty to prevent the eruption of hostilities: for instance, during the Ugandan occupation of Ituri in the DRC, Uganda acknowledged its responsibility as an occupying power to protect the local population from the violence of the ongoing non-international armed conflict in that area.[151] Since Article 43 HR embodies obligations of conduct,[152] the occupying power bears the burden to prove that it has done everything feasible to ensure and restore public order when dealing with the occurrence of hostilities, having undertaken diligently any available law-enforcement measures to prevent such hostilities. It follows that the occupying power may not lawfully resume the hostilities or open new hostilities in the occupied territory without, at the same time, violating Article 43 HR,[153] except for cases in which the occupying power manages to demonstrate that the resumption of hostilities is the only feasible means to restore and ensure public order. Indeed, since Article 43 HR embodies obligations of conduct to be implemented in light of the due diligence principle, it may happen that the occupying power is compelled to resort to hostilities by the activity of the armed resistance itself. However, when there are other feasible means to restore and ensure public order, although Article 43 HR may not prevent the occupying power from actually resuming hostilities, it does provide a source of international responsibility if the occupying power does. Accordingly, these legal constraints upon the occupying power regarding the resort to the conduct of hostilities in the occupied territory strongly support the view that the law-enforcement model is the preferential paradigm under which the occupying power may resort to armed force.[154] The conduct of hostilities is a residual model that may

---

[151] See Sixth Report of the Secretary-General on UN Mission in DRC, S/2001/128, 12 February 2001, para. 27. For the coexistence of a non-international armed conflict and a situation of occupation, see *infra*, Section 5.4.3.

[152] See *supra*, Section 5.3.1.

[153] See Louise Doswald-Beck, 'The Right to Life in Armed Conflict: Does International Humanitarian Law Provide All the Answers?' (2006) 88 IRRC 881, 893; Pertile, 'L'adozione', 309; Otto, *Targeted*, 447.

[154] See Pertile, 'L'adozione', 309; Murray, *Practitioners' Guide*, 99–100.

be invoked only under exceptional circumstances, which are addressed in Section 5.6, below.

The prevalence of the law-enforcement paradigm is not at odds with the conclusion that situations of occupation maintain an ongoing armed conflict over the occupied territory. Indeed, the law of occupation explicitly introduces in the law of armed conflict the special regime regarding the maintenance and restoration of public order in the occupied territory, which demands the application of the law-enforcement model, usually discarded in the course of an armed conflict in favour of the conduct of hostilities.[155] This regime, compelling the resort to law enforcement, is *lex specialis* with regard to the general law of armed conflict, including conduct of hostilities, and it prevails as long as the situation is one that should be addressed through law enforcement,[156] notwithstanding the ongoing existence of an armed conflict in the occupied territory.[157] Although the international human rights law paradigm governing law enforcement thus completes the law of occupation, nonetheless, international humanitarian law remains the main legal framework requiring the application of law-enforcement standards.[158] Accordingly, the failure to resort to law enforcement is at the same time a violation of the law of occupation and, independently, a violation of the international human rights obligations binding the occupying power.

In conclusion, the law of occupation demands the occupying power to ensure and restore public order in the occupied territory largely through the same means the ousted sovereign would have employed. This inclination is explicit in the law of occupation with regard to the criminal system already existing in the occupied territory and the judiciary. However, arguably, the same rationale regulates the use of armed force: just as the ousted sovereign would have employed armed force to restore and ensure public order only pursuant to the law-enforcement paradigm, so the occupying power must apply as far as possible that same paradigm. It is not happenstance that many occupying powers have employed the local police or have trained new units of local police in order to ensure and restore public order. The

---

[155] See Andrea Carcano, 'On the Relationship between International Humanitarian Law and Human Rights Law in Times of Belligerent Occupation: Not Yet a Coherent Framework' in Erika de Wet & Jann Kleffner (eds.), *Convergence and Conflicts of Human Rights and International Humanitarian Law in Military Operations* (Pretoria University Law Press 2014) 121, 144.

[156] As a consequence, this author disagrees with the view that the normative model pertaining to the conduct of hostilities is *lex specialis* with regard to that pertaining to law enforcement (Melzer, *Targeted Killing*, 277; Schmitt, 'Iraq', 364–5).

[157] For more on the interplay between law enforcement and conduct of hostilities, see *infra*, Section 5.6.

[158] Ferraro, 'The Law', 288.

prevalence of law enforcement is supported by the fact that, pursuant to Article 43 HR, the occupying power may not resume hostilities in the occupied territory by itself, since this conduct would amount to a violation of the law of occupation.

5.4. THE RELATIONSHIP BETWEEN HOSTILITIES AND OCCUPATION

5.4.1. *Defining 'Hostilities' under International Humanitarian Law*

International humanitarian law conventions do not define the terms 'act of hostility', 'hostilities', and 'conduct of hostilities'. Nonetheless, the term 'hostilities' is frequently employed in international humanitarian law conventions, for instance with regard to the commencing of hostilities, conduct of hostilities, persons taking or not taking part in hostilities, suspension of hostilities, termination of hostilities, and so on.[159]

Moreover, most military manuals and domestic legislation pertaining to armed conflict fail to define what constitutes hostilities. For instance, the US Military Manual only acknowledges the link between the use of means and methods of warfare and the conduct of hostilities.[160] Even a document aiming to provide a glossary of the terms employed in the law of armed conflict such as the NATO Glossary of Terms and Definitions does not define hostilities, although this expression is employed in a number of definitions collected in the document.[161]

Some useful elements to define hostilities may be drawn from the debate regarding the definition of 'direct participation of civilians in hostilities' under Article 51(3) AP I, particularly in the framework of the ICRC's mission to disseminate the knowledge of international humanitarian law. For instance, according to the commentary to AP I published under the ICRC's auspices, 'hostile acts' are 'acts which by their nature and purpose are intended to cause actual harm to the personnel and equipment of the armed forces'.[162] Similarly, in non-international armed conflict, 'hostilities' are defined as 'acts of war that by their nature or purpose struck at the personnel and matériel of enemy armed forces'.[163] These definitions attracted the criticism of the Supreme Court of Israel, which, rightly, pointed out

---

[159] Just as examples, see common Art. 3(1) GCs; Art. 17 GC I; Art. 33 GC II; Title Section II and Arts. 21(3), 67, 118, 119 GC III; Arts. 49(2), 130, 133, 134, 135 GC IV; Arts. 33, 34, 40, 43(2), 45, 47, 51(3), 59, 60 AP I and Title Part IV, Section I AP I; Arts. 4 and 13(3) AP II.
[160] US Military Manual, section 5.1.
[161] NATO Glossary of Terms and Definitions, AAP-06, Edition 2013.
[162] Sandoz, Swinarski, & Zimmermann (eds.), *Commentary*, para. 1942.
[163] Ibid., para. 4788.

5.4. The Relationship between Hostilities and Occupation

that acts of hostility should encompass also conduct against civilians.[164] The remarks of the Supreme Court of Israel did not go unnoticed by the ICRC, which included acts conducted against protected persons in the definition of hostilities embodied in the 2009 Interpretive Guidance on the Notion of Direct Participation in Hostilities under International Humanitarian Law.[165] The Interpretive Guidance goes on to define hostilities as 'the (collective) resort by the parties to the conflict to means and methods of injuring the enemy'.[166]

There is a general consensus among scholars that an 'act of hostility' is a resort to the means and methods of warfare to harm the enemy, while 'hostilities' refers to the sum of acts of hostility occurring in certain armed conflict.[167] For instance, Pietro Verri defines hostilities as 'acts of violence by a belligerent against an enemy in order to put an end to his resistance and impose obedience',[168] while Jean Salmon defines *hostilités* as '[e]nsemble des actes offensifs ou défensifs et des opérations militaires accomplis par un belligérant dans le cadre d'un conflit armé'.[169] Melzer emphasises the collective nature of the concept 'hostilities', suggesting that, '[g]enerally speaking, the concept of hostilities is equivalent to *the sum of all conduct regulated by the law of hostilities*, namely the choice of and use by the parties to an armed conflict of means and methods of injuring the enemy'.[170] Straightforwardly, Melzer and Gaggioli affirm that '[t]he generic concept of hostilities refers to the resort to means and methods of warfare between parties to an armed conflict'.[171] Similarly, the Tallinn Manual 2.0 on the International Law Applicable to Cyber Operations posits that '[h]ostilities presuppose the collective application of means and methods of warfare'.[172]

On the basis of the wide consensus among scholars on the definition of hostilities, some general considerations may be drawn regarding the latitude of the concept. The concept of hostilities refers to the resort to means and methods of warfare. Even if hostilities may occur only in the framework

---

[164] *Targeted Killings* case, para. 33 ('It seems that acts which by nature and objective are intended to cause damage to civilians should be added to that definition').
[165] See Nils Melzer, *Interpretive Guidance on the Notion of Direct Participation in Hostilities under International Humanitarian Law* (ICRC 2009) ('*Interpretive Guidance*') 16.
[166] Ibid., 43.
[167] Melzer, *Targeted Killing*, 273.
[168] Pietro Verri, *Dictionary of the International Law of Armed Conflict* (ICRC 1992) 57.
[169] Jean Salmon (ed.), *Dictionnaire de droit international public* (Bruylant 2001) 652, 550.
[170] Melzer, *Targeted Killing*, 269 (emphasis added).
[171] Melzer & Gaggioli, 'Conceptual', 70.
[172] Michael N. Schmitt (ed.), *Tallinn Manual 2.0 on the International Law Applicable to Cyber Operations* (Cambridge University Press 2017) 383.

of an armed conflict,[173] it is clear that a number of activities occurring in an armed conflict are *not* acts of hostility: this is the case with such law-enforcement operations as those aimed at restoring and ensuring public order in occupied territory, or those pertaining to the detention of prisoners of war.[174] On the other hand, 'hostilities' seem to be a concept broader than 'attack', which, under Article 49(1) AP I, is defined as an 'act[] of violence against the adversary, whether in offence or in defence'. The definition of attack seems to be characterised by the restrictive element of 'violence',[175] which is not present in every conduct that amounts to an act of hostility.[176] Accordingly, not every 'act of hostility' is an 'attack' under international humanitarian law, which seems to consider 'attacks' as a specific, and non-exhaustive, kind of acts of hostility.[177] Rather, the term 'hostilities' appears similar to the concept of 'military operations', which is broader than 'attack' and is not defined by international humanitarian law.[178] In fact, the terms 'hostilities' and 'military operations' have been employed as synonyms by prominent authors.[179]

From this survey of contemporary thought, one may define hostilities as the collective resort to means and methods of warfare against the enemy. Since occupation is a situation of actual authority over enemy territory and the law of occupation confers on the occupying power the means to restore and ensure public order and to provide for its own security, it is necessary to investigate whether the outbreak of hostilities in the occupied territory, with the application of means and methods of warfare, is compatible with the state of occupation itself or, rather, whether it terminates the occupation.

---

[173] If there is no armed conflict, international humanitarian law is not applicable, including the rules referring to hostilities.

[174] See Melzer & Gaggioli, 'Conceptual', 71.

[175] Sandoz, Swinarski, & Zimmermann (eds.), Commentary, para. 1880 (according to which, 'attack' involves 'combat action').

[176] See Marco Roscini, *Cyber Operations and the Use of Force in International Law* (Oxford University Press 2014) 178. See also Sandoz, Swinarski, & Zimmermann (eds.), Commentary, para. 1943; Dinstein, *Conduct*, 2.

[177] For a list of 'military operations short of violence', see US Military Manual, section 5.2.2.1. For a discussion whether and under which circumstances intelligence gathering operations may amount to acts of hostility, even if they do not involve violence, see Marco Longobardo, '(New) Cyber Exploitation and (Old) International Humanitarian Law' (2017) 77 ZaöRV 809, 828-33.

[178] See Stefan Oeter, 'Methods and Means of Combat' in Dieter Fleck (ed.), *The Handbook of International Humanitarian Law* (3rd edn, Oxford University Press 2013) 115, 166.

[179] See, e.g., Melzer, *Targeted Killing*, 271-5 (with many references to international practice).

5.4.2. The Practice of Hostilities in Occupied Territories

International practice demonstrates that hostilities in the sense of international humanitarian law may occur in times of occupation. In several cases, occupying powers have employed means and methods of warfare in the course of armed confrontations with resistance forces resorting to the same violent conduct. The following examples of state practice are sufficient to illuminate a trend in international practice.

The OPT has been the theatre of recurring hostilities for over half a century of occupation. For instance, during the Second Intifada, Palestinian armed groups conducted guerrilla warfare against Israeli military and civilians objectives,[180] leading to an exceptionally muscular Israeli response encompassing the recourse to means and methods of warfare.[181] More recently, the three large-scale military operations in the Gaza Strip were characterised by intense recourse to means and methods of warfare by both Israel and Palestinian armed groups: the operation Cast Lead (2009), which involved the employment of aerial airstrikes and heavy artillery,[182] was triggered by the launch of a large number of rockets and mortars against Israeli civilian and military objectives;[183] in the operation Pillar of Clouds (2012), Israel employed, in a robust and proactive manner, means and methods of warfare[184] in response to the firing of rockets and mortars from the Gaza Strip,[185] while intense hostilities occurred during operation Protective Edge (2014), wherein the firing of a number of mortars and rockets from the Gaza Strip[186] was matched with heavy Israeli airstrikes and the employment of artillery.[187] Since 2007, the Gaza Strip has been locked in an ongoing blockade, which should be considered an act of hostility as blockades are generally considered to be methods of warfare.[188]

---

[180] See Catignani, *Israeli Counter-Insurgency*, 104–6.
[181] Ibid., 108.
[182] Israel, *The Operation in Gaza*, paras. 83–8; Goldstone Report, paras. 333–51.
[183] The numbers differ depending on the accounts. See Israel, *The Operation in Gaza*, para. 41; Goldstone Report, paras. 1600–9. For a legal evaluation of the firing of such weapons, see Marco Pertile, 'Le violazioni del diritto umanitario commesse da Hamas durante l'operazione Piombo fuso' (2009) 3 DUDI 333.
[184] IDF, Operation 'Pillar of Defense', 4; HRC, Report of the UN High Commissioner for Human Rights on the Implementation of Human Rights Council Resolutions S-9/1 and S-12/1, paras. 7–12.
[185] IDF, Operation 'Pillar of Defense', 3.
[186] 2014 Gaza Report, paras. 59–92; Israel, *The 2014 Gaza Operation*, para. 16.
[187] 2014 Gaza Report, paras. 111–86.
[188] See Declaration concerning the Laws of Naval War, 26 February 1909; Louise Doswald-Beck (ed.), *San Remo Manual on International Law Applicable to Armed Conflicts at Sea* (Cambridge University Press 1995) paras. 93–104; Wolff Heintschel von Heinegg, 'Blockade' in *MPEPIL online* (2015).

In addition, hostilities affected the province of Ituri, in DRC, during the Ugandan occupation. Indeed, the region was at the centre of the so-called 'Second Congo War', often labelled as the 'Africa's World War' because of the involvement of a number of states as well as myriad non-state armed groups that fought out of ethnic hatred and to gain access to areas containing natural resources between August 1998 until July 2003.[189] As the ICC found out, an ongoing non-international armed conflict between several armed groups was already underway in the area when the occupation commenced,[190] and the hostilities lasted long after the establishment of the occupation.[191]

Similarly, actual hostilities took place during the occupation of Iraq both in the areas controlled by the United Kingdom and those controlled by the United States. In particular, after less intense armed confrontations, in the fall of 2003, in order to respond to major attacks on CPA forces, the United States launched a very robust military campaign called operation Iron Hammer, which resulted in the destruction of many buildings in Baghdad and involved the employment of heavy artillery.[192] US military records confirm the occurrence of hostilities in occupied Iraq, demonstrating that, as of 30 June 2004, a number of violent attacks against CPA forces occurred, including 'five anti-aircraft attacks, 12 grenade attacks, 101 attacks using improvised explosive devices, 52 attempted attacks using improvised explosive devices, 145 mortar attacks, 147 rocket propelled grenade attacks, 535 shootings and 53 others'.[193]

Accordingly, even this cursory overview demonstrates that hostilities may occur during occupations. The crux is whether such hostilities terminate the state of occupation.

5.4.3. The Compatibility of Hostilities with a Situation of Occupation: Hostilities within the Occupation versus Hostilities Terminating the Occupation

As already noted, occupation is a peculiar situation in which, in the context of an armed conflict, a state acquires the duty of ensuring public order and civil life within an enemy territory on the basis of the exercise of actual

---

[189] See Louise Arimatsu, 'The Democratic Republic of the Congo 1993–2010' in Wilmshurst (ed.), *Classification*, 146, 167–72.
[190] See *Prosecutor v. Lubanga*, Judgment pursuant to Art. 74, paras. 561–5.
[191] See *Prosecutor v. Katanga*, Judgment pursuant to Art. 74, para. 433.
[192] See US Army, Center of the Law and Military Operations, *Legal Lessons Learned from Afghanistan and Iraq: Vol. II* (2005) 11–12.
[193] ECtHR, *Al Skeini* et al. v. *UK*, para. 23.

authority over that area. The fact of the occupation may be established only when the battle is over: in the words of the ICTY, normally during occupations 'the enemy's forces have surrendered, been defeated or withdrawn. In this respect, battle areas may not be considered as occupied territory'.[194] The law of occupation itself requires the exercise of actual authority over the occupied territory in order to allow the occupying power to comply with its international humanitarian law obligations. Consequently, international case law and state practice generally support the distinction between a situation of occupation, which triggers the application of the law of occupation, and mere invasion, which does not trigger the application of the law of occupation. Although the determination of the exact moment in which an invasion becomes an occupation is troublesome, the very existence of such a distinction between occupation and invasion appears soundly rooted in international law.[195]

On this basis, one could contend that the resumption of hostilities in the occupied territory, with the renewed employment of means and methods of warfare, automatically brings to an end the occupation. Indeed, it is difficult to reconcile the idea of the occupying power's actual authority with the employment of means and methods of warfare: on the one hand, the resumption of hostilities against the occupying power may be seen as evidence of the occupying power's inability to control the territory from which the hostilities originate; on the other, the occupying power's need to resort to means and methods of warfare would imply that the means provided by the law of occupation to face threats from the occupied territory, i.e., law-enforcement measures, are no longer effective. The view that hostilities terminate *ipso facto* the occupation, which has been labelled 'either/or approach',[196] has been advocated by some scholars arguing that 'either a territory is occupied, or it is in a state of "hot" armed conflict so that the law on the conduct of hostilities is applicable. In an armed conflict, there is no control, and where there is control and thus occupation, there is no armed conflict'.[197] Following this view, '[t]he law of occupation applies to the areas over which the occupying power exercises effective control. It does not apply to situations where the adversary's army is still capable of fighting, thereby precluding the exclusive control of the would-be occupying power'.[198] Similarly, the occupying power's need to resort

---

[194] *Prosecutor v. Naletilić*, para. 217.
[195] See *supra*, Section 2.3.2.
[196] Ferraro (ed.), *Expert Meeting*, 112–13.
[197] Paulus, 'UN Missions', section 2.I.
[198] Orakhelashvili, 'The Interaction', 164.

to means or methods of warfare, at least in the peculiar circumstances of Gaza Strip, has been interpreted as evidence of the non-occupied status of the area by some commentators.[199]

On the other hand, international humanitarian law conventions, international and domestic case law, and state practice suggests that the occurrence of hostilities does not terminate, *ipso facto*, the occupation.

From some references in international humanitarian law conventions, it is clear that the drafters of those treaties did not consider hostilities and occupation to be mutually exclusive. For instance, Article 5(2) GC IV regulates the treatments of protected persons that, in occupied territory, are detained 'under definite suspicion of *activity hostile to the security of the occupying power*'.[200] Similarly, both Articles 5(2) and 68(3) GC IV deal with acts of espionage and sabotage in occupied territory, which are methods of warfare. Furthermore, Article 4(A)(2) GC III considers prisoners of war '[m]embers of other militias and members of other volunteer corps … belonging to a Party to the conflict and operating in or outside their own territory, *even if this territory is occupied*';[201] as observed by a leading commentator, this provision implicitly recognises that hostilities may happen in occupied territory because '[i]f any organized resistance barred occupation, such resistance fighters would by definition never find themselves in an occupied territory'.[202] In addition, the law of occupation itself embodies provisions suggesting the occurrence of hostilities in the occupied territory: for instance, Articles 49(2) and (5) IV refers to 'imperative military reasons', Article 53 GC IV refers to 'military operations', which is synonymous with hostilities, and Article 6(3) GC IV refers to 'military operations' within the occupied territory.[203]

A similar conclusion is supported by international and domestic case law. This issue was addressed by the US Military Tribunal at Nuremberg with regard to the German occupation of Greece and Yugoslavia during WWII. The tribunal, dealing with robust armed resistance to the German occupation

---

[199] See Shany, 'Faraway', 382; Benvenisti, *The International Law*, 211–12. *Contra*, see Pasquale De Sena, 'Ancora a proposito di Gaza' (2014) 1 *Quaderni di SIDIblog* 64, 69–70, according to whom the employment of armed force by Israel in the Gaza Strip demonstrates Israel's control over the area. The present author considers the Gaza Strip still under occupation, for the reasons expressed *supra*, Section 2.3.2.

[200] Emphasis added.

[201] Emphasis added.

[202] Sassòli, 'Concept', 1396.

[203] This interpretation of Article 6(3) GC IV is explained *supra*, Section 2.4.2.

5.4. The Relationship between Hostilities and Occupation 201

that was as intense as in a military campaign,[204] concluded that the resistance did not bring the occupation to an end. The Tribunal argued that:

> While it is true that the partisans were able to control sections of these countries at various times, it is established that the Germans could at any time they desired assume physical control of any part of the country. The control of the resistance forces was temporary only and not such as would deprive the German Armed Forces of its status of an occupant.[205]

In the opinion of the US Military Tribunal, then, the existence of actual hostilities in the occupied territory did not terminate automatically the occupation where such hostilities only created a situation of temporary control by resistance forces.

Some decades later, the ICTY addressed this issue, affirming that 'sporadic local resistance, even successful, does not affect the reality of occupation'.[206] However, in the same decision, dealing with the merits of the specific case regarding the destruction of properties, the ICTY affirmed that, since 'many soldiers refused to give up their weapons', as long as fighting continued, a specific area may not be considered 'under occupation beyond any reasonable doubt'.[207] This paragraph may be read in two different ways. On the one hand, the ICTY could have affirmed that the existence of actual fighting prevented the establishment of a situation of occupation. However, this interpretation would contradict the previous statement regarding the role of 'sporadic local resistance, even successful', which is the theoretical premise of the specific findings regarding the destruction of properties.[208] An alternative interpretation of the paragraph regarding the destruction of properties suggest that the ICTY may have meant that the absolute existence of a state of occupation before the complete end of fighting was *not sufficiently established*; following this idea, the ICTY would not have contradicted itself regarding sporadic resistance within the occupation but, rather, would have only acknowledged that, in the specific circumstances of that case, the prosecution had failed to prove the existence of an occupation. This conclusion is supported by the reference to the existence of occupation 'beyond any reasonable doubt', which is the standard of proof specifically required in criminal prosecution. In addition, in 2017, the ICTY restated the view that hostilities may occur in occupied

---

[204] *Hostage* case, 56.
[205] Ibid.
[206] *Prosecutor v. Naletilić*, para. 217. See, also, *Prosecutor v. Prlić* et al., para. 320.
[207] *Prosecutor v. Naletilić*, para. 587.
[208] Ibid., para. 222.

territory in a case wherein the Court unambiguously affirmed that '[t]he fact that a territory is occupied does not exclude the possibility that hostilities may resume. If the occupying power continues to maintain control of the territory in spite of resistance and sporadic fighting, the territory is still considered occupied'.[209] Accordingly, the ICTY likely concurred with the US Military Tribunal that hostilities may be conducted in occupied territory without ending the occupation.

The ICC took the same view in relation to the Ugandan occupation of the Congolese province of Ituri. The Court affirmed that the existence of an ongoing non-international armed conflict in the occupied territory does not prevent the creation of a situation of occupation, concluding that Ituri was under occupation notwithstanding the ongoing hostilities.[210] Indeed, the Court was more concerned with assessing whether the fact of the occupation altered the original classification of the preexisting non-international armed conflict, an issue that is addressed in Section 5.5.3.3. However, the Court never questioned the termination of the occupation due to the occurrence of hostilities.

Additionally, the Supreme Court of Israel specified on a number of occasions that hostilities have occurred in the context of the occupation of the OPT. With regard to the response to the Second Intifada, the Court held that '[t]hese combat operations ... are not regular police operations, but embody all the characteristics of armed conflict',[211] affirming at the same time, that '[t]he general point of departure of all parties – which is also our point of departure – is that Israel holds the area in belligerent occupation'.[212] The same operations have been defined as 'combat activities' in another decision,[213] while yet another decision employed the terms 'armed conflict'[214] and 'military operations'.[215] Clearly, in the Court's view, the occurrence of hostilities does not terminate, *ipso facto*, the occupation.

Finally, the possibility of the existence of hostilities within the occupied territory is recognised by most military manuals. For instance, the UK Military Manual affirms that '[t]he existence within an occupied area of a defended

---

[209] See *Prosecutor v. Prlić* et al., para. 319 (references omitted).
[210] See *Prosecutor v. Lubanga*, Decision on Confirmation of Charges, para. 220; *Prosecutor v. Katanga*, Decision on Confirmation of Charges, para. 240.
[211] *Beit Sourik* case, para. 2. See also *Targeted Killings* case, para. 16.
[212] Ibid., para. 23.
[213] HCJ 3114/02, 3115/02, 3116/02, *Barake v. Minister of Defence* (14 April 2002), unofficial English translation available at elyon1.court.gov.il/Files_ENG/02/140/031/A02/02031140.A02.pdf, paras. 1, 2, and 12.
[214] *Mara'abe* case, para. 1.
[215] Ibid., para. 2.

5.4. The Relationship between Hostilities and Occupation

zone makes no difference so long as it is surrounded and effectively cut off'.[216] More clearly, the US Military Manual provides that '[a]n occupation may be effective despite the existence of areas in the enemy state that are temporarily controlled by enemy forces or pockets of resistance', also in cases of 'defended location ... still controlled by enemy forces' within the occupied territory, and of 'intermittent insurgent attacks or temporary seizures of territory by resistance forces'.[217] This view is also supported by a number of scholars.[218]

At the end of the day, the problem of whether hostilities are *ipso facto* incompatible with a state of occupation raises the question of which authority may be considered effective in order to create the fact of the occupation. Since this topic has already been explored in a previous Section 2.3, it will suffice to recall here that the test regarding the establishment of an occupation is somewhat stricter that the test regarding the termination of an occupation, as there is a presumption in favour of the existence of the occupation once actual authority has been secured.[219] The same rationale applies to the existence of hostilities: in dealing with the establishment of an occupation, as in the case before the ICTY, the occurrence of hostilities suggests that the territory is not yet occupied; on the contrary, when an occupation has been already established, as in the case before the US Military Tribunal, then the occurrence of sporadic hostilities does not terminate *ipso facto* the occupation.

However, a caveat is necessary. Affirming that hostilities and occupation may coexist should not be seen as an argument to overthrow the factual nature of occupation. In fact, the resumption of hostilities in the occupied territory may lead to the termination of the occupation. However, there is no automatism between the happenstance of hostilities and the termination of occupation: indeed, hostilities may be of such a character that the occupied territory may no longer be considered to be under the authority of the occupying power, pursuant to Article 42 HR. As affirmed by the aforementioned US Military Tribunal in another decision, when 'partisans had wrested considerable territory from the ... occupant, and ... military combat action of some dimensions was required to reoccupy those areas', then '[i]n reconquering enemy territory which the occupant has lost to the enemy, he is not carrying out a police performance but a regular act of war'.[220] State practice offers some practical examples. For instance, during WWII, the Nazi occupation of the

---

[216] UK Military Manual, section 11.3.2.
[217] US Military Manual, section 11.2.2.1 (references omitted).
[218] See Melzer, *Targeted Killing*, 156–7; Dinstein, *The International Law*, 46.
[219] See, in particular, *supra*, Section 2.3.3.
[220] US Military Tribunal, In re *Ohlendorf* et al. (10 April 1948), 15 ILR 656, 662.

northern part of Italy lasted until the Allies, with the support of local partisans, succeeded in ousting the Germans from Italian territory. More recently, the hostilities against Iraq at the time of the occupation of Kuwait led to the termination of that occupation. However, in both cases, the occupation did not end due to the fact of the hostilities alone, but rather, the hostilities contributed to the termination of hostile authority over those portions of territory.

Clearly, the distinction between hostilities occurring within the occupied territory and hostilities leading to the termination of occupation is not an easy one to make. The US Military Tribunal relied on the ability of 'the Germans [to] at any time they desired assume physical control of any part of the country' as the decisive test to consider some portions of Greece and Yugoslavia still under occupation notwithstanding intense resistance activity.[221] However, the US Military Tribunal did not offer any element supporting the claim that the German loss of control was only temporary and that the Germans could have regained it at their will – nor does this statement seem to take into account the factual nature of occupation as spelt out in Article 42 HR;[222] following a reasoning contrary to that of the US Military Tribunal, one could argue that those portions of territory had been under occupation, then they were no longer occupied for a time, and then became occupied again. More correctly, the emphasis should be on the authority exercised over a territory *notwithstanding* the occurrence of hostilities: for instance, South Africa was considered an occupying power in Namibia despite SWAPO's success in securing military control over portions of that territory for temporary period of time.[223] Similarly, in the case of the OPT during the two intifadas, even if some portions of territories were the theatre of intense hostilities against Israel, nonetheless the occupying power managed to maintain the occupation[224] thanks to its very engagement in the hostilities, and through the power exercised over water, electricity, and similar supplies in those areas.

In conclusion, hostilities and occupation are not mutually exclusive. Hostilities in occupied territory may evidence a loss of control on the part of the occupying power and may lead to the termination of the occupation if the occupying power is no longer able to exercise authority over that territory. However, there is no inevitability between the occurrence of hostilities and the termination of occupation.

---

[221] *Hostage* case, 56.
[222] For some critical remarks on this reasoning, see Benvenisti, *The International Law*, 47; Sassòli, 'Concept', 1396–7.
[223] See Larsdotter, 'Fighting', 1028.
[224] Disntein, *The International Law*, 45.

5.5. THE CLASSIFICATION OF HOSTILITIES IN THE OCCUPIED TERRITORY

5.5.1. Preliminary Remarks

The identification of the *jus in bello* rules governing the conduct of hostilities has attracted some debate between supporters of the application of the law of international armed conflict and those supporting the application of the law of non-international armed conflict.[225] This issue may be parsed into two main aspects: the international humanitarian law rules regulating hostilities between the occupying power and the ousted sovereign, and the regulation of hostilities between the occupying power and armed groups not belonging to the ousted sovereign's armed forces. The latter situation of hostilities involving armed groups not affiliated with the ousted sovereign is certainly more irksome.

The difficulty in identifying the most adequate rules of international humanitarian law applicable to hostilities in occupied territory brought to the underestimation of the relevance of such identification. For instance, it has been argued that, since the progressive convergence between the laws on non-international and international armed conflict, the partition between these two branches should be overcome,[226] and, consequently, the classification of hostilities in occupied territory would be less relevant now than in the past.[227] Israel[228] and some UN practice[229] have endorsed this approach. However, although the convergence between the two branches of international law, especially with regard to customary international law, may not be denied, some differences still remain, for instance with regard to captured combatants.[230] Moreover, the determination of the applicable international

---

[225] *De lege lata, tertium non datur. De lege ferenda,* some authors have envisaged the creation of a third category which would be relevant also for hostilities occurring within the occupied territory (see, e.g., Geoffrey Corn & Eric Talbot Jensen, 'Transnational Armed Conflict: A "Principled" Approach to the Regulation of Counter-Terror Combat Operations' (2009) 42 IsLR 46; Claus Kreß, 'Some Reflections on the International Legal Framework Governing Transnational Armed Conflicts' (2010) 15 JCSL 245).

[226] See James G. Stewart, 'Towards a Single Definition of Armed Conflict in International Humanitarian Law: A Critique of Internationalization of Armed Conflict' (2003) 85 IRRC 313; Emily Crawford, 'Unequal before the Law: The Case for the Elimination of the Distinction between International and Non-International Armed Conflict' (2007) 20 LJIL 441.

[227] See, e.g., Pertile, 'L'adozione', 308, fn. 46.

[228] See Israel, *The Operation in Gaza,* para. 30; Israel, *The 2014 Gaza Operation,* para. 233.

[229] See Goldstone Report, paras. 280–3; 2014 Gaza Report, para. 35.

[230] The status of prisoner of war is not available in non-international armed conflicts. On the ontological differences between the laws on international and non-international armed conflicts, see Rogier Bartels, 'Timelines, Borderlines and Conflicts: The Historical Evolution of

humanitarian law is still relevant under the ICC Statute, which provides slightly different lists of war crimes on the basis of their link with an international or a non-international armed conflict.[231] It follows that the identification of the international humanitarian law rules applicable to hostilities, on the basis of their international or non-international character, is not moot, but rather, such an examination is useful for a better understanding of the rules pertaining to the use of armed force in occupied territory.

5.5.2. The Rules Applicable to Hostilities between the Occupying Power and the Ousted Sovereign

In the case of hostilities between the occupying power and the ousted sovereign of the occupied territory, the classification of the armed conflict is relatively easy: since a situation of occupation may be created only during an international armed conflict and its main effect is preserving the existence of a state of ongoing armed conflict on the occupied territory, it is clear that the rules on international armed conflict apply.[232] This conclusion is also consistent with the fact that, usually, the occupation is established in the course of hostilities between two states, the occupying power and the sovereign of the occupied territory; indeed, interstate conflicts are regulated by definition by the law of international armed conflict.[233]

State practice and international case law support the contention that the law of international armed conflict regulates interstate conflicts, and consequently, hostilities between the occupying power and the sovereign of the occupied territory. For instance, the international and domestic case law that dealt with the Nazi war crimes committed during WWII supports the argument that the law of international armed conflict applied to situations of occupation. In the context of trials focusing on a number of alleged war

---

the Legal Divide between International and Non-International Armed Conflicts' (2009) 91 IRRC 35.
[231] See Art. 8 ICC Statute.
[232] See Ronzitti, *Le guerre*, 21, fn. 3, and 32; Kolb & Vité, *Le droit*, 351; Dapo Akande, 'Classification of Armed Conflicts: Relevant Legal Concepts' in Wilmshurst (ed.), *Classification*, 32, 46; Annoni, *L'occupazione*, 225; Ferraro (ed.), *Expert Meeting*, 124; Murray, *Practitioners' Guide*, 117.
[233] According to common Art. 2(1), the GC applies to 'all cases of declared war or of any other armed conflict which may arise between two or more of the High Contracting Parties'. Accordingly, 'the identity of the actors involved in the hostilities – States – will therefore define the international character of the armed conflict. In this regard, statehood remains the baseline against which the existence of an armed conflict under Article 2(1) will be measured' (Tristan Ferraro & Lindsay Cameron, 'Article 2: Application of the Convention' in ICRC, *Updated Commentary on the First Geneva Convention*, para. 221).

crimes pertaining to hostilities within occupied territory, these courts tested the legality of Nazi conduct against the law of international armed conflict. The reference to the international character of WWII is not explicit in those judgments; however, prior to 1949, the only extant law on armed conflict was that pertaining to international armed conflicts, since the rules on non-international armed conflict were codified only by common Article 3 GCs.[234] It follows that hostilities within the occupied territory were considered subject to the rules on international armed conflict or they would not have been examined under the law of armed conflict at all. More recently, the CPA confirmed the applicability of the law of international armed conflict during the occupation of Iraq, including those provisions that have no correspondence in the law on non-international armed conflict, such as the rules pertaining to prisoners of war.[235]

The determination of whether the hostilities occurring in the occupied territory in fact involve the occupying power and the ousted sovereign is crucial. This assessment may be difficult since, in situations of occupation, usually the armed forces of the ousted sovereign are dismantled. Different international law rules may be relevant in this determination.

First, since international humanitarian law regulates the conduct of the belligerents' armed forces, one should verify whether international humanitarian law clarifies when acts of hostility involve a certain state. According to Article 3 IV 1907 Hague Convention, a belligerent is 'responsible for all acts committed by persons forming part of its armed forces'. Armed forces may be comprised of both combatants and non-combatants.[236] According to the HR, '[i]n countries where militia or volunteer corps constitute the army, or form part of it, they are included under the denomination "army"', as long as they are under a responsible command, wear a fixed distinctive emblem, carry arms openly, and respect international humanitarian law.[237] Accordingly, armed forces encompasses 'all organized armed forces, groups and units which are

[234] See Sandesh Sivakumaran, *The Law of Non-International Armed Conflict* (Oxford University Press 2012) 105–235; Dinstein, *Non-International Armed Conflicts*, 20–57; Lindsey Cameron et al., 'Article 3: Conflicts Not of an International Character' in ICRC, *Updated Commentary*, para. 351.
[235] See Written Submission from the Coalition Provisional Authority to the United Nations High Commissioner for Human Rights, 28 May 2004, reprinted in Talmon (ed.), *The Occupation*, 1040, 1043; UK Foreign and Commonwealth Office, Letter to the Clerk of the House of Commons Foreign Affair Committee, 24 June 2004, in Talmon (ed.), *The Occupation*, 571; Sandra L. Hodgkinson, 'Detention Operations: A Strategic View' in Geoffrey S. Corn, Rachel E. Van Landingham, & Shane R. Reeves (eds.), *US Military Operations: Law, Policy, and Practice* (Oxford University Press 2015) 275, 294.
[236] Art. 3 HR.
[237] Art. 1 HR.

under a command responsible to that Party for the conduct of its subordinates, even if that Party is represented by a government or an authority not recognized by an adverse Party. Such armed forces shall be subject to an internal disciplinary system'.[238] Indeed, the ousted sovereign is still considered a party to the original armed conflict in the sense of international humanitarian law even if it has lost control over the territory due to the occupation.[239] However, the meaning of the expression 'belonging to a Party' is not clarified, and until recent times, it has received scant attention in legal scholarship.[240]

It could be worth dividing the members of the armed force in two subgroups, for which different rules apply regarding their affiliation to a state. On the one hand, *de jure* members of the ousted sovereign's armed force are those individuals who belong to that specific armed force in light of relevant domestic legislation.[241] Accordingly, any act of hostility between such individuals and the occupying power is regulated by the law on international armed conflict as it involve the two states.

However, in situations of involvement of irregular forces, it is more difficult to discern whether they belong to a party to the conflict or not since domestic legislation does not play any significant role. Such situations are not infrequent since '[i]t is natural that, in international armed conflicts, the Government which previously possessed an occupied area should encourage and take under its wing the irregular forces which continue fighting within the borders of the country'.[242] In the past, such situations were practically resolved through some proclamations promulgated by the belligerents in order to specify which armed groups belonged to their armed forces;[243] however, the drafters of the GCs rejected the proposal to consider the emanation of such declarations mandatory.[244]

There are two different ways in which this issue has been addressed, one on the basis of autonomous primary customary international law rules pertaining to the classification of the armed conflict, and one on the basis of the law of state responsibility. In spite of the overlapping between the two strands of reasoning in some judicial decisions, they deserve a separate analysis.

---

[238] Art. 43 API.
[239] See Sandoz, Swinarski, & Zimmermann (eds.), *Commentary*, para. 1661.
[240] See Israel, Military Court Sitting in Ramallah, *Military Prosecutor v. Kassem* et al., 476.
[241] See Melzer, *Interpretive Guidance*, 25, 31; Sean Watts, 'Who Is a Prisoner of War?' in Clapham, Gaeta, & Sassòli (eds.), *The 1949 Geneva Conventions*, 879, 897.
[242] Israel, Military Court Sitting in Ramallah, *Military Prosecutor v. Kassem* et al., 476–7.
[243] See, e.g., the Dutch Royal Emergency Decree of September 1944, quoted in Israel, Military Court Sitting in Ramallah, *Military Prosecutor v. Kassem* et al., 477. See, also, the practice mentioned by Annoni, *L'occupazione*, 255, fn. 455 (emphasis added).
[244] See Watts, 'Who Is', 898.

One view supports the idea that the 'belonging' requirement should be constructed as a primary international humanitarian law rule based on a factual relationship between the individuals fighting against the occupying power (or any other actor in a different scenario) and the ousted sovereign (or another state outside situations of occupation). According to an Israeli Military Court, in order to consider some combatants 'belonging to a Party' of the armed conflict, 'a *"command relationship"* should exist between such Government and the fighting forces', so that 'a continuing responsibility exists of the Government and the commanders of its army for those who fight in its name and on its behalf'.[245] Similarly, Article 43(1) AP I posits that '[t]he armed forces of a Party to a conflict consist of all organized armed forces, groups and units *which are under a command responsible to that Party for the conduct of its subordinates*, even if that Party is represented by a government or an authority not recognized by an adverse Party';[246] a number of authors suggest that this criterion refers to irregular armed forces as well.[247] The identification of a command relationship with the requirement of belonging to an armed force is, however, contradicted by Article 4(A)(2) GC III, which, with reference to the different topic of the entitlement to prisoner-of-war status, provides that an individual must belong to a party of the armed conflict *and* be under a command, thus implying that the two conditions are distinctive.[248] However, the most thorny issue is defining which level of control is sufficient to fulfil the belonging requirement. According to the celebrated Pictet's commentary, the belonging requirement is satisfied when there is 'a *de facto* relationship between the resistance organization and the party to international law which is in a state of war, but the existence of this relationship is sufficient. It may find expression merely by tacit agreement, if the operations are such as to indicate clearly for which side the resistance organization is fighting'.[249] This view has been supported by some other authors,[250] to the extent that some commentators have argued that the concept of belonging would be very

---

[245] Israel, Military Court Sitting in Ramallah, *Military Prosecutor v. Kassem* et al., 477.
[246] Emphasis added.
[247] See Sandoz, Swinarski, & Zimmermann (eds.), *Commentary*, para. 1672. See also Michael Bothe, Karl Josef Partsch, & Waldemar A. Solf (eds.), *New Rules for Victims of Armed Conflicts* (Martinus Nijhoff 1982) 234; Dapo Akande, 'Clearing the Fog of War? The ICRC's Interpretive Guidance on Direct Participation in Hostilities' (2010) 59 ICLQ 180, 184.
[248] See Watts, 'Who Is', 897.
[249] Jean Pictet, *Commentary to III Geneva Convention* (ICRC 1960) 57.
[250] See Katherine del Mar, 'The Requirement of "Belonging" under International Humanitarian Law' (2010) 21 EJIL 105, 111–13; Rogier Bartels, 'Terrorist Groups as Parties to an Armed Conflict' (2017) 47 *Collegium* 56, 61.

similar to that of allegiance.[251] However, the main risk with this approach is the potential to enlarge excessively the category of those belonging to a party.

Although this author concurs with the idea that the relevant test according to which individuals belong to a state in the sense of the law of armed conflict is a primary rule rather than a secondary rule on state responsibility, the generic requirement of an allegiance risks to create the paradoxical situation of some individuals belonging to the armed forces of a state without its consent or knowledge. Accordingly, a more stringent test must be identified. The case law of the ICTY, in relation to armed activities conducted by individuals not considered to be organs under domestic law and organised in armed groups, offers the right answer to this issue. The ICTY's Appeals Chamber, in its famous reasoning of the *Tadić* case with regard to the classification of the armed conflicts occurring in the former Yugoslavia, affirmed that the 'overall control' of a state over irregular armed forces is sufficient to consider those forces belonging to the state. According to the Appeals Chamber, in cases of military armed groups involved in an armed conflict, one has to take into account Article 4(A)(2) GC III, which pertains to the entitlement to the status of prisoner of war.[252] This rule refers to armed forces 'belonging to a state', an expression which is not defined by international humanitarian law. Accordingly, the Appeals Chamber resorted to the law on international responsibility and, after having reviewed international practice and case law, affirmed that the conduct of an organised armed group should be attributed to a state if the armed group acted under the 'overall control' of that state.[253] Despite some initial reactions,[254] the 'overall control' test is recognised today

---

[251] See, e.g., Robert Kolb, *Ius in bello: le droit international des conflits armés: précis* (Helbing & Lichtenhahn 2003) 160.
[252] ICTY, *Prosecutor v. Tadić*, IT-94-1-A, Appeals Chamber, 15 July 1999, para. 92.
[253] Ibid., para. 145:

> In the case at issue, given that the Bosnian Serb armed forces constituted a 'military organization', the control of the FRY authorities over these armed forces required by international law for considering the armed conflict to be international was overall control going beyond the mere financing and equipping of such forces and involving also participation in the planning and supervision of military operations. By contrast, international rules do not require that such control should extend to the issuance of specific orders or instructions relating to single military actions, whether or not such actions were contrary to international humanitarian law.

See also para. 138.

[254] See, e.g., Claus Kreß, 'L'organe *de facto* en droit international public: réflexions sur l'imputation à l'état de l'acte d'un particulier à la lumière des développements récents' (2001) 105 RGDIP 93, 112–16; André J. J. de Hoogh, 'Articles 4 and 8 of the 2001 ILC Articles on State Responsibility, the Tadic Case and Attribution of Acts of Bosnian Serb Authorities to the Federal Republic of Yugoslavia' (2002) 72 British YIL 255; Giulio Bartolini, 'Il concetto di controllo

as the relevant test under customary international law to ascertain whether an armed group acted on behalf of a state in order to qualify an armed conflict as international or non-international, as demonstrated by subsequent case law of the ICTY[255] and the ICC.[256] The ICJ itself, while maintaining a different position regarding the issue of attribution under the law of international responsibility, acknowledged that 'as the "overall control" test is employed to determine whether or not an armed conflict is international, which was the sole question which the Appeals Chamber was called upon to decide, it may well be that the test is applicable and suitable'.[257] Accordingly, in order to qualify hostilities occurring in occupied territory, the 'overall control' test is relevant to determine whether organised armed groups belong to the ousted sovereign.[258] Accordingly, despite the fact that the *Tadić* decision was argued at the same time on the basis of the belonging requirement and of the law of state responsibility,[259] the 'overall control' test constitutes the relevant primary rule regulating the cases in which individuals belong to a state forthe classification of an armed conflict.[260]

For the sake of completeness, it is worth pointing out that there is a second view, according to which the law on international responsibility regulates whether an armed conflict is international or non-international. Indeed, some international practice and case law suggests that, if hostilities are attributable to two or more states, then the armed conflict is international in character. For instance, according to the aforementioned Israeli Military Court, 'an opposite party must exist to *bear responsibility for the acts of its forces, regular and irregular*. We agree that the [GC III] applies to military forces (in the wide sense of

---

sulle attività di individui quale presupposto della responsabilità dello Stato' in Marina Spinedi, Alessandra Gianelli, & Maria Luisa Alaimo (eds.), *La codificazione della responsabilità internazionale degli Stati alla prova dei fatti* (Giuffré 2006) 25.

[255] See *Prosecutor v. Aleksovski*, IT-95-14/1-A, Appeals Chamber, 24 March 2000, paras. 131–4; *Prosecutor v. Delalić* et al., IT-96-21-A, Appeals Chamber, 20 February 2001, para. 26; *Prosecutor v. Kordić and Čerkez*, IT-94-1-A, 17 December 2004, paras. 306–8; *Prosecutor v. Mladić*, IT-09-92-T, 22 November 2017, para. 3014.

[256] See *Prosecutor v. Lubanga*, Decision on Confirmation of Charges, para. 221; *Prosecutor v. Lubanga*, Judgment pursuant to Art. 74, para. 541; *Prosecutor v. Katanga*, Trial Chamber, Judgment pursuant to Art. 74, para. 1178; *Prosecutor v. Bemba Gombo*, para. 130.

[257] *Bosnian Genocide* case, para. 404.

[258] See Ferraro (ed.), *Expert Meeting*, 127; Roscini, *Cyber Operations*, 138–40; Ferraro & Cameron, 'Article 2', paras. 270–3.

[259] One of the judges of the bench that pronounced that decision in the *Tadić* case voiced his discontent about the ICJ's reasoning, arguing that the test spelled in the ICTY's decision was not confined to the classification of the armed conflict only (Antonio Cassese, 'The Nicaragua and *Tadić* Tests Revisited in Light of the ICJ Judgment on Genocide in Bosnia' (2007) 18 EJIL 649).

[260] See Roscini, *Cyber Operations*, 138–9.

the term) which, *as regards responsibility under International Law, belong to a State engaged in armed conflict* with another State'.[261] Following this view, only acts attributable to a party of the armed conflicts are committed by members of its armed forces.[262] On the basis of the rules of attribution of international responsibility,[263] states are primarily responsible for acts committed by their organs, an expression that includes 'any person or entity which has that status in accordance with the internal law of the State'.[264] Accordingly, acts of hostility against the occupying power involving members of the armed forces of the ousted sovereign are interstate hostilities regulated by the law on international armed conflict both under international humanitarian law and the law on international responsibility. In addition, the law on international responsibility, under certain circumstances, considers that the conduct of individuals who are not organs under domestic legislation may be, nonetheless, attributed to a state. This is the case of individuals placed under complete dependence of a state.[265] Moreover, according to Article 8 DARS, '[t]he conduct of a person or group of persons shall be considered an act of a State under international law if the person or group of persons is in fact acting on the instructions of, or under the direction or control of, that State in carrying out the conduct'. The case law of the ICJ confirms the assertion that 'effective control' over individuals triggers state responsibility. In particular, in the *Nicaragua* v. *USA* case, the Court affirmed that '[f]or this conduct to give rise to legal responsibility of [a state], it would in principle have to be proved that that State had effective control of the military or paramilitary operations in the course of which

---

[261] Israel, Military Court Sitting in Ramallah, *Military Prosecutor* v. *Kassem* et al., 477 (emphases added).

[262] See, also, Italy, Supreme Military Tribunal, *In re Keppler*, 197–9.

[263] Clearly, a thorough analysis of the rules on attribution is beyond the purview of this book. A summary of the debate may be read in the DARS, with Commentary, and in the many reports prepared by the ILC's special rapporteurs between 1956 and 2001 (these reports are available at legal.un.org/ilc/guide/9_6.shtml). Among the most prominent studies in this field and for further references, see Dioniso Anzilotti, *Teoria generale della responsabilità dello Stato nel diritto internazionale* (Lumachi Libraio 1902) 153–87; Roberto Ago, 'Le délit international' (1939) 68 RCADI 415, 450–98; Ian Brownlie, *System of the Law of Nations. State Responsibility, Part I* (Clarendon Press 1983) 132–66; Luigi Condorelli, 'L'imputation a l'état d'un fait internationalement illicite: solutions classiques et nouvelles tendances' (1984) 189 RCADI 9; Haritini Dipla, *La responsabilité de l'Etat pour violation des droits de l'homme: problèmes d'imputation* (Pedone 1994); Paolo Palchetti, *L'organo di fatto dello Stato nell'illecito internazionale* (Giuffré 2007); James Crawford, *State Responsibility: The General Part* (Cambridge University Press 2013) 113–214; Gaetano Arangio-Ruiz, *State Responsibility Revisited: The Factual Nature of the Attribution of Conduct to the State* (Giuffré 2017).

[264] See Art. 4 DARS.

[265] See *Nicaragua* v. *USA*, paras. 109–10; *Bosnian Genocide* case, para. 392.

5.5. The Classification of Hostilities in the Occupied Territory 213

the alleged violations were committed'.[266] Similarly, in the *Bosnian Genocide* case, the ICJ reiterated that

> it has to be proved that [the armed groups] acted in accordance with that State's instructions or under its "effective control". It must however be shown that this "effective control" was exercised, or that the State's instructions were given, in respect of each operation in which the alleged violations occurred, not generally in respect of the overall actions taken by the persons or groups of persons having committed the violations.[267]

Accordingly, following the view that links the classification of an armed conflict to attribution under the law of international responsibility, if individuals placed under the dependence or the effective control of the ousted sovereign fight against the occupying power, then the law on international armed conflict applies.

Finally, some authors have investigated whether Article 9 DARS may be relevant in order to attribute conduct of non-state armed groups to the ousted sovereign, with the consequence that the hostilities conducted by them against the occupying power should be regulated by the law on international armed conflict.[268] Article 9 DARS posits that:

> The conduct of a person or group of persons shall be considered an act of a state under international law if the person or group of persons is in fact exercising elements of the governmental authority in the absence or default of the official authorities and in circumstances such as to call for the exercise of those elements of authority.

Should this rule be applicable to acts of armed resistance against the occupying power, hostilities between armed groups and the occupying power in the occupied territory would be attributed to the ousted sovereign, and thus they would be regulated by the law on international armed conflict. As affirmed by the DARS commentary, this provision deals with exceptional cases 'such as during revolution, armed conflict or *foreign occupation*, where the regular authorities dissolve, are disintegrating, have been suppressed or are for the time being inoperative'.[269] However, this rule of attribution is applicable only in 'the situation of a total collapse of the state apparatus'[270] and 'in the absence

---

[266] See *Nicaragua v. USA*, para. 115.
[267] *Bosnian Genocide* case, para. 400.
[268] See Knut Dörmann & Laurent Colassis, 'International Humanitarian Law in the Iraq Conflict' (2004) 47 German YIL 293, 320–1; Mégret, 'Grandeur', 411.
[269] DARS, commentary to Article 9, para. 1 (emphasis added).
[270] Ibid., para. 5.

of any constituted authority'.[271] The typical situation is that of the *levée en masse*,[272] when the local population of an invaded territory rises against the enemy in order to defend the territory and repeal the invasion.[273] However, this rule is not applicable in cases of existing occupations where, by definition, an authority exercising governmental functions on the occupied territory *does exist* in the form of the occupying power's administration. Accordingly, as demonstrated also by the complete lack of relevant state practice, Article 9 DARS may not be employed in order to attribute hostilities involving armed groups to the ousted sovereign.

Clearly, all the relevant rules on attribution cover cases in which individuals should be considered as belonging to a state's armed forces; accordingly, if an act of hostility is attributable to a state, very likely the author of that act belongs to the armed forces of that states.[274] However, the 'overall control' test embodied in a primary customary international law rule is broader than the tests codified by DARS with regard to state responsibility. On the basis of the above observations, it is possible to conclude that hostilities in occupied territory are regulated by the law on international armed conflict if such hostilities involve the armed forces of the ousted sovereign, including irregular forces who belong to the ousted sovereign under the primary rule of the 'overall control' test spelt out by the ICTY.

However, armed groups very often act outside any control of the ousted sovereign. In similar situations, the identification of the rules governing the hostilities in occupied territory may be more challenging.

5.5.3. The Rules Pertaining to Hostilities between the Occupying Power and Armed Groups Not Belonging to the Ousted Sovereign

5.5.3.1. The Thesis of the Application of the Rules on Non-International Armed Conflict

Some UN practice[275] and a number of authors have advanced the idea that hostilities between the occupying power and armed groups not belonging to the ousted sovereign are regulated by the law of non-international armed conflict

---

[271] Ibid., para. 6.
[272] Ibid., para. 2. See Olivier De Frouville, 'Attribution of Conduct to the State: Private Individuals' in Crawford, Pellet, & Olleson (eds.), *The Law*, 257, 273.
[273] See Art. 2 HR and Art. 4(A)(6) GC III.
[274] See Melzer, *Interpretive Guidance*, 23.
[275] Question of the Violation of Human Rights in the Occupied Arab Territories, Including Palestine: Report of the Human Rights Inquiry Commission Established Pursuant to Commission Resolution S-5/1 of 19 October 2000, 16 March 2001, para. 39.

since international armed conflict are only fought between states.[276] It would follow in turn that every time hostilities in occupied territory do not involve two states, as in the case of armed resistance not affiliated to the ousted sovereign or operating from occupied territories not belonging to any state before the occupation, the law on non-international armed conflict should apply.

This idea posits that the classification of an armed conflict depends on the status of the belligerents. A non-international armed conflict would exist whenever there is a protracted resort to armed force between a state and organised non-state actor *irrespective of whether the violence occurs within or without the territory of the state*. Following this approach, as long as armed groups do not belong to the armed force of any state, the hostilities against the occupying power should fall under the law on non-international armed conflict. The fact that the classification of an armed conflict depends on the status of the parties is supported by a number of authoritative elements. For instance, this conclusion has been implied by the *Hamdan* case in which the US Supreme Court applied common Article 3 GCs to the armed conflict between the US and the Taliban as non-international.[277] The Court, however, never explicitly characterised that armed conflict as non-international, leaving the door open to a different classification.[278] Moreover, the idea that an armed conflict between a state and a non-state actor is regulated by the law on non-international armed conflict is authoritatively supported by the most recent ICRC commentary on the GCs, according to which 'armed confrontations, meeting the requisite intensity threshold, between a state and a non-state armed group which operates from the territory of a second, neighbouring state ... if the non-state armed group does not act on behalf of the second state ... should be regarded as a non-international armed conflict'.[279] Following this view, the fact that common Article 3 GCs and Article 1(1) AP II mention that non-international armed conflict should occur in the territory of *a* High Contracting Party should not be constructed as implying that the armed conflict must be confined to the territory of the state against which the armed group fights, but rather, that it may

---

[276] See Ben-Naftali & Michaeli, 'We Must', 255–9; Milanovic, 'Lessons', 381–6; David Kretzmer, 'Targeted Killing of Suspected Terrorists: Extra-Judicial Executions or Legitimate Means of Defence?' (2005) 16 EJIL 171, 210–11; Alessandra Annoni, 'Esecuzioni mirate di sospetti terroristi e diritto alla vita' (2008) 91 RDI 991, 1006–9; Arai-Takahashi, *The Law*, 297–304; Russell Buchan, 'The International Law of Naval Blockade and Israel's Interception of the *Mavi Marmara*' (2011) 58 NILR 209, 216–32; Douglas Guilfoyle, 'The *Mavi Marmara* Incident and Blockade in Armed Conflict' (2011) 81 British YIL 171, 181–91; Ferraro (ed.), *Expert Meeting*, 127; Ben Saul, 'Many Small Wars: The Classification of Armed Conflicts in the Non-Self-Governing Territory of Western Sahara (Spanish Sahara) in 1974–1976' (2016) 2 African YIHL 86, section 5.
[277] *Hamdan v. Rumsfeld*, (2006) 548 US 557, 630–1.
[278] Milanovic, 'Lessons', 377–81.
[279] Cameron et al., 'Article 3', para. 477.

be waged from the territory of *another* state party.[280] Similarly, the US Military Manual considers that non-international armed conflicts 'are classified as such simply *based on the status of the parties* to the conflict, and sometimes occur in more than one state. The mere fact that an armed conflict occurs in more than one state and thus may be characterised as international "in scope" does not render it "international in character"'.[281] Some UN practice[282] and some authoritative private codifications[283] support this view. Even in light of the plummeting involvement of non-state actors in cross-border hostilities, this view appears to be the most widely accepted today.[284]

As a consequence of this view, the status of the parties involved in the hostilities in occupied territory determines the rules governing the resort to armed force and, if the armed group does not belong to the armed force of any state, the rules on non-international armed conflict shall apply in occupied territory. Some authors have suggested that the Separate Opinion of Judge Kooijmans in the *Wall* Opinion, which denied any international character to the armed attacks launched by Palestinian armed groups, would support this idea.[285] In addition, one author has argued that the hostilities between Israel and Palestinian armed groups must be regarded as regulated by the law on non-international armed conflict because:

> (i) the occupying power is the only state for decades to exercise exclusive effective control over the territory; (ii) no other state is laying claim to the territory; and (iii) the insurgents themselves are not purporting to fight on behalf of any other state, nor is their struggle directly related to the initial international armed conflict.[286]

[280] It is worth pointing out that, today, every state in the world is party to the GCs.
[281] US Military Manual, section 17.1.1.2 (emphasis added).
[282] HRC, Report of the Special Rapporteur on the Promotion and Protection of Human Rights and Fundamental Freedoms while Countering Terrorism, A/HRC/6/17/Add.3, 22 November 2007, para. 8.
[283] See Schmitt (ed.), *Tallinn Manual 2.0*, 386.
[284] See, e.g., Liesbeth Zegveld, *Accountability of Armed Opposition Groups in International Law* (Cambridge University Press 2002) 136; Derek Jinks, 'September 11 and the Laws of War' (2003) 28 Yale JIL 1, 38–41; Kretzmer, 'Targeted Killing', 171, 195; Vité, 'Typology', 92; Melzer, *Targeted Killing*, 261; Marco Sassòli, 'The Role of Human Rights and International Humanitarian Law in New Types of Armed Conflicts' in Ben-Naftali (ed.), *International*, 34, 55–6; Sivakumaran, *The Law*, 229–31; Andreas Zimmermann & Robin Geiß, 'Article 8 para. 2 (c)–(f) and para. 3: War Crimes Committed in an Armed Conflict Not of an International Character' in Otto Triffterer & Kai Ambos (eds.), *The Rome Statute of the International Criminal Court: A Commentary* (3rd edn, CH Beck-Hart-Nomos 2016) 528, 541; Murray, *Practitioners' Guide*, section 2.07; Thilo Marauhn & Zacharie F. Ntoubandi, 'Armed Conflict, Non International' in *MPEPIL online* (2016) para. 14; Salerno, *Diritto*, 280.
[285] *Wall* opinion, Separate Opinion of Judg Kooijmans, para. 36, which has been mentioned, e.g., by Kretzmer, 'Targeted Killing', 210, fn. 176.
[286] Milanovic, 'Lessons', 385–6.

5.5. The Classification of Hostilities in the Occupied Territory

Another commentator has relied on the fact that no armed group in the OPT has been fighting on behalf of any state, whether the parties to the original armed conflict in 1967 or the state of Palestine – if any such exists – in order to affirm the applicability of rules on non-international armed conflict in times of occupation.[287]

In this author's view, the described approach is subject to criticism. Without repeating here the already expressed remarks on this reasoning,[288] it should be noted that Judge Kooijmans's opinion on the non-international character of the Palestinian attacks was not shared by any other judges, and that Judge Kooijmans never entered the debate regarding the applicable *jus in bello*. Moreover, the fact that a non-international armed conflict may exist outside the borders of the involved state can be contested in light of some textual elements and international case law – which are examined subsequently – suggesting that only intrastate hostilities may be qualified as non-international armed conflicts.[289] Following this view – which, however, this author does not consider to be conclusive – the law on non-international armed conflict would not apply since the occupied territory may not be considered annexed to the occupying power's territory.

However, the main objection to the application of the law on non-international armed conflict is that the supporters of this view do not take into account at all the existence of a situation of occupation. *Prima facie*, one could wonder how it could be that a situation – the occupation – that may be created only in an international armed conflict would require the application of the law on non-international armed conflict. Several critics of the non-international armed conflict argument have pointed out this inconsistency.[290] The most common answer to this criticism is that the ICJ and the ICTY have recognised that an international armed conflict may coexist with one or more non-international armed conflicts.[291] However, to the best of this author's knowledge, never has an international court affirmed that the occupying power may be involved, simultaneously, in both international and non-international armed conflicts in the occupied territory. It is not strange that the reference to the aforementioned international case law is approached cautiously by one of the strongest supporters of the application of the law on non-international armed conflict, according to whom the involvement of

---

[287] Mastorodimos, 'The Character', 457–8.
[288] See *supra*, Section 3.2.3.2.
[289] See *infra*, Section 5.5.3.2.
[290] See Cassese, *International Law*, 420; Watkin, 'Use of Force', 293; Zimmermann & Geiß, 'Article 8', 540.
[291] See *Nicaragua v. USA*, para. 219; ICTY, *Prosecutor v. Tadić*, Appeal Chamber's Judgment, para. 84.

the occupying power into a non-international armed conflict 'is not *entirely* contradictory'.[292]

Additionally, there are practical reasons not to apply the law on non-international armed conflict to hostilities occurring within the occupied territory. Although 'there are significant similarities to insurgencies in a non-international armed conflict',[293] hostilities in the occupied territory are, in principle, regulated by the law on international armed conflict if they involve armed forces belonging to the ousted sovereign or acting under its overall control. Accordingly, the distinction between non-international armed conflicts within the occupied territory and hostilities linked to the original armed conflict would impose upon the occupying power the burden to make a threefold distinction: not only must it distinguish between law enforcement and conduct of hostilities, but also between different types of hostilities on the basis of the personal status of the enemy fighters (i.e., depending on whether they 'belong' to the ousted sovereign). Such a distinction is highly impracticable, as demonstrated by the practice related to the occupation of Iraq, wherein it was tremendously difficult to distinguish between hostilities involving the remnant of Saddam Hussein's regime and independent armed groups. As has been very clearly explained, since '[t]hese groups, often acting as co-belligerents, fight the same occupying power ... [i]t is difficult to see what advantage is gained in seeking to subdivide this conflict into different categories in what is an integrated operational and security environment involving protection of the same population'.[294]

For all these reasons, the majority of scholars have rejected the idea that the law on non-international armed conflict regulates hostilities between the occupying power and armed groups not belonging to the ousted sovereign. A variety of different explanations have been advanced to support the idea that the law on international armed conflict should apply.

5.5.3.2. Different Arguments for the Application of Rules on International Armed Conflict

Although many states have expressed the view that hostilities between the occupying power and armed groups are regulated by the law on international armed conflict,[295] these same states have not offered any legal reasoning to

---

[292] Milanovic, 'Lessons', 386 (emphasis added).
[293] Watkin, 'Maintaining', 186.
[294] Watkin, 'Use of Force', 292.
[295] See the position of Syria (S/PV.4503, 18); Algeria (S/PV.4503, 20); Jordan (S/PV.4503, 26); Tunisia (S/PV.4506, 6); Saudi Arabia (S/PV.4506, 18–19); Libya (S/PV.6060, 7); Indonesia

substantiate this view. Conversely, a number of authors have advanced interesting arguments explaining why hostilities between the occupying power and armed groups, including in cases of absence of any previous sovereign, are regulated by the law on international armed conflict. An analysis of the different approaches advanced in international scholarship may contribute to identifying the most pertinent legal framework.

One argument advanced by some scholars is that the law on international armed conflict is applicable if the armed groups that fight against the occupying power are fighting for the self-determination of the people dwelling in the occupied territory.[296] Indeed, according to Article 1(4) AP I, 'armed conflicts in which peoples are fighting against colonial domination and alien occupation and against racist régimes in the exercise of their right of self-determination' should be considered international in character. Despite the fact that Article 1(4) AP I was drafted with the situations of Namibia and the OPT in mind,[297] many author argues that this provision does not refer to occupied territory: one author, for instance, has argued that occupation is already regulated by the law of international armed conflict, so that the reference to 'alien occupation' in Article 1(4) AP I must refer to different situations,[298] while other authors have suggested that the reference to 'alien occupation' pertains to 'cases of partial or total occupation of a territory which has not yet been fully formed as a state'.[299] In addition, this provision was considered not applicable to the occupations of Namibia and the OPT due to the lack of any ratification by South Africa[300] and Israel,[301] given that most authors take the view that Article 1(4) AP I does

---

(S/PV.6060, 10); Burkina Faso (S/PV.6060, 15); Costa Rica (S/PV.6060, 16); Egypt (S/PV.6060, 18); Cuba (A/67/PV.47, 3–4); Palestine (S/PV.7214, 4); Namibia (S/PV.7222, 45); Iran (S/PV.7222, 56); Bangladesh (S/PV.7222, 62).

[296] See Zimmermann, 'Abiding', 55–7; Zimmermann & Geiß, 'Article 8', 540.
[297] See Ronzitti, *Le guerre*, 34, 203.
[298] Ibid., 33–4, and Ronzitti, *Diritto*, 145.
[299] See Sandoz, Swinarski, & Zimmermann (eds.), *Commentary*, para. 112. See also Bothe, Partsch, & Solf (eds.), *New*, 51–2 (referring to 'cases in which a High Contracting Party occupies territories of a State which is not a [High Contracting Party], or territories with a controversial international law status').
[300] South African domestic courts affirmed the non-correspondence to customary international law of the rule embodied in Art. 1(4) AP I in a number of decisions. See, e.g., the Supreme Court decisions in the cases S v. *Sagarius en andere* 1983 (1) SA 833 (SWA), S v. *Mogoerane et al.* (TPD) 6 August 1982, published in (1983) *Lawyers for Human Rights Bulletin* 118.
[301] According to some authors, Israel could be seen as a persistent object to the crystallisation of a rule of customary international law corresponding to Art. 1(4) AP I (Cassese, 'Wars', 322; Andreas Zimmerman, 'Responsibility for Violations of International Humanitarian Law, International Criminal Law and Human Rights Law – Synergy and Conflict?' in Wolff Heintschel von Heinegg & Volker Epping (eds.), *International Humanitarian Law Facing New Challenges* (Springer 2007) 215, 218).

not reflect customary international law.[302] However, in principle, following this view, Article 1(4) AP I might be employed to consider the rules on international armed conflict applicable to hostilities occurring in the occupied territory if the occupying power is a party to the AP I, and as long as the movement of national liberation fighting against the occupying power has issued a declaration of acceptance of the law on international armed conflicts.[303]

Despite the fact that some states have claimed that the fight against an occupying power is inherently a war of national liberation,[304] this author does not share the view that Article 1(4) AP I is the right answer to the problems pertaining to the classification of hostilities in occupied territory. In this author's view, since the situations of Namibia and OPT – to regulate which this provision was envisaged – fall into the contemporary definition of occupation adopted in this book,[305] they do not need a different regulation from traditional occupations which are outside the scope of Article 1(4) AP I. In fact by the time Article 1(4) AP I was adopted, some authors had already suggested, rightly, that the Namibian and Palestinian situations fell into the already accepted definition of occupation and, thus, under common Article 2 GCs.[306] Accordingly, Article 1(4) AP I would create a different regime for some specific situations of occupation when there is no reason to regulate differently the same situations; it is not a chance the fact that this provision, which was adopted mainly for ideological reasons, was never applied with respect of occupied territory.[307]

Indeed, there are serious practical issues that render the application of Article 1(4) AP I to hostilities occurring within occupied territory particularly irksome. For instance, Article 1(4) AP I refers only to national liberation movements operating in the occupied territory, so that conduct of armed groups

---

[302] See, e.g., Ronzitti, *Diritto*, 144–5; Dinstein, *The Conduct*, 37. Cassese had suggested initially that the provision was in line with customary international law ('Wars of National Liberation and Humanitarian Law' in Swinarski (ed.), *Études*, 313, 322), but he rejected this assumption in more recent works due to lack of corresponding state practice (Cassese, *Self-Determination*, 203–4).

[303] See Art. 96(3) AP I, and Sivakumaran, *The Law*, 220–1, for a detailed analysis of this provision. So far, only POLISARIO has issued successfully such a declaration (see Swiss Federal Council, Notification to the Governments of the states Parties to the Geneva Conventions of 12 August 1949 for the Protection of War Victims, 26 June 2015, www.eda.admin.ch/content/dam/eda/fr/documents/aussenpolitik/voelkerrecht/geneve/150626-GENEVE_en.pdf).

[304] See the position of Iran, S/PV.4506, 11. With reference to the Soviet occupation of Afghanistan, see Reisman, 'The Resistance'.

[305] See *supra*, Section 1.3.

[306] See Richard R. Baxter, 'Humanitarian Law or Humanitarian Politics? The 1974 Diplomatic Conference on Humanitarian Law' (1975) 16 Harvard ILJ 1, 14–15. See, also, Edward Kwakwa, 'The Namibian Conflict: A Discussion of the *Jus ad Bellum* and the *Jus in Bello*' (1988) 9 New York Law School JICL 195, 216–20.

[307] This author believes that such a provision may play a more significant role in relation of struggles for self-determination outside occupied territory, such as in a colonial context.

that do not enjoy this status would not be regulated by the law on international armed conflict.[308] Moreover, it is not easy to discern who is a member of a movement of national liberation since the affiliation to an armed group, even in the law of non-international armed conflict, is a largely debated question.[309] Considering Article 1(4) AP I the decisive factor would be very impractical for the occupying power, which would be required to discern between the following scenarios in order to apply the correct legal framework: (i) situations requiring law enforcement (not directly regulated by international humanitarian law rules on the conduct of hostilities); (ii) hostilities involving the ousted sovereign (per se regulated by the law on international armed conflict); (iii) hostilities involving members of national liberation movements (regulated by the law on international armed conflict only if the occupying power is party to the AP I and the movement has enacted the declaration under Article 96(3) AP I); and (iv) hostilities with armed groups not belonging to the ousted sovereign nor affiliated with any national liberation movements (regulated by the law on non-international armed conflict). In addition, there is no consensus on the threshold that would be necessary to apply Article 1(4) AP I: some authors have argued that, since the hostilities at hand are to be considered regulated by the law on international armed conflict, the same threshold of international armed conflict (i.e., whatever use of armed force) should apply;[310] however, this conclusion is not consistent with the fact that, considering Article 1(4) AP I the determining factor between the law on non-internal armed conflict and the law on international armed conflict, the hostilities in occupied territory would be, in origin, non-international in character, and therefore would need to reach the threshold of non-international armed conflict before being considered international in character due to the legitimacy of their aim.[311] For all these reasons, Article 1(4) AP I does not appear decisive in qualifying the nature of hostilities in the occupied territory.

A second argument in favour of the application of the law on international armed conflict derives from a different understanding of the geographical scope of non-international armed conflicts. According to this approach, a non-international armed conflict may exist only *within* the territory of one state that is also a party to that conflict or, at least, it must originate from the

---

[308] Zimmermann & Geiß, 'Article 8', 540.
[309] On this topic, outside the scope of this book, see, generally, Michael N. Schmitt, 'The Status of Opposition Fighters in a Non-International Armed Conflict' (2012) 88 ILS 119; Annyssa Bellal, 'ICRC Commentary of Common Article 3: Some Questions Relating to Organized Armed Groups and the Applicability of IHL', EJIL: Talk!, 5 October 2017.
[310] See Sandoz, Swinarski, & Zimmermann (eds.), *Commentary*, paras. 114–15; Abi-Saab, 'Wars', 413–14; Sivakumaran, *The Law*, 217.
[311] See Paolo Benvenuti, 'Movimenti insurrezionali e Protocolli aggiuntivi alla Convenzione di Ginevra del 1949' (1981) 64 RDI 513, 523–4.

territory of one state party to the conflict even if it may 'spill over' and assume a partially cross-border nature.[312] It follows that, since the occupied territory is, ontologically, not part of the occupying power's territory, an armed conflict between the occupying power and armed groups in the occupied territory may not be qualified as non-international. This geographical understanding of non-international armed conflicts is supported by a number of elements. For instance, common Article 3 GCs, generally considered the main provision on non-international armed conflicts, regards 'armed conflict not of an international character *occurring in the territory of one of the High Contracting Parties*'.[313] The authoritative Pictet's commentary stressed that non-international armed conflicts are conflicts 'which are in many respects similar to an international war, but *take place within the confines of a single country*'.[314] Similarly, Article 1(1) AP II refers to armed conflicts 'which take place in the territory of a High Contracting Party between *its* armed forces ... and armed groups'.[315] Consistently, the famous definition of non-international armed conflict in the *Tadić* case refers to 'protracted armed violence between governmental authorities and organized armed groups or between such groups *within a State*'.[316] The ICTR adopted the same approach,[317] as well as the ICC.[318] For instance, a Trial Chamber held that a non-international armed conflict 'takes place within the confines of a State'.[319] Furthermore, the idea that non-international armed conflicts may occur only within the territory of a state is supported by some UN practice,[320] authoritative non-binding codifications,[321] some military manuals,[322] and

---

[312] See Arts. 1 and 7 Statute of the ICTR, text in (1994) 33 ILM 1598.
[313] Emphasis added.
[314] Pictet (ed.), *Commentary to IV Geneva Convention*, 36.
[315] Emphasis added.
[316] ICTY, *Prosecutor v. Tadić*, Decision on the Defence Motion, para. 70.
[317] ICTR, *Prosecutor v. Musema*, ICTR-96-13-A, Trial's Chamber Judgment and Sentence, 27 January 2000, para. 248.
[318] The aforementioned passage of the *Tadić* judgment is cited, without further commentary, in the case *Prosecutor v. Bemba*, Judgment pursuant to Art. 74, para. 128.
[319] *The Prosecutor v. Bemba Gombo*, ICC-01/05-01/08, Decision Pursuant to Article 61(7)(a) and (b) of the Rome Statute on the Charges, 15 June 2009, para. 231. See also para. 146.
[320] See Commission of Inquiry on Lebanon, Report pursuant to Human Rights Council resolution S-2/1, A/HRC/3/2, 23 November 2006, paras. 50–62.
[321] See IDI, Resolution on the Application of International Humanitarian Law and Fundamental Human Rights, in Armed Conflicts in which Non-State Entities are Parties, Session of Berlin (1999), Art. 1; Michael N. Schmitt, Yoram Dinstein, & Charles Garraway (eds.), *The Manual on the Law of Non-International Armed Conflict with Commentary* (International Institute of Humanitarian Law 2006) 2.
[322] See UK Military Manual, section 15.2; Spanish Military Manual, section 1.2.b.(2); German Military Manual, section 1301.

many commentators.[323] Following this approach, since the occupied territory is definitely not part of the occupying power's territory, the hostilities between the occupying power and armed groups in occupied territory may not be qualified as non-international,[324] as confirmed by the Supreme Court of Israel[325] and by some UN practice.[326] Although this view correctly takes into account the fact that the occupied territory may not be equated with the occupying power's territory, however, as already mentioned in the previous subsection, the view that a non-international armed conflict may exist only within the territory of the belligerent state is considered outdated by most recent authorities, especially in light of the increased involvement of non-state actors in cross-border violence.[327] Accordingly, today it is not possible to maintain that an armed conflict between a non-state actor and a state is non-international in character merely because the armed confrontations occur outside the state's borders.

Additionally, some commentators have argued that the law on international armed conflict should apply for policy reasons. For instance, Cassese held that the law on international armed conflict should govern hostilities in occupied territory since it provides a higher level of protection to civilians. Cassese argued that:

> The object and purpose of international humanitarian law impose that in case of doubt the protection deriving from this body to be *as extensive as possible*, and it is indisputable that the protection accorded by the rules on international conflicts is much broader than that relating to internal conflicts.[328]

[323] Theodor Meron, 'On the Inadequate Reach of Humanitarian and Human Rights Law and the Need for a New Instrument' (1983) 77 AJIL 589, 593; Lindsay Moir, *The Law of Internal Armed Conflict* (Cambridge University Press 2002) 31; Cassese, *International Law*, 420; Bartolini, 'Le eliminazioni', 626; Annoni, *L'occupazione*, 235; Dinstein, *Non-International Armed Conflicts*, 24–5; Dieter Fleck, 'The Law of Non-International Armed Conflict' in Fleck (ed.), *Handbook*, 581, 584–5; Martha M. Bradley, 'Expanding the Borders of Common Article 3 in Non-International Armed Conflicts: Amending Its Geographical Application Through Subsequent Practice?' (2017) 64 NILR 375.

[324] See Cassese, *International Law*, 420; Lubell, 'The ICJ', 297, fn. 68; Otto, *Targeted Killings*, 450.

[325] See *Targeted Killings* case, para. 18; *Al-Bassiouni v. Prime Minister*, paras. 12–15; HCJ 201/09 *Physicians for Human Rights v. Prime Minister*, 19 January 2009, para. 14, unofficial English translation available at elyon1.court.gov.il/files_eng/09/010/002/n07/09002010.n07.pdf; *A and B v. State of Israel*, CrimA 6659/06, CrimA 1757/07, CrimA 8228/07 and CrimA 3261/08, 11 June 2008, para. 9) quoted in Guilfoyle, 'The *Mavi Marmara*', 185, fn. 77).

[326] Report of the Secretary-General's Panel of Inquiry on the 31 May 2010 Flotilla Incident, September 2011, para. 73, available at www.un.org/News/dh/infocus/middle_east/Gaza_Flotilla_Panel_Report.pdf.

[327] See *supra*, Section 5.5.3.1.

[328] Cassese, *International Law*, 420 (emphasis in the original).

Other scholars share the view espoused in Cassese's opinion.[329] It is difficult to overlook the desirability of such an approach that, rightly, draws on the faultiness of the law on non-international armed conflict, especially of that codified in international humanitarian law conventions. However, the fact that the law on international armed conflict provides more protection does not per se justify a different classification of an armed conflict.[330] Perhaps, if there were no applicable rules of *jus in bello* at all, then it might be argued that the protective reach of the Martens Clause might allow the analogical application of the most protective rules, that is the law on international armed conflict.[331] However, it is not so clear that hostilities in the occupied territory are 'cases not covered by' existing rules on international law.[332]

Finally, a number of authors believe that the law on international armed conflict is applicable since the occupation may be created only in a situation of international armed conflict and is regulated by the same branch of *jus in bello*.[333] Apparently, this is the view of the ICJ, which in the *Wall* opinion evaluated whether to apply Article 23(g) HR, which regulates the conduct of hostilities in international armed conflict.[334] Similarly, in the *DRC v. Uganda* case, the ICJ applied the rules on international armed conflict to hostilities occurring in the occupied Congolese province of Ituri even if they involved non-state actors.[335] In addition, according to the Israeli report investigating the boarding of the vessel *Mavi Marmara* in 2010, '[s]ince an occupation can only exist within the context of an international armed conflict, the position that the Gaza Strip is subject to an occupation necessarily leads to the conclusion

---

[329] See Benvenuti, 'Judicial Review', xiv; Bartolini 'Le eliminazioni', 628; Helen Keller & Magdalena Forowicz, 'A Tightrope Walk between Legality and Legitimacy: An Analysis of the Israeli Supreme Court's Judgment on Targeted Killing' (2008) 21 LJIL 185, 193.

[330] See Guilfoyle, 'The *Mavi Marmara*', 187.

[331] The employment of the so-called Martens Clause in order to support the application by analogy of international humanitarian law to cases not explicitly covered by the relevant rules has been famously advanced by Cassese, 'The Martens Clause', 189–90, 212–13.

[332] Preamble HR; Art. 1(1) AP I.

[333] See, e.g., Reisman & Silk, 'Which Law', 483; Cassese, *International Law*, 420; Dinstein, *The International Law*, 100; Andrea Gioia, 'La lotta al terrorismo tra diritto di guerra e diritti dell'uomo' in Gargiulo & Vitucci (eds.), *La tutela*, 179–89, fn. 26; Kolb & Vité, *Le droit*, 352; Schmitt, 'Iraq', 364–5; Scobbie, 'Gaza', 295; Wolff Heintschel von Heinegg, 'Methods and Means of Naval Warfare in Non-International Armed Conflicts' (2012) 88 ILS 211, 228; Watkin, 'Use of Force', 293; Zamir, *Classification*, 166.

[334] *Wall* opinion, para. 124. The Court rejected the application of Art. 23(g) HR on the basis of a reasoning unrelated to the classification of the hostilities as international or non-international. See *infra*, Section 6.3.2.2.

[335] For this reading, see Akande, 'Classification', 48.

5.5. The Classification of Hostilities in the Occupied Territory 225

that the conflict in the Gaza Strip is international in character'.[336] This view is supported also by some UN practice[337] and by the ICC OTP.[338] This idea was applied by the ICC Pre-Trial Chamber I in the *Lubanga* and *Katanga* trials when, due to the occupation, the law on international armed conflict was considered applicable to any armed conflict in the occupied territory, including those armed conflicts between non-state armed groups that had commenced before the occupation;[339] subsequently, however, the ICC Trial Chambers have rejected these findings, affirming that non-international armed conflicts may coexist with an international armed conflict within a situation of occupation.[340]

The idea that the law on international armed conflict should govern every hostility occurring in occupied territory is based on the fact that an occupation may be created only during an international armed conflict and that the occupation preserves the existence of that armed conflict. This approach is very close to the correct one since it emphasises that the occupation itself imposes the application of the law on international armed conflict. Accordingly, when an occupation exists, the usual rules governing the classification of an armed conflict are not applicable. However, while reaching this correct conclusion, the authors supporting this view, so far, have failed to explain the normative basis according to which every hostility involving the occupying power should be regulated by the law on international armed conflict, even in cases of armed confrontations against non-state actors. Indeed, absent the occupation, a state may be involved in international and non-international armed conflicts simultaneously, as confirmed by authoritative international case law.[341] So far, no convincing answer has been provided to the question of why this

---

[336] The Public Commission to Examine the Maritime Incident of 31 May 2010: The Turkel Commission (2011) para. 41, available at www.jewishvirtuallibrary.org/jsource/Society_&_Culture/TurkelCommission.pdf (see also para. 44).

[337] See Goldstone Report, para. 77 (discussing the applicability of the status of prisoner of war, which exists only in international armed conflict); Report of the International Fact-Finding Mission to Investigate Violations of International Law, Including International Humanitarian and Human Rights Law, Resulting from the Israeli Attacks on the Flotilla of Ships Carrying Humanitarian Assistance, A/HRC/15/21, 27 September 2010, paras. 62–6.

[338] See ICC, OTP, Situation on Registered Vessels of Comoros, para. 16; OTP, Report on Preliminary Examination Activities (2016) para. 158 (with reference to Crimea).

[339] *Prosecutor v. Lubanga*, Decision on Confirmation of Charges, para. 220; *Prosecutor v. Katanga*, Decision on Confirmation of Charges, para. 240.

[340] See *Prosecutor v. Lubanga*, Judgment pursuant to Art. 74, para. 563; *Prosecutor v. Katanga*, Judgment pursuant to Art. 74, para. 1226.

[341] See *Nicaragua v. USA*, para. 219; ICTY, *Prosecutor v. Tadić*, Appeal Chamber's Judgment, para. 84. See also Report of the International Commission of Inquiry on Libya, A/HRC/19/68, 2 March 2012, para. 28.

principle is not applicable to hostilities involving the occupying power. The next subsection provides a legal explanation based on the law of occupation and the rationales behind the rules on international and non-international armed conflicts.

5.5.3.3. The Application of Rules on International Armed Conflicts as a Consequence of the Occupation Itself

The conundrum regarding the classification of the hostilities within a situation of occupation may be solved with reference to the law of occupation in its entirety and, in particular, to the principle guiding the occupying power's administration. A close look at the principles at the basis of the law on non-international armed conflict reveals their incompatibility with the exercise of occupying power's functions. Historical reasons demonstrate that the drafters of the GC IV considered hostilities in the occupied territory to be governed by the law on international armed conflict. Accordingly, it is argued here that a differentiation must be drawn between hostilities involving the occupying power, which are regulated by the law on international armed conflict, and hostilities between armed groups in the occupied territory, which are regulated by the law on non-international armed conflict as outside occupied territory.

The law of occupation itself requires the application of the law on international armed conflict. Essentially, the law of occupation regulates the conduct of the occupying power. Accordingly, it is a *lex specialis* in relation to other rules of international humanitarian law not specifically dealing with situations of occupation. As has been observed, 'the relevant question is not what type of conflict exists between the state and the non-state group but what law applies to the acts of an occupying power within occupied territory'.[342] Indeed, the law of occupation puts restraints on the occupying power not only with respect to the ousted sovereign, but also in relation to the local population of the occupied territory, which clearly cannot be classified as a state actor per se.[343] One of the basic tenets of the law of occupation is that the occupying power is prevented from acquiring sovereignty over the occupied territory, and instead has to distinguish itself from the true sovereign of that territory. This assumption is reflected by the fact that every time the occupying power is required to act in the place of the ousted sovereign, the law of occupation provides for a specific enabling norm, Article 43 HR being the most important one.

---

[342] Akande, 'Classification', 47.
[343] Ibid. On the holders of the legal interests protected by the law of occupation, see *supra*, Section 2.6.

5.5. The Classification of Hostilities in the Occupied Territory

However, the law of occupation is incompatible with the rationale behind the law on non-international armed conflict. In cases of non-international armed conflicts, territorial states have a *jus puniendi* against insurgents. This *jus puniendi* derives from the states' sovereignty. In the past, only acts of sovereign entities could be seen as legitimate acts of war; accordingly, no international status was recognised for non-state actors fighting.[344] Still today, when a state's conduct in non-international armed conflict is constrained by a number of international law rules, international humanitarian law acknowledges the right of this state to punish as criminals individuals involved in a non-international armed conflict against themselves.[345] As is well known, insurgents, if captured, do not enjoy the status of prisoners of war but may be punished because their conduct against the central authorities is considered criminal under domestic law.[346] This *jus puniendi* is not created by international law, but rather is based on the pact of allegiance between the sovereign and its population pursuant to domestic legislation. International law only acknowledges the existence of a similar *jus puniendi* and, with the exception of situations of recognition of belligerency or legitimate struggles under Article 1(4) AP I, requires other states to abstain from any interference with this internal matter.[347]

Conversely, the occupying power does not enjoy such an inherent *jus puniendi* in occupied territory. Since the occupying power has no sovereignty over the inhabitants of the occupied territory, it lacks any domestic *jus puniendi* over the local population in cases of resort to armed force. As already demonstrated, the local population is free from any duty of obedience or allegiance to the occupying power.[348] To fill the absence of an inherent (because sovereign) *jus puniendi* upon the occupying power, the law of occupation had to bestow upon the occupying power an *additional* source of punitive powers, through the rules codified in Article 43 HR and Article 64 GC IV. This source of *jus puniendi*[349] is international in character and it is not a consequence of the territorial sovereignty of a state; rather, these rules specifically grant the occupying power the means to ensure its own security and to restore

---

[344] See Emily Crawford, *The Treatment of Combatants and Insurgents under the Law of Armed Conflict* (Oxford University Press 2010) 68–74.
[345] See Art. 3(1) AP II. See, also, US Military Manual, section 17.4.1.
[346] See, e.g., UK Military Manual, 15.6.3; US Military Manual, section 17.4.1.1. See also Cassese, *International Law*, 429; Ronzitti, *Diritto*, 144.
[347] See Art. 3(2) AP II.
[348] See *supra*, Section 4.2.2.
[349] As explained afore, the law of occupation confers 'faculties' rather than 'rights' to the occupying power (see *supra*, Section 2.6). Accordingly, the expression *jus puniendi* with reference to the occupying power should be read as 'faculty of punishing'.

and ensure public order during the temporary situation of the occupation.[350] Absent these provisions, the occupying power would be prevented from criminalising the activities of the resistance since such conduct falls outside the occupying power's sovereign *jus puniendi*.[351]

Now, it is necessary to understand why the drafters of the law of occupation decided to adopt rules allowing the occupying power to exercise its *jus puniendi*. Indeed, should they have considered hostilities in occupied territory to be non-international in character, there would have been no need to provide for this additional source of *jus puniendi*, since states' faculty to criminalise acts of resistance would have been inherent in cases of non-international armed conflicts. Arguably, the only way to understand the necessity of such explicit provisions regarding the occupying power's *jus puniendi* is to acknowledge that the drafters of GC IV believed that situations of occupation were ontologically different from non-international armed conflicts. Indeed, if the drafters had thought that similar hostilities were regulated by the law on non-international armed conflict, these armed confrontations would have been subject to such *jus puniendi* even in the absence of explicit international law provisions. Consequently, the need for such clauses enabling the occupying power to punish acts against its own security demonstrates unequivocally that hostilities in the occupied territory, irrespective of the nature of the actors involved, are regulated by the law on international armed conflict if involving the occupying power.

The counterargument that states did provide for such additional sources of the occupying power's *jus puniendi* because they failed to envisage hostilities not involving the ousted sovereign is fallacious for historical reasons. In fact, the drafters of the GC IV clearly had in mind the possibility of hostilities within the occupied territory involving non-state actors not affiliated to the occupied state, thanks to the experience of partisan wars during WWII.

The application of the law on international armed conflict to every hostility involving the occupying power in occupied territory is not at odds with the aforementioned case law regarding the coexistence of international and non-international armed conflicts, since the relevant decisions have never regarded armed conflicts involving the occupying power in occupied territory; rather, an international armed conflict may coexist with a non-international armed conflict in occupied territory if the latter involves two or more non-state actors. Indeed, the classification of a non-international armed conflict

---

[350] See *supra*, Section 5.3.2.
[351] According to one author, 'applying the law of non-international armed conflict would actually highlight the "criminal" nature of the insurgent activities' against the occupying power (Watkin, 'Use of Force', 291).

between two or more non-state actors is not affected by the establishment of an occupation for two reasons: first, the lack of any direct involvement of the occupying power prevents any relevance of the law of occupation in that situation; second, there is no involvement of any state's *jus puniendi* when hostilities occur between armed groups. Accordingly, there is no reason to consider that an existing non-international armed conflict should become international merely because of a subsequent occupation of that area, as the ICC Trial Chambers openly affirmed.[352] Similarly, if two or more non-state actors are involved in protracted armed violence against each other, then a non-international armed conflict may arise in an occupied territory after the commencement of the occupation.[353] The most cited example of this possibility is that of Hamas and Fatah, the two main factions within the PNA, which have occasionally resorted to violence amongst themselves since 2006.[354]

In conclusion, the need for explicit provisions enabling the occupying power to punish acts against its own security is at odds with the theoretical premises of the law on non-international armed conflict, according to which the territorial state has the right to punish those acts without needing any international law permission to do so. Accordingly, the presence of such clauses in the law of occupation demonstrates that the drafters of the GC IV did consider hostilities occurring in the occupied territory to be regulated by the law on international armed conflict as long as hostilities involve the occupying power.

5.6. THE INTERPLAY BETWEEN LAW ENFORCEMENT AND CONDUCT OF HOSTILITIES IN OCCUPIED TERRITORY

5.6.1. *The Main Theories Regarding the Interplay between Law Enforcement and Conduct of Hostilities*

The occurrence of hostilities in occupied territory requires the application of the conduct of hostilities paradigm along with the law-enforcement paradigm. As mentioned afore, the law of occupation favours recourse to law enforcement in order to restore and ensure public order and guarantee the security of the occupying power. Accordingly, the resort to conduct of hostilities must be

---

[352] See *Prosecutor v. Lubanga*, Judgment pursuant to Art. 74, para. 563; *Prosecutor v. Katanga*, Judgment pursuant to Art. 74, para. 1226.
[353] See Andreas Paulus & Mindia Vashakmadze, 'Asymmetrical War and the Notion of Armed Conflict: A Tentative Conceptualization (2009) 91 IRRC 95, 115.
[354] See Akande, 'Classification', 48. For a description of the violence between Hamas and Fatah, see Goldstone Report, paras. 1345–68, 1550–75.

constructed as exceptional in light of the law of occupation. However, when hostilities occur, law enforcement and conduct of hostilities are not mutually exclusive, but rather, are both applicable in principle to the use of armed force in occupied territory.[355] In light of the differences between law enforcement and conduct of hostilities, it is necessary to identify the rules governing their interplay and the factors allowing the occupying power to switch from the default applicable paradigm (law enforcement) to the exceptional one (conduct of hostilities).

The interplay between the two paradigms has been described in a number of ways. On the basis of the paradigm chosen, the assessment of the occupying powers' conduct will be different, since different legal standards are at stake. The entire debate focuses on the identification of the elements contributing to the distinction between situations requiring law enforcement and those following the conduct of hostilities paradigm – that is, those 'conversion factors' on which the law of occupation is totally silent.[356] Many criteria have been suggested, all of which are based on the assumption that, due to the lack of a specific discipline regarding the use of armed force in the law of occupation, a situation-based approach is needed in order to understand which legal regime is applicable to operations involving the use of armed force.[357] The basic assumption at the heart of every suggested criteria is that less intense armed violence may be dealt with by law enforcement, while more intense armed confrontations require the conduct of hostilities. This solution is confirmed by state practice: for instance, in occupied Namibia, South Africa ensured public order and addressed SWAPO's armed resistance mainly through its criminal system and police force; however, when SWAPO guerrilla tactics intensified and gained support from other insurgent movements in the neighbouring states, the South African Defence Force started undertaking military operations.[358] The main problem is the precise identification of the factors allowing such a shift between applicable models.

According to some authors, situations of occupation may be classified in two different sub-categories: so-called situations of 'calm occupation', in which the occupying power may employ armed force in order to maintain public order following law enforcement, and so-called situations of 'violent' or 'troubled'

---

[355] See Dieter Fleck, 'Law Enforcement and the Conduct of Hostilities: Two Supplementing or Mutually Excluding Legal Paradigms?' in Fischer-Lescano et al. (eds.), *Frieden*, 391; Charles H. D. Garraway, 'Armed Conflict and Law Enforcement: Is There a Legal Divide?' in Mariëlle Matthee, Brigit Toebes, & Marcel Brus (eds.), *Armed Conflict and International Law: In Search of the Human Face* (Springer 2013) 259.

[356] See Ferraro (ed.), *Expert Meeting*, 114.

[357] See Watkin, 'Maintaining', 192–3.

[358] Dale, 'The Armed Forces', 67–9; Larsdotter, 'Fighting', 1030.

occupation, in which the occupying power addresses the occurrence of hostilities in the occupied territory.[359] Despite the fact that this distinction has been employed by some scholars,[360] it must be handled with care. As the situations of the OPT and of occupied Iraq demonstrate, it is not easy to distinguish between territories that are under 'calm occupation' and those under 'violent occupation', since the occupying power may face very different threats in the same territory. Moreover, there could be an unexpected resumption of hostilities in an occupied territory where the occupying power has never faced any significant threats before and which, accordingly, was classified as being under 'calm occupation'. Consequently, the distinction between 'calm' and 'violent' occupations only has a descriptive value. Such a distinction is not static, but rather is relevant only *hic et nunc* as long as the factual circumstances do not change.

Another criterion to distinguish between law enforcement and conduct of hostilities is the existence of a nexus with the broader armed conflict of which the situation of occupation is only a portion. As one author has suggested, 'the law of armed conflict fully governs the conduct of hostilities, detention of prisoners of war, and other activities with a direct nexus to the conflict; applicable human rights law ... will generally govern actions taken by the occupying power pursuant to its law-enforcement and governance responsibilities'.[361] Interestingly, this approach links the applicability of the rules pertaining to the conduct of hostilities to the existence of a 'direct nexus' with the original armed conflict, of which the occupation is only a portion. Although this argument may appear logical, however, it contains crucial flaws that make it difficult to apply. For instance, it is not clear what the 'direct nexus' is, although theories regarding the direct participation of civilians in hostilities could contribute to clarifying this expression.[362] Additionally, such a test would impose on the occupying power's armed forces the burden of finding out in advance whether the attacks against them are linked to the broader armed conflict. Moreover, if this test were applied too rigorously, it would compel the occupying power to address hostilities not linked to the original armed conflict through law enforcement, notwithstanding the actual nature of the hostilities.

---

[359] See, generally, Ferraro (ed.), *Expert Meeting*, 114.
[360] See, e.g., Doswald-Beck, 'The Right', 892–4; Arai-Takahashi, *The Law*, 311; Otto, *Targeted Killings*, 442–52; Jelena Pejic, 'Conflict Classification and the Law Applicable to Detention and the Use of Force' in Wilmshurst (ed.), *Classification*, 80, 109; Watkin, 'Use of Force', 276–83; Roscini, *Cyber Operations*, 145, fn. 174.
[361] Schmitt, 'Iraq', 364–5. See also Michael N. Schmitt & Charles H. B. Garraway, 'Occupation Policy in Iraq and International Law' (2004) 9 *International Peacekeeping: The Yearbook of International Peace Operations* 27, 31.
[362] Melzer, *Interpretive Guidance*, 58.

Similarly, some scholars have suggested a 'sliding scale' approach wherein, when disorders reach a certain intensity, there would be a smooth transition from the law-enforcement model to the conduct-of-hostilities model.[363] This approach was discussed at a meeting convened by the ICRC, wherein some experts showed different views regarding the relevant factors to be taken into account. The nature of the threat was mentioned as one of the sub-factors relevant in assessing whether a certain situation may be treated through law enforcement or through conduct of hostilities: if a threat emanates from insurgent groups, whether combatants, members of organised armed groups, or individuals directly participating in hostilities, then the threat may be dealt with under the conduct-of-hostilities model.[364] This assumption links the model of dealing with a threat to the status of the individuals involved within the meaning of international humanitarian law. This solution works in relation to threats posed by individuals affiliated with the ousted sovereign or belonging to organised armed groups, which may be dealt with through conduct of hostilities. However, in relation to civilians taking direct part in the hostilities, determining in advance the nature of the threat may be difficult under particular circumstances.[365] In fact, it would be impracticable to require the occupying power to verify in advance whether the threat originates from individuals affiliated with an armed group, and only after this determination, to decide which model it will employ to react against it. The assessment of the entitlement to the prisoner-of-war status is different, since the captured combatant may be questioned regarding their status and other investigations may be carried out.

Other scholars have advanced additional sub-criteria regarding the interplay between law enforcement and conduct of hostilities. For instance, some experts have contended that the intensity of the control exercised by the occupying power is relevant since, in areas where the occupying power is 'firmly in control', law enforcement should apply, while the conduct-of-hostilities model should be available only in areas where occupying forces have less firm control.[366] However, this apparently reasonable solution is based on some incorrect assumptions. While it is true that in situations of less stringent control the local population may resume hostilities more easily than in cases of a higher degree of control, it is true as well that a higher degree of control

---

[363] See Ferraro (ed.), *Expert Meeting*, 113–15.
[364] Ibid., 114. See also Kolb & Vité, *Le droit*, 360; Watkin, 'Maintaining', 193.
[365] Ferraro (ed.), *Expert Meeting*, 114, fn. 5 (suggesting the example of soldiers at a checkpoint requested to respond to persons of unknown status who were driving towards them in a suspicious manner); Gloria Gaggioli (ed.), *Expert Meeting on the Use of Force in Armed Conflicts: Interplay between the Conduct of Hostilities and Law Enforcement Paradigms* (ICRC 2013) 8–9, 26.
[366] Ferraro (ed.), *Expert Meeting*, 114. See also Watkin, 'Maintaining', 187–8.

5.6. Law Enforcement and Conduct of Hostilities 233

is required in situations where hostilities are more frequent, while a lesser degree of control could be the response to a relatively calm area.[367] All in all, if the degree of control exercised is not sufficient to maintain order pursuant to Article 43 HR, legally speaking, this is not a reason to shift from law enforcement to conduct of hostilities, but rather, the occupying power should take all feasible measures to solidify its control and implement its obligations under Article 43 HR.[368]

Another view considers that the duration of the occupation should be an additional criterion since, 'when the occupation endured, the "conduct-of-hostilities" model would come to be gradually replaced by the law enforcement model', following the fact that 'violence between the occupying forces and local armed forces and/or organized insurgent groups should subside with the passage of time'.[369] This is wishful thinking, since it presumes that prolonged occupations are calmer than brief occupations, when practice shows that this assumption is incorrect. For instance, the most prolonged occupation post-WWII, the occupation of the OPT, has faced recurrent escalations of violence over many years since its commencement in 1967, as demonstrated by the two intifadas (1989 and 2000) and the three operations against the Gaza Strip (2009, 2012, 2014).[370] On the other hand, other prolonged occupations have faced few hostilities after the firm establishment of the occupying power's authority, as in the case of Northern Cyprus under the TRNC. Accordingly, practice shows that the duration of the occupation is not per se relevant to the determination of the applicable paradigm. More generally, the entire 'sliding scale' approach, albeit attractive, presents many problems regarding its practical application, especially since it is not easy to determine when exactly a situation being dealt with under the law-enforcement model escalates to such intensity as to require a conduct-of-hostilities response.

Another approach, labelled 'jump theory', suggests that the differences between law enforcement and conduct of hostilities are too great to allow a smooth transition between the two paradigms; rather, a specific condition should be required to activate the application of the conduct-of-hostilities paradigm, especially in cases in which the armed confrontations involve individuals not belonging to the armed forces of the ousted sovereign of the occupied territory.[371] In similar cases, it has been suggested that such a threshold could be identified in the criteria normally employed in order to assess the

---

[367] See US Military Manual, section 11.2.2.1.
[368] See Pertile, 'L'adozione', 324–5.
[369] Ferraro (ed.), *Expert Meeting*, 114.
[370] Ibid.
[371] Ibid., 115.

existence of a non-international armed conflict.[372] As affirmed by the ICTY, a non-international armed conflict pursuant to common Article 3 GCs exists whenever there is 'protracted armed violence between governmental authorities and organized armed groups or between such groups within a state',[373] if such armed violence meets the requisite elements of: (i) intensity; (ii) large-scale nature; and (iii) protracted duration.[374] According to this view, whenever the armed confrontation within the occupied territory meets these criteria, the occupying power is entitled to resort to the conduct-of-hostilities model. The clever rationale behind this reasoning posits that, since the occupying power acts in the place of the ousted government, it is appropriate to consider that the occupying power may switch from law enforcement to conduct of hostilities under the same conditions that the ousted sovereign would have had to meet – that is, following the rules about the existence of a non-international armed conflict. On a practical level, this view clearly prevents the occupying power from resorting to the conduct of hostilities in cases that should be addressed under the law-enforcement model, such as 'banditry, unorganized and short-lived insurrections, or terrorist activities, which are not subject to international humanitarian law',[375] and of 'internal disturbances and tensions, such as riots, isolated and sporadic acts of violence and other acts of a similar nature, as not being armed conflicts'.[376] Since the law of occupation never refers to the criteria pertaining to the existence of a non-international armed conflict, most commentators prudently specify that the non-international armed conflict threshold should be applied not *de jure*, but as mere guidance in the case by case assessment of the best operational model to employ.[377] However, such a conclusion is not satisfactory, since it fails to explain the

---

[372] See Doswald-Beck, 'The Right', 893–4; Ferraro (ed.), *Expert Meeting*, 115, 122–3; Murray, *Practitioners' Guide*, 116; Michael John-Hopkins, *The Rule of Law in Crisis and Conflict Grey Zones: Regulating the Use of Force in a Global Information Environment* (Routledge 2017) 120–1.

[373] ICTY, *Prosecutor v. Tadić*, Decision on the Defence Motion, para. 70.

[374] Ibid.; ICTY, *Prosecutor v. Tadić*, Opinion and Judgment (Trial Chamber), para. 562–8. The determination of the existence of a non-international armed conflict, however, is not straightforward, since international case law is not consistent with regard to the relevant criteria. This assessment is further complicated by the fact that Art. 1(1) AP II embodies a higher threshold of application, with additional requirements. On this topic, which is beyond the purview of this book, see, generally, Moir, *The Law*, 34–52; Anthony Cullen, *The Concept of Non-International Armed Conflict in International Humanitarian Law* (Cambridge University Press 2010); Sivakumaran, *The Law*, 105–235; Dinstein, *Non-International Armed Conflicts*, 20–57; Cameron et al., 'Article 3', paras. 421–44.

[375] ICTY, *Prosecutor v Tadić*, Opinion and Judgment (Trial Chamber), para. 562.

[376] Art. 1(2) APII.

[377] Doswald-Beck, 'The Right', 894; Pertile, 'L'adozione', 309; Watkin, 'Use of Force', 291.

5.6. Law Enforcement and Conduct of Hostilities 235

legal, rather than political, reasons to apply the non-international armed conflict threshold.

5.6.2. A New Way to Look at the Interplay between the Two Paradigms

The theories regarding the interplay between the conduct-of-hostilities and law-enforcement models examined so far provide useful practical guidance. In particular, it is unquestionable that the assessment regarding which model is applicable has to be made case by case on the basis of the facts pertaining to the specific situation in which the use of armed force is required. Similarly, it is possible to affirm without doubt that threats posed by individuals belonging to the ousted sovereign's armed forces may be dealt with directly through conduct of hostilities, without any requirement of intensity or organisation.

However, the aforementioned theories provide less useful guidance in relation to threats originating from individuals not affiliated with the ousted sovereign. In particular, the application of the threshold of non-international armed conflict should be undertaken in the context of the normative dimension of the use of armed force in occupied territory: the issue is the identification of a norm allowing the occupying power to employ the factual indicators corresponding to the existence of a non-international armed conflict in order to resort to the conduct of hostilities. The application of certain factors as a matter of policy and for operational purposes does not fully satisfy a legal analysis of the use of armed force in occupied territory. Suffice it to say that resorting to these factors as a matter of policy would render the decision to resort to conduct of hostilities non-justiciable since there would be no legal parameter referring to the switch from law enforcement to conduct of hostilities. Accordingly, it may be useful to approach this issue from an entirely different normative perspective.

As has already been affirmed, the state of occupation may be created only in an international armed conflict, and it preserves the existence of that armed conflict over the occupied territory. In the course of an armed conflict, the parties may resort to hostilities – that is, the employment of means and methods of warfare, irrespectively of any assessment regarding the level of violence of the armed confrontation in question. Accordingly, setting aside the aforementioned hypothesis of a new armed conflict occurring in the occupied territory, apparently, the occupying power may resort to the conduct of hostilities whenever it deems this model necessary in order to restore and ensure public order and provide for its own security – the only aims allowing the occupying power to employ armed force in the occupied territory under the law of occupation.[378] However, although the conduct of hostilities is the model typically applicable to the use of armed force during an armed conflict, the peace-like governmental functions bestowed upon the occupying power, at odds with the inherently hostile character of the occupation, strongly contradict the conclusion that the occupying power may resort at will to conduct of hostilities, particularly because such an assumption could severely endanger the local population of the occupied territory. To solve this conundrum, it is necessary to identify a norm that makes a distinction between situations governed by law enforcement and situations governed by the conduct of hostilities in the context of an ongoing armed conflict over the occupied territory. This rule should be part of international humanitarian law, since it would directly affect the application of other international humanitarian law rules.

This author believes that the solution to this normative conundrum is, again, provided by Article 43 HR and its corollaries, which prevent the occupying power from resorting to the conduct of hostilities in those cases in which the ousted sovereign would be prevented from doing so. In the normative system created by this provision and other implementing and specifying rules such as Article 64 GC IV, the occupying power has to act as the ousted sovereign would have with regard to the maintenance and restoration of public order. As already noted, since the law of occupation introduces a peacetime model in a situation of occupation, which would apply when the occupying power is engaged in law-enforcement operations, the law-enforcement paradigm is the one preferred in occupied territory and that there is a presumption in favour of the applicability of law enforcement.[379] However, the law of occupation may be read as forcing the occupying power to act as the ousted sovereign even with regard to the conduct of hostilities: as a government may resort to means and methods of warfare during peacetime only when a non-international armed conflict exists, similarly, the law of occupation bars the occupying power from resorting to means and methods of warfare in situations in which the ousted sovereign would have been prevented from doing so.[380] In other words, the law of occupation, insulating as far as possible the governmental activities of the occupying power from the surrounding situation of armed conflict, not only imposes on the occupying power the same conditions regarding law enforcement that the ousted sovereign would have had, but also

---

[378] The idea that Article 43 HR limits the occupying power's faculty to employ armed force in the occupied territory has been discussed *supra*, Section 5.3.1.

[379] See *supra*, Section 5.3.3.2.

[380] The similarities between the situation of the occupying power and a state involved in a non-international armed conflict with regard to the interplay between law enforcement and conduct of hostilities has been noted by a number of authors (see Garraway, 'Occupation' 277; Gioia, 'La lotta', 171, 179–80; Watkin, 'Maintaining', 186).

preserves the same conditions regarding the possibility of conducting hostilities. It is insufficient to affirm that Article 43 HR demands the preferential application of law enforcement; the law of occupation also removes situations domestically addressed through law enforcement from those situations to which the occupying power may react through means and methods of warfare. Consequently, it is true that the deciding factor between law enforcement and conduct of hostilities is the existence of armed confrontations of the same nature as those of a non-international armed conflict. This assumption, however, is a direct consequence of the rationale behind the provisions pertaining the administration of occupied territory, Article 43 HR being at the forefront. More precisely, this is not a case of analogical application of the threshold of non-international armed conflict in the situation of occupation with regard to the occupying power's faculty to resort to the conduct of hostilities paradigm. Rather, in a situation of occupation, the resort to the conduct of hostilities paradigm would be allowed *in principle* due to the existence of an ongoing armed conflict. However, *the law of occupation* prevents the occupying power from resorting to the conduct of hostilities in those cases in which the ousted sovereign would be prevented from doing so. As already mentioned,[381] this conclusion does not imply that the *law* on non-international armed conflict regulates such hostilities, but rather, that the threshold to apply the *model* of the conduct of hostilities is the one typical of non-international armed conflict, thanks to the law of occupation.

This reading of the functioning of the law of occupation attempts to maintain the balance between the hostile character of the occupation and the need to govern the occupied territory even when the use of armed force is required. Moreover, the suggested approach also has a geographical corollary: if hostilities are limited to a certain area, nonetheless, the law of occupation bars the occupying power from resorting to the conduct of hostilities in the whole occupied territory. This conclusion may prove especially useful since it is unclear whether the rules on the conduct of hostilities apply to the entire territory of the belligerents or, rather, are limited to the so-called 'conflict zone'.[382]

---

[381] This author has argued that the law on international armed conflict regulates such hostilities *supra*, Section 5.5.3.3.

[382] The most authoritative determination of the scope of application of international humanitarian law is provided by ICTY, *Prosecutor v. Tadić*, Decision on the Defence Motion, para. 68, according to which:

> Although the Geneva Conventions are silent as to the geographical scope of international "armed conflicts," the provisions suggest that at least *some of the provisions* of the Conventions *apply to the entire territory of the Parties to the conflict*, not just to the vicinity of actual hostilities. Certainly, *some of the provisions are clearly bound up with the hostilities and the geographical scope of those provisions should be so limited'* (emphases added).

The proposed approach is consistent with the main tenets of the law of occupation, as prescribed by Article 43 HR itself. Indeed, such an interpretation would have been discarded if it could have created conflicts with the principles inspiring the law of occupation, such as the temporary nature of the occupation, the principle of non-annexation, and the protection of the local population. However, not one of these principles is violated by the proposed reading. Instead, the proposed approach rejects the view of the applicability of the threshold pertaining to non-international armed conflicts as such, which would have placed the occupying power in exactly the same role as that of a sovereign state within its territory. On the contrary, this approach confirms that the law of occupation *artificially* tames the waging of the ongoing armed conflict in the occupied territory, compelling the occupying power to temporarily act as the ousted sovereign. Consequently, this approach enhances the protection of the local population of the occupied territory since it prevents the occupying power from employing means and methods of warfare in situations that the ousted sovereign would have addressed through law enforcement.

In conclusion, the same reasoning, according to which the law of occupation prescribes to the occupying power the restoration and maintenance of public order under the same conditions as the ousted sovereign, is applicable to the conduct of hostilities. Although, at a practical level, the switch from law enforcement to conduct of hostilities is determined by the existence of armed confrontation of the same level as a non-international armed conflict in purely domestic situations, this conclusion is not the result of the transplant of a normative threshold belonging to a subsystem into a different one, but is rather a direct consequence of the basic tenets of the law of occupation regarding the administration of occupied territory.

5.7. CONCLUSIONS

The difficult balance struck by the law of occupation between the inherently hostile character of the occupation and the need to fill the governmental gap left by the ousted sovereign reaches a critical point when the use of armed force

---

This statement seems to suggest that the rules on the conduct of hostilities are applicable only to the conflict zone (Gaggioli (ed.), *Expert Meeting*, 17); however, such a concept is often criticised as lacking support in international humanitarian law conventions and state practice, resulting in a vague and arbitrary concept (Gaggioli (ed.), *Expert Meeting*, 22). For more on this, see Katja Schöberl, 'The Geographical Scope of Application of the Conventions' in Clapham, Gaeta, & Sassòli (eds.), *The 1949 Geneva Conventions*, 67.

is required. The fact that the occupation is a kind of armed conflict would suggest the application of the rules on the conduct of hostilities, whereas duty to restore and ensure public order upon the occupying power hints that a governmental-like approach based on law enforcement is more appropriate.

To solve this conundrum, one must look at the law of occupation in its entirety. Even if the law of occupation does not address explicitly the way in which armed force may be employed in occupied territory, nonetheless it offers important clues. The basic principle is that the occupying power must act as the ousted sovereign would have had to. Indeed, the law of occupation favours the maintenance and restoration of public order through the same non-forcible measures that the ousted sovereign would have had to employ, as demonstrated by the HR and GC IV's provisions regarding criminal law and the judicial system. State practice and international case law demonstrate that the same rationale applies to measures involving the use of armed force. Accordingly, the law of occupation demands that the occupying power shall apply the operational and legal paradigm of law enforcement when dealing with restoration and maintenance of public order. Notwithstanding the situation of occupation, law enforcement is regulated by domestic and international human rights standards. State practice demonstrates a significant trend favouring the performance of law-enforcement responsibilities by the local police of the occupied territory, pursuant to the domestic legislation in force prior to the occupation. However, when law enforcement is conducted by the armed forces of the occupying power, international human rights law, rather than international humanitarian law, regulates the use of armed force.

However, it may happen that, notwithstanding the exercise of law-enforcement responsibilities by the occupying power, hostilities occur in occupied territory. In these cases, it is necessary to distinguish between hostilities terminating the occupation and hostilities disrupting public order without terminating the occupation. State practice demonstrates a number of episodes of both kinds. When hostilities involve the occupying power in occupied territory, the law on international armed conflict must apply to the conduct of hostilities on the basis of the different theoretical premises of the law of occupation and the law on non-international armed conflict.

If hostilities occur within occupied territory, the occupying power may resort to the model of conduct of hostilities only when the armed confrontation in the occupied territory reaches the threshold of a non-international armed conflict; the occupying power must address armed confrontations below this threshold through law enforcement. This solution is not a sort of analogical application of the law on non-international armed conflict in a situation of occupation, but rather, it is a direct consequence of the aforementioned principle of continuity between the means at disposal of the ousted sovereign and those allowed to the occupying power. As the ousted sovereign would have been able to resort to conduct of hostilities only if violence reached a certain threshold, similarly, under that threshold, the principle of continuity forces the occupying power to refrain from conduct of hostilities in favour of law enforcement.

6

The Regulation of the Use of Armed Force in Occupied Territory in Light of the Right to Life

[W]ars were fifty years earlier. Now the Nebular Regions required merely the acts of occupation and taxation. Previously there had been words to gain ... and now there was little left to do but to contend with single men.[1]

6.1. INTRODUCTION

After having shown that two different paradigms may coexist in occupied territory, law enforcement and conduct of hostilities, and having examined the rules governing their interplay, it is necessary now to turn to the restraints these two paradigms impose on the use of armed force in occupied territory, particularly with respect to the right to life of the individuals involved.

During law enforcement operations, international and domestic human rights law, both of which allow deprivation of life only as a last resort measure when there is no other alternative way to protect a legal interest of the same value (for instance, in case of personal self-defence), protect the right to life. Conversely, during the conduct of hostilities, two different rationales must be taken into account: on the one hand, that at the base of international humanitarian law, which accepts the killing of enemy combatants, and on the other, that behind applicable international human rights law, which provides a stronger protection for the right to life. The following subsections explore the different legal paradigms applicable to the use of armed force during law enforcement operations and conduct of hostilities in light of the right to life. In particular, this chapter first illustrates each legal paradigm as applicable outside situations of occupation, and then goes on to examine the peculiarities of the application of each legal paradigm in situations of occupation.

---

[1] Isaac Asimov, *The Stars, Like Dust* (Tom Doherty 1951) 43.

6.2. LAW ENFORCEMENT AND THE USE OF ARMED FORCE IN OCCUPIED TERRITORY

6.2.1. *The Right to Life in Law Enforcement Operations*

The use of armed force in law enforcement operations is governed by a normative paradigm based on human rights law standards. In particular, international human rights law protects the right to life during law enforcement operations so that lethal armed force may be employed only as a last resort measure.

In peacetime, domestic and international human rights law regulate law enforcement operations. According to the UN Code of Conduct for Law Enforcement Officials, '[i]n the performance of their duty, law enforcement officials shall respect and protect human dignity and maintain and uphold the human rights of all persons'.[2] The UN Basic Principles on the Use of Force and Firearms by Law Enforcement Officials states that 'the use of force and firearms by law enforcement officials should be commensurate with due respect for human rights'.[3] The European Code of Police Ethics clearly affirms that '[p]olice operation must always be conducted in accordance with the national law and international standards accepted by the country'.[4]

With regard to the use of armed force during law enforcement operations, the most delicate issue pertains to respect for the right to life, which may be seriously affected by the use of armed force. A number of international law conventions protect the right to life. For instance, Article 6(1) ICCPR establishes this right at a universal level, providing that '[e]very human being has the inherent right to life. This right shall be protected by law. No one shall be *arbitrarily* deprived of his life'.[5] This right is also enshrined in most regional international human rights instruments. For instance, Article 4(1) ACHR affirms that '[e]very person has the right to have his life respected. This right shall be protected by law and, in general, from the moment of conception. No one shall be *arbitrarily* deprived of his life'.[6] Article 4 ACHPR posits that '[h]uman beings are inviolable. Every human being shall be entitled to respect for his life and the integrity of his person. No one may be *arbitrarily* deprived

---

[2] Art. 2 Code of Conduct for Law Enforcement Officials.
[3] Basic Principles on the Use of Force and Firearms by Law Enforcement Officials, A/CONF.144/28/Rev.l (1990), preamb para. 7.
[4] Art. 3. See also the provisions pertaining to specific rights mentioned in Arts. 35, 36, 40, 41, 43, and 44.
[5] Emphasis added.
[6] Emphasis added.

6.2. Law Enforcement and the Use of Armed Force in Occupied Territory 243

of this right'.[7] Other regional international human rights law treaties embody similar provisions.[8]

All these instruments permit the deprivation of the right to life if it is not *arbitrary*.[9] According to the CCPR, a death is arbitrary if the action of police is not 'necessary in their own defence or that of others, or [it is not] necessary to effect the arrest or prevent the escape of the persons concerned'[10] and if the police's use of armed force is 'disproportionate to the requirements of law enforcement'.[11] A deprivation of life is arbitrary even if the killing is not voluntary, but rather, occurs in the course of riot control.[12] The main example of legitimate use of armed force is personal self-defence against an immediate threat which may not be addressed in a less harmful way.[13]

The IACtHR offers a compressive view on which are the requirements of the use of armed force by law enforcement officials in order to respect the right to life:

> The *use of force* by law enforcement officials must be defined by *exceptionality* and must be planned and *proportionally* limited by the authorities ... [F]orce or coercive means can only be used *once all other methods of control have been exhausted and have failed*. The use of *lethal force and firearms* against individuals by law enforcement officials – which *must be forbidden as a general rule* – is only justified in *even more extraordinary cases*. The exceptional circumstances under which firearms and lethal force may be used shall be *determined by the law and restrictively construed*, so that they are used to the *minimum extent* possible in all circumstances and never exceed the use which is *"absolutely necessary"* in relation to the force or threat to be repealed. When excessive force is used, any resulting deprivation of life is arbitrary. The use of force must be *limited by the principles of proportionality, necessity and humanity*. Excessive or disproportionate use of force by law enforcement officials that result in the loss of life may therefore amount to arbitrary deprivations of life. The principle of necessity justifies only those measures of military violence which are *not forbidden by international law*

---

[7] Emphasis added.
[8] See, e.g., Art. 5 ArCHR
[9] On the origins and meaning of this clause, see C. K. Boyle, 'The Concept of Arbitrary Deprivation of Life' in B. G. Ramcharan (ed.), *The Right to Life in International Law* (Martinus Nijhoff 1985) 221; Marco Pedrazzi, 'The Protection of the Right to Life in Law-Enforcement Operations' in Bernardo Cortese (ed.), *Studi in onore di Laura Picchio Forlati* (Giappichelli 2014) 105.
[10] *Suárez de Guerrero v. Colombia* (45/79) para. 13.2.
[11] Ibid., para. 13.3. See also Basic Principles on the Use of Force and Firearms by Law Enforcement Officials, Article 10.
[12] See, e.g., *Umateliev v. Kyrgyzstan* (127/04); *Domínguez v. Paraguay* (1828/08).
[13] For more on this, see Hessbruegge, *Human Rights*, 91–234.

and which are *relevant and proportionate* to ensure the prompt subjugation of the enemy with the least possible cost of human and economic resources.[14]

The IACtHR's view is particularly interesting because it makes a distinction between the exceptional use of armed force by law enforcement officials and their ever more exceptional use of *lethal* armed force, which should be in principle considered unlawful.

Contrary to other international human rights law conventions, the ECHR does not refer to the arbitrariness of the deprivation of life. Instead, Article 2 ECHR affirms that '[e]veryone's right to life shall be protected by law. No one shall be deprived of his life intentionally save in the execution of a sentence of a court following his conviction of a crime for which this penalty is provided by law'. However, the provision goes on to specify that deprivation of life is permitted 'when it results from the use of force which is no more than *absolutely necessary*: (a) in defence of any person from unlawful violence; (b) in order to effect a lawful arrest or to prevent the escape of a person lawfully detained; (c) in action lawfully taken for the purpose of quelling a riot or insurrection'.[15] Accordingly, the main test is that of the absolute necessity of the deprivation of life in cases of defence from violence, lawful arrests, and lawful actions of riot control. The ECtHR clarified that the use of force 'must be no more than "absolutely necessary"'[16] and that violations of Article 2 ECHR must be assessed through 'the most careful scrutiny, particularly where deliberate lethal force is used, taking into consideration not only the actions of the agents of the state who actually administer the force but also all the surrounding circumstances including such matters as the planning and control of the actions under examination'.[17] In order to comply with the ECHR, 'policing operations must be sufficiently regulated by [national law], within the framework of a system of adequate and effective safeguards against arbitrariness and abuse of force, and even against avoidable accident'.[18] In particular, armed force should not be used if there are other available means to defend one's life or to capture someone who violated or threatened the right to life.[19]

---

[14] See *Zambrano Vélez* et al. v. *Ecuador* (Merits, Reparations and Costs) 4 July 2007, IACtHR, series C no. 166, paras. 83–5 (emphases added, references omitted). See, also, *Montero-Aranguren* et al. v. *Venezuela*, (Preliminary Objection, Merits, Reparations and Costs) 5 July 2006, IACtHR, series C no. 150, paras. 67–9.

[15] Emphasis added.

[16] *McCann* v. *UK* (Application no. 18984/91), 27 September 1995, para. 148.

[17] Ibid., 150.

[18] *Finogenov* et al. v. *Russia* (Application nos 18299/03 and 27311/03), 20 December 2011, para. 207.

[19] Ibid., 219.

The relevance of the right to life for law enforcement operations is confirmed by the aforementioned UN Basic Principles, which are useful guidelines for states regarding their obligations in law enforcement operations.[20] Article 9 summarises the way to respect the right to life during law enforcement operations as follows:

> Law enforcement officials shall not use firearms against persons except in self-defence or defence of others against the imminent threat of death or serious injury, to prevent the perpetration of a particularly serious crime involving grave threat to life, to arrest a person presenting such a danger and resisting their authority, or to prevent his or her escape, and only when less extreme means are insufficient to achieve these objectives. *In any event, intentional lethal use of firearms may only be made when strictly unavoidable in order to protect life.*[21]

Clearly, this document posits that law enforcement agents may employ lethal force only in order to protect their own right to life or the right to life of others, as well as in relation to the commission of crimes that violate or seriously endanger the right to life. In any case, the resort to lethal force is only a last-resort solution.

All the aforementioned binding and non-binding sources and documents, as well as the relevant case law, demonstrate that the resort to armed force, particularly lethal force, is threat-based:[22] armed force must be absolutely necessary in the light of the threat and proportionate to the same. In law-enforcement operations, the principle of necessity means that the use of lethal armed force is a last-resort measure, while proportionality dictates that armed force may be employed 'only in proportion to the immediate threat posed by the target'.[23] As emphasised in a subsequent subsection, proportionality and necessity in international human rights law are very different from proportionality and necessity in international humanitarian law.[24]

In addition, international human rights law requires the criminalisation of any arbitrary deprivation of the right to life and, consequently, diligent, expeditious, and impartial investigations when death occurs in the course of law enforcement operations. According to the ECtHR, '[t]he obligation to protect

---

[20] For an overview of the usage that the ECtHR did of this document, see Schabas, *The European Convention*, 130–1.
[21] Emphasis added.
[22] Garraway, 'Occupation', 277.
[23] Michael Newton & Larry May, *Proportionality in International Law* (Oxford University Press 2015) 249. See also Gaggioli (ed.), *Expert Meeting*; Casey-Maley & Connolly, *Police*, 92–3.
[24] See *infra*, Section 6.3.2.2 to the right to life during

the right to life ... requires by implication that there should be some form of effective official investigation when individuals have been killed as a result of the use of force by, *inter alios*, agents of the State'.[25] The ECtHR described the requirements of these investigations: they must be effective, independent, objective, accessible to the families of victims, and prompt.[26] Other international human rights courts and mechanisms have confirmed the existence of a similar duty to investigate deaths that occur when state's agents are involved.[27]

Even this cursory look at international instruments, practice, and case law, suggests some conclusions about the use of armed force with respect to the right to life during law enforcement operations. In principle, killing in law-enforcement operations should be avoided to the maximum extent possible: law-enforcement agents may resort to lethal armed force only as a last-resort solution, and every killing requires accurate and impartial scrutiny regarding its lawfulness under national and international standards. Although the law of occupation requires the application of this legal framework, the hostile context of an occupation characterised by an ongoing armed conflict poses some practical and legal challenges to the application of this international human rights law-based regime.

6.2.2. The Application of the Law Enforcement Paradigm in Occupied Territory

The application of the law-enforcement paradigm in times of occupation is challenging, due to the hostile nature of the foreign authority. In a situation of occupation, the international human rights law framework governing law enforcement is complemented by international humanitarian law, on the basis of the aforementioned theory of the cumulative application of these two branches of international law. Two scenarios can be distinguished: first,

---

[25] *McCann v. UK*, para. 161. See, also, *Kaya v. Turkey* (Application no. 22535/93), 28 March 2000, para. 102; *Tagayeva et al. v. Russia* (Application no. 26562/07 and others), 13 April 2017, para. 496.

[26] See the detailed analysis in *Armani Da Silva v. UK* (Application no. 5878/08), 30 March 2016, paras. 231–9.

[27] See, e.g., IACtHR, *Velásquez Rodríguez v. Honduras*, Merits, 29 July 1988, Series C no. 4 (1988), para. 166; ACmHPR, *Commission Nationale des Droits de l'Homme et des Libertés v. Chad* (79/92) and *Zimbabwe NGO Human Rights Forum v. Zimbabwe* (245/02), para. 153. For an analysis of the different approaches, see Vera Rusinova, 'The Duty to Investigate the Death of Persons Arrested and/or Detained by Public Authorities' in Tomuschat, Lagrange, & Oeter (eds.), *The Right*, 65; Philip Leach, Rachel Murray, & Clara Sandoval, 'The Duty to Investigate Right to Life Violations across Three Regional Systems: Harmonisation or Fragmentation of International Human Rights Law?' in Buckley, Donald, & Leach (eds.), *Towards Convergence*, 33.

6.2. Law Enforcement and the Use of Armed Force in Occupied Territory 247

law-enforcement operations conducted by *the police of the occupied territory*, which should be subject to the human rights provisions embodied in the law in force in the occupied territory prior to the occupation, including any applicable international human rights law obligations binding the ousted sovereign; second, law enforcement operations conducted *by the occupying power*, which must comply with the rules on law enforcement embodied in the law of occupation and international human rights law binding the occupying power. The occupying power and the sovereign of the occupied territory may be bound by different international human rights treaty law. In the case of the occupation of Iraq, for instance, the ECHR constituted the legal framework of law enforcement operations conducted only by the UK as occupying power,[28] since Iraq was not (and could not have been) party to that treaty.[29]

The ECtHR, dealing with the conduct of the UK in occupied Iraq, held that the right to life of individuals under the occupying power's jurisdiction may not be discarded on the basis of the occupation only; rather, the same exceptions to the right to life applicable in peacetime govern law-enforcement activities in times of occupation.[30] This is also true with regard to the procedural obligations to investigate cases of death caused by state agents.[31] Similarly, the UN High Commissioner for Human Rights, with regard to killings that occurred in occupied Crimea, applied the ICCPR's peacetime standards regarding the effectiveness of Russian investigations.[32] Likewise, the UN Secretary-General affirmed that:

> In the West Bank, Israeli forces act in a law-enforcement capacity and are therefore bound by article 6 [ICCPR] and article 43 [HR], in addition to general principles on the use of force by law enforcement officials, including the principles of necessity and proportionality contained in the Basic Principles on the Use of Force and Firearms by Law Enforcement Officials ... and the Code of Conduct for Law Enforcement Officials ... Independent, prompt and effective investigations into such incidents are critical to ensure accountability for deaths and injuries. Should negligent or unlawful behaviour be identified during such investigations, judicial and/or disciplinary proceedings should be initiated against those responsible.[33]

---

[28] See ECtHR, *Al-Skeini* case.
[29] According to Art. 101 ECHR, only states members of the Council of Europe may become party of the ECHR.
[30] See *Al Skeini* case, para. 162.
[31] Ibid., para. 164.
[32] UN High Commissioner for Human Rights, Situation of Human Rights in the Temporarily Occupied Autonomous Republic of Crimea and the City of Sevastopol (Ukraine), 25 September 2017, paras. 80–3.
[33] UN Secretary-General, Israel Practices affecting the Human Rights of the Palestinian People in the Occupied Palestinian Territory, including East Jerusalem, 14 September 2012, para. 17.

Accordingly, both UN practice and the ECtHR's case law support the view that law enforcement in times of occupation is regulated by the same standards applicable in peacetime. The main issue is to make the law-enforcement model and normative paradigm to fit the situations of occupation, which are characterised by the hostility of the local population.

The Israeli judiciary has acknowledged the justiciability, in light of domestic and international human rights law standards pertaining to the right to life, of law enforcement operations conducted in the OPT in the 2017 *Elor Azaria* case.[34] The case regarded the conviction of an Israeli medic sergeant for an incident that occurred in Hebron on 24 March 2006, when two Palestinians attacked some Israeli soldiers standing at an inspection post and, as a result, one of the Palestinians was hit and killed outright, while the second Palestinian was wounded, and left lying at the scene; a few minutes after the Palestinians' shooting, the medic Elor Azaria arrived at the scene of the incident and killed the wounded Palestinian by firing a single bullet at his head.[35] Indicted for manslaughter, Elor Azaria pleaded guilty, claiming that he had acted on the fear that the Palestinian was carrying an explosive device.[36] Elor Azaria was sentenced to eighteen months of prison[37] and his appeal was dismissed. This case is important because the Israeli judiciary evaluated Elor Azaria's conduct in light of the domestic law provisions regulating the right to life in peacetime, which are in line with international standards. For instance, the accused's claim regarding putative self-defence was analysed, and rejected, on the basis of the immediacy of the threat addressed,[38] the proportionality the response adopted,[39] and the availability of non-lethal measures to address that threat, with no mention of conducting hostilities under international humanitarian law.[40] Notwithstanding any consideration regarding the appropriateness of the penalty, the decisions in the *Elor Azaria* case point toward the correct direction of analysing the use of armed force

---

[34] Israel, Military Court of the Central District, *Military Prosecutor* v. *Sergent Elor Azaria*, 4 January 2017 (on file with the author); Military Court of Appeals, *Sergent Elor Azaria* v. *Military Prosecutor*, 7 July 2017 (on file with the author).

[35] Military Court of Appeals, *Sergent Elor Azaria* v. *Military Prosecutor*, para. 2.

[36] Ibid., para. 3.

[37] See Israel, Military Court of the Central District, *Military Prosecutor* v. *Sergent Elor Azaria*, 21 February 2017, para. 93 (on file with the author).

[38] Military Court of the Central District, *Military Prosecutor* v. *Sergent Elor Azaria*, para. 173; Military Court of Appeals, *Sergent Elor Azaria* v. *Military Prosecutor*, para. 113.

[39] Military Court of the Central District, *Military Prosecutor* v. *Sergent Elor Azaria*, para. 174; Military Court of Appeals, *Sergent Elor Azaria* v. *Military Prosecutor*, para. 113.

[40] Military Court of the Central District, *Military Prosecutor* v. *Sergent Elor Azaria*, para. 175; Military Court of Appeals, *Sergent Elor Azaria* v. *Military Prosecutor*, para. 113.

6.2. Law Enforcement and the Use of Armed Force in Occupied Territory 249

in occupied territory through the lens of domestic and international human rights law.[41]

The British rules of engagement in occupied Iraq provide further useful insight. British soldiers could employ lethal armed force beyond self-defence, but the soldiers were warned that they were 'to use no more force than absolutely necessary' for the protection of human life, when a person was committing or about to commit an act likely to endanger life and there was no other way to prevent the danger, after having provided, if possible, an adequate warning.[42] These rules appear respectful of the right to life as applicable in law-enforcement operations. A scrutiny of the rules of engagement of the US army shows that the USA envisaged two different scenarios: riot control and use of armed force. The two scenarios do not correspond exactly to the distinction between law enforcement and conduct of hostilities. With regard to riot control, these rules posit that force may be employed in self-defence and 'graduated force should be used when the situation permits and it is reasonable and practicable to do so. The use of force should be necessary, proportional, and reasonable in intensity, duration, and magnitude'.[43] The same rules of conduct require the shouting of warnings and suggest a preference for non-lethal methods (such as detention) to deal with a threat.[44] However, the rules refer generically to 'hostile act' or demonstrations of 'hostile intent' as justification to employ lethal force, and let the soldiers to assess case by case whether a graduated use of armed force is permissible according to 'time and circumstances'.[45] Such vague terms and the latitude conferred on the soldiers' judgment widen the role of the subjective perception of the involved soldiers beyond that usually provided by international human rights law conventions.

One of the most challenging scenarios regarding the use of armed force in law enforcement operations is the maintenance of public order during demonstrations against the occupying power.[46] State practice demonstrates

---

[41] It has been reported that the sentence was subsequently reduced by four months (Amos Arel, 'Israeli Army Chief Cuts Hebron Shooter's Sentence by Four Months', *Haaretz*, 27 September 2017, www.haaretz.com/israel-news/1.814579). On the legal and political situation surrounding this case, with particular reference to the sense of impunity that pertains to similar incidents in the OPT, see Emily Schaeffer Omer-Man, 'Extrajudicial Killing with Near Impunity: Excessive Force in Israeli Law Enforcement against Palestinians' (2017) 35 Boston University ILJ 116.
[42] The British rules of engagement in Iraq are quoted ECtHR, Al-Skeini para. 24.
[43] Section 3.C.(3)(A) of the rules of engagement published by WikiLeaks and available at file.wikileaks.org/file/us-iraq-rules-of-engagement.pdf
[44] Ibid., section 3.G.(1).
[45] Ibid.
[46] Robert Kolb, '"Condotta delle ostilità" e "mantenimento dell'ordine": due concetti chiave della definizione dei rapporti tra diritto internazionale umanitario e diritti umani' in Di Stefano & Sapienza (eds.), *La tutela*, 67, 69; Gaggioli (ed.), *Expert Meeting*, 1.

that such situations may pose threats to the occupying power's security: for instance, demonstrators may throw stones or use other weapons against law enforcement officials. Such demonstrations may escalate into riots that could severely affect the security of the occupying power and its authority over the occupied territory.

International humanitarian law takes a very prudent stance regarding such demonstrations. On the one hand, international humanitarian law does not recognise as legitimate combatants every inhabitant of the occupied territory revolting against the occupying power, restricting the possibility of the *levée en masse* only before the occupation is established.[47] Accordingly, the faculty of the occupying power to maintain public order in these contexts is uncontested. However, since international humanitarian law does not consider demonstrations, even if violent, to be direct participation of civilians in hostilities,[48] the occupying power must ensure public order during such demonstrations primarily through law enforcement, which is presumed to be the applicable operational and legal paradigm.[49]

It should be noted that most international human rights law conventions do not refer expressly to this scenario. Only Article 2(2)(c) ECHR contemplates deprivation of life 'in action lawfully taken for the purpose of quelling a riot or insurrection'. Applying this provision to demonstrations against the occupation and the occupying power in North Cyprus, the ECtHR held that law enforcement officials dealing with such demonstrations are bound by the same rules regulating the right to life in other law-enforcement scenarios.[50] The existence of a violent demonstration may influence the assessment of the threat against law enforcement officials or other individuals, and, thus, of the necessity of resorting to armed force and the proportionality of the response. However, the ECtHR does not assess these elements in a different way because of the situation of occupation. In particular, the ECtHR affirmed that the same rules governing the right to life are applicable '[e]ven though the fact that the demonstrators, who had sticks and iron bars, were throwing stones at the [occupying] Turkish forces carried the risk of potentially more violent developments'.[51]

---

[47] See *supra*, Section 4.2.1.
[48] See Melzer, *Interpretive Guidance*, 63; Annoni, *L'occupazione*, 231; Gaggioli (ed.), *Expert Meeting*, 24.
[49] See Gaggioli (ed.), *Expert Meeting*, 25; Annoni, *L'occupazione*, 231.
[50] *Solomou et al. v. Turkey* (Application no. 36832/97), 24 June 2008, para. 78; *Isaak et al. v. Turkey* (Application no. 44587/98), 24 June 2008, paras. 116–19; *Andreou v. Turkey* (Application no. 45653/99), 27 October 2009, paras. 54–5.
[51] *Andreou v. Turkey*, para. 54.

6.2. Law Enforcement and the Use of Armed Force in Occupied Territory

The practice of the OPT is particularly interesting since it shows an evolution of the regulations regarding the use of armed force by Israeli officials. Before the First Intifada, lethal armed force against the civilian population was allowed only as last resort in self-defence or in defence of other individuals under the protection of a law-enforcement official, as long as the harm inflicted was proportionate to the harm suffered or threatened.[52] Accordingly, law-enforcement officials could employ firearms only as response to explosive gunfire attacks, while they had to respond to other attacks with non-lethal means with firearms 'only when there exists a real and immediate danger to their lives', after having warned the opponents of the possibility of responding with firearms and having fired a warning shot.[53] These rules are generally in line with international human rights standards on the use of armed force in law enforcement operations. However, after March 1988, when the demonstrations at the heart of the First Intifada spread, the Israeli Minister of Defence declared that the rules on the use of armed force had been changed to allow the shooting of Palestinians attacking with non-lethal means.[54] It has been reported that this change of policy caused a dramatic increase in Palestinian casualties that went largely uninvestigated and unpunished.[55] Despite the fact that the IDF was advised to employ less lethal plastic bullets rather than lead bullets,[56] it is clear that the use of armed force was authorised beyond cases of absolute necessity and strict proportionality, in violation of international human rights law.

During the Second Intifada, Israel further altered the rules of engagement in order to allow even more liberal resort to armed force. It has been reported that new open-fire regulations were adopted, expanding the range of situations in which soldiers may open fire: the new situations included firing without warning at Palestinian suspects, and the use of firearms in operations initiated by the IDF and in preventive actions.[57] This practice does not comply with the legal

---

[52] See Section 22 Israeli Penal Code, quoted in B'Tselem, *The Use of Firearms by the Security Forces in the Occupied Territories* (1990) 7.
[53] See the Israeli regulation on these of firearms quoted by B'Tselem, The Use of Firearms by the Security Forces in the Occupied Territories (1990) 7. 9–14. See also Human Rights Watch, *The Israeli Army and the Intifada* (1990) 17–22, available at www.hrw.org/sites/default/files/report_pdf/israel_intifada_0890.pdf
[54] See Ilan Peleg, *Human Rights in the West Bank and Gaza: Legacy and Politics* (Syracuse University Press 1995) 109–10.
[55] Ibid., 110; Human Rights Watch, *The Israeli*, 33–88; B'Tselem, *The Killing of Palestinian Children and the Open-Fire Regulations* (1993), available at www.btselem.org/download/199306_killing_of_children_eng.pdf
[56] B'Tselem, *The Use*, 17–21; Human Rights Watch, *The Israeli*, 26–32.
[57] See B'Tselem, *Trigger Happy: Unjustified Shooting and Violation of the Open-Fire Regulations during the al-Aqsa Intifada* (2002) 6–8.

paradigm pertaining to law-enforcement operations, since armed force may be employed with lethal consequences beyond cases of absolute necessity and strict proportionality.[58] However, it should be noted that *some* armed confrontations during the Second Intifada likely fall outside the paradigm of law enforcement, and into the paradigm of the conduct of hostilities; as already noted, the assessment regarding the model to employ must be done case by case.[59] However, there is room to argue that, during the Second Intifada, some people were shot during a number of demonstrations that may not be considered situations of hostilities, without any effective judicial scrutiny of these deaths.[60]

In addition, the occurrence of hostilities in *one portion* of the occupied territory does not allow the occupying power to disregard the law enforcement paradigm in relation to demonstrations occurring in a *different area* of the occupied territory and not falling into the definition of hostilities. Where the occupying power delegates the bulk of maintenance of public order to the local police, this distinction is easier to respect, since the actors involved in the two scenarios are different. Conversely, when the occupying power's armed forces are tasked with both the conduct of hostilities and law enforcement, the risk of a violation of international human rights law pertaining to law-enforcement is higher. For instance, Israel failed to respect the law-enforcement paradigm during some demonstrations in the West Bank that occurred at the time of the Israeli military operation Cast Lead against the Gaza Strip in 2009, when Israel applied a new regulation regarding the use of lethal force adopted in 2006; this regulation provides for a more stringent regime regarding the use of lethal force when the authorities have to face disorders involving Israeli citizens, while it allows more relaxed standards when the disorders involve only Palestinians: in the first case, rubber and live ammunitions may be employed only in violent manifestations posing a 'clear and imminent danger', while the existence of a more generic danger to the 'physical integrity' of soldiers is sufficient to trigger the use of lethal armed force if there are only Palestinians involved.[61] It has been reported that this policy resulted in the death of a high number of Palestinians,[62] without any subsequent effective investigations,[63] in violation of the right to life pursuant to Article 6 ICCPR.[64] Similarly, during

[58] See Pertile, 'Fighting', 280.
[59] See *supra*, Section 5.6.
[60] See B'Tselem, *Trigger Happy*, 16–18.
[61] The 2006 regulation is quoted and commented by Orna Ben-Naftali, 'PathoLAWgical Occupation: Normalizing the Exceptional Case of the Occupied Palestinian Territory and Other Legal Pathologies' in Ben-Naftali (ed.), *International*, 129, 184
[62] Goldstone Report, paras. 1381–404.
[63] Ibid., paras. 1405–9.
[64] Ibid., 1430–1.

the operation Protective Edge, a number of demonstrations in the West Bank were quelled through the use of armed force, resulting in the death of twenty-seven Palestinians and the injury of over 3,100 individuals.[65] The HRC correctly classified these operations as law-enforcement,[66] and found that Israel had used firearms and live ammunitions in riot control beyond self-defence and situations of absolute necessity.[67] This conduct is considered to be out of line with the aforementioned UN Basic Principles[68] and a violation of the right to life binding upon Israel thanks to Article 6 ICCPR.[69]

This cursory scrutiny of state practice supports the view that military forces are often inadequate to exercise law-enforcement responsibilities, which must be enacted through international human rights law. Especially in situations of violent demonstrations, armed forces personnel tend to apply the paradigm they are more familiar with, that of the conduct of hostilities. The British Army itself has confirmed the unpreparedness of the armed forces to conduct law enforcement activities in occupied territory.[70] However, legally speaking, the paradigm of law enforcement, based on international human rights law, must be applicable to law-enforcement operations notwithstanding who conducts them. Accordingly, the occupying powers have a responsibility to employ personnel fit for law enforcement and able to restore and ensure public order while respecting international human rights.[71]

6.3. THE USE OF ARMED FORCE DURING THE CONDUCT OF HOSTILITIES IN OCCUPIED TERRITORY

6.3.1. *The Legal Paradigm of the Conduct of Hostilities*

To understand better the rules on the use of armed force in occupied territory when hostilities occur, and to determine the level of protection offered for the right to life under those circumstances, it is necessary to summarise briefly the international humanitarian law rules pertaining to the conduct of hostilities.

The rules on the conduct of hostilities in international armed conflict are mainly embodied in the HR and in the AP I. Notwithstanding the lack of

---

[65] See OCHA, The Monthly Humanitarian Bulletin (June–August 2014): Sharp Increase in Clashes and Casualties across the West Bank, available at www.ochaopt.org/content/sharp-increase-clashes-and-casualties-across-west-bank
[66] 2014 Gaza Report, 153, and paras. 544–6.
[67] Ibid., paras. 543–4.
[68] Ibid., paras. 545.
[69] Ibid., paras. 546.
[70] UK, Ministry of Defence, *Aitken Report* (2008), quoted in *Al Skeini* case, para. 24.
[71] See Sassòli, 'Legislation', 668.

universal ratification of AP I, the rules governing the conduct of hostilities embodied therein are commonly considered to be part of international customary law.[72] As already mentioned, these rules strike a delicate balance between two different exigencies: on the one hand, the principle of military necessity, that is the belligerents' interest in gaining military advantage and, eventually, in attaining victory;[73] on the other, the principle of humanity, which tries to reduce as far as possible the negative impact of the hostilities on civilians, while at the same time proscribing some conduct considered inherently heinous even if directed against enemy combatants.[74]

With respect to the right to life, the main difference between international humanitarian law and international human rights law is that international humanitarian law does not prohibit the death of individuals during hostilities as such. Rather, the rules on the conduct of hostilities make a distinction between lawful and unlawful killings on the basis of the status of the targeted individual. The basic tenet of the conduct of hostilities is that enemy combatants may be lawfully targeted and killed, whereas civilians[75] and persons *hors de combat*[76] must not be targeted, even as a matter of reprisals.[77] This rule is part of the principle of distinction, according to which '[i]n order to ensure respect for and protection of the civilian population and civilian objects, the Parties to the conflict shall at all times distinguish between the civilian population and combatants and between civilian objects and military objectives and accordingly shall direct their operations only against military objectives'.[78] The protection of civilians requires states to abstain from indiscriminate attacks.[79] Accordingly, the status of the target is the main criterion governing the use of armed force during the conduct of hostilities.[80] The distinction between civilians and

---

[72] See, generally, Henckaerts & Doswald-Beck (eds.), *Customary* vol. I.
[73] On this principle, see, generally, Gabriella Venturini, *Necessità e proporzionalità nell'uso della forza militare in diritto internazionale* (Giuffrè 1988) and 'Necessity in the Law of Armed Conflict and in International Criminal Law' (2010) 41 Netherlands YIL 45; Laura Salvadego, *Struttura e funzioni della necessità militare nel diritto internazionale* (Giappichelli 2012); Etienne Henry, *Le principe de nécessité militaire: Histoire et actualité d'une norme fondamentale du droit international humanitaire* (Pedone 2016).
[74] For more on this, see *supra*, Section 2.2.
[75] See Art. 51(1) and (2) AP I.
[76] See Art. 41 AP I.
[77] Art. 51(6) AP I.
[78] Art. 48 AP I.
[79] See Art. 51(4) and (5) AP I.
[80] For more on this and for further references, see, generally, William H. Boothby, *The Law of Targeting* (Oxford University Press 2012); Dinstein, *The Conduct*, 102–6; Paul A. L. Ducheine, Michael N. Schmitt, & Frans P. B. Osinga (eds.), *Targeting: The Challenges of Modern Warfare* (Springer 2016).

6.3. Use of Armed Force

combatants may not be an easy one to make: although international humanitarian law prescribes some distinctive emblems that the combatants must wear in order to be distinguishable from civilians, sometimes combatants fail to comply with these prescriptions, especially in occupied territory, and, as a result, they are deprived of prisoner-of-war status.[81] According to Article 43(2) AP I, '[m]embers of the armed forces of a Party to a conflict (other than medical personnel and chaplains ...) are combatants';[82] this rule, which reflects customary international law,[83] refers to the definition of armed forces already examined.[84] According to Article 50(1) AP I, civilians are those individuals who are not combatants, who are protected against attacks 'unless and for such time as they take a direct part in hostilities';[85] accordingly, civilians who take direct part in the hostilities may be targeted lawfully.[86] As confirmed with regard to the occupation of the OPT by the Supreme Court of Israel, individuals who are not combatants and who take direct part in the hostilities remain civilians, even if they may be targeted.[87] International humanitarian law conventions do not embody any reference to what is considered direct participation of civilians in hostilities. The ICRC's detailed review of state practice considers that a civilian may be targeted if three requirements are cumulatively met: (i) the civilian's conduct must cause the enemy a certain threshold of harm; (ii) there must be a direct causal link between the act and the harm; (iii) the act must have a nexus to an armed conflict.[88]

In addition, international humanitarian law allows the death of civilians in other circumstances. In particular, the unintended death of civilians is admissible if such casualties occur in the course of an attack against a military objective and as long as the deaths are 'not excessive' in relation to the expected

---

[81] See Art. 1 HR; Art. 4 GC III; Art. 44(3) AP I.
[82] Art. 43(2) AP I. See, also, US Military Manual, section 5.7.2.
[83] See Henckaerts & Doswald-Beck (eds.), *Customary* vol. I, 11; Akande, 'Clearing the Fog', 185.
[84] See *supra*, Section 5.5.2.
[85] Art. 51(3) AP I.
[86] On this topic, see generally Giulio Bartolini, 'The Participation of Civilians in Hostilities' in Michael J. Matheson & Djamchid Momtaz (eds.), *Rules and Institutions of International Humanitarian Law Put to the Test of Recent Armed Conflicts* (Brill 2010) 321; Melzer, *Interpretive Guidance*; Emily Crawford, *Identifying the Enemy: Civilian Participation in Armed Conflict* (Oxford University Press 2015); Disntein, *The Conduct*, 174–81.
[87] *Targeted Killings* case, para. 28. The Court, rightly, ruled out the existence of a third category beside combatants and civilians, that of 'unlawful combatants'. This aspect of the Court's decision attracted general favour (see Benvenuti, 'Judicial Review', XVI; Cassese, 'On Some Merits', 343–4; but see Orna Ben-Naftali & Keren R. Michaeli, '*Public Committee against Torture in Israel v. Government of Israel*. Case No HCJ 769/02' (2007) 101 AJIL 459, 464). For more on the treatment of civilians involved in armed resistance against the occupying power, see *supra*, Section 4.2.3.
[88] Melzer, *Interpretive Guidance*, 16.

military advantage.[89] The respect for this rule is often labelled as the 'principle of proportionality', while the unintended civilian casualties are often euphemistically labelled 'collateral damage'.[90]

In order to comply with the principles of distinction and proportionality, the belligerents must take precautions both if they attack[91] and when they are attacked.[92] In particular, those who plan and conduct an attack must verify the nature of the target and whether the consequences of the attack would be excessive in light of the expected military advantage, choosing the means and methods of warfare that are able to minimise civilian casualties, suspending the attack in case the likely unintended harm to civilians is excessive in comparison with the military advantage expected.[93] In addition, the belligerent who is attacking, whenever possible, must provide in advance of the attack adequate warnings to the civilian population.[94]

The aforementioned rules allow the direct targeting of an enemy combatant and their killing as long as the safeguards for the civilians' right to life are observed. The ICRC proposed introducing further international humanitarian law restrains to the faculty to kill combatants on the base of the principles of humanity and necessity, according to which 'the kind and degree of force which is permissible against persons not entitled to protection against direct attack *must not exceed what is actually necessary to accomplish a legitimate military purpose in the prevailing circumstances*'.[95] This idea met with harsh criticism[96] and some support;[97] suffice it to say now that, as argued below,

---

[89] According to Art. 51(5)(b) AP I, indiscriminate attacks refers to 'attack[s] which may be expected to cause incidental loss of civilian life, injury to civilians, damage to civilian objects, or a combination thereof, which would be excessive in relation to the concrete and direct military advantage anticipated'.

[90] On the assessment of proportionality in targeting, see, generally, Cannizzaro, 'Proportionality'; Newton & May, *Proportionality*, 85–120,155–75; Dinstein, *Conduct*, 149–63.

[91] See Art. 57 AP I. On the relationship between this provision and the principles of proportionality and distinction, as well as for further references on the principle of precaution, see Marco Longobardo, 'L'obbligo per gli Stati di assumere tutte le informazioni necessarie prima di un attacco ai sensi del diritto internazionale umanitario fra nuove e vecchie forme di intelligence' in Andrea Spagnolo & Stefano Saluzzo (eds.), *La responsabilità degli Stati e delle organizzazioni internazionali: nuove fattispecie e problemi di attribuzione e di accertamento* (Ledizioni 2017) 37.

[92] See Art. 58 AP I.

[93] Art. 57(2)(a) AP I.

[94] Art. 57(2)(c).

[95] See Melzer, *Interpretive Guidance*, 77 (emphasis added). See also Ibid., 78–9.

[96] See, US Military Manual, section 5.7.1. See, also, W. Hays Parks, 'Part IX of the ICRC Direct Participation in Hostilities Study: No Mandate, No Expertise, and Legally Incorrect' (2009–10) 42 New York University JIL & Policy 769, 783–830; Akande, 'Clearing the Fog', 191–2; Jann K. Kleffner, 'Section IX of the ICRC Interpretive Guidance on Direct Participation in Hostilities: The End of *Jus in Bello* Proportionality as We Know It' (2012) 45 IsLR 35; Dinstein, *Conduct*, 42.

[97] See Ryan Goodman, 'The Power to Kill or Capture Enemy Combatants' (2013) 24 EJIL 819.

a similar result may be achieved through the interpretation of international humanitarian law in light of applicable international human rights law.[98]

International humanitarian law requires investigations of deaths that occur in the course of hostilities only with regard to specific cases. The duty to criminalise war crimes[99] embodies an obligation to investigate any deaths that occurred as the result of the commission of an alleged war crime.[100] Accordingly, international humanitarian law demands an investigation where there are reasonable bases to believe that the civilian population or individual civilians have been made wilfully the object of attack, an indiscriminate attack has been launched wilfully against the civilian population or civilian objects, a protected person has been targeted wilfully or has been killed wilfully – since all of these examples of unlawful use of armed force are considered war crimes.[101] However, despite these specific exceptions and other similar instances where the commission of a war crime is claimed, there is no duty under international humanitarian law to investigate every killing.

Recent state practice shows that states are more engaged in the investigation of deaths that occur during the conduct of the hostilities, regardless of the presence of claims pertaining to the commission of war crimes. This significant trend is the result of the contextual application of international human rights law, along with international humanitarian law. Since international human rights law requires investigation when life is deprived, states are required more and more to provide investigations regarding deaths that occur during hostilities under applicable international human rights law.[102]

This extremely brief glance at the right to life under international humanitarian law pertaining to the conduct of hostilities demonstrates that the protection offered to individuals is radically different from that offered to them under the law-enforcement model, particularly with regard to enemy combatants. However, in occupied territory, both models are applicable. In addition, international human rights law is applicable in the occupied territory along with international humanitarian law. Accordingly, it is necessary to coordinate

---

[98] See *infra*, Section 6.3.2.2.
[99] See Arts. 49 and 50 GC I; Arts. 50 and 51 GC II; Arts. 129 and 130 GC III; Arts. 146 and 147 GC IV; Arts. 85, 86, and 87 AP I.
[100] For more on this, see Michael N. Schmitt, 'Investigating Violations of International Law in Armed Conflict' (2011) 2 *Harvard National Security Journal* 31, 35–48; Gaggioli (ed.), *Expert Meeting*, 49; Francoise J. Hampson, 'An Investigation of Alleged Violations of the Law of Armed Conflict' (2016) 46 IYHR 1, 12–18.
[101] Gaggioli (ed.), *Expert Meeting*, 49. See also *Targeted Killings* case, para. 40.
[102] See the practice analysed and reviewed by Schmitt, 'Investigating Violations', 48–82; Hampson, 'An Investigation', 18–27; Luca Gervasoni, 'A Contextual-Functional Approach to Investigations into Right to Life Violations in Armed Conflict' (2017) 36 *Zoom-In Questions of International Law* 5.

the rules on the conduct of hostilities and the inherent hostile character of the occupation in order to verify whether the killing of an individual in occupied territory is lawful.

6.3.2. The Application of the Legal Paradigm Pertaining to Conduct of Hostilities in Occupied Territory

6.3.2.1. The Law of Occupation versus the Law on the Conduct of Hostilities

One of the main issues regarding the legal framework applicable to hostilities in occupied territory is whether the situation of occupation affects the application of the rules on the conduct of hostilities under international humanitarian law. Two commentators in particular have authoritatively advocated the idea that the law of occupation impacts the rules on the conduct of hostilities in occupied territory. According to Orna Ben-Naftali and Keren Michaeli, the rules pertaining to the conduct of hostilities codified by AP I, such as the definition of combatants and the direct participation of civilians in hostilities, are not applicable as such in occupied territory, where GC IV governs the status of individuals under the occupying power's authority.[103] These authors argue that the 'logic' at the basis of GC IV and AP I is different,[104] and that, accordingly, the fact that the law of occupation does not regulate conduct of hostilities does not allow the application of AP I's rules.[105] However, these authors do not reach the logical conclusion of their reasoning based on the inherent differences between situations of occupation and conduct of hostilities, that would be the inapplicability of the law on the conduct of hostilities as such due to the prevalence of the law of occupation as *lex specialis*. In the words of the two authors, 'that the Convention rejects the legality of compromising the physical integrity of any person belonging to the occupied population [is] an interpretation that coheres with the primary concern of the Convention, [but] is nevertheless unlikely because would entail a prohibition on any act of justified self-defense on the part of the occupying power'.[106] According to this view, the silence of GC IV regarding the regulation of the conduct of hostilities and the different 'logic' at the basis of GC IV and AP I would impact the *interpretation* of the rules on the conduct of hostilities: 'The law of occupation, while embracing the principles of

---

[103] See Ben-Naftali & Michaeli, 'Public Committee', 463–5.
[104] Ibid., 464. See also the brief critical remarks of Kathleen Cavanaugh, 'Rewriting the Law: The Case of Israel and the Occupied Territories' in Wippman & Evangelista (eds.), New Wars, 227, 250.
[105] Ben-Nafali & Michaeli, 'Public Committee', 465.
[106] Ben-Naftali & Michaeli, 'We Must', 282.

a legitimate military target, should nonetheless put an emphasis on a different set of considerations, tilting the balance of interests against those of the occupying power and in favor of the inhabitants of the occupied territory'.[107] The source of this new regulation would be found in Articles 4 and 5 GC IV regarding protected persons, as well as in applicable international human rights law.[108]

Although such an approach is extremely desirable because it enhances the protection of the local population of the occupied territory, there is no support for it in state practice or in domestic or international case law. Rather, AP I was envisaged as an instrument to bridge the gap between the so-called 'Hague Law', pertaining to the conduct of hostilities and codified by the HR, and the so-called 'Geneva Law', pertaining to the protection of civilians and individuals *hors de combat*, mainly codified in the GCs. AP I takes into account the situation of hostilities in the occupied territory thanks to Article 44(3) AP I, which prescribes less stringent requirements for individuals in occupied territory in order to be considered legitimate combatants and, thus, prisoners of war if captured. Accordingly, the drafters of AP I were aware of the peculiarities of hostilities in occupied territory, and it is applicable during occupations.[109] Clearly, the two aforementioned authors consider that Article 44(3) AP I reduces rather than widens the protection of the population of occupied territories;[110] nonetheless, there is no room to argue that the rules on the conduct of hostilities should be 'adjusted' in occupied territory in order to take into account the occupation in a different fashion than outside occupied territory. Simply, the AP I does not support this view since it does not regulate differently the protection of civilians from the effects of hostilities depending on the existence of a situation of occupation. It is not happenstance that the two aforementioned authors stress that AP I, including its rules of conduct of hostilities, is not applicable to their case study, the OPT, for a number of reasons that are not examined here.[111] However, there is nothing in the AP I to suggest that its rule on the conduct of hostilities should apply differently in situations of occupation.[112]

---

[107] Ibid.
[108] Ibid., 282 and 288–92; Ben-Naftali & Michaeli, '*Public Committee*', 465.
[109] Melzer, *Targeted Killing*, 157.
[110] Ben-Naftali & Michaeli, '*Public Committee*', 464–5.
[111] Ibid., 463–4.
[112] However, even in cases of occupying powers not bound by the AP I, the two authors' reasoning is unconvincing since the rules pertaining to the conduct of hostilities embodied therein are unanimously considered to be reflective of customary international law. Even the idea that hostilities in occupied territory should be regulated under the law on non-international armed conflict, thus rejecting radically the applicability of AP I and corresponding customary rules, does not determine a different outcome: the aforementioned two authors fail to demonstrate that customary international rules of the law on non-international armed conflict

In light of this reasoning, the rules on the conduct of hostilities are the same for hostilities occurring within and without the occupied territory. There is only one notable exception: in the rare event of a rule pertaining to the conduct of hostilities *embodied in the law of occupation*, this rule would prevail over a more generic rule on the conduct of hostilities not specifically addressing occupations on the basis of the principle of *lex specialis*. The regulation of the protection of property is the most clear example of this peculiar relationship between the law of occupation and the rules on the conduct of hostilities since international humanitarian law governs protection of property in an occupied territory and during the course of hostilities in slightly different ways. According to the aforementioned Article 53 GC IV, '[a]ny destruction by the occupying power of real or personal property belonging individually or collectively to private persons ... is prohibited, except where such destruction is rendered absolutely necessary by military operations'. This rule is specifically dedicated to situations of occupation. According to the ICJ, this rule is applicable to every destruction of property occurring in occupied territory, even if property is destroyed in the course of military actions undertaken against non-state actors resorting to means and methods of warfare against the occupying power.[113] In ruling so, the Court seemed to discard the application of the rule pertaining to the protection of property in the course of the conduct of hostilities, Article 23(g) HR, according to which enemy's property is protected 'unless such destruction or seizure be imperatively demanded by the necessities of war'. It is worth pointing out that the test embodied in Article 53 GC IV (absolute necessity for military operations) is narrower than the test envisaged by Article 23(g) HR (which refers to more generic 'necessities of war'). Some authors criticised the ICJ's stance, arguing that the application of Article 53 GC IV instead of Article 23(g) HR implies the ICJ's failure to acknowledge the existence of hostilities in occupied territory.[114] Following this view, the Supreme Court of Israel considered that Article 23(g) HR is the rule governing the use of armed force resulting in the destruction of property if hostilities exist in the occupied territory.[115] In this author's view, there is an

---

addressing the conduct of hostilities in occupied territory, with a more protective reach regard the local population, exist. Indeed, the current discourse on customary rules on the conduct of hostilities focuses on the *convergence* between rules pertaining to international and non-international armed conflict, without any reference to the fact that hostilities occur within or without occupied territory (see, generally, Henckaerts & Doswald-Beck (eds.), *Customary International Humanitarian Law* vol. I).

[113] See *Wall* opinion, paras. 132 and 135.
[114] See David Kretzmer, 'The Advisory Opinion: The Light Treatment of International Humanitarian Law' (2005) 99 AJIL 88 .
[115] See *Beit Sourik* case, paras. 32 and 35.

alternate reading of the ICJ's application of Article 53 GC IV: in fact, this provision refers to military operations, an expression which, as already noted, is equivalent to hostilities.[116] Consequently, both Article 53 GC IV and Article 23(g) HR regulate the destruction of property during the conduct of hostilities;[117] accordingly, since the two provisions provide different tests, Article 53 GC IV, which was adopted specifically to address situations of occupations, must be applied as the relevant *lex specialis* to situations of occupation.[118] However, with the exception of the destruction of property, the rules adopted to regulate the conduct of hostilities outside occupied territory are applicable in occupied territory, since the law of occupation does not provide any other specific regulation in conflict with that pertaining to the conduct of hostilities.

6.3.2.2. The Interplay between International Humanitarian Law and International Human Rights Law for the Conduct of Hostilities in Occupied Territory

Another important issue regarding the conduct of hostilities concerns the difference between *jus in bello* rules pertaining to the use of armed force and international human rights law rules pertaining to the right to life that are applicable in occupied territory thanks to the exercise of state extraterritorial jurisdiction. The protection of the human right to life in situations of armed conflict has raised many legal problems.[119] Due to the restricted purview of this book, only the specific issues pertaining to occupations are addressed here, solely with reference to the law on international armed conflict.[120]

---

[116] See *supra*, Section 5.4.1.
[117] The scope of Art. 53 GC IV is so broad that it governs destruction of property both in law enforcement and during the conduct of hostilities in occupied territory. Only in the latter scenario is destruction of property permitted if absolutely necessary.
[118] Some authors support the applicability of Art. 53 GC IV instead of Art. 23(g) HR (see, e.g., Pertile, 'Legal Consequences', 134–5; Giulia Pinzauti, 'Aspetti problematici della legittimità del "muro" in Palestina: il caso *Beit Sourik*' (2005) 88 RDI 441, 450) without, however, exploring the issue of the legal framework pertaining to the destruction of property during hostilities occurring in occupied territory.
[119] On the right to life in the conduct of hostilities, see, among others, Gaggioli & Kolb, 'A Right'; Vera Gowlland-Debbas, 'The Right to Life and the Relationship between Human Rights and Humanitarian Law' in Tomuschat, Lagrange, & Oeter (eds.), *The Right*, 121; Marco Pedrazzi, 'La protezione del diritto alla vita tra diritto internazionale umanitario e tutela internazionale dei diritti umani' in Di Stefano & Sapienza (eds.), *La tutela*, 79; Gaggioli (ed.), *Expert Meeting*; William A. Schabas, 'The Right to Life' in Clapham & Gaeta (eds.), *The Oxford Handbook*, 365.
[120] For an overview of the right to life in non-international armed conflicts, see Marco Sassòli & Laura M. Olson, 'The Relationship between International Humanitarian and Human Rights Law Where It Matters: Admissible Killing and Internment of Fighters in Non-International

As already mentioned, international humanitarian law considers admissible the death of individuals in military operations as long as the belligerents respect the principle of distinction (according to which only combatants and civilians taking direct part in the hostilities may be targeted), the principle of proportionality (according to which the death of civilians is admissible if it is proportionate to the expected military advantage), and the principle of precaution (imposing on the belligerents the duty to take all feasible measures to minimise the impact of military operations upon civilians). The application of the principles of proportionality and necessity is radically different under international humanitarian law and international human rights law. As already mentioned, necessity in international humanitarian law refers to the legitimate aim to gain a military advantage, while, under international human rights law, necessity refers to the use of armed force as a last resort. Similarly, under international humanitarian law, the assessment of the proportionality of the armed force employed must take into account the military advantage expected compared to the unintended harm to civilians and civilian objects;[121] conversely, the principle of proportionality under international human rights law posits that armed force is legitimate only in light of a preventive balancing between the threat posed by the individual and the potential harm to this individual, as well as to bystanders.[122] Accordingly, while the use of armed force is permitted under international humanitarian law on the basis of the status of the target (combatants may be killed), international human rights law requires the assessment of the threat posed by the target. The application of these two branches of the law in a separate way may lead to very different legal assessments. Just to mention a very clear-cut example, according to the traditional view on international humanitarian law, an enemy combatant may be killed if caught asleep under international humanitarian law, while such a killing would be arbitrary and, thus, unlawful, under international human rights law since a sleeping enemy is not able to pose a sufficient threat.[123]

During the conduct of hostilities in occupied territory, both international human rights law and international humanitarian law must be taken into account. In order to reconcile the opposite *weltanschauungen* at the bases of the two sets of rules pertaining to the use of armed force, it is necessary to recall the principles regulating the relationship

---

Armed Conflicts' (2008) 90 IRRC 599; Juliet Chevalier-Watts, 'Has Human Rights Law become *Lex Specialis* for the European Court of Human Rights in Right to Life Cases Arising from Internal Armed Conflicts?' (2010) 14 *The International Journal of Human Rights* 584.

[121] Article 51(5)(b) AP I.
[122] See *supra*, Section 6.2.1.
[123] See Garraway, 'Occupation', 277.

6.3. Use of Armed Force

between international human rights law and international humanitarian law already explored.[124]

The rules on treaty interpretation and, in particular, the systemic integration technique envisaged by Article 31(3)(c) VCLT, must be taken into account in order to interpret and apply the two branches of international law in a coherent way. This solution is particularly convenient when dealing with international human rights law conventions prohibiting 'arbitrary' deprivations of the rights to life, such as in the ICCPR and the ACHR. With regard to the conduct of the hostilities, the ICJ affirmed that, in times of armed conflict, the arbitrariness of a killing should be assessed in light of relevant rules of international humanitarian law, which constitute the interpretive context of these dispositions; accordingly, the use of armed force in compliance with international humanitarian law may not be considered an arbitrary deprivation of the right to life under international human rights law.[125] This approach, operating a sort of *renvoi* to international humanitarian law,[126] is shared by the CCPR so that the recent draft General Comment no. 36 on the Right to Life affirms that:

> Uses of lethal force authorized and regulated by and complying with international humanitarian law are, in principle, not arbitrary. By contrast, practices inconsistent with international humanitarian law, entailing a risk to the lives of civilians and persons hors de combat, including the targeting of civilians and civilian objects, indiscriminate attacks, failure to apply adequate measures of precaution to prevent collateral death of civilians, and the use of human shields, violate article 6 of the Covenant.[127]

Such an interpretation permits the avoidance of normative conflicts between international humanitarian law and international human rights law, providing an adequate answer to the conundrum of the parallel application of the two regimes.

The situation is more complex with regard to the right to life enshrined in the ECHR, which does not refer to the arbitrariness of the deprivation of life. The lack of such reference prevents any recourse to international humanitarian law according to the aforementioned technique of *renvoi*. Accordingly, providing an interpretation of the right to life under the ECHR that is not inconsistent with international humanitarian law is not easy; the risk of distorting the protection of the ECHR is very real. The ECtHR openly avoided

---

[124] See *supra*, Section 2.5.
[125] See *Nuclear Weapons* opinion, para. 25.
[126] See *supra*, Section 2.5.3.
[127] Draft General Comment no. 36, para. 67.

dealing with this issue in the *Bankovic* case, arguing that aerial bombings are not an exercise of a state's jurisdiction and, accordingly, they were not sufficient to trigger the application of the ECHR under Article 1.[128] This unsatisfactory opinion will not be examined here in detail as the case is largely outside the purview of this book;[129] suffice it to say that such an approach is not applicable in situations of occupation where a state exercises its jurisdiction extraterritorially by definition.

Article 2 ECHR must be interpreted taking into account international humanitarian law. According to the ECtHr's decision in the *Varnava* case, 'Article 2 must be interpreted in so far as possible in light of the general principles of international law, including the rules of international humanitarian law which play an indispensable and universally-accepted role in mitigating the savagery and inhumanity of armed conflict'.[130] The case law of the ECtHR on the right to life in armed conflict attempted to interpret the ECHR taking into account the peculiarities of an armed conflict. For instance, in the *Ergi* case, the Court, having acknowledged the existence of hostilities,[131] affirmed that state responsibility exists if a state 'fail[s] to take all feasible precautions in the choice of means and methods of a security operation mounted against an opposing group with a view to avoiding and, in any event, to minimising, incidental loss of civilian life.'[132] It is clear that the Court read the *jus in bello* principle of precaution into Article 2 ECHR, even if the judgment prefers not to refer to international humanitarian law. Significantly, in the *Khamzayev* case, the Court acknowledged the occurrence of unintended deaths in the conduct of hostilities, implicitly referring to the rule on collateral damage under international humanitarian law.[133]

However, the interpretation of international human rights law in light of international humanitarian law is not always an easy path when dealing with the right to life: for instance, in the *Issayeva* cases, absent any derogation under Article 15 ECHR, the Court affirmed that the cases had to be assessed under

---

[128] *Bankovič v. Belgium*, paras. 74–82.
[129] The capacity to kill an individual is considered an exercise of state jurisdiction by those authors who consider that state jurisdiction is exercised where there is effective control over individuals; indeed, it is indisputable that the capacity to kill an individual by the state is an exercise of public powers that may affect individual rights. For more on this, see De Sena, *La nozione*, 135–9; Milanovic, *Extraterritorial*, 19–53.
[130] *Varnava* et al. v. *Turkey*, para. 185.
[131] *Ergi* v. *Turkey* (Application no. 40/1993/435/514), 28 July 1998, para. 85.
[132] Ibid., para. 79
[133] *Khamzayev* et al. v. *Russia* (Application no. 1503/02), 3 May 2011, para. 178.

the usual legal background.[134] Accordingly, Russia attempted, unsuccessfully, to justify some military operations during a non-international armed conflict on the basis of the exception of personal self-defence under Article 2(2)(a) ECHR.[135] If the applicable rules were those of international humanitarian law, likely Russia would have argued the cases in a different way.[136]

Consequently, according to the ECtHR's case law, the conduct of hostilities, even in occupied territory, is not only subject to international humanitarian law but, also, to international human rights law. In the specific case of the ECHR, the protective scope of the right to life under Article 2 may narrow significantly the right to resort to armed force since it is impossible to *renvoyer* to international humanitarian law. The recent ECtHR reading of international human rights law obligations in light of international humanitarian law standards reduces the differences between the two branches, altering the balance between military necessity and humanity embodied in the *jus in bello* rules pertaining to the conduct of hostilities. Accordingly, states parties to the ECHR have two options: they may conduct hostilities both in conformity with the right to life under the ECHR and international humanitarian law, enhancing the progressive humanisation of the law on the conduct of hostilities;[137] or, rather, they may derogate from the right to life under the ECHR thanks to Article 15 ECHR. This provision allows states to derogate from the right to life in time of war 'in respect of deaths resulting from lawful acts of war'. Although there is some debate regarding the interpretation of this expression, which has never been addressed by the ECtHR,[138] arguably, 'lawful acts of war' implies that derogations to the right to life are admissible only if deprivation of life occurs in the context of military operations complying with international humanitarian law.[139] However,

---

[134] *Isayeva v. Russia* (Application no. 57950/00), 24 February 2005, para. 191. See, also, *Khamzayev et al. v. Russia*, para. 187.

[135] *Isayeva v. Russia*, paras. 169–200; *Isayeva et al. v. Russia* (Application nos 57947/00, 57948/00, 57949/00), 24 February 2005, paras. 179–201.

[136] However, in those cases, likely Russian conduct was illegal also under international humanitarian law, as explained by Gaggioli & Kolb, 'A Right', 141–4.

[137] Some authors advocate that such an application of international human rights law along with international humanitarian law reinforces the already protective scope of international humanitarian law, which should be construed as emphasising the principle of humanity (see, e.g., Eyal Benvenisti, 'Human Dignity in Combat: The Duty to Spare Enemy Civilians' (2006) 39 IsLR 81; Gaggioli & Kolb, 'A Right', 143–4; Schabas, *The European Convention*, 158).

[138] Schabas, *The European Convention*, 601.

[139] Gaggioli & Kolb, 'A Right', 126; Milanovic, *Extraterritorial Application*, 255; Rusen Ergec & Jacques Velu, *Convention européenne des droits de l'homme* (2nd edn, Bruylant 2014) 234; Clapham, 'The Complex Relationship', 712–13. *Contra*, see Schabas, *The European Convention*, 602, according to whom this expression refers primarily to *jus ad bellum*.

absent such a derogation, the conduct of hostilities must comply both with international humanitarian law and the ECHR since, as already observed, the theory of the prevalence of international humanitarian law as *lex specialis* is incorrect.

In state practice, the decision of the Supreme Court of Israel in the *Targeted Killings* case is particularly relevant since the Court took into account international human rights law – even if the outcome of its reasoning is not fully convincing. First, it must be pointed out that the Court acknowledged the existence of hostilities in the OPT, including in the West Bank, which, in the Court's view, is under occupation.[140] Initially, the Court affirmed that international human rights law is applicable only to fill lacunae in international humanitarian law applicable to international armed conflict,[141] and performed a detailed survey of the *jus in bello* rules on the conduct of hostilities.[142] However, at the end of the reasoning, the Court affirmed that:

> [A] civilian taking a direct part in hostilities *cannot be attacked* at such time as he is doing so, *if a less harmful means can be employed*. In our domestic law, that rule is called for by the principle of proportionality. Indeed, *among the military means, one must choose the means whose harm to the human rights of the harmed person is smallest*. Thus, *if a terrorist taking a direct part in hostilities can be arrested, interrogated, and tried, those are the means which should be employed. Trial is preferable to use of force*. A rule-of-law state employs, to the extent possible, *procedures of law and not procedures of force* ... Arrest, investigation, and trial are not means which can always be used. At times the possibility does not exist whatsoever; at times it involves a risk so great to the lives of the soldiers, that it is not required. However, it is *a possibility which should always be considered*. It might actually be particularly practical under the conditions of belligerent occupation, in which the army controls the area in which the operation takes place, and in which arrest, investigation, and trial are at times realizable possibilities. Of course, given the circumstances of a certain case, that possibility might not exist. At times, its harm to nearby innocent civilians might be greater than that caused by refraining from it. In that state of affairs, it should not be used. Third, after an attack on a civilian suspected of taking an active part, at such time, in hostilities, a thorough investigation regarding the precision of the identification of the target and the circumstances of the attack upon him is to be performed (retroactively). That investigation must be independent.[143]

---

[140] *Targeted Killings* case, para. 16.
[141] Ibid., para. 18.
[142] Ibid., paras. 16–46.
[143] Ibid., para. 40 (references omitted, emphases added). See also Cassese, *International Law*, 442.

As is clearly demonstrated by reference to international human rights case law, this passage is directly inspired by the principles and rules of international human rights law rather than by international humanitarian law.[144] As mentioned before, international humanitarian law does not demand the capture rather than the killing of civilians taking direct part in the hostilities – who, simply, may be killed *while involved in the hostilities*; nor does it favour the trial of the enemy over their killing. Similarly, beyond the occurrence of war crimes, international humanitarian law does not prescribe any duty to investigate every death that occurs in the course of hostilities. By contrast, as already mentioned, the right to life under international human rights law conventions requires the capture rather than the killing of individuals, to employ less harmful means against threats, and to effectively investigate every death that occurs under the state's jurisdiction, especially when state officials are involved. With these differences in mind, it seems that the Supreme Court of Israel's approach in the *Targeted Killings* case merges international humanitarian law and international human rights law standards in relation to extrajudicial killings.[145] However, even so, this decision fails to acknowledge that two different scenarios may occur: law enforcement and conduct of hostilities. The Court's approach may be considered desirable and, finally, correct, only if restricted to the conduct of hostilities: if, and only if, the occupying power may lawfully resort to the conduct of hostilities, the parallel application of the two branches of international law could further the humanisation of the recourse to armed force.[146] However, since international and domestic human rights law primarily regulates the use of armed force with respect to law-enforcement operations, then, if a situation falls into the scope of law enforcement, the legal reasoning of the Supreme Court of Israel is not applicable and the right to life should be guaranteed only by the more protective rules of international human rights law. Accordingly, the failure of the Supreme Court of Israel to clearly distinguish these two scenarios risks undermining rather than enhancing the protection of the right to life in occupied territory.[147] Accordingly, the *Targeted Killings* case presents an interesting and progressive approach only if its findings are restricted to situations of hostility occurring in occupied territory.

Another complex issue in state practice regarding the right to life in the context of the conduct of hostilities in occupied territory pertains to violent

---

[144] This passage was subsequently echoed by the Interpretive Guidance, section IX.
[145] See Ferraro (ed.), *Expert Meeting*, 115.
[146] See Cassese, 'On Some Merits'.
[147] See the criticisms to this judgment by Benvenuti, 'Judicial Review', xiv; Bartolini 'Le eliminazioni', 625–6.

demonstrations against the occupying power. As already mentioned, these activities, in principle, should be addressed through law enforcement.[148] However, it may happen that the model of the conduct of hostilities becomes applicable. For instance, if combatants infiltrate the demonstration in order to attack the occupying power's law enforcement officials, then the conduct of hostilities model and legal framework is applicable to similar demonstrations.[149] In such circumstances, the identification of the factors allowing the resort to the conduct of hostilities is not easy. When similar demonstrations deteriorate into acts of hostility, it is crucial to maintain that the presumed applicable operational and legal paradigm is that of law enforcement. Accordingly, it is possible to resort to the conduct of hostilities only when combatants have infiltrated civilian groups or if civilians take direct part in the hostilities under Article 51(3) AP I – that is, when there are acts of hostility causing a certain threshold of harm and directly linked to an armed conflict. In such cases, civilians who take part in such demonstrations without causing sufficient harm may not be targeted under international humanitarian law. However, at a practical level, most rules of engagement adopt an 'escalation of force procedure',[150] which blends the distinction between law enforcement and conduct of hostilities, allowing the shift from one paradigm to the other on the basis of the subjective perception of the threat to the involved occupying power's officials.[151]

6.4. CONCLUSIONS

It is not easy to identify any one single regime regulating the use of armed force in occupied territory; rather, the distinction between law enforcement and conduct of hostilities is crucial. In situations of law enforcement, international human rights law is the main legal framework governing the use of armed force. Accordingly, the right to life is protected so that the armed force may be employed lawfully only as a last resort measure. In the conduct of hostilities, international humanitarian law rules on hostilities are generally applicable in occupied territory, along with international human rights law. Accordingly, the use of lethal armed force is permitted if the target is an enemy combatant or a civilian taking direct part in the hostilities, while it is prohibited in the case of civilians or individuals *hors de combat*. However, the contextual application of international humanitarian law and international human rights

---

[148] See *supra*, Section 6.2.2.
[149] See the discussion summarised in Gaggioli (ed.), *Expert Meeting*, 24–9.
[150] Ibid., 27.
[151] Ibid.

6.4. Conclusions

law demands a complementary interpretation of the two branches. Under the ICCPR and the ACHR, every deprivation of life that occurs in line with international humanitarian law should not be considered arbitrary. In the context of the ECHR, Article 2 has been interpreted as encompassing to a certain extent the principles governing the conduct of hostilities, offering, however, a more protective regime than that provided by international humanitarian law alone.

In the specific circumstances of occupied territory, the occupying power must use armed force with the same constraints that limit peacetime law enforcement. Accordingly, even during an occupation, the use of armed force and the consequent deprivation of the right to life should be regarded as last-resort measures. However, should hostilities occur, the occupying power may lawfully resort to the conduct of hostility rules. Situations such as violent demonstrations and riots may be challenging with regard to determining the relevant regime. However, the presumption in favour of the application of law enforcement should guide the occupying power's conduct even in similar circumstances. To properly address this challenge, the occupying power may find it useful to deploy the local police, if feasible, since their lack of affiliation to the occupying power and their experience in maintaining public order could prove a significant asset when violent demonstrations occur.

7

General Conclusions

The dialogue of the occupying power and the occupied territory ... is that of two people at war, enemies, equal sovereigns; that of Ulysses and Hector, but in a devastated Troy.[1]

At the end of this work, it is necessary to acknowledge that the use of armed force is a common phenomenon in situations of occupation and that international law does regulate it. Despite the scant interest that this topic has attracted in international scholarship for decades (as demonstrated by the survey provided in Section 1.2), the idea that occupying powers exercise unregulated authority over the occupied territory is definitively over, and it is time to study this topic in a comprehensive way. Indeed, the law of occupation, coupled with other rules of applicable international law, offers a highly sophisticated legal framework governing the use of armed force in occupied territory; this legal framework has developed progressively in order to constrain the inherently hostile relationship that accompanies every occupation. As this book has striven to demonstrate, the use of armed force in occupied territory does not lie in a deregulated limbo, but is, rather, fully governed by international law.

One of the main challenges of the application of the relevant rules of international law to armed confrontations occurring in occupied territory is the reluctance of states to acknowledge their position as occupying powers. As demonstrated in Section 1.3, situations of occupations are not as rare as is often affirmed. Even beyond the clear-cut examples of the occupations of the OPT, Northern Cyprus, and Iraq in 2003–4, there are many other situations in which the law of occupation applies, regardless of any acknowledgement of this by the occupying powers. Accordingly, every time armed force is employed in one of these contexts, its use should be regulated in the way that is described in this book.

[1] Pellet, 'The Destruction', 173.

As affirmed in Chapter 2, occupation triggers the application of the body of international law referred to as the law of occupation. The constitutive elements of the fact of the occupation are: exercise of actual authority by one state engaged in an international armed conflict against another state, over one part of the territory of the latter; loss of authority by the latter over that part of territory; and lack of consent by the state whose territory is controlled. State practice has evolved so that today such an authority may be exercised by states directly or through controlled entities or armed groups, as well as by international organisations, irrespective of whether the occupied territory belonged to any state prior to the occupation. The acknowledgement of the situation of occupation is entirely irrelevant for the application of the law of occupation, but factual uncertainty may arise with regard to the amount of authority required to establish an occupation. In situations where armed resistance exists, where territories do not belong to any state prior to the occupation, and where the occupying power is not present with boots on the ground in specific areas, occupying powers are particularly reluctant to apply the law of occupation. Nevertheless, as demonstrated in Section 2.3, the law of occupation does in fact apply.

The basic tenets of the law of occupation are that the occupying power does not acquire sovereignty over the occupied territory, and that, therefore, its administration is temporary in nature. As demonstrated in Chapter 2, the entire law of occupation addresses the delicate equilibrium between different interests when, as a consequence of an international armed conflict, a hostile state is required to govern a portion of territory. On the one hand, the law of occupation is tasked with preventing the occupying power from annexing the occupied territory; however, the law of occupation must allow the occupying power to administer the occupied territory. Accordingly, the law of occupation offers balanced solutions that take into account both the inherently hostile character of the occupation and the government-like aspect of the occupying power's administration. At the same time, the law of occupation protects the interests of the local population as well, limiting the occupying power's administration if it infringes upon protected persons' rights.

In order to better satisfy all the interests at stake, the law of occupation is envisaged, in principle, as an open system, where other branches of international law are still applicable. This feature is particularly relevant with regard to the application of international human rights law. As described in Section 2.5, the relationship between the law of occupation and international human rights law should be constructed as that of mutually complementary regimes, applying codified rules of treaty interpretation in order to avoid normative conflicts as far as possible.

As explained in Chapter 3, the law of occupation does not allow the application of *jus ad bellum*. Accordingly, the occupying power and the ousted sovereign may not invoke *jus ad bellum* with regard to armed force employed within the occupied territory. This conclusion, which is supported by the ICJ's case law, is not a consequence of this author's opinion regarding the different issue of the right to self-defence against non-state actors' armed attacks; indeed, the huge debate on this topic, examined in Section 3.2, is not the proper context in which to address the issue of self-defence within occupied territory. *Jus ad bellum* may not be invoked in relation to armed force employed in occupied territory because it is 'irrelevant', since the law of occupation, as explained in Section 3.4, preserves the existence of a situation of ongoing armed conflict in occupied territory. Taking into account this premise, it is logical to conclude that *jus ad bellum* is irrelevant since it regulates only the beginning of armed conflicts. Accordingly, the occupying power may not invoke *jus ad bellum* and self-defence in order to undertake actions that are not allowed by the law of occupation, which is the primary framework applicable to the use of armed force in occupied territory.

Chapter 4 explores the evolution of international law with regard to the legitimacy of armed resistance against the occupying power. During the process of the codification of international humanitarian law, the divergent views of smaller states and more powerful states have long barred the codification of any rules in favour of or against armed resistance. However, international humanitarian law has evolved so that today the existence of armed resistance in occupied territory is openly acknowledged by international humanitarian law conventions, which do not prohibit it, but rather, under certain circumstances, grant prisoner-of-war status to those involved in armed resistance. The same evolution has affected the alleged existence of a duty of obedience of the population of the occupied territory, which is not considered to be consistent with contemporary international humanitarian law. Accordingly, as demonstrated in Section 4.2, international humanitarian law offers a source of legitimacy, even if not a proper right, to armed resistance against the occupying power.

Similarly, Section 4.3 demonstrates that the principle of self-determination of peoples supports the legitimacy of armed resistance against the occupying power since, as demonstrated by state practice and case law, the population of an occupied territory enjoys the right of self-determination. However, international law allows only national liberation movements that are recognised as representative of one people to resort to armed force; moreover, there is a significant trend that favours peaceful means of struggle to put the occupation to an end. Accordingly, state practice regarding the legitimacy of armed resistance in occupied territory is restricted only to those cases where the occupying power refuses to negotiate and maintain a territory under occupation for an extended period of time. International law does not recognise a 'right to resist' the occupying power, but rather, international humanitarian law and the principle of self-determination of peoples support the legitimacy of armed resistance against the occupying power as long as it is conducted in accordance with international law.

However, exploring the relevance of *jus ad bellum* and of the rules regarding the legitimacy of armed resistance does not conclude the analysis of the legal framework governing the use of armed force in occupied territory. Rather, the law of occupation provides useful guidance. As explained in Chapter 5, the regulation of the use of armed force in occupied territory may be inferred by the rules governing the occupying power's administration. Two different paradigms are applicable in occupied territory: law enforcement, which is based on international human rights standards and is typical of the exercise of governmental functions, and conduct of hostilities, which normally applies in armed conflict and is regulated by international humanitarian law and international human rights law. Even if the law of occupation does not address explicitly the way in which armed force may be employed in occupied territory, the interplay between these two paradigms may be explained with reference to the balance struck by the law of occupation between its inherently hostile character and the need to fill the governmental gap left by the ousted sovereign. As explained in Section 5.3.1, the law of occupation imposes upon the occupying power the duty to restore and ensure public order in the occupied territory, demanding that the occupying power employs, as far as possible, the same means that the ousted sovereign would have employed (Section 5.3.2). State practice and international case law demonstrate that the same rationale applies to the use of armed force which, as far as possible, should be conducted as the ousted sovereign would have done – that is, law enforcement (Section 5.3.3.2). In addition, state practice demonstrates a significant trend favouring the performance of law-enforcement responsibilities by the local police of the occupied territory, pursuant to the domestic legislation in force prior to the occupation.

However, state practice shows that, notwithstanding the exercise of law-enforcement responsibilities by the occupying power, hostilities may occur in occupied territory, as explained in Section 5.4.2. In these cases, it is necessary to distinguish between hostilities terminating the occupation and hostilities disrupting public order without terminating the occupation. In cases of hostilities within occupied territory, international law permits the occupying power to resort to the model of conduct of hostilities only when a specific armed confrontation reaches the threshold of a non-international armed conflict, while armed confrontations below this threshold fall into those that should be addressed through law enforcement. As demonstrated in Section 5.6.2, this solution does not rely on the analogical application of the law on non-international armed conflict in a situation of occupation, but rather, it is a direct consequence of the aforementioned principle of continuity between the means at the disposal of the ousted sovereign and those allowed to the occupying power. As the ousted sovereign would have been able to resort to conduct of hostilities only if violence reached a certain threshold, similarly, under that threshold, the principle of continuity requires the occupying power to refrain from conduct of hostilities.

Section 5.5 investigates the issue of which rules of international humanitarian law must apply to the conduct of hostilities in occupied territory. To this end, it is possible to envisage two different scenarios: hostilities involving the occupying power and the ousted sovereign, which are unanimously considered to be regulated by the law on international armed conflict, and hostilities between the occupying power and armed groups not belonging to the armed forces of the ousted sovereign, which have sparked a significant debate that is analysed in Section 5.5.3. This author demonstrates that the law on international armed conflict must apply as the sole regime governing the conduct of the occupying power in the occupied territory. Indeed, as demonstrated by state practice, at the time of the drafting of the GC IV, states believed that hostilities within the occupied territory were regulated by the law on international armed conflict. This conclusion is in line with one of the main features of the law on non-international armed conflict: the state's *jus puniendi* regarding the insurgent. The law of occupation does not consider that the occupying power has such an inherent right, but rather, offers an *additional* source of legitimacy to the occupying power's punishment of acts of armed resistance under Article 64 GC IV. Consequently, as Section 5.5.3.3 demonstrates, the drafters of GC IV considered hostilities in occupied territory to be regulated by the law on international armed conflict.

As demonstrated in Chapter 6, the distinction between law enforcement and conduct of hostilities is important because armed force is regulated in a different way depending on the paradigm employed. Since in situations of law enforcement, international human rights law is the main legal framework governing the use of armed force, the right to life is protected to the extent that armed force may be employed lawfully only as a last-resort measure. Under the conduct-of-hostilities paradigm, though, international humanitarian law rules on hostilities are generally applicable in occupied territory, along with international human rights law, and, accordingly, the use of lethal armed force is permitted if the target is an enemy combatant or a civilian taking direct part in the hostilities, while it is prohibited in the case of civilians or individuals *hors de combat*. However, the contextual application of international humanitarian law and international human rights law demands a complementary interpretation of the two branches. In the specific circumstance of occupied territory, the occupying power must use armed force with the same constraints that limit peacetime law-enforcement activities. Accordingly, the deprivation of the right to life as a consequence of the use of armed force is permissible only as last resort. The presumption in favour of the application of law enforcement should guide the occupying power's conduct in situations such as violent demonstrations and riots, wherein the boundaries between law enforcement and conduct of hostilities are subtle. To properly address this challenge, the occupying power may find it useful to deploy the local police, if feasible, since their lack of affiliation with the occupying power and their experience in maintaining public order could prove a significant asset when violent demonstrations occur.

In conclusion, and with recent and less recent armed confrontations in occupied territories in mind, this author believes that the use of armed force in occupied territory is in fact regulated by international law, and by the law of occupation in particular. The main problem is the implementation of the legal framework described in this book, especially in cases where the occupying powers deny the existence of a situation of occupation. However, domestic justice and international justice, both in the form of state dispute-settlement and international criminal law, have passed judgment on the legality of the use of armed force in occupied territory on a number of occasions. This consideration should be an incentive to further explore the topic at the centre of this book and a disincentive to violate the legal framework pertaining to the use of armed force in occupied territory.

Select Bibliography

Abi-Saab, Georges, 'Wars of National Liberation in the Geneva Conventions and Protocols' (1979) 65 *RCADI* 353.
Ago, Roberto, *Il requisito dell'effettività dell'occupazione in diritto internazionale* (Anonima Romana Editore 1934).
'Le délit international' (1939) 68 *RCADI* 415.
'Occupazione bellica dell'Italia e Trattato Lateranense' (1946) 2 *CS* 130.
'Nota a *In re Keppler*' (1953) 36 *RDI* 200.
Ahmed, Dawood I., 'Defending Weak States against the "Unwilling or Unable" Doctrine of Self-Defense' (2013) 9 *JIL & International Relations* 1.
Akande, Dapo, 'Clearing the Fog of War? The ICRC's Interpretive Guidance on Direct Participation in Hostilities' (2010) 59 *ICLQ* 180.
'Classification of Armed Conflicts: Relevant Legal Concepts' in Elizabeth Wilmshurst (ed.), *International Law and the Classification of Conflicts* (Oxford University Press 2012) 32.
'Is Israel's Use of Force in Gaza Covered by the *Jus Ad Bellum*?', EJIL: Talk!, 22 August 2014.
Akehurst, Michael, 'The Hierarchy of the Sources of International Law' (1974–5) 47 *British YIL* 273.
Amirante, Aldo, *Occupazione Bellica* (Edizioni Scientifiche Italiane 2007).
Andenas, Mads & Bjorge, Eirik (eds.), *A Farewell to Fragmentation: Reassertion and Convergence in International Law* (Cambridge University Press 2015).
Annoni, Alessandra, 'Esecuzioni mirate di sospetti terroristi e diritto alla vita' (2008) 91 *RDI* 991.
L'occupazione "ostile" nel diritto internazionale contemporaneo (Giappichelli 2012).
Anzilotti, Dioniso, *Teoria generale della responsabilità dello Stato nel diritto internazionale* (Lumachi Libraio 1902).
Arai-Takahashi, Yutaka, 'Fair Trial Guarantees in Occupied Territory the Interplay between International Humanitarian Law and Human Rights Law' in Roberta Arnold & Noëlle Quénivet (eds.), *International Humanitarian Law and Human Rights Law Towards a New Merger in International Law* (Brill 2008) 455.
The Law of Occupation: Continuity and Change of International Humanitarian Law, and Its Interaction with International Human Rights Law (Martinus Nijhoff 2009).

'Law-Making and the Judicial Guarantees in Occupied Territories' in Andrew Clapham, Paola Gaeta, & Marco Sassòli (eds.), *The 1949 Geneva Conventions: A Commentary* (Oxford University Press 2015) 1421.

'Protection of Private Property' in Andrew Clapham, Paola Gaeta, & Marco Sassòli (eds.), *The 1949 Geneva Conventions: A Commentary* (Oxford University Press 2015) 1515.

Arangio-Ruiz, Gaetano, 'The Normative Role of the General Assembly of the United Nations and the Declaration of Principles of Friendly Relations: With an Appendix on The Concept of International Law and the Theory of International Organisation' (1972-III) 137 *RCADI* 409.

'Autodeterminazione (diritto dei popoli alla)' in *Enciclopedia giuridica* (Treccani 1988) 1.

'On the Security Council's "Law-Making"' (2000) 83 *RDI* 609.

State Responsibility Revisited: The Factual Nature of the Attribution of Conduct to the State (Giuffré 2017).

Arcari, Maurizio, 'L'intervention armée contre l'Iraq et la question de l'autorisation du Conseil de Sécurité' (2003) 19 *ADI* 5.

'Violazione del divieto di uso della forza, aggressione o attacco armato in relazione all'intervento militare della Russia in Crimea?' (2014) 8 *DUDI* 473.

Arimatsu, Louise, 'The Democratic Republic of the Congo 1993–2010' in Elizabeth Wilmshurst (ed.), *International Law and the Classification of Conflicts* (Oxford University Press 2012) 146.

Arnold, Roberta & Quénivet, Noëlle (eds.), *International Humanitarian Law and Human Rights Law: Towards a New Merger in International Law* (Brill 2008).

Aust, Anthony, *Handbook of International Law* (2nd edn, Cambridge University Press 2010).

Baker, Bartholomew Sherston, *Halleck's International Law* vol. II (C. K. Paul & Co. 1878).

Balladore Pallieri, Giorgio, *Diritto Bellico* (2nd edn, Cedam 1954).

Balmond, Louis, 'Etat Palestinien' in Thierry Garcia (ed.), *La Palestine: d'un etat non membre de l'organisation des Nations Unies a un etat souverain?* (Pedone 2015) 5.

Banks, William, *Counterinsurgency Law: New Directions in Asymmetric Warfare* (Oxford University Press 2013).

Barberis, Julio A., 'Nouvelles questions concernant la personnalité juridique international' (1983) 179 *RCADI* 145.

Barile, Giuseppe, 'Tendenze e sviluppi della recente dottrina italiana di diritto internazionale pubblico (1944–1951)' (1952) 4 *CS* 397.

Barnidge, Robert P., Jr, *Self-Determination, Statehood, and the Law of Negotiation: The Case of Palestine* (Hart 2016).

Bartels, Rogier, 'Timelines, Borderlines and Conflicts: The Historical Evolution of the Legal Divide between International and Non-International Armed Conflicts' (2009) 91 *IRRC* 35.

'Terrorist Groups as Parties to an Armed Conflict' (2017) 47 *Collegium* 56.

Bartolini, Giulio, 'I *targeted killings* di appartenenti a gruppi terroristici tra diritto internazionale umanitario e diritti umani' in Pietro Gargiulo & Maria Chiara Vitucci (eds.), *La tutela dei diritti umani nella lotta e nella guerra al terrorismo* (Editoriale Scientifica 2009) 273.

'Il concetto di controllo sulle attività di individui quale presupposto della responsabilità dello Stato' in Marina Spinedi, Alessandra Gianelli, & Maria Luisa Alaimo (eds.), *La codificazione della responsabilità internazionale degli Stati alla prova dei fatti* (Giuffré 2006) 25.

'Le eliminazioni mirate di appartenenti a gruppi terroristici al vaglio della Corte suprema d'Israele' (2007) 1 *DUDI* 623.

'The Participation of Civilians in Hostilities' in Michael J. Matheson & Djamchid Momtaz (eds.), *Rules and Institutions of International Humanitarian Law Put to the Test of Recent Armed Conflicts* (Brill 2010) 321.

'The Impact of Fascism on the Italian Doctrine of International Law' (2012) 14 *Journal of History of International Law* 237.

Bastid Burdeau, Geneviève, 'Les références au droit international' in SFDI, *Les compétences de l'Etat en droit international* (Pedone 2006) 161.

Baxter, Richard R., 'The Duty of Obedience to the Belligerent Occupant' (1950) 27 *British YIL* 235.

'So-Called "Unprivileged Belligerency": Spies, Guerrillas and Saboteurs' (1951) 28 *British YIL* 323.

'Humanitarian Law or Humanitarian Politics? The 1974 Diplomatic Conference on Humanitarian Law' (1975) 16 *Harvard ILJ* 1.

Bayley, David H. & Perito, R. M., *The Police in War: Fighting Insurgency, Terrorism, and Violent Crime* (Lynne Rienner Publishers 2010).

Bellal, Annyssa, 'ICRC Commentary of Common Article 3: Some Questions Relating to Organized Armed Groups and the Applicability of IHL', *EJIL: Talk!*, 5 October 2017.

Ben-Naftali, Orna, '"A la Recherche du Temps Perdu": Rethinking Article 6 of the Fourth Geneva Convention in the Light of the Legal Consequences of the Construction of a Wall in the Occupied Palestinian Territory Advisory Opinion' (2005) 38 *IsLR* 212.

'PathoLAWgical Occupation: Normalizing the Exceptional Case of the Occupied Palestinian Territory and Other Legal Pathologies' in Orna Ben-Naftali (ed.), *International Humanitarian Law and International Human Rights Law: Pas de Deux* (Oxford University Press 2011) 129.

'Belligerent Occupation: A Plea for the Establishment of an International Supervisory Mechanism' in Antonio Cassese (ed.), *Realizing Utopia: The Future of International Law* (Oxford University Press 2012) 538.

Ben-Naftali, Orna, Gross, Aeyal M., & Michaeli, Keren R., 'Illegal Occupation: Framing the Occupied Palestinian Territory' (2005) 23 *Berkeley JIL* 551.

Ben-Naftali, Orna & Michaeli, Keren R., 'We Must Not Make a Scarecrow of the Law: A Legal Analysis of the Israeli Policy of Targeted Killings' (2003) 36 *Cornell ILJ* 233.

'*Public Committee against Torture in Israel v Government of Israel*. Case No HCJ 769/02' (2007) 101 *AJIL* 459.

Ben-Naftali, Orna & Shany, Yuval, 'Living in Denial: The Application of Human Rights in the Occupied Territories' (2004) 37 *IsLR* 17.

Benvenisti, Eyal, 'The Applicability of Human Rights Conventions to Israel and to the Occupied Territories' (1992) 26 *IsLR* 24.

The International Law of Occupation (Princeton University Press 1993).

'The Israeli-Palestinian Declaration of Principles: A Framework for Future Settlement' (1993) 4 *EJIL* 542.

'Human Dignity in Combat: The Duty to Spare Enemy Civilians' (2006) 39 *IsLR* 81.
'Occupation, Belligerent' in *MPEPIL online* (2009).
'The Law on the Unilateral Termination of Occupation' in Andreas Zimmermann & Thomas Giegerich (eds.), *Veröffentlichungen des Walther-Schücking-Instituts für Internationales Recht an der Universität Kiel* (Kiel University Press 2009) 371.
The International Law of Occupation (2nd edn, Oxford University Press 2012).
'An Article That Changed the Course of History?' (2017) 50 *IsLR* 269.
Benvenisti, Eyal & Keinan, Guy, 'The Occupation of Iraq: A Reassessment' (2010) 86 *ILS* 263.
Benvenuti, Paolo, 'Movimenti insurrezionali e Protocolli aggiuntivi alla Convenzione di Ginevra del 1949' (1981) 64 *RDI* 513.
'Ensuring Observance of International Humanitarian Law: Function, Extent and Limits of the Obligation of Third States to Ensure Respect for International Humanitarian Law' (1989–90) *Yearbook of the International Institute of Humanitarian Law* 27.
'Le respect du droit international humanitaire par les forces des Nations Unies: la circulaire du Secrétaire Général' (2001) 105 *RGDIP* 355.
'Judicial Review nella guerra al terrorismo nella decisione della Corte suprema israeliana sui targeted killings' (2007) 19 *Diritto pubblico comparato ed europeo* XIII.
'La tutela dei diritti umani e il diritto internazionale umanitario' in Adriana Di Stefano & Rosario Sapienza (eds.), *La tutela dei diritti umani e il diritto internazionale* (Editoriale Scientifica 2012) 53.
Bernardini, Aldo, 'Iraq: illecita occupazione, resistenza popolare, autodeterminazione irakena' (2003) *RCGI* 29.
Besson, Samantha, 'The Extraterritoriality of the European Convention on Human Rights: Why Human Rights Depend on Jurisdiction and What Jurisdiction Amounts To' (2012) 25 *LJIL* 857.
Bhuta, Nehal, 'The Antinomies of Transformative Occupation' (2005) 16 *EJIL* 721.
(ed.), *The Frontiers of Human Rights: Extraterritoriality and Its Challenges* (Oxford University Press 2016).
Bianchi, Andrea, 'Dismantling the Wall: The ICJ's Advisory Opinion and Its Likely Impact on International Law' (2004) 47 *German YIL* 343.
Bianchi, Andrea & Naqvi, Yasmin, *International Humanitarian Law and Terrorism* (Hart 2011).
Bílková, Veronika, 'The Use of Force by the Russian Federation in Crimea' (2015) 75 *ZaöRV* 27.
Bisharat, George, Crawley, Timothy, Elturk, Sar, & James, Carey, et al., 'Israel's Invasion of Gaza in International Law' (2009) 38 *Denver JIL & Policy* 41.
Bjorge, Erik, *The Evolutionary Interpretation of Treaties* (Oxford University Press 2014).
Blokker, Niels, 'Is the Authorization Authorized? Powers and Practice of the UN Security Council to Authorize the Use of Force by "Coalitions of the Able and Willing"' (2000) 11 *EJIL* 541.
Blum, Yehuda Z., 'The Missing Reversioner: Reflections on the Status of Judea and Samaria' (1968) 3 *IsLR* 279.
Blunt, Gwilym David, 'Is There a Human Right to Resistance?' (2017) 39 *Human Rights Quarterly* 860.
Boas, Gideon, *Public International Law* (Edward Elgar 2012).

Bockel, Alain, 'Le retrait israélien de Gaza et ses conséquences sur le droit international' (2005) 51 *AFDI* 16.
'Gaza: le processus de paix en question' (2009) 55 *AFDI* 173.
'Le retrait israélien de Gaza et ses conséquences sur le droit international' (2005) 51 *AFDI* 16.
Boisson De Chazournes, Laurence & Condorelli, Luigi, 'Common Article 1 of the Geneva Conventions Revisited: Protecting Collective Interests' (2000) 82 *IRRC* 67.
Bonfils, Henri & Fauchille, Paul, *Manuel de droit international public* (7th edn, Rousseau 1914).
Boon, Kristen E., 'Obligations of the New Occupier: The Contours of a *Jus Post Bellum*' (2009) 31 *Loyola of Los Angeles International & Comparative Law Review* 60.
Boothby, William H., *The Law of Targeting* (Oxford University Press 2012).
Bothe, Michael, 'Occupation, Belligerent' in Rudolf Bernhardt (ed.), *Encyclopedia of Public International Law* vol. IV (North-Holland 1982) 64.
'Terrorism and the Legality of Pre-emptive Force' (2003) 14 *EJIL* 234.
'Effective Control during Invasion: A Practical View on the Application Threshold of the Law of Occupation' (2012) 94 *IRRC* 37.
'The Current Status of Crimea: Russian Territory, Occupied Territory or What?' (2014) 53 *MLLWR* 99.
Bothe, Michael, Partsch, Karl Josef, & Solf, Waldemar A. (eds.), *New Rules for Victims of Armed Conflicts* (Martinus Nijhoff 1982).
Bowett, Derek William, *Self-Defence in International Law* (Manchester University Press 1959).
United Nations Forces: A Legal Study of United Nations Practice (Stevens and Sons 1964).
Boyle, C. K., 'The Concept of Arbitrary Deprivation of Life' in B. G. Ramcharan (ed.), *The Right to Life in International Law* (Martinus Nijhoff 1985).
Boyle, Francis A., 'The Creation of the State of Palestine' (1990) 1 *EJIL* 307.
Bradley, Martha M., 'Expanding the Borders of Common Article 3 in Non-International Armed Conflicts: Amending Its Geographical Application Through Subsequent Practice?' (2017) 64 *NILR* 375.
Brown, Davis, 'Use of Force against Terrorism after September 11th: State Responsibility, Self-Defence and Other Responses' (2003) 11 *Cardozo JICL* 1.
Brownlie, Ian, *International Law and the Use of Force by States* (Clarendon Press 1968).
'Legal Status of Natural Resources in International Law' (1979-I) 162 *RCADI* 249.
System of the Law of Nations. State Responsibility, Part I (Clarendon Press 1983).
Brown Scott, James (ed.), *The Proceedings of the Hague Peace Conferences: Translation of the Original Texts* (Carnegie Endowment for International Peace 1920).
Buchan, Russel, 'The International Law of Naval Blockade and Israel's Interception of the *Mavi Marmara*' (2011) 58 *NILR* 209.
International Law and the Construction of the Liberal Peace (Hart 2013).
Buckley, Carla, Donald, Alice, & Leach, Philip (eds.), *Towards Convergence in International Human Rights Law: Approaches of Regional and International Systems* (Brill 2017).
Buignon, François, '*Jus ad Bellum, Jus in Bello* and Non-International Armed Conflicts' (2003) 6 *YIHL* 167.
Burgenberg, Marc & Hobe, Stephan (eds.), *Permanent Sovereignty over Natural Resources* (Springer 2015).

Calvo, Carlos, *Le droit international théorique et pratique* vol. IV (5th edn, Russeau 1896).
Cameron, Lindsey, Demeyere, Bruno, & Henckaerts, Jean-Marie, et al., 'Article 3: Conflicts Not of an International Character' in ICRC, *Updated Commentary on the First Geneva Convention* (ICRC 2016).
Campanelli, Danio, 'The Law of Military Occupation Put to the Test of Human Rights Law' (2008) 90 *IRRC* 653.
Cannizzaro, Enzo, 'Contextualizing Proportionality: *Jus ad Bellum* and *Jus in Bello* in the Lebanese War' (2006) 88 *IRRC* 779.
    'Entités non-étatiques et régime international de l'emploi de la force: une étude sur le cas de la réaction israélienne au Liban' (2007) 110 *RGDIP* 333.
    'Proportionality in the Law of Armed Conflicts' in Andrew Clapham & Paola Gaeta (eds.), *The Oxford Handbook of International Law in Armed Conflict* (Oxford University Press 2014) 332.
    Diritto Internazionale (3rd edn, Giappichelli 2016).
Canor, Iris, 'When *Jus ad Bellum* Meets *Jus in Bello*: The Occupier's Right of Self-Defence against Terrorism Stemming from Occupied Territories' (2006) 19 *LJIL* 129.
Cansacchi, Giorgio, 'Occupazione bellica' in *Novissimo Digesto Italiano* vol. XI (UTET 1965) 744.
Capotorti, Francesco, *L'occupazione nel diritto di guerra* (Jovene 1949).
Carcano, Andrea, *L'occupazione dell'Iraq nel diritto internazionale* (Giuffrè 2009).
    'On the Relationship between International Humanitarian Law and Human Rights Law in Times of Belligerent Occupation: Not Yet a Coherent Framework' in Erika de Wet & Jann Kleffner (eds.), *Convergence and Conflicts of Human Rights and International Humanitarian Law in Military Operations* (Pretoria University Law Press 2014) 121.
    The Transformation of Occupied Territory in International Law (Brill 2015).
Cardona Llorens, Jorge, 'Le principe du droit des peuples à disposer d'eux-mêmes et l'occupation étrangère' in Nicolas Angelet, Olivier Corten, Eric David, & Pierre Klein (eds.), *Droit du pouvoir, pouvoir du droit: Mélanges offerts à Jean Salmon* (Bruylant 2007) 855.
Casey-Maslen, Stuart & Connolly, Sean, *Police Use of Force under International Law* (Cambridge University Press 2017).
Cassese, Antonio, 'The Genova Protocols of 1977 on the Humanitarian Law of Armed Conflict and Customary International Law' (1984) 3 *UCLA Pacific Basin Law Journal* 55.
    'Wars of National Liberation and Humanitarian Law' in Christophe Swinarski (ed.), *Études et essais sur le droit international humanitaire et sur les principes de la Croix-Rouge en l'honneur de Jean Pictet* (ICRC 1984) 313.
    'Legal Considerations on the International Status of Jerusalem' (1986) 3 *Palestine YIL* 13.
    'Powers and Duties of an Occupant in Relation to Land and Natural Resources' in Emma Playfair (ed.), *International Law and the Administration of Occupied Territories* (Clarendon Press 1992) 419.
    The Self-Determination of Peoples: A Legal Reappraisal (Cambridge University Press 1996).
    'The Martens Clause: Half a Loaf or Simply Pie in the Sky?' (2000) 11 *EJIL* 187.

'Article 51' in Jean-Pierre Cot, Alain Pellet, & Mathias Forteau (eds.), *La Charte des Nations Unies: Commentaire article par article* (3rd edn, Economica 2005) 1329.
International Law (2nd edn, Oxford University Press 2005) 24.
'On Some Merits of the Israeli Judgment on Targeted Killings' (2007) 5 *JICJ* 339.
'The *Nicaragua* and *Tadić* Tests Revisited in Light of the ICJ Judgment on Genocide in Bosnia' (2007) 18 *EJIL* 649.
Diritto internazionale (3rd edn, Il Mulino 2017, Micaela Frulli (ed.)).

Cataldi, Giuseppe, 'Le deroghe ai diritti mani in stato di emergenza' in Laura Pineschi (ed.), *La tutela internazionale dei diritti umani: norme, garanzie, prassi* (Giuffrè 2006) 752.

Catignani, Sergio, *Israeli Counter-Insurgency and the Intifadas: Dilemmas of a Conventional Army* (Routledge 2008).

Cavanaugh, Kathleen, 'Rewriting the Law: The Case of Israel and the Occupied Territories' in David H. Wippman & Michael Evangelista (eds.), *New Wars, New Laws? Applying Laws of War in 21st Century Conflicts* (Martinus Nijhoff 2005) 227.
'The Israeli Military Court System in the West Bank and Gaza' (2007) 12 *JCSL* 197.

Cerone, John, 'Minding the Gap: Outlining KFOR Accountability in Post-Conflict Kosovo' (2001) 12 *EJIL* 469.

Challine, Paul, *Le droit international public dans la jurisprudence française de 1789 à 1848* (Loviton 1934).

Chesterman, Simon, *You, The People. The United Nations, Transitional Administrations, and State-Building* (Oxford University Press 2004).

Chevalier-Watts, Juliet, 'Has Human Rights Law become *Lex Specialis* for the European Court of Human Rights in Right to Life Cases Arising from Internal Armed Conflicts?' (2010) 14 *The International Journal of Human Rights* 584.

Chinkin, Christine, 'Normative Developments in the International Legal System' in Dinah Shelton (ed.), *Commitment and Compliance: The Role of Non-Binding Norms in the International Legal System* (Oxford University Press 2000) 21.
'Laws of Occupation' in Neville Botha, Michèle Olivier, & Delarey van Tonder (eds.), *Multilateralism and International Law with Western Sahara as a Case Study* (Unisa Press 2010) 167.

Christakis, Théodore, *Le droit à l'autodétermination en dehors de situations de décolonisation* (Pedone 1999).
'Self-Determination, Territorial Integrity and Fait Accompli in the Case of Crimea' (2015) 75 *ZaöRV* 75.

Chrysostomides, Kypros, *The Republic of Cyprus: A Study in International Law* (Kluwer Law International 2000).

Cimiotta, Emanuele, 'Conflitto armato nella Repubblica Democratica del Congo e principio della sovranità permanente degli Stati sulle proprie risorse naturali' in Aldo Ligustro & Giorgio Sacerdoti (eds.), *Problemi e tendenze del diritto internazionale dell'economia: Liber amicorum in onore di Paolo Picone* (Editoriale Scientifica 2011) 55.

Clapham, Andrea, 'The Complex Relationship between the 1949 Geneva Conventions and International Human Rights Law' in Andrew Clapham, Paola Gaeta, & Marco Sassòli (eds.), *The 1949 Geneva Conventions: A Commentary* (Oxford University Press 2015) 701.

Clarke, Ben, 'The Judicial Status of Civilian Resistance to Foreign Occupation under the Law of Nations and Contemporary International Law' (2005) 7 *University of Notre Dame Australia Law Review* 1.

Cohen, Esther, *Human Rights in the Israeli-Occupied Territories, 1967–1982* (Manchester University Press 1985).

Combacau, Jean, 'Obligations de résultat et obligations de comportement: quelques questions et pas de réponse' in Daniel Bardonnet, Jean Combacau, Michel Virally, & Prosper Weil (eds.), *Mélanges offerts a Paul Reuter* (Pedone 1981) 181.

Condorelli, Luigi, 'Le droit international face à l'autodéterminacion du Sahara Occidental'(1978) 33 *CI* 396.

'L'imputation a l'état d'un fait internationalement illicite: solutions classiques et nouvelles tendances' (1984) 189 *RCADI* 9.

'Le azioni dell'ONU e l'applicazione del diritto internazionale umanitario: il bollettino del Segretario generale del 6 agosto 1999' (1999) 92 *RDI* 1049.

'Les attentats du 11 septembre et leurs suites: où va le droit international?' (2001) 105 *RGDIP* 829.

Condorelli, Luigi & Boisson De Chazournes, Laurence, 'Quelques remarques à propos de l'obligation des États de «respecter et faire respecter» le droit international humanitaire «en toutes circonstances»' in Christophe Swinarski (ed.), *Études et essais sur le droit international humanitaire et sur les principes de la Croix-Rouge en l'honneur de Jean Pictet* (ICRC 1984) 17.

Conforti, Benedetto, 'Obblighi di mezzi e obblighi di risultato nelle convenzioni di diritto uniforme' in Tullio Treves, Fausto Pocar, Tullio Scovazzi, & Roberta Clerici (eds.), *Studi in memoria di Mario Giuliano* (Cedam 1989) 373.

'Unité et fragmentation du droit international: "Glissez, mortels, n'appuyez pas"!' (2007) *RGDIP* 5.

Diritto internazionale (10th edn, Editoriale Scientifica 2014).

Conforti, Benedetto & Focarelli, Carlo, *The Law and Practice of the United Nations* (6th edn, Brill 2016).

Coomans, Fons & Kamminga, Menno (eds.), *Extraterritorial Application of Human Rights Treaties* (Intersentia 2004).

Corn, Geoffrey & Jensen, Eric Talbot, 'Transnational Armed Conflict: A "Principled" Approach to the Regulation of Counter-Terror Combat Operations' (2009) 42 *IsLR* 46.

Corsi, Alessandro, *L'occupazione militare in tempo di guerra* (Forzani & Co 1882).

Corten, Olivier, 'Iraqi Freedom: peut-on admettre l'argument de l'"autorisation implicte" du Conseil de Sécurité?' (2003) 36 *RBDI* 205.

'Déclarations unilatérales d'indépendance et reconnaissances prématurées: du Kosovo à l'Ossétie du sud et à l'Abkhazie' (2008) 112 *RGDIP* 721.

The Law Against War: The Prohibition on the Use of Force in Contemporary International Law (Hart 2010).

'Territorial Integrity Narrowly Interpreted: Reasserting the Classical Inter-State Paradigm of International Law' (2011) 24 *LJIL* 87.

'L'applicabilité problématique du droit de légitime défense au sens de l'article 51 de la Charte des Nations Unies aux relatons entre la Palestine et Israël' (2012) 45 *RBDI* 67.

'La rébellion et le droit international: le principe de neutralité en tension' (2014) 374 *RCADI* 53.

Corten, Olivier & Dubuisson, François, 'Operation "liberté immuable": une extension abusive du concept de légitime défense' (2002) 106 *RGDIP* 51.

Corso, Noemi, 'Occupazione militare e tutela della proprietà privata' in Adriana Di Stefano & Rosario Sapienza (eds.), *La tutela dei diritti umani e il diritto internazionale* (Editoriale Scientifica 2012) 115.

'A props de l'applicability du droit de l'occupation militaries aux forces des Nations Unies' (2013) 23 *RSDIE* 609.

Crawford, Emily, 'Unequal before the Law: The Case for the Elimination of the Distinction between International and Non-International Armed Conflict (2007) 20 *LJIL* 441.

The Treatment of Combatants and Insurgents under the Law of Armed Conflict (Oxford University Press 2010).

Identifying the Enemy: Civilian Participation in Armed Conflict (Oxford University Press 2015).

Crawford, James, 'The Creation of the State of Palestine: Too Much too Soon?' (1990) 1 *EJIL* 307.

'Israel (1948–1949) and Palestine (1988–1999): Two Studies in the Creation of States' in Guy S. Goodwin-Gill & Stefan Talmon (eds.), *The Reality of International Law: Essays in Honour of Ian Brownlie* (Clarendon Press 1999) 95.

The Creation of States in International Law (2nd edn, Oxford University Press 2006).

Brownlie's Principles of Public International Law (8th edn, Oxford University Press 2012).

State Responsibility: The General Part (Cambridge University Press 2013).

Crawford, James & Nevill, Penelope, 'Relations between International Courts and Tribunals: The "Regime Problem"' in Margaret A. Young (ed.), *Regime Interaction in International Law: Facing Fragmentation* (2012) 235.

Crawford, James & Nicholson, Rowan, 'The Continued Relevance of Traditional Rules and Institutions Relating to the Use of Force' in Mark Weller (ed.), *The Oxford Handbook of the Use of Force in International Law* (Oxford University Press 2015) 86.

Crema, Luigi, *La prassi successiva e l'interpretazione del diritto internazionale scritto* (Giuffrè 2017).

Cryer, Robert, 'The Fine Art of Friendship: *Jus in Bello* in Afghanistan' (2002) 7 *JCSL* 37.

Cullen, Anthony, *The Concept of Non-International Armed Conflict in International Humanitarian Law* (Cambridge University Press 2010).

Curti Gialdino, Carlo, 'Occupazione bellica' in *Enciclopedia del Diritto* vol. XXIX (Giuffrè 1979) 720.

Curtis, Michael, 'International Law and the Territories' (1991) 32 *Harvard ILJ* 457.

Cuyckens, Hanne, 'Is Israel Still an Occupying Power in Gaza?' (2016) 63 *NILR* 275.

Revisiting the Law of Occupation (Brill 2017).

Czaplinski, W. & Danilenko, G., 'Conflict of Norms in International Law' (1990) 21 *NILR* 3.

D'Argent, Pierre, 'Non-Renunciation of Rights Provided by the Conventions' in Andrew Clapham, Paola Gaeta, & Marco Sassòli (eds.), *The 1949 Geneva Conventions: A Commentary* (Oxford University Press 2015) 145.

D'Aspremont, Jean. 'La légitimité des rebelles en droit international' (Interest Group on Peace and Security – ESIL Heidelberg Meeting 2008) 5, available at papers.ssrn.com/sol3/papers.cfm?abstract_id=1266047

D'Aspremont, Jean & Tranchez, Elodie, 'The Quest for Non-Conflictual Coexistence of International Human Rights Law and Humanitarian Law: Which Role for the *Lex Specialis* Principle?' in Robert Kolb & Gloria Gaggioli (eds.), *Research Handbook on Human Rights and Humanitarian Law* (Edward Elger 2013) 223.

Da Costa, Karen, *The Extraterritorial Application of Selected Human Rights Treaties* (Brill 2012).

Dale, Richard, 'The Armed Forces as an Instrument of South African Policy in Namibia' (1980) 18 *The Journal of Modern African Studies* 57.

––––– 'Melding War and Politics in Namibia: South Africa's Counterinsurgency Campaign, 1966–1989' (1993) 20 *Armed Forces and Society* 7.

Darcy, Shane, 'Punitive House Demolitions, the Prohibitions of Collective Punishment, and the Supreme Court of Israel' (2003) 21 *Penn State International LR* 477.

––––– 'Collective Punishment Receives a Judicial Imprimatur', *EJIL: Talk!*, 21 August 2014.

Darcy, Shane & Reynolds, John, 'An Enduring Occupation: The Status of the Gaza Strip from the Perspective of International Humanitarian Law' (2010) 15 *JCSL* 211.

David, Eric, 'Le statut étatique de la Palestine' (2009) 20 *I diritti dell'uomo. Cronache e battaglie* 42.

Davidson, Tyler & Gibson, Kathleen, 'Expert Meeting on Security Detention Report: Speaker's Summary: Security Detention and Israel' (2009) 40 *Case Western Reserve JIL* 323.

Davis, George B., *The Elements of International Law, with an Account of Its Origin, Sources and Historical Development* (3rd edn, Harper & Brothers 1908) 329.

Dawidowicz, Martin, 'The Obligation of Non-Recognition of an Unlawful Situation' in James Crawford, Alain Pellet, & Simon Olleson (eds.), *The Law of International Responsibility* (Oxford University Press 2010) 683.

––––– 'Trading Fish or Human Rights in Western Sahara' in Duncan French (ed.), *Statehood and Self-Determination* (Cambridge University Press 2013) 272.

De Frouville, Olivier, 'Attribution of Conduct to the State: Private Individuals' in James Crawford, Alain Pellet, & Simon Olleson (eds.), *The Law of International Responsibility* (Oxford University Press 2010) 257.

De Hoogh, André J. J., 'Articles 4 and 8 of the 2001 ILC Articles on State Responsibility, the Tadic Case and Attribution of Acts of Bosnian Serb Authorities to the Federal Republic of Yugoslavia' (2002) 72 *British YIL* 255.

De Mulinen, Frédéric, *Handbook on the Law of War for Armed Forces* (ICRC 1987).

De Sena, Pasquale, *La nozione di giurisdizione statale nei trattati sui diritti dell'uomo* (Giappichelli 2002).

––––– 'Le Conseil de sécurité et le contrôle du juge' in Joël Rideau, Constance Grewe, Louis Balmond, & Maurizio Arcari (eds.), *Sanctions ciblées et protections juridictionnelles des droits fondamentaux dans l'Union européenne* (Bruylant 2010) 43.

––––– 'Ancora a proposito di Gaza' (2014) 1 *Quaderni di SIDIblog* 64.

'Prassi, consuetudine e principi nel campo dei diritti dell'uomo. Riflessioni internazionalistiche' (2014) 34 *Ragion pratica* 511.

De Vattel, Emer, *Le droit des gens* (London 1758).

De Visscher, Charles, 'L'occupation de guerre' (1918) 34 *LQR* 72.

de Visser, Lieneke Eloff, 'Winning Hearts and Minds: Legitimacy in the Namibian War for Independence' (2013) 24 *Small Wars & Insurgencies* 712.

De Waxel, Platon, *L'armée d'invasion et la population* (Kruger 1874).

De Wet, Erika, 'The Direct Administration of Territories by the United Nations and Its Member States in the Post-Cold War Era: Legal Bases and Implications for National Law' (2004) 8 *MPYUNL* 291.

De Wet, Erika & Vidmar, Jure, 'Conflitti tra paradigmi internazionali: gerarchia versus integrazione sistemica' (2015) 20 *Ars interpretandi* 119.

Debuisson, François, 'L'applicabilité du droit de légitime défense dans les rapports entre Israël at le Territoire palestinien occupé' in Jean-Philippe Kot (ed.), *Palestine and International Law, New Approaches* (Birzeit University Press 2011) 89.

Deeks, Ashley S., '"Unwilling or Unable": Toward a Normative Framework for Extraterritorial Self-Defense' (2012) 52 *Virginia JIL* 483.

del Mar, Katherine, 'The Requirement of "Belonging" under International Humanitarian Law' (2010) 21 *EJIL* 105.

Della Morte, Gabriele, 'Sulla giurisprudenza italiana in tema di terrorismo internazionale' (2009) 92 *RDI* 443.

Demotses, James A., 'Israeli Actions in Response to the Intifada: Necessary Security Measures or Violations of International Law?' (1992) 16 *Suffolk Transnational Law Review* 92.

Denis, Catherine, *Le pouvoir normative du Conseil de Security des Nations Unies: Portée et limites* (Bruylant 2004).

Dennis, Michael J., 'Application of Human Rights Treaties Extraterritorially in Times of Armed Conflict and Military Occupation' (2005) 99 *AJIL* 119.

Di Blase, Antonietta, 'The Role of the Host State's Consent with Regard to Non-Coercive Actions by the United Nations' in Antonio Cassese (ed.), *United Nations Peace Keeping: Legal Essays* (Sijthoff & Noordhoff 1978) 55.

Dikker Hupkes, S. D., *What Constitutes Occupation? Israel as the Occupying Power in the Gaza Strip after the Disengangement* (EM Meijers Instituut 2007).

Dinstein, Yoram, 'The International Law of Belligerent Occupation and Human Rights' (1978) 8 *IYBR* 104.

'The Israeli Supreme Court and the Law of Belligerent Occupation: Demolitions and Sealing off of Houses' (1999) 29 *IYHR* 285.

'Legislation under Article 43 of the Hague Regulations: Belligerent Occupation and Peacebuilding', Program on Humanitarian Policy and Conflict Research Harvard University, 1 *Occasional Paper Series* (Fall 2004) 2, available at www.hpcrresearch.org/sites/default/files/publications/OccasionalPaper1.pdf

The International Law of Belligerent Occupation (Cambridge University Press 2009).

Non-International Armed Conflicts in International Law (Cambridge University Press 2014).

War, Aggression and Self-Defence (6th edn, Cambridge University Press 2017).

Dipla, Haritini, *La responsabilité de l'Etat pour violation des droits de l'homme: problèmes d'imputation* (Pedone 1994).

Distefano, Giovanni, 'L'interprétation évolutive de la norme internationale' (2011) 115 *RGDIP* 373.
  Use of Force' in Andrew Clapham & Paola Gaeta (eds.), *The Oxford Handbook of International Law in Armed Conflict* (Oxford University Press 2014) 545.
Distefano, Marcella (ed.), *Il principio di autodeterminazione dei popoli alla prova del nuovo millennio* (CEDAM 2014).
Dörmann, Knut, 'The Legal Situation of "Unlawful/Unprivileged" Combatants' (2005) 85 *IRRC* 45.
Dörmann, Knut & Colassis, Laurent, 'International Humanitarian Law in the Iraq Conflict' (2004) 47 *German YIL* 293.
Dörr, Oliver, 'Use of Force, Prohibition of' in *MPEPIL online* (2015).
  'Article 31 – General Rule of Interpretation' in Oliver Dörr & Kirsten Schmalenbach (eds.), *Vienna Convention on the Law of Treaties: A Commentary* (2nd edn, Springer 2018) 559.
Dörr, Oliver & Randelzhofer, Albrecht, 'Article 2(4)' in Bruno Simma, Daniel-Erasmus Khan, Georg Nolte, & Andreas Paulus (eds.), *The Charter of the United Nations. A Commentary* (3rd edn, Oxford University Press 2012) 200.
Doswald-Beck, Louise (ed.), *San Remo Manual on International Law Applicable to Armed Conflicts at Sea* (Cambridge University Press 1995).
  'The Right to Life in Armed Conflict: Does International Humanitarian Law Provide All the Answers?' (2006) 88 *IRRC* 881.
Drew, Catriona, 'Self-Determination, Population Transfer and the Middle East Peace Accords' in Stephen Bowen (ed.), *Human Rights, Self-determination and Political Change in the Palestinian Occupied Territories* (Kluwer Law 1997) 119.
Ducheine, Paul A. L., Schmitt, Michael N., & Osinga, Frans P. B. (eds.), *Targeting: The Challenges of Modern Warfare* (Springer 2016).
Dugard, John, 'The Organisation of African Unity and Colonialism: An Inquiry into the Plea of Self-Defence as a Justification for the Use of Force in the Eradication of Colonialism' (1967) 16 *ICLQ* 157.
  'SWAPO: The *Jus ad Bellum* and the *Jus in Bello*' (1976) 93 *South African Law Journal* 144.
  Recognition and the United States (Cambridge University Press 1987).
  'Enforcement of Human Rights in the West Bank and Gaza Strip' in Emma Playfair (ed.), *International Law and the Administration of Occupied Territories* (Clarendon Press 1992) 461.
Dupuy, Pierre-Marie, 'Reviewing the Difficulties of Codification: On Ago's Classification of Obligations of Means and Obligations of Result in Relation to State Responsibility' (1999) 10 *EJIL* 371.
  'L'unité de l'ordre juridique international' (2002) 297 *RCADI* 9.
  'Evolutionary Interpretation of Treaties: Between Memory and Prophecy' in Enzo Cannizzaro (ed.), *The Law of Treaties beyond the Vienna Convention* (Oxford University Press 2011) 123.
Economidés, Constantin P., 'Content of the Obligation: Obligations of Means and Obligations of Result' in James Crawford, Alain Pellet, & Simon Olleson (eds.), *The Law of International Responsibility* (Oxford University Press 2010) 371.
Emanuelli, Claude, *Les action militaires de l'ONU et le droit international humanitaire* (Wilson et Lafleur Itéé 1995).

van Engeland, Anicée, 'Protection of Public Property' in Andrew Clapham, Paola Gaeta, & Marco Sassòli (eds.), *The 1949 Geneva Conventions: A Commentary* (Oxford University Press 2015) 1535.

Epshtain, Itay, 'Setting a Time Limit: The Case for a Protocol on Prolonged Occupation', 11 May 2013, available at phap.org/system/files/article_pdf/Epshtain-ProlongedOccupation_0.pdf

Ergec, Rusen & Velu, Jacques, *Convention européenne des droits de l'homme* (2nd edn, Bruylant 2014).

Fabbricotti, Alberta, 'Legittima difesa e autodeterminazione dei popoli' in Alessandra Lanciotti & Attila Tanzi (eds.), *Uso della forza e legittima difesa nel diritto internazionale contemporaneo* (Jovene 2012) 255.

Falk, Richard A., 'Some Legal Reflections on Prolonged Israeli Occupation of Gaza and the West Bank' (1989) 2 *Journal of Refugee Studies* 40.

Falk, Richard A. & Weston, Burns H., 'The Relevance of International Law to Palestinian Rights in the West Bank and Gaza: In Legal Defense of the Intifada' (1991) 32 *Harvard ILJ* 129.

Fauchille, Paul, *Traité de droit international public* vol. II (Russeau 1921).

Feilchenfeld, Ernst H., *The International Economy Law of Belligerent Occupation* (Carnegie Endowment for International Peace 1942) 9.

Ferraro, Tristan, 'Determining the Beginning and End of an Occupation under International Humanitarian Law' (2012) 94 *IRRC* 133.

— (ed.), *Expert Meeting: Occupation and Other Forms of Administration of Foreign Territory* (ICRC 2012).

— 'The Applicability and Application of International Humanitarian Law to Multinational Forces' (2013) 95 *IRRC* 561.

— 'The Law of Occupation and Human Rights Law: Some Selected Issues' in Robert Kolb & Gloria Gaggioli (eds.), *Research Handbook on Human Rights and Humanitarian Law* (Edward Elger 2013) 273.

Ferraro, Tristan & Cameron, Lindsay, 'Article 2: Application of the Convention' in ICRC, *Updated Commentary on the First Geneva Convention* (ICRC 2016).

Finkelstein, Claire, Ohlin, Jens David, & Altman, Andrew (eds.), *Targeted Killings: Law and Morality in an Asymmetrical World* (Oxford University Press 2012).

Fiore, Pasquale, *Trattato di diritto internazionale pubblico* vols. I, III (3rd edn, Unione Tipografica Editrice 1891).

Fitzpatrick, Joan, 'Jurisdiction of Military Commissions and the Ambiguous War on Terrorism' (2002) 96 *AJIL* 345.

Fleck, Dieter, 'The Protocols Additional to the Geneva Conventions and Customary International Law' (1990) 29 *MLLWR* 497.

— 'Law Enforcement and the Conduct of Hostilities: Two Supplementing or Mutually Excluding Legal Paradigms?' in Andreas Fischer-Lescano, Hans-Peter Gasser, Thilo Marauhn, & Natalino Ronzitti (eds.), *Frieden in Freiheit, Peace in liberty, Paix en liberté – Festschrift fur Michal Bothe zum 70. Geburtstag* (Nomos 2008) 391.

— 'The Law of Non-International Armed Conflict' in Dieter Fleck (ed.), *The Handbook of International Humanitarian Law* (3rd edn, Oxford University Press 2013) 581.

Focarelli, Carlo, 'Common Article 1 of the 1949 Geneva Conventions: A Soap Bubble?' (2010) 21 *EJIL* 125.

International Law as Social Construct: The Struggle for Global Justice (Oxford University Press 2012).
Ford, W. J., 'Resistance Movements in Occupied Territory' (1956) 3 *NILR* 355.
Fox, Gregory H., *Humanitarian Occupation* (Cambridge University Press 2008).
Fraenkel, Ernst, *Military Occupation and the Rule of Law: Occupational Government in the Rhineland 1918–1923* (Oxford University Press 1944).
Franck, Thomas M., 'The Stealing of the Sahara' (1976) 70 *AJIL* 694.
  'Terrorism and the Right of Self-Defence' (2001) 95 *AJIL* 839.
  Recourse to Force: State Action against Threats and Armed Attacks (Cambridge University Press 2002).
French, Duncan (ed.), *Statehood and Self-Determination* (Cambridge University Press 2013).
Frigessi di Rattalma, Marco, 'Qualche riflessione sull'azione bellica in Afghanistan e la legittima difesa' in Andrea Giardina & Flavia Lattanzi (eds.), *Studi di diritto internazionale in onore di Gaetano Arangio-Ruiz* vol. III (Editoriale Scientifica 2003) 1623.
Frigo, Manlio, 'La sovranità permanente degli Stati sulle risorse naturali' in Paolo Picone & Giorgio Sacerdoti (eds.), *Diritto internazionale dell'economia* (Franco Angeli 1982) 245.
  'La protezione dei beni culturali nei territori occupati. Il divieto di esportare i beni culturali da un territorio occupato e gli obblighi di restituzione' in Paolo Benvenuti & Rosario Sapienza (eds.), *La tutela internazionale dei beni culturali nei conflitti armati* (Giuffrè 2007) 103.
Frowein, Jochen A., 'The Relationship between Human Rights Regimes and Regimes of Belligerent Occupation' (1998) 28 *IHYR* 1.
Frulli, Micaela, *Le operazioni di peacekeeping delle Nazioni Unite: continuità di un modello normativo* (Editoriale Scientifica 2012).
Gaeta, Paola, 'Are Victims of Serious Violations of International Humanitarian Law Entitled to Compensation?' in Orna Ben-Naftali (ed.), *International Humanitarian Law and International Human Rights Law: Pas de Deux* (Oxford University Press 2011) 305.
Gaggioli, Gloria (ed.), *Expert Meeting on the Use of Force in Armed Conflicts: Interplay between the Conduct of Hostilities and Law Enforcement Paradigms* (ICRC 2013).
Gaggioli, Gloria & Kolb, Robert, 'A Right to Life in Armed Conflicts? The Contribution of the European Court of Human Rights' (2007) 37 *IYHR* 115.
Gainsborough, J. R., *The Arab-Israeli Conflict* (Gower 1986).
Gaja, Giorgio, 'Il Consiglio di sicurezza di fronte all'occupazione del Kuwait: il significato di un'autorizzazione' (1990) 73 *RDI* 696.
  'Use of Force Made or Authorized by the United Nations' in Christian Tomuschat (ed.), (*The United Nations at Age Fifty. A Legal Perspective* (Nijhoff 1995) 39.
  'Combating Terrorism: Issues of *Jus ad Bellum* and *Jus in Bello*: The Case of Afghanistan' in Wolfgang Benedek & Alice Yotopoulos-Marangopoulos (eds.), *Anti-Terrorist Measures and Human Rights* (Brill 2004) 161.
  'The Protection of General Interests in the International Community' (2012) 364 *RCADI* 9.
Gargiulo, Pietro, 'Uso della forza (diritto internazionale)' in *Enciclopedia del Diritto* (Giuffrè 2012) 1367.

Garraway, Charles H. D., 'Armed Conflict and Law Enforcement: Is There a Legal Divide?' in Mariëlle Matthee, Brigit Toebes, & Marcel Brus (eds.), *Armed Conflict and International Law: In Search of the Human Face* (Springer 2013) 259.

'Occupation Responsibilities and Constraints' in Howard M. Hensel (ed.), *The Legitimate Use of Military Force* (Ashgate 2008) 263.

'The Duties of the Occupying Power: An Overview of the Recent Developments in the Law of Occupation' in Julia Race & Patrick Sutter (eds.), *Facets and Practices of State-Building* (Martinus Nijhoff 2009) 179.

'War and Peace: Where Is the Divide?' (2012) 88 *ILS* 93.

Gasser, Hans-Peter, 'Acts of Terror, "Terrorism" and International Humanitarian Law' (2002) 84 *ICRC* 547.

Gasser, Hans-Peter & Dörmann, Knut, 'Protection of the Civilian Population' in Dieter Fleck (ed.), *The Handbook of International Humanitarian Law* (3rd edn, Oxford University Press 2013) 231.

Gattini, Andrea, 'Occupazione bellica' in Sabino Cassese (ed.), *Dizionario di diritto pubblico* (Giuffrè 2006) 3889.

Geiß, Robin, 'Russia's Annexation of Crimea: The Mills of International Law Grind Slowly but They Do Grind' (2015) 91 *ILS* 425.

'The Obligation to Respect and to Ensure Respect for the Conventions' in Andrew Clapham, Paola Gaeta, & Marco Sassòli (eds.), *The 1949 Geneva Conventions: A Commentary* (Oxford University Press 2015) 111.

Gentili, Alberico, *De Iure Belli Libri Tres* vol. III (London 1612), English translation by John C. Rolfe (Clarendon Press 1933).

Gerson, Allan, *Israel, the West Bank and International Law* (Frank Case 1978).

Gervasoni, Luca, 'A Contextual-Functional Approach to Investigations into Right to Life Violations in Armed Conflict' (2017) 36 *Zoom-In Questions of International Law* 5.

Giacca, Gilles, *Economic, Social and Cultural Rights in Armed Conflict* (Oxford University Press 2014).

Gigerich, Thomas, 'Article 60' in Oliver Dörr & Kirsten Schmalenbach (eds.), *Vienna Convention on the Law of Treaties: A Commentary* (2nd edn, Springer 2018) 1095.

Giladi, Rotem, 'The *Jus Ad Bellum/Jus In Bello* Distinction and the Law of Occupation' (2008) 41 *IsLR* 246.

Gill, Terry D., 'Legal and Some Political Limitations on the Power of the UN Security Council to Exercise Its Enforcement Powers under Chapter VII of the Charter' (1995) 26 *Netherlands YIL* 33.

'The Law of Belligerent Occupation: The Distinction between Invasion and Occupation of Disputed Territory' in Andrea de Guttry, Harry G. Post, & Gabriella Venturini (eds.), *The 1998–2000 War between Eritrea and Ethiopia* (TMC Asser Press 2009) 365.

Gillespie, Alexander, *A History of the Laws of War* vols I–II (Hart 2011).

Gioia, Andrea, 'Terrorismo internazionale, crimini di guerra e crimini contro l'umanità' (2004) 87 *RDI* 5.

'Terroristi o combattenti: un'alternativa credibile alla luce del diritto internazionale?' (2007) 29 *Ragion Pratica* 355.

'La lotta al terrorismo tra diritto di guerra e diritti dell'uomo' in Pietro Gargiulo & Maria Chiara Vitucci (eds.), *La tutela dei diritti umani nella lotta e nella guerra al terrorismo* (Editoriale Scientifica 2009) 171.

'The Belligerent Occupation of Territory' in Andrea de Guttry, Harry G. Post, & Gabriella Venturini (eds.), *The 1998–2000 War between Eritrea and Ethiopia* (TMC Asser Press 2009) 351.

'The Role of the European Court of Human Rights in Monitoring Compliance with Humanitarian Law in Armed Conflict' in Orna Ben-Naftali (ed.), *International Humanitarian Law and International Human Rights Law: Pas de Deux* (Oxford University Press 2011) 201.

Manuale di diritto internazionale (5th edn, Giuffrè 2015).

von Glahn, Gerhard, *The Occupation of Enemy Territory: A Commentary on the Law and Practice of Belligerent Occupation* (University of Minnesota Press 1957).

'Taxation under Belligerent Occupation' in Emma Playfair (ed.), *International Law and the Administration of Occupied Territories* (Clarendon Press 1992) 341.

Goodman, Davis P., 'The Need of Fundamental Change in the Law of Occupation' (1985) 37 *Stanford LR* 1573.

Goodman, Ryan, 'The Power to Kill or Capture Enemy Combatants' (2013) 24 *EJIL* 819.

Gorelick, Robert E., 'Wars of National Liberation: *Jus ad Bellum*' (1979) 11 *Case Western Reserve JIL* 71.

Gowlland-Debbas, Vera, 'The Right to Life and the Relationship between Human Rights and Humanitarian Law' in Christian Tomuschat, Evelyne Lagrange, & Stefan Oeter (eds.), *The Right to Life* (Brill 2010) 121.

Graber, Doris Appel, *The Development of the Law of Belligerent Occupation 1863–1914: A Historical Survey* (Columbia University Press 1949).

Gradoni, Lorenzo, 'Il lato oscuro dell'articolo 103 della Carta delle Nazioni Unite' in Massimo Meccarelli, Paolo Palchetti, & Carlo Sotis (eds.), *Le regole dell'eccezione. Un dialogo interdisciplinare a partire dalla questione del terrorismo* (eum 2011) 263.

Grant, Thomas D., *Aggression against Ukraine: Territory, Responsibility, and International Law* (Palgrave Macmillan 2015).

Gray, Christine, *International Law and the Use of Force* (3rd edn, Oxford University Press 2008).

'The Use of Force and the International Legal Order' in Malcolm D. Evans (ed.), *International Law* (4th edn, Oxford University Press 2014) 61.

Green, James A., *The International Court of Justice and Self-Defence in International Law* (Hart 2009).

Greenspan, Morris, *The Modern Law of Land Warfare* (University of California Press 1950).

Greenwood, Christopher, 'The Relationship between *Ius ad Bellum* and *Ius in Bello*' (1983) 9 *Review of International Studies* 221.

'Customary Law Status of the 1977 Geneva Protocols' in Astrid J. M. Delissen & Gerald Jacob Tanja (eds.), *Humanitarian Law of Armed Conflict: Challenges Ahead – Essays in Honor of Frits Kalshoven* (Martinus Nijhoff 1991) 93.

'The Administration of Occupied Territory in International Law' in Emma Playfair (ed.), *International Law and the Administration of Occupied Territories* (Clarendon Press 1992) 241.

'Self-Defence' in *MPEPIL online* (2011).

Greppi, Edoardo, 'Diritto internazionale umanitario dei conflitti armati e diritti umani: profili di una convergenza' (1996) 51 *CI* 473.
'To What Extent Do the International Rules on Human Rights Matter?' in Fausto Pocar, Marco Pedrazzi, & Micaela Frulli (eds.), *War Crimes and the Conduct of Hostilities: Challenges to Adjudication and Investigation* (Edward Elgar 2013) 38.
Grignon, Julia, 'The Geneva Conventions and the End of Occupation' in Andrew Clapham, Paola Gaeta, & Marco Sassòli (eds.), *The 1949 Geneva Conventions: A Commentary* (Oxford University Press 2015) 1575.
Gross, Aeyal M., 'The Construction of a Wall between The Hague and Jerusalem: The Enforcement and Limits of Humanitarian Law and the Structure of Occupation' (2006) 19 *LJIL* 393.
'Human Proportions: Are Human Rights the Emperor's New Clothes of the International Law of Occupation?' (2007) 18 *EJIL* 1.
The Writing on the Wall: Rethinking the International Law of Occupation (Cambridge University Press 2017).
Grotius, Hugo, *De jure belli ac pacis libri tres* (Paris 1625), English translation by Francis W. Kelsey, On the Law of War and Peace vol. III (Oceana 1964).
Guarino, Giancarlo, *La questione della Palestina nel diritto internazionale* (Giappichelli 1994).
'The Palestine Liberation Organization and Its Evolution as a National Liberation Movement' (2008) 10 *RCGI* 13.
Guellali, Anna, '*Lex specialis*, droit international humanitaire et droits de l'homme: leur interaction dans le nouveaux conflits armés' (2007) 111 *RGDIP* 539.
Guelle, Jules, *Precis des lois de la guerre sur terre* vol. 1 (Pedone Laurel 1884).
Guggenheim, Paul, *Traité de Droit international public* vol. II (Georg & Cie 1954).
Guilfoyle, Douglas, 'The *Mavi Marmara* Incident and Blockade in Armed Conflict' (2011) 81 *British YIL* 171.
Gutteridge, Joyce A. C., 'The Geneva Conventions of 1949' (1949) 26 *British YIL* 294.
Hall, William E., *A Treatise on International Law* (4th edn, Clarendon Press 1895).
Hampson, Françoise J., 'The Relationship between International Humanitarian Law and Human Rights Law from the Perspective of a Human Rights Treaty' (2008) 90 *IRRC* 549.
'Afghanistan 2001–2010' in Elizabeth Wilmshurst (ed.), *International Law and the Classification of Conflicts* (Oxford University Press 2012) 242.
'An Investigation of Alleged Violations of the Law of Armed Conflict' (2016) 46 *IYHR* 1.
Hamrouni, Maïa-Oumeïma, 'Les juridictions européennes et l'article 103 de la charte des Nations Unies' (2017) 120 *RGDIP* 769.
Harpaz, Guy, 'When Does a Court Systematically Deviate from Its Own Principles? The Adjudication by the Israel Supreme Court of House Demolitions in the Occupied Palestinian Territories' (2015) 31 *LJIL* 28.
Heffter, August W., *Das Europäische Völkerrecht der Gegenwart* (Schroeder 1844), French translation by Jules Bergson, *Le droit international de l'Europe* (Cotillon 1873).
Heintschel von Heinegg, Wolff, 'Methods and Means of Naval Warfare in Non-International Armed Conflicts' (2012) 88 *ILS* 211.
'Blockade' in *MPEPIL online* (2015).
Henckaerts, Jean-Marie, 'Article 1: Respect and Ensure Respect' in ICRC, *Updated Commentary on the First Geneva Convention* (ICRC/Cambridge University Press 2016) 35.

Henckaerts, Jean-Marie & Doswald-Beck, Louise (eds.), *Customary International Humanitarian Law* vol. I (Cambridge University Press 2005).

Henderson, Christian & Green, James A., 'The *Jus ad Bellum* and Entities Short of Statehood in the Report on the Conflict in Georgia' (2010) 59 *ICLQ* 129.

Henry, Etienne, *Le principe de nécessité militaire: Histoire et actualité d'une norme fondamentale du droit international humanitaire* (Pedone 2016).

Hessbruegge, Jan Arno, *Human Rights and Personal Self-Defense in International Law* (Oxford University Press 2017).

Heyns, Christof, Akande, Dapo, Hill-Cawthorne, Lawrence, & Chengeta, Thompson, 'The International Legal Framework Regulating the Use of Armed Drones' (2016) 65 *ICLQ* 791.

Higgins, Roslyn, 'Derogations under Human Rights Treaties' (1976–7) 48 *British YIL* 281.
Problems and Process: International Law and How We Use It (Clarendon Press 1995).

Higgins, Roslyn, Webb, Philippa, Akande, Dapo, Sivakumaran, Sandesh, & Sloan, James, *Oppenheim's International Law: United Nations* vol. II (Oxford University Press 2017).

Hilpold, Peter, 'Ukraine, Crimea and New International Law: Balancing International Law with Arguments Drawn from History' (2015) 14 *CJIL* 237.

Hodgkinson, Sandra L., 'Detention Operations: A Strategic View' in Geoffrey S. Corn, Rachel E. Van Landingham, & Shane R. Reeves (eds.), *US Military Operations: Law, Policy, and Practice* (Oxford University Press 2015) 275.

Hoffman, Michael H., 'Terrorists Are Unlawful Belligerents, Not Unlawful Combatants: A Distinction with Implications for the Future of International Humanitarian Law' (2002) 34 *Case Western Reserve JIL* 227.

Iglesias Velasco, Alfonso J., 'El Estatuto jurìdico-internacional de Jerusalén' (1999) 48 *Afers Internacional* 75.
'El marco jurídico de las operaciones de mantenimiento de la paz de Naciones Unidas' (1/2005) *Foro, Nueva época* 127.

Imseis, Ardi, 'Critical Reflections on the International Humanitarian Law Aspects of the ICJ Wall Advisory Opinion' (2005) 99 *AJIL* 102.

Ingravallo, Ivan, 'L'azione internazionale per la ricostruzione dell'Afghanistan' (2004) 59 *CI* 525.
Il Consiglio di sicurezza e l'amministrazione diretta dei territori (Editoriale Scientifica 2008) 1.

Ivanel, Bogdan, 'Puppet States: A Growing Trend of Covert Occupation' (2015) 18 *YIHL* 43.

Jellinek, Georg, *L'état moderne et son droit* vol. II, Théorie juridique de l'État (Giard & Brière 1913).

Jenks, Wilfred, 'The Conflict of Law-Making Treaties' (1953) 30 *British YIL* 401.

Jinks, Derek, 'September 11 and the Laws of War' (2003) 28 *Yale JIL* 1.

John-Hopkins, Michael, *The Rule of Law in Crisis and Conflict Grey Zones: Regulating the Use of Force in a Global Information Environment* (Routledge 2017).

Johnstone, Ian, 'Managing Consent in Contemporary Peacekeeping Operations' (2011) 18 *International Peacekeeping* 168.

Jung, Youngjin, 'In Pursuit of Reconstructing Iraq: Does Self-Determination Matter?' (2004–5) 33 *Denver Journal of International Law & Politics* 53.

Kalandarishvili-Mueller, Natia, 'On the Occasion of the Five-Year Anniversary of the Russian-Georgian War: Is Georgia Occupied?', *EJIL: Talk!*, 1 October 2013.
'The Status of the Territory Unchanged: Russia's Treaties with Abkhazia and South Ossetia, Georgia', *Opinio Juris*, 20 April 2015.
Kälin, Walter, *Human Rights in Times of Occupation: The Case of Kuwait* (Law Books of Europe 1994).
Kammerhofer, Jörg, 'The *Armed Activities* Case and Non-State Actors in Self-Defence' (2007) 20 *LJIL* 89.
Kamminga, Menno T. & Scheinin, Martin (eds.), *The Impact of Human Rights Law on General International Law* (Oxford University Press 2009).
Karl, Wolfram, 'Treaties, Conflict Between' in Rudolf Bernhardt (ed.), *Encyclopedia of Public International Law* vol. IV (North-Holland 1990) 935.
Kattan, Victor, 'The Legality of the West Bank Wall: Israel's High Court of Justice v. the International Court of Justice' (2007) 40 *Vanderbilt Journal of Transnational Law* 1425.
'Operation Cast Lead: Use of Force Discourse and *Jus ad Bellum* Controversies' (2009) 15 *Palestine YIL* 95.
Keller, Helen & Forowicz, Magdalena, 'A Tightrope Walk between Legality and Legitimacy: An Analysis of the Israeli Supreme Court's Judgment on Targeted Killing' (2008) 21 *LJIL* 185.
Kelly, Michael J., 'Iraq and the Law of Occupation: New Tests for an Old Law' (2003) 6 *YIHL* 127.
Kelsen, Hans, *The Law of the United Nations* (Stevens & Sons 1950).
Principles of International Law (2nd edn, Holt, Rinehart and Winston 1966).
Kleffner, Jann K., 'Section IX of the ICRC Interpretive Guidance on Direct Participation in Hostilities: The End of *Jus in Bello* Proportionality as We Know It' (2012) 45 *IsLR* 35.
Klein, Pierre, 'Le droit international à l'épreuve du terrorisme' (2006) 321 *RCADI* 203.
Knop, Karen, *Diversity and Self-Determination in International Law* (Cambridge University Press 2002).
Koivurova, Timo, 'Due Diligence' in *MPEPIL online* (2010).
Kolb, Robert, 'The Relationship between International Humanitarian Law and Human Rights Law: A Brief History of the 1948 Universal Declaration of Human Rights and the 1949 Geneva Conventions' (1998) 38 *IRRC* 409.
'Etude sur l'occupation et sur l'article 47 de la IVeme Convention de Genève du 12 août 1949 relative à la protection des personnes civiles en temps de guerre: le degré d'intangibilité des droits en territoire occupé' (2002) 10 *African YIL* 267.
Ius in bello: le droit international des conflits armés: précis (Helbing & Lichtenhahn 2003).
'Occupation in Iraq since 2003 and the Powers of the UN Security Council' (2008) 98 *IRRC* 29.
'"Condotta delle ostilità" e "mantenimento dell'ordine": due concetti chiave della definizione dei rapporti tra diritto internazionale umanitario e diritti umani' in Adriana Di Stefano & Rosario Sapienza (eds.), *La tutela dei diritti umani e il diritto internazionale* (Editoriale Scientifica 2012) 67.
'Human Rights and Humanitarian Law' in *MPEPIL online* (2013).
'L'article 103 de la Charte des Nations Unies' (2013) 367 *RCADI* 9.

Advanced Introduction to International Humanitarian Law (Edward Elgar 2014).
Kolb, Robert & Gaggioli, Gloria (eds.), *Research Handbook on Human Rights and Humanitarian Law* (Edward Elger 2013).
Kolb, Robert & Hyde, Robert, *An Introduction to the International Law of Armed Conflicts* (Hart 2008).
Kolb, Robert, Porretto, Gabriele, & Vité, Sylvain, *L'application du droit international humanitaire et des droits de l'homme aux organisations internationales. Forces de paix et administrations civiles transitoires* (Bruylant 2005).
Kolb, Robert & Vité, Sylvain, *Le droit de l'occupation militaire: Perspectives historiques et enjeux juridiques actuelles* (Bruylant 2009).
Koreen, Amy J., 'The Palestinian Uprising of December 1987: An Examination under International Humanitarian Law' (1992) 37 *Touro Journal of Transnational Law* 197.
Korman, Sharon, *The Right of Conquest: The Acquisition of Territory by Force in International Law and Practice* (Clarendon Press 1996).
Koskenniemi, Martti, 'Occupation and Sovereignty: Still a Useful Distinction?' in Ola Engdahl & Pål Wrange (eds.), *Law at War: The Law as It Was and the Law as It Should Be* (Brill 2008) 163.
'Occupied Zone: A Zone of "Reasonableness?"' (2008) 41 *IsLR* 13.
Koutroulis, Vaios, 'Mythes et réalités de l'application du droit international humanitaire aux occupations dites "transformatives"' (2007) 40 *RBDI* 365.
Le début et la fin de l'application du droit de l'occupation (Pedone 2010).
Les relations entre le jus contra bellum et le jus in bello: étanchéité absolue ou vases communicants? (PhD Dissertation, Université Libre de Bruxelles 2011).
'Of Occupation, *Jus ad Bellum* and *Jus in Bello*: A Reply to Solon Solomon's "The Great Oxymoron: *Jus in Bello* Violations as Legitimate Non-Forcible Measures of Self-Defense: The Post-Disengagement Israeli Measures towards Gaza as a Case Study"' (2011) 10 *CJIL* 897.
'The Application of International Humanitarian Law and International Human Rights Law in Situation of Prolonged Occupation: Only a Matter of Time?' (2012) 94 *IRRC* 165.
'And Yet It Exists: In Defence of the "Equality of Belligerents" Principle' (2013) 26 *LJIL* 449.
Kreß, Claus, 'L'organe *de facto* en droit international public: réflexions sur l'imputation à l'état de l'acte d'un particulier à la lumière des développements récents' (2001) 105 *RGDIP* 93.
'Some Reflections on the International Legal Framework Governing Transnational Armed Conflicts' (2010) 15 *JCSL* 245.
Krebs, Shiri, 'Lifting the Veil of Secrecy: Judicial Review of Administrative Detentions in the Israeli Supreme Court' (2012) 45 *Vanderbilt Journal of Transnational Law* 639.
Kretzmer, David, 'The Advisory Opinion: The Light Treatment of International Humanitarian Law' (2005) 99 *AJIL* 88.
The Occupation of Justice: The Supreme Court of Israel and the Occupied Territories (State University of New York Press 2002).
'Targeted Killing of Suspected Terrorists: Extra-Judicial Executions or Legitimate Means of Defence?' (2005) 16 *EJIL* 171.
Krüger, Heiko, *The Nagorno-Karabakh Conflict: A Legal Analysis* (Springer 2010).
Kulesza, Joanna, *Due Diligence in International Law* (Brill 2016).

Kwakwa, Edward, 'The Namibian Conflict: A Discussion of the *Jus ad Bellum* and the *Jus in Bello*' (1988) 9 *New York Law School JICL* 195, 216–20.
Lamberti Zanardi, Pierluigi, *La legittima difesa nel diritto internazionale* (Giuffrè 1972).
'Indirect Military Aggression' in Antonio Cassese (ed.), *The Current Legal Regulation of the Use of Force* (Martinus Nijhoff 1986) 111.
Lanciotti, Alessandra & Tanzi, Attila (eds.), *Uso della forza e legittima difesa nel diritto internazionale contemporaneo* (Jovene 2012).
Langille, Benjamin, 'It's Instant Custom: How the Bush Doctrine Became Law after the Terrorist Attacks of September 11, 2001' (2003) 26 *Boston College International & Comparative Law Review* 145.
Lapidoth, Ruth, 'Jerusalem and the Peace Process' (1994) 28 *IsLR* 402.
Larsdotter, Kersti, 'Fighting Transnational Insurgents: The South African Defence Force in Namibia, 1966–1989' (2014) 37 *SCT* 1024.
Lattanzi, Flavia, 'Autodeterminazione dei popoli' in *Digesto delle discipline pubblicistiche* (UTET 1987) 4.
'Il confine fra diritto internazionale umanitario e diritti dell'uomo' in Andrea Giardina & Flavia Lattanzi (eds.), *Studi di diritto internazionale in onore di Gaetano Arangio-Ruiz* vol. III (Editoriale Scientifica 2004) 1985.
Lauterpacht, Hersh, *Oppenheim's International Law. A Treatise, vol. II: Disputes, War and Neutrality* (7th edn, Longmans 1952).
Lazarus, Claude, 'Le Statut International des Mouvements de Libération Nationale à l'Organisation des Nations Unies' (1974) 20 *AFDI* 173.
Leach, Philip, Murray, Rachel, & Sandoval, Clara, 'The Duty to Investigate Right to Life Violations across Three Regional Systems: Harmonisation or Fragmentation of International Human Rights Law?' in Carla Buckley, Alice Donald, & Philip Leach (eds.), *Towards Convergence in International Human Rights Law: Approaches of Regional and International Systems* (Brill 2017) 33.
Lemkin, Raphael, *Axis Rule in Occupied Europe: Laws of Occupation, Analysis of Government, Proposals for Redress* (Carnegie Endowment for International Peace 1944).
Lesaffer, Randall, 'The Classical Law of Nations (1500–1800)' in Alexander Orakhelashvili (ed.), *Research Handbook on the Theory and History of International Law* (Edward Elgar 2011) 408.
Lieber, Francis, 'Guerrilla Parties, Considered with Reference to the Laws and Usages of War' in *Miscellaneous Writings* vol. II (Lippincott & Co 1881) 277.
Lieblich, Eliav, 'Reflections on the Israeli Report on the Gaza Conflict', *Just Security*, 24 June 2015.
Lillich, Richard B., 'The Growing Importance of Customary International Human Rights Law' (1995–6) 25 *Georgia JICL* 1.
Linderfalk, Ulf, 'The Principle of Rational Decision-Making as Applied to the Identification of Normative Conflicts in International Law' (2013) 73 *ZaöRV* 591.
Lindroos, Anja, 'Addressing Norm Conflicts in a Fragmented Legal System: The Doctrine of *Lex Specialis*' (2005) 74 *NJIL* 27.
Locke, John, *Two Treatises of Government* (1689) (London 1821).

Longobardo, Marco, 'La recente adesione palestinese alle convenzioni di diritto umanitario e ai principali trattati a tutela dei diritti dell'uomo' (2014) 1 *Ordine internazionale e diritti umani* 771.

'Lo Stato di Palestina: emersione fattuale e autodeterminazione dei popoli prima e dopo il riconoscimento dello status di Stato non membro delle Nazioni Unite' in Marcella Distefano (ed.), *Il principio di autodeterminazione dei popoli alla prova del nuovo millennio* (CEDAM 2014) 9.

'Some Developments in the Prosecution of International Crimes Committed in Palestine: Any Real News?' (2015) 35 *Polish YIL* 109.

'The Palestinian Right to Exploit the Dead Sea Coastline for Tourism' (2015) 58 *German YIL* 317.

'State Responsibility for International Humanitarian Law Violations by Private Actors in Occupied Territories and the Exploitation of Natural Resources' (2016) 63 *NILR* 251.

'(New) Cyber Exploitation and (Old) International Humanitarian Law' (2017) 77 *ZaöRV* 809.

'L'obbligo per gli Stati di assumere tutte le informazioni necessarie prima di un attacco ai sensi del diritto internazionale umanitario fra nuove e vecchie forme di intelligence' in Andrea Spagnolo & Stefano Saluzzo (eds.), *La responsabilità degli Stati e delle organizzazioni internazionali: nuove fattispecie e problemi di attribuzione e di accertamento* (Ledizioni 2017) 37.

López-Jacoiste Díaz, Eugenia, 'Algunas reflexiones sobre la Opinión Consultiva sobre el Muro de Israel: la solución está en Ramalla y Gaza y no en la Haya o Manhattan' (2004) 20 *ADI* 467.

Lowe, Vaughan, 'The Wall in the Occupied Palestinian Territory' in Laurence Boisson de Chazournes & Marcelo Kohen (eds.), *International Law and the Quest for Implementation: Liber Amicorum Vera Gowlland-Debbas* (Martinus Nijhoff 2010) 309.

Lozano Contreras, José Fernando, *La noción de debida diligencia en derecho internacional public* (Atelier 2006).

Lubell, Noam, 'The ICJ Advisory Opinion and the Separation Barrier: A Troublesome Route' (2005) 35 *IYHR* 283.

Extraterritorial Use of Force against Non-State Actors (Oxford University Press 2010).

'Human Rights Obligations in Military Occupation' (2012) 94 *IRRC* 317.

'The War (?) against A-Qaeda' in Elizabeth Wilmshurst (ed.), *International Law and the Classification of Conflicts* (Oxford University Press 2012) 421.

Malanczuk, Peter, 'Israel: Status, Territory and Occupied Territories' in Rudolf Bernhardt (ed.), *Encyclopedia of Public International Law* (North-Holland 1990) 149.

'Some Basic Aspects of the Agreements between Israel and the PLO from the Perspective of International Law' (1996) 7 *EJIL* 485.

Mallison, W. Thomas & Jabri, R. A. 'Juridical Characteristics of Belligerent Occupation and the Resort to Resistance by the Civilian Population: Doctrinal Development and Continuity' (1974) 42 *George Washington Law Review* 185.

Mallisson, W. Thomas & Mallisson, Sally V., *The Palestine Problem in International Law and World Order* (Longman 1986).

Mancini, Marina, *Stato di guerra e conflitto armato nel diritto internazionale* (Giappichelli 2009).

'Conseguenze giuridiche dell'attribuzione alla Palestina dello status di Stato osservatore presso le Nazioni Unite' (2013) 96 *RDI* 100.

'The Effects of a State of War or Armed Conflict' in Mark Weller (ed.), *The Oxford Handbook of the Use of Force in International Law* (Oxford University Press 2015) 988.

Marauhn, Thilo & Ntoubandi, Zacharie F., 'Armed Conflict, Non International' in *MPEPIL online* (2016).

Marcelli, Fabio, 'Gli accordi fra Israele e OLP nel diritto internazionale' (1994) 77 *RDI* 430.

Marchesi, Antonio, *Obblighi di condotta e obblighi di risultato: contributo allo studio degli obblighi internazionali* (Giuffré 2003).

Marchisio, Sergio, *L'ONU: il diritto delle Nazioni Unite* (2nd edn, Il Mulino 2012).

Marinoni, Mario, 'Della natura giuridica dell'occupazione bellica' (1910) 5 *RDI* 181.

Martínez Guillem, Ramón, 'La participación de fuerzas policiales en las operaciones de mantenimiento de la paz' in Consuelo Ramón Chornet (ed.), *El derecho internacional humanitario ante los nuevos conflictos armados* (Tirant lo Blanch 2002) 159.

Maside Miranda, Luis, 'Cuestiones relativas a la *occupatio bellica*' (2004) 8 *Anuario da Facultade de Dereito da Universidade da Coruña* 461.

Mastorodimos, Konstantinos, 'How and When Do Military Occupations End?' (2009) 21 *Sri Lanka JIL* 109.

'The Character of the Conflict in Gaza: Another Argument towards Abolishing the Distinction between International and Non-International Armed Conflicts' (2010) 12 *International Community Law Review* 437.

Maurer, Peter, 'Challenges to International Humanitarian Law: Israel's Occupation Policy' (2012) 94 *IRRC* 1504.

McDougal, Myres S. & Feliciano, Florentino P., *Law and Minimum World Public Order: The Legal Regulation of International Coercion* (Yale University Press 1961).

McNair, Arnold, 'Les effects de la guerre sur les traités' (1937) 59 *RCADI* 527.

Mégret, Frédéric, 'Grandeur et déclin de l'idée de résistance à l'occupation: réflexions à propos de la légitimité des "insurgés"' (2008) 41 *RBDI* 382.

Melzer, Nils, *Targeted Killings in International Law* (Cambridge University Press 2008).

Interpretive Guidance on the Notion of Direct Participation in Hostilities under International Humanitarian Law (ICRC 2009).

International Humanitarian Law: A Comprehensive Introduction (ICRC 2016).

Melzer, Nils & Gaggioli, Gloria, 'Conceptual Distinction and Overlaps between Law Enforcement and the Conduct of Hostilities' in Terry D. Gill & Dieter Fleck (eds.), *The Handbook of the International Law of Military Operations* (2nd edn, Oxford University Press 2015) 63.

Meron, Theodor, 'The Applicability of Multilateral Conventions to Occupied Territories' (1978) 72 *AJIL* 542.

'On the Inadequate Reach of Humanitarian and Human Rights Law and the Need for a New Instrument' (1983) 77 *AJIL* 589.

'The Geneva Conventions as Customary Law' (1987) 81 *AJIL* 348.

Human Rights and Humanitarian Norms as Customary Law (Oxford University Press 1989).

'The Humanization of Humanitarian Law' (2000) 94 *AJIL* 239.

The Humanization of International Law (Brill 2006).

'Opinion: Settlement in the Administered Territory' (18 September 1967), reprinted in Iain Scobbie & Sarah Hibbin, *The Israel-Palestine Conflict in International Law: Territorial Issues* (SOAS 2009) 116.

'The West Bank and International Humanitarian Law on the Eve of the Fiftieth Anniversary of the Six-Day War' (2017) 111 *AJIL* 357.
L'occupazione bellica (Giuffrè 1949).
Migliazza, Alessandro, 'L'évolution de la réglementation de la guerre à la lumière de la sauvegarde des droits de l'Homme' (1972) 137 *RCADI* 141.
'Occupazione bellica' in *Enciclopedia Giuridica* vol. XXI (Treccani 1990) 1.
Milano, Enrico, 'Diplomatic Protection and Human Rights before the International Court of Justice: Re-fashioning Tradition?' (2004) 35 *Netherlands YIL* 85.
Unlawful Territorial Situations in International Law – Reconciling Effectiveness, Legality and Legitimacy (Brill 2005).
'Il ricorso all'uso della forza nei confronti di attori non statali' in Alessandra Lanciotti & Attila Tanzi (eds.), *Uso della forza e legittima difesa nel diritto internazionale contemporaneo* (Jovene 2012) 105.
Formazione dello Stato e processi di State-Building nel diritto internazionale: Kosovo 1999–2013 (Editoriale Scientifica 2013).
'Occupation' in André Nollkaemper & Ilias Plakokefalos (eds.), *The Practice of Shared Responsibility* (Cambridge University Press 2017).
Milanovic, Marko, 'Lessons for Human Rights and Humanitarian Law in the War on Terror: Comparing *Hamdan* and the Israeli *Targeted Killings* Case' (2007) 89 *IRRC* 373.
'A Follow-Up on Israel and Gaza', *EJIL: Talk!*, 3 January 2009.
'A Norm Conflict Perspective on the Relationship between International Humanitarian Law and Human Rights Law' (2010) 14 *JCSL* 459.
Extraterritorial Application of Human Rights Treaties: Law, Principles, and Policy (Oxford University Press 2011).
'European Court Decides That Israel Is Not Occupying Gaza', *EJIL: Talk!*, 17 June 2015.
'The Lost Origins of *Lex Specialis*: Rethinking the Relationship between Human Rights and International Humanitarian Law' in Jens David Ohlin (ed.), *Theoretical Boundaries of Armed Conflict and Human Rights* (Cambridge University Press 2016) 78.
'Accounting for the Complexity of the Law Applicable to Modern Armed Conflicts' in Christopher Ford, Shane Reeves, & Winston Williams (eds.), *Complex Battlespaces: The Law of Armed Conflict and the Dynamics of Modern Warfare* (Oxford University Press forthcoming) 7, draft available at papers.ssrn.com/sol3/papers.cfm?abstract_id=2963575
Moghadam, Assaf, 'Palestinian Suicide Terrorism in the Second Intifada: Motivations and Organizational Aspects' (2003) 65 *SCT* 65.
Moir, Lindsay, *The Law of Internal Armed Conflict* (Cambridge University Press 2002).
Mona, Rishmawi, 'The Administration of the West Bank under Israeli Rule' in Emma Playfair (ed.), *International Law and the Administration of Occupied Territories* (Clarendon Press 1992) 267.
Monaco, Riccardo, 'Le recenti annessioni territoriali al Regno d'Italia e il problema del diritto interlocale' (1941) 2 *Stato e diritto* 188.
Moodrick-Even Khen, Hilly, 'Having It Both Ways: The Question of Legal Regimes in Gaza and the West Bank' (2011) 16 *Israel Studies* 55.
Morris, Benny, *One State, Two States: Resolving the Israel/Palestine Conflict* (Yale University Press 2009).
Moussa, Jasmine, 'Can *Jus ad Bellum* Override *Jus in Bello*? Reaffirming the Separation of the Two Bodies of Law' (2008) 90 *IRRC* 963.

Murphy, John F., 'Afghanistan: Hard Choices and the Future of International Law' (2009) 85 *ILS* 79.

Murphy, Sean D., 'Assessing the Legality of Invading Iraq' (2003–4) 92 *The Georgetown Law Journal* 173.

'Self-Defense and the Israeli *Wall* Advisory Opinion: An *Ipse Dixit* from the ICJ?' (2005) 99 *AJIL* 62.

'Terrorism and the Concept of "Armed Attack" in Article 51 of the U.N. Charter' (2002) 43 *Harvard ILJ* 41.

Murphy, Shannonbrooke, 'Unique in International Human Rights Law: Article 20(2) and the Right to Resist in the African Charter on Human and Peoples' Rights' (2011) 11 *African Human Rights Law Journal* 465.

Murray, Christina, 'The 1977 Geneva Protocols and Conflict in Southern Africa' (1984) 33 *ICLQ* 462.

'The Status of the ANC and SWAPO and International Humanitarian Law' (1983) 100 *South African Law Journal* 402.

Murray, Darragh, 'How International Humanitarian Law Treaties Bind Non-State Armed Groups' (2015) 20 *JCSL* 101.

Practitioners' Guide to Human Rights Law in Armed Conflict (Elizabeth Wilmshurst, Francoise Hampson, Charles Garraway, Noam Lubell, & Dapo Akande (consultant eds.)) (Oxford University Press 2016).

Nabulsi, Karma, *Traditions of War: Occupation, Resistance and the Law* (Oxford University Press 1999).

Newton, Michael & May, Larry, *Proportionality in International Law* (Oxford University Press 2015).

Nieto-Navia, Rafael, 'International Peremptory Norms (*Jus Cogens*) and International Humanitarian Law' in Lal Chand Vohrah, Fausto Pocar, Yvonne Featherstone et al.(eds.), *Man's Inhumanity to Man: Essays on International Law in Honour of Antonio Cassese* (Kluwer Law International 2003) 595.

Nigro, Raffaella, *La definizione di terrorismo nel diritto internazionale* (Editoriale Scientifica 2013).

Nolte, Georg, *Treaties and Subsequent Practice* (Oxford University Press 2013).

Noto, Maria Chiara, 'Le sanzioni del Consiglio di sicurezza e il terrorismo internazionale nella giurisprudenza penale nazionale: il caso *Daki*' (2008) 44 *RDIPP* 732.

Oberleitner, Gerd, *Human Rights in Armed Conflict: Law, Practice, Policy* (Cambridge University Press 2015).

O'Brian, William, 'Reprisals, Deterrence and Self-Defense in Counterterror Operations' (1990) 30 *Virginia JIL* 421.

O'Connell, Mary Ellen, 'The Prohibition of the Use of Force' in Nigel D. White & Christian Henderson (eds.), *Research Handbook on International Conflict and Security Law* (Edward Elgar 2013) 89.

Oeter, Stefan, 'Self-Determination' in Bruno Simma, Daniel-Erasmus Khan, Georg Nolte, & Andreas Paulus (eds.), *The Charter of the United Nations. A Commentary* (3rd edn, Oxford University Press 2012) 313.

'Methods and Means of Combat' in Dieter Fleck (ed.), *The Handbook of International Humanitarian Law* (3rd edn, Oxford University Press 2013) 115.

Ohlin, Jens David, 'The Right to Exist and the Right to Resist' in Fernando R. Tesón (ed.), *The Theory of Self-Determination* (Cambridge University Press 2016) 70.

O'Keefe, Roger. 'Legal Consequences of the Construction of a Wall in the Occupied Palestinian Territory: A Commentary' (2004) 37 *RBDI* 92.

Okimoto, Keiichiro, 'The Cumulative Requirements of *Jus ad Bellum* and *Jus in Bello* in the Context of Self-Defense' (2012) 11 *CJIL* 45.

Oppenheim, Lassa, 'The Legal Relations between an Occupying Power and the Inhabitants' (1907) 37 *LQR* 363.

'On War Treason' (1917) 33 *LQR* 266.

Orakhelashvili, Alexander, 'Legal Consequences of the Construction of a Wall in the Occupied Palestinian Territory: Opinion and Reaction' (2006) 11 *JCSL* 119.

'Overlap and Convergence: The Interaction between *Jus ad Bellum* and *Jus in Bello*' (2007) 12 *JCSL* 157.

'The Interaction between Human Rights and Humanitarian Law: Fragmentation, Conflict, Parallelism, or Convergence?' (2008) 19 *EJIL* 125.

Otto, Roland, *Targeted Killings and International Law* (Springer 2012).

Paddeu, Federica I., 'Use of Force against Non-State Actors and the Circumstance Precluding Wrongfulness of Self-Defence' (2017) 30 *LJIL* 93.

Palchetti, Paolo, *L'organo di fatto dello Stato nell'illecito internazionale* (Giuffré 2007).

'La participation de la Palestine à la procédure devant la Cour internationale de Justice' in Thierry Garcia (ed.), *La Palestine: d'un etat non membre de l'organisation des Nations Unies a un etat souverain?* (Pedone 2015) 75.

Palmisano, Giuseppe, 'Autodeterminazione dei popoli' in *Enciclopedia del Diritto. Annali* vol. V (Giuffrè 2012) 81.

Papa, Maria Irene, *I rapporti tra la Corte internazionale di giustizia e il Consiglio di sicurezza* (CEDAM 2006).

'Protezione diplomatica, diritti umani e obblighi *erga omnes*' (2008) 91 *RDI* 669.

Parameswaran, Katharina, 'The Use of Military Force and the Applicable Standards of Force Governing Police Operations in Occupied Territories' (2006) 45 *MLLWR* 249.

Parks, W. Hays, 'Part IX of the ICRC Direct Participation in Hostilities Study: No Mandate, No Expertise, and Legally Incorrect' (2009–10) 42 *New York University JIL & Policy* 769.

Paulus, Andreas, 'UN Missions and the Law of Occupation' in Andreas von Arnauld, Nele Matz-Lück, & Kerstin Odendahl (eds.), *100 Years of Peace through Law: Past and Future* (Duncker & Humblot 2015) 237.

Paulus, Andreas & Leiß, Johann Ruben, 'Article 103' in Bruno Simma, Daniel-Erasmus Khan, Georg Nolte, & Andreas Paulus (eds.), *The Charter of the United Nations. A Commentary* vol. II (3rd edn, Oxford University Press 2012) 2110.

Paulus, Andreas & Vashakmadze, Mindia, 'Asymmetrical War and the Notion of Armed Conflict: A Tentative Conceptualization (2009) 91 *IRRC* 95.

Pauwelyn, Joost, *Conflict of Norms in Public International Law* (Cambridge University Press 2003).

Pedrazzi, Marco, 'La protezione del diritto alla vita tra diritto internazionale umanitario e tutela internazionale dei diritti umani' in Adriana Di Stefano & Rosario Sapienza (eds.), *La tutela dei diritti umani e il diritto internazionale* (Editoriale Scientifica 2012) 79.

'The Protection of the Right to Life in Law-Enforcement Operations' in Bernardo Cortese (ed.), *Studi in onore di Laura Picchio Forlati* (Giappichelli 2014) 105.

Pejic, Jelena, 'Procedural Principles and Safeguards for Internment/Administrative Detention in Armed Conflict and Other Situations of Violence' (2005) 87 *IRRC* 375.
'Conflict Classification and the Law Applicable to Detention and the Use of Force' in Elizabeth Wilmshurst (ed.), *International Law and the Classification of Conflicts* (Oxford University Press 2012) 80.
Peleg, Ilan, *Human Rights in the West Bank and Gaza: Legacy and Politics* (Syracuse University Press 1995).
Pellet, Alain, 'The Destruction of Troy Will Not Take Place' in Emma Playfair (ed.), *International Law and the Administration of Occupied Territories* (Clarendon Press 1992) 169.
'The Palestinian Declaration and the Jurisdiction of the International Criminal Court' (2010) 8 *JCSL* 981.
'Response to Koh and Buchwald's Article: Don Quixote and Sancho Panza Tilt at Windmills' (2015) 109 *AJIL* 557.
Perina, Alexandra, 'Legal Bases for Coalition Combat Operations in Iraq, May 2003-Present' (2010) 86 *ILS* 81.
Pertile, Marco, '"Legal Consequences of the Construction of a Wall in the Occupied Palestinian Territory": A Missed Opportunity for International Humanitarian Law?' (2004) 14 *Italian YIL* 121.
'L'adozione di misure contro il terrorismo nei territori occupati: i poteri e gli obblighi delle potenze occupanti' in Pietro Gargiulo & Maria Chiara Vitucci (eds.), *La tutela dei diritti umani nella lotta e nella guerra al terrorismo* (Editoriale Scientifica 2009) 295.
'Le violazioni del diritto umanitario commesse da Hamas durante l'operazione Piombo fuso' (2009) 3 *DUDI* 333.
La relazione tra risorse naturali e conflitti armati nel diritto internazionale (CEDAM 2012).
'Il principio di proporzionalità tra diritto umanitario e diritti umani' in Adriana Di Stefano & Rosario Sapienza (eds.), *La tutela dei diritti umani e il diritto internazionale* (Editoriale Scientifica 2012) 159.
'Fighting Terror within the Law? Terrorism, Counterterrorism and Military Occupations' in Fausto Pocar, Marco Pedrazzi, & Micaela Frulli (eds.), *War Crimes and the Conduct of Hostilities: Challenges to Adjudication and Investigation* (Edward Elgar 2013) 276.
Peters, Anne, 'The Crimean Vote of March 2014 as an Abuse of the Institution of the Territorial Referendum', in Christian Calliess (ed.), *Liber Amicorum für Torsten Stein zum 70. Geburtstag* (Nomos 2015) 278.
Picone, Paolo, 'La guerra contro l'Iraq e le degenerazioni dell'unilateralismo' (2003) 86 *RDI* 329.
'Le autorizzazioni all'uso della forza tra sistema delle Nazioni Unite e diritto internazionale generale' (2005) 88 *RDI* 5.
'The Distinction between *Jus Cogens* and Obligations *Erga Omnes*' in Enzo Cannizzaro (ed.), *The Law of Treaties beyond the Vienna Convention* (Oxford University Press 2011) 411.
Comunità internazionale e obblighi erga omnes (3rd edn, Jovene 2013).
'L'insostenibile leggerezza dell'art 51 della Carta dell'ONU' (2016) 99 *RDI* 7.

Pictet, Jean (ed.), *Commentary to IV Geneva Convention* (ICRC 1958).
  (ed.), *Commentary to III Geneva Convention* (ICRC 1960) 57.
  (ed.), *Humanitarian Law and the Protection of War Victims* (Sijthoff 1975).
Pillet, Antoine, *Les lois actuelles de guerre* (Rousseau 1898).
Pinzauti, Giulia, 'Aspetti problematici della legittimità del "muro" in Palestina: il caso *Beit Sourik*' (2005) 88 *RDI* 441.
Pisillo Mazzeschi, Riccardo, *'Due Diligence' e responsabilità internazionale degli Stati* (Giuffré 1989).
  'The Due Diligence Rule and the Nature of International Responsibility of States' (1992) 35 *German YIL* 9.
Pocar, Fausto, 'To What Extent Is Protocol I Customary International Law?' (2002) 78 *ILS* 337.
Poissonnier, Ghislain, 'La Palestine, État non-membre observateur de l'Organisation des Nations Unies' (2013) 140 *JDI* 427.
Pradier-Fodéré, Paul, *Traité de Droit International Public Européen* vol. VII (Pedone 1897).
Pronto, Arnold, 'The Effect of War on Law – What Happens to Their Treaties When States Go to War' (2013) 2 *Cambridge JICL* 227.
Prost, Mario, *The Concept of Unity in Public International Law* (Hart 2012).
Provost, René, *International Human Rights and Humanitarian Law* (Cambridge University Press 2002).
von Pufendorf, Samuel, *Two Books of the Elements of Universal Jurisprudence* (1660), English translation by William Abbott Oldfather, Thomas Behme (ed.) (Liberty Fund 2009) 393.
Quigley, John, 'The Relation between Human Rights Law and the Law of Belligerent Occupation: Does an Occupied Population Have a Right to Freedom of Assembly and Expression?' (1989) 12 *Boston College International and Comparative Law Review* 1.
  'Punitive Demolition of Houses: A Study in International Rights Protection' (1992–3) 5 *St Thomas Law Review* 359.
  'The PLO-Israeli Interim Agreements and the Geneva Civilians Convention' in Stephen Bowen (ed.), *Human Rights, Self-Determination and Political Change in the Palestinian Occupied Territories* (Kluwer Law 1997) 25.
  The Case for Palestine: An International Law Perspective (2nd edn, Duke University Press 2005).
  The Statehood of Palestine: International Law in the Middle East Conflict (Cambridge University Press 2010).
  The Six-Day War and Israeli Self-Defense: Questioning the Legal Basis for Preventive War (Cambridge University Press 2013).
Ragazzi, Maurizio, *The Concept of International Obligations Erga Omnes* (Oxford University Press 1997).
Randelzhofer, Albrecht & Nolte, Georg, 'Article 51' in Bruno Simma, Daniel-Erasmus Khan, Georg Nolte, & Andreas Paulus (eds.), *The Charter of the United Nations: A Commentary* (3rd edn, Oxford University Press 2012) 1397.
Ratner, Steven R., 'Foreign Occupation and International Territorial Administration: The Challenges of Convergence' (2005) 16 *EJIL* 695.

Reisman, W. Michael, 'The Resistance in Afghanistan is Engaged in a War of National Liberation' (1987) 81 *AJIL* 906.
Reisman, Michael W. & Silk, James, 'Which Law Applies to the Afghan Conflict?' (1988) 82 *AJIL* 459.
Rivier, Raphaële, 'Conséquences juridiques de l'édification d'un mur dans le territoire palestinien occupé, Cour internationale de Justice, avis consultatif du 9 juillet 2004' (2004) 50 *AFDI* 292.
Roberts, Adam, 'What Is a Military Occupation?' (1984) 55 *British YIL* 251.
  'Prolonged Military Occupation: The Israeli-Occupied Territories since 1967' (1990) 84 *AJIL* 44.
  'The End of Occupation: Iraq 2004' (2005) 54 *ICLQ* 27.
  'Transformative Military Occupation: Applying the Laws of War and Human Rights' (2006) 100 *AJIL* 580.
  'Occupation, Military, Termination of' in *MPEPIL Law online* (2009).
  'Resistance to Military Occupation: An Enduring Problem in International Law' (2017) 111 *AJIL Unbound* 45.
Rodley, Nigel, Shany, Yuval, & Ronen, Yaël (eds.), 'Special Issue on the Palestine Mandate' (2016) 49 *IsLR* 285.
Roger, Anthony, 'Combatant Status' in Elizabeth Wilmhurst & Susan Breau (eds.), *Perspectives on the ICRC Study on Customary International Humanitarian Law* (Cambridge University Press 2007) 101.
Rolin, Albéric, *Le droit moderne de la guerre* vol. I (Albert Dewit 1920).
Ronen, Yaël, 'Illegal Occupation and Its Consequences' (2008) 41 *IsLR* 201.
  'Recognition of the State of Palestine: Still Too Much Too Soon?' in Christine Chinkin & Freya Baetens (eds.), *Sovereignty, Statehood and State Responsibility: Essays in Honour of James Crawford* (Cambridge University Press 2015) 229.
Ronzitti, Natalino, *Le guerre di liberazione nazionale e il diritto internazionale* (Pacini Editore 1974).
  'Resort to Force in Wars of National Liberation' in Antonio Cassese (ed.), *Current Problems of International Law* (Giuffrè 1975) 319.
  'The 2006 Conflict in Lebanon and International Law' (2006) 16 *Italian YIL* 3.
  'The Expanding Law of Self-Defence' (2006) 11 *JCSL* 343.
  Il conflitto del Nagorno-Karabakh e il diritto internazionale (Giappichelli 2014).
  Diritto internazionale dei conflitti armati (Giappichelli 2017).
Roscini, Marco, *Cyber Operations and the Use of Force in International Law* (Oxford University Press 2014).
  'On the "Inherent" Character of the Right of States to Self-Defence' (2015) 4 *Cambridge JICL* 634.
Rousseau, Jean-Jacque, *Contrat social ou principes du droit publique* (2nd edn, Bureaux de la Publication 1865).
Ruiz Colomé, M. Angeles, *Guerras civiles y guerras coloniales* (Eurolex 1996).
Rusinova, Vera, 'The Duty to Investigate the Death of Persons Arrested and/or Detained by Public Authorities' in Christian Tomuschat, Evelyne Lagrange, & Stefan Oeter (eds.), *The Right to Life* (Brill 2010) 65.

Ruys, Tom, *'Armed Attack' and Article 51 of the UN Charter* (Cambridge University Press 2011).

Ryngaert, Cedric & Van de Meulebroucke, Anneleen, 'Enhancing and Enforcing Compliance with International Humanitarian Law by Non-State Armed Groups: An Inquiry into some Mechanisms' (2010) 16 *JCSL* 443.

Sadat-Akhavi, Seyed-Ali, *Methods of Resolving Conflicts between Treaties* (Brill 2003).

Salerno, Francesco, 'Il nemico "legittimo combattente" all'origine del diritto internazionale dei conflitti armati' (2009) 38 *Quaderni Fiorentini* 1417.

Diritto internazionale: Principi e norme (4th edn, Cedam 2017).

Salmon, Jean (ed.), *Dictionnaire de droit international public* (Bruylant 2001) 652.

'Les colonies de peuplement israéliennes en territoire palestinien occupé au regard de l'avis consultatif de la Cour internationale de Justice du 9 juillet 2004' in Andreas Fischer-Lescano, Hans-Peter Gasser, Thilo Marauhn, & Natalino Ronzitti. (eds.), *Frieden in Freiheit, Peace in liberty, Paix en liberté – Festschrift fur Michal Bothe zum 70. Geburtstag* (Nomos 2008) 285.

'La qualité d'Etat de la Palestine' (2012) 45 *RBDI* 13.

Salvadego, Laura, *Struttura e funzioni della necessità militare nel diritto internazionale* (Giappichelli 2012).

Samson, Elizabeth, 'Is Gaza Occupied? Redefining the Status of Gaza under International Law' (2010) 25 *American University ILR* 915.

Sandoz, Yves, Swinarski, Christophe, & Zimmermann, Bruno (eds.), *Commentary on the Additional Protocols of 8 June 1977 to the Geneva Conventions of 12 August 1949* (Martinus Nijhoff 1987).

Sassòli, Marco, 'Droit international pénal et droit pénal interne: le cas des territoires se trouvant sous administration internationale' in Marc Henzelin & Robert Roth (eds.), *Le droit pénal à l'épreuve de l'internationalisation* (Bruylant 2002) 119.

'Use and Abuse of the Laws of War in the "War on Terrorism"' (2004) 22 *Law and Inequality* 195.

'Legislation and Maintenance of Public Order and Civil Life by Occupying Powers' (2005) 16 *EJIL* 661.

'Terrorism and War' (2006) 4 *JICJ* 959.

'*Ius ad Bellum* and *Ius in Bello* – The Separation between the Legality of the Use of Force and Humanitarian Rules to Be Respected in Warfare: Crucial or Outdated?' in Michael N. Schmitt & Jelena Pejic (eds.), *International Law and Armed Conflict: Exploring the Faultlines* (Martinus Nijhoff 2007) 241.

'The Role of Human Rights and International Humanitarian Law in New Types of Armed Conflicts' in Orna Ben-Naftali (ed.), *International Humanitarian Law and International Human Rights Law: Pas de Deux* (Oxford University Press 2011) 34.

'A Plea in Defence of Pictet and the Inhabitants of Territories under Invasion: The Case for the Applicability of the Fourth Geneva Convention during the Invasion Phase' (2012) 94 *IRRC* 42.

'Concept and the Beginning of Occupation' in Andrew Clapham, Paola Gaeta, & Marco Sassòli (eds.), *The 1949 Geneva Conventions: A Commentary* (Oxford University Press 2015) 1390.

'The International Legal Framework for Stability Operations: When May International Forces Attack or Detain Someone in Afghanistan?' (2009) 85 *ILS* 431.

Sassòli, Marco & Olson, Laura M., 'The Relationship between International Humanitarian and Human Rights Law Where It Matters: Admissible Killing and Internment of Fighters in Non-International Armed Conflicts' (2008) 90 *IRRC* 599.

Saul, Ben, *Defining Terrorism in International Law* (Oxford University Press 2008).

'The Status of Western Sahara as Occupied Territory under International Humanitarian Law and the Exploitation of Natural Resources' (2015) 27 *Global Change* 301.

'Many Small Wars: The Classification of Armed Conflicts in the Non-Self-Governing Territory of Western Sahara (Spanish Sahara) in 1974–1976' (2016) 2 *African YIHL* 86.

Saul, Matthew, 'The Impact of the Legal Right to Self-Determination on the Law of Occupation as a Framework for Post-Conflict State Reconstruction' in Noëlle Quénivet & Shilan Shah-Davis (eds.), *International Law and Armed Conflict* (TMC Asser 2010) 398.

Sayed, Hani, 'The Fictions of the Illegal Occupation in the West Bank and Gaza' (2014) 16 *Oregon Review of International Law* 79.

Scelles, Georges, 'Observations' (1957-I) 47 *Annuaire de l'IDI* 578.

Schabas, William A., '*Lex Specialis*? Belt and Suspenders? The Parallel Operation of Human Rights Law and the Law of Armed Conflict, and the Conundrum of *Jus ad Bellum*' (2007) 40 *IsLR* 592.

'The Right to Life' in Andrew Clapham & Paola Gaeta (eds.), *The Oxford Handbook of International Law in Armed Conflict* (Oxford University Press 2014) 365.

The European Convention on Human Rights: A Commentary (Oxford University Press 2015).

Schaeffer Omer-Man, Emily, 'Extrajudicial Killing with Near Impunity: Excessive Force in Israeli Law Enforcement against Palestinians' (2017) 35 *Boston University ILJ* 116.

Scharf, Michael P., *Customary International Law in Times of Fundamental Change: Recognizing Grotian Moments* (Cambridge University Press 2013).

Schindler, Dietrict & Toman, Jiri (eds.), *The Laws of Armed Conflicts* (Martinus Nijhoff 1988).

Schmitt, Carl, *Der Nomos der Erde im Völkerrecht des Jus Publicum Europaeum* (Duncker & Humblot 1950), English translation by G. L. Ulmen, *The Nomos of the Earth* (Telos Press 2006).

Theorie des Partisanen, Zwischenbemerkung zum Begriff des Politischen (Duncker & Humblot 1963).

Schmitt, Michael N., 'Responding to Transnational Terrorism under the *Jus ad Bellum*: A Normative Framework' in Michael N. Schmitt & Jelena Pejic (eds.), *International Law and Armed Conflict: Exploring the Faultlines* (Martinus Nijhoff 2007) 157.

'Debellatio' in *MPEPIL* (2009).

'Investigating Violations of International Law in Armed Conflict' (2011) 2 *Harvard National Security Journal* 31.

'Iraq (2003 onwards)' in Elizabeth Wilmshurst (ed.), *International Law and the Classification of Conflicts* (Oxford University Press 2012) 356.

'The Status of Opposition Fighters in a Non-International Armed Conflict' (2012) 88 *ILS* 119.

(ed.), *Tallinn Manual 2.0 on the International Law Applicable to Cyber Operations* (Cambridge University Press 2017).

Schmitt, Michael N., Dinstein, Yoram, & Garraway, Charles (eds.), *The Manual on the Law of Non-International Armed Conflict with Commentary* (International Institute of Humanitarian Law 2006).

Schmitt, Michael N. & Garraway, Charles H. B., 'Occupation Policy in Iraq and International Law' (2004) 9 *International Peacekeeping: The Yearbook of International Peace Operations* 27.

Schöberl, Katja, 'The Geographical Scope of Application of the Conventions' in Andrew Clapham, Paola Gaeta, & Marco Sassòli (eds.), *The 1949 Geneva Conventions: A Commentary* (Oxford University Press 2015) 67.

Schrijver, Nico J., *Sovereignty over Natural Resources: Balancing Rights and Duties* (Cambridge University Press 1997).

'Article 2, Paragraphe 4' in Jean-Pierre Cot, Alain Pellet, & Mathias Forteau (eds.), *La Charte des Nations Unies: commentaire article par article* vol. II (3rd edn, Economica 2005) 437.

'The Ban on the Use of Force in the UN Charter' in Mark Weller (ed.), *The Oxford Handbook of the Use of Force in International Law* (Oxford University Press 2015) 465.

Schwarzenberger, Georg, *International Law as Applied by International Courts and Tribunals* vol. II (Stevens & Sons 1968).

Schwenk, Edmund H., 'Legislative Power of the Military Occupant under Article 43, Hague Regulations' (1945) 54 *Yale Law Journal* 393.

Scobbie, Iain, 'Natural Resources and Belligerent Occupation: Mutation Through Permanent Sovereignty' in Stephen Bowen (ed.), *Human Rights, Self-Determination and Political Change in the Palestinian Occupied Territories* (Kluwer Law 1997) 221.

'An Intimate Disengagement: Israel's Withdrawal from Gaza, the Law of Occupation and of Self-Determination' (2004–5) 11 *Yearbook of Islamic and Middle Eastern Law* 3.

'Words My Mother Never Taught Me: "In Defense of the International Court"' (2005) 99 *AJIL* 76.

'Principle or Pragmatics? The Relationship between Human Rights Law and the Law of Armed Conflict' (2010) 14 *JCSL* 449.

'Gaza', in Elizabeth Wilmshurst (ed.), *International Law and the Classification of Conflicts* (Oxford University Press 2012) 280.

'International Law and the Prolonged Occupation of Palestine', 22 May 2015, available at papers.ssrn.com/sol3/papers.cfm?abstract_id=2611130

'Prolonged Occupation and Article 6(3) of the Fourth Geneva Convention: Why the International Court Got It Wrong Substantively and Procedurally', *EJIL: Talk!*, 16 June 2015.

Seatsu, Francesco, 'On the Interpretation of Derogation Provisions in Regional Human Rights Treaties in Light of Non-Binding Sources of International Humanitarian Law' (2011) 4 *Inter-American and European Human Rights Journal* 3.

Sereni, Angelo Piero, *Diritto internazionale, vol. IV: Conflitti internazionali* (Giuffrè 1965).

Seršić, Maja, 'Due Diligence: Fault-based Responsibility or Autonomous Standard?' in Rüdiger Wolfrum, Maja Seršić, & Trpimir M Šošić (eds.), *Contemporary Developments in International Law: Essays in Honour of Budislav Vukas* (Brill 2016) 151.

Shamgar, Meir, 'The Observance of International Law in the Administered Territories' (1971) 1 *IYHR* 262.

'Legal Concepts and Problems of the Israeli Military Government: The Initial Stage' in Meir Shamgar (ed.), *Military Government in the Territories Administrated by Israel 1967–1980* (Hebrew University of Jerusalem Press 1982) 13.
Shany, Yuval, 'Faraway, So Close: The Legal Status of Gaza after Israel's Disengagement' (2005) 8 *YIHL* 369.
Shehadeh, Raja, *From Occupation to Interim Accords: Israel and the Palestinian Territories* (Kluwer Law 1997).
Sherman, Matt & Paul, Josh, 'The Role of Police in Counterinsurgency Operations in Iraq, 2003–2006' in C. Christine Fair & Sumit Ganguly (eds.), *Policing Insurgencies: Cops as Counterinsurgents* (2014) 227.
Shlaim, Avi, *Israel and Palestine: Reappraisals, Revisions, Refutations* (Verso 2009).
Shy, John & Collier, Thomas W., 'Revolutionary War' in Peter Paret (ed.), *Makers of Modern Strategy from Machiavelli to the Nuclear Age* (Princeton University Press 1986) 833.
Sicilianos, Linos-Alexandre, *Les réactions décentralisées à l'illicite* (LGDJ 1990).
  'Entre multilatéralisme et unilatéralisme: l'autorisation par le Conseil de sécurité de recourir à la force' (2009) 339 *RCADI* 9.
  'The Classification of Obligations and the Multilateral Dimension of the Relations of International Responsibility' (2002) 13 *EJIL* 1127.
  'L'articulation enter droit international humanitaire et droits de l'homme dans la jurisprudence de la Cour européenne des droits de l'homme' (2017) 27 *RSDIE* 3.
Simma, Bruno, 'From Bilateralism to Community Interest in International Law' (1994) 250 *RCADI* 217.
Simma, Bruno & Alston, Philip, 'The Sources of Human Rights Law: Custom, Jus Cogens, and General Principles' (1988–9) 12 *Australian YIL* 82.
Simma, Bruno & Tams, Christian J., 'Article 60 – Convention de 1969' in Olivier Corten & Pierre Klein (eds.), *Les Conventions de Vienne sur le droit des traités: Commentaire article par article* (Bruyilant 2006) 2131.
Simpson, Gerry, 'International Law in Diplomatic History' in James Crawford & Martti Koskenniemi (eds.), *The Cambridge Companion to International Law* (Cambridge University Press 2012) 25.
Singer, Joel, 'The Establishment of a Civil Administration in the Areas Administered by Israel' (1982) 12 *IYHR* 259.
Sitaraman, Ganesh, *The Counterinsurgent's Constitution: Law in the Age of Small Wars* (Oxford University Press 2013).
Sivakumaran, Sandesh, 'Binding Armed Opposition Groups' (2006) 55 *ICLQ* 369.
  'Re-envisaging the International Law of Internal Armed Conflict' (2011) 22 *EJIL* 219.
  The Law of Non-International Armed Conflict (Oxford University Press 2012).
  'The Influence of Teachings of Publicists on the Development of International Law' (2017) 66 *ICLQ* 1.
Sloane, Robert D., 'The Cost of Conflation: Preserving the Dualism of *Jus ad Bellum* and *Jus in Bello* in the Contemporary Law of War' (2009) 34 *Yale JIL* 48.
Slonim, Solomon, *South West Africa and the United Nations: An International Mandate in Dispute* (The John Hopkins University Press 1973).
Solis, Gary D., 'Law of War Issues in Ground Hostilities in Afghanistan' (2009) 85 *ILS* 219.

Solomon, Solon, 'The Great Oxymoron: *Jus In Bello* Violations as Legitimate Non-Forcible Measures of Self-Defense: The Post-Disengagement Israeli Measures towards Gaza as a Case Study' (2010) 9 *CJIL* 501.
  'Occupied or Not: The Question of Gaza's Legal Status after the Israeli Disengagement' (2011) 19 *Cardozo JICL* 59.
Spaight, G. M., *War Rights on Land* (MacMillan & Co 1911).
Spoerri, Philip, 'The Law of Occupation' in Andrew Clapham & Paola Gaeta (eds.), *The Oxford Handbook of International Law in Armed Conflict* (Oxford University Press 2014) 182.
Stahn, Carsten, 'Terrorist Acts as "Armed Attack": The Right to Self-Defense, Article 51 (1/2) of the UN Charter, and International Terrorism' (Summer/Fall 2003) 27 *The Fletcher Forum of World Affairs* 35.
  '"Jus ad Bellum", "Jus in Bello" ... "Jus post Bellum"? – Rethinking the Conception of the Law of Armed Force' (2006) 17 *EJIL* 921.
  The Law and Practice of International Territorial Administration: Versailles to Iraq and Beyond (Cambridge University Press 2008).
Starita, Massimo, 'L'occupation de l'Iraq, le Conseil de Sécurité, le droit de la guerre et le droit des peuples à disposer d'eux-mêmes' (2004) 108 *RGDIP* 883.
Stephanopoulos, Nicholas, 'Israel's Legal Obligations to Gaza After the Pullout' (2006) 31 *Yale JIL* 524.
Stewart, James G., 'Towards a Single Definition of Armed Conflict in International Humanitarian Law: A Critique of Internationalized Armed Conflict' (2003) 85 *IRRC* 313.
Stirk, Peter M. R., 'The Concept of Military Occupation in the Era of the French Revolutionary and Napoleonic Wars' (2015) 3 *Comparative Legal History* 60.
Stone, Julius, *Legal Controls of International Conflict* (Rinehart and Co. 1954).
Summers, James, *Peoples and International Law* (2nd edn, Brill 2013).
Talmon, Stefan, 'Diplomacy under Occupation: The Status of Diplomatic Missions in Occupied Iraq' (2006) 6 *Anuario Mexicano de Derecho Internacional* 461.
  'The Duty Not to "Recognize as Lawful" a Situation Created by the Illegal Use of Force or Other Serious Breaches of a *Jus Cogens* Obligation: An Obligation without Real Substance?' in Christian Tomuschat & Jean-Marc Thouvenin (eds.), *The Fundamental Rules of the International Legal Order: Jus Cogens and Obligations Erga Omnes Obligations* (Martinus Nijhoff 2006) 99.
  'A Plurality of Responsible Actors: International Responsibility for Acts of the Provisional Coalition Authority in Iraq' in Phil Shiner & Andrew Williams (eds.), *The Iraq War and International Law* (Hart 2008) 185.
  (ed.), *The Occupation of Iraq, vol. II: The Official Documents of the Coalition Provisional Authority and the Iraqi Governing Council* (Hart 2013).
Tams, Christian J., *Enforcing Obligations Erga Omnes in International Law* (Cambridge University Press 2005).
  'Light Treatment of a Complex Problem: The Law of Self-Defence in the *Wall* Case' (2005) 16 *EJIL* 963.
  'The Use of Force against Terrorists' (2009) 20 *EJIL* 359.
Tancredi, Antonello, 'Autodeterminazione dei popoli' in Sabino Cassese (ed.), *Dizionario di diritto pubblico* (Giuffrè 2006) 568.

'Il problema della legittima difesa nei confronti di milizie non statali alla luce dell'ultima crisi tra Israele e Libano' (2007) 90 *RDI* 909.

'Neither Authorized nor Prohibited? Secession and International Law after Kosovo, South Ossetia and Abkhazia' (2008) 18 *Italian YIL* 37.

'Crisi in Crimea, referendum ed autodeterminazione dei popoli' (2014) 8 *DUDI* 480.

'The Russian Annexation of the Crimea: Questions Relating to the Use of Force' (2014) 1 *Zoom In – Questions of International Law* 10.

'Le droit a l'autodétermination du peuple Palestinien' in Thierry Garcia (ed.), *La Palestine: d'un etat non membre de l'organisation des Nations Unies a un etat souverain?* (Pedone 2015) 33.

Tanzi, Attila, 'Riflessioni introduttive per un dibattito sull'uso della forza armata e la legittima difesa nel diritto internazionale contemporaneo' in Alessandra Lanciotti & Attila Tanzi (eds.), *Uso della forza e legittima difesa nel diritto internazionale contemporaneo* (Jovene 2012) 1.

Tesón, Fernando R. (ed.), *The Theory of Self-Determination* (Cambridge University Press 2016).

Theodoropoulos, Christos, 'Support for SWAPO's War of Liberation in International Law' (1979) 26 *Africa Today* 39.

Thirlway, Hugh, 'Human Rights in Customary Law: An Attempt to Define Some of the Issues' (2015) 28 *LJIL* 495.

Thouvenin, Jean-Marc, 'Article 103' in Jean-Pierre Cot, Alain Pellet, & Mathias Forteau (eds.), *La Charte des Nations Unies: commentaire article par article* vol. II (3rd edn, Economica 2005) 2133.

Tignino, Mara, *L'eau et la guerre: éléments pour un régime juridique* (Bruylant 2011).

Todeschini, Vito, 'The ICCPR in Armed Conflict: An Appraisal of the Human Rights Committee's Engagement with International Humanitarian Law' (2017) 35 *Nordic Journal of Human Rights* 203.

Tomuschat, Christian (ed.), *Modern Law of Self-Determination* (Martinus Nijhoff 1993).

'Prohibition of Settlements' in Andrew Clapham, Paola Gaeta, & Marco Sassòli (eds.), *The 1949 Geneva Conventions: A Commentary* (Oxford University Press 2015) 1551.

Tomuschat, Christian & Thouvenin, Jean-Marc (eds.), *The Fundamental Rules of the International Legal Order: Jus Cogens and Obligations Erga Omnes* (Brill 2006).

Trapp, Kimberley N., 'Back to the Basics: Necessity, Proportionality, and the Right of Self-Defence against Non-State Terrorist Actors' (2007) 56 *ICLQ* 141.

State Responsibility for International Terrorism (Oxford University Press 2011).

'Can Non-State Actors Mount an Armed Attack?' in Mark Weller (ed.), *The Oxford Handbook of the Use of Force in International Law* (Oxford University Press 2015) 679.

Treves, Tullio, *Diritto internazionale: problemi fondamentali* (Giuffrè 2005).

'Fragmentation of International Law: The Judicial Perspective' (2007) 23 *CS* 821.

'The Security Council as Legislator' in Aristotle Constantinides & Nikos Zaikos (eds.), *The Diversity of International Law: Essays in Honour of Professor Kalliopi K Koufa* (Brill 2009) 61.

Trigeaud, Laurent, 'L'opération Bordure protectrice menée par Israël dans la Bande de Gaza (8 juillet – 26 août 2014)' (2014) *AFDI* 171.

'L'influence des reconnaissances d'Etat sur la formation des engagements conventionnels' (2015) 119 *RGDIP* 571.

Tsagourias, Nicholas, 'Self-Defence against Non-State Actors: The Interaction between Self-Defence as a Primary Rule and Self-Defence as a Secondary Rule' (2016) 29 *LJIL* 801.

Turns, David, 'The Law of Armed Conflict (International Humanitarian Law)' in Malcolm D. Evans (ed.), *International Law* (4th edn, Oxford University Press 2014) 821.

——— 'Jus ad Pacem in Bello? Afghanistan, Stability Operations and the International Laws Relating to Armed Conflict' (2009) 85 *ILS* 387.

Tzanakopoulos, Antonios, *Disobeying the Security Council: Countermeasures against Wrongful Sanctions* (Oxford University Press 2011).

Udina, Manlio, 'Lo smembramento della Jugoslavia' (1941) 5 *Diritto internazionale* 3.

Ulfstein, Geir, 'More Focus on *Jus ad Bellum* in Gaza', *Just Security*, 12 August 2014.

Valles Cavia, Antonio, 'El concepto de acto terrorista y el comportamiento de fuerzas armadas durante un conflicto armado' (2017) 57 *Revista de Derecho Comunitario Europeo* 689.

Van Steenberghe, Raphaël, 'Self-Defence in Response to Attacks by Non-State Actors in the Light of Recent State Practice: A Step Forward?' (2010) 23 *LJIL* 183.

Venturini, Gabriella, *Necessità e proporzionalità nell'uso della forza militare in diritto internazionale* (Giuffrè 1988).

——— 'L'operazione militare di Israele contro Gaza e il diritto internazionale umanitario' (2009) 3 *DUDI* 309.

——— 'Necessity in the Law of Armed Conflict and in International Criminal Law' (2010) 41 *Netherlands YIL* 45.

Verri, Pietro, *Dictionary of the International Law of Armed Conflict* (ICRC 1992).

Viarengo, Ilaria, 'Deroghe e restrizioni alla tutela dei diritti umani nei sistemi internazionali di garanzia' (2005) 88 *RDI* 955.

Vidmar, Jure, 'Palestine and the Conceptual Problem of Implicit Statehood' (2013) 12 *CJIL* 19.

——— 'The Annexation of Crimea and the Boundaries of the Will of the People' (2015) 16 *German Law Journal* 365.

Vierucci, Luisa, 'Prisoners of War or Protected Persons *qua* Unlawful Combatants? The Judicial Safeguards to Which Guantanamo Bay Detainees Are Entitled' (2003) 1 *JICJ* 284.

——— 'Sul principio di proporzionalità a Gaza, ovvero quando il fine non giustifica i mezzi' (2009) 3 *DUDI* 319.

Villalpando, Santiago, *L'émergence de la communauté internationale dans la responsabilité des États* (PUF 2005).

Villani, Ugo, 'Lo status di Gerusalemme nel diritto internazionale' (1999) 54 *CI* 217.

——— *L'ONU e la crisi del Golfo* (3rd edn, Cacucci 2005).

Villiger, Mark E., *Commentary on the Vienna Convention on the Law of Treaties* (Martinus Nijhoff 2009).

Vité, Sylvain, 'L'applicabilité du droit international de l'occupation militaire aux activités des organisations internationales' (2004) 86 *IRRC* 9.

——— 'Typology of Armed Conflicts in International Humanitarian Law: Legal Concepts and Actual Situations' (2009) 91 *IRRC* 69.

Vitucci, Maria Chiara, *Sovranità e amministrazioni territoriali* (Editoriale Scientifica 2012).

Vranes, Erich, 'The Definition of "Norm Conflict" in International Law and Legal Theory' (2006) 17 *EJIL* 395.
Waibel, Michael, 'Falkland Islands/Islas Malvinas' in *MPEPIL online* (2011).
Walker, Georg K., 'The Crisis over Kuwait, August 1990 – February 1991' (1991) 1 *Duke Journal of Comparative and International Law* 25.
Walker, Phillip James, 'Iraq and Occupation' in David H. Wippman & Michael Evangelista (eds.), *New Wars, New Laws? Applying Laws of War in 21st Century Conflicts* (Martinus Nijhoff 2005) 259.
Watkin, Kenneth, 'Maintaining Law and Order during Occupation: Breaking the Normative Chains' (2008) 41 *IsLR* 175.
  'Use of Force during Occupation: Law Enforcement and Conduct of Hostilities' (2012) 94 *IRRC* 267.
  Fighting at the Legal Boundaries: Controlling the Use of Force in Contemporary Conflict (Oxford University Press 2016).
Watson, Geoffrey R., *The Oslo Accords: International Law and the Israeli-Palestinian Agreements* (Oxford University Press 2000).
Watts, Arthur, 'Israeli Wall Advisory Opinion (Legal Consequences of the Construction of a Wall in the Occupied Palestinian Territory)' in *MPEPIL online* (2007).
Watts, Sean, 'Who Is a Prisoner of War?' in Andrew Clapham, Paola Gaeta, & Marco Sassòli (eds.), *The 1949 Geneva Conventions: A Commentary* (Oxford University Press 2015) 879.
Wedgwood, Ruth, 'Responding to Terrorism: The Strikes against Bin Laden' (1999) 24 *Yale JIL* 568.
  'The ICJ Advisory Opinion on the Israeli Security Fence and the Limits of Self-Defense' (2005) 99 *AJIL* 52.
Weill, Sharon, 'The Judicial Arm of the Occupation: The Israeli Military Courts in the Occupied Territories' (2007) 89 *IRRC* 395.
Weill, Sharon & Azarova, Valentina, 'The 2014 Gaza War: Reflections on *Jus Ad Bellum*, *Jus in Bello*, and Accountability' in Annyssa Bellal (ed.), *The War Report: Armed Conflict in 2014* (Oxford University Press 2015) 360.
Weissbrodt, David & Bergquist, Amy, 'Extraordinary Rendition and the Humanitarian Law of War and Occupation' (2007) 47 *Virginia JIL* 295.
Weller, Marc, *Iraq and the Use of Force in International Law* (Oxford University Press 2010).
Wheatom, Henry, *Elements of International Law* (3rd edn, Lea & Blanchard 1846).
Wilde, Ralph, *International Territorial Administration* (Oxford University Press 2008).
  'Complementing Occupation Law: Selective Judicial Treatment of the Suitability of Human Rights Norms' (2009) 42 *IsLR* 80.
Wilson, Heather A., *International Law and the Use of Force by National Liberation Movements* (Clarendon Press 1988).
Wolfrum, Rüdiger, 'International Administration in Post-Conflict Situations by the United Nations and Other International Actors' (2005) 9 *MPYUNL* 649.
Zachary, Shlomy, 'Between the Geneva Conventions: Where Does the Unlawful Combatant Belong?' (2005) 38 *IsLR* 378.
Zambrano, Valentina, *Il principio di sovranità permanente dei popoli sulle risorse naturali tra vecchie e nuove violazioni* (Giuffrè 2009).

Zamir, Noam, *Classification of Conflicts in International Humanitarian Law* (Edward Elgar 2017).

Zappalà, Salvatore, 'Can Legality Trump Effectiveness in Today's International Law?' in Antonio Cassese (ed.), *Realizing Utopia: The Future of International Law* (Oxford University Press 2012) 105.

Zegveld, Liesbeth, *Accountability of Armed Opposition Groups in International Law* (Cambridge University Press 2002).

Ziccardi, Pietro, 'Occupazione bellica ed amministrazione della giustizia' (1948) *Temi* 488.

Ziccardi Capaldo, Giuliana, *Le situazioni territoriali illegittime nel diritto internazionale* (Editoriale Scientifica 1977).

Ziegler, Andreas & Boie, Bertram, 'The Relationship between International Trade Law and International Human Rights Law' in Erika De Wet & Jure Vidmar (eds.), *Hierarchy in International Law: The Place of Human Rights* (Oxford University Press 2012) 272.

Zimmermann, Andreas, 'Responsibility for Violations of International Humanitarian Law, International Criminal Law and Human Rights Law – Synergy and Conflict?' in Wolff Heintschel von Heinegg & Volker Epping (eds.), *International Humanitarian Law Facing New Challenges* (Springer 2007) 215.

'The Second Lebanon War: *Jus ad Bellum, Jus in Bello* and the Issue of Proportionality' (2007) 11 *MPYUNL* 99.

'Abiding by and Enforcing International Humanitarian Law in Asymmetric Warfare: The Case of Operation Cast Lead' (2011) 31 *Polish YIL* 47.

Zimmermann, Andreas & Geiß, Robin, 'Article 8 para. 2 (c)–(f) and para. 3: War Crimes Committed in an Armed Conflict Not of an International Character' in Otto Triffterer & Kai Ambos (eds.), *The Rome Statute of the International Criminal Court: A Commentary* (3rd edn, CH Beck-Hart-Nomos 2016) 528.

Zwanenburg, Marten, 'Challenging the Pictet Theory' (2012) 94 *IRRC* 30.

Index

Abkhazia, 18, 90
ACHPR, 67, 80, 150, 152, 242
administrative detention, 183, 184
Afghanistan
    Enduring Freedom, operation, 15, 104
    Soviet occupation, 13–14, 151, 167
    US occupation, 15–17, 41, 91
aggression, crime of, 2, 119
aggression, definition of, 2, 119, 154
American Civil War, 23, 34, 142
AP I
    ban on annexation, 48
    customary status, 43, 146, 254
    relationship with GC IV, 51, 146, 258–59
    relationship with international human rights law, 64, 72
    self-determination of peoples, principle of, 34, 153, 219–21
AP II, 72, 194, 215, 222, 227, 234

Basic Principles on the Use of Force and Firearms by Law Enforcement Officials, 242, 247
belligerency, recognition of, 34
Ben-Naftali, Orna & Michaeli, Keren, 258–59
blockade, 197
Brussels Declaration, 23, 143, 169

Cassese, Antonio, 223–24
civilians
    direct participation in hostilities, 194, 195, 231, 250, 255, 258
    immunity from attacks, 254
    protection in occupied territory, 21, 27, 52, 64, 72, 84, 254–56, 254–56
    protection in occupied territory, 26
    protection in occupied territory, 259
Code of Conduct for Law Enforcement Officials, 185, 242, 247
collective punishment, 6, 176, 177, 182, 184
combatants
    definition, 146, 209, 255, 258
    levée en masse, 250
    resistance forces, 143, 145, 148, 259
conduct of hostilities
    classification, 205–29
    definition of hostilities, 194–96
    demonstrations, 267–68
    hostilities in occupied territory, 197–204
    interplay with law enforcement, 229–38
    interplay with law of occupation, 258–61
    legal paradigm, 253–58
    right to life in occupied territory and, 261–68
Congress of Vienna (1815), 22
CPA
    de-Ba'athification measures, 59, 173
    protection of diplomatic facilities, 174
    restoration of security and stability, 171
    self-defence, 91
    use of armed force by, 3, 198
Crimea, 18–19, 56, 120, 247
cultural property, protection of, 43

De Vattel, Emer, 26
death penalty, 82, 139, 181
debellatio, 23, 25, 83
diplomatic protection, 26
distinction, principle of, 26, 254, 262
DRC, occupation of, 15, 66, 192, 198, 202, 224
due diligence, 106, 172, 192

East Timor, 12, 85, 121, 151, 190
ECHR
   applicability in armed conflict and occupation, 67, 247, 263–64
   demonstrations, 250
   derogation clauses, 82
   extraterritorial application, 67–69
   interplay with international humanitarian law, 71–72, 78–79, 184, 247, 263–64
   right to life, 244, 247, 263–66
EECC, 15
effectiveness, principle of, 124
enlistment, prohibition of, 178
equality of belligerents, principle of, 29, 157
erga omnes, obligations
   definition, 84
   law of occupation as, 86, 140
   principle of self-determination of peoples as, 50
   prohibition of aggression as, 50
erga omnes partes, obligations
   definition, 84
   law of occupation as, 86, 140
espionage, 86, 147, 149, 200

fair trial in occupied territory, 181, 182, 183
Fatah, 229
Fiore, Pasquale, 138
forcible transfers and deportations, prohibition of, 177, 184
franc tireurs, 142
Franco-Prussian War (1970-1971), 142–43
freedom of expression, 77
French Revolution, 20, 22

GC III, 145, 146, 147, 200, 209, 210
GC IV
   alteration of the law in force, 58, 170, 181
   continuity of criminal law system, 178, 187–88
   continuity of public officials, 187–88
   customary status, 43
   invasion and, 38–39
   protection of individuals, 27
   relationship with AP I, 51, 146, 258–59
   relationship with HR, 59, 187
   special agreements, 45, 46, 72, 84, 148
Georgia, 17–18, 67, 90, 120
Germany (post-WWII occupation of), 59
Germany (WWII occupation by), 177
Golan Heights, 153

Halleck, HW, 138
Hamas, 94, 97, 98, 114, 229
Hezbollah, 104, 113, 114
hostages, taking of, 6, 161, 177, 178, 184
house demolition, 182
HR
   as balancing of different legal interests, 84
   customary status, 43
human shields, 263
humanity, principle of, 27, 64, 254

ICCPR
   applicability in armed conflict and occupation, 67, 82, 150
   extraterritorial application, 68
   interplay with international humanitarian law, 81, 184, 263
   right to life, 78, 82, 242, 247, 252, 253, 263, 269
   self-determination of peoples, principle of, 149, 150
ICESCR
   applicability in armed conflict and occupation, 69, 150
   extraterritorial application, 69
   self-determination of peoples, principle of, 149, 150
ICJ
   applicability of international human rights law in armed conflict, 66–67
   self-defence within occupied territory, 99–101

Index

ILC
  DARS, 49, 105, 108, 157, 212–14
  fragmentation of international law, 62
  international armed conflict
    as requirement for belligerent occupation, 21, 30, 33, 54, 142, 206
    coexistence with non-international armed conflict, 192, 198, 225
    definition, 206, 212
  international armed conflict, law on
    applicability to hostilities within occupied territory, 206–14, 229
    applicability to wars of national liberation, 153
    differences with the law on non-international armed conflict, 205
  international human rights law
    applicability in occupied territory, 45, 62–82, 182, 183
    conduct of hostilities in occupied territory and, 261–68
    convergence with international humanitarian law, 64, 257
    customary status of, 69–71
    derogation clauses, 45, 65, 72, 73, 82, 264, 265
    differences with international humanitarian law, 64–65, 254, 263
    extraterritorial application, 69, 70, 261, 264
    interplay with law of occupation, 71–80
    jurisdiction, definition of, 67–69
    maintenance of public order in occupied territory and, 59, 182, 183, 186, 246–53
    use of armed force in law enforcement and, 246–53
  international humanitarian law
    applicability to UN peacekeeping forces, 31
    permissive versus prohibitive character of, 86–87, 148
Iraq
  insurgency, 167, 168, 173
  Iraqi Freedom operation, 2
  maintenance of public order, 167, 168, 171, 173, 178, 189, 190, 191
  occupation of, 17
  rules of engagement, 249

  SC's impact on the law of occupation, 41, 46–47
  self-defence in occupied territory, 91
  termination of occupation, 41
  terrorism, 180
Israel
  civilian settlements in occupied territory, 57
  rules of engagement, 250–53
  self-defence, 91–99, 104, 113
  Six-Day War, 2, 10, 131
  Supreme Court of, 8, 11, 36, 52, 55, 56, 57, 84, 92, 94, 100, 132, 146, 172, 175, 180, 183, 184, 194, 202, 223, 255, 260, 266, 267
  wall, 51, 93, 99, 101

jus cogens
  law of occupation as, 47
  principle of self-determination of peoples as, 50, 157, 158
  prohibition of aggression as, 50
  SC and, 47

Kolb, Robert & Vité, Silvayn, 185
Kuwait, 6, 14, 119, 126, 129, 204

law enforcement
  applicability in occupied territory, 186–87, 188–92, 246–53
  definition, 185
  function of, 184–86
  interplay with conduct of hostilities, 229–38
  legal paradigm, 186, 242–46
  presumption of applicability, 187–88, 192–93
  right to life, 242–46, 246–53
legality of occupation
  illegal occupation, 151, 158
  interplay between *jus in bello* and *jus ad bellum*, 29
  principle of self-determination of peoples, 151
lex specialis principle, 46, 72–77, 114–16, 193, 226, 258, 260, 261

Lieber Code
  background, 142, 147
  codification of the law of occupation, 23
  illegality of armed resistance, 142, 144

mandate, 10, 178, 191
Martens Clause, 144, 224
Mavi Marmara, 224
Melzer, Nils & Gaggioli, Gloria, 185, 195
military necessity, 254, 265

Nagorno-Karabakh, 14–15
Namibia (South West Africa), 10, 123, 150, 155, 174, 180, 191, 204, 219, 220, 230
natural resources management, 44, 50, 60
non-international armed conflict
  definition, 215–16, 223
  threshold, 215
non-international armed conflict, law on
  applicability to hostilities within occupied territory, 214–18
  jus puniendi, 226–28
normative conflicts, 46, 71–76, 76, 77, 115–16, 263
Northern Cyprus, Turkish occupation of, 12, 122, 233

obedience, duty of
  contractual-like relationship, 138, 139–40
  duty of allegiance, 139, 140
  duty to *pati*, 139
  lack of, 137–41
obligations of conduct, 173, 192
occupatio pacifica, 30
occupation, law of
  administration of occupied territory, 53–62, 169–76
  annexation, prohibition of, 48–50
  codification, 23
  conservationist principle, 57–62, 179, 187–88, 191–92
  customary status, 43
  evolution, 21–28
  jus cogens status, 47
  sources, 43–44
  temporal scope, 51–52
  temporariness, 50–51, 52
occupation, situation of
  'actual authority', 35, 39, 203
  'effective control', 35
  boots on the ground, 36–38
  commencement, 29
  definition, 29
  factual character, 29, 34, 35, 39, 42, 203
  insurgents as Occupying Powers, 33–34
  international organisations as Occupying Powers, 30–33
  invasion, difference with, 38–39
  sporadic armed resistance, 36, 198–204
  termination, 39–41, 203
  terminological issues, 42–43
OPT
  Cast Lead, operation, 3, 8, 94, 168, 197, 252
  conduct of hostilities, 266–67
  Defensive Wall, operation, 91
  East Jerusalem, 10
  First Intifada, 6, 168, 251
  Gaza Strip, 3, 10, 11, 37, 39, 95, 114, 132, 190, 197, 200, 233
  Israeli-PLO agreements, 46, 70, 190
  law enforcement, 247, 248, 250–53
  occupied status, 10–12, 52, 56, 85, 109, 112, 220
  Pillar of Clouds, operation, 3, 8, 197
  Protective Edge, operation, 3, 8, 197
  Second Intifada, 6, 8, 91, 167, 168, 197, 202, 251, 252
  West Bank, 3, 10, 168, 190, 252
Oxford Manual 1880, 23, 143

partisan, 167, 169, 201, 203, 228
peacekeeping, 13, 32
permanent sovereignty over natural resources, principle of, 44, 154
Pictet, Jean, 209, 222
pillage, 61
PLO, 46, 155, 158
police
  allegiance of local police to the Occupying Power, 189

continuity of functions, 166, 179, 247
cooperation between the local police and the Occupying Power, 70, 188–91
local police and Occupying Power's legislation, 190
POLISARIO, 13, 155
precaution, principle of, 256, 262, 264
prisoner of war status, 143, 145, 146, 147, 149, 163, 200, 209, 210, 227, 232, 259, 273
prolonged occupation, 52, 63, 157, 233
property, protection of, 26, 45, 50, 57, 60–61, 148, 182–83, 260–61
proportionality, principle of
international human rights law, 243, 245, 247, 248, 250
international humanitarian law, 93, 256, 262
jus ad bellum, 93, 107
protected persons, 45, 57, 58, 72, 140, 148, 200, 259, 271
puppet regimes, 14, 17, 30, 41, 56, 90

relief operations, 60, 84
reprisals, 140, 177, 254
resistance, armed
compatibility with occupation, 36, 198–204
legitimacy of armed resistance in light of counter-terrorism conventions, 159–62
legitimacy of armed resistance in light of international humanitarian law, 149
legitimacy of armed resistance in light of the human right to resist, 152
legitimacy of armed resistance in light of the principle of self-determination of peoples, 149–59
levée en masse, 136–37
restoration/maintenance of public order, duty of
demonstrations, 249–53
obligation of conduct, 171, 192
Occupying Power's security, 170–71
private actors' violations, 174
protection of diplomatic facilities, 174
protection of UN facilities, 174
use of armed force, 176
Rousseau, Jean-Jacque, 27

Salmon, Jean, 195
self-defence
against non-State actors, 112–14
armed attack by non-State actors, 101–10
armed attacks from within occupied territory as internal phenomena, 111–12
circumstance precluding the wrongfulness of an act, 108, 157
Israeli wall, 99–101
self-determination of peoples, principle of
applicability in occupied territory, 44, 150–51
classification of hostilities in occupied territory, 153, 219–21
definition, 49
illegal occupation, 151, 157–58
as *jus cogens*, 49, 158
legitimacy of armed resistance in occupied territory, 149–59, 163–64
national liberation movements, 155, 156, 158, 220
as obligation *erga omnes*, 50, 85
prohibition of annexation, 22, 25, 49, 118
self-defence, 122–25
terrorism, 162
wars of national liberation, 151–59, 219–21
South Ossetia, 18, 90, 120
state of ongoing armed conflict, 95, 97, 99, 126–33, 166, 193, 236, 237, 238, 246
state of war, 66, 127–28, 129, 133, 209
State responsibility
failure to prevent armed attacks as rule of attribution, 105–6
ILC rules on attribution, 211–14
'overall control' test, 211
SWAPO, 123, 155, 180, 191, 204, 230

targeted killings, 8, 248–49, 266–67
terra nullius, 24

terrorism
  global war against terrorism, 130
  international humanitarian law and, 161
  law enforcement, 179, 181, 182, 191
  legitimacy of armed resistance in occupied territory, 159–62
  Occupying Powers' legislation, 179–81
  self-defence against terrorism, 93
  self-determination of peoples, principle of, 161–62
transfer of civilians of the Occupying Power into the occupied territory, 50, 57
transformative occupation, 59
Transnistria, 17
treaty interpretation
  evolutionary interpretation, 53
  systemic integration, 77, 78, 80, 263

Ukraine, 18–19, 66, 121
unlawful combatants, 146, 255
use of armed force, prohibition of, 3, 88, 101, 102, 103, 107, 112–13, 126, 133

Verri, Pietro, 195

war rebellion, 142
war treason, 142
Western Sahara, 12–13, 151, 155
Westphalia (1648), Peace of, 21

Yugoslavia, occupation of, 15, 210

CPSIA information can be obtained
at www.ICGtesting.com
Printed in the USA
LVHW080411250220
648027LV00011BA/118